REAL-TIME SYSTEMS, ARCHITECTURE, SCHEDULING, AND APPLICATION

Edited by **Seyed Morteza Babamir**

Real-Time Systems, Architecture, Scheduling, and Application
Edited by Seyed Morteza Babamir

Published by InTech
Janeza Trdine 9, 51000 Rijeka, Croatia

Publishing Process Manager Maja Bozicevic

Technical Editor Teodora Smiljanic

Cover Designer InTech Design Team

Additional hard copies can be obtained from orders@intechopen.com

Real-Time Systems, Architecture, Scheduling, and Application,
Edited by Seyed Morteza Babamir
p. cm.
ISBN 978-953-51-0510-7

For EU product safety concerns:
IN TECH d.o.o., Prolaz Marije Krucifikse Kozulić 3, 51000 Rijeka, Croatia,
info@intechopen.com or visit our website at intechopen.com.

Meet the editor

Dr Seyed Morteza Babamir received BS degree in Software Engineering from Ferdowsi University of Meshhad and MS and PhD degrees in Software Engineering from Tarbiat Modares University in 2002 and 2007 respectively. He was a researcher at Iran Aircraft Industries, Tehran City, Iran, from 1987 to 1993, head of Computer Center in University of Kashan, Kashan, Iran, from 1997 to 1999 and haed of Computer Engineering Department in University of Kashan from 2002 to 2005. Since 2007, he has been an assistant professor of Department of Computer Engineering in University of Kashan, Kashan, Iran. He authored one book in Software Testing, 4 book chapters, 14 journal papers and more than 40 international and internal conference papers. He is the managing director of Soft Computing Journal published by supporting University of Kashan, Kashan, Iran. Dr. Babamir is a member of the ACM.

Contents

Preface

Real-Time Systems are computing systems that must meet their temporal specification. In computer science, real-time or reactive computing is the study of hardware and software systems that are subject to a real-time constraint called deadline, which the system should respect it in its response to events. Real-time systems, in fact, must guarantee response within strict time constraints. Real-time systems often appear as critical systems such as mission critical ones. The anti-lock brakes system on a car, for instance, is a real-time computing system where the real-time constraint is the brakes release time to prevent the wheel from locking. Real-time software may use synchronous programming languages, real-time operating systems and real-time networks providing essential frameworks for constructing real-time software applications.

Since correctness of a real-time operation depends not only on its logical correctness but also on the time in which the operation is carried out, real-time systems are classified by three types of deadlines: (1) Hard where missing a deadline leads to total system failure, (2) Firm where missing a deadline is tolerable, but it may degrade quality of system services and (3) Soft where deadlines are tolerable to be half extended. Therefore, the goal of a hard real-time system is to ensure that all deadlines are met; however, that of a soft real-time system is to ensure that a deadline is nearly met or a subset of deadlines is met. Maximizing the number of met deadlines or maximizing the number of met deadlines for high priority tasks and minimizing the lateness of tasks are the concerned goals in the soft real-time systems. Embedded systems like car engine control system, medical systems (such as heart pacemakers), industrial process controllers, video game systems and vector graphics are hard real-time systems having hard requirements. A car engine control system, for instance, is a hard real-time system where a delayed signal may cause engine failure or damage. Multitasking systems are another type of real-time systems where the scheduling policies are a matter of concern. Typical policies are Priority driven or Preemptive scheduling, Earliest Deadline First and Overlay scheduling, such as Adaptive Partition Scheduling.

This book stresses architecture, scheduling, specification and verification and real world applications of real-time systems. It includes a cross-fertilization of ideas and concepts between the academic and industrial worlds. The book starts with a section

(Chapters 1 to 4) on real-time architectures and continues with a section (Chapters 5 and 6) on specification and verification of real-time systems, a section on real-time scheduling algorithms (Chapters 7 to 9) and ends with a section (Chapters 10 to 15) on some real world application of real-time systems.

Section 1 consisting of Chapters 1 to 4 deals with architectures of real-time systems. Chapter 1 presents realizing the networking applications by means of DSP microcomputer architecture (Blackfin microcomputer) supported by an operating system kernel (Visual DSP Kernel) and lightweight IP protocol stack (LWIP suite). Moreover, the chapter provides the frameworks for telecommunications applications development and for performance evaluation. A VoIP (Voice over IP) system, as a complex networking application example, is illustrated based on adaptive multi-rate codec.

Chapter 2 discusses some development efforts to identify general terms and metrics that are necessary to track a system's upcoming evolutionary phases. It presents higher-level analyses of these metrics by examples of several years of systems development track history and in multiple projects. Based on observations, it tries to derive a preliminary methodology to formulate system dynamics towards their evolution.

Chapter 3 elaborates concept of mode and includes a number of current views of modes and addresses previous work on modes in real-time systems. It extends the current schedulability analysis associated with mode changes in static priority preemptive based scheduling. It derives analysis that includes tasks executing across a mode change with deadlines larger than their period.

Chapter 4 addresses the problem of providing temporal isolation to components in an integrated system. Temporal isolation allows to develop and verify the components independently and concurrently and then to integrate them into a system. To provide true temporal isolation when components execute on a shared processor, this chapter tries to address this problem by means of a hierarchical scheduling framework (HSF). HSF provides the means for the integration of independently developed and analyzed components into a predictable real-time system. A component is defined by a set of tasks, a local scheduler and a server defining the component's time budget (i.e. its share of the processing time) and its replenishment policy.

Section 2 consisting of Chapters 5 and 6 discusses specification and verification issues in real-time systems. Chapter 5 deals with specification and verification in UML known as a semiformal language. The chapter presents a formal interpretation of a set of sequence diagrams with time constraints. The formal interpretation is used to constructing programming tools for supporting validation of systems behavior specification and prototyping of the systems. The chapter demonstrates how the set of scenarios specifying system behavior may be derived from the set of sequence diagrams and how this set may be analyzed against its consistency and completeness.

Also, this chapter proposes an approach to specify real-time systems having some features. To this end, it extends the UML sequence diagrams with new kinds of stereotypes and the notion of monitoring scenarios is introduced. Monitoring scenarios are also specified by sequence diagrams used to define liveness and safety properties.

Chapter 6 provides a method for specifying and stating real-time software using *Timed Automata* and Real-time Logic respectively. Then, the chapter deals with obtaining the safety constraints from *reachability graph* of Timed Automata extracted from the problem specification and then the constraints are stated in Real-time Logic propositions. These propositions showing safety constraints are used for verification of the system behavior. To show the effectiveness of the proposed method, the chapter sets it forth for a real-time system called Rail Road Crossing Control. This chapter also includes a brief explanation of Timed Automata and Real-time Logic and a method is presented to simulate Timed Automata in Real-time logic.

Section 3 consisting of Chapters 7 to 9 deals with scheduling discussion in real-time systems. Chapter 7 addresses the problem of handling overload conditions in real-time systems. The conditions are critical situations in which the computational demand requested by some application exceeds the processor capacity. If not properly handled, an overload can cause sudden performance degradation or a system crash. The chapter, in fact, aims to claim that a real-time system should be designed to anticipate and tolerate unexpected overload situations.

Chapter 8 discusses concurrency control method where transactions access real-time data. The chapter first reviews concurrency control protocols proposed in real-time database systems and describes some concurrency control algorithms for accessing temporal data. Then, it deals with analysing validity of active real-time systems and effects real-time data on the concurrency control. Based on characteristics of temporal data, a concurrency control algorithm called "real-time concurrency control algorithm based on Data-deadline" is put forward.

Chapters 9 discusses hard real-time paradigm. Most scheduling algorithms developed for soft and firm real-time systems and they lack the ability to enforce constraints on the upper limit of deadline misses. However, without such enforcement, violation of time constraint may occur. If consecutive instances of a task fail to complete before their deadlines, the system will eventually fail. Although firm deadlines can occasionally be missed, there is normally an upper limit on the number of misses within a defined interval. The hard real-time paradigm is well established and it has received considerable attention by researchers and practitioners within academia and industry.

Section 4 consisting of chapters 10 to 15 proposes applications of real-time systems. Chapter 10 proposes the security issue in Unmanned Wireless Sensor Networks (UWSNs) as an application of real-time systems. Such networks should collect small size and secure data in real-time manner. However, since sensor nodes are small and low power with low storage, classical algorithms maybe inapplicable and so they cannot guarantee the security of the data. This problem is very critical in the new generation of WSNs called UWSNs. Moreover, since disconnected networks in UWSNs are established in critical or military environments, sink or collector sensors are unable to gather data in real-time manner. Also, the network may be leaved unattended and may periodically be visited. This issue is subject to some threats such as discovering and compromising sensor nodes by adversary without detection or injection of some invalid data to the network. In such setting the main challenge is giving an assurance that data survive for long time. This chapter aims to propose a scheme that shares generated data and encode them to provide confidentiality and integrity.

Chapter 11 proposes an application of image processing where ensemble statistical binary classifiers whose function is to make a binary decision on whether an image region is an object of interest or not. The methods of interest include mainly the AdaBoost method whose original purpose was to fuse a small number of relatively well working so-called weak classifiers into one better working, so-called strong classifier. This approach was further developed into an approach that instead of a small number of relatively well working weak classifiers took into account a large number of simple functions and selected a suitable weak classifiers automatically from these functions. The AdaBoost approach has been further refined and modified to WaldBoost which was based on Wald's sequential decision making combined with AdaBoost.

Chapter 12 proposes the application of energy consumption and performance evaluation of protocols in an ad hoc network. This chapter is a research where mobile ad hoc networks are described and some routing protocols are explained. During simulation, different results are given by changing the selected parameters. In this chapter, mobile ad Hoc networks are described and some of important routing protocols are studied. The results obtained from the assessment and comparisons on energy consumption are shown for some protocols. Based on obtained results, among others, two protocols show better performance than other.

Chapter 13 proposes the application of real-time motion estimation. Motion estimation is a low-level vision task managing a number of applications like sport tracking, surveillance, security, industrial inspection, robotics, navigation and optics. This chapter introduces different motion estimation systems and their implementation when real-time is required. Three systems regarding low-level and midlevel vision domain are explained. Three different case studies of real-time optical flow systems developed by the authors are presented. Then, the analysis of performance and resources consumed by each one of three real-time implementations are discussed.

Chapter 14 focuses on description of exposure systems used for data acquisition that is exposure to radiofrequency electromagnetic fields in bio-electromagnetic investigations. Such systems are referred to as real-time and able to generate and control electromagnetic field and are suitable to be used in experiments where data acquisition has to be carried out simultaneously with the exposure. In biomedicine, the real-time concept is applied to both fast calculation of some parameters of biomedical and the experimental acquisition of physiological data simultaneously. In this chapter, real-time exposure systems are used to acquire fast biological responses, in milliseconds in order to study possible health effects due to electromagnetic exposure. The aim of this chapter is to merge a well-assessed design procedure of radiofrequency exposure systems with the requirements emerging from real-time investigations. It is provided that how to adapt the general rules for exposure system design to real-time systems.

Finally, Chapter 15 proposes a real-time application in fast movement of eye called *saccade*. It discusses a wavelets-based technique for the estimation of blinking and saccade time moments, using continuous wavelet transformation. The estimation of the blink and Electrooculography bio-signals is important for the real-time human–computer interaction systems. This chapter is proposed because: (1) previous work related to the optimization approach using the blinking and eye movement model was not well fitted for the real-time processing and (2) computation requirements are high. The reduction of computation time is obtained by the selection of the more efficient evolutionary operators and it is reduced by reduction of the number of processed samples. In this chapter, performance analyses of the algorithm and latency behaviour are considered.

Seyed Morteza Babamir
Assistant Professor of University of Kashan, Kashan,
Iran

Part 1

Architectures

1

Networking Applications for Embedded Systems

Sorin Zoican
Politehnica University of Bucharest
Romania

1. Introduction

The chapter is organized as follows: a briefly introduction that motivate the necessity of networking embedded systems, a background section which illustrates the basic resources used to accomplish the networking embedded systems (Blackfin microcomputer, Visual DSP Kernel and LWIP suite), two sections that discuss the frameworks for networking application development and performance evaluation, and conclusion. A VoIP system based on AMR codec is illustrated, as a complex networking application example.

Embedded networking applications are now more and more used to send out multimedia content (audio and image) over wired or wireless networks. Control applications and sensor networks are additional areas where adding network means is desirable. More or fewer all systems connected to the Internet communicate using the IP protocol stack (Deborah Estrin, 2001, Gregory Pottie and William Kaiser, 2005). Owing to the supremacy of IP networks, many networked embedded systems are connected to such networks and therefore must be able to communicate using such protocols. However, the IP protocol suite is often apparent to be "heavyweight" in that an achievement of the protocols requires many memory resources and processing power (Adam Dunkels, 2005). The understanding that the IP protocols would require large memory leads to using large microprocessors. If the IP protocol stack is carried out using lesser amount of memory, then smaller microprocessors could be chosen. This would not only make the resulting systems less expensive to manufacture, but would also enable a whole class of smaller embedded systems to communicate using the IP protocol. On the other hand, if the microprocessor is large, and the IP protocol uses less memory then more complex applications may be accomplished.

For the embedded systems, the cost is a limiting element that constrains the resources such as memory and processor capabilities. As a result, many embedded systems do not have more than a few tens kilobytes of memory that make impractical to run the TCP/IP from Linux or Windows. The main difficulty is the memory constraint. The processing power is not quite a difficult problem owing to current technology improvements. The solution to the dilemma of running TCP/IP inside constrained memory limits is developing a very small TCP/IP implementation capable to run on a system with very little memory, called "lightweight" IP (LWIP). The LWIP was carried out for a powerful microcomputer, Blackfin BF5xx (Analog Devices Inc., ADI) using the EZ-KIT LITE BF5xx evaluation boards.

Making an embedded system for networking applications require detailed knowledge of hardware and software resources needed to develop it. Architectural elements such as computational units, address units, control units and memory management are presented for a correct evaluation of the computational power of Blackfin family processors used in complex networking applications that include digital signal processing like as voice-over IP system. The LWIP protocol stack benefits of many operating system primitives. Well understanding of the operating system kernel functioning, such as scheduling, semaphore, memory management, is necessary for writing the software needed in networking applications. The LWIP implementation for Blackfin family must be detailed while the networking application uses the protocol stack resources (functions, memory allocation).

2. Background

This section shows the elements that help achieve an embedded system with LWIP capabilities: the Blackfin microcomputer, as hardware support, the Visual DSP Kernel (VDK) real-time operating system kernel, as software support and LWIP protocol stack.

2.1 Blackfin microcomputer

The Blackfin microcomputer is a 16-bit fixed-point processor based on the micro-signal architecture (MSA) core, developed in cooperation by Analog Devices and Intel. Low-cost and high performance features make Blackfin suitable for computationally applications including video equipment and third-generation cell phones (Sorin Zoican, 2008). The Blackfin microcomputer may have embedded Ethernet and controller area network. The Figure 1 illustrated the Blackfin general architecture (Analog Devices, 2006).

The MSA is designed to attain high-speed digital signal performance and top power efficiency. This architecture combines the best capabilities of microcontroller and DSP processor into a single programming model. A dynamic power management circuit continually monitors the running software and dynamically adjusts the voltage and the frequency at which the core runs. As a result, power consumption and performance for real-time applications, such node in sensor networks, are optimized.. The Blackfin core combines dual multiply-accumulate (MAC) units, an orthogonal reduced instruction-set computer (RISC) instruction set, single instruction, multiple data (SIMD) programming capabilities, and multimedia processing features into a unified architecture. As shown in Figure 1, the Blackfin BF5xx processor includes system peripherals such as parallel peripheral interface (PPI), serial peripheral interface (SPI), serial ports (SPORTs), general-purpose timers, universal asynchronous receiver transmitter (UART), real-time clock (RTC), watchdog timer, and general-purpose input/output (I/O) ports. The Blackfin processor has a direct memory access (DMA) controller that efficiently transfers data between external devices/memories and the internal memories without processor involvement. Blackfin processors offer L1 cache memory for fast accessing of both data and instructions.

Blackfin processors have well-to-do peripheral supports, memory management unit (MMU), and RISC-like instructions, usually found in many high-end microcontrollers. These processors have high-speed buses and highly developed computational units that support variable-length arithmetic operations in hardware. These features make the Blackfin processors appropriate to replace other high-end DSPs and MCUs. The Blackfin processor uses a modified Harvard architecture, which allows multiple memory accesses per clock cycle. The Blackfin processor instruction set is optimized so 16-bit operation codes are the frequently used instructions. Complex DSP instructions are encoded into 32-bit operation codes like multifunction instructions. Blackfin microcomputers bear a limited multi-issue facility, where a 32-bit instruction can be issued in parallel with two 16-bit instructions. The programmer can use several core resources in a single instruction cycle. The Blackfin architecture supports instructions that control vector operations. We take advantage of these instructions to carry out concurrent operations on multiple 16-bit values (add, subtract, multiply, shift, negate, pack, and search instructions).

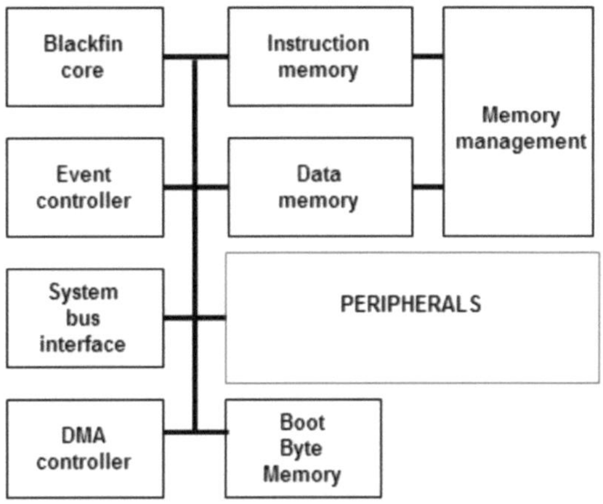

a)

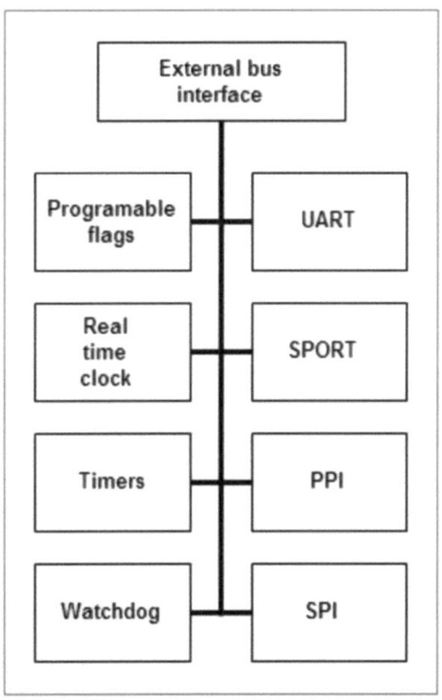

b)

Fig. 1. a) Overall Blackfin architecture; b) The Blackfin peripherals

The Blackfin microcomputers family includes dual-core processors, such as the ADSP-BF561 microcomputer. Besides to other features, dual-core processors append a new facet to application development. Each dual-core Blackfin processor has two Blackfin cores, A and B, each with internal L1 memory. The two cores have a common internal memory shared between them. The cores share access to external memory. Each core functions autonomously: they have their reset address, Event Vector Table, instruction and data caches. On reset, core A starts running from its reset address, whereas core B is disabled. Core B starts running when it is enabled by core A. When core B starts running, it starts running its application, from its reset address. Having one application per core the complete potential of the dual-core Blackfin processor is exploiting. Effectively, two single core applications are building autonomously, and run in parallel on the processor. The common memory areas, both internal and external, are each subdivided into three areas: a section dedicated to core A, a section dedicated to core B, and a shared section.

Figure 2 shows that the core architecture consists of three main units: the address arithmetic unit, the data arithmetic unit, and the control unit.

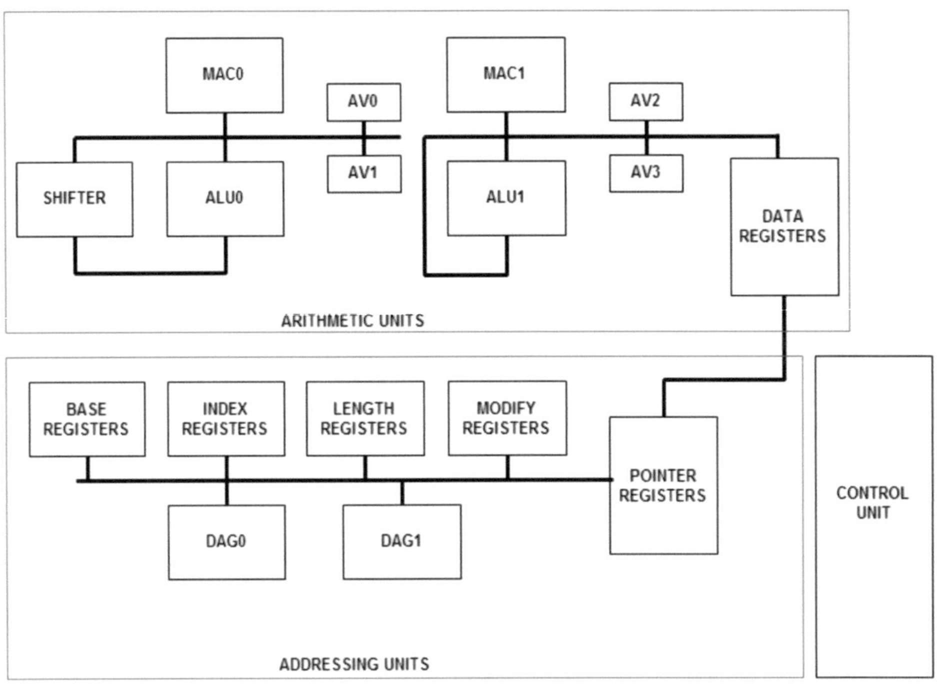

Fig. 2. The Blackfin core

The arithmetic unit supports SIMD operation and it has Load/Store architecture. The assembler instruction syntax is algebraic; it is insightful and makes it simple to understand what the instruction does. Figure 3 illustrates several of arithmetic instruction efficiently executed in a single cycle. The video ALUs offer parallel computational power for video operations – quad 8-bit add/subtract, quad 8-bit average, SAA (Subtract-Absolute-Accumulate). Quad 8-bit ALU instruction takes one cycle to complete.

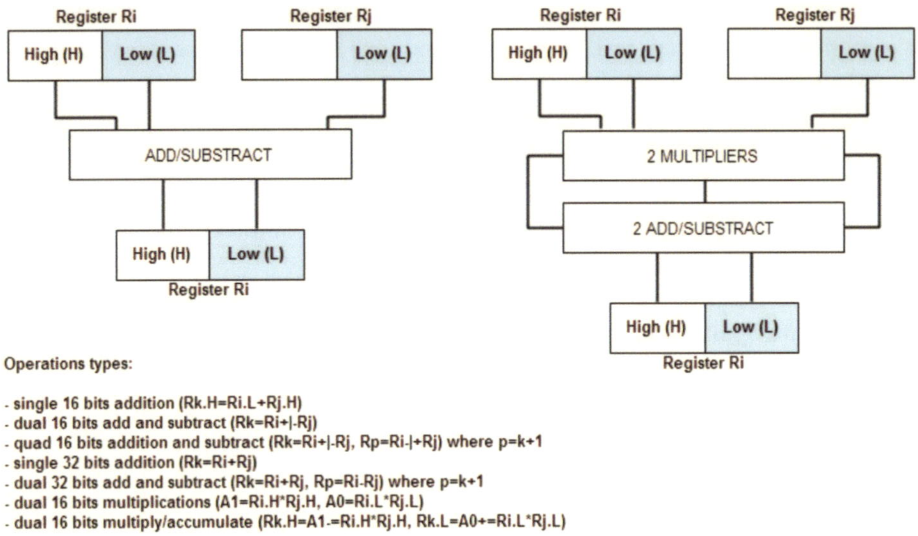

Fig. 3. Blackfin arithmetic instructions

A program sequencer controls the instruction execution flow, which includes instruction alignment and instruction decoding. The Blackfin processor supports two loops with two sets of loop counters, loop top and loop bottom registers to handle looping. Hardware counters calculate the loop condition.

Blackfin sequencer manages events that include: interrupts (hardware and software), exceptions (error situation or service related). Despite the Blackfin processor has a Harvard architecture, it has a single memory map shared between data and instruction memory. Instead of using a single large memory, the Blackfin processor supports a hierarchical memory model as shown in Figure 4. The L1 data and instruction memory are placed on the chip and are generally smaller but faster than the L2 external memory, which has a superior capacity. As a result, transmission data from memory to registers in the Blackfin processor is set in a hierarchy from the slowest memory (L2) to the fastest memory (L1).

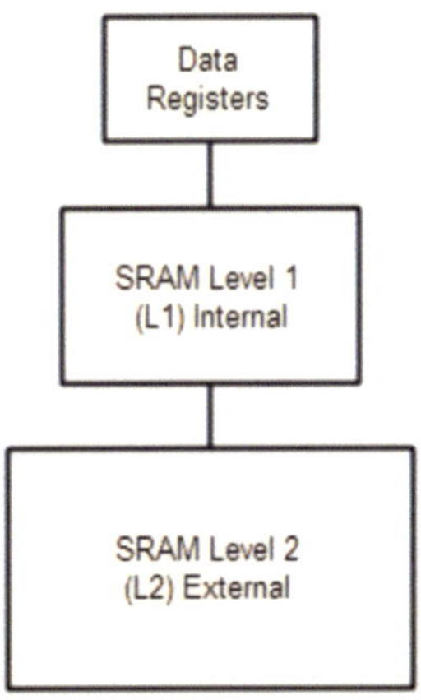

Fig. 4. Blackfin memory model

The justification following hierarchy memory is based on three principles: (1) the principle of building the common case fast, where code and data that have to be accessed repeatedly are stored in the fastest memory; (2) the principle of locality, where the program reuse instructions and data that have been used in recent times; and (3) the principle of smaller is faster, where smaller memory has faster access time.

All the shown features, make the Blackfin microcomputers family an ideal candidate to develop the embedded real-time system, which can run complex applications including networking applications with LWIP support.

2.2 The real-time operating system Visual DSP Kernel (VDK)

Other problem that must be solved, for networking applications, is to develop an operating system that knows how to run on the embedded system.

The resource restrictions and application characteristics of embedded systems put particular requirements on the operating systems running on the embedded system. The applications are usually event-based: the application performs nearly all of its work in reply to external events. Early researches into operating systems for sensor networks identified the requirements and proposed a system, called TinyOS, which solved many problems. Yet, in the TinyOS, a set of features normally found in larger operating systems, such as multithreading and run-time module loading is not accomplished. The multithreading and run-time loading of modules is wanted features of an operating system for embedded systems with networking applications.

The VDK includes the features above and runs in the resource limitations of a sensor node, and thus show that these features are feasible for sensor node operating systems. This section illustrates the main characteristics of a real-time kernel for DSP processors. The real-time kernel Visual DSP Kernel (VDK), produced by Analog Devices, is illustrated (Analog Devices 2, 2007).

The Visual DSP kernel is a strong real-time operating system kernel. It provides critical kernel features. Features include a completely preemptive scheduler (time slicing and cooperative scheduling are as well supported), thread creation, semaphores, interrupt management, interthread messaging, events, and memory administration (memory pools and multiple heaps). In multiprocessors environments, messaging is provided.

Processes are created by a primitive operating system call, which makes memory allocation for process execution.

Real-time operating system for DSP applications manage signal processor resources and have the following functions:

1. Process scheduling according to the priority given to each. The processes having all resources available less CPU is placed in a ready queue.
2. Communication between interdependent processes.
3. Synchronization process with the external environment and other processes.
4. Exclusive use of shared resources.

The real-time kernel state diagram is illustrated in Figure 5.

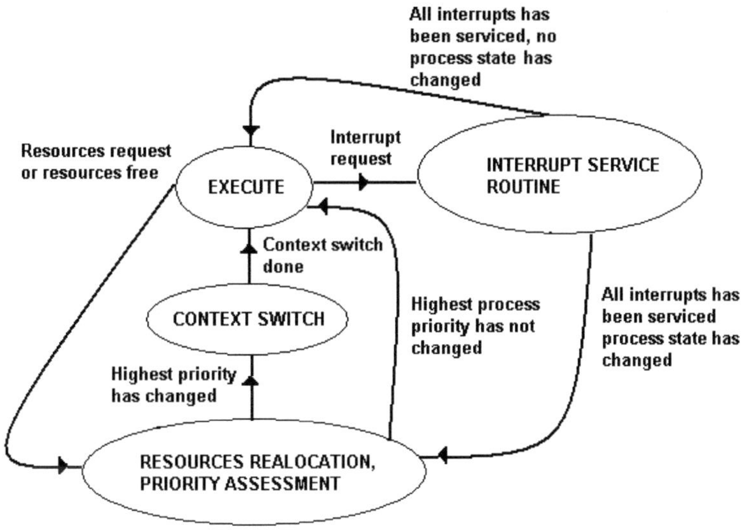

Fig. 5. The real-time kernel state diagram

Execution of the processes will be based on the priority (dynamically allocated) associated with each process. In VDK, three methods of scheduling can be defined: cooperative scheduling, uniform time division (round robin) and preemptive scheduling. Cooperative scheduling is involved for processes with the same priority. Each process takes the DSP processor and passes it, on own initiative, to the next process. The running process will yield the processor by calling a primitive system; the suspended process will be placed in the ready queue in the last position. The round robin scheduling assigns to processes with equal priority equal length time quantum for execution.

Semaphores, events and I/O flags are used to achieve communication and synchronization between processes. A process waiting a signal may continue execution (whether the signal is available) or can enter the blocking state whether the signal is not available. The process will unlock when the signal becomes available or when a timer expires. Semaphores are global variables in the system; therefore, they are available to any process. A semaphore is a data structure that can be used to:

- Control access to shared system resources
- Allow synchronization of processes
- Periodic executions of processes

The semaphore may be posted or it may be pending. Pending the semaphore means testing its value with zero. If the semaphore is zero then the process increases the semaphore value and access the shared resource, otherwise the process waits. When the process has finished using the shared resource it posts the semaphore. Posting a semaphore means that its value is decremented and the resource is make available. Processes interact with semaphores by real-time kernel routines for both semaphores pending and post.

The VDK kernel has all the necessary features to support the LWIP protocol stack development (memory management, semaphores and process scheduling).

2.3 The LWIP implementation on Blackfin microcontrollers

In embedded system architecture, RAM is the most demanding resource. With only a little RAM available for the TCP/IP stack to use, mechanisms used in conventional TCP/IP cannot be straight applied (Adam Dunkels, 2007).

Two memory management solutions may be chosen: dynamic buffers or single global buffer. For first memory management solution, the memory for storing connection state and packets is dynamically allocated from a global group of available memory blocks.

The second memory management solution does not use dynamic memory allocation. As an alternative, it uses a single global buffer for storing packets and has an unchanging table for holding connection state.

The total memory used for LWIP implementations depends deeply on the applications of the particular device in which the implementations are to be run. The memory arrangement determines both the amount of traffic the system should be capable to handle and the maximum of concurrent connections. A device that will be transported large e-mails while running a web server with extremely dynamic web pages and multiple concurrent clients need more RAM than an undemanding Telnet server. TCP/IP implementation with as small as 200 bytes of RAM is achievable, but such a pattern will provide very low throughput and will allow few of simultaneous connections.

The LWIP stack, (Analog Devices 2, 2010), uses the dynamic memory allocations, with VDK support. A general framework for network applications development, based on LWIP implementation, will be defined in the next section. The LWIP stack package on Analog Devices Blackfin family of processors uses a standardized driver interface to permit it to be used with different Ethernet controllers. The drivers are each accomplished as part of the Analog Devices Inc. (ADI) driver model and use the System Services Libraries (SSL). The stack provides the standard BSD socket API to the application and has been planned to decouple it from both the working environment and the particular network interface being used. The stack is connected to the nearby environment by two standardized interfaces (TCP wrapper and LWIP library) accomplished as a different library for separate environment shown in Figure 6.

The kernel API abstracts the operating system services. The kernel abstraction simplifies the movement of LWIP stack to different operating system environments. The fundamental services contain synchronization services, interrupt services, and timer based callback services (Analog Devices 1, 2007).

Blackfin processors can take benefit of the system service library (SSL), which provides reliable, easy C language access to Blackfin features: the interrupt manager, direct memory access (DMA), and power management units. Clock frequency and voltage can be changed without difficulty at run time through a set of simple APIs. Interrupt handling is fired at the time of the event, or delayed to a time of the application's choosing. A device manager integrates device drivers for on-chip and off-chip peripherals. The SSL is operating system neutral and can be run as a separate or with a real-time operating system (RTOS).

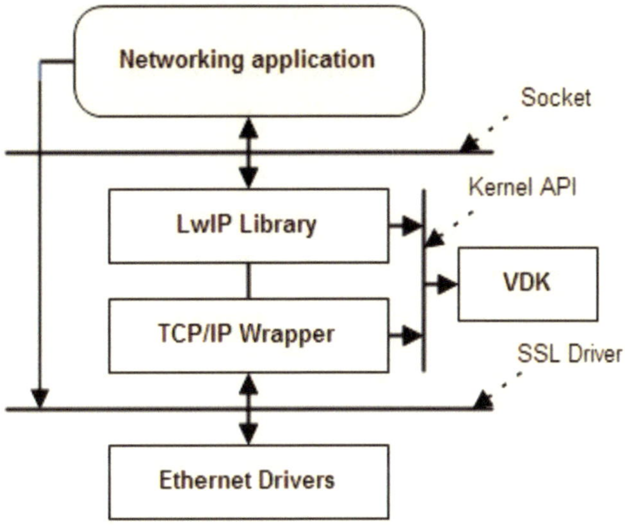

Fig. 6. The Analog Devices LWIP architecture

3. The framework of networking applications for telecommunications development using LWIP and VDK

This section presents a framework for networking applications for telecommunications. Such applications involve complex computation (for example, digital signal processing).

In the proposed framework, the programmer must be aware of all capabilities of Blackfin family (arithmetic instructions, addressing mode, hardware loops, interrupts and memory management) presented in section 3.

The LWIP stack can be run also as a task in a multitasking system or as the main program in a single tasking system. In both cases, the main control loop, illustrated in Figure 7, performs two operations repeatedly: check whether a packet has arrived from the network and check whether a periodic timeout has occurred. This pattern will be used in the framework for application development and performance evaluation.

An application that requirements to use the LWIP stack with VDK is responsible for creating a VDK thread type that the LWIP stack will use to create any threads that it requires during operation. The application also has to initialize several system service library components besides to creating an instance of the driver for the appropriate Ethernet controller.

The steps involved in creating an application that uses the LWIP stack can be summarized as (Analog Devices 2, 2010):

1. Specifying the header file for the socket API
2. Guarantee that enough VDK semaphores are configured
3. Initialize the SSL interrupt and device driver managers
4. Initialize and set up the kernel API library
5. Open the device driver for the Ethernet MAC controller and pass the handle for the driver to the LWIP stack

6. Configure external bus interface unit (EBIU) controller to provide DMA priority over processor
7. Provide the MAC address that will be used by the device driver
8. Give memory to the device driver to enable it to bear the appropriate number of concurrent reads and writes
9. Inform the device driver library that the Ethernet driver will use the dataflow method
10. Initialize and build up the LWIP stack supplying memory for the stack to use as its internal heap
11. Tell the Ethernet driver that it should now start to run
12. Wait for the physical link to be established

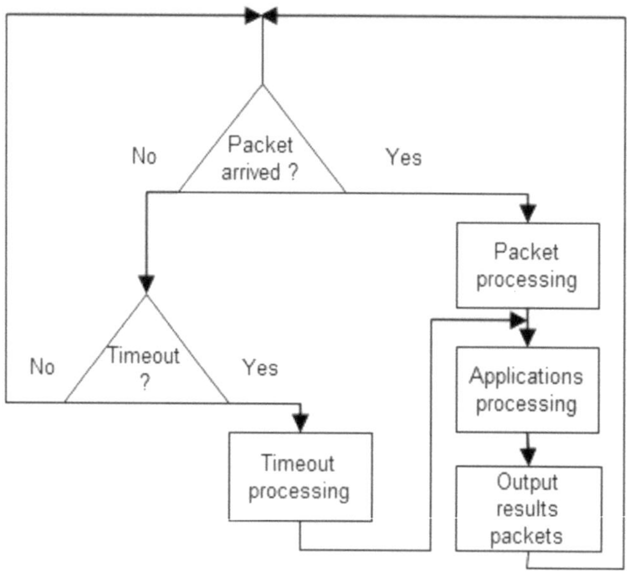

Fig. 7. The main control loop for LWIP stack

The framework for networking applications for telecommunications is based on the following assumptions (Sorin Zoican, 2011):

- there are two groups of tasks: the first manage digital processing of analog signals (such as audio or video samples) and the second deals with packets processing among the network (receive and transmit packets)
- the first group has complex tasks and the second group has less complex tasks
- block processing may be necessarily
- the system should work in real-time
- there are two type of information: signals, constituted by samples of analog signals, and data, constituted by binary results which will be transferred over network

These tasks will be scheduled using the VDK primitives (illustrated in section 3). All the scheduling methods are involved: cooperative scheduling for collaborative tasks, round robin scheduling for equal priority tasks, and preemptive scheduling for higher priority tasks. Several system tasks will be created to interact with network card using system service library, as it is stated in section 3.

If it is necessarily, two independent applications may be carried out using a dual core microcontroller such as Blackfin BF561. The application in the fist core implements the tasks of first group and the application in the second core may implements some simple tasks in the first group and the networking tasks (these tasks are less complex). This strategy was validated by implementing a voice-over IP system based on an adaptive multirate (AMR) codec (Redwan Salami et al., 2002). In the first group (tasks A) consider an AMR encoder and in the second group (task B) consider an AMR decoder, the setting of the codec rate and the packet processing that consists of receiving and transmitting packets over network using UDP protocol (Johan Sjöberg et al., 2002).

The AMR codec has high computational demands. Many specific signal processing operations must be completed in real time. The Blackfin powerful instruction set (as can observe in Figure 3), memory management, events control and the peripherals included in its architecture make realizable a real-time implementation of the both AMR codec and networking processing in a VoIP embedded system.

A technique called *switching buffers* was involved, to ensure a real-time functioning of the communication system (Woon-Seng Gan. and Sen M. Kuo, 2007). In this technique, there are pairs of input and output buffers that will be switched periodically. One pair of buffers is used for processing and the other pair is used for receiving the inputs and sending previous results.

For the particular case of AMR-VoIP system, the following buffers are defined:

- Signal_RX[0] and Signal_RX[1] - for input frames
- Signal_TX[0] and Signal_TX[1] - for output frames
- Data_RX[0] and Data_RX[1] - for coder results
- Data_TX[0] and Data_TX[1] - for decoder inputs

The input frames have N sample length each and the coder/decoder results buffer have length of M results each. Two flags, *flag_A* and *flag_B*, are defined to control the program flow in the core A and core B. A variable *counter* is defined to manage the sample frames acquisition. An interrupt is generated by the audio analog to digital converter (ADC) every input speech sample. The interrupt routine service acquires the new sample, store it in the current signal input buffer and transmit to the digital to analog converter (DAC) the signal sample from current output buffer. After N signal samples have been acquired, the signal and data buffers will be switched. A necessary condition for real-time operating is that the acquisition time for input current frame must be greater than the processing time of this frame. The buffers, flags and counter, above defined, are shared resources of the two cores in the Blackfin microcomputers. Figures 8 to 12 illustrated the switching buffer technique, flowcharts of core A, core B and interrupt service routine, respectively. The variables *i* and *j* are the acquisition buffer and the processing buffer indexes. The networking processing is illustrated in Figure 13.

The application code, written in C, may be optimized for speed (Analog Devices 1, 2010). Several techniques for C optimizations were used:

- build-in functions for fractional data
- using circular buffers and hardware controlled loops

- interprocedural analysis (IPA) - the compiler sees the entire source files used in a final link at compilation time and to use that information while optimizing

The most computational expensive block in the voice-over IP, based on AMR codec, is the AMR encoder, carried out in core A. The rest of computations, (AMR decoder, setting AMR rate at each frame and the networking processing) are less computational expensive.

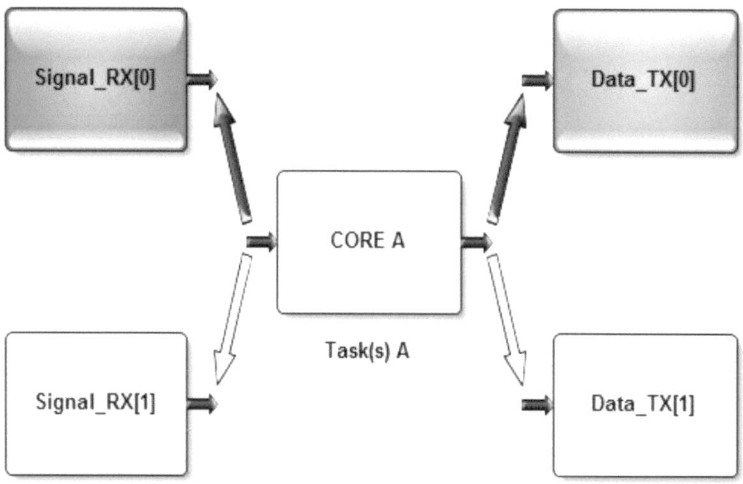

Fig. 8. Switching buffers technique in core A

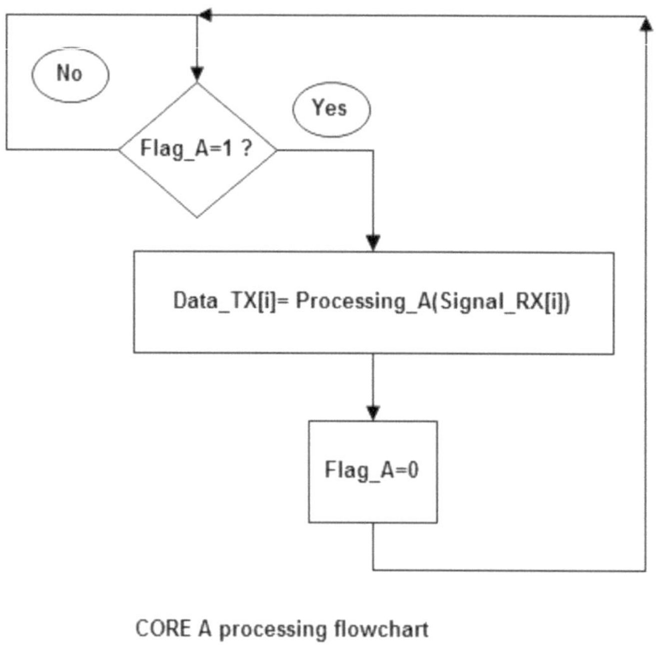

Fig. 9. Program flowchart in core A

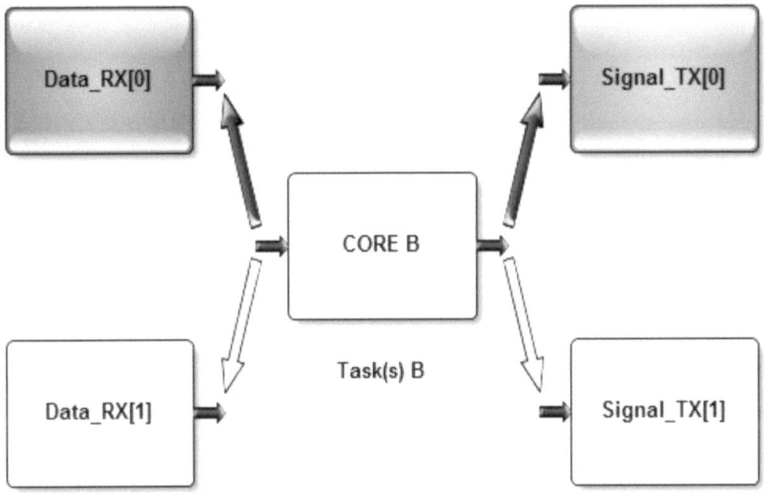

Fig. 10. Switching buffers technique in core B

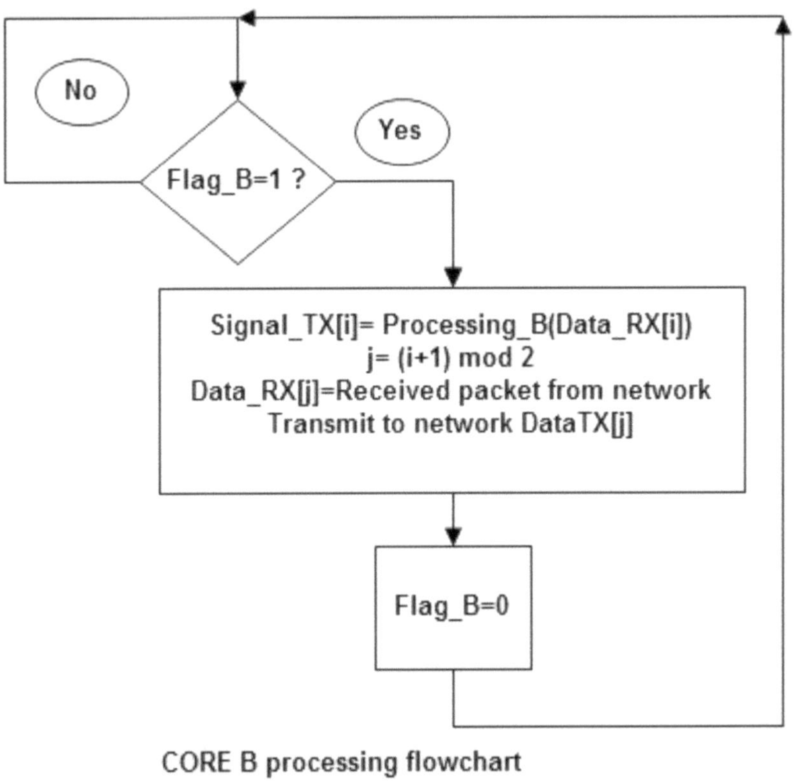

Fig. 11. Program flowchart in core B

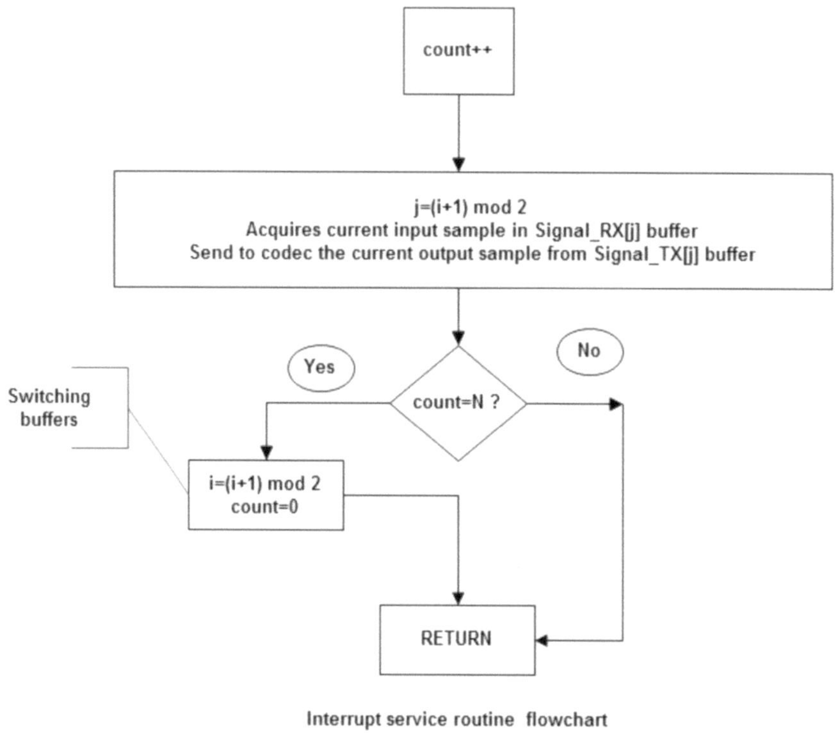

Fig. 12. ISR flowchart

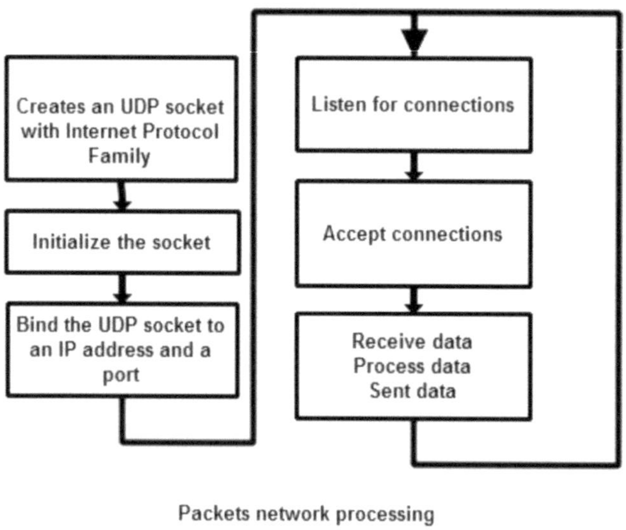

Fig. 13. Network processing flowchart

The optimized execution time can be seen in Table 1. In this table one can observe that the processing time is less than frame acquisition time of 20 milliseconds and therefore the VoIP system works in real-time.

MODE	AMR Codec--Execution time (Dual core Blackfin Processors)			
	CORE A		CORE B	
	Cycles	Milliseconds	Cycles	Milliseconds
MR475 4.75 Kbit/s	13593292	18.12	1783754	2.38
MR515 5.15 Kbit/s	10673898	14.23	1756316	2.34
MR59 5.90 Kbit/s	12141920	16.19	1743907	2.33
MR67 6.70 Kbit/s	14376904	19.17	1745566	2.33
MR74 7.40 Kbit/s	13584752	18.11	1752102	2.34
MR795 7.95 Kbit/s	14025496	18.70	1830429	2.44
MR102 10.20 Kbit/s	14200042	18.93	1813014	2.42
MR122 12.20 Kbit/s	14685916	19.58	1887733	2.52

Table 1. Execution time for AMR codec

The proposed strategy may be used as a framework for various applications, especially for applications in sensor networks, that requires fast computation, lower power consumption and network (fixed or mobile) connectivity.

4. LWIP performance evaluation

This section presents the framework in which performance evaluation was performed. Two test programs were developed: a client program and a server program. The client connect to the server and send continually data requests, while the server listen for connections, accept it and send a replay message to the clients. More than ten client instances were started to evaluate the performance of the LWIP connection with high load.

The client and server flowcharts are illustrated in Figures 14 and 15, respectively.

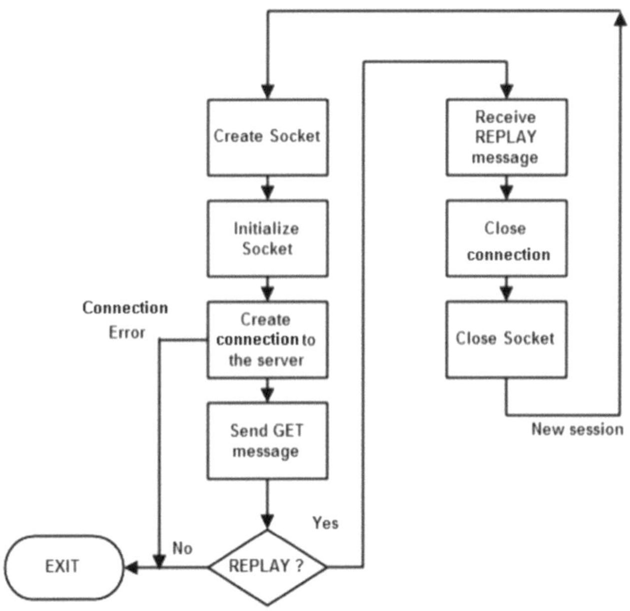

Fig. 14. Client flowchart

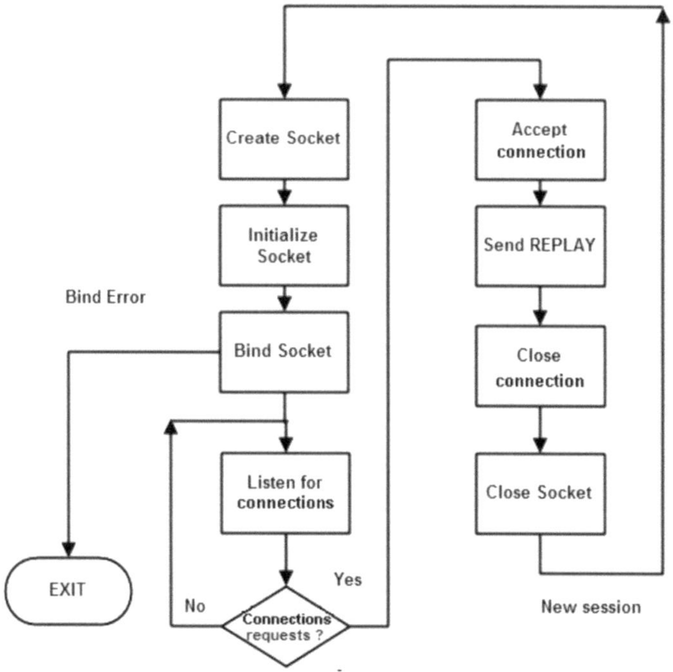

Fig. 15. Server flowchart

The clients were run on a personal computer (PC) with Windows operating system and they were written in C language using Visual 2008 Studio. The WinSock2.0 library was used for manage the network connections, sending and receiving the packets over network. The server has two versions: one developed under Windows operating system (as the clients) and the second developed using the LWIP stack protocol under the VDK operating system kernel, presented in the section 3. The embedded server was written using the LWIP API functions (Analog Devices 2, 2010) and benefits of VDK support as it specify above.

The clients and server programs were run, both on PC and Blackfin BF537 evaluation board and the packets transferred over the network was captured using the network analyzer Wireshark. The following sequence that shows the flow of a TCP connection was used to measure the connection time and the response time between clients and server:

1. The server creates the listener socket waiting for remote clients to connect.
2. The client call *connect ()* socket function to start the TCP handshake (SYN, SYN/ACK, ACK).
3. The server call *accept ()* socket function to accept the connection request.
4. The client and server issue the *read ()* and *write ()* socket functions to exchange data over the socket.
5. Either the server or the client decides to close the socket that causes the occurrence of the sequences FIN and ACK.
6. The server either closes the listener socket or repeats beginning with step 2 to accept another connection from a remote client.

The packets, transferred between clients and server, were analyzed for SYN, SYN/ACK ACK and FIN flags. The time between TCP flags SYN and SYN/ACK was measured to determine the connection time of the clients to the server. The time between the GET and REPLAY messages was measured to determine the response time. The results, both for embedded server and PC server, are illustrated in Figures 16 and 17.

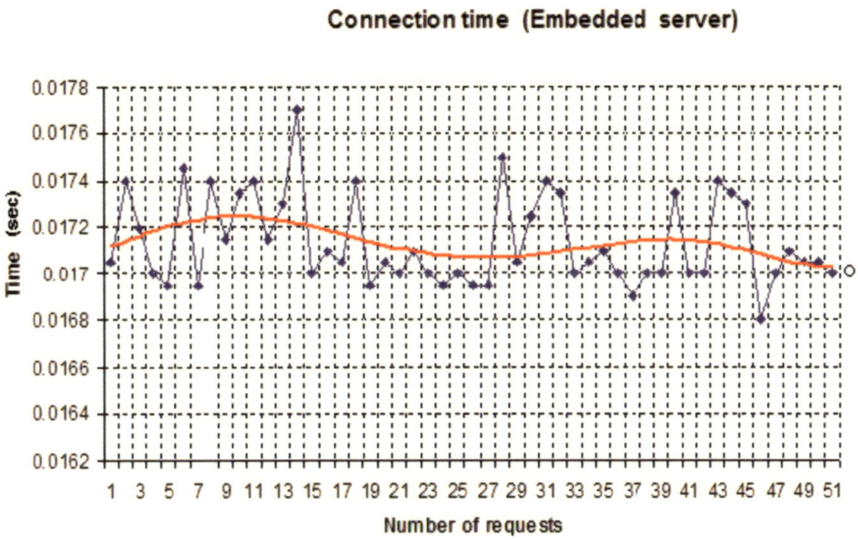

a)

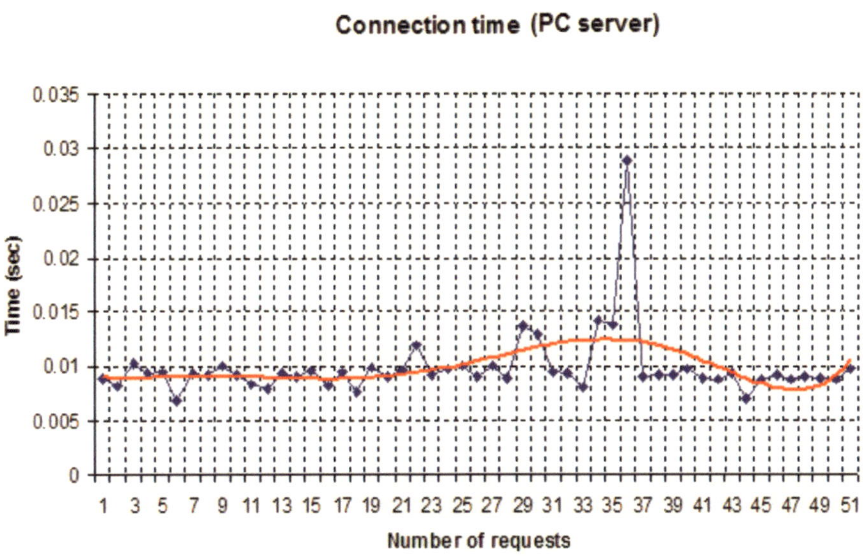

b)

Fig. 16. The connection time: a) Embedded server; b) PC server (red line is a trend line)

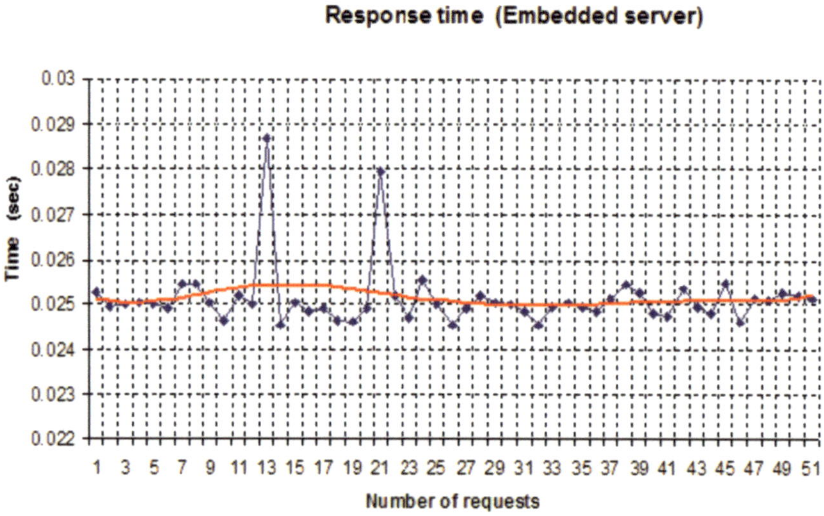

a)

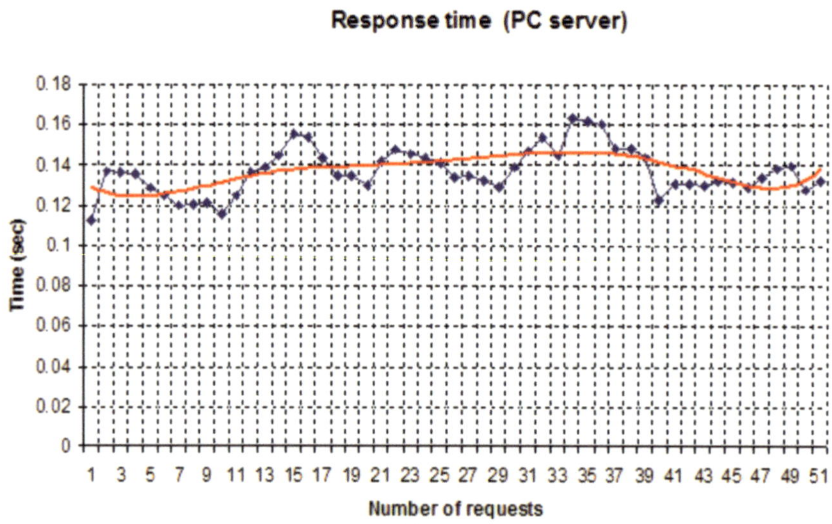

b)

Fig. 17. The response time: a) Embedded server; b) PC server (red line is a trend line)

Accordingly with these figures, the embedded server has a slower connection time. That is happened due the LWIP has a limited memory buffers and involves a slow memory management mechanism. The clients and the PC server were run on the same PCs (Windows XP 32 bits, 100Mbps network interface). In both situations, up to ten clients were run without connection error.

Comparing the connection and the response time, one can observe that the differences between the TCP and LWIP implementation are not critical, for absolute values. The values obtained with LWIP implementation are very good; the connection time is similar for

Blackfin implementation and PC implementation. The response time depends of the traffic load on the PC, but it is good for both implementations.

Due the limited memory and the memory management used in LWIP implementation, the connection time and response time are slower than in personal computers, but they remain still acceptable.

Several system threads are created to interface the network card with the Blackfin core using the SSL library. These threads were created using the VDK primitives. This approach allows the clients to run concurrently and therefore the connection time and response time will be decreased. The processor load is about 30% (considering up to ten clients that require connections). Figure 18 illustrates the system threads and processor load.

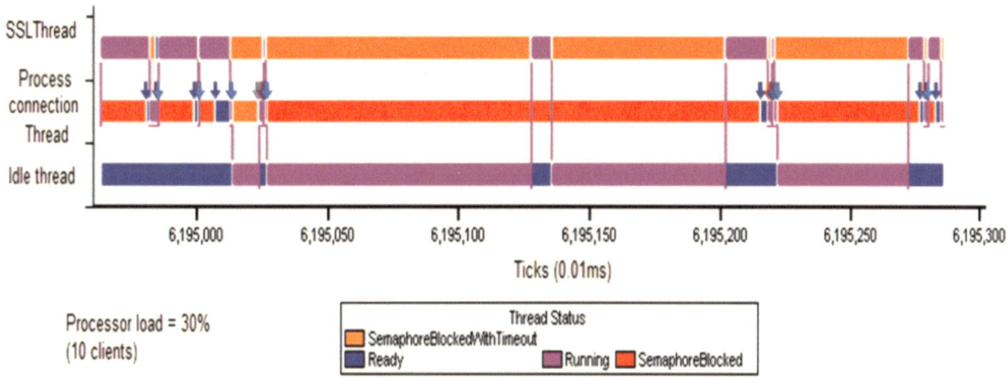

Fig. 18. Threads and processor load

5. Conclusion

The chapter presents a strategy for networking real-time applications development--based on Blackfin microcomputers family, VDK operating kernel and LWIP stack protocol--and evaluates the performance of the lightweight TCP/IP protocol stack for embedded systems. Its applications reside in sensor networks in which the sensors may be connected directly to the Internet. This strategy may be used for various complex applications such digital signal processing in sensor network. The overall performance is similar to the performance of the implementation of the TCP/IP protocol stack in PCs. The connection time and response time are slower in the LWIP implementation, comparing with typical TCP/IP implementation, but they are acceptable. A real-time implementation of network applications, such as voice--over IP system, is exemplified, using a dual core microcomputer and a practical approach to achieve a real-time functioning is provided. Future work will investigate the real-time functionality of presented strategy in multimedia applications.

6. Acknowledgement

This work has benefited the support of FP7 project ALICANTE–FP7–ICT–2009–4 no. 248652.

7. References

Deborah Estrin (2001). Embedded Everywhere: A Research Agenda for Networked Systems of Embedded Computers, National Academy Press, ISBN 0-309-07568-8

Redwan Salami et al. (2002). The Adaptive Multi-Rate Codec: History and Performance, IEEE Speech Coding Workshop, Tsukuba, Japan, pp. 144–146

Johan Sjöberg et al. (2002). Real-Time Transport Protocol (RTP) Payload Format and File Storage Format for the Adaptive Multi-Rate (AMR) and Adaptive Multi-Rate Wideband (AMR-WB) Audio Codecs, IETF RFC 3267

Gregory Pottie and William Kaiser (2005). Principles of Embedded Networked Systems Design, Cambridge University Press, ISBN 9780521840125

Adam Dunkels (2005). Towards TCP/IP for Wireless Sensor Networks, Ed. Arkitektkopia, Vasteras, Sweden, ISBN 91-88834-96-4

Analog Devices (2006). ADSP-BF533: Blackfin Embedded Processor DataSheet, Rev. C., www.analog.com

Analog Devices 1 (2007). VisualDSP++ 5.0 Device Drivers and System Services Manual for Blackfin Processors, www.analog.com

Analog Devices 2 (2007). VisualDSP 5.0 Kernel (VDK) Users Guide, www.analog.com

Adam Dunkels (2007). Programming Memory-Constrained Networked Embedded Systems, SICS Dissertation Series 47, Ed. Arkitektkopia, Vasteras, Sweden, ISSN 1101-1335

Woon-Seng Gan. and Sen M. Kuo, (2007). Embedded Signal Processing with the Micro Signal Architecture, Wiley-Interscience, ISBN 978-0471738411

Sorin Zoican (2008). The Role of Programmable Digital Signal Processors (DSP) for 3G Mobile Communication Systems, Acta Tehnica Napocensis, Electronic and Telecommunications, vol. 49, no. 3, 2008, pp.49-56

Analog Devices 1 (2010). VisualDSP++ 5.0 C/C++ Compiler and Library Manual for Blackfin Processors, www.analog.com

Analog Devices 2 (2010). LWIP user guide, www.analog.com

Sorin Zoican (2011). The Adaptive Multirate Speech Codec: Deployment Strategy Using the Blackfin Microcomputer", Sped 2011 - The proceedings of 6th Conference on Speech Technology and Human - Computer Dialogue, Brasov, Romania, pp. 81-84.

Additional readings

John Proakis, Charles Rader, and Fuyun Ling (1992). Advanced Topics in Digital Signal Processing, Prentice Hall, ISBN: 0-02-396841-9

Arnold Berger (2001), Embedded Systems Design: An Introduction to Processes, Tools and Techniques, CPM Books, ISBN 1-800-788-3123

John Catsoulis and O'Reilly (2005). Designing Embedded Hardware, O'Reilly Media, ISBN 0-596-00755-8

Douglas Comer (1993). Internetworking with TCP/IP - Principles, Protocols and Architecture, Prentice Hall, 1993, ISBN 86-7991-142-9

2

Dynamics of System Evolution

Ashirul Mubin[1], Rezwanur Rahman[1] and Daniel Ray[2]
[1]*University of Alabama, Tuscaloosa, AL,*
[2]*The University of Virginia's College at Wise, Wise, VA,*
USA

1. Introduction

A system is built to serve a common purpose of an organization or a network; it usually consists of a set of operations, interfaces for inputs and outputs, and a group of users with direct or indirect interactions. Systems exist in nature as well as in virtually any conceivable area of human society (Dori, 2003). We are surrounded by systems which undergo changes over time and experience some sort of evolutionary pressure. In order to formulate a system with its specifications, a complete set of updated requirements is established before delving further into the development process. Here the presumption is that, based on the specified requirements, the system would adequately serve the underlying community within its predefined life cycle. However, like any other objects or materials, the system will gradually become outdated over an extended period of time (unless any newly emerged requirements are addressed); this is due to the changes in its surrounding environment, which includes end users, groups of people involved through meetings or other common interests, their mutual interactions with other systems or exchange of information through social networks, related auxiliary or dependent systems and its type of services to the community. In the end, the system will lose its value over a period of time and it is a common fact, but unavoidable scenario, unless explicit measures are taken for re-configuring the system with new specifications. In other words, the current expiring features need to be replaced with newly emerged requirements so that it can maintain its efficacy and remain competitive in the market. Traditional systems do not have such capabilities to address emerging requirements. These systems either need to be thoroughly re-engineered, or simply replaced with a new system. Both of these options are very expensive in all aspects. With the help of a *"Wrapper system,"* if a system can identify these upcoming requirements and able to direct necessary changes into the system itself by dynamically adjusting its specifications, then it will be in a good standing to extend its life cycle, and maintain a higher level of user satisfaction through its dynamic configurations. A wrapper system is a real-time system itself; it is a carefully formulated meta-structure to address dynamic configurability. In this setup, the target system can be termed an *"Evolvable system"* which, via its adaptability, gradually makes a valuable return of investment over an extended software lifetime.

Normally, when a system is built and deployed into a production environment, it becomes very difficult to change or upgrade it. Additionally, to take down the service for maintenance or upgrade without the complete knowledge of the problem scope, is also very expensive. Several examples of these non-evolvable traditional systems are listed below:

- *Vending Machines* -- lack the ability to track purchase rates, assess current inventory and automatically notify when it is necessary to reorder. These also lack the ability to capture the underlying changing patterns of seasonal purchasing habits for that locality.
- *Microwave Ovens* -- lack the ability to assess the weight-volume of the food, and the intensity or duration of cooking, and it cannot track heating patterns of meals in a household.
- *Elevator systems* -- lack the ability to learn and communicate with other elevators, to assess load balancing, deduce operation schedules based on usage patterns and cannot notify when it is the right time for maintenance.
- *OBD Code Readers* -- lack the ability to suggest the probable cause(s) of the problem from previous history, predict any upcoming related issues, or inform the manufacturer with the estimated fault rate of certain parts so that their next model can eliminate any such issues in the future.
- *Document Management Systems* -- lack the ability to generalize the identification of input locations of data fields in the paper-based forms with the help of OCR-texts accordingly and cannot suggest probable filing destinations in the database.
- *Security System of Buildings* -- lacks the ability to identify and track object movements or sounds generated from certain areas, and to capture occupancy patterns by observing and comparing over a period of time.

Without the options for reconfigurations to meet these shortfalls, the above mentioned systems cannot be termed as evolvable systems since it will be very difficult to make necessary changes outside of their preset functionalities. Such rigid and non-configurable systems will become outdated at some point and will need to be replaced with newer versions. Otherwise, some continued laborious support will need to be provided to go on with the current settings. To avoid this, a system should be as dynamically reconfigurable as possible. It opens up a wide range of opportunities to address many emerging requirements through fine tuning specifications from any desirable perspective.

Building a system itself is not enough; the main exhaustive part emerges from the great effort to sustain and keep pace with ongoing demands. Surveys indicate that on average as much as 70% of projects software budget is devoted to maintenance activity over the life of the software (Port, 1988; Bennet, 1990). Maintenance of any system is inevitable, either to enhance the system by altering its functionality, or to adapt the system to cope with the changes in the environment; to correct newly discovered errors, or to update the system in anticipation of any future problems. Therefore, it is becoming increasingly important to consider future system maintenance activity as it is designed and developed (Ferneley, 1998).

Our area of concentration for the study of system dynamics focuses on software-driven processes in general, because they have the capability of automatically collecting system's pre-configured meta-data from various junction points in the workflow, as well as from its surrounding environment. It can also provide real-time analytics and the flexibilities in deducing meta-models for dynamic configuration of system specifications. Having a supporting sub-system can also enable the architects, designers, developers and stakeholders to have real-time snap-shots of system states. At any instant of time they can view how well the system is performing its services, examine the current workload of the system, track the history of system usage patterns, and detemine imminent changes. Moreover, it can provide clear insight into the system and collect important feedbacks and analytics for necessary changes being applied into the system. These capabilities are the *primary constituent elements* of an evolvable system. In this way, a newly built system is expected to have a way to adapt with any additional future requirements that were imperceptible at the time of initial system design. These new requirements gradually emerge by frequent and recurring usages of the system surrounded by an operating environment over a long period of time.

The primary goal here is to be able to address these newly emerged requirements and then apply them into the system already in production so that it can continue to meet the incremental needs of the end users. To implement such versatile capabilities into a system requires a set of additional supporting components that will efficiently capture detailed system usage patterns throughout its operating workflow and, implicitly collect new system requirements from users by survey agents, automated collection of system usage patterns, and random voluntary feedback over a period of time. It is vital to look for any evolutionary changes, or indications through carefully analyzing the meta-data collected from the system. The objective is to be able to reflect in its behavior any ongoing changes in the surrounding environment so that it may continue to serve satisfactorily with a high value of return in the competitive market.

In this chapter, we discuss the development efforts to identify general terms and metrics that are necessary to track a system's upcoming evolutionary phases. We present higher-level analyses of these metrics through examples of several years of systems development track history and usage data in multiple projects in order to discover any significant implications of applying new changes towards their extended system lifecycle. Based on our rigorous observation, we also derived a preliminary methodology to formulate system dynamics towards their evolution, which can be followed or modified as needed for the purpose of building evolvable systems.

2. Evolvable systems

Evolution is often an intrinsic, feedback-driven, property of a software-based system. The meta-structure (as mentioned in Section 1), within which a system evolves, contains a number of feedback relationships (we will see more details in Section 3). The organization and environmental feedbacks transmit the evolutionary pressure to yield the continuing change in the process. The rate at which a program executes, the frequency of usage, user interactions with the operating environment, and economic and social dependencies of external processes on the system in production-all these cause its deficiencies be exposed over a period of time (Lehman, 1980). Therefore, these deficiencies to eventually become newly emerged system requirements that need be addressed to ensure the sustainability of the system.

Program maintenance is generally used to describe all changes made to a system after its deployment. With maturity of software development practices, maintainability of the resulting products (i.e. software-driven systems) has become one of the most important concerns in recent years. This is because we need systems to be evolvable to avoid any failed investments. Evolutionary behavior relates to attributes of relevant software processes, their components and relevant domains or environment. Attributes (such as system size, complexity, efforts applied, and the rate of changes) reflect aspects of its evolutionary behavior. Measurement or estimation of these attributes has provided a basis for the study of software evolution dynamics (Ramil & Lehman, 1999). By classifying programs according to their relationship to the environment in which they are executed, the sources of evolutionary pressure on computer-based applications and programs can be identified (Lehman, 1980).

The dynamic evolutionary nature of computer-based applications, the software that implements them, and the process that produces, introduce the concept of system lifecycle management as a whole. In studying system evolution, the repetitive phenomena that define a lifecycle can be observed on different time scales representing various levels of abstractions (Lehman, 1980). The laws of system evolution include: (1) continuing change, (2) increasing complexity, (3) system dynamicity (which is subject to measures of system attributes that are self-regulating with statistically determinable trends and invariance.), (4) conservation of the organizational stability, and (5) conservation of familiarity (Lehman, 1980). Since they arise from the habits and practices of users and organizations, their modification or change requires involving the surrounding environment, and cross into the realm of sociology, economics and management.

Each system can evolve differently, based on the type of its functionalities, services and the way it is used or consumed by the users. Therefore, the impact of foreseeable evolutionary changes varies with the nature of the system itself. For example recurring usage cycles (eg. yearly event), continuous roll-over usages (eg. viewlist online), or aperiodic/ad-hoc usage (eg. on-demand services).

2.1 Prerequisites of evolvable system

Like the dynamic evolutionary nature of complex social networks or economic systems and the processes of their subsistence, any software-driven system should have enabling processes to sustain itself over a longer period of time. For a system to be evolvable, it needs to be more flexible in interaction with not only the end users, but also various self-contained meta-data collecting agents or data-loggers (Lehman, 1986). These might include automated survey agents, probing points, or task request history (Mubin & Luo, 2010a). Table 1 lists some of the desirable characteristics of an evolvable system.

The characteristics mentioned in Table 1 strongly suggest that there should be a wrapper system responsible for both collecting meta-data, as well as applying the desired changes. Such a wrapper system should be built in parallel to the system itself (Mubin & Luo, 2010b) with equal emphasis.

System Characteristics	Descriptions
Encourage a high-degree of user involvements	Involve users in various phases of system development life cycle (including post development activities) and deployment activities; distribute significant real-time system usage statistics to the users while using the system; present analytical summary reports at the relevant areas in the system workflow to enable users to become more aware of the dynamicity of the system components and their interactions.
Actively participate in system feedbacks	Users are informed with ongoing development and new upcoming changes, and infrequent requests for feedbacks or suggestions from them. It can also implicitly encourage them to drop few responses to very simple questions at their will, while traversing through the system workflow.
Experience of uniqueness	System is able to personalize each user's experience based on the system usage patterns from activity log; this would help a user to feel as if it is molded towards his/her own expectations from the service provider.
Ability to provide current system state	The meta-structure should be able to provide instant pictures of the system from various viewpoints. This dynamicity is also a form of self-advertisement, as it tends to attract all user groups, developers and stakeholders where they are able to view real-time results of interests; and thereby help all in the community to further promote the services in a more guided way.
Flexibility in the incorporation of new features	User is both aware of necessary changes and is engaged with the system's flexibility and openness for incorporating new adjustments in the future.

Table 1. Desirable Characteristics of an Evolvable System

3. Operational environment

Conceptual models are the means by which software intensive systems are conceived, architected, designed, and built (Dori, 2003). To realize such a conceptual model, we introduce a wrapper system that interacts with the system itself and its surrounding environment. This interaction is a great source of valuable indications about the system dynamics. A system cannot be successful unless it can effectively communicate with its environment. Therefore, it is important to establish a controlled link between the system and the environment (Lehman, 1986) and collect the interaction behavior as completely and efficiently as possible. Data should be collected from any sort of direct/indirect feedbacks, inquiries, error logs, usage patterns, and real-time analytics - all with timestamps saved into knowledgebase so that the underlying meta-structure is able to produce meaningful insights about the system's current state, performance, and any noticeable changes in the usage patterns. Cultural changes, over a period of time (in the surrounding environment) also affect how users view and perform their works and interact with other groups of users and service providers.

3.1 System reconfiguration

Systems and models are intimately related. Modeling is a set of abstract artifacts representing systems (Dori, 2003). Therefore, we can develop a meta-model while designing a system that will abstract out the system specifications by carrying over the underlying adjustable parameters. This mechanism may impose additional tasks at the developers end, and will incur further expenses; however it will open up a wide door for any future adjustments without the need for refactoring or overhauling the system. Thus, it is a valuable investment to the more contolled software maintenance activities. Such a wrapper system provides direct interactions among the system users, surrounding environment, and the service providers. This link (or communication path) enables the environmental responses on new changes that need to be applied as feedback into the system. Figure 1 shows an example of such placement of a wrapper system. A set of automated survey-agents and probing stations (Mubin & Luo, 2010a) are responsible for capturing various usage factors from the system itself (such as, access rates, feature ranks, utilization factors, path traversals), from its operational environment (such as, system users, work habits, workstations, workspaces, user feedbacks, new system requirements, user satisfaction index), and from the external environment (with influential factors).

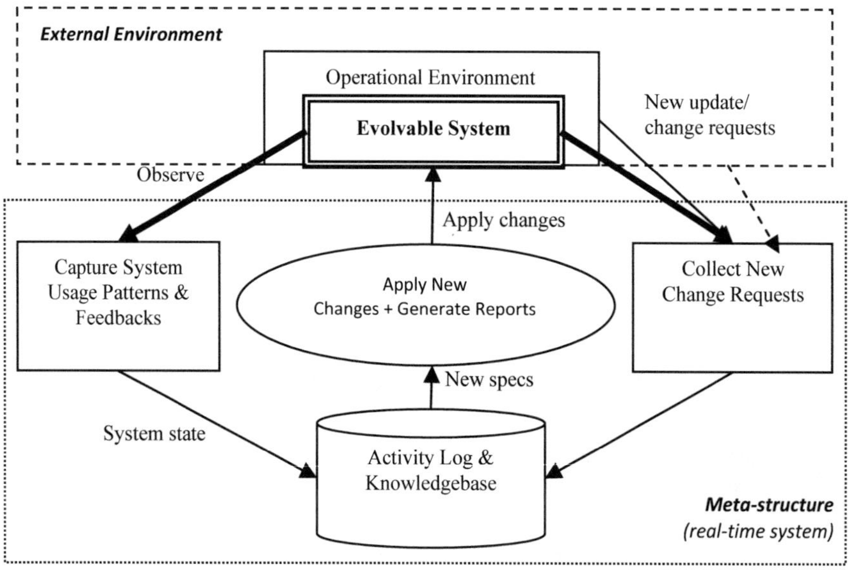

Fig. 1. Setup of a Real-Time Meta-Structure for a System to become Evolvable

3.2 Real time feedback

The feedback concept is at the heart of the system dynamics approach (System Dynamics Society); it emphasizes a continuous view that strives to look beyond regular services to see the underlying dynamic patterns. In our setup, there are four feedback loops in the proposed operational environment through the meta-structure: (1) system usage activities are observed, and quantified into utilization factors, satisfaction indices and system state; and the knowledge base identifies whether there are any noticeable changes, and instructs the application of this change into the system, if necessary. Similarly, any change or update requests from the (2) system (3) operational environment, and (4) external influences are also applied through the service queue. Thus, over a period of time, outcomes from these activities will result in the corresponding *loop dominance*, which are then traced back into the knowledge base. The responses of such a meta-structure not only depend on logical inferences, but also on the physical instant from which the outputs are produced.

4. System dynamics

The central concept of system dynamics is the idea of two-way causation or feedback (Meadows and Robinson, 2002); it is assumed that social or individual decisions are made on the basis of the *flow* of information about the system state or environment surrounding the decision makers. The decisions lead to actions that are intended to change the state of the system. New information about the system state then produces further decisions and changes. Each such closed chain of causal relationships forms a *feedback loop*. System dynamics models are made up of such loops linked together (as shown in figure 1).

In other words, system dynamics include a set of concepts, representational techniques, and beliefs that make it into a definite modeling paradigm. It emphasizes a *continuous view* (Richardson, 1999) and looks for *causality* that underlies the longer-term patterns of change in systems. Here, the focus is on the general dynamic tendencies; under what conditions the system as a whole is stable or unstable, oscillating, growing, declining, self-correcting, or in equilibrium state (Meadows and Robinson, 2002). Properties of dynamic problems contain quantities that vary over time; such variability is described by the *causality*, which influences a closed system with *feedback loops*. Thus, dynamic systems are characterized by interdependence, mutual interaction, information feedback and circular causality. Every system experiences a number of changes over time and only in keeping detailed track-records of these behavioral changes can visualize the system dynamics. Therefore, the core objective is to tool the wrapper system so that we can capture dynamic system behavior, track any change history and discover correlations, as well as analyze and act upon it for better service for end users and thereby extend the system lifecycle.

4.1 Background of dynamic system behavior

As mentioned earlier, each dynamic system should consist of one or more loops running over a period of time as a part of its lifecycle. The items that affect other items in the system but are not themselves affected by anything in the system are called exogenous items. These exogenous disturbances are seen as the triggers of system behavior. *Positive loops* tend to amplify any disturbance and to produce exponential growth: if the cause increases, the effect increases and if the cause decreases, the effect decreases. *Negative loops* tend to counteract any disturbance and to move the system toward an equilibrium point: if the cause increases, the effect decreases and vice versa. Stable conditions will exist when negative loops dominate positive loops. Non-linear relationships can cause feedback loops to vary in strength, depending on the state of the rest of the system. The dominating loop might also shift over time; linked non-linear feedback loops form the patterns of shifting loop dominance. Under some conditions one part of the system is very active, and under other conditions, another set of relationships takes control and shifts the entire system behavior; i.e. one particular loop is always responsible for the overall behavior of that system.

The timing of system behavior depends on the presence of system elements that create inertia or delays. These inertial elements are referred to as state variables (see section 4.2). Each state is an accumulation (*stock*) of information. System elements representing the decision, action, or change in a state variable are indicated by a *flow* of information to/from a state variable. Also, there could be time-delays in information flows, and we need to look for any lagged relationships in the system.

4.2 Transition of system states

A system state can be defined as a report on system status from different perspectives for an instant of time. For example, the current performance rate of the system, how well the system is doing in terms of its user satisfaction or system value, or what is the current condition at the workflow nodes in the system graph (i.e. utilization factors) and so on. By observing system states and their transitions over a period of time, we can analyze the causes behind each transition, re-assign edge probabilities in the workflow to fine tune each transition and formulate system behavior accordingly.

As explained in figure 1, after running through one or more recurring cycles during the initialization phase of a system in production, the underlying knowledge base will begin to identify the system's state of transition, in terms of its variations in system value. Based on the specific conditions or causes (such as task requests arrival rates, task completion rates, changes in user satisfaction index, or system access rates) this, in turn, will trigger a state transition and indicate whether any newly captured requirements need to be placed in the service queue. After application of these new changes into the system by the server (a process that performs the new service requests, not necessarily automatic), the wrapper-system will continue to observe the new state and will mark any changes in the system value or in the user satisfaction levels by repeating the process.

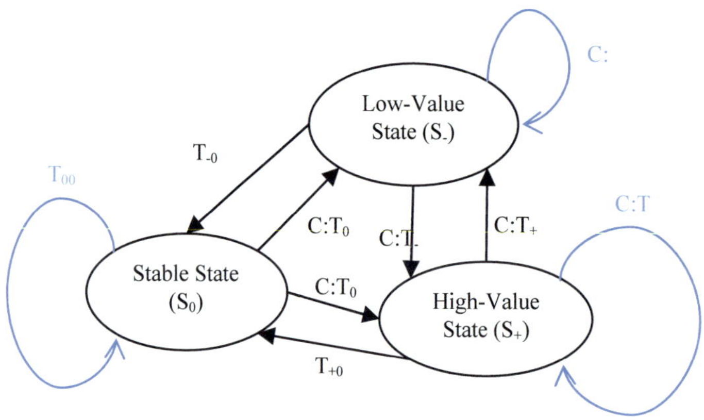

Fig. 2. Schematic diagram of an Evolvable System based on concepts of Finite State Machines

To maintain the system in a stable state (and avoid any reduction in system-value), a state-machine, as shown in figure 2, can be established to build an Ordinal Response Model (such as -2, -1, 0, +1, +2 to indicate system status and new transition) so that a state transition can be triggered to notify any inception phase of an upcoming evolution, the end of an evolutionary change or positive/negative loop dominances. There are three states of relative system value: stable state (S_0), downward or lower state (S_-), and upward or higher state (S_+). Based on this, we can deduce nine possible state transitions, labeled with combinations of $T_{[0,\,-,\,+]}$, as described in figure 2. Each transition is associated with one or more causes ($C_{T0..Tn}$). These may include task request arrival rates, task completion rates, delay in addressing requested changes due to complexity, applying new features into the system, changes in system access rates, variations in feature rank, utilization factors, etc.

The primary assumption is that the persistent dynamic tendencies of any system arise from its internal causal structure. With no causes or activities, the system will come back to a stable state. One or more causes will initiate a trigger, which in turn may cause another trigger from that point. Based on the collected data from survey-agents, probing stations and other means (Mubin & Luo, 2010a) the knowledgebase is responsible for identifying a cause in $\{C_{T0}..C_{Tn}\}$, where C_{T0} being no cause (nothing significant happened). The influential cause(s) of the transition, as well as the factor(s) in the operational environment, are archived into the knowledgebase for contextual analyses at a later point. Based on further statistical analyses of the current system and past track records each transition is associated with a *transition* probability. This may help the system avoid overshoot issues against a preset threshold value. Out of three different states, there are nine possible state transitions (see table 2) which can be mapped into an "acceptability" matrix, where each cell is a response-indicator for the current system dynamics of an evolutionary phase.

Transition due to occurrences of a set of causes, in $\{C_{T0}..C_{Tn}\}$	*Destination State*		
Begin State	Stable (S_0)	High-Value State (S_+)	Low-Value State (S_-)
Stable (S_0)	T_{00}: Okay (nothing significant happened)	T_{0+}: Good (High-yield)	T_{0-}: Bad (trigger)
High-Value State (S_+)	T_{+0}: Okay (new stable state)	T_{++}: Good	T_{+-}: Bad (trigger)
Low-Value State (S_-)	T_{-0}: Good (new stable state)	T_{-+}: Good (Ideal case)	T_{--}: Bad (trigger)

Table 2. Evaluation of State Transition Matrix for Acceptability Measure

Ideally, we would expect the system to maintain either at a stable state or at a higher-value state. However, due to environmetal factors, we cannot ensure such elevated states. Rather, the system would often experience low-value state over a period of time. Based on all system related feedbacks, new task requests, and applying new changes if a system experiences low-value state for a time period, we may need to reconfigure the meta-structure to generate a trigger. System architects, analysts and stakeholders would observe that the system runs for a while and then fine tune these speficications according to their expectations.

5. Measurement metrics for system evolution

We need to be able to instrument a system so that it becomes sensitive to any changes in software characteristics. Any appropriate measurement is a catalyst for improvement, it helps in system advancements, and improves the system's bottom line (Dekkers & McQuaid, 2002). The users' behaviors and contributions towards using a system's service(s) should be the integral measurement collected. A software-driven system's characteristics, usage and task request history, and its surrounding environment are all useful in measuring the quality and maintainability of that system (Coleman, et el., 1994). Measurements of these characteristics can be incorporated into system dynamics which can then be properly utilized as input to the upcoming evolutionary phases. It is always beneficial to outline the purpose and scope of the measurements within the context of system evolution. In addition, the metrics concerned with the measurement of an evolvable system's attributes will themselves be evolved, as needed. In addition to measuring the software itself, we would like to measure how the system impacts its users, as well as how the incremental additions to the system configurations influence the performance over a longer period of time. In summary, the set of measurement metrics are not fixed; instead it is up to the system's architect and stakeholders to pick and define any necessary metrics deemed useful upon careful observations or experimentations.

5.1 Classification of metrics

A system that meets the needs of its users will reinforce satisfaction with the major elements of that system (Ives et el., 1983). Otherwise, the system value will continue to degrade. Metrics can be used to specify what we want, to predict what we can expect to get, to measure what we've got, and to control variations between desired and actually attained values of various attributes of software products (Sherif et el., 1988). Metrics-based meta-structures help in fact-finding and process-selection decisions. At the component level, these models can be used to monitor any changes to the system as they occur, then fine tune their values. Also these help to predict fault-prone components (Coleman, et el., 1994). In other words, we can also analyze the values of metrics to generate a trigger that will indicate an inception phase of an upcoming system evolution.

For the purpose of studying system dynamics, we need to make the measurement a part of the overall development process and investigate three possible categories of metrics: (1) metrics of workflow graph, (2) metrics of system usage, and (3) metrics of development activities. The following sections discuss these classes of metrics in detail. Later in the chapter we will provide case studies on applying some of these metrics and their outcomes.

5.1.1 Metrics of workflow graph

Given any system or process, we can draw its information flow graph. The major elements in the information flow analysis can be determined at the system design time. The availability of this quantitative measure early in the system development process allows the system structure to be corrected with the least cost.

Also, by observing the communication patterns among the system components, we can define measurements for complexity, module coupling, level interactions, and stress points (Henry & Kafura, 1981). Figure 3 gives a simple example of mapping a system workflow into an equivalent graph model, with nodes (based on corresponding processes or decision points) and edges (based on the control flow paths). Hence, a general rule for mapping workflow processes, decision points and control paths can be defined by the system management team with the main objective that covers all areas with a set of nodes and edges of a graph model and apply various metrics related to graph models (such as McCabe's Cyclomatic index). Then at the junction points in the workflow, we may place data-loggers (Lehman, 1986) or, more specifically, probing stations or survey agents (Mubin & Luo, 2010a).

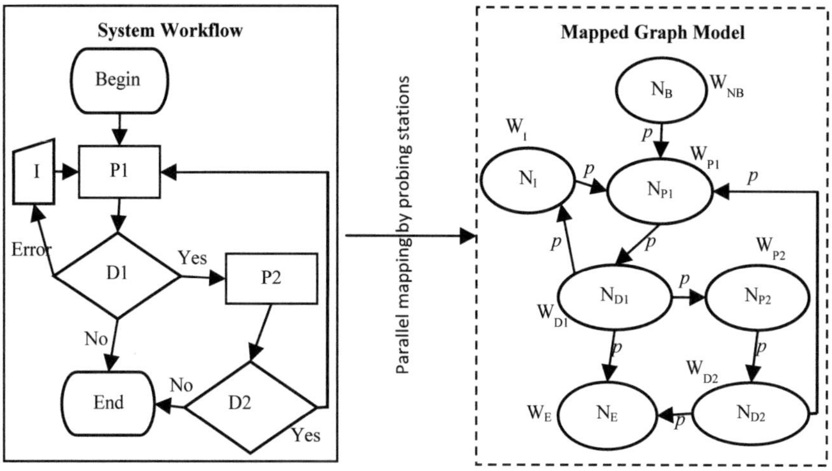

Fig. 3. Mapping of system workflow into an equivalent graph model with transition probabilities and process weights

5.1.2 Metrics of system usage

From the mapped model, we can now introduce a set of system usage metrics to help assess system dynamics. As denoted in the figure 3, each node (N_i) is assigned with a weight (W_{Ni}) calculated from its constituent set of features. A node may or may not contain components with features of concerns. If not, the weight will be zero. The chance of traversing through an edge from one node to another is based on the desired usage patterns and branching factors from which the initial probabilities (P_E) are assigned. The functionality of a process may be assigned a Feature Rank (FR_i), which is based on its significance of contribution into the service provided by the system as defined by the stakeholders and its expected usage frequency. Feature Utilization (FU_i) is the number of times a feature is actually used within a predefined usage cycle. A feature may be more under-utilized than expected, or over-utilized. The User Satisfaction Index or USI (Mubin et el., 2009) is a quantitative indicator of the overall satisfaction of using the system during a predefined time frame. With the combination of USI's for all groups of users, we may deduce a quantitative system value and compare it against other metrics for overall assessment of system evolution. As mentioned earlier, for an evolvable system measurement metrics should be configured in a way so that they can be re-adjusted or fine tuned as needed.

Suitable weights for nodes (i.e. different components or characteristics) can be assigned based on how important it is in the overall system evaluation metrics. For example, the functionality, reliability, usability, and efficiency of a system can be assigned weights 4, 4, 3 and 2, respectively. Here, weight value measures from 1 (poor) to 4 (high) (Jeanrenaud & Romanazzi, 1994). In a similar way, for any desired set of metrics we may use ordinal values for generating indexes. We need to identify whether a feature is being over-utilized or under-utilized than expected by the system architect or analyst. Increased value of a Feature Rank may be due to its over-utilization. Thus, it will impact on USI and on system's overall value. Similarly, decreased value of a Feature Rank could be from the under-utilization and will impact on the USI and system value, as well.

Class	List of Metrics	Description
1. Metrics from Graph Model	Weight of Edge	Probability that the sustem user or control flow will visit this path while using the system, E_N = p (path traversal)
	Weight of Node	$W_N = \sum_{i=0..m} \{ (FR_{Ni} * FU_{Ni}) / (\sum FU_{0..N})\}$, where m is number of features in this node's (N) equivalent process in the system
	Work-flow Nodes & Interconnections (Mubin & Luo, 2010a)	• Decision Nodes $\{D_i\}$ have one or more output branches that end up in a sub-process $\{P_i\}$ • Probing Stations $\{PS_i\}$ mark each branching areas and collect contextual data • Feature Rank $\{FR_i\}$ is an index and can be calculated in a way that is suitable for the architects to assess the utility of a certain feature or component of the system • Interconnection rules: $D_i \rightarrow \{PS_{1..n}\} \rightarrow P_j$ ………… (1) $P_i \rightarrow \{FR_i\} \rightarrow D_i$ ………… (2) • Branching Factor (%), based on rule (1) and (2) mentioned above • Locality of Change-requests: Map of change request areas in the system work-flow
2. System Usage Metrics	Feature Utilization	FU is the usage frequency of system features in the workflow tree
	Feature Rank	$FR_{i+1} = FR_i + \{(FU_{i+1} - FU_i) / FU_i\}$, where, FR_0 is assigned as mentioned in table 1, and $FU_0 = 0$; i indicates previous run cycle.
	System's overall value, SV	$SV = \sum_{i=1..n} \{(USI_i * f_i) / \sum_{j=1..n} f_j \}$, where n is the number of users in the system, and f_j is the number of cycles completed by user j.
3. Development Activity Metrics	Task Requests, TR	Average Inter-arrival time Frequency of Task Arrivals Task Request Priority Tasks in Multi-project environment (out-of-scope)
	Task Completion (or Service) Time, TC	Frequency of Task Completions Wait-time/ Idle-Time/ Latent-Time Service-Time & Deployment-Time Allocated time for a task in multi-project environment (out-of-scope)
	Task Complexity	Complexity = f(service-time, priority, USI-change, man-hour, nature of task)
	System State	A system's state can be viewed from different perspectives; and can give absolute, abstract or recurring metrics.

Table 3. System metrics necessary for managing evolvable systems

5.1.3 Metrics of development activities

In addition to system usage metrics, we also need to focus on the metrics that will help track all sorts of system development activities such as; new change requests, requests to add new features in a system component, and task completion rates based on the environment setup described in Section 3. Depending on the system's functionalities, we need to deduce a specific set of metrics to drive the meta-structure (wrapper-system) in the surrounding environment of the system so that its knowledgebase will be able to generate necessary supporting configurations to guide the subsequent evolutionary phases and provide appropriate suggestions for applying new changes and analyzing the changing patterns throughout the system lifecycle. Table 3 lists a summary of these sets of metrics.

In order to find comparative measurements of metrics so that we can visualize the impact of system dynamics we apply normalization and then plot the normalized measurements against each other.

5.2 Indicator metrics

Mapped nodes in the graph model are either processing nodes or decision nodes (figure 3). Decision paths reflect how the users are making choices and thus directly impacts on "Edge Probabilities", based on the variations in Edge Probabilities the analysts may decide to rearrange the workflow in favor of currently used paths thus changing the branching factors as well as the underlying graph model.

Probing stations can collect node visit frequencies which will identify the popularity of workflow locations and, more specifically, certain features of the system. Feature Utilization (FU) frequency directly impacts the feature's rank. Variations in the rank are major indicators in identifying any redundant components (for elimination), under-utilized features (may need advertisements) and over-utilized features (that need to be efficient). With the changing rank in features each node's weight will vary. For certain nodes with no significant features the weight will eventually be reducded to zero and will have no contributions in the system value.

User satisfaction index (USI) reflects the outcome experience of a user or a group of users. A declining USI is a driving force to initiate major revisions into the system to meet newly emerged requirements. Overall system value is something that the stakeholders, architects, analysts and developers keep their eyes on. Based on the type of services provided they will derive a composite formula or index that best describes a system's overall performance at a particular instant of time. For example, a highly significant feature may yield a lesser system value during low usage activity for that cycle time.

5.3 Dependencies of metrics

It is beneficial to categorize system metrics into dependent and independent metrics. There should be clear precedence relationships among the dependent metrics in terms of their logical ordering of causes, events or development activities. If necessary, such dependencies can be artificially manipulated by associating one or more attributes such as priority level, task complexity, urgency, service queue re-ordering, etc. For example, priority of a certain activity can be put to a halt if a new higher priority activity arrives in the service queue. In general, we can establish a set of primary measures from which other attributes could be derived. That is, having recorded the primary measures associated with a given process, one could reconstruct evolutionary behavior depicted by them and by secondary measures where the later could be obtained by some combinations of the primary measures (Ramil & Lehman, 1999).

6. Evolutionary phases

An evolutionary phase is a transition from the current state of the system configuration to the next stage with newly system features applied into the system. There could be major changes or simple minor adjustments. System architects and stakeholders may pre-set the threshold on defining the degree of "evolutionary phases" specific to a system's functionalities or services provided to the end users. As a simple example of a one-dimensional measure the receipt of X or greater number of "feature-adding" task-requests within one cycle will trigger an inception phase and prepare for an upcoming evolution. The number X can vary based on the type and service of the underlying system. Such measures can be made composite to incorporate other necessary measurement metrics.

6.1 System evaluation

A solid framework should be established that collects all necessary metrics for the purpose of system evaluation as a prerequisite to the study of system evolution. According to the ISO 14598 (1999) "Information Technology - Software Product Evaluation," there are four phases that the evaluation process should follow: (1) requirements, (2) specification, (3) design and (4) execution. We can classify and rearrange system metrics to cover these areas in the right order and then the underlying meta-structure will collect and generate system evaluations for any instant of time, as described in figure 1. System evaluation should have the flexibility to include new measures as it passes through evolutionary phases.

6.2 Evolutionary factors

It is critical to observe the system within the operational environment over a period of time to identify and derive possible causes or key evolutionary factors covering the system dynamics. For this purpose we need to capture emerging requirements, shifts of usage patterns, changing service retention policies, changes in satisfaction levels (or composite system values), changing influences from the surrounding environment, and so on. Collectively, the comparative analysis of the metrics within each cycle with the knowledge base will suggest necessary system evolution. It is the responsibility of the system architect or analysts (along with stakeholders) to devise their own policies and threshold measures for determining the trigger for the next evolutionary phase. Over a period of time the knowledgebase will have sufficient historical data for generating a system's dynamic specifications (in terms of configuration values, development stages, changing patterns, and timing) to address the requests for newly desired features in the system. The process of system evolution itself may be generalized for the repeating evolutionary phases observed over a period of time. This will help to *predict* further evolutions.

7. Implications of updating or applying new changes

Empirical evidence has suggested a relationship between the application of design measurements and future software maintainability (Grady, 1994). Establishing a meta-structure with a repository of historical measures of various metrics provides in depth analytics for software maintainability. Such a meta-structure serves as a link between the system users' needs and the developer team's activities for both system development and process improvements. Understanding the reasons for variability in the data provides a powerful decision tool. Naturally, real data will have variations. Efforts need to be given to understand the causes of variations in the collected data sets. Since any positive process improvement changes deliver better positive results the objective here is to improve the process and thereby maintain system value at higher level.

Newly added desirable features requested by system users or added by the developer team should nominally add value to the system. Therefore, such activities raise the level of overall satisfaction in user expectations. Evaluation of the track history of development activities within a system usage cycle can be captured through the changing rates of accumulating task completions compared with the cumulative system values. These cumulative system values may a composite estimation that is based on the accumulation of changes in identified USIs, superimposed with system access rates, for example

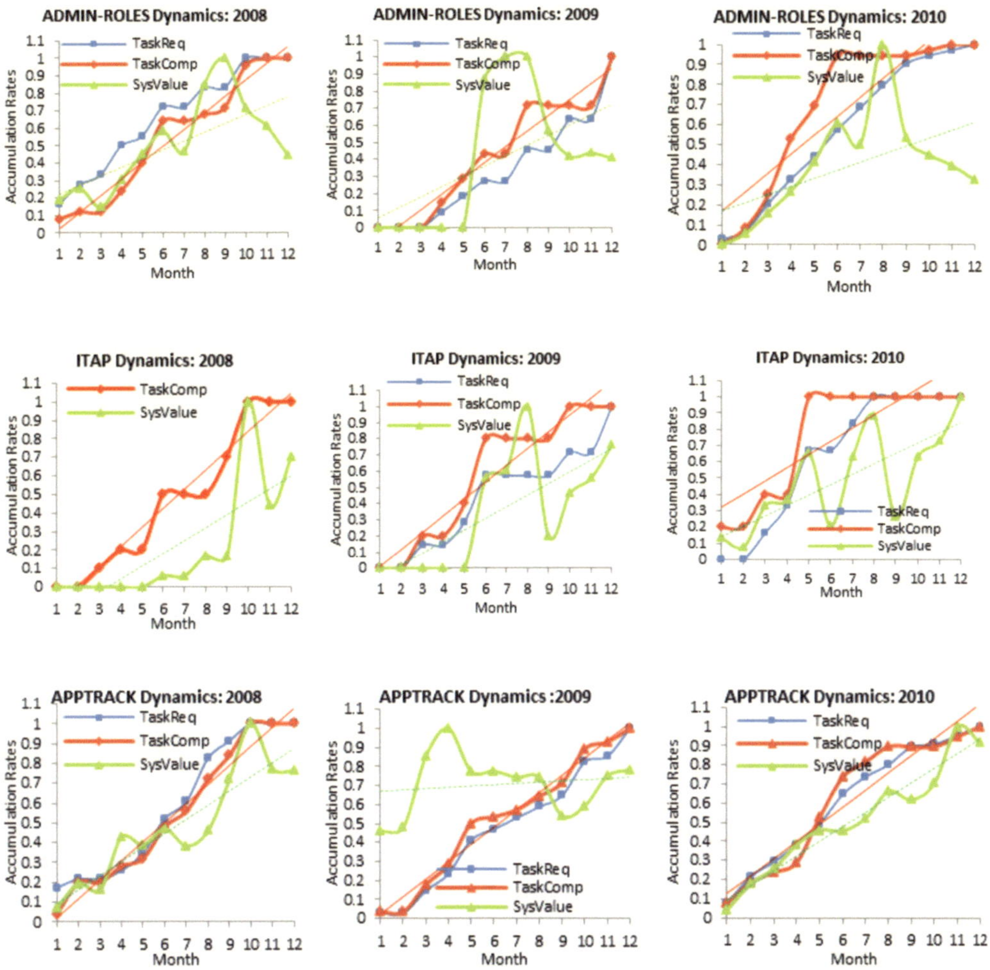

Fig. 4. Identifying possible state transitions in various systems from intersecting points within a yearly cycle

For example, figure 4 shows the *normalized* data plots (for side-by-side comparison) of the last several years for three development projects for a university administrative office. These are illustrated by different services: **ADMIN-ROLES** (to manage graduate administrative roles across the campus), **ITAP** (registration and scoring system for international teaching assistant program) and **APPTRACK** (a sub-system to manage graduate applications data online). ADMIN-ROLES and APPTRACK are moderate sized projects that run throughout the year. ITAP is a comparatively smaller sized project with seasonal usage patterns.

Referencing the state diagram mentioned in figure 2, we can compare the variations in the system value (as the state transitions T_i in the matrix) throughout the yearly cycle. We use the changing values of accumulating Task Requests or Task Completion rates as the underlying cause, because Task completion rates have a more direct impact on the users and overall system values. We have also generated the trend lines to observe the significance of the intersecting points (see figure 4), as well as their regression analyses in table 4.

ADMIN-ROLES					
Year	R2	sERR	sigF	p-V	Correl.
2000	0.507	0.194	0.009	0.009	0.713
2009	0.369	0.333	0.036	0.035	0.608
2010	0.593	0.179	0.003	0.003	0.769
ITAP					
Year	R2	sERR	sigF	p-V	Correl.
2000	0.707	0.185	0.001	0.001	0. 841
2009	0.656	0.218	0.001	0.001	0.810
2010	0.459	0.233	0.015	0.015	0.677
APPTRACK					
Year	R2	sERR	sigF	p-V	Correl.
2000	0.877	0.103	0.000	0.000	0.936
2009	0.027	0.165	0.606	0.606	0.165
2010	0.837	0.121	0.000	0.000	0.915

Table 4. Regression Analyses: Task Completion (TC) vs. System Value (SV)

7.1 System assessment

By selecting significant metrics, developers may derive their own system value that best reflects the current condition of the system state based on the type of services and its influence in the surrounding environment. We calculated the system value (SV) as a composite metric of system access rates with the accumulating perceived USI changes that emerged due to task completions over a yearly cycle. Higher demands for system usage should put more values in SV. Ideally, we'd expect a transition of T_{++} due to expected positive impact of any incremental development activities. However, the scenario is often not the same for real data sets.

In comparing the accumulating rates of task completions (TC) with the rate of variations in system value (SV) in normalized plots (as shown in fig. 4), first we are interested in the intersecting points indicating that TC and SV have the same rates. Second, for the segments between the intersections, our focus is on the transition of SV. As described in the following sections we see wide variations in the patterns for different projects in respective plots.

7.1.1 Assessment of ADMIN-ROLES

Although ADMIN-ROLES is a yearly usage system (with roll-over), higher activities are concentrated during the months of August and September. We noticed that there were four intersecting points in 2008 where the SV transitions occurred between the segments were T_{+-}, T_{++}, T_{-+} and T_{+-}, respectively. The causes $C_{1..n}$ include the access patterns and the perceived changes in USI values over a year. At the intersecting points, the rates are the same and ideally we would expect the same rate of change in both TC and SV. However, due to various environmental factors both of these metrics vary and their patterns change during the segmented time frame. Moreover, the projected trend lines intersecting in 2008 and 2009 yearly cycles indicate the instability in system state. But, in 2010 there were no intersections with increasing disparity between TC and SV. Regression analyses in table 4 shows close ties between TC and SV in 2008 and 2010 and incidcates environmental disturbances in 2009.

7.1.2 Assessment of ITAP

ITAP has seasonal usage patterns, and showed a scenario rather parallel activities. Brief intersections occured where the transition pattern was T_{+-} in that segment. During the last three years, the trend lines did not intersect at all and TC > SV was maintained across these years. The regression analyses in table 4 also support the consistent and stonger connections between TC and SV.

7.1.3 Assessment of APPTRACK

APPTRACK also has a rolling usage patterns. Again, regression analyses shows close ties between TC and SV in 2008 and 2010 and incidcates either environmental disturbances or large changes in usage patterns in 2009.

In summary, thorough analyses of a carefully designed set of relevant metrics, as well as the underlying development track history, open up many possible experiments for closely studying system dynamics over a period of time. Upon maturity, these metrics of measurements would form the foundation for developing futher statistical models to drive a set of tools for managing evolvable systems.

8. System usage patterns

One of the basic patterns that we would like to know is how frequently a system is being used or accessed over each cycle (with sufficiently long periods between cycles). Then if we can compare this for several consecutive cycles, we can capture more details on how the behavior is changing over a period of time along with possible causes. For example, figure 5 demonstrates such activities over the last four years. If we closely observe the changing patterns we can summarize that ADMIN-ROLES has had *horizontal shifts,* meaning that users have changed their habit of system usage time over the yearly cycle even though the overall access volume remained same. For APPTRACK we see that there had been *vertical shifts* over the last several years indicating that the system has become more/less popular. For GTA-WS and ITAP systems, there are clear signs of seasonal activities that repeat over each yearly cycle.

These access rates can be superimposed with the accumulated USI values that are related to applying new changes into the system. This would represent a more meaningful output of overall system values as demonstrated in figure 4. We present another example of system usage patterns that compares the actual usage versus the expected usage patterns. As proposed in figure 3, we can assign the probabilities of using certain features in the workflow paths. Figure 6 demonstrates such mapping of partial workflow paths of the system ADMIN-ROLES. Initially we would expect that under normal circumstances, a user may take one of the five possible options (so 0.2 is the probability to access one option). Then at the next level (from *Node4* to *Node4.1*), there is just one possibility with probability 1.0; and from Node4.1 there are three options with probability 0.33 probability each.

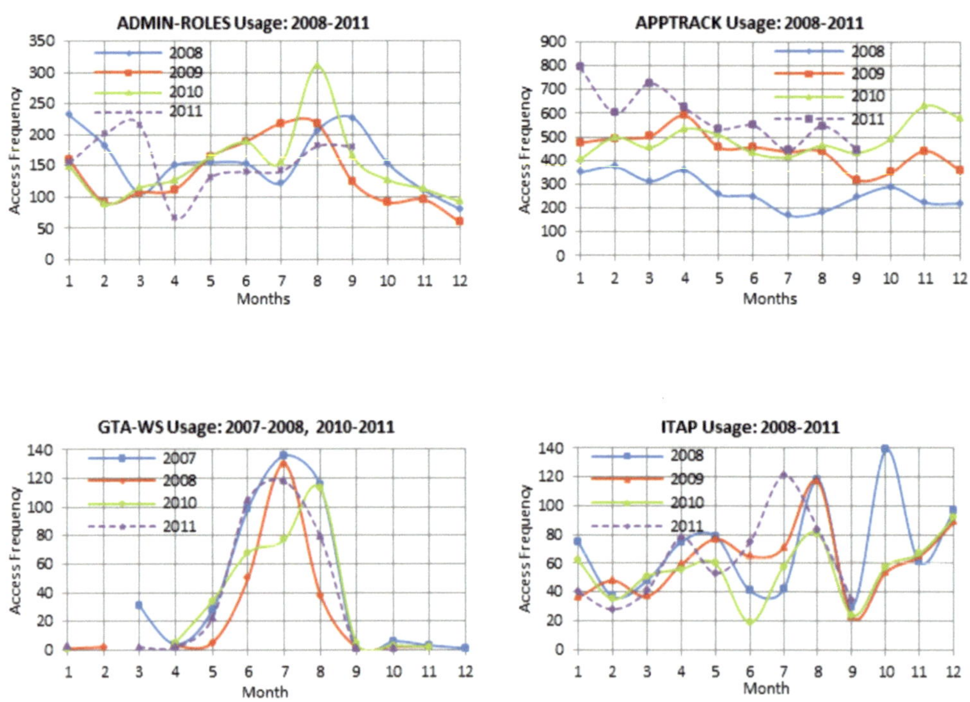

Fig. 5. Various patterns of system access frequencies

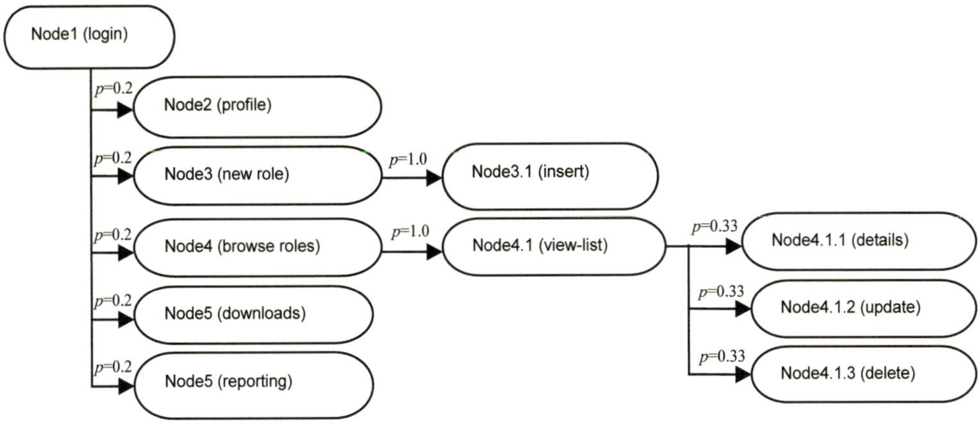

Fig. 6. Example of a mapped graph of partial workflow nodes in ADMIN-ROLES

Therefore, the chance of utilizing feature of *Node4.1.2* will be, p=0.2 x 1.0 x 0.33 = 0.066. Figure 7 compares the scenario for three activities; ACT_INS, ACT_UPD and ACT_DEL.

As we can see from the regression analyses (see table 5), there are close correlations between the actual usage patterns and the expected usage patterns. This experiment reveals that our expected usage pattern of ACT_UPD is almost 8.7 times higher, although the relative usage rates coincide with each other. (Notice the R^2, *p*-Value and Correlation for this activity in table 5). For ACT_INS and ACT_DEL the outputs look correct in terms of estimations. Therefore, the result suggests that in order to achieve the expected system behavior we need to adjust the pre-assigned probabilities to these three leaf nodes in the graph.

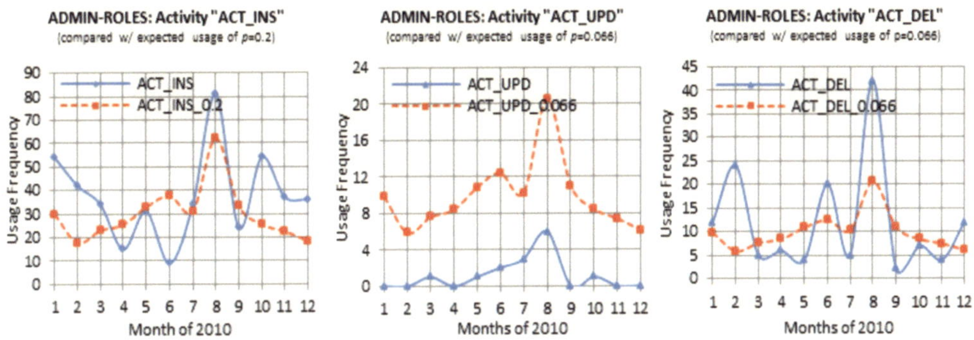

Fig. 7. Usage activities of specific features comparing to estimated probabilities

ADMIN-ROLES	R^2	sERR	sigF	p-Value	Correlation
ACT_INS	0.2066	0.1745	0.1375	0.0243	0.4546
ACT_UPD	0.7529	0.3415	0.0002	0.0000	0.8677
ACT_DEL	0.4149	0.0812	0.0237	0.0002	0.6441

Table 5. Regression Analyses three ADMIN-ROLES Features

In summary, we may follow these experiments to calibrate the processes, thereby adapting the values of multiplicative constants, probabilities, etc. to the empirical data for the environment of our particular system. However, over a longer period of time the environment itself may change significantly. Therefore, these calibrated values need to be reviewed and re-adjusted recurringly as the system evolves over time.

9. Formulating system dynamics as a process

Implementing an effective measurement program as a meta-structure of its parent system is a big challenge. And overcoming these challenges is worthwhile, because such measures provide insights into the system behavior. Such implementation also improves the ability to plan and track systems evolutionary progress and needed for addressing risks/problems much earlier (Clark, 2002). Therefore, we need to have an underlying methodology that can be applied to formulate a process for evolvable systems. Typically this would include the study and observation of selected set of metrics, development track history, changes in usage track history, and so on. In the previous sections of this chapter, we attempted to explain the necessary elements of such a process in detail. Although the resulting evolution of software mostly appears to be driven and controlled by human decisions, managerial edict and developer's judgement, yet a high-level generalized pseudo code for such a process can be developed, as presented in fig. 8. This is in conformance with the system dynamics approach suggested by Richardson (Richardson, 1999).

10. Benefits & limitations

System dynamics methods recognize that the real-world is a non-linear web of feedback processes with significant delays and is usually not in equilibrium. We can seek the causes of problems by the interactions of real-world feedback loops. System dynamics provides a way-of-thinking (a paradigm) and associated communication and software driven tools to help design policies that provide durable solutions to pressing problems. Capturing a system's dynamic behavior has a number of significant benefits that include a clear insight into the system, increased control over maintaining and upgrading the system, the capability for better and more timely services, lower maintenance cost, and the ability to progressively maintain satisfactory system outcomes. Therefore, the user retention rates are often high. In addition, the supporting meta-structure also tends to provide significantly more controlled administration and higher manageability towards building reconfigurable systems. Any additional data that can be generated by the meta-system can be utilized further toward supporting or providing credence for additional experts' opinion. It can help us better understand how a problem grew up over time and assist us in finding a long-lasting solutions to the problem.

The vital observations of system update requests and usage activities, as described in this chapter, depend on a number of factors. These include: the operational environment, groups of users performing similar functions within a somewhat common time frame, any relevant external influences on the work environment, and the functionality of the system itself.

```
Status SystemDynamics(SystemSpecifications-Initial)
BEGIN
        WrapperSystem ← SetupMetaStructure(SystemSpecifications-Initial)
        ThisSystem ← SystemConfiguration(WrapperSystem) // dynamically configure the system
        System_Initialization(ThisSystem)
        BEGIN
                // in tabular format, collect the complete system workflow paths
                SystemControlFlowPath ← GetControlFlow(ThisSystem)
                // prepare equivalent graph model from the system with initial weights
                SystemGraph ← GenerateGraphModel(SystemControlFlowPath, Node_Weights,
                Edge_Values)
                // environment setup: System Usage
                Setup_Probing_Stations(SystemControlFlowPath, SystemGraph)
                // environment setup: collect update/change requests
                Setup_TaskActivity_Stations(SystemControlFlowPath, TaskRequest_Template,
                TaskCompletion_Template)
        END
        // interconnect the flow with feedback loops (circular causality)
        WHILE (System is running)
        BEGIN
           FOR EACH [TIME-CYCLE] IN System-Lifecycle
           BEGIN
                // get dynamic system behavior and state (feedback loops)
                sysState ← GetSystemState(TimestampNow)
                sysUsage ← GetSystemUsage(TimestampNow)
                sysTasks ← GetSystemTasks(TimestampNow)
                // formulate model: identify stock (or accumulations) & info flows (rates)
                Knowledgebase ← Record_System_Dynamics(sysState, sysUsage, sysTasks)
                // get system status for evaluation
                SystemStatus ← SystemEvaluation(Knowledgebase, TimeStampNow)
                SWITCH (SystemStatus)
                BEGIN
                        CASE "EVOLUTION":
                                PrevSpecs ← SystemSpecifications-Initial
                                // derive policy insights
                                NewSpecs ← GenerateNewSpec(Knowledgebase)
                                Apply_New_Changes(PrevSpecs, NewSpecs)
                                // save changes resulting from model-based updates
                                Knowledgebase ← Record_New_Changes(PrevSpecs, NewSpecs)
                                // recursive call
                                RETURN SystemDynamics(NewSpecs)
                        CASE "INCEPTION":
                                Prep_Inception_Phase(Knowledgebase, ThisSystem)
                        CASE "SYSVALUE_INC": // save data on incremental SV
                                thisINC ← Generate_Change_Report(Knowledgebase,
                                prevCHANGE,    TimeStampNow)
                                thisCHANGE ← thisINC
                        CASE "SYSVALUE_DEC": // save data on declining SV
                                thisDEC ← Generate_Change_Report(Knowledgebase,
                                prevCHANGE, TimeStampNow)
                                thisCHANGE ← thisDEC
                        CASE "NOCHANGE": continue loop
                END SWITCH
                Prep_Next_Iteration(Knowledgebase)
           END FOR
        Prep_Next_Cycle(ThisSystem, SystemSpecifications-Revised)
        END WHILE
        RETURN SystemStatus
END
```

Fig. 8. A high-level pseudo-code for a generalized process of system evolution

Although the majority of systems fall under these scenarios, there are a number of other classes of systems where a meta-structure either cannot be established or the establishment of such a structure would be cost-prohibitive. For these classes of systems, such evaluations may not support the discovery of system behavior or impact based on updated request history.

In addition, many systems will not allow suggested changes to be applied until the system is shut down for some prolonged period of time. Thus, frequent update requests will not be possible. In addition, due to time, money or manpower restrictions, many developers may not venture through setting up such a closely coupled meta-structure within the surrounding system environment.

11. Conclusion

We can think of the meta-structure attached to the system itself as a measurement program. There is a growing awareness that such systems pay off but not without some investment of both time and resources. As the benefits of applying meta-models become more evident, the establishment of such structure will become more essential for evolvable systems to retain their value to a satisfactory level and to remain competitive in the market. With the growing experiences and maturing systems, multi-dimensional data will become available for further research. This, in turn, will make it possible to develop better models. Although it is typically too costly to run carefully controlled experiments on capturing meta-data covering the entire development cycles, it is definitely worth the investment for any long-running systems. Certain meta-level system development practices must be established so that we can fully understand the system, manage it in a more cost-effective way, and readily adapt to a changing environment. Although our proposed model does not cover every aspect, it opens up a wide range of options for the system architects or stakeholders to deduce their own sets of metrics and to utilize these measures to fine-tune systems to extend their lifecycles. Eventually, the systems being instrumented to support software evolution will become more complex with higher capabilities to configure themselves with more feature-rich services. Thus, a growing proportion of resources will continue to be needed for maintenance of these systems.

12. Future research

Building evolvable systems is a considerable challenge and undertaking the issues of developing evolvable systems and then formulating methods to maintain their extended life-cycles are quite large and time consuming initiatives. Given this, some future research on the selected areas of system evolution can be outlined as follows:

- Automated ways to to update system objects, processes and codes needs to be investigated further
- In-depth studies of psychological impact on USI during each system upgrade will help refine the calculation of system value and focus on the influential evolutionary factors only. (Halstead's effort metrics and Cyclomatic complexity of workflow graph can be used to predict psychological complexity)
- Applying further statistical analyses (such as vector and velocity measures for comparing TC and SV curves, applying differentiation on the system value, etc.) on the accumulated historical data in the knowledgebase will direct accurate prediction of evolvable cycles by imposing probabilities at the state-transition points.
- Applying proper design patterns to probing stations and survey agents across the workflow will make the overall process more mature and reconfigurable.
- Because each update request needs to be addressed and implemented into the system, a corresponding queuing server model for more complex multi-project development environment can be built based on queuing theories.

- Each system will need initialization time to configure itself and fine-tune with correct parametric values - thus a novel approach needs to be sought to generalize the initiation process with necessary delay at each the inception phase of evolution.

13. Acknowledgement

We express our sincere gratitude to the Dean's Office of The Graduate School at The University of Alabama for supporting the underlying infrastructure of servers, development tools and the systems development track history records.

14. References

Bennet, K. H. (1990), *An Introduction to Software Maintenance,* Information and Software Technology, 32(4)

Clark, B. (2002). *Eight Secrets of Software Measurement,* IEEE Software, September/October 2002

Coleman, D.; Ash, D.; Lowther, B.; Oman, P. (1994), *Using Metrics to Evaluate Software System Maintenability,* IEEE Computer, August 1994.

Dekkers, C.; McQuaid, P. (2002). *The Dangers of Using Software Metrics,* IT Pro, March/April 2002, IEEE

Dori, D. (2003), *Conceptual Modeling and System Architecting,* Communications of the ACM, October 2003, 46 (10).

Ferneley, E. H. (1999), *Design Metrics as an Aid to Software Maintenance: An Empirical Study,* John Wiley & Sons, Ltd.

Grady, R. B. (1994), *Hewlett-Packard - successfully applying software metrics,* IEEE Computer, 27(9)

Henry, S.; Kafura, D. (1981). *Software Structure Metrics Based on Information Flow,* IEEE Transaction on Software Engineering, Vol. SE-7, No. 5, Sep. 1981

Ives, B.; Olson, M.; Bardoui J. (1983), *The measurement of User Information Satisfaction,* Communications of the ACM, 26(10), October 1983

Jeanrenaud, A.; Romanazzi, P. (1994). *Software Product Evaluation Metrics: A methodological approach,* Transaction on Information and Communications technologies

Lehman, M. (1980), *Programs, Life Cycles, and Laws of Software Evolution,* Proceedings of the IEEE, 68 (9), Sep. 1980

Mubin, A.; Luo, Z. (2010a), *Low Overhead and High Yield Integrated Surveys,* Proceedings of ACM SIGUCCS Fall 2010

Mubin, A.; Luo, Z. (2010b), *Building a Reconfigurable System with Integrated Meta-Model,* Proceedings of International Multi-Conference on Engineering and Technological Innovation 2010

Mubin, A.; Ray, D.; Rahman, R. (2009), *Architecting an Evolvable System by Iterative Object Process Modeling,* Proceedings of IEEE and World Congress on Computer Science and Information Engineering (CSIE), 2009.

Port, O. (1988), *The Software Trap – automate or else,* Business Week, Special Report, 9(1)

Ramil, J.; Lehman, M. (1999), *Challenges facing Data Collection for Support and Study of Software Evolution Process,* ICSE 99 Workshop on Empirical Studies of Software Development and Evolution

Richardson, G. (1999), *System Dynamics* (in Encyclopedia of Operations Research and Information Science), Kluwer Acadmics Publishers

Sherif, Y. S.; Ng, E.; Steinbacher, J. (1988), *Computer Software Development: Quality Attributes, Measurements, and Metrics*, John Wiley & Sons, Inc.

System Dynamics Society: http://www.systemdynamics.org

3

Schedulability Analysis of Mode Changes with Arbitrary Deadlines

Paulo Martins[1,2], I. G. Hidalgo[2], M. A. Carvalho[2], A. de Angelis[2], V. Timóteo[2], R. Moraes[2], E. Ursini[2] and Udo Fritzke Jr[3]
[1]*Chaminade University*
[2]*Universidade Estadual de Campinas (UNICAMP)*
[3]*PUC Minas*
[1]*USA*
[2,3]*Brazil*

1. Introduction

Modern real-time systems are required to operate in complex applications and dynamically adapt to a wide range of changes in the environment. One strategy that allows the implementation of these systems in complex scenarios is the partitioning of their applications into modes of operation. Flexibility of operation is achieved by having the system execute in several modes of operation and undergo transitions between modes in response to external or internal events. A mode of operation can be seen as a specific configuration of the computational resources that is optimal for the operational phase that the system executes. As conditions in the environment change, resource allocations may become inadequate. Therefore, the system must reconfigure itself through a mode change, reallocating its resources in an efficient manner. A classic example of modes lies in the area of aviation where most aircraft undergo at least three basic modes of operation: take-off, level-flight, and landing modes. Having the system designed with a single mode of operation does not explore the fact that some operations, and thus resource usage, are mutually exclusive. The allocation of all these resources, as if they could be needed at the same time, leads to inefficiency. More importantly, the resulting system is not scalable. The so called "*all-modes-in-one*" system is usually feasible for simple systems with limited functionality.

Flexible modal real-time systems must guarantee by means of schedulability analysis that all tasks complete before their deadlines. Current literature in schedulability analysis for mode changes requires that all task deadlines are less than or equal to the tasks periods (Pedro & Burns, 1998; Real & Crespo, 2004). Allowing task deadlines to be less than task periods is useful for many real-time applications (Tindell et al., 1994). However, in some real-time applications an instance of a task is allowed to arrive before its previous invocation has finished. In such case the task can be delayed until its previous invocation terminates.

This chapter extends the current schedulability analysis associated with mode changes in static priority pre-emptive based scheduling. In particular, it derives analysis that includes tasks executing across a mode change with deadlines larger than their period (arbitrary deadlines).

The rest of this chapter is organized as follows: section 2 elaborates on the concept of modes. We include a number of current views of modes and provide a working definition. In section 3 we introduce the computational model and assumptions. In section 4 we address previous work on modes in real-time systems. The schedulability analysis of mode changes with arbitrary deadlines is then derived in section 5. Section 6 shows an example of the applicability analysis. Finally, in section 7 we present our concluding remarks.

2. Definition of modes

The discussion on the concept of modes of operation appears more comprehensively in the literature of human-computer interaction and human-automation interaction (aviation and cockpit design). Modes have been commonly associated with the idea of functions, states, behavior, and schedule, depending on the research field. In real-time systems, since most work involving modes focus on the schedulability analysis of mode changes, this discussion has been limited.

The most widespread notion of modes is related to functionality. One example is the work in safety-critical systems by Papadopoulos (1996): a mode is defined by the *"set of active functions that the system is prepared to deliver while operating in that mode"*. As modes represent functions, they may be arranged hierarchically. This is due to the fact that functionality can be refined down to lower level functions, leading to a hierarchical graph of the functional space. Another example is given by Norman (1981): *"Every control system that can perform a variety of functions has modes: the more functions, the more modes."*

In human-computer interaction and interfacing, modes are seen as *special states*. Howe (1997) remarks that *"a mode is a general state, usually used with an adjective describing the state"*. They are states that are extended over time and with some specific activity being carried out. Interface modes are defined by Tesler (1981) as *"a state of the user interface that lasts for a period of time. It is not associated with any particular (display) object and has no role other than to place an interpretation of operator input "*. According to Poller & Garter (1984), modes are the application's interpretation of the user's input. Therefore, a mode change occurs whenever there is a change of the interpretation of the same inputs.

In human-automation interaction (e.g. aviation psychology and cockpit interface design), modes are described as behavior of a certain component of the system, such as the interface. In particular, Degani et al. (1999) describe a mode as *the manner of behavior of a given system*. A system may have multiple mutually exclusive ways of behaving. Each behavior is defined by the system's input, output, and states. A mode change consists of an evolution from one pattern of behavior to another as a function of time. Transitions between modes are triggered by events in the environment: the way such systems behave reflects the transformation of the environment (Degani & Kirlik, 1995).

In the literature of real-time systems modes have been regarded as a collection of tasks, or schedule (e.g. Real (2000); Tindell, Burns & Wellings (1992)). For Fohler (1994) a schedule is a set of processes or messages (literally a *collection of objects*), characterized by its inherent timing parameters. These objects may have access to a shared resource according to a pre-defined policy. A mode change is a change in the task set, by means of replacement, addition or removal of tasks.

In computer science in general, modes have been described by the executable code or program (downloaded or memory resident) that is active under execution. Therefore, any change in the executable code reflects a change in the operational mode. A mode has also been regarded as the configuration of the system during a particular phase of operation, meaning how different system resources may be physically or logically arranged. For example, as noted by Degani et al. (1999): *"we define a mode as a machine configuration that corresponds to a unique behavior"*. A system may dynamically change its configuration in order to achieve a better performance. A classic example is load balancing in distributed systems, where reconfiguration is achieved through process migration.

From the definitions above, we can summarize the idea of a mode of operation as the system's behavior while executing a given schedule. The notion of behavior is used to address modes when dealing with the higher levels of abstraction of a real-time system, such as the application or the interface design. Function and performance are two fundamental components of the behavior of a real-time system. A real-time system delivers a function with a certain performance attribute attached to it. A change either in the functionality or in the performance of the system characterizes a change in behavior. A change in behavior is noticed by changing the performance level while keeping the functional set, or likewise by changing the functional set while keeping the systems' performance. Taking these remarks into consideration a mode can be comprehensively defined as follows (Martins & Burns, 2008):

"A mode of a real-time system is defined by the behavior of the system, described by a set of allowable functions and their performance attributes, and hence by a single schedule, containing a set of processes and their timing parameters".

Clearly, the definition of a mode depends upon the field of application and the level of abstraction considered. At the lower levels of abstraction of a real-time system, the notion of a single schedule is suitable to define a mode, since we are interested in applying schedulability analysis to guarantee the predictability of the real-time system. Nevertheless, the idea of schedule very often is a too low-level concept, and therefore devoid of meaning when addressing the end user application concerns. Therefore, as we are searching for a comprehensive definition of modes for real-time systems, we also associate our definition of modes with the idea of behavior. The behavior of the system is bounded to a restricted set of operations that it is allowed to perform when it executes in a specific mode. It constrains the actions that the system is not ready to deliver while in that mode. It also constrains the behavior that the system may exhibit. Unlike states, a mode does not limit its variable values directly. It may be regarded as the system's behavior resulting from its execution through a progression of states. Nevertheless, it is not always possible to map a group of states to a particular mode. Whereas in simple systems the modes and states can be more easily associated, in a complex real-time distributed system it may be difficult (and perhaps not necessary) to related both. Therefore it ensues, from the above definition of modes, that a change from a source mode A to a target mode B occurs in response to the need to change the system's functionality or adjust its performance. We adopt the following definition for a mode change of a uniprocessor system (Martins & Burns, 2008):

"A mode change of a real-time system is defined as a change in the behavior exhibited by the system, accompanied by a change in the scheduling activity of the system."

Many real-time systems in fact run a fixed task set. Processes executed in mutually exclusive modes are treated as if they could run at the same time, and grouped into a single schedule. Consequently, resources have to be allocated as if they could be requested at the same time, although this is an impossible scenario. This approach may be appropriate for simple real-time systems. However, for large and complex real-time systems this may result in significant reduction in efficiency of the system and sub-utilization of system resources. From a software engineering perspective, this approach denies the principles of modularization and separation of concerns, since it allows unrelated modes (and unrelated schedules) of a system to be treated and designed as if they were instead a single mode and schedule, although they may be logically independent, mutually exclusive or both.

3. Computational model and assumptions

We shall consider a set of periodic or sporadic tasks $\tau = \{\tau_1, \tau_2, ...\tau_i, ..\tau_p\}$ per mode. Each task τ_i is characterized by the tuple $S_i = \{T_i, D_i, C_i, P_i\}$, where: 1) T_i and D_i are respectively the period of task τ_i (or, if a sporadic task, the minimum inter-arrival time between successive tasks of the stream i) and the deadline; 2) C_i is the worst-case execution time (WCET) of the task τ_i. This value is deemed to contain the overheads due to context switching. Moreover, the values of C_i, D_i and T_i are such that $C_i < D_i \leq T_i$. In subsection 5.2 we remove the restriction that $D_i \leq T_i$; 3) P_i represents the priority of task τ_i , assigned according to the Deadline Monotonic Scheduling algorithm.

Throughout this chapter, we use the notation $C_{i(O)}$,$C_{i(A)}$ and $C_{i(N)}$ when referring to the worst-case computational time of an old-mode completed task, an aborted task, and a new-mode task, respectively. τ_i denotes a task for which we are finding the worst-case response time (WCRT) and τ_j denotes a higher-priority task. We use the term *steady-state analysis* to refer to the body of schedulability analysis of single-mode systems, where the task set is fixed and there are no mode changes. We also use the notation:

- $\forall\ \tau_{j(O)}\ hp\ \tau_i$: set of old-mode tasks τ_j with priority higher than task τ_i;
- $\forall\ \tau_{j(A)}\ hp\ \tau_i$: set of aborted tasks τ_j with priority higher than task τ_i;
- $\forall\ \tau_{j(N)}\ hp\ \tau_i$: set of new-mode tasks τ_j with priority higher than task τ_i.

The mode-change model is based on the following assumptions:

- Tasks are executed in a uniprocessor system;
- Tasks are not permitted to voluntarily suspend themselves during an invocation (so, for example, tasks are not allowed to execute internal Ada-like delay statements);
- There are fixed task sets before and after the mode change;
- The worst-case response time of a generic task τ_i (WCRT), denoted R_i, is the longest time ever taken by that τ_i from the time it arrives until the time it completes its required computation;

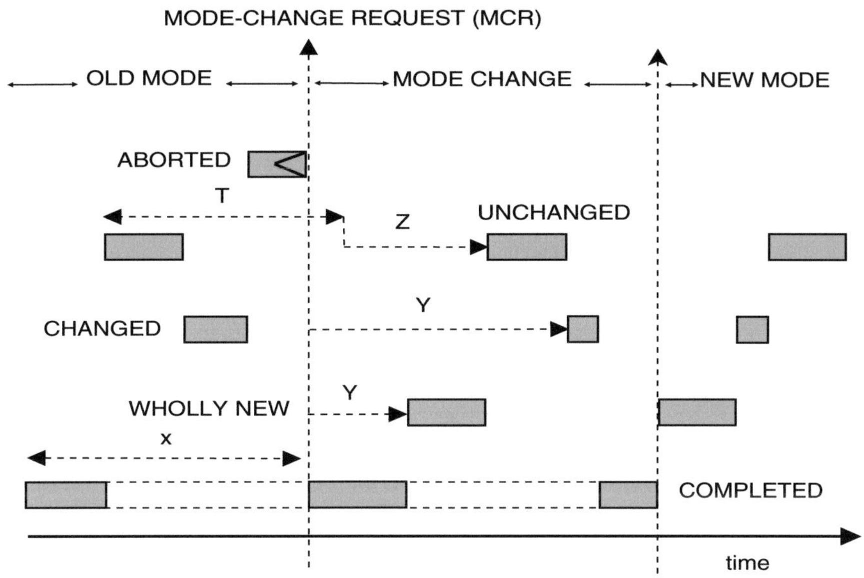

Fig. 1. Mode-Change Model (Pedro, 1999; Real & Crespo, 2004)

- Tasks are scheduled with time offsets during the mode change only. This time phasing between tasks may or may not hold after the mode change.

A *mode-change request (MCR)* is the event that triggers a transition from an old mode of operation to a new one. The window x is the phasing between the MCR and the activation of task τ_i. A MCR may not be preempted by another MCR. The mode-change model comprises of five types of tasks (Fig. 1):

- *Old-mode completed tasks,* $\tau_{i(O)}$: These tasks are released in the old mode, i.e. before the arrival of the MCR. They need to advance their execution into the transition window in order to finish execution. Old-mode completed tasks cannot be simply aborted as they would leave the system in an inconsistent state. Once they complete during the transition, there are no further releases. They are used to model the behavior of the system in the old mode that is no longer needed in the new mode.
- *Old-mode aborted tasks,* $\tau_{i(A)}$: These tasks are also released prior to the MCR. They need to be immediately discarded after the MCR in order to release allocated resources back to the system. The behavior they implement is no longer needed in the new mode of operation.
- *New-mode changed tasks,* $\tau_{i(C)}$: These tasks are released during the transition, with an offset Y from the MCR. This class models the behavior that is changed in the new mode. Changed new-mode tasks have a modified timing parameter compared to their corresponding old-mode version, such as changed worst-case execution time (C), period (T), or priority (P).
- *New-mode unchanged tasks,* $\tau_{i(U)}$: These tasks are released during the transition window, with an offset Z, from the end of the period of their corresponding old-mode version. They model the behavior of the application that is not changed across the mode change and in the new mode. Their timing parameters are the same as the preceding old-mode version.

- *Wholly new task*, $\tau_{i(W)}$: These tasks are released during the transition window with an offset Y. They are used to model the behavior that is totally new, i.e. has no equivalent in the old-mode of operation.

With respect to the way tasks are executed across a mode change, they are classified as: 1)Tasks with mode-change periodicity: these tasks are executed across the mode change and maintain their activation pace, and 2) Tasks without mode-change periodicity: these tasks do not preserve their activation pace across a mode change.

The mode-change latency is usually an important performance criterion when dealing with mode changes. We often seek to minimize the latency since during the mode change the system may deliver only partial functionality at the expenses of more critical services. The mode change latency is defined as:

"A window starting with the arrival of the mode-change request (MCR) and ending when the set of new-mode tasks have completed their first execution and the set of old-mode tasks have completed their last execution".

In the following section we review background work on schedulability analysis of mode changes using the fixed-priority preemptive scheduling approach.

4. Background

A number of mode-change protocols have been proposed and classified into synchronous or asynchronous protocols. Synchronous mode-change protocols complete the old-mode tasks before any new task start execution. Synchronous protocols do not require schedulability analysis. On the other hand, asynchronous protocols allow new-mode tasks to begin execution while old-mode tasks are still running. Asynchronous protocols may reduce the mode-change latency, but may have reduced schedulability, since the processing load is larger. These protocols do require schedulability analysis, since old-mode tasks will interfere with the execution of new-mode tasks and vice-versa.

Two types of mode-change protocols can be defined regarding the way unchanged tasks are executed: 1) Protocols with periodicity are protocols where unchanged tasks preserve their activation pace or periodicity. Under these protocols, tasks are executed independently of the mode change in progress; 2) On the other hand, the activation of unchanged tasks may be delayed by protocols without periodicity. Their rate of activation is affected by the transition. The loss of periodicity may be necessary to guarantee the feasibility of the mode change or to preserve data consistency.

The *idle time protocol* (Tindell & Alonso, 1996) delays the execution of any *MCR* until an idle time, where there is no CPU load (activity). It is a simple, synchronous protocol. A mode change task detects the idle time and performs the mode change, by suspending all old mode tasks and activating the new mode ones. The disadvantage is the delay in waiting for the idle time, especially when there may be new-mode tasks with short deadlines waiting to be executed.

The *maximum period offset protocol* (Bailey, 1993) delays all tasks for the time corresponding to the period of the least frequent task in both modes. Being a synchronous protocol, it has the advantage of simplicity, and the fact that is does not require schedulability analysis. The disadvantage of this protocol is its poor promptness, with an even larger mode-change delay than the idle time protocol.

The *minimum single offset protocol* (without periodicity) (Real, 2000) applies an offset Y to all new mode tasks. The offset is the sum of the worst-case execution time of all old-mode tasks that have been released (but not completed) before the arrival of the MCR. This protocol also suffers from poor promptness, but incurs in less mode-change latency compared to the maximum period offset protocol, since all the old-mode tasks execute only once.

The *minimum single offset protocol* (with periodicity) (Real, 2000) similarly applies an offset Y to all new mode tasks. The offset is large enough to accommodate the old mode tasks and all unchanged tasks that need to preserve their periodicity. The disadvantage of this protocol is poor promptness, which is worse than the previous protocol. The protocol is also synchronous and dispenses schedulability analysis.

In the *asynchronous mode-change protocol with periodicity* presented by Tindell, Burns & Wellings (1992), old-mode tasks are allowed to complete their last activation upon the arrival of a MCR, but are no longer released during the mode change. The mode-change model does not include aborted tasks. Wholly new tasks are released after a sufficient offset Y after the MCR. New-mode changed tasks are released right after the end of the period of the corresponding old-mode task. Because only wholly new tasks can be introduced with an offset, the ability to make any transition schedulable is reduced.

Pedro & Burns (1998) introduced an asynchronous protocol without periodicity, which included aborted tasks in the mode-change model. Considering that in this protocol all new-mode tasks can have offsets, it is relatively easy to find a schedulable transition. The schedulability analysis is relatively simplified compared to that of Tindell, Burns & Wellings (1992), since the number of time windows to analyze is lower than in the previous protocol.

Real (2000) proposes an asynchronous protocol with periodicity that merges the advantages of the last two protocols. The mode-change model is similar to that of Pedro & Burns (1998). Nevertheless, an offset Z is introduced for unchanged tasks, relative to the end of the period of the corresponding old-mode task. An offset $Z = 0$ means that the unchanged task is introduced immediately after the end of the period of its corresponding old-mode version. The inclusion of this offset allows the desired periodicity for unchanged tasks. However, when the task set is unschedulable, it is possible to lose periodicity in order to gain schedulability by increasing the value of Z.

5. Schedulability analysis of mode changes

In the following subsection we review previous work on mode changes with deadlines less than or equal to periods, before we relax this constraint.

5.1 Mode changes with deadlines less than or equal to periods

We must find the WCRT for both old-mode tasks and new-mode tasks defined in the mode-change model. We first consider analysis for the old-mode task set. The analysis gives exact (both necessary and sufficient) bounds on the worst-case response time of each task.

5.1.1 Analysis of old-mode tasks

Old-mode tasks suffer the interference from higher-priority aborted tasks before the mode change, and from higher-priority completed tasks before and after the mode change (Fig. 1). During the mode change, old-mode tasks are also preempted by higher-priority new-mode tasks. Clearly, there is no interference from aborted tasks during the transition. We now show the interference terms for each type of task.

5.1.1.1 Interference from higher-priority old-mode completed tasks

Old-mode, higher-priority completed tasks τ_j will interfere with task τ_i mostly over the interval x. This interference extends to the mode-change window as the higher-priority tasks still run in order to complete their execution. The total interference is formulated as the ceiling function of x/T_j as follows:

$$I_{hp(O)} = \sum_{\forall\, \tau_{j(O)}\ hp\ \tau_i} \left\lceil \frac{x}{T_j} \right\rceil C_j \tag{1}$$

5.1.1.2 Interference from higher-priority aborted tasks

Aborted tasks will interfere over a lower-priority task τ_i during the interval x. Within the interval x there is an integral number of periods T_j of the higher-priority aborted task τ_j, and therefore a set of instances that complete their execution. It is only the last release that runs across the *MCR* and has to be aborted. The interference from completed releases of task τ_j before the *MCR* is given by:

$$\sum_{\forall\, \tau_{j(A)}\ hp\ \tau_i} \left\lfloor \frac{x}{T_j} \right\rfloor C_j \tag{2}$$

We also need to consider the amount of aborted execution time of a higher-priority task in the old mode: This occurs during the remaining time w_{rem}, which is a fraction of the period of the aborted task preceding the *MCR*, and is given by:

$$w_{rem} = x - \left\lfloor \frac{x}{T_j} \right\rfloor T_j \tag{3}$$

The *remaining time* w_{rem} can be large enough to: 1) allow only a partial execution of the task τ_j (equation (4)), since $w_{rem} < C_j$, or 2) accommodate an additional execution of the higher-priority aborted task (equation (5)), since $w_{rem} \geq C_j$):

$$0 < x - \left\lfloor \frac{x}{T_j} \right\rfloor T_j < C_j \tag{4}$$

$$C_j \leq x - \left\lfloor \frac{x}{T_j} \right\rfloor T_j \leq T_j \tag{5}$$

In the first case (eq. 4), $w_{rem} < C_j$ and the interference is the minimum value between C_j and w_{rem}, since there is only a partial execution of the aborted task (i.e. $I_{hp(A)rem} = \min(w_{rem}, C_j)$.

In the second case (eq. 5), $w_{rem} \geq C_j$ and there is another full execution of the task within w_{rem}: it is not really necessary to abort the task. The remaining time is greater than C_j but less than the period. Again the interference is the minimum value between C_j and w_{rem}. Once the task completes there is no further releases in the remaining time. Therefore, the amount of interference is C_j. In any case, the partial interference is always the minimum of the intervals w_{rem} and C_j. Therefore, the amount of partial (or aborted) interference is given by:

$$I_{hp(A)rem} = \min\left(x - \left\lfloor \frac{x}{T_j} \right\rfloor T_j, C_j \right) \tag{6}$$

Combining both terms (6) and (2), the total interference from higher-priority aborted tasks is:

$$I_{hp(A)} = \sum_{\forall \tau_{j(A)}\ hp\ \tau_i} \left(\left\lfloor \frac{x}{T_j} \right\rfloor C_j + \min\left(x - \left\lfloor \frac{x}{T_j} \right\rfloor T_j, C_j \right) \right) \tag{7}$$

5.1.1.3 Interference from higher-priority new-mode tasks

Higher-priority new-mode tasks do not preserve their mode-change periodicity. The analysis must account for the fact that these tasks are released with an offset Y_j from the MCR. Their interference interval is therefore reduced to $w_i - x - Y_j$ and expressed as:

$$I_{hp(N)} = \sum_{\forall \tau_{j(N)}\ hp\ \tau_i} \left\lceil \frac{w_i - x - Y_j}{T_j} \right\rceil_0 C_j \tag{8}$$

5.1.1.4 Interference from higher-priority unchanged new-mode tasks

As discussed in section 3, unchanged new-mode tasks preserve the mode-change periodicity. This term is derived by Real & Crespo (2004), and given by:

$$I_{hp(N)\_per} = \sum_{\forall \tau_{j(U)}\ hp\ \tau_i} \left\lceil \frac{w_i(x) - \lceil \frac{x}{T_j} \rceil T_j - Z_j}{T_j} \right\rceil_0 C_j \tag{9}$$

Combining all the interference terms, we obtain the total interference suffered from the old-mode task τ_i across the mode change:

$$I_{mc} = \sum_{\forall \tau_{j(O)}\ hp\ \tau_i} \left\lceil \frac{x}{T_j} \right\rceil C_j + \sum_{\forall \tau_{j(A)}\ hp\ \tau_i} \left(\left\lfloor \frac{x}{T_j} \right\rfloor C_j + \min\left(x - \left\lfloor \frac{x}{T_j} \right\rfloor T_j, C_j \right) \right) + \sum_{\forall \tau_{j(N)}\ hp\ \tau_i} \left\lceil \frac{w_i - x - Y_j}{T_j} \right\rceil_0 C_j + \sum_{\forall \tau_{j(U)}\ hp\ \tau_i} \left\lceil \frac{w_i(x) - \lceil \frac{x}{T_j} \rceil T_j - Z_j}{T_j} \right\rceil_0 C_j \tag{10}$$

By adding the Worst-Case Execution Time (WCET) C_i of the old-mode task being analyzed, we obtain the *WCRT* of task τ_i as follows:

$$w_i(x) = C_i + \sum_{\forall\, \tau_{j(O)}\ hp\ \tau_i} \left\lceil \frac{x}{T_j} \right\rceil C_j + \sum_{\forall\, \tau_{j(A)}\ hp\ \tau_i} \left\lfloor \frac{x}{T_j} \right\rfloor C_j + \min\left(x - \left\lfloor \frac{x}{T_j} \right\rfloor T_j, C_j \right) + \sum_{\forall\, \tau_{j(N)}\ hp\ \tau_i} \left\lceil \frac{w_i - x - Y_j}{T_j} \right\rceil_0 C_j + \sum_{\forall\, \tau_{j(U)}\ hp\ \tau_i} \left\lceil \frac{w_i(x) - \lceil \frac{x}{T_j} \rceil T_j - Z_j}{T_j} \right\rceil_0 C_j \quad (11)$$

The solution to equation (11) is obtained by forming a recurrence equation on w_i, to find the smallest positive integer that satisfies it. Since many values of x give the same WCRT, the significant values of x are the ones that lead to new values for the ceiling and floor functions. The set of significant values x is the set of all positive values in the domain of $w_i(x)$ such that:

$$x\ \epsilon\ (0, \epsilon, T_j + \epsilon, 2T_j + \epsilon, 3T_j + \epsilon, ..R_i^{ss})\ \forall\ \tau_{j(O)}\ hp\ \tau_i \text{ and}$$
$$x\ \epsilon\ (0, C_j, T_j + C_j, 2T_j + C_j, ..R_i^{ss})\ \forall\ \tau_{j(A)}\ hp\ \tau_i \quad (12)$$

where ϵ is the time quantum, which we assume to be 1 and R_i^{ss} is the steady-state WCRT of task τ_i.

5.1.2 Analysis of new-mode tasks

In the worst-case scenario, all old-mode tasks are released momentarily before the mode change, thus sharing a critical instant with the window w_i. The interference from higher-priority new-mode tasks upon a new-mode task τ_i must account for the offset of the interfering task, during which there is no interference. The interference from unchanged new-mode tasks must account for the offset Z_j, from the end of the period of the preceding old-mode version. The worst-case response time of a new-mode task across a mode change is given by: (Pedro & Burns, 1998; Real & Crespo, 2004)

$$w_i = C_{i(N)} + \sum_{\forall\, \tau_{j(O)}\ hp\ \tau_i} C_j + \sum_{\forall\, \tau_{j(N)}\ hp\ \tau_i} \left\lceil \frac{w_i - Y_j}{T_j} \right\rceil_0 C_j + \sum_{\forall\, \tau_{j(U)}\ hp\ \tau_i} \left(C_j + \left\lceil \frac{w_i - T_j - Z_j}{T_j} \right\rceil_0 C_j \right) \quad (13)$$

This equation must also be solved using recurrence relation as before. Considering that task τ_i is released with an offset Y_i after the mode change, then to obtain the value of R_i window w_i must be decreased by Y_i:

$$R_i = w_i - Y_i \quad (14)$$

If the expression $w_i - C_{i(n)} \leq Y_i$ holds, the amount of interference over new-mode task τ_i is smaller than the value of its mode-change offset Y_i. Therefore, the new-mode task τ_i is released in the steady state after all old-mode tasks have completed.

We now turn to the analysis of tasks across a mode change with arbitrary deadlines.

5.2 Mode-changes with arbitrary deadlines

Lehoczky describes qualitative analysis which can determine the worst-case response time of a given task with such arbitrary deadlines (Lehoczky, 1990). Tindell et al. (1994) derived analysis from that of M. & Pandya (1986) and using the approach of Lehoczky, for static priority pre-emptive systems that permit tasks to have arbitrary deadlines, release jitter, and behave as sporadically periodic tasks. His analysis illustrates how using a window approach to finding worst-case response times for these tasks is an appropriate way of obtaining an analysis tailored to the behavior of real-time tasks. In single mode, steady-state systems, the busy period $w_{i,q}$ for a task τ_i with arbitrary deadlines is calculated as follows (Tindell et al., 1994):

$$w_{i,q} = (q+1)C_i + I_{hp} \tag{15}$$

Where the term I_{hp} is the interference from higher-priority tasks, and q is the number of instances of task τ_i during the *busy period*. Equation 15 is the basis to extend current analysis of mode changes to allow arbitrary deadlines. Therefore, for the analysis of mode changes with arbitrary deadlines, we need to: 1) review the notion of busy period in the light of mode changes, specifically the definition of the beginning and end of the busy period; 2) find the number of instances q of a task τ_i to be analyzed, and 3) determine the amount of interference from higher-priority computation (I_{hp}), as follows:

- *Busy periods*: A *level-i* busy period is defined as *the maximum time for which a processor executes tasks of priority greater than or equal to the priority of task τ_i*. Lehoczky shows how the worst-case response time of a task τ_i can be found by examining a number of busy periods, each starting at an arrival of task τ_i (hence some multiple of T_i before the current invocation of task τ_i). The busy period ends when a lower-priority task is able to begin execution. To find the worst-case response time, all invocations of task τ_i in this busy period must be examined. In Fig. 2 task τ_i completes when the given busy period finishes, but arrives at some point in time after the start of the busy period. By knowing the width of the busy period and when the busy period starts (relative to arrival of task τ_i) then we can find the corresponding response time. The width of the busy period is equal to the higher-priority computation that is released in it. The WCRT of task τ_i is the longest of the response times corresponding to each of the examined busy periods. In the next section we discuss the beginning and end of the busy period regarding a mode change.
- *Number of instances to analyze*: If a task has a $WCRT$ greater than its period, then the possibility exists for a task to re-arrive before the previous invocation has completed. In this case we assume that the new arrival is deemed to have a lower priority, and is therefore delayed from executing until after the previous invocation terminates. Fig. 3 illustrates the response time of a task τ_i, with its deadline larger than its period, executing across a mode change as an old-mode completed task. The MCR arrives during the execution of an arbitrary invocation of task τ_i. To facilitate the analysis we assume, without loss of generality, that the MCR arrives while the third invocation of task τ_i is under execution. In a busy period without a mode change, the 4th and 5th invocations are released and execute regularly. However, with the arrival of a MCR, the 4th and the 5th invocations do not need to be released anymore, according to the mode-change model. The cancellation of both the 4th and the 5th releases will shorten the length of the busy period, causing the lower-priority task (*task low*) to begin execution earlier. Therefore, we need to apply the

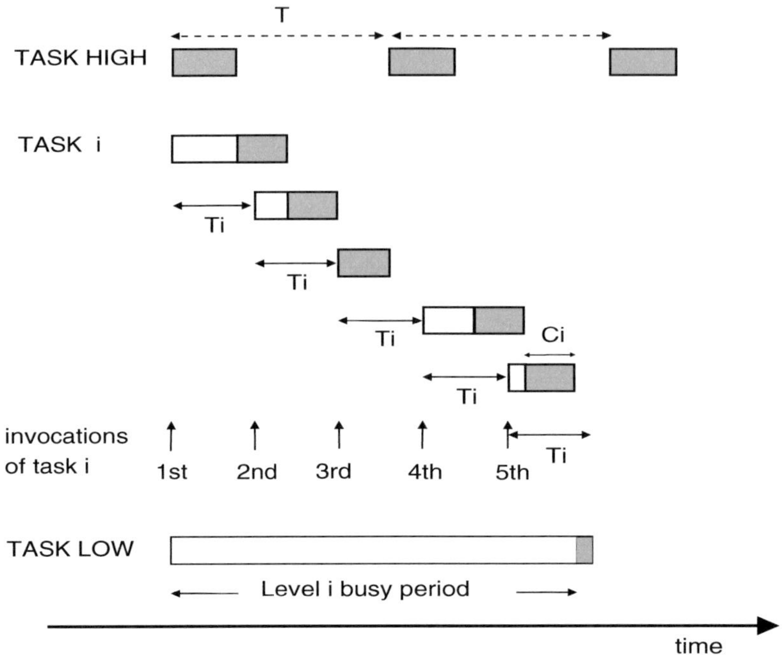

Fig. 2. A level *i* busy period (Lehoczky, 1990), (Tindell et al., 1994)

schedulability analysis only for the first three invocations. However, it is only the third invocation that needs to be analyzed using mode-change analysis. The first and second invocations can be analyzed using the steady-state equations derived by Tindell et al. (1994).

- *Higher-priority interference*: Fig. 2 also illustrates a higher-priority unchanged task (T_{high}). Clearly, other types of tasks such as wholly new and changed new-mode tasks may interfere with the execution of task τ_i. While an invocation of T_{high} may be delayed by a previous invocation, the number of instances of T_{high} interfering with task τ_i is not affected by the introduction of arbitrary deadlines. Therefore, the calculation of higher-priority computation under the assumption of arbitrary deadlines remains the same as the one from previous work (Real & Crespo, 2004).

We now look at the analysis of old-mode tasks.

5.2.1 Analysis of old-mode tasks

We begin by extending the notion of busy period for old-mode tasks: *A level "i" busy period for an old-mode task across a mode change is defined as the maximum time for which a processor executes tasks of priority greater than or equal to the priority of task. A busy period begins at a time x before the arrival of a mode-change request (MCR). The busy period ends during the transition, with the completion of the last invocation q of task τ_i before the steady-state new mode, when a lower-priority task is able to begin execution.*

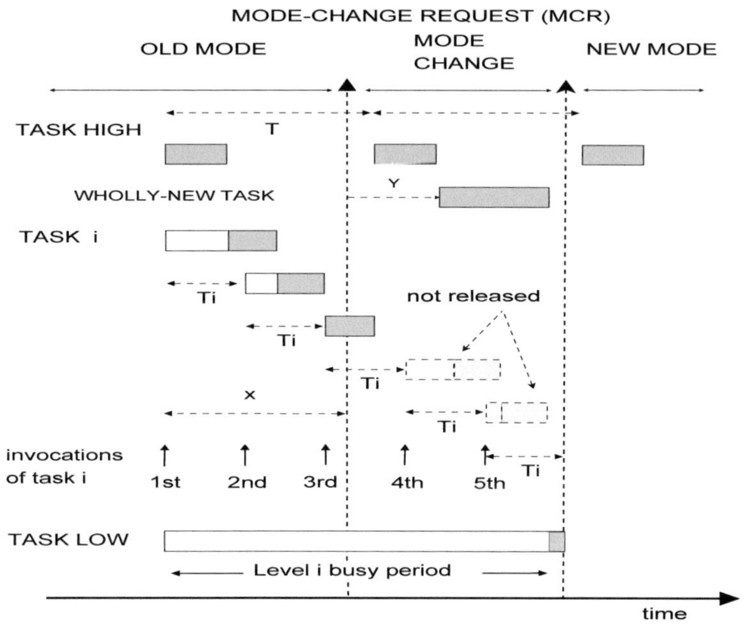

Fig. 3. Mode-Change with Arbitrary Deadlines

From the definition of latency of mode changes (section 3), it follows that the end of the busy period falls inside the mode-change window. This is because task τ_{low} is an old-mode completed and the mode change is not over until all the old-mode tasks have completed.

Consider the three instances of task τ_i before the *MCR* in Fig. 3. Instances 1 and 2 are called the steady-mode instances, since they are released and completed before the *MCR*. We are interested in finding the *WCRT* for the third instance, the *old-mode completed instance*, which runs across the *MCR* and executes through the mode change. When the old-mode completed invocation begins, the steady-mode invocations have already completed. Therefore, their schedulability is guaranteed by steady-state analysis (Audsley et al., 1993).

By defining the beginning and the end of the busy period as above we can reuse the work from Pedro & Burns (1998) and Real (2000) by including in their analysis the multiple *WCET*s introduced by the steady-mode releases (i.e. previous invocations of task τ_i) during window x. In our example, the third invocation is delayed by the first and second invocations.

There are no further releases of the old-mode completed task after the *MCR*, according to the mode-change protocol. As we increase the value of x in the analysis, more steady-state invocations of task τ_i appear before the *MCR*, potentially delaying the old-mode completed task τ_i. The impact of a mode change on the analysis of old-mode tasks is that there are less releases of task τ_i to be analyzed than in steady-state analysis. The number of instances q of task τ_i that need to be analyzed before the mode change is given by:

$$q_i = \left\lceil \frac{x}{T_i} \right\rceil \qquad (16)$$

and it is only the last invocation that requires mode-change analysis. The interference suffered by the mode-changing task includes the types of tasks from the mode-change model, i.e. old-mode aborted, old-mode completed, new-mode changed, unchanged and wholly-new tasks as previously analyzed. Taking these remarks into consideration, the analysis of a mode-change for an old-mode task with arbitrary deadlines is given by:

$$w_i(x) = (q+1)C_i + \sum_{\forall\, \tau_{j(O)}\ hp\ \tau_i} \left\lceil \frac{x}{T_j} \right\rceil C_j + \sum_{\forall\, \tau_{j(A)}\ hp\ \tau_i} \left(\left\lfloor \frac{x}{T_j} \right\rfloor C_j + \min\left(x - \left\lfloor \frac{x}{T_j} \right\rfloor T_j, C_j \right) \right) +$$

$$\sum_{\forall\, \tau_{j(N)}\ hp\ \tau_i} \left\lceil \frac{w_i(x) - x - Y_j}{T_j} \right\rceil_0 C_j + \sum_{\forall\, \tau_{j(U)}\ hp\ \tau_i} \left\lceil \frac{w_i(x) - \lceil \frac{x}{T_j} \rceil T_j - Z_j}{T_j} \right\rceil_0 C_j \quad (17)$$

In single-mode, steady-state systems, windows for increasing values of q need to be determined. The sequence is finite, however, because the search can stop if a level i busy period is found which finishes before task τ_i starts (i.e. the processor is released to process lower-priority tasks) - since the processor is executing lower priority tasks there can be no impact on task τ_i from previous invocations of task τ_i in busy periods starting earlier. The above iteration over increasing values of q can stop if:

$$w_i(q) < (q+1)T_i \quad (18)$$

The response time corresponding to the window starting qT_i before the current invocation of task τ_i is therefore given by:

$$(w_i(q) - qT_i) \quad (19)$$

Now, as mentioned above, the worst-case response time can occur at any one of these response times, and thus the WCRT is given by:

$$r_i = \max(w_i(q) - qT_i) \quad q = 1, 2, 3.. \left\lceil \frac{x}{T_i} \right\rceil \quad (20)$$

In the analysis with arbitrary deadlines and single mode systems, windows for increasing values of q need to be determined; variable x is not present in the analysis. In the WCRT analysis of mode changes with deadlines less than or equal to periods we need to apply all significant values of x, and the analysis is not a function of q. Clearly, the analysis of tasks with arbitrary deadlines across a mode change is a function of both x and q, and q is limited by x (for old-mode tasks).

5.2.2 Analysis of new-mode tasks

A level i busy period for a new-mode task is defined as: *The maximum time for which a processor executes tasks of priority greater than or equal to the priority of task τ_i. A busy period begins with the arrival of a mode-change request MCR. It ends when a task with lower priority than τ_i is able to begin execution during the mode-change window.*

As seen in section 5.2, the pattern of interference from higher computation over τ_i is not affected by the introduction of arbitrary deadlines. As with the analysis for old-mode tasks, the new-mode task is delayed by its previous invocations. Therefore, equation (13) is reformulated as follows:

$$w_i = (q+1)C_{i(N)} + \sum_{\forall\, \tau_{j(O)}\ hp\ \tau_i} C_j + \sum_{\forall\, \tau_{j(N)}\ hp\ \tau_i} \left\lceil \frac{w_i - Y_j}{T_j} \right\rceil_0 C_j + \sum_{\forall\, \tau_{j(U)}\ hp\ \tau_i} \left(C_j + \left\lceil \frac{w_i - T_j - Z_j}{T_j} \right\rceil_0 C_j \right) \quad (21)$$

Unlike the analysis of old-mode tasks, which limits the number of busy periods to be examined by $\lceil \frac{x}{T_i} \rceil$, in the analysis of new-mode tasks the number of instances q to be inspected has no direct correlation with the beginning or end of the mode change. The above iteration over increasing values of q can stop if:

$$w_i(q) < (q+1)T_i \quad (22)$$

The first qT of level i busy period falls before the current invocation of task τ_i is released. The response time corresponding to the given level i busy period starting time qt before the current invocation of task τ_i is therefore given by: $w_{i,q} - qt$. The response time can occur at any one of these response times, and thus the worst-case response time is given by:

$$R_i = w_{i,q} - qt - Y_i \quad (23)$$

Where $q = \{0, 1, 2...\}$. This equation specifies an infinite number of busy periods. Only a finite number need to be examined because the search can stop if a level i busy period is found which finishes before the invocation of task τ_i following the current one. The longest busy period that needs to be examined is bounded by the LCM of task periods.

6. Example

In this section we present an example of the mode change analysis based upon the Generic Avionics Platform (GAP) task set described by Locke et al. (1991). We consider the example of two modes of aircraft operation: *Level flight* and *Defense Mode*, described in tables 1 and 2 respectively (Pedro, 1999), and we analyze the schedulability of the transition from level-flight to defense mode. The level-flight mode contains four tasks which are not originally defined in the GAP set: auto_pilot, mission_advisor, fuelling_management and display_graphic_2. The task set used in the defense mode is the original task set defined (Locke et al., 1991), except that the Timer_Interrupt task has been removed.

Tasks printed in boldface in table 1 denote completed old-mode tasks that are replaced by the corresponding boldfaced wholly-new tasks in table 2 (e.g. Weapon_Release replaces Auto_Pilot). Tasks in the defense mode are carried out as new-mode changed tasks. Display _Hook_Update is an aborted task. In order to increase the schedulability of the task set, all new-mode tasks lose their periodicity during the transition. Table 3 illustrates the

τ	Behavior	τ	Behavior
$\tau_{1(O)}$	**Auto_pilot**	$\tau_{19(O)}$	Tracking_Target_Upd
$\tau_{3(O}$	Radar_Tracking_Filter	$\tau_{21(O)}$	**Display_Graphic_2 ***
$\tau_{5(O)}$	RWR_Contact_Mgmt	$\tau_{23(O)}$	Nav_Steering_Cmds
$\tau_{7(O)}$	Data_Bus_Poll_Device	$\tau_{25(O)}$	Display_Stores_Updates
$\tau_{9(O)}$	**Mission_advisor ***	$\tau_{27(O)}$	Display_Keyset
$\tau_{11(O)}$	**Fuelling_Mgmt ***	$\tau_{29(O)}$	Display_Stat_Update
$\tau_{13(O)}$	Nav_Update	$\tau_{31(O)}$	BET_E_Status_Update
$\tau_{15(O)}$	Display_Graphic_1	$\tau_{33(O)}$	Nav_Status
$\tau_{17(A)}$	Display_Hook_Update	—	—

Table 1. Task Set Description in Aircraft Level-Flight Mode

schedulability analysis for the mode change from the level-flight mode to the defense mode. Each column represents the period T, deadline D, $WCET$ C, priority P, the worst-case arrival time for an old-mode task x, the steady-state response time for a task in the old mode $R^{ss}_{i(O)}$, the $WCRT$ of a task during the mode change $R_{i(mc)}$ and the steady-state WCRT of a new-mode task $R^{ss}_{i(N)}$. Tasks with a lower value of P have a higher priority. All times are specified in milliseconds with a multiplication factor of 10.

The latency of the mode change is given by new-mode task $\tau_{34(c)}$, which completes its first execution at time 21400 (i.e. $R_i(n) + Y_i$ = 2140 ms) after the MCR. The worst-case response times of all tasks are less than the deadlines, and hence the task set is schedulable across the mode change.

τ	Behavior	τ	Behavior
$\tau_{2(W)}$	**Weapon_Release ***	$\tau_{20(C)}$	Tracking_Target_Upd
$\tau_{4(C)}$	Radar_Tracking_Filter	$\tau_{22(W)}$	**Weapon_Protocol ***
$\tau_{6(C)}$	RWR_Contact_Mgmt	$\tau_{24(C)}$	Nav_Steering_Cmds
$\tau_{8(C)}$	Data_Bus_Poll_Device	$\tau_{26(C)}$	Display_Stores_Updates
$\tau_{10(W)}$	**Weapon_Aiming ***	$\tau_{28(C)}$	Display_Keyset
$\tau_{12(W)}$	**Radar_Target_Update**	$\tau_{30(C)}$	Display_Stat_Update
$\tau_{14(C)}$	Nav_Update	$\tau_{32(C)}$	BET_E_Status_Update
$\tau_{16(C)}$	Display_Graphic	$\tau_{34(C)}$	Nav_Status
$\tau_{18(C)}$	Display_Hook_Update	—	—

Table 2. Task Set Description in Aircraft Defense Mode

If task WCRT's are much less than their periods (i.e. $R_i << T_i$) then the analysis will converge immediately for values of $q = 0$. There are no extra invocations (q = 1,2,3..) in the busy period. Task $\tau_{13(O)}$ is an exception: it has a period T_{13} = 1100 and deadline D_{13} = 1550 (D > T). Its WCRT is 1227 and it occurs when the task arrives at time x = 801 before the MCR. In the worst-case, $\tau_{13(O)}$ is delayed by one single invocation (i.e. q = 1) before the MCR, but it is still able to meet its deadline.

τ	T	D	C	P	Y	x	$R^{ss}_{i(O)}$	$R_{i(mc)}$	$R^{ss}_{i(N)}$	TEST
$\tau_{1(O)}$	1000	50	10	1	—	0	10	10	—	sched.
$\tau_{2(W)}$	2000	50	30	1	0	0	—	40	30	sched.
$\tau_{3(O)}$	2000	1200	200	12	—	601	742	862	—	sched.
$\tau_{4(C}$	250	60	20	2	2000	0	—	50	50	sched.
$\tau_{5(O)}$	2000	1400	5	13	—	601	747	897	—	sched.
$\tau_{6(C}$	250	120	50	3	2000	0	—	100	100	sched.
$\tau_{7(O)}$	400	400	10	4	—	1	100	130	—	sched.
$\tau_{8(C)}$	400	400	10	4	400	0	—	110	110	sched.
$\tau_{9(O)}$	600	450	20	5	—	1	120	150	—	sched.
$\tau_{10(W)}$	500	450	30	5	0	0	—	180	140	sched.
$\tau_{11(O)}$	800	500	50	6	—	1	170	230	—	sched.
$\tau_{12(W)}$	500	500	50	6	0	0	—	280	190	sched.
$\tau_{13(O)}$	1100	1550	80	15	—	801	977	1227	—	sched.
$\tau_{14(C)}$	590	590	80	7	1650	0	—	340	340	sched.
$\tau_{15(O)}$	1700	1600	40	16	—	1001	1107	1227	—	sched.
$\tau_{16(C)}$	800	600	90	8	1700	0	—	440	440	sched.
$\tau_{17(A)}$	1700	1650	100	17	—	1001	1237	1367	—	—
$\tau_{18(C)}$	800	700	20	9	1700	0	—	460	460	sched.
$\tau_{19(O)}$	2000	800	30	10	—	251	342	452	—	sched.
$\tau_{20(C)}$	1000	800	50	10	2000	0	—	740	740	sched.
$\tau_{21(O)}$	3000	900	90	11	—	401	442	552	—	sched.
$\tau_{22(W)}$	2000	900	10	11	0	0	—	482	750	sched.
$\tau_{23(O)}$	250	60	20	2	—	1	30	60	—	sched.
$\tau_{24(C)}$	2000	1200	30	12	250	0	—	542	970	sched.
$\tau_{25(O)}$	250	120	60	3	—	1	90	120	—	sched.
$\tau_{26(C)}$	2000	1400	10	13	250	0	—	567	980	sched.
$\tau_{27(O)}$	3000	1500	10	14	—	801	897	1017	—	sched.
$\tau_{28(C)}$	2000	1500	10	14	3000	0	—	990	990	sched.
$\tau_{29(O)}$	4000	590	30	7	—	1	200	310	—	sched.
$\tau_{30(C)}$	2000	1550	30	15	4000	0	—	1380	1380	sched.
$\tau_{31(O)}$	20000	600	15	8	—	1	215	325	—	sched.
$\tau_{32(C)}$	10000	1600	10	16	20000	0	—	1390	1390	sched.
$\tau_{33(O)}$	20000	700	17	9	—	1	232	342	—	sched.
$\tau_{34(C)}$	10000	1650	10	17	20000	0	—	1400	1400	sched.

Table 3. Feasibility Analysis of GAP Task Set Across a Mode Change

7. Summary and discussion

Before we discuss the schedulability analysis of tasks across a mode change, we must define what a mode of operation is in real-time systems and what a mode change from a source to a target mode represents. In the first part of this chapter we have surveyed the literature and presented a number of views on the notion of modes, before formulating our definition for real-time systems.

The second focus of this work was on guaranteeing hard real-time tasks with arbitrary deadlines that execute through a mode change. Original work on schedulability analysis for real-time tasks across mode changes assumes that all task have deadlines less than or equal to their periods. This work relaxed this constraint, by allowing tasks to have arbitrary deadlines. It also showed the generality of the analysis presented by Tindell et al. (1994) on arbitrary deadlines: when proper busy periods are considered, schedulability analysis for fixed-priority preemptive systems is amenable to extensions such as the one presented in this chapter. From another perspective, the schedulability results of mode changes by Pedro & Burns (1998) and Real & Crespo (2004) can be extended to allow for arbitrary deadlines without major modifications to their original analysis.

In order to introduce arbitrary deadlines in the schedulability analysis of mode changes of Pedro & Burns (1998) and Real & Crespo (2004) we had to consider: 1) The definition of busy periods in the light of mode changes; 2) The amount of higher-priority computation; 3) The number of instances q of the task being analyzed τ_i, and 4) The delays from earlier invocations of task τ_i. Therefore, we introduced the following modifications to the original analysis:

1. Readjusted the beginning of the busy period with regard to the arrival of the MCR and adopted the basic definition as given by Lehoczky (1990);
2. Maintained the calculation of the interference from higher-priority tasks: the introduction of arbitrary deadlines does not change the amount of interference from higher-priority tasks. Clearly, higher-priority tasks can be delayed by their previous invocations, but this does not change the calculation of the higher-priority computational load;
3. Changed the number of instances q to be inspected: For old-mode tasks, the arrival of the MCR changes the number of busy periods to be inspected. In the schedulability analysis of mode changes, the condition $w < (q+1)T_i$ can be reached much earlier than in the corresponding analysis of steady-state (single-mode) systems. It occurs long before the LCM of tasks and it depends on the value of x. In addition, the mode-change analysis refers only to the last invocation of task τ_i before the MCR: the preceding invocations do not cross the mode-change and merely delay task τ_i. For new-mode tasks we analyze a number of invocations q until the condition $w < (q+1)T_i$ is satisfied;
4. Maintained the delay of previous invocations of the task being analyzed in the analysis of both old-mode tasks and new-mode ones: Because we considered that the previous instance of task τ_i has higher priority than the new release, it will not preempt but instead delay the execution of the instance being analyzed.

This work will allow us to investigate more complex systems and applications that require mode changes using arbitrary deadlines. A good example is the schedulability analysis of the *Controller Area Network (CAN)* (Davis et al., 2007), which is based on arbitrary deadlines, but assumes a fixed message set with one single mode of operation. Before we tackle the schedulability analysis of messages across a mode change in a CAN bus, we need to be familiar with the schedulability analysis of mode changes with arbitrary deadlines, such as the one derived in this chapter.

8. References

Audsley, N., Burns, A., Richardson, M., Tindell, K. & Wellings, A. J. (1993). Applying new scheduling theory to static priority pre-emptive scheduling, *Software Engineering Journal* 8: 284–292.

Bailey, C. M. (1993). Hard real time operating system kernel: Investigation of mode change, task 14 deliverable on estsec contract 9198/90/nl/sf, *Technical report*, British Aerospace Systems Ltd.

Davis, R. I., Burns, A., Bril, R., & Lukkien, J. (2007). Controller area network (can) schedulability analysis: Refuted, revisited and revised, *Real-Time Systems* 35: 239–272.

Degani, A. & Kirlik, A. (1995). Modes in human-automation interaction:initial observations about a modelling approach, *Proceedings of the IEEE International Conference on Systems, Man, and Cybernetics (SMC)*, pp. 1–15.

Degani, A., Shafto, M. & Kirlik, A. (1999). Modes in human-machine systems: Review, classification, and application, *International Journal of Aviation Psychology* 9(2): 125–138.

Fohler, G. J. (1994). *Flexibility in Statically Scheduled Hard Real-Time Systems*, PhD thesis, Technische Universitat Wien, Institut fur Technische Informatik.

Howe, D. (1997). Free On-line Dictionary of Computing. http://wombat.doc.ic.ac.uk /foldoc /index.html.

Lehoczky, J. (1990). Fixed priority scheduling of periodic task set with arbitrary deadlines, *Proceedings of the 11th Real Time Systems Symposium*, pp. 201–209.

Locke, C. D., Vogel, D. & Mesler, T. (1991). Building a Predictable Avionics Platform in Ada: A Case Study, *Proceedings of the 12th Real-Time Systems Symposium (Dec.)*, pp. 181–189.

M., J. & Pandya, P. (1986). Finding response times in a real-time system, *BCS Computer Journal* 29(05): 390–395.

Martins, P. & Burns, A. (2008). On the meaning of modes in uniprocessor real-time systems, *Proceedings of the 2008 ACM symposium on Applied computing*, SAC '08, ACM, New York, NY, USA, pp. 324–325.
URL: *http://doi.acm.org/10.1145/1363686.1363770*

Norman, D. A. (1981). Categorization of action slips, *Psychological Review* 1(88): 1–15.

Papadopoulos, Y. (1996). Real-Time Safety Administration by Using Safety Cases, *Technical Report Oct*, The University of York, Computer Science,2nd Year Thesis Proposal.

Pedro, P. (1999). *Schedulability of Mode Changes in Flexible Real-Time Distributed Systems*, PhD thesis, The University of York.

Pedro, P. & Burns, A. (1998). Schedulability analysis for mode changes in flexible real-time systems, *Real-Time Systems, 1998. Proceedings. 10th Euromicro Workshop on*, pp. 172 –179.

Poller, M. F. & Garter, S. K. (1984). The Effects of Modes on Text Editing by Experienced Editor Users, *Human Factors*, Vol. 26(4), pp. 449–462.

Real, J. (2000). *Protocolos de Cambio de Modo para Sistemas de Tiempo Real*, PhD thesis, Universidad Politecnica de Valencia.

Real, J. & Crespo, A. (2004). Mode change protocols for real-time systems: A survey and a new proposal, *Real-Time Systems* 26: 161–197. 10.1023/B:TIME.0000016129.97430.c6. URL: *http://dx.doi.org/10.1023/B:TIME.0000016129.97430.c6*

Tesler, L. (1981). The SmallTalk Environment, *Byte Magazine*, Vol. 6(8), pp. 90–147.

Tindell, K. & Alonso, A. (1996). A Very Simple Protocol for Mode Changes in Priority Preemptive Systems, *Technical report*, Universidad Politécnica de Madrid.

Tindell, K., Burns, A. & Wellings, A. (1994). An Extendible Approach for Analysing Fixed Priority Hard Real-Time Tasks, *Journal of Real-Time Systems* 6(2): 133–151.

Tindell, K. W., Burns, A. & Wellings, A. (1992). Mode changes in priority pre-emptively scheduled systems, *Technical Report RTSS92-TBW*, Department of Computer Science.

Tindell, K. W., Burns, A. & Wellings, A. J. (1992). Mode changes in priority pre-emptively scheduled systems, *Proceedings of the Real Time Systems Symposium*, pp. 100–109.

4

An Efficient Hierarchical Scheduling Framework for the Automotive Domain

Mike Holenderski, Reinder J. Bril and Johan J. Lukkien
Eindhoven University of Technology
The Netherlands

1. Introduction

Modern real-time systems have become exceedingly complex. A typical car is controlled by over 100 million lines of code executing on close to 100 Electronic Control Units (ECU). With more and more functions being implemented in software, the traditional approach of implementing each function (such as engine control, ABS, windows control) on a dedicated ECU is no longer viable, due to increased manufacturing costs, weight, power consumption, and decreased reliability and serviceability (Nolte et al., 2009). With the ECUs having increasingly more processing power, it has become feasible to integrate several functions on a single ECU. However, this introduces the challenge of supporting independent and concurrent development and analysis of individual functions which are later to be integrated on a shared platform. A popular approach in the industry and literature is component based engineering, where the complete system is divided into smaller software components which can be developed independently. The Automotive Open System Architecture (AUTOSAR) (AUTOSAR, 2011) standard is an example of such an approach in the automotive domain. It relies on a formal specification of component interfaces to verify the functional properties of their composition. Many functions in automotive systems, however, also have real-time constraints, meaning that their correct behavior is not only dependent on their functional correctness but also their temporal correctness. AUTOSAR does not provide temporal isolation between components. Verifying the temporal properties of an integrated system requires complete knowledge of all functions comprising the components mapped to the same ECU, and therefore violates the requirement for independent development and analysis.

In this chapter we address the problem of providing temporal isolation to components in an integrated system. Ideally, temporal isolation allows to develop and verify the components independently (and concurrently), and then to seamlessly integrate them into a system which is functioning correctly from both a functional and timing perspective (Nolte, 2011; Shin & Lee, 2008). The question is how to provide true temporal isolation when components execute on a shared processor. We address this problem by means of an hierarchical scheduling framework (HSF).

An HSF provides the means for the integration of independently developed and analyzed components into a predictable real-time system. A component is defined by a set of tasks, a local scheduler and a *server*, which defines the component's time budget (i.e. its share of the processing time) and its replenishment policy.

An HSF-enabled platform should provide the following general functionalities:

1. Interface for the creation of servers and assigning tasks to servers.
2. *Virtual timers*, which are relative to a components's budget consumption, as well as *global timers*, which are relative to a fixed point in time.
3. Local scheduling of tasks within a component, and global scheduling of components on the system level.

In this chapter we focus on providing temporal isolation and preventing interference between components. We aim at satisfying the following additional requirement:

4. Expiration of events local to a component, such as the arrival of periodic tasks, should not interfere with other components. In particular, the handling of the events local to inactive components should be deferred until the corresponding component is activated. The time required to handle them should be accounted to the corresponding component, rather than the currently active one.

These requirements should be met by a modular and extensible design, with low performance overhead and minimal modifications to the underlying RTOS. It should exhibit predictable overhead, while remaining efficient to support resource-constrained embedded systems in the automotive domain.

Real-time applications will often require support for periodic task arrival. Periodic tasks rely on timers to represent their arrival time. For servers, we also need timers representing the replenishment and depletion of a budget. Vital, and a starting point for our design, is therefore the support for simple timers (or timed events), i.e. the assumption that an event can be set to arrive at a certain time. This simple timer support is typically available in an off-the-shelf Real-Time Operating System (RTOS) (Labrosse, 2002). Some RTOSes provide much more functionality (for which our work then provides an efficient realization) but other systems provide just that. As a result, the emphasis lies with the management of timers. The timer management should support long event interarrival times and long lifetime of the system at a low overhead.

Contributions

We first present the design of a general timer management system, which is based on Relative Timed Event Queues (RELTEQ) (Holenderski et al., 2009), an efficient timer management system targeted at embedded systems. Pending timers are stored in a queue sorted on the expiration time, where the expiration time of each timer is stored relative to the previous timer in the queue. This representation makes it possible to reduce the memory requirements for storing the expiration times, making it ideal for resource constrained embedded systems. We have implemented RELTEQ within μC/OS-II, and showed that it also reduces the processor overhead compared to the existing timer implementation.

We then leverage RELTEQ to implement periodic tasks and design an efficient HSF. The proposed HSF extension of RELTEQ supports various servers (including the polling, idling-periodic, deferrable and constant-bandwidth servers), and provides access to both virtual and global timers. It supports independent development of components by separating the global and local scheduling, and allowing each server to define a dedicated scheduler. The HSF design provides a mechanism for tasks to monitor their server's remaining budget, and addresses the system overheads inherent to an HSF implementation. It provides temporal isolation and limits the interference of inactive servers on the system level. Moreover, it avoids recalculating the expiration of virtual events upon every server switch and thus reduces the worst-case scheduler overhead.

The proposed design is evaluated based on an implementation within μC/OS-II, a commercial operating system used in the automotive domain. The results demonstrate low overheads of the design and minimal interference between the components.

In this chapter we focus on the means for implementing a HSF. The corresponding analysis falls outside of the scope.

Outline

Section 2 discusses related work, followed by the system model description in Section 3. Section 4 introduces RELTEQ, describing its provided interface, underlying data structures, and algorithms for fast insertion and deletion of timed events. Subsequently, the RELTEQ interface is used to implement periodic tasks in Section 5 and fixed-priority servers in Section 6. The servers form an integral part of the HSF presented in Section 7. In Section 8 the HSF design is evaluated based on an implementation on top of a commercial operating system. Section 9 concludes this chapter.

2. Related work

In this section we discuss the work related to timer management, HSFs in general, and HSFs in automotive systems.

2.1 Timer management

The two most common ways to represent the timestamps of pending timers are: *absolute* timestamps are relative to a fixed point in time (e.g. January 1st, 1900), while *relative* timestamps are relative to a variable point in time (e.g. the last tick of a periodic timer).

In (Oikawa & Rajkumar, 1999; Palopoli et al., 2009) each timer consists of a 64-bit absolute timestamp and a 32-bit overflow counter. The timers are stored in a sorted linked list. A timer Interrupt Service Routine (ISR) checks for any expiring timers, and performs the actual enforcement, replenishment, and priority adjustments. In (Oikawa & Rajkumar, 1999) the timer ISR is driven by a one-shot high resolution timer which is programmed directly. Palopoli et al. (2009) use the Linux timer interface, and therefore their temporal granularity and latency depend on the underlying Linux kernel.

The Eswaran et al. (2005) implementation is based on the POSIX time structure timeval, with two 32-bit numbers to represent seconds/nanoseconds. The authors assume the absolute timestamp value is large enough such that it will practically not overflow.

Carlini & Buttazzo (2003) present the Implicit Circular Timers Overflow Handler (ICTOH), which is an efficient time representation of absolute deadlines in a circular time model. It assumes a periodic timer and absolute time representation. It's main contribution is handling the overflow of the time due to a fixed-size bit representation of time. It requires managing the overflow at every time comparison and is limited to timing constraints which do not exceed 2^{n-1}, where n is the number of bits of the time representation. Buttazzo & Gai (2006) present an implementation of an EDF scheduler based on ICTOH for the ERIKA Enterprise kernel (Evidence, n.d.) and focus on minimizing the tick handler overhead.

The μC/OS-II (Labrosse, 2002) real-time operating system stores timestamps relative to the current time. The timers are stored in an unordered queue. It assumes a periodic timer, and at every tick it decrements the timestamp of all pending timers. A timer expires when its timestamp reaches 0. Timestamps are represented as 16-bit integers. The lifetime of their queue is therefore 2^{16} ticks.

In (Holenderski et al., 2009) we introduced Relative Timed Event Queues (RELTEQ), which is a timed event management component targeted at embedded operating systems. It supports long event interarrival time (compared to the size of the bit representation for a single timestamp), long lifetime of the event queue, and low memory and processor overheads. By using extra "dummy" events it avoids the need to handle overflows at every comparison due to a fixed bit-length time representation, and allows to vary the size of the time representation to trade the processor overhead for handling dummy events for the memory overhead due to time representation. Similar to (Engler et al., 1995; Kim et al., 2000), our RELTEQ implementation is tick based, driven by a periodic hardware timer.

2.2 Hierarchical scheduling frameworks

HSFs are closely related to resource reservations. Mercer et al. (1994) introduce the notion of processor reservations, aiming at providing temporal isolation for individual components comprising a real-time system. Rajkumar et al. (1998) identify four mechanisms which are required to implement such reservations: *admission control*, *scheduling*, *monitoring* and *enforcement*. Run-time monitoring of the consumed resources is intrinsic to realizing correct implementation of the scheduling and enforcement rules. Monitoring of real-time systems can be classified as synchronous or asynchronous (Chodrow et al., 1991). In the synchronous case, a constraint (e.g worst-case execution time) is examined by the task itself. In the asynchronous case, a constraint is monitored by a separate task. The approaches in (Chodrow et al., 1991) are based on program annotations and, hence, are synchronous. In reservation-based systems, however, monitoring should be asynchronous to guarantee enforcement without relying on cooperation from tasks. Moreover, monitoring should not interfere with task execution, but should be part of the operating system or middleware that hosts the real-time application. Our HSF takes the asynchronous monitoring approach.

Shin & Lee (2003) introduce the periodic resource model, allowing the integration of independently analyzed components in compositional hard real-time systems. Their resource is specified by a pair (Π_i, Θ_i), where Π_i is its replenishment period and Θ_i is its capacity. They also describe the schedulability analysis for a HSF based on the periodic resource model under the Earliest Deadline First and Rate Monotonic scheduling algorithms. While the periodic-idling server Davis & Burns (2005) conforms to the periodic resource model, the deferrable (Strosnider et al., 1995) and polling (Lehoczky et al., 1987) servers do not. The HSF presented in this chapter supports various two-level hierarchical processor scheduling mechanisms, including the polling, periodic idling, deferrable servers, and constant-bandwidth (Abeni & Buttazzo, 1998) servers. We have reported on the benefits of our constant-bandwidth server implementation in (van den Heuvel et al., 2011). In this chapter we focus on the underlying timer management and illustrate it with fixed-priority servers.

2.2.1 HSF implementations

Saewong et al. (2002) present the implementation and analysis of an HSF based on deferrable and sporadic servers using an hierarchical rate-monotonic and deadline-monotonic scheduler, as used in systems such as the Resource Kernel (Rajkumar et al., 1998).

Inam et al. (2011) present a FreeRTOS implementation of an HSF, which is based on our earlier work in (Holenderski et al., 2010). It supports temporal isolation for fixed-priority global and local scheduling of independent tasks, including the support for the idling-periodic and deferrable servers. Their goal is to minimize the changes to the underlying OS. Consequently they rely on absolute timers provided by FreeRTOS. They do not address virtual timers. The HSF presented in this chapter relies on relative times, which allow for an efficient implementation of virtual timers. Also, our HSF implementation is modular and supports both fixed-priority as well as EDF scheduling on both global and local levels, as well as constant-bandwidth servers.

Kim et al. (2000) propose a two-level HSF called the SPIRIT uKernel, which provides a separation between components by using partitions. Each partition executes a component, and uses the Fixed-Priority Scheduling (FPS) policy as a local scheduler to schedule the component's tasks. An offline schedule is used to schedule the partitions on a global level.

Behnam et al. (2008) present an implementation of a HSF based on the periodic resource model in the VxWorks operating system. They keep track of budget depletion by using separate event queues for each server in the HSF by means of absolute times. Whenever a server is activated (or switched in), an event indicating the depletion of the budget, i.e. the current time plus the remaining budget, is added to the server event queue. On preemption of a server, the remaining budget is updated according to the time passed since the last server release and the budget depletion event is removed from the server event queue. When the server's budget depletion event expires, the server is removed from the server ready queue, i.e. it will not be rescheduled until the replenishment of its budget.

Oikawa & Rajkumar (1999), describe the design and implementation of Linux/RK, an implementation of a resource kernel (Portable RK) within the Linux kernel. They minimize the modifications to the Linux kernel by introducing a small number of call back hooks for identifying context switches, with the remainder of the implementation residing in an independent kernel module. Linux/RK introduces the notion of a resource set, which is a set of processor reservations. Once a resource set is created, one or more processes can be attached to it to share its reservations. Although reservations are periodic, periodic tasks inside reservations are not supported. The system employs a replenishment timer for each processor reservation, and a global enforcement timer which expires when the currently running reservation runs out of budget. Whenever a reservation is switched in the enforcement timer is set to its remaining budget. Whenever a reservation is switched out, the enforcement timer is cancelled, and the remaining budget is recalculated.

AQuoSA (Palopoli et al., 2009) also provides the Linux kernel with EDF scheduling and various well-known resource reservation mechanisms, including the constant bandwidth server. Processor reservations are provided as servers, where a server can contain one or more tasks. Periodic tasks are supported by providing an API to sleep until the next period. Similar to Oikawa & Rajkumar (1999) it requires a kernel patch to provide for scheduling hooks and updates the remaining budget and the enforcement timers upon every server switch.

Faggioli et al. (2009) present an implementation of the Earliest Deadline First (EDF) and constant bandwidth servers for the Linux kernel, with support for multicore platforms. It is implemented directly into the Linux kernel. Each task is assigned a period (equal to its relative deadline) and a budget. When a task exceeds its budget, it is stopped until its next period expires and its budget is replenished. This provides temporal protection, as the task behaves like a hard reservation. Each task is assigned a timer, which is activated whenever a task is switched in, by recalculating the deadline event for the task.

Eswaran et al. (2005) describe Nano-RK, a reservation-based RTOS targeted for use in resource-constrained wireless sensor networks. It supports fixed-priority preemptive multitasking, as well as resource reservations for processor, network, sensor and energy. Only one task can be assigned to each processor reservation. Nano-RK also provides explicit support for periodic tasks, where a task can wait for its next period. Each task contains a timestamp for its next period, next replenishment and remaining budget. A one-shot timer drives the timer ISR, which (i) loops through all tasks, to update their timestamps and handle the expired events, and (ii) sets the one-shot timer to the next wakeup time.

Unlike the work presented in (Behnam et al., 2008), which implements a HSF on top of a commercial operating system, and in (Faggioli et al., 2009; Oikawa & Rajkumar, 1999; Palopoli et al., 2009), which implement reservations within Linux, our design for HSF is integrated within a RTOS targeted at embedded systems. Kim et al. (2000) describe a micro-kernel with a two-level HSF and time-triggered scheduling on the global level.

Our design aims at efficiency, in terms of memory and processor overheads, while minimizing the modifications of the underlying RTOS. Unlike Behnam et al. (2008); Oikawa & Rajkumar (1999); Palopoli et al. (2009) it avoids recalculating the expiration of local server events, such as budget depletion, upon every server switch. It also limits the interference of inactive servers on system level by deferring the handling of their local events until they are switched in. While Behnam et al. (2008) present an approach for limiting interference of periodic idling servers, to the best of our knowledge, our work is the first to also cover deferrable servers.

2.3 Hierarchical scheduling in automotive systems

Asberg et al. (2009) make first steps towards using hierarchical scheduling in the AUTOSAR standard. They sketch what it would take to enable the integration of software components by providing temporal isolation between the AUTOSAR components. In (Nolte et al., 2009) they extend their work to systems where components share logical resources, and describe how to apply the SIRAP protocol (Behnam et al., 2007) for synchronizing access to resources shared between tasks belonging to different components. In this work we consider independent components and focus on minimizing the interference between components due to them sharing the timer management system.

3. System model

In this paper we assume a system is composed of independently developed and analyzed components. A components consists of a set of tasks which implement the desired application, a local scheduler, and a server. There is a one-to-one mapping between components and servers.

3.1 Tasks

We consider a set Γ of periodic tasks, where each task $\tau_i \in \Gamma$ is specified by a tuple (i, ϕ_i, T_i, C_i), where i is a fixed priority (smaller i means higher priority), ϕ_i is the task's phasing, T_i is the interarrival time between two consecutive jobs, and C_i is its worst-case execution time. Tasks are preemptive and independent.

3.2 Servers

We consider a set of servers Σ, where each server $\sigma_i \in \Sigma$ is specified by a tuple (i, Π_i, Θ_i), where i is the priority (smaller i means higher priority), Π_i is its replenishment period and Θ_i is its capacity. During runtime, its available budget β_i may vary. Every Π_i time units β_i is replenished to Θ_i. When a server is running, every time unit its available budget β_i is decremented by one.

The mapping of tasks to servers is given by $\gamma(\sigma_i) \subseteq \Gamma$ which defines the set of tasks mapped to server σ_i. We assume that each task is mapped to exactly one server. A task $\tau_j \in \gamma(\sigma_i)$ which is mapped to server σ_i can execute only when $\beta_i > 0$.

3.2.1 Deferrable server

The deferrable server Strosnider et al. (1995) is bandwidth preserving. This means that when a server is switched out because none of its tasks are ready, it will preserve its budget to handle tasks which may become ready later. A deferrable server can be in one of the states shown in Figure 1. A server in the *running* state is said to be *active*, and in either *ready*, *waiting* or *depleted* state is said to be *inactive*. A change from inactive to active or vice-versa is accompanied by the server being *switched in* or *switched out*, respectively.

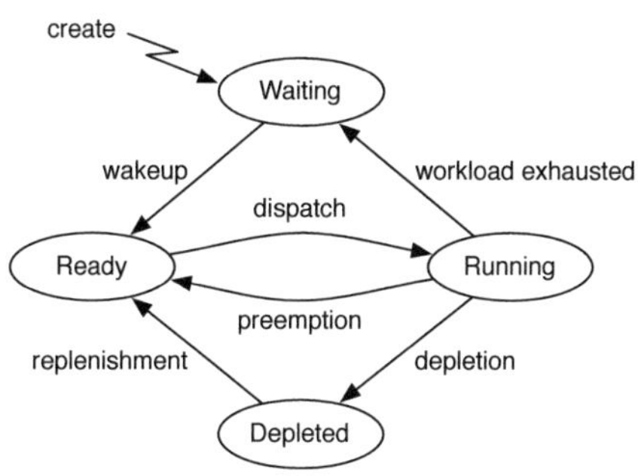

Fig. 1. State transition diagram for the deferrable server. The replenishment transitions from the Ready, Running and Waiting states pointing to the same state are not shown.

A server σ_i is created in the waiting state, with $\beta_i = \Theta_i$. When it is dispatched by the scheduler it moves to running state. A running server may become inactive for one of three reasons:

- It may be preempted by a higher priority server, upon which it preserves its budget and moves to the ready state.
- It may have available budget $\beta_i > 0$, but none of its tasks in $\gamma(\sigma_i)$ may be ready to run, upon which it preserves its budget and moves to the waiting state.
- Its budget may become depleted, upon which it moves to the depleted state.

When a depleted server is replenished it moves to the ready state and becomes eligible to run. A waiting server may be woken up by a newly arrived periodic task or a delay event.

3.2.2 Idling periodic server

When the idling periodic server Davis & Burns (2005) is replenished and none of its tasks are ready, then it idles its budget away until either a proper task arrives or the budget depletes. An idling periodic server follows the state transition diagram in Figure 1, however, due to its idling nature it will never reach the waiting state (and can therefore be regarded as created in ready state).

3.3 Hierarchical scheduling

In two-level hierarchical scheduling one can identify a global scheduler which is responsible for selecting a component. The component is then free to use any local scheduler to select a task to run.

In order to facilitate the reuse of existing components when integrating them to form larger systems, the platform should support (at least) fixed-priority preemptive scheduling at the local level within components (since it is a de-facto standard in the industry). To give the system designer the most freedom it should support arbitrary schedulers at the global level. In this paper we will focus on a fixed-priority scheduler on both local and global level.

3.4 Timed events

The platform needs to support at least the following timed events: task delay, arrival of a periodic task, server replenishment and server depletion.

Events local to server σ_i, such as the arrival of periodic tasks $\tau_j \in \gamma(\sigma_i)$, should not interfere with other servers, unless they wake a server, i.e. the time required to handle them should be accounted to σ_i, rather than the currently running server. In particular, handling the events local to inactive servers should not interfere with the currently active server and should be deferred until the corresponding server is switched in.

4. RELTEQ

To implement the desired extensions in μC/OS-II we needed a general mechanism for different kinds of timed events, exhibiting low runtime overheads. This mechanism should be expressive enough to easily implement higher level primitives, such as periodic tasks, fixed-priority servers and two-level fixed-priority scheduling.

4.1 RELTEQ time model

RELTEQ stores the arrival times of future events relative to each other, by expressing their time *relative to their previous event*. The arrival time of the head event is relative to the current time[1], as shown in Figure 2.

[1] Later in this chapter we will use RELTEQ queues as an underlying data structure for different purposes. We will relax the queue definition: all event times will be expressed relative to their previous event, but the head event will not necessarily be relative to "now".

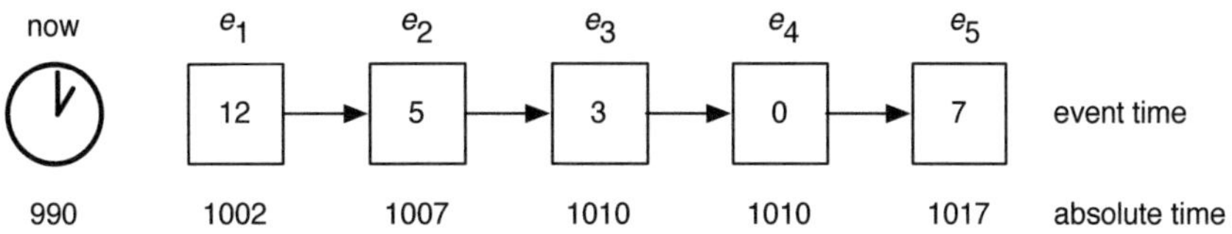

Fig. 2. Example of the RELTEQ event queue.

Unbounded interarrival time between events

One of our requirements is for long event interarrival times with respect to time representation. In other words, given d as the largest value that can be represented for a fixed bit-length time representation, we want to be able to express events which are kd time units apart, for some parameter $k > 1$.

For an n-bit time representation, the maximum interval between two consecutive events in the queue is $2^n - 1$ time units[2]. Using k events, we can therefore represent event interarrival time of at most $k(2^n - 1)$. RELTEQ improves this interval even further and allows for an *arbitrarily long interval* between *any* two events by inserting "dummy" events, as shown in Figure 3.

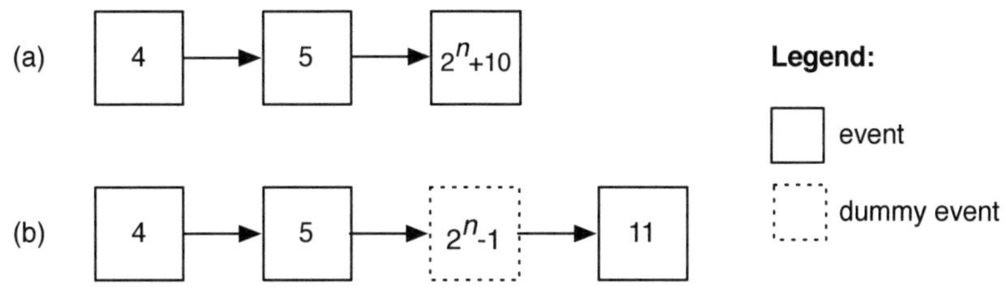

Fig. 3. Example of (a) an overflowing relative event time (b) RELTEQ inserting a dummy event with time $2^n - 1$ to handle the overflow.

If t represents the event time of the last event in the queue, then an event e_i with a time larger than $2^n - 1$ relative to t can be inserted by first inserting dummy events with time $2^n - 1$ at the end of the queue until the remaining relative time of e_i is smaller or equal to $2^n - 1$.

In general, dummy events act as placeholders in queues and can be assigned any time in the interval $[0, 2^n - 1]$.

4.2 RELTEQ data structures

A RELTEQ *event* is specified by the tuple $(kind, time, data)$. The *kind* field identifies the event kind, e.g. a delay or the arrival of a periodic task. *time* is the event time. *data* points to additional data that may be required to handle the event and depends on the event kind. For example, a delay event will point to the task which is to be resumed after the delay event expires. Decrementing an event means decrementing its event time and incrementing an event means incrementing its event time. We will use a dot notation to represent individual fields in the data structures, e.g. $e_i.time$ is the event time of event e_i.

A RELTEQ *queue* is a list of RELTEQ events. *Head*(q_i) represents the head event in queue q_i.

[2] With n bits we can represent 2^n distinct numbers. Since we start at 0, the largest one is $2^n - 1$.

4.3 RELTEQ tick handler

While RELTEQ is not restricted to any specific hardware timer, in this chapter we assume a periodic timer which invokes the *tick handler*, outlined in Figure 4.

The tick handler is responsible for managing the *system queue*, which is a RELTEQ queue keeping track of all the timed events in the system. At every tick of the periodic timer the time of the head event in the queue is decremented. When the time of the head event is 0, then the events with time equal to 0 are popped from the queue and handled.

The scheduler is called at the end of the tick handler, but only in case an event was handled. If no event was handled the currently running task is resumed straightway.

The behavior of a RELTEQ tick handler is summarized in Figure 4.

```
Head(system).time := Head(system).time - 1;
if Head(system).time = 0 then
   while Head(system).time = 0 do
      HandleEvent(Head(system));
      PopEvent(system);
   end while
   Schedule();
end if
```

Fig. 4. Pseudocode for the RELTEQ tick handler.

How an event is handled by *HandleEvent()* depends on its kind. E.g. a *delay event* will resume the delayed task. In general, the event handler will often use the basic RELTEQ primitives, as described in the following sections.

Note that the tick granularity dictates the granularity of any timed events driven by the tick handler: e.g. a server's budget can be depleted only upon a tick. High resolution one-shot timers (e.g. High Precision Event Timer) provide a fine grained alternative to periodic ticks. In case these are present, RELTEQ can easily take advantage of the fine time granularity by setting the timer to the expiration of the earliest event among the active queues. The tick based approach was chosen due to lack of hardware support for high resolution one-shot timers on our example platform. In case such a one-shot timer is available, our RELTEQ based approach can be easily modified to take advantage of it.

4.4 Basic RELTEQ primitives

Three operations can be performed on an event queue: a new event can be inserted, the head event can be popped, and an arbitrary event in the queue can be deleted.

NewEvent(k, t, p) Creates and returns a new event e_i with $e_i.kind = k$, $e_i.time = t$, and $e_i.data = p$.

InsertEvent(q_i, e_j) When a new event e_j with absolute time t_j is inserted into the event queue q_i, the queue is traversed accumulating the relative times of the events until a later event e_k is found, with absolute time $t_k \geq t_j$. When such an event is found, then (i) e_j is inserted before e_k, (ii) its time $e_j.time$ is set relative to the previous event, and (iii) the arrival time of e_k is set relative to e_j (i.e. $t_k - t_j$). If no later event was found, then e_j is appended at the end of the queue, and its time is set relative to the previous event.

PopEvent(q_i) When an event is popped from a queue it is simply removed from the head of the queue q_i. It is not handled at this point.

DeleteEvent(q_i, e_j) Since all events in a queue are stored relative to each other, the time $e_j.time$ of any event $e_j \in q_i$ is critical for the integrity of the events later in the queue. Therefore, before an event e_j is removed from q_i, its event time $e_j.time$ is added to the following event in q_i.

Note that the addition could overflow. In such case, instead of adding $e_j.time$ to the following event in q_i, the kind of e_j is set to a dummy event and the event is not removed. If e_j is the last event in q_i then it is simply removed, together with any dummy events preceding it.

4.5 Event queue implementation

The most straightforward queue implementation is probably a doubly linked list. The time complexity of the *InsertEvent()* operation is then linear in the number of events in the queue, while the complexity of the *DeleteEvent()* and *PopEvent()* operations is constant.

The linear time complexity of the insert operation may be inconvenient for large event queues. An alternative implementation based on a heap or a balanced binary tree may seem more appropriate, as it promises logarithmic time operations. However, as the following theorem states, the relative time representation coupled with the requirement for long event interarrival times (compared to the time representation) make such an implementation impossible.

Theorem 4.1. *Assume that the maximum value we can represent in the time representation is d and also assume that we store times in a tree using relative values no greater than d. Finally, assume that any two events in the tree are at most kd apart in real time, for some parameter k. Then a logarithmic time retrieval of an event from a tree is not possible.*

Proof. If there are k events, the largest time span these k events can represent is kd time units, i.e., the time difference between the first and last event can be at most kd units. If we are to obtain this value by summing over a path this path has to be of length k which leads to a linear representation. This argument pertains to any representation that sums contributions over a path. □

We can illustrate Theorem 4.1 using dummy events: assuming that we start at time 0, the real time of a newly inserted event is at most kd. We would need to insert dummy events until a root path can contain this value. This means we would need to add dummy events until there is a root path of length k.

Conversely, if we assume a tree representation, then we would like to obtain kd as a sum of $\log(k)$ events. If we assume an even distribution over all events, which is the best case with respect to the number of bits required for the time representation, then each event time will be equal to $\frac{k}{\log(k)}d$. This means that $\left\lceil \log\left(\frac{k}{\log(k)}\right)\right\rceil$ extra bits are needed. Therefore, in a tree implementation one cannot limit the time representation to a given fixed value, independent of kd (i.e. the tree span).

In order to satisfy our initial requirement for long event interarrival time, we chose for a linked-list implementation of RELTEQ queues. In future work we look into relaxing this requirement.

5. Periodic tasks

The task concept is an abstraction of a program text. There are roughly three approaches to periodic tasks, depending on the primitives the operating system provides. Figure 5 illustrates the possible implementations of periodic tasks, where function $f_i()$ represents the body of task τ_i (i.e. the actual work done during each job of task τ_i).

Task τ_i :
$k := 0;$
while *true* **do**
  $now := GetTime();$
  $DelayFor(\phi_i + k * T_i - now);$
  $k := k + 1;$
  $f_i();$
end while

(a)

Registration:
$TaskMakePeriodic(\tau_i, \phi_i, T_i);$

Task τ_i :
while *true* **do**
  $TaskWaitPeriod();$
  $f_i();$
end while

(b)

Registration:
$RegisterPeriodic(f_i(), \phi_i, T_i);$

(c)

Fig. 5. Possible implementations of a periodic task.

In Figure 5.a, the periodic behavior is programmed explicitly while in Figure 5.b this periodicity is implicit. The first syntax is typical for a system without support for periodicity, like μC/OS-II. It provides two methods for managing time: $GetTime()$ which returns the current time, and $DelayFor(t)$ which delays the execution of the current task for t time units relative to the time when the method was called. As an important downside, the approach in Figure 5.a may give rise to jitter, when the task is preempted between $now := GetTime()$ and $DelayFor()$.

In order to go from Figure 5.a to 5.c we extract the periodic timer management from the task in two functions: a registration of the task as periodic and a synchronization with the timer system. A straightforward implementation of *TaskWaitPeriod()* is a suspension on a semaphore. Note that we wait at the beginning of the while loop body (rather than at the end) in case $\phi_i > 0$. Going from interface in Figure 5.b to 5.c is now a simple implementation issue.

Note that the task structure described in Figure 5.b guarantees that a job will not start before the previous job has completed, and therefore makes sure that two jobs of the same task will not overlap if the first job's response time exceeds the task's period.

RELTEQ primitives for periodic tasks

In order to provide the periodic task interface in 5.b, we need to implement a timer which expires periodically and triggers the task waiting inside the *TaskWaitPeriod()* call.

To support periodic tasks we introduce a new kind of RELTEQ events: a *period event*. Each period event e_i points to a task τ_i. The expiration of a period event e_i indicates the arrival of a periodic task τ_i upon which (i) the event time of the e_i is set to T_i and reinserted into the system queue using *InsertEvent()*, and (ii) the semaphore blocking τ_i is raised.

To support periodic tasks we have equipped each task with three additional variables: *TaskPeriod*, expressed in the number of ticks, *TaskPeriodSemaphore*, pointing to the semaphore guarding the release of the task, and *TaskPeriodEvent*, pointing to a RELTEQ period event. For efficiency reasons we have added these directly to the Task Control Block (TCB), which is the μC/OS-II structure storing the state information about a task. Our extensions could, however, reside in a separate structure pointing back to the original TCB.

A task τ_i is made periodic by calling *TaskMakePeriodic*(τ_i, ϕ_i, T_i), which

1. sets the *TaskPeriod* to T_i,
2. removes the *TaskPeriodEvent* from the system queue using *DeleteEvent()*, in case it was already inserted by a previous call to *TaskMakePeriodic()*, otherwise creates a new period event using *NewEvent*(*period*, T_i, τ_i) and assigns it to *TaskPeriodEvent*.
3. sets the event time of the *TaskPeriodEvent* to ϕ_i if $\phi_i > 0$ or T_i if $\phi_i = 0$, and inserts it into the system queue.

6. Servers

A server σ_i is created using *ServerCreate*($\Pi_i, \Theta_i, kind$), where *kind* specifies whether the server is *idling periodic* or *deferrable*. A task τ_i is mapped to server σ_i using *ServerAddTask*(σ_i, τ_i).

In Section 4.3 we have introduced a system queue, which keeps track of pending timed events. For handling periodic tasks assigned to servers we could reuse the system queue. However, this would mean that the tick handler would process the expiration of events local to inactive servers within the budget of the running server.

In order to limit the interference from inactive servers we would like to separate the events belonging to different servers. For this purpose we introduce additional RELTEQ queues for each server. We start this section by introducing additional primitives for manipulating queues, followed by describing how to use these in order to implement fixed-priority servers.

6.1 RELTEQ primitives for servers

We introduce the notion of a pool of queues, and define two pools: *active queues* and *inactive queues*. They are implemented as lists of RELTEQ queues. Conceptually, at every tick of the periodic timer the heads of all active queues are decremented. The inactive queues are left untouched.

To support servers we extend RELTEQ with the following methods:

***ActivateQueue*(q_i)** Moves queue q_i from the inactive pool to the active pool.

***DeactivateQueue*(q_i)** Moves queue q_i from the active pool to the inactive pool.

***IncrementQueue*(q_i)** Increments the head event in queue q_i by 1. Time overflows are handled by setting the overflowing event to $2^n - 1$ and inserting a new dummy event at the head of the queue with time equal to the overflow (i.e. 1).

***SyncQueueUntilEvent*(q_i, q_j, e_k)** Synchronizes queue q_i with queue q_j until event $e_k \in q_j$, by conceptually computing the absolute time of e_k, and then popping and handling all the events in q_i which have occurred during that time interval.

6.2 Limiting interference of inactive servers

To support servers, we add an additional *server queue* for *each* server σ_i, denoted by $\sigma_i.sq$, to keep track of the events local to the server, i.e. delays and periodic arrival of tasks $\tau_j \in \gamma(\sigma_i)$. At any time at most one server can be active; all other servers are inactive. The additional server queues make sure that the events local to inactive servers do not interfere with the currently active server.

When a server σ_i is switched in its server queue is activated by calling *ActivateQueue*($\sigma_i.sq$). In this new configuration the hardware timer drives two event queues:

1. the *system queue*, keeping track of system events, i.e. the replenishment of periodic servers,
2. the *server queue* of the *active* server, keeping track of the events local to a particular server, i.e. the delays and the arrival of periodic tasks belonging to the server.

When the active server is switched out (e.g. a higher priority server is resumed, or the active server gets depleted) then the active server queue is deactivated by calling *DeactivateQueue*($\sigma_i.sq$). As a result, the queue of the switched out server will be "paused", and the queue of the switched in server will be "resumed". The system queue is never deactivated.

To keep track of the time which has passed since the last server switch, we introduce a *stopwatch*. The stopwatch is basically a counter, which is incremented with every tick. In order to handle time overflows discussed in Section 4.1, we represent the stopwatch as a RELTEQ queue and use *IncrementQueue(stopwatch)* to increment it.

During the time when a server is inactive, several other servers may be switched in and out. Therefore, next to keeping track of time since the last server switch, for each server we also need to keep track of how long it was inactive, i.e the time since that particular server was switched out. Rather than storing a separate counter for each server, we multiplex the stopwatches for all servers onto the single stopwatch which we have already introduced, exploiting the RELTEQ approach. We do this by inserting a *stopwatch event*, denoted by $\sigma_i.se$, at the head of the stopwatch queue using *InsertEvent(stopwatch,* $\sigma_i.se$*)* whenever server σ_i is switched out. The event points to the server and its time is initially set to 0. The behavior of the tick handler with respect to the stopwatch remains unchanged: upon every tick the head event in the stopwatch queue is incremented using *IncrementQueue(stopwatch)*.

During runtime the stopwatch queue will contain one stopwatch event for every inactive server (the stopwatch event for the currently active server is removed when the server is switched in). The semantics of the stopwatch queue is defined as follows: the accumulated time from the head of the queue until (and including) a stopwatch event $\sigma_i.se$ represents the time the server σ_i was switched out.

When a server σ_i is switched in, its server queue is synchronized with the stopwatch using *SyncQueuesUntilEvent*($\sigma_i.sq$*, stopwatch,* $\sigma_i.se$), which handles all the events in $\sigma_i.sq$ which might have occurred during the time the server was switched out. It accumulates the time in the stopwatch queue until the stopwatch event $\sigma_i.se$ and handles all the events in $\sigma_i.sq$ which have expired during that time. Then $\sigma_i.se$ is removed from the stopwatch queue. When σ_i is switched out, $\sigma_i.se$ with time 0 is inserted at the head of the stopwatch queue.

6.2.1 Example of the stopwatch behavior

The stopwatch queue is a great example of RELTEQ's strength. It provides an efficient and concise mechanism for keeping track of the inactive time for *all* servers. Figure 6 demonstrates the behavior of the stopwatch queue for an example system consisting of three servers *A*, *B* and *C*. It illustrates the state of the stopwatch queue at different moments during execution, before the currently running server is switched out and after the next server is switched in.

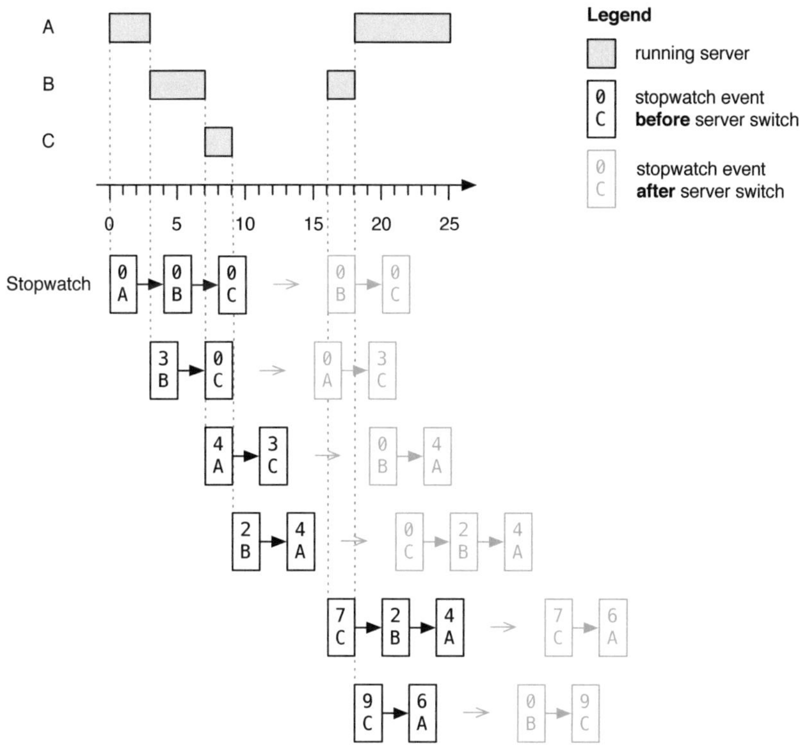

Fig. 6. Example of the stopwatch queue.

Initially, when server σ_i is created, a stopwatch event $\sigma_i.se$ with time 0 is inserted into the stopwatch queue. At time 0 server *A* is switched in and its stopwatch event is removed. While server *A* is running, the tick handler increments the head of the stopwatch queue, which happens to be the stopwatch event of server *B*. At time 3, when server *A* is switched out and server *B* is switched in, server *B* synchronizes its absolute queue with the stopwatch queue until and including *B.se*, *B.se* is deleted, and *A.se* with time 0 is inserted. Note that when *B.se* is deleted, its time is added to *C.se*.

At time 7 server C is switched in, its absolute queue is synchronized with time $4 + 3 = 7$, after which *C.se* is deleted, and *B.se* with time 0 is inserted.

At time 9, since no server is switched in, no synchronization is taking place and no stopwatch event is deleted. Only stopwatch event *C.se* with time 0 is inserted, since server C is switched out.

At time 16, when server *B* is switched in and its stopwatch event *B.se* is deleted, the time of *B.se* is added to *C.se*.

6.2.2 Deferrable server

When the workload of a deferrable server σ_i is exhausted, i.e. there are no ready tasks in $\gamma(\sigma_i)$, then the server is switched out and its server queue $\sigma_i.sq$ is deactivated. Consequently, any periodic task which could wake up the server to consume any remaining budget cannot be noticed. One could alleviate this problem by keeping its server queue active when σ_i is switched out. This, however, would make the tick handler overhead linear in the number of deferrable servers, since a tick handler decrements the head events in all active queues (see Section 6.6).

Instead, in order to limit the interference of inactive deferrable servers, when a deferrable server σ_i is switched out and it has no workload pending (i.e. no tasks in $\gamma(\sigma_i)$ are ready), we deactivate the σ_i's server queue, change its state to waiting, and insert a *wakeup event*, denoted as $\sigma_i.we$, into the system queue. The wakeup event has its *data* pointing to σ_i and time equal to the arrival of the first event in $\sigma_i.sq$. When the wakeup event expires, the σ_i's state is set to the ready state. This way handling the events inside $\sigma_i.sq$ is deferred until σ_i is switched in.

When a deferrable server is switched in while it is in the waiting state, its wakeup event $\sigma_i.we$ is removed from the system queue.

6.2.3 Idling periodic server

An idling periodic server is a special kind of a deferrable server containing an idle task (with lowest priority). The idle task is switched in if no higher priority task is ready, effectively idling away the remaining capacity. In order to save memory needed for storing the task control block and the stack of the idle task, one idle task is shared between all idling periodic servers in the system.

6.3 Virtual timers

When the server budget is depleted an event must be triggered, to guarantee that a server does not exceed its budget. We present a general approach for handling budget depletion and introduce the notion of *virtual timers*, which are events relative to server's budget consumption.

We can implement virtual timers by adding a *virtual server queue* for *each* server, denoted by $\sigma_i.vq$. Similarly to the server queues introduced earlier, when a server is switched in, its virtual server queue is activated. The difference is that the virtual server queue is not synchronized with the stopwatch queue, since during the inactive period a server does not consume any of its budget. When a server is switched out, its virtual server queue is deactivated.

The relative time representation by RELTEQ allows for a more efficient virtual queue activation than an absolute time representation does. An absolute time representation (e.g. in (Behnam et al., 2008; Inam et al., 2011)) requires to recompute the expiration time for *all* the events in a virtual server queue upon switching in the corresponding server, which is linear in the number of events. In our RELTEQ-based virtual queues the events are stored relative to each other and their expiration times do not need to be recomputed upon queue activation. Note that it will never be necessary to handle an expired virtual event upon queue activation, since such an event would have been already handled before the corresponding server was switched out. Therefore, our HSF design exhibits a constant time activation of a virtual server queue.

6.4 Switching servers

The methods for switching servers in and out are summarized in Figures 7 and 8.

SyncQueuesUntilEvent(σ_i*.sq, stopwatch,* σ_i*.se);*
ActivateQueue(σ_i*.sq);*
ActivateQueue(σ_i*.vq);*
if $\sigma_i.we \neq \emptyset$ **then**
  DeleteEvent(system, σ_i*.we);*
  $\sigma_i.we = \emptyset$;
end if

Fig. 7. Pseudocode for *ServerSwitchIn*(σ_i).

DeleteEvent(stopwatch, σ_i*.se);*
σ_i*.se = NewEvent(stopwatch, 0,* σ_i*);*
InsertEvent(stopwatch, σ_i*.se);*
DeactivateQueue(σ_i*.sq);*
DeactivateQueue(σ_i*.vq);*
if $\sigma_i.readyTasks = \emptyset$ **then**
  σ_i*.we = NewEvent(wakeup, Head(*σ_i*.sq).time,* σ_i*);*
  InsertEvent(system, σ_i*.we);*
end if

Fig. 8. Pseudocode for *ServerSwitchOut*(σ_i).

6.5 Server replenishment and depletion

We introduce two additional RELTEQ event kinds to support servers: *budget replenishment* and *budget depletion*. When a server σ_i is created, a replenishment event e_j is inserted into the *system queue*, with $e_j.data$ pointing to σ_i and $e_j.time$ equal to the server's replenishment period Π_i. When e_j expires, $e_j.time$ is updated to Π_i and it is inserted into the system queue.

Upon replenishment, the server's depletion event e_j is inserted into its *virtual server queue*, with $e_j.data$ pointing to σ_i and $e_j.time$ equal to the server's capacity Θ_i. If the server was not depleted yet, then the old depletion event is removed from the virtual server queue using *DeleteEvent*($\sigma_i.vq$, e_j).

6.6 RELTEQ tick handler with support for servers

An example of the RELTEQ queues managed by the tick handler in the proposed RELTEQ extension with servers is summarized in Figure 9. Conceptually, every tick the stopwatch queue is incremented and the heads of the system queue, the active server queue and the active virtual server queue are decremented. If the head of any queue becomes 0, then their head event is popped and handled until the queue is exhausted or the head event has time larger than 0.

Actually, rather than decrementing the head of each active queue and checking whether it is 0, a *CurrentTime* counter is incremented and compared to the *Earliesttime*, which is set whenever the head of an active queue changes. If they are equal, then (i) the *CurrentTime* is subtracted from the heads of all the active queues, (ii) any head event with time 0 is popped and handled,

(iii) *CurrentTime* is set to 0, and (iv) *Earliesttime* is set to the earliest time among the heads of all active queues[3].

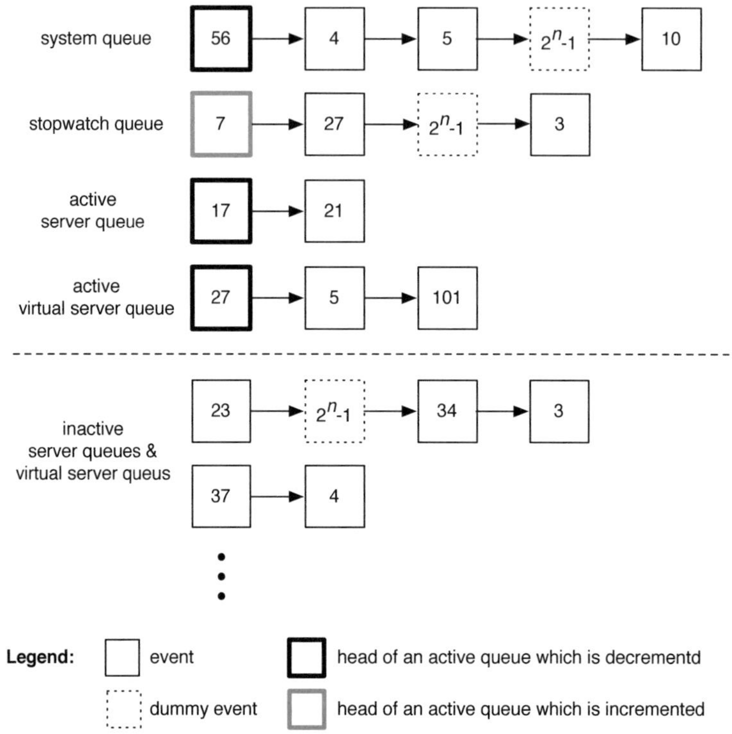

Fig. 9. Example of the RELTEQ queues managed by the tick handler.

The behavior of a RELTEQ tick handler supporting servers is summarized in Figure 10.

> *IncrementQueue*(*stopwatch*);
> *CurrentTime* := *CurrentTime* + 1;
> **if** *Earliesttime* = *CurrentTime* **then**
>   **for all** $q \in activequeues$ **do**
>   *Head*(q).*time* := *Head*(q).*time* − *CurrentTime*;
>   **while** *Head*(q).*time* = 0 **do**
>   *HandleEvent*(*Head*(q));
>   *PopEvent*(q);
>   **end while**
>   **end for**
>   *CurrentTime* := 0;
>   *Earliesttime* := *Earliest*(*activequeues*);
>   *Schedule*();
> **end if**

Fig. 10. Pseudocode for the RELTEQ tick handler supporting hierarchical scheduling.

Note that at any moment in time there are at most four active queues, as shown in Figure 9.

[3] Note that the *time* of any event will never become negative.

6.7 Summary

We have described a generic framework for supporting servers, which is tick based (Section 4.3) and limits the interference of inactive servers on system level (Section 6.2). The interference of inactive servers which are either ready or depleted was limited by means of a combination of inactive server queues and a stopwatch queue. Deactivating server queues of waiting servers was made possible by inserting a wakeup event into the system queue, in order to wake up the server upon the arrival of a periodic task while the server is switched out.

7. Hierarchical scheduling

Rajkumar et al. (1998) identified four ingredients necessary for guaranteeing resource provisions: admission, monitoring, scheduling and enforcement. In this section we describe how our implementation of HSF addresses each of them.

7.1 Admission

We allow admission of new components only during the integration, not during runtime. The admission testing requires analysis for hierarchical systems, which is outside the scope of this chapter.

7.2 Monitoring

There are two reasons for monitoring the budget consumption of servers: (i) handle the budget depletion and (ii) allow the assigned tasks to track and adapt to the available budget.

In order to notice the moment when a server becomes depleted we have introduced a virtual *depletion event* for every server, which is inserted into its virtual server queue. When the depletion event expires, then (i) the server's capacity is set to 0, (ii) its state is set to depleted, and (iii) the scheduler is called.

In order to allow tasks $\tau_j \in \gamma(\sigma_i)$ to track the server budget β_i we equipped each server with a *budget counter*. Upon every tick the budget counter of the currently active server is decremented by one. The depletion event will make sure that a depleted server is switched out before the counter becomes negative. We also added the *ServerBudget()* method, which can be called by any task.

ServerBudget(σ_i) Returns the current value of β_i, which represents the lower bound on the processor time that server σ_i will receive within the next interval of Π_i time units.

7.3 Scheduling

The μC/OS-II the scheduler does two things: (i) select the highest priority ready task, and (ii) in case it is different from the currently running one, do a context switch. Our hierarchical scheduler replaces the original *OS_SchedNew()* method, which is used by the μC/OS-II scheduler to select the highest priority ready task.

It first uses the *global scheduler HighestReadyServer()* to select the highest priority ready server, and then the server's *local scheduler HighestReadyTask()*, which selects the highest priority ready task belonging to that server. This approach allows to implement different global and local schedulers, and also different schedulers in each server. Our fixed-priority global scheduler is shown in Figure 11.

$highestServer := HighestReadyServer();$
if $highestServer \neq currentServer$ **then**
  if $currentServer \neq \emptyset$ **then**
    $ServerSwitchOut(currentServer);$
  end if
  if $highestServer \neq \emptyset$ **then**
    $ServerSwitchIn(highestServer);$
  end if
  $currentServer := highestServer;$
end if
if $currentServer \neq \emptyset$ **then**
  return $currentServer.HighestReadyTask();$
else
  return $idleTask;$
end if

Fig. 11. Pseudocode for the hierarchical scheduler.

The *currentServer* is a global variable referring to the currently active server. Initially $currentServer = \emptyset$, where $\emptyset$ refers to a null pointer.

The scheduler first determines the highest priority ready server. Then, if the server is different from the currently active server, a server switch is performed, composed of 3 steps:

1. If there is a currently active server, then it is switched out, using *ServerSwitchOut()* described in Section 6.4.
2. If there is a ready server, then it is switched in, using *ServerSwitchIn()* described in Section 6.4.
3. The *currentServer* is updated.

Finally the highest priority task in the currently active server is selected, using the current server's local scheduler *HighestReadyTask()*. If no server is active, then the idle task is returned.

7.4 Enforcement

When a server becomes depleted during the execution of one of its tasks (i.e. if a depletion event expires), the task will be preempted and the server will be switched out. This is possible, since we assume preemptive and independent tasks.

8. Evalulation

In this section we evaluate the modularity, memory footprint and performance of the HSF extension for RELTEQ. We chose a linked-list as the data structure underlying our RELTEQ queues and implemented the proposed design within μC/OS-II.

8.1 Modularity and memory footprint

The design of RELTEQ and the HSF extension is modular, allowing to enable or disable the support for HSF and different server types during compilation with a single compiler directive for each extension.

The complete RELTEQ implementation including the HSF extension is 1610 lines of code (excluding comments and blank lines), compared to 8330 lines of the original μC/OS-II. 105 lines of code were inserted into the original μC/OS-II code, out of which 60 were conditional compilation directives allowing to easily enable and disable our extensions. No original code was deleted or modified. Note that the RELTEQ+HSF code can replace the existing timing mechanisms in μC/OS-II, and that it provides a framework for easy implementation of other scheduler and servers types.

The 105 lines of code represent the effort required to port RELTEQ+HSF to another operating system. Such porting requires (i) redirecting the tick handler to the RELTEQ handler, (ii) redirecting the method responsible for selecting the the highest priority task to the HSF scheduler, and (iii) identifying when tasks become ready or blocked.

The code memory footprint of RELTEQ+HSF is 8KB, compared to 32KB of the original μC/OS-II. The additional data memory foot print for an application consisting of 6 servers with 6 tasks each is 5KB, compared to 47KB for an application consisting of 36 tasks (with a stack of 128B each) in the original μC/OS-II.

8.2 Performance analysis

In this section we evaluate the system overheads of our extensions, in particular the overheads of the scheduler and the tick handler. We express the overhead in terms of the maximum number of events inside the queues which need to be handled in a single invocation of the scheduler or the tick handler, times the maximum overhead for handling a single event.

8.2.1 Handling a single event

Handling different events will result in different overheads.

- When a dummy event expires, it is simply removed from the head of the queue. Hence, handling it requires $O(1)$ time.
- When a task period event expires, an event representing the next periodic arrival is inserted into the corresponding server queue. In this section we assume a linked-list implementation, and consequently insertion is linear in the number of events in a queue. Note that we could delay inserting the next period event until the task completes, as at most one job of a task may be running at a time. This would reduce the handling of a periodic arrival to constant time, albeit at the additional cost of keeping track for each task of the time since its arrival, which would be taken into account when inserting the next period event. However, if we would like to monitor whether tasks complete before their deadline, then we will need to insert a deadline event into $\sigma_i.sq$ anyway. Hence the time for handling an event inside of a server queue is linear in the number of events in a server queue. Since there are at most two events per task in a server queue (period and deadline events), handling a period event is linear in the maximum number of tasks assigned to a server, i.e. $O(m(\sigma_i))$.

- When a task deadline event expires, it is simply removed from the head of the queue an the system is notified that a deadline was missed. Hence, handling it requires $O(1)$ time.
- When a server replenishment event expires, an event representing the next replenishment is inserted into the system queue[4]. Since there are at most two events in the system queue per server (replenishment and wakeup event), handling a replenishment event is linear in the number of servers, i.e $O(|\Sigma|)$.
- When a server depletion event expires, it is simply removed from the queue. Hence, handling it requires $O(1)$ time.

8.2.2 Scheduler

Our HSF supports different global and local schedulers. For the sake of a fair comparison with the μC/OS-II which implements a fixed-priority scheduler, we also assume fixed-priority global and local schedulers in this section. For both global and local scheduling we can reuse the bitmap-based approach implemented by μC/OS-II, which has a constant time overhead for selecting the highest priority ready task as well as indicating that a task is ready or not (Labrosse, 2002). Consequently, in our HSF we can select the highest priority server and task within a server in constant time.

Once a highest priority server σ_i is selected, the overhead of switching in the server depends on the number of events inside the stopwatch queue and σ_i's server queue (which needs to be synchronized with the stopwatch), and the overhead of selecting the highest priority task.

The stopwatch queue contains one stopwatch event for each inactive server. The length of the stopwatch queue is therefore bounded by $|\Sigma| + d_s$, where $|\Sigma|$ is the number of servers, and $d_s = \max_{\sigma_i \in \Sigma} \left\lfloor \frac{t_s(\sigma_i)}{2^n - 1} \right\rfloor$ is the maximum number of dummy events inside the stopwatch queue. $t_s(\sigma_i)$ is the longest time interval that a server can be switched out, and $2^n - 1$ is the largest relative time which can be represented with n bits.

The only local events are a task delay and the arrival of a periodic task. Also, each task can wait for at most one timed event at a time. The number of events inside the server queue is therefore bounded by $m(\sigma_i) + d_l(\sigma_i)$, where $m(\sigma_i)$ is the maximum number of tasks assigned to server σ_i, and $d_l(\sigma_i) = \left\lfloor \frac{t_l(\sigma_i)}{2^n - 1} \right\rfloor$ is the maximum number of dummy events local to the server queue $\sigma_i.sq$. $t_l(\sigma_i)$ is the longest time interval between any two events inside of $\sigma_i.sq$ (e.g. the longest task period or the longest task delay).

The complexity of the scheduler is therefore $O(|\Sigma| + d_s + m(\sigma_i) + d_l(\sigma_i))$. Note that the maximum numbers of dummy events d_s and $d_l(\sigma_i)$) can be determined at design time.

8.2.3 Tick handler

The tick handler synchronizes all active queues with the current time, and (in case an event was handled) calls the scheduler. The active queues are comprised of the system queue and two queues for the server σ_i which is active at the time the tick handler is invoked (its server queue $\sigma_i.sq$ and virtual server queue $\sigma_i.vq$).

[4] Inserting the next replenishment event could be deferred until the server is depleted, at a similar cost and benefit to deferring the insertion of the task period event.

The system queue contains only replenishment and wakeup events. Its size is therefore proportional to $|\Sigma| + d_g$, where $d_g = \left\lfloor \frac{t_g}{2^n-1} \right\rfloor$ is the maximum number of dummy events inside the global system queue. t_g is the longest time interval between any two events inside the global system queue (i.e. the longest server period).

The size of $\sigma_i.sq$ is linear in the number of tasks assigned to the server. Similarly, since $\sigma_i.vq$ contains one depletion event and at most one virtual timer for each task, its size is linear in the number of tasks assigned to the server.

Therefore, when server σ_i is active at the time the tick handler is invoked, the tick handler will need to handle $t_t(\sigma_i) = |\Sigma| + d_g + m(\sigma_i) + d_l(\sigma_i)$ events. The complexity of the tick handler is therefore $O(\max_{\sigma_i \in \Sigma} m(\sigma_i) t_t(\sigma_i))$. Note that the tick handler overhead depends only on tasks belonging to the server σ_i which is active at the time of the tick. It does not depend on tasks belonging to other servers.

8.2.4 Experimental results

In Section 6.2 we introduced wakeup events in order to limit the interference due to inactive servers. In order to validate this approach we have also implemented a variant of the HSF scheduler which avoids using wakeup events and instead, whenever a deferrable server σ_i is switched out, it keeps the server queue $\sigma_i.sq$ active. Consequently, the scheduler does not need to synchronize the server queue when switching in a server. However, this overhead is shifted to the tick handler, which needs to handle the expired events in all the server queues from inactive deferrable servers. In the following discussion we refer to this approach as *without limited interference*, as opposed to *with limited interference* based on wakeup events.

Figures 12.a to 12.e compare the two variants. We have varied the number of deferrable servers and the number of tasks assigned to each server (all servers had the same number of tasks). The server replenishment periods and the task periods were all set to the same value (100ms), to exhibit the maximum overhead by having all tasks arrive at the same time. Each task had a computation time of 1ms and each server had a capacity of 7ms. We have run the setup within the cycle-accurate hardware simulator for the OpenRISC 1000 architecture OpenCores (2010). We have set the processor clock to 345MHz and the tick to 1KHz, which is inline with the platform used by our industrial partner. Each experiment was run for an integral number of task periods.

Figures 12.a and 12.b show the maximum measured overheads of the scheduler and the tick handler, while Figures 12.c and 12.d show the total overhead of the scheduler and the tick handler in terms of processor utilization. The figures demonstrate that wakeup events reduce the tick overhead, at the cost of increasing the scheduler overhead, by effectively shifting the overhead of handling server's local events from the tick handler to the scheduler. Since the scheduler overhead is accounted to the server which is switched in, as the number of servers and tasks per server increase, so does the advantage of the limited interference approach. Figure 12.e combines Figures 12.c and 12.d and verifies that the additional overhead due to the wakeup events in the limited interference approach is negligible.

Figure 12.f compares the system overheads of our HSF extension to the standard μC/OS-II implementation. As the standard μC/OS-II does not implement hierarchical scheduling, we have implemented a flat system containing the same number of tasks with the same parameters as in Figures 12.a and 12.b. The results demonstrate the temporal isolation and

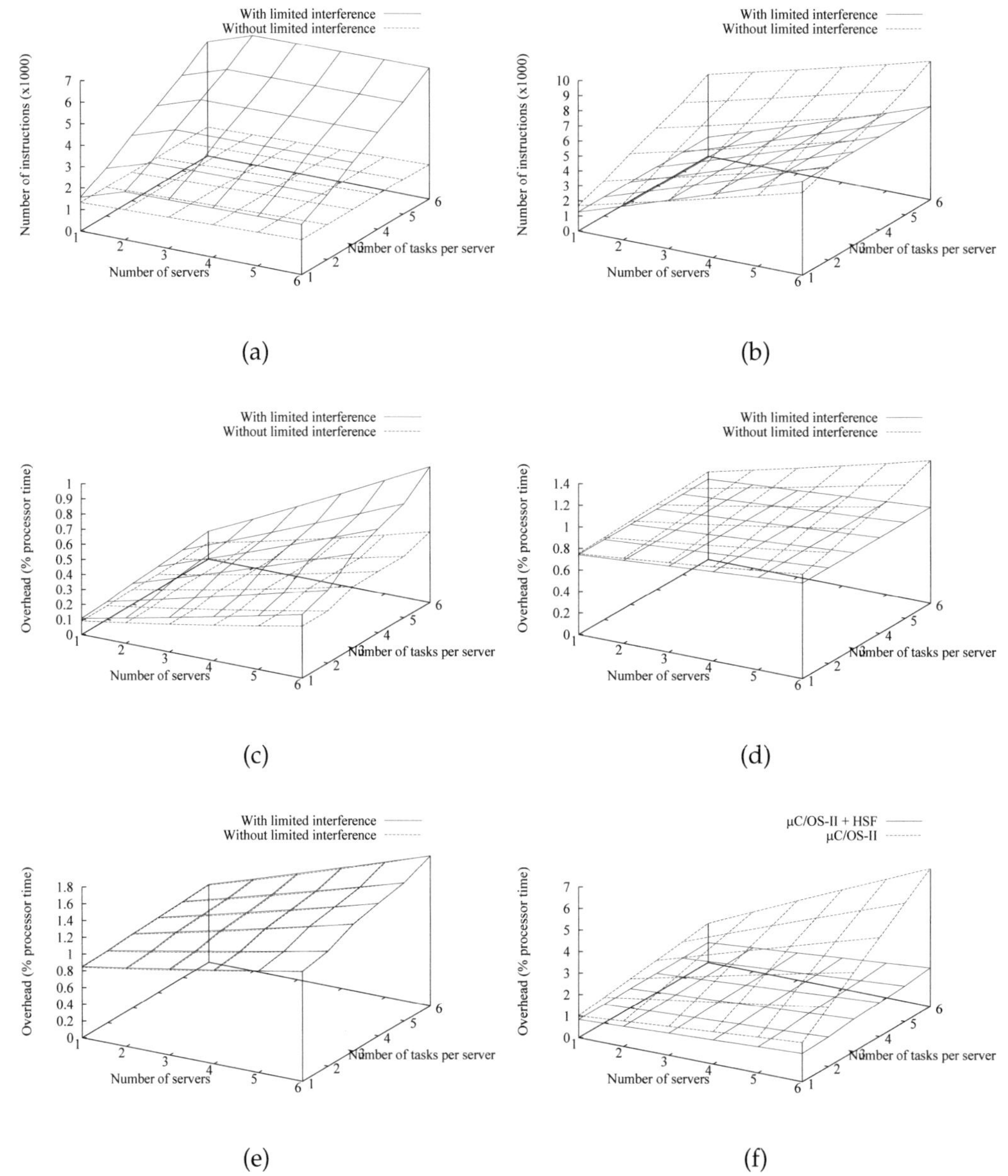

Fig. 12. (a) maximum overhead of the (local + global) scheduler, (b) maximum overhead of the tick handler, (c) total overhead of the scheduler, (d) total overhead of the tick handler, (e) and (f) total overhead of the tick handler and the scheduler.

efficiency of our HSF implementation. While the standard μC/OS-II scans through all tasks on each tick to see if any task delay has expired, in the HSF extension the tick handler needs to consider only head event in the server queue of the currently running server.

Figure 13 compares the best-case and worst-case measured overheads of the scheduler and tick handler between μC/OS-II with our extensions, compared to the standard μC/OS-II, for which we have implemented a flat system containing the same number of tasks with the same parameters as for the μC/OS-II+HSF case.

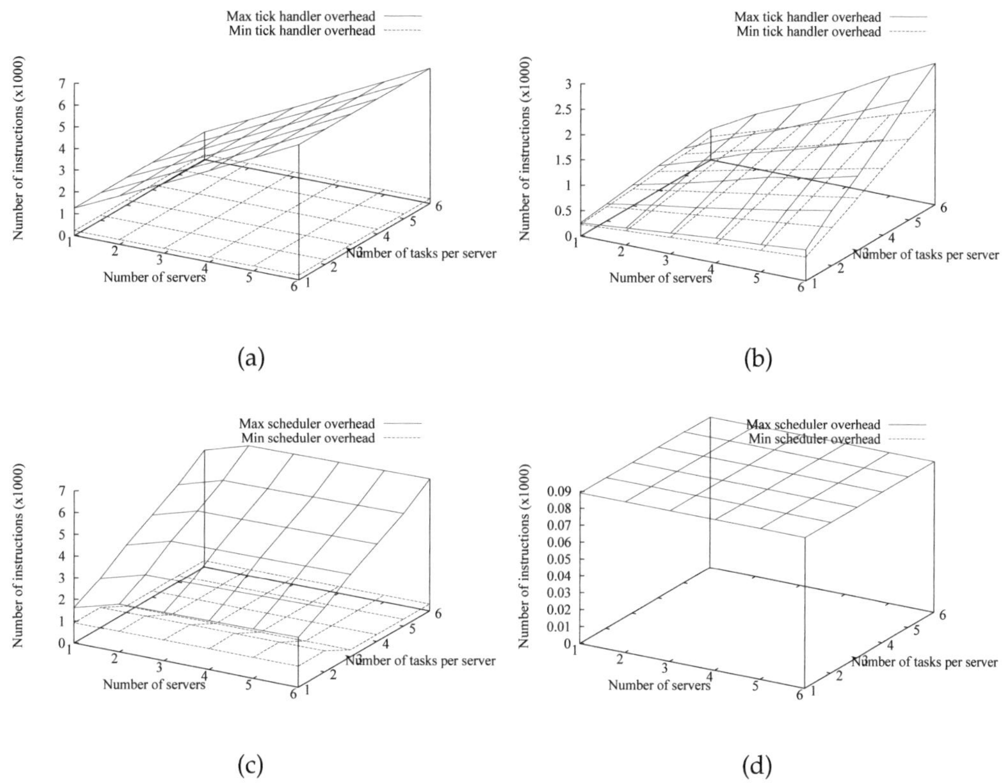

Fig. 13. (a) tick handler overhead in μC/OS-II+HSF, (b) tick handler overhead in μC/OS-II, (c) scheduler overhead in μC/OS-II+HSF, (d) scheduler overhead in μC/OS-II.

The figure shows that both scheduler and tick handler suffer larger execution time jitter under μC/OS-II+HSF, than the standard μC/OS-II. In the best case the μC/OS-II+HSF tick handler needs to decrement only the head of the system queue, while in μC/OS-II the tick hander traverses all the tasks in the system and for each one it checks whether its timer has expired.

In a system with small utilization of individual tasks and servers (as was the case in our experiments), most local events will arrive while the server is switched out. Since handling local events is deferred until the server is switched in and its server queue synchronized with the stopwatch queue, it explains why the worst-case tick handler overhead is increasing with the number of servers and the worst-case scheduler overhead is increasing with the number of tasks per server.

9. Conclusions

We have presented an efficient, modular and extendible design for enhancing a real-time operating system with a two-level HSF. It relies on Relative Timed Event Queues (RELTEQ), a general timer management system targeting embedded systems. Our design supports various server types (including polling, idling periodic, deferrable and constant-bandwidth servers), and global and virtual timers. It supports fixed-priority and EDF schedulers on both local and global level. It provides temporal isolation between components and limits the interference of inactive servers on the active server, by means of wakeup events and a combination of inactive server queues with a stopwatch. We have evaluated a fixed-priority based implementation of our RELTEQ and HSF within the μC/OS-II real-time operating system used in the automotive domain. The results demonstrate that our approach exhibits low performance overhead and limits the necessary modifications of the underlying operating system.

We have assumed a linked-list implementation of our RELTEQ queues, and indicated the challenges of a tree-based implementation due to the relative time representation. In the future we want to investigate in more detail other advanced data structures for implementing RELTEQ queues.

10. References

Abeni, L. & Buttazzo, G. (1998). Integrating multimedia applications in hard real-time systems, *Real-Time Systems Symposium (RTSS)*, pp. 4–14.

Asberg, M., Behnam, M., Nemati, F. & Nolte, T. (2009). Towards hierarchical scheduling in AUTOSAR, *Emerging Technologies Factory Automation (ETFA)*, pp. 1 –8.

AUTOSAR (2011). Automotive open system architecture (AUTOSAR). URL: *http://www.autosar.org*

Behnam, M., Nolte, T., Shin, I., Åsberg, M. & Bril, R. J. (2008). Towards hierarchical scheduling on top of VxWorks, *International Workshop on Operating Systems Platforms for Embedded Real-Time Applications (OSPERT)*, pp. 63–72.

Behnam, M., Shin, I., Nolte, T. & Nolin, M. (2007). Sirap: a synchronization protocol for hierarchical resource sharingin real-time open systems, *International Conference on Embedded Software (EMSOFT)*, pp. 279–288.

Buttazzo, G. & Gai, P. (2006). Efficient EDF implementation for small embedded systems, *International Workshop on Operating Systems Platforms for Embedded Real-Time Applications (OSPERT)*.

Carlini, A. & Buttazzo, G. C. (2003). An efficient time representation for real-time embedded systems, *ACM Symposium on Applied Computing*, pp. 705–712.

Chodrow, S., Jahanian, F. & Donner, M. (1991). Run-time monitoring of real-time systems, *Real-Time Systems Symposium (RTSS)*, pp. 74–83.

Davis, R. I. & Burns, A. (2005). Hierarchical fixed priority pre-emptive scheduling, *Real-Time Systems Symposium (RTSS)*, pp. 389–398.

Engler, D. R., Kaashoek, M. F. & O'Toole, Jr., J. (1995). Exokernel: an operating system architecture for application-level resource management, *Symposium on Operating Systems Principles (SOSP)*, pp. 251–266.

Eswaran, A., Rowe, A. & Rajkumar, R. (2005). Nano-RK: An energy-aware resource-centric RTOS for sensor networks, *Real-Time Systems Symposium (RTSS)*, pp. 256–265.

Evidence (n.d.). ERIKA Enterprise: Open Source RTOS for single- and multi-core applications. URL: *http://www.evidence.eu.com*

Faggioli, D., Trimarchi, M., Checconi, F. & Scordino, C. (2009). An EDF scheduling class for the linux kernel, *Real-Time Linux Workshop*.

Holenderski, M., Cools, W., Bril, R. J. & Lukkien, J. J. (2009). Multiplexing real-time timed events, *Emerging Technologies and Factory Automation (ETFA)*, pp. 1718–1721.

Holenderski, M., Cools, W., Bril, R. J. & Lukkien, J. J. (2010). Extending an open-source real-time operating system with hierarchical scheduling, *Technical Report CS-report 10-10*, Eindhoven University of Technology.

Inam, R., Maki-Turja, J., Sjodin, M., Ashjaei, S. & Afshar, S. (2011). Support for hierarchical scheduling in freertos, *Emerging Technologies Factory Automation (ETFA)*, pp. 1 –10.

Kim, D., Lee, Y.-H. & Younis, M. (2000). SPIRIT-μKernel for strongly partitioned real-time systems, *Real-Time Systems and Applications (RTCSA)*, pp. 73–80.

Labrosse, J. J. (2002). *MicroC/OS-II: The Real Time Kernel*, 2nd edition edn, CMP Books.

Lehoczky, J. P., Sha, L. & Strosnider, J. K. (1987). Enhanced aperiodic responsiveness in hard real-time environments, *Real-Time Systems Symposium (RTSS)*, pp. 261–270.

Mercer, C., Rajkumar, R. & Zelenka, J. (1994). Temporal protection in real-time operating systems, *IEEE Workshop on Real-Time Operating Systems and Software*, pp. 79–83.

Nolte, T. (2011). Compositionality and CPS from a platform perspective, *Embedded and Real-Time Computing Systems and Applications (RTCSA)*, Vol. 2, pp. 57 –60.

Nolte, T., Shin, I., Behnam, M. & Sjödin, M. (2009). A synchronization protocol for temporal isolation of software components in vehicular systems, *IEEE Transactions on Industrial Informatics* 5(4): 375–387.

Oikawa, S. & Rajkumar, R. (1999). Portable RK: a portable resource kernel for guaranteed and enforced timing behavior, *Real-Time Technology and Applications Symposium (RTAS)*, pp. 111–120.

OpenCores (2010). Openrisc 1000: Architectural simulator. URL: *http://opencores.org/openrisc,or1ksim*

Palopoli, L., Cucinotta, T., Marzario, L. & Lipari, G. (2009). Aquosa—adaptive quality of service architecture, *Software – Practice and Experience* 39(1): 1–31.

Rajkumar, R., Juvva, K., Molano, A. & Oikawa, S. (1998). Resource kernels: A resource-centric approach to real-time and multimedia systems, *Conference on Multimedia Computing and Networking (CMCN)*, pp. 150–164.

Saewong, S., Rajkumar, R. R., Lehoczky, J. P. & Klein, M. H. (2002). Analysis of hierarchical fixed-priority scheduling, *Euromicro Conference on Real-Time Systems (ECRTS)*, p. 173.

Shin, I. & Lee, I. (2003). Periodic resource model for compositional real-time guarantees, *Real-Time Systems Symposium (RTSS)*, pp. 2–13.

Shin, I. & Lee, I. (2008). Compositional real-time scheduling framework with periodic model, *ACM Transactions on Embedded Computing Systems* 7: 30:1–30:39.

Strosnider, J. K., Lehoczky, J. P. & Sha, L. (1995). The deferrable server algorithm for enhanced aperiodic responsiveness in hard real-time environments, *IEEE Transactions on Computers* 44(1): 73–91.

van den Heuvel, M. M. H. P., Holenderski, M., Bril, R. J. & Lukkien, J. J. (2011). Constant-bandwidth supply for priority processing, *IEEE Transactions on Consumer Electronics* 57(2): 873–881.

van den Heuvel, M. M. H. P., Holenderski, M., Cools, W., Bril, R. J. & Lukkien, J. J. (2009). Virtual timers in hierarchical real-time systems, *Work in Progress session of the Real-time Systems Symposium (RTSS).*

Part 2

Specification and Verification

5

Specification and Validation of Real-Time Systems Using UML Sequence Diagrams

Zbigniew Huzar and Anita Walkowiak
Wrocław University of Technology, Institute of Informatics
Poland

1. Introduction

UML (OMG, 2011) is considered as a contemporary standard in information systems development. Being a graphical modeling language it offers a family of diagrams that may be used for specification and designing of information systems. Sequence diagrams, being a part of the family, are very often used to specify functional requirements of the developed systems and are typically associated with the use case realizations in the logical view of the system under development. They show how actors involved in the scenario representing a use case realization cooperate with system's objects. Therefore, the meaning of a sequence diagram is a set of scenarios, each describing interaction between objects of the designed system and its environment. Semantics of sequence diagrams is defined informally in plain language, and, additionally, the definition is limited to the interpretation of single diagrams. But in nontrivial cases a set of sequence diagrams is necessary to give a complete specification of the system's behavior, and therefore the interpretation of the set of such diagrams is needed. Since UML has informal semantics, a set of sequence diagrams brings some interpretation problems. The problem becomes even more difficult when the real-time systems are designed when numerous time constraints are associated with the diagrams.

Hence, the primary aim of the chapter is to give a precise interpretation of a set of sequence diagrams with time constraints. The formal interpretation is necessary to construct programming tools supporting validation of the systems' behavior specification, and possibly prototyping of the systems. The chapter demonstrates how the set of scenarios specifying system's behavior may be derived from the set of sequence diagrams, and how this set may be analyzed against its consistency and completeness.

Another aim of the chapter is to propose an approach to real-time systems specification. Real-time systems have some peculiarities. For example, a typical task for a real-time system is to track the events from its environment and then responding to them, within imposed time constraints, through the generation of new events targeted to the environment. To follow such schemata, we propose to extend the UML sequence diagrams with new kinds of stereotyped combined fragments.

A specific methodological aspect of real-time system specification is also considered. Namely, very often, in addition to an explicit description of the behavior of the system, additional properties such as safety and liveness, are taken into account. Usually, the properties are expressed in modal logics. We propose to use sequence diagrams to express them, to obtain in this way uniformity of means for a system specification. For this purpose, the notion of monitoring scenarios is introduced. Monitoring scenarios are specified by sequence diagrams, and are used to define liveness and safety properties of the system's behavior.

In the chapter, the proposed semantics of extended sequence diagrams is explained, and an example of a simple system specification and its analysis are presented. The analysis is done by means of the prototype of a programming tool that enables analysis of system's behavior against consistency and completeness as well as checking its liveness and safety properties.

The chapter is organized as follows.

Section 2 presents how UML sequence diagrams are defined, and also introduces new kinds of combined fragments that are used to define extended sequence diagrams. A set of extended sequence diagrams is used to represent the behavior of a real-time system.

Section 3 outlines our approach to specification of the real-time systems. The approach uses class diagrams to represent the structural aspect, and a set of sequence diagrams to represent the behavioral aspect of the specified system. A specific feature of the approach is a possibility to extend the behavior specification with additional monitoring diagrams - sequence diagrams - representing forbidden and expected behaviors. In this way we introduce some redundancy to the behavior specification, which enables checking safety and liveness of system's behavior. The approach is illustrated by a simple example.

In Section 4, an informal semantics of real-time system specification is explained; a notion of the graph of possible scenarios is defined. The graph is derived from the set of extended sequence diagrams, and defines a set of possible scenarios representing system's behavior.

System's specification requires validation with respect to consistency, definiteness and completeness. These properties are defined and discussed in Section 5.

Section 6 is the main section of the chapter. It formalizes semantics of a set of extended sequence diagrams. First, it defines a set of basic notions, and next it formally presents construction of the graph of possible scenarios which are semantics of a set of sequence diagrams.

Section 7 ends the chapter with concluding remarks.

2. Sequence diagrams in UML

Features of real-time systems define some requirements put on the system development process, and in consequence, on specification language used in this process. The language, in which the specification is expressed, should be characterized by the right power of expression (allowing a description of real-time systems, and development of system models for the assumed point of view), and should be abstract (allowing an appropriate level of detail description). Additionally, the language should be supported by programming tools enabling validation (confirmation that the informal user's needs are met) and verification (checking the specification against a set of properties: consistency, completeness, determinism) of specifications.

There are several languages that enable real-time systems specification, but we focus on UML, especially on UML sequence diagrams that are drawn from Message Sequence Charts (ITU-T, 2004; Cleaveland & Sengupta, 2006). UML 2.4 sequence diagrams provide mechanisms for specification of time properties (OMG, 2011).

A sequence diagram represents an interaction - a set of communications among objects arranged visually in time order. The diagram shows the objects with their lifelines participating in an interaction, and the sequences of exchanged messages, but it does not show object relationships. So, the diagram forms an interaction that consists of objects' lifelines and messages exchanged between the lifelines. For each message there are two events: sending and receiving.

The newest version of UML 2.4.1 enables explicit handling of real-time events on sequence diagrams. The basic mechanisms are: observation of current time, especially observation of time of an event occurrence, and observation of duration of message transmission. As in the previous versions of UML, time constraints may be specified - see Fig.1. The constraints may take into account times of sending and receiving a message, duration of a message transmission, times of occurring of selected events etc.

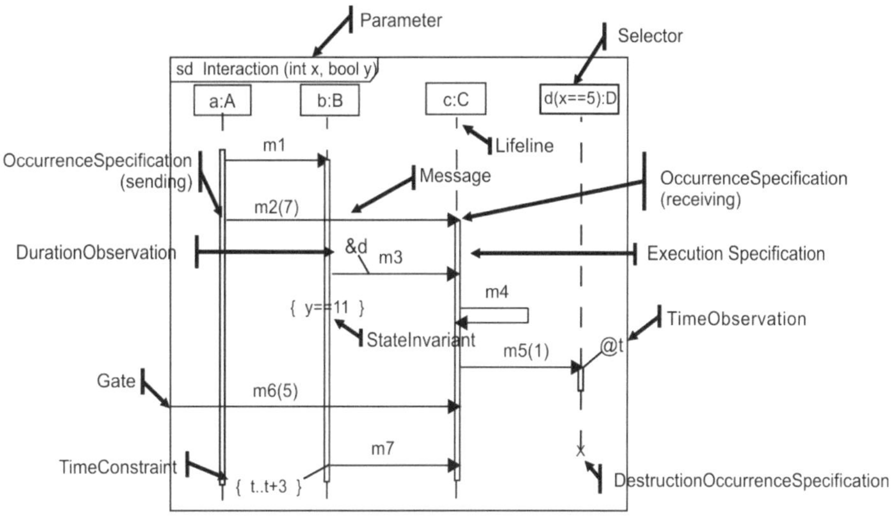

Fig. 1. Sequence diagram with time constraints

Sequence diagrams can exist in a descriptor form (describing all possible scenarios) and in an instance form (describing one actual scenario). The descriptor form uses combined fragments that are shown as nested regions within a sequence diagram. A combined fragment defines an expression of interaction fragments. A combined fragment is defined by an interaction operator and corresponding interaction operands. There are a number of combined fragments for representing contingent behavior, such as conditionals, loops, and so on. A combined fragment has a keyword, e.g., *alt, break, par, loop, seq, strict,* that specifies its type. Depending on the keyword, there are one or more embedded operands, each of which is a structured subfragment of the overall interaction. A combined fragment may also have zero or more gates, which specify the interface between the combined fragment and other parts of the interaction.

Following specific features of real-time systems, a new combined fragment is introduced. It is a composition of two new stereotypes «action» and «reaction» applied to arguments of the combined fragment with operator *strict* (Fig. 2a). This combined fragment expresses a typical cooperation schema between a computer system and its environment: the system should respond to signals received from the environment. The argument with the stereotype «action» specifies a message or a sequence of messages that represent a stimulus from the environment, and the argument with the stereotype «reaction» specifies a message or a sequence of messages that represent the system response. Both arguments are linked via strict sequencing operator which means that if the scenario represented by the argument «action» is executed then the scenario represented by the argument «reaction» must occur.

The other two combined fragments presented in Fig. 2b and 2c are new stereotypes of *assert* and *neg* combined fragments. The fragments are used to define liveness and safety properties, respectively, of the specified system. The first one means that if the execution reaches the beginning of the construct, then the behavior of the fragment, as an expected behavior of the specified system, must occur. The second one defines the behavior of the fragment, as a forbidden behavior of the system, may not occur.

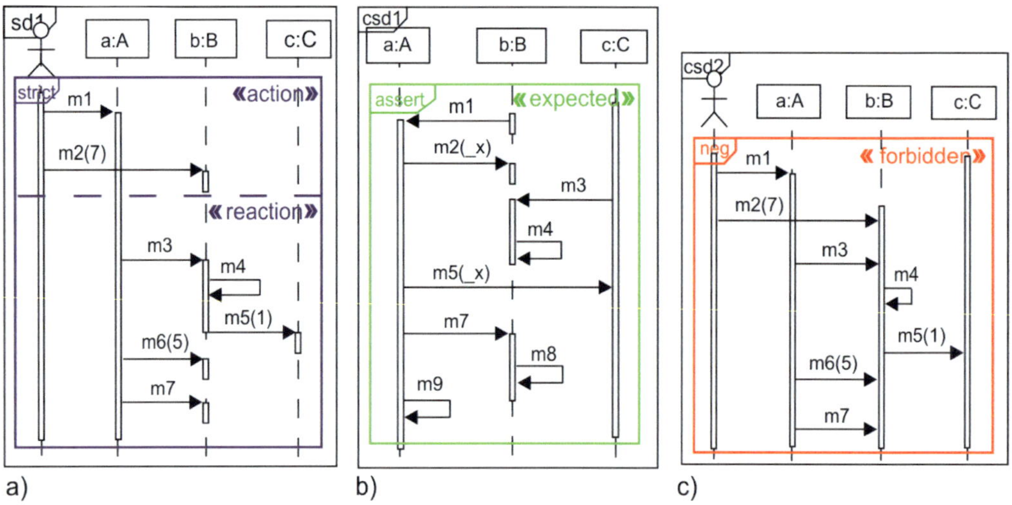

Fig. 2. Examples of sequence diagram with specific combined fragments

3. Real-time system specification

In the presented approach to system specification we define the system as a pair of two elements: the system structure that expresses the static aspect, and its behavior that presents the dynamic aspect of the system. Specification of the static aspect *sSpec* is expressed by UML class and objects diagrams while specification of the behavioral aspect *bSpec* – by a set of extended UML sequence diagrams. So, the system specification is defined as:

$$Spec_{UML} = \langle sSpec, bSpec \rangle$$

In a typical approach, one would expect that the set of sequence diagrams *bSpec* will specify only the desired behavior of the developed system. Usually, such a set of sequence diagrams reflects a family of user stories; each describing a scenario or scenarios represented by a sequence diagram.

The peculiarity of the proposed approach lies in that the set of diagrams may contain also additional diagrams called monitoring diagrams. The idea to use the monitoring diagrams comes from the postulate, that we expect high level of credibility of specification of each system, and especially specification of the real-time system. The monitoring diagrams introduce some redundancy to the specification and, in this way, increase its credibility. So, the behavioral aspect *bSpec* consists of two sets of sequence diagrams:

$$bSpec = Sd_{spec} \cup Sd_{monit}$$

where the set Sd_{spec} specifies the desired behavior of the system, and the set Sd_{monit} defines monitored behaviors. The monitored behaviors may in turn be split into forbidden and expected behaviors, namely:

$$Sd_{monit} = Sd_{forbidden} \cup Sd_{expected}.$$

The forbidden behaviors represent the safety property of the developed system, i.e., they express the fact that the undesirable situation will not appear during system execution (the system does not reach unacceptable states).

The expected behaviors represent the liveness property of the system, i.e., express the fact that if some situation is required it will happen eventually during the system execution (the system reaches desirable states).

The liveness and safety properties (Nissanke, 1997) are usually expressed in a language of modal logics (Manna & Pnueli, 1992; Manna & Pnueli, 1995). Having a model or a system's prototype, one examines whether the model or prototype complies with specified properties (*model checking*). Peculiarity of the presented approach is to use sequence diagrams to express these both properties. In this way we obtain the possibility of specifying the system's behavior and its properties using a uniform mechanism of sequence diagrams.

An example of a system specification is presented below. The example specifies a simple real-time system which controls and monitors a bakery. Fig. 3 presents a class diagram representing components of the system.

The behavior of the system is described by three user stories represented in Figs. 4, 5 and 6.

The first user story is presented on three sequence diagrams - Fig. 4. They describe reaction of the system when the main switch of the control panel is clicked to on or to off. When the main switch of the control panel is clicked to on, the main light should be turned on and the console background color should be changed to green. When the switch is clicked to off, the light should be turned off, and the console background color should be changed to white.

The second user story is presented on two sequence diagrams - Fig. 5. The story relates to an alarm situation when the current temperature of the bakery exceeds the permissible temperature for some period of time. In reaction to the situation the main light on the console is changed to red, and next, alternatively, the controller switches off the system, or the user decides about switching off or setting a new permissible temperature.

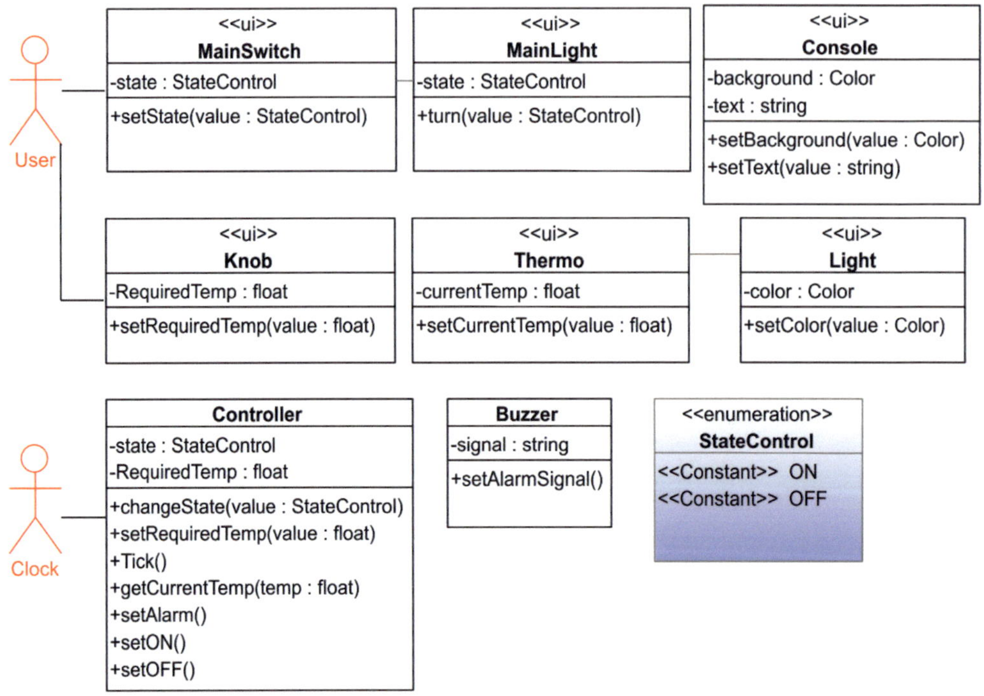

Fig. 3. Class diagram for the example

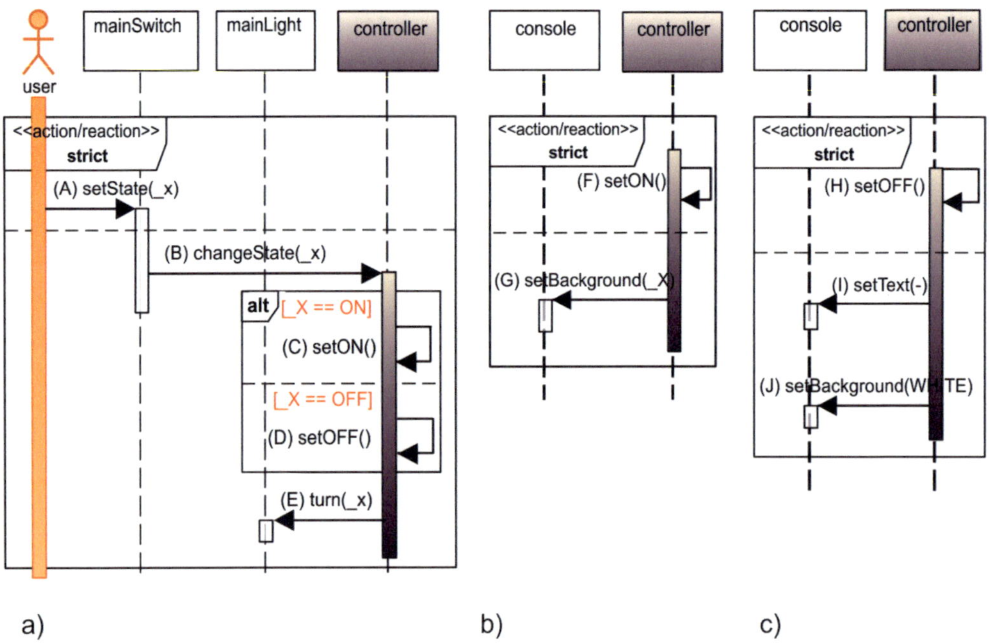

Fig. 4. Sequence diagrams – representation of the first user story

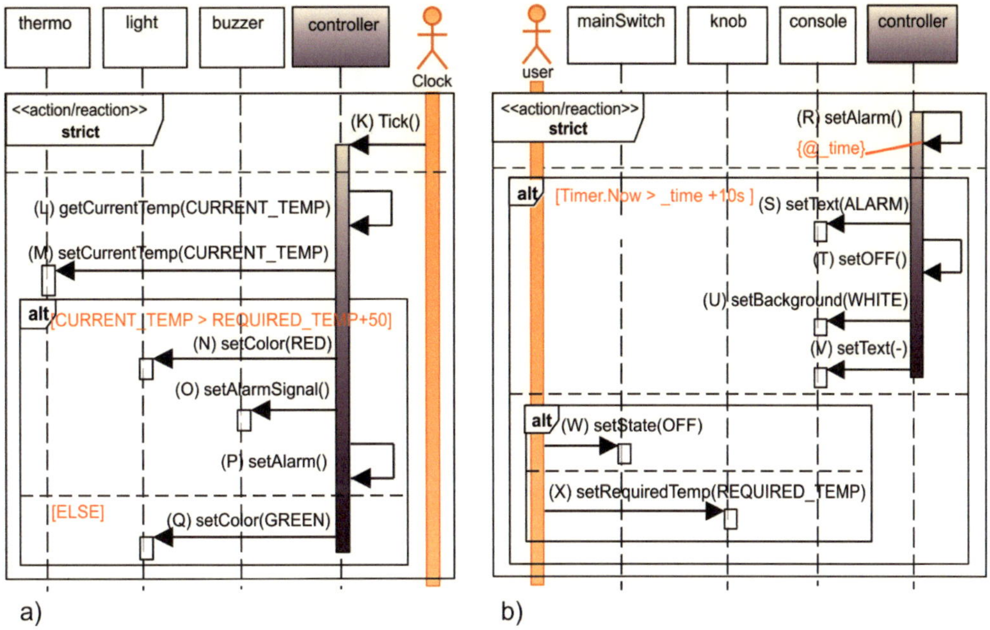

Fig. 5. Sequence diagrams – representation of the second user story

The last, a very simple user story – Fig. 6 – describes reaction of the system on setting a new permissible temperature by the user.

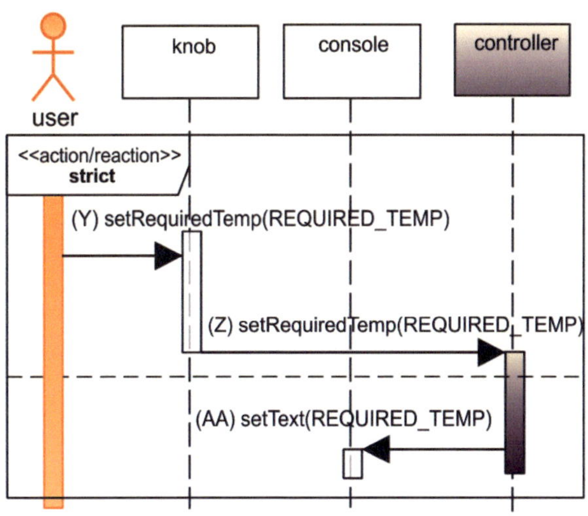

Fig. 6. Sequence diagrams – representation of the third user story

Two sequence diagrams in Fig. 7 represent the expected and forbidden behaviors of the specified system. The scenario from Fig. 7b should belong to the set of expected scenarios of the system, while the scenario from Fig. 7a should not belong to this set of scenarios.

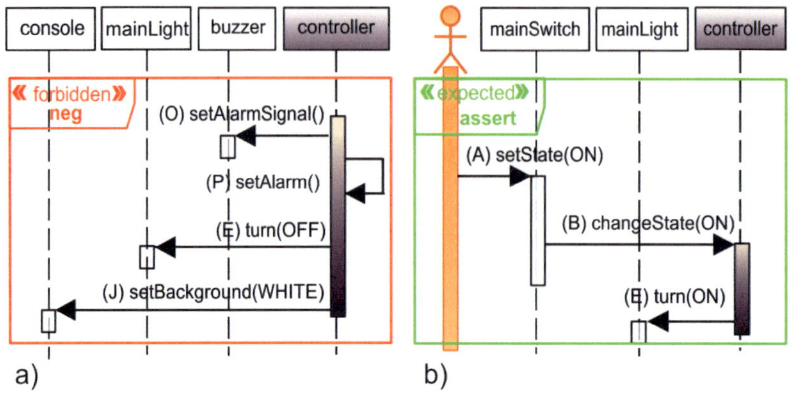

Fig. 7. Sequence diagrams - representation of expected and forbidden behaviors

4. Informal semantics of a set of sequence diagrams

The definition of UML presented in the standard (OMG, 2011) is informal. Lack of formal semantics brings ambiguity problems (Harel & Maoz, 2008; Störrle, 2004), especially in the case of automation of system development process and design of tools supporting the process. Furthermore, the possibility of UML model-checking is limited to syntax verification. To allow analysis of the properties of the spetcification formulated in UML, we propose a transformation of the specification - a set of sequence diagrams - to the abstract model which describes the behavior of the modeled system as a graph of possible scenarios (Fig. 8).

The graph of possible scenarios consists of nodes and arcs. Nodes represent system's configurations, meaning its states. Arcs represent events that cause transitions between configurations. Events may represent message sending or message receiving, time events and synchronization events. The latter are related to entering into or exiting from the combined fragments or their arguments.

The structure of the graph is similar to a tree. The root of the tree represents an initial configuration, in general, while leafs represent final configurations. It is possible however for some leafs to return to the initial configuration what is formally represented by an arc labeled with an artificial event δ. It is also possible to have loops for some configurations. The loops are labeled by synchronization events that do not change system configurations. A sequence of transitions starting from the initial configuration (a scenario) may be finite or infinite. The set of all sequences of transitions defines the set of possible scenarios of interactions between the system and its environment.

Fig. 8 presents only a fragment of the graph of possible scenarios for our exemplary specification. The graph contains only selected scenarios that are derived from the specification. The labels on arcs are symbols of messages taken from the sequence diagrams.

Now, semantics of the set of sequence diagrams may be defined as the set of all scenarios - sequences of events - generated by this graph. The scenarios are derived from fragments of interactions represented by single diagrams. On the basis of the set of sequence diagrams the graph expressing all derived scenarios is constructed.

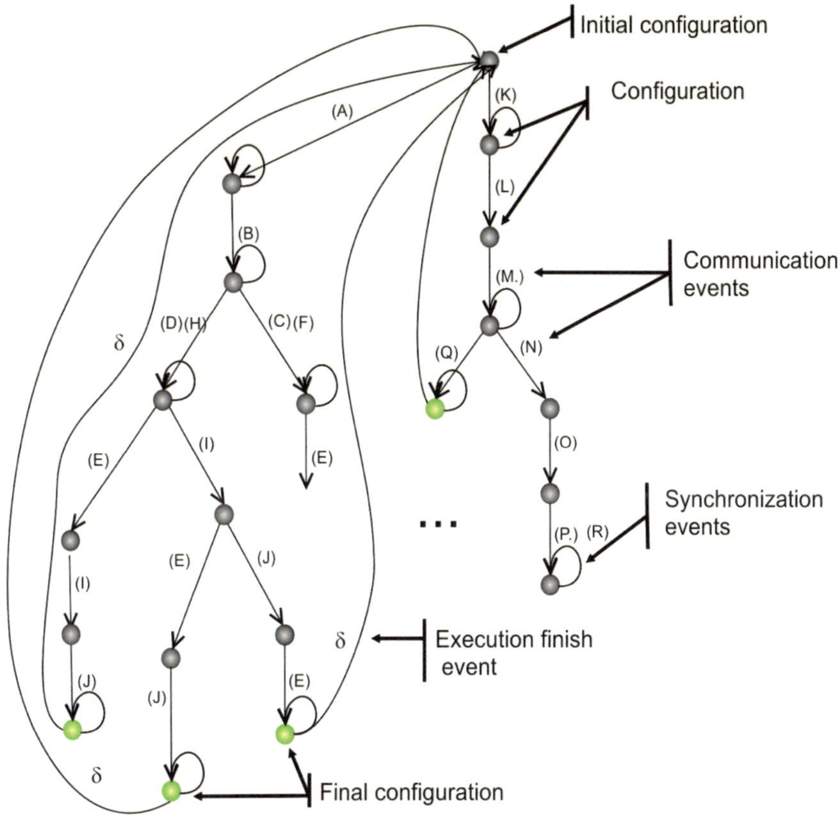

Fig. 8. Fragments of the graph of possible scenarios

The algorithm constructs the graph while walking from one location to another location along the lifelines on the sequence diagrams. A location is a time point on an object's lifeline with attached event, e.g. sending or receiving message. A set which for each lifeline of a given single diagram contains its location constitutes a snapshot of the diagram.

The snapshot represents current progress of the behavior modeled by the sequence diagram. The diagram together with its snapshot and the values of currently exchanged messages constitute a live copy of the diagram. The set of live copies of all diagrams which are involved into common scenario, i.e. operate on the same messages, determines a configuration. A configuration is changing when an event appears.

Of course, construction of the graph has to take into account all possible relationships between scenarios presented by individual sequence diagrams. In particular, in the first place, a consistency between scenarios has to be checked. The algorithm of the graph construction is presented in details in Section 6.

5. Specification properties

Each specification should be unambiguous and a complete formulation of the user's requirements. We check the specification against the following three properties: definiteness, consistency and completeness. Definiteness and consistency may be checked automatically whereas it is not possible for completeness. Completeness refers to the domain of application and therefore it requires domain expertise; it can also be validated experimentally.

As our specifications are executable, the experiments are possible and the user observing system's behavior may decide on completeness of the specification. Nevertheless, some aspects of completeness may be checked automatically. For example, if a sequence diagram contains a message being the system response, a stimulating action is expected.

The notions of definiteness and consistency as defined below may be automatically checked. Consistency is essential and indispensable property of the specification. General definition of consistency is given in (Huzar & Walkowiak, 2010). Here, we concentrate on partial orders of exchanged messages defined by different sequence diagrams. Two orders are consistent, if the sequences determined by matching messages are the same. Consistency of specification means that partial message orders, determined by different sequence diagrams defining one scenario of interactions between the system and its environment, are consistent.

The specification is undefined if there is at least one undefined transition in a scenario derived from the set of sequence diagrams. A transition may be undefined due to an undefined value of exchanged messages.

The algorithm constructing the graph of possible scenarios is extended by the analysis of consistency, definiteness and completeness of the specification.

The analysis of the specification is carried out during the configuration transformations. Particular configurations are processed until the following appears:

- the end of interaction being a reaction to a stimulus from the environment is reached (the set of live copies of the reached configuration is empty),
- inconsistency in the message orders,
- identification of the events, which refer to indefinite values of messages (indefiniteness),
- identification of the messages exchanged between the system elements or the messages sent from the system to its environment such that they appear in activation part of a sequence diagram and there is not another sequence diagram which contains the same messages in reaction part (incompleteness).

Now we consider consistency, definiteness and completeness of the exemplary specification.

The sequence diagrams in Figs. 4c and 5b represent fragments of the same scenario of the interaction between the system and its environment. The scenario specifies the system response to the situation when the bakery temperature exceeds the desired temperature by 50^0 C by 10 seconds from the time of its detection.

Observe that there is a contradiction in ordering of the matching messages *setBackgound*(WHITE) and *setText*(-) on these diagrams. According to the diagram in Fig. 5b when the alarm is detected, the display's background is change to white and next its content is reset. According to the diagram in Fig. 4c, in this situation the controller changes its state to OFF, and the display's content is reset, and next its background is changed to white.

Using of the variable in the message C, Fig. 4b, changing display's background, results in specification indefiniteness - lack of an event, which allows defining the value of the considered variable during the execution. The variable is not symbolic (its value isn't assigned by the environment), and none of diagrams activated during the transformation (which forms the considered interaction scenario) contains any matched message which value would be assigned to the considered variable.

The message in the activation part of the combined fragment in Fig. 6 informing about a change of the temperature requested by the user (message Z), entails incompleteness of the specification. The message specifies system's reaction to the action from its environment and therefore links two different fragments of the same scenario. However, there is no another diagram containing this message in its reaction part.

The complete graph of all possible scenarios with the results of its analysis is given in Fig. 9.

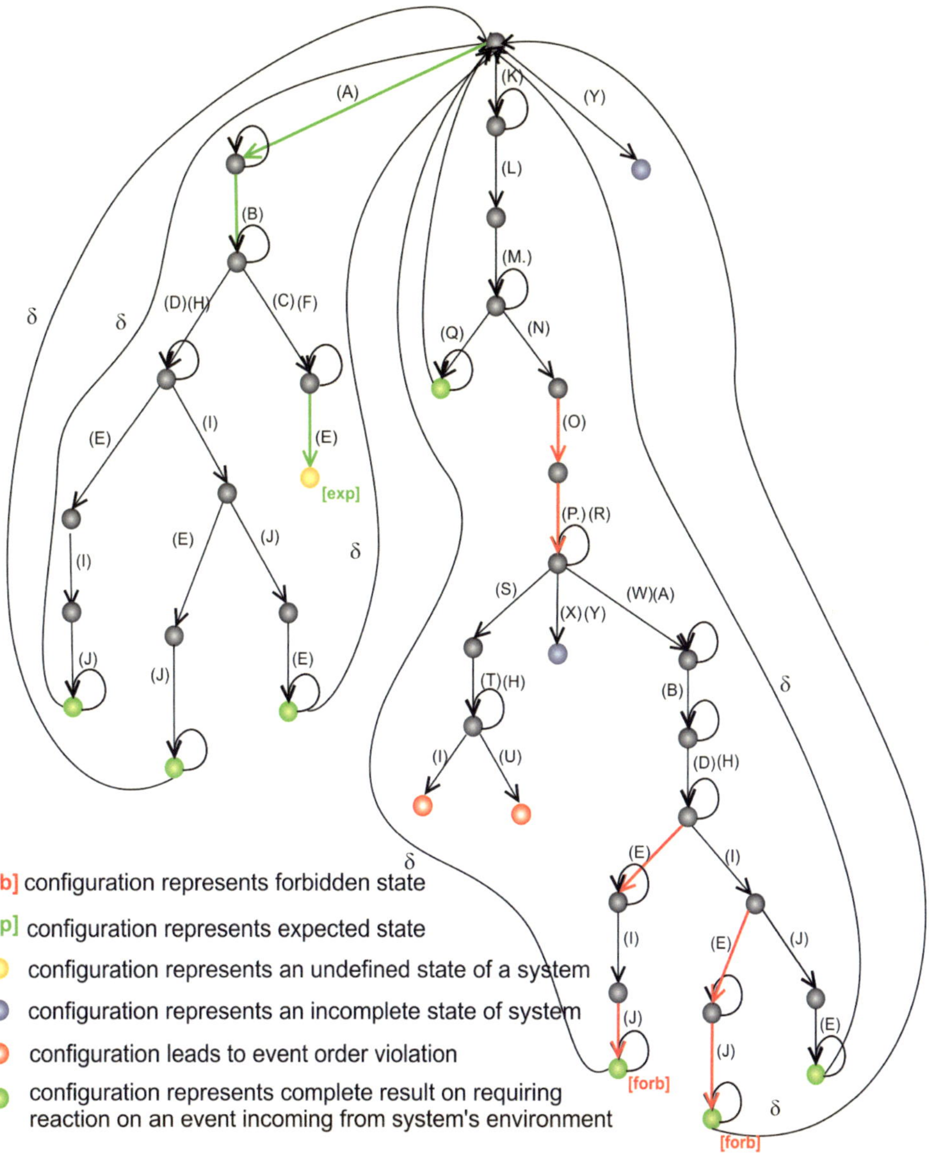

Fig. 9. Complete (interpreted) graph of possible scenarios

6. Graph of possible scenarios

The Section gives formal definitions (subsection 6.1) that are necessary to present formally construction of the graph of possible scenarios (subsection 6.2). In this way formal semantics of a set of extended sequence diagram is defined.

6.1 Basic definitions

In the definitions given below we introduce basic meta-classes from the meta-model of the extended sequence diagram. For the sake of simplicity we will treat the meta-classes as sets of specific elements. Therefore the notation *e* : *M*, where *e* is a name of an element, and *M* is a name of a meta-class, will be read: *e* is an instance of the meta-class *M*, or *e* is an element of the set *M*.

We will use dotted notation: if *e* is some element and *p* is its property then the expression *e.p* means the value of the property *p* of the element *e*.

Notation and meta-elements of the system specification

$\perp$	An undefined value
$DataType$	A family of data types, each defined as a set of values and set of operations over the set of values; $d{:}\,DataType$ denotes the data type d from this family
Ω_d	A set of values of the data type $d{:}\,DataType$
Ω	A set of values of all data types: $\bigcup_{d:DataType}\Omega_d$
$Attribute$	A set of attributes, each defined as: $\langle name{:}\,String, d{:}\,DataType\rangle$
$Parameter$	A set of formal parameters; each defined as: $\langle name{:}\,String, d{:}\,DataType\rangle$
$Operation$	A set of operations, each defined as: $\langle name{:}\,String, parm{:}\,Parameter\rangle$
$ClassifierType$	The enumeration type of classifiers: $\{actor, external, ui, internal\}$
$Classifier$	A set of classifiers, each defined as: $\langle name{:}\,String, A{:}\,Attribute[*], O{:}\,Operation[*], type{:}\,ClassifierType\rangle$
$ClassifierModel$	A set of classifier models, each defined as: $\langle D{:}\,DataType[*], C{:}\,Classifier[*]\rangle$
$Instance$	A set of instances, each defined as: $\langle name{:}\,String, c{:}\,Classifier\rangle$
$InstanceModel$	A set of instances' models, each defined as: $\langle I{:}\,Instance[*]\rangle$
$StructureSpecification$	A set of system structure specifications, each defined as: $\langle cM{:}\,ClassifierModel, iM{:}\,InstanceModel\rangle$
$Environment$	A set of instances in the system's environment
$Time$	A set of time points
$LifeLine$	A set of life lines, each defined as: $\langle i{:}\,Instance, T{:}\,Time[*], t_0{:}\,Time\rangle$
$Variable$	A set of variables at a sequence diagram, each defined as: $\langle name{:}\,String, d{:}\,DataType, \omega, \Phi\rangle$, where: ω=& means symbolic (dynamically defined) variable, ω=⊥ means undefined variable, and $\Phi \subseteq \Omega_d \cup I$ – defines the set of values that cannot be assigned to the variable; initially $\Phi = \emptyset$; if $\Phi \neq \emptyset$ then $\omega \in \{\perp, \&\}$.
$Message$	A set of messages, each defined as: $\langle l_{src}{:}\,LifeLine, l_{dst}{:}\,LifeLine, o{:}\,Operation, arg{:}\,Variable, sendEvent{:}\,ComEvent, recvEvent{:}\,ComEvent\rangle$
$Operator$	A set of operators of combined fragments: $\{alt, par, strict, assert, neg\}$

$CombinedFragmentArgument$	A set of arguments of a combined fragment
$CombinedFragment$	A set of combined fragments, each defined as: $\langle oper: Operator, CfL: LifeLine[*], CfA: CombinedFragmentArgument[*], guard: String\rangle$
$Event$	A set of events at a sequence diagram, each defined as: $\langle eventTime: Time[*]\rangle$
$ComEventType$	A set of types of communication events: $\{send, recv\}$
$ComEvent$	A set of communication events associated with message sending or receiving, each defined as: $\langle msg: Message, type: ComEventType\rangle$
$SyncEventType$	A set of types of synchronization events: $\{entry, exit\}$
$SyncEvent$	A set of synchronization events associated with an entry into or exit from a combined fragment or its argument, each defined as: $\langle f: CombinedFragment \cup CombinedFragmentArgument, type: SyncEventType\rangle$
$SequenceDiagram$	A set of sequence diagrams, each defined as: $\langle name: String, L: LifeLine[*], Var: Variable[*], Msg: Message[*], Cf: CombinedFragment[*], cf_0: CombinedFragment, E_{com}: ComEvent[*], E_{sync}: SyncEvent[*]\rangle$
$BehaviourSpecification$	A set of system behavior specifications, each defined as: $\langle Sd_{spec}: SequenceDiagram[*], Sd_{monit}: SequenceDiagram[*] = Sd_{forbidden} \cup Sd_{expected}\rangle$
src	The function $src: Message \longrightarrow Instance$ yields the instance which sends a message: $src(msg) = msg.l_{src}.i$
dst	The function $dst: Message \longrightarrow Instance$ yields the instance which receives a message: $dst(msg) = msg.l_{dst}.i$
$action$	The function $action: SequenceDiagram \longrightarrow CombinedFragmentArgument$ for a given sequence diagram, yields the argument of a combined fragment stereotyped by «*action*»
$reaction$	The function $reaction: SequenceDiagram \longrightarrow CombinedFragmentArgument$ for a given sequence diagram, yields the argument of a combined fragment stereotyped by «*reaction*»
$enclosing$	The function $enclosing: Message \cup Event \cup CombinedFragment \longrightarrow CombinedFragmentArgument \cup \{\perp\}$ for a given specification element, yields an argument of the combined fragment in which the element is nested directly; if there is no such an argument the function returns $\perp$
$allEnclosing$	The function $allEnclosing: Message \cup Event \cup CombinedFragment \longrightarrow 2^{CombinedFragmentArgument}$ for a given specification element, yields a list of arguments of all combined fragment in which the element is nested:
$\preccurlyeq_{sd} \subseteq Time^2$	A partial ordering relations defined on the set of time points at lifelines of a given extended sequence diagram
$\preccurlyeq_{sd} \subseteq Event^2$	A partial ordering relations defined on the set of events of a given extended sequence diagram

The series of the following definitions refines some notions, e.g. snapshot, configuration, which were informally introduced in Section 4.

Definition 6.1.1

A snapshot of a sequence diagram sd, noted $s_{sd}: Snapshot$, is defined as the set:

$$s_{sd} = \{\langle l, t\rangle \mid l \in sd.L, t \in l.T\} \quad (6.1.1)$$

where:

- l - is a lifeline of an object from the diagram *sd*, and
- t - is a time instance at the lifeline l representing time of a communication event or a synchronization event on entry to or exit from a combined fragment.

The function $initial: SequenceDiagram \longrightarrow Snapshot$ yields an initial snapshot of a sequence diagram.

An example of a snapshot of a sequence diagram is presented in Fig. 10.

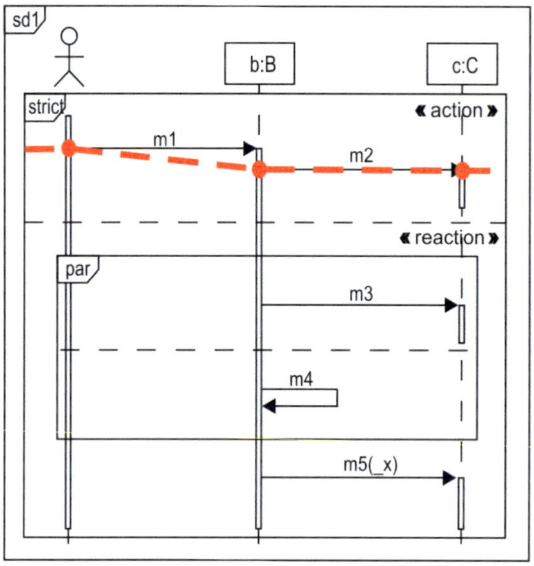

Fig. 10. An example of a snapshot

Let $l.t_i$ means the i-th time point at the life line l of the sequence diagram.

Definition 6.1.2

A set of time points $T \subseteq \bigcup_{l \in sd.L} l.T$ is said to be closed when:

$$\forall_{l \in sd.L}: \forall_{l.t_x \in T}: y \leq x \iff l.t_y \in T \quad (6.1.2)$$

Definition 6.1.3

A lower closure $\downarrow s_{sd}$ of a snapshot s_{sd} is defined as the minimal closed set of time points of the diagram *sd* which contains all points of the snapshot.

A snapshot s_{sd} is correct if:

$$\forall_{\langle l,t\rangle \in s_{sd}}: \forall_{t' \in l.T}: t' \preccurlyeq_{sd} t \iff t' \in \downarrow s_{sd} \quad (6.1.3)$$

Definition 6.1.4

An active copy of the sequence diagram *sd*, noted lc_{sd}: *LiveCopy*, is defined as the triple:

$$lc_{sd} = \langle sd, s_{sd}, mode \rangle \quad (6.1.4)$$

where:

- *sd* – is a copy of the sequence diagram with the valuation of its variables,
- s_{sd} – a snapshot of the sequence diagram showing the progress of the behavior described by the diagram, and
- $mode \in \{action, reaction, check\}$ – a state of the active copy. The active copy is in the *action* state if realizes behavior specified in the activation part of the diagram, in the *reaction* state if realizes behavior specified in the reactive part of the sequence diagram, and in the *check* state if realizes behavior specified by the monitoring diagram.

Let an active copy and a variable with the valuation established for the active copy be given (see example in Fig. 11). Then, the function $val{:}\, LiveCopy \times Variable \longrightarrow \Omega \cup \{\perp, \&\}$ yields a value of a given variable, the function $forbiddenVal{:}\, LiveCopy \times Variable \longrightarrow 2^{\Omega \cup \{\perp,\&\}}$, yields a set of forbidden values for a given variable, and the function $free{:}\, LiveCopy \times Variable \longrightarrow \{true, false\}$ indicates by *true* or *false* whether valuation of the variable is undefined.

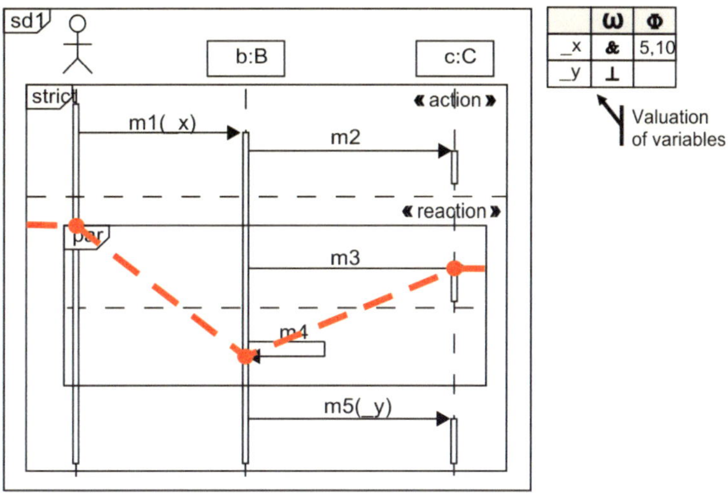

Fig. 11. An example of an active copy

If an active copy is known and a given event happens then by applying the function $advance{:}\, LiveCopy \times Event \longrightarrow LiveCopy$ a new active copy is defined.

Definition 6.1.5

A configuration of a set of sequence diagrams, noted *conf*: *Configuration*, is defined as the tuple:

$$conf = \langle e, Lc_{spec}, Lc_{forbidden}, Lc_{expected}, context, time_{context}, guards, Forbidden, Expected, type \rangle \quad (6.1.5)$$

where:

- e – is a communication event which causes a transition to a new state represented by the configuration, $e = \perp$ for the initial configuration,
- Lc_{spec} – a subset of active copies of the sequence diagrams specifying required behavior,
- $Lc_{forbidden}$ – a subset of active copies of the sequence diagrams specifying forbidden behavior,
- $Lc_{expected}$ – a subset of active copies of the sequence diagrams specifying expected behavior,
- $context$ – a set of bound variables, which values are agreed during a transition to the configuration,
- $time\_context$ – a set of time instants of the event e and other events associated with e,
- $guards$ – a condition for realization of the communication event e,
- $Forbidden$ – a set of sequence diagrams specifying forbidden behavior,
- $Expected$ – a set of sequence diagrams specifying expected behavior,
- $type \in \{complete, violating, undefined, incomplete, \perp\}$ – type of the final configuration; $complete$ – indicates that the configuration is the result of a completely executed reaction to the event incoming from system's environment; $violating$ – indicates whether the configuration leads to the violation of event order; $undefined$ – indicates whether the configuration represents an undefined state of a system; $incomplete$ – indicates whether the configuration represents an incomplete state of system; $\perp$ indicates the leaf-configuration.

An example of a configuration of a set of sequence diagrams is presented in Fig. 12.

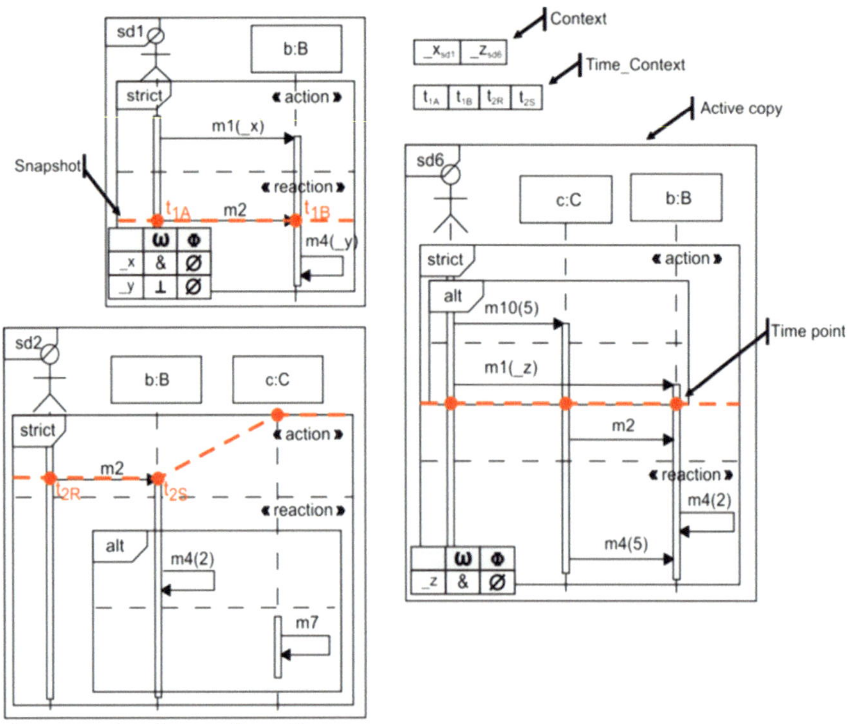

Fig. 12. An example of a configuration

The function $areConnect: Configuration \times Variable \times Variable \longrightarrow \{true, false\}$ returns $true$ if the variables are bound, and $false$ otherwise.

Definition 6.1.6

An event *e* is a **first event** in the diagram *sd* if it belongs to the set of communication events of the diagram, and it is a message sending event, and there are no other events that precede *e* in the sense of the relation $\preccurlyeq_{sd}$:

$$e \in sd.E_{first} \Leftrightarrow \left(e \in sd.E_{com} \wedge e.type = send \wedge \nexists_{e' \in sd.E_{com}}: e' \preccurlyeq_{sd} e\right) \qquad (6.1.6)$$

Examples of first events for sequence diagrams are presented in Fig. 13.

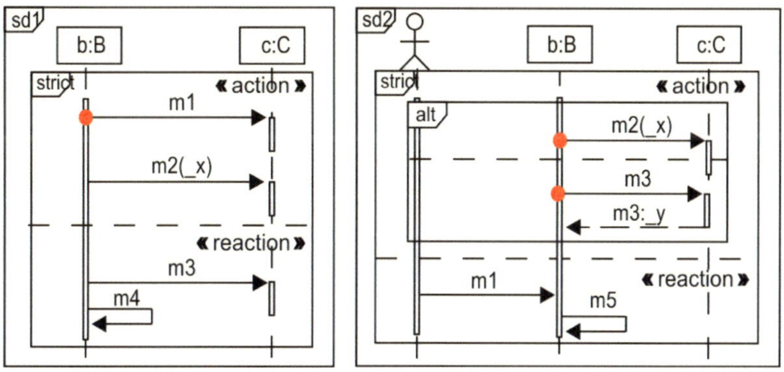

Fig. 13. Examples of first events for the sequence diagrams

Definition 6.1.7

An event *e* is an **initial event** of the sequence diagram *sd* if it belongs to the set of first events of the diagram and it is message event which is sent by the environment of the system:

$$e \in sd.E_{init} \Leftrightarrow \left(e \in sd.E_{first} \wedge src(e.msg) \in Environment\right) \qquad (6.1.7)$$

An example of an initial event for a sequence diagram is presented in Fig. 14.

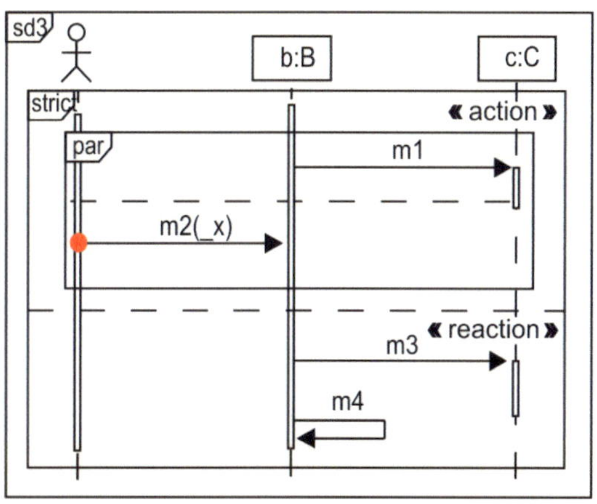

Fig. 14. An example of the initial event for the sequence diagram

Definition 6.1.8

An event e is **enabled** in the active copy lc if it belongs to the set of events of the diagram $lc.sd$, and the time points of the snapshot for all lifelines representing instances participating in realization of the event e directly precede e, and there is no a such event e' that proceeds e (does not belong to the lower closure of the snapshot $\downharpoonleft lc.s_{sd}$).

If e is a communication event sending a message and e'' is a communication event receiving the message then e'' is enabled in the snapshot representing realization of the event e:

$$e \in lc.E_{enabled} \Leftrightarrow \tag{6.1.8}$$

$$\Big(e \in lc.sd.E_{com} \cup lc.sd.E_{sync} \wedge \nexists_{e' \in lc.sd.E_{com} \cup lc.sd.E_{sync}}: (e' \prec_{sd} e \wedge e' \notin \downharpoonleft lc.s_{sd}) \wedge (e.type = send \Rightarrow e.msg.recvEvent \in advance(lc.s_{sd}, e).E_{enabled})\Big)$$

An example of time point associated with an enabled event for an active copy of a sequence diagram is presented in Fig. 15.

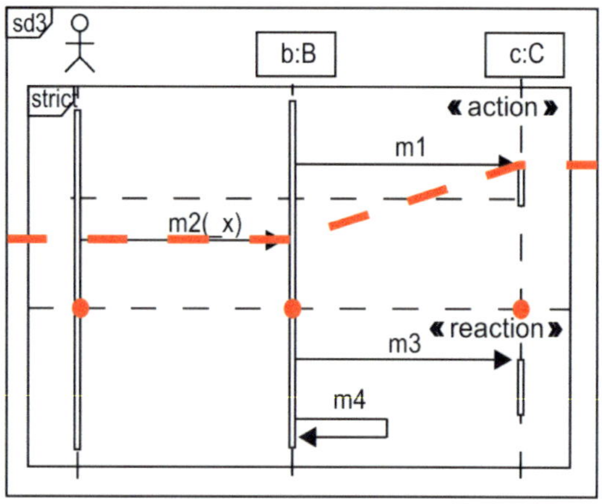

Fig. 15. An example of time point associated with an enabled event for an active copy

Definition 6.1.9

An event e **causes a transition** of the active copy lc if:

- it belongs to the set of enabled events for the active copy, and
- if it is associated with the message sending by the system then it also belongs to the scenario representing system's reaction (part «*reaction*») and the variable to which it refers has defined value:

$$e \in lc.E_{advanced} \Leftrightarrow \tag{6.1.9}$$

$$e \in lc.E_{enabled} \wedge$$

$$\Big(e \in lc.sd.E_{com} \wedge src(e.msg) \notin Environment \Rightarrow \big(reaction(lc.sd) \in allEnclosing(e) \wedge (e.msg.arg \neq \perp \Rightarrow val(lc, e.msg.arg.\omega) \neq \perp)\big)\Big)$$

An example of time point associated with an event causing transition for an active copy of a sequence diagram is presented in Fig. 16.

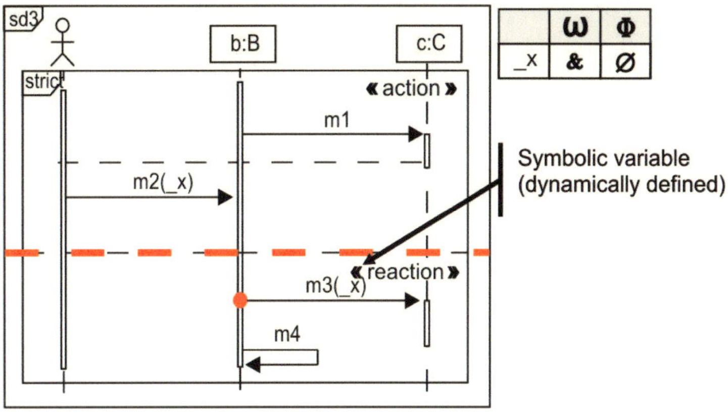

Fig. 16. An example of a time point associated with the event causing transition for an exemplary active copy

Definition 6.1.10

An event e is **reachable** for the active copy lc if it is the enabled communication event for the copy or if there exists a synchronization event e' such that e is reachable for the active copy representing realization of the event e':

$$e \in lc.E_{reachable} \Leftrightarrow \tag{6.1.10}$$

$$\left(e \in lc.sd.E_{com} \wedge \left(e \in lc.E_{enabled} \vee \exists_{e' \in lc.sd.E_{sync}}: e \in advance(lc, e').E_{reachable}\right)\right)$$

An example of a time point associated with the reachable event for an active copy is presented in Fig. 17.

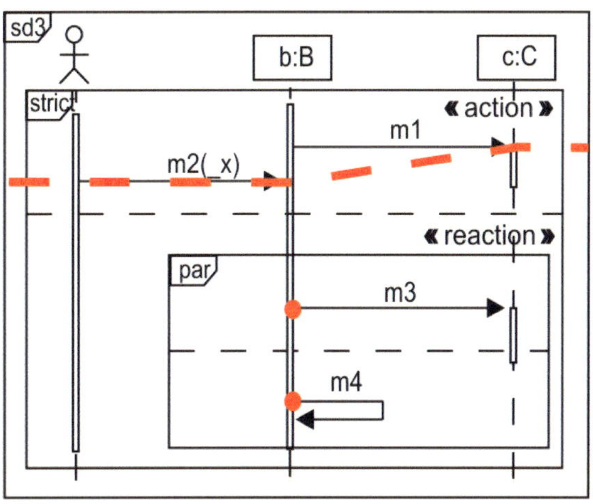

Fig. 17. An example of a time point associated with the reachable event for an exemplary active copy

Definition 6.1.11

An event e **violates events' ordering** of the active copy lc if it belongs to the set of obligatory communication events of the diagram $lc.sd$, but it is not reachable for the copy:

$$e \in lc.E_{violating} \Leftrightarrow \tag{6.1.11}$$

$$\left(e \in lc.sd.E_{com} \wedge e \notin lc.E_{reachable} \wedge \nexists_{cfa \in lc.sd.Cf_{alt}.CfA}: cfa \in allEnclosing(e)\right)$$

An example of time points associated with violating events for an exemplary active copy is presented in Fig. 18.

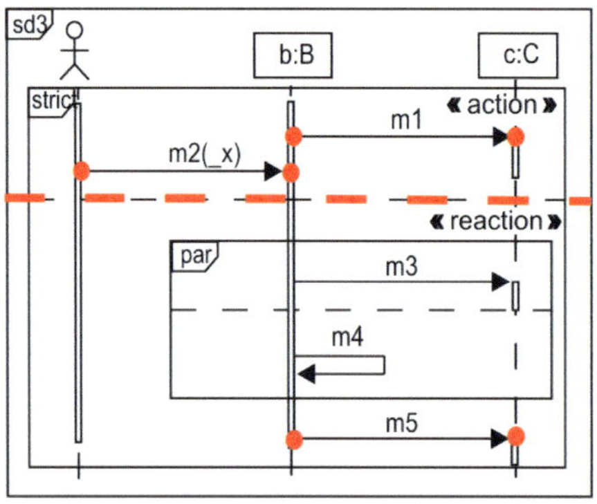

Fig. 18. An example of time points associated with the violating events for an exemplary active copy

Definition 6.1.12

A **variable** var' is ***weak-unifiable*** with a variable var in a given configuration if:

- its value is not defined,
- has the same value as the variable var, for symbolic variable the variables are bound,
- the value of the variable var' is defined dynamically, the value of the variable var is defined statically and does not belong to the set of forbidden values of the variable var':

$$\begin{aligned} match_{w-unif}(var', var) \stackrel{\text{def}}{=} (&var'.\omega = \perp \vee \\ &\left(var'.\omega = var.\omega \wedge \left(var'.\omega = \& \Rightarrow areConnect(var', var)\right)\right) \vee \\ &(var'.\omega = \& \wedge var.\omega \notin \{\perp, \&\} \wedge var.\omega \notin var'.\Phi)) \end{aligned} \tag{6.1.12}$$

Definition 6.1.13

A **variable** var' is ***strict-unifiable*** with a variable var if has the same value, for symbolic variable the variables are bound:

$$match_{s-unif}(var', var) \stackrel{\text{def}}{=}$$

$$\left(var'.\omega = var.\omega \wedge \left(var'.\omega = \& \Rightarrow areConnect(var', var)\right)\right) \tag{6.1.13}$$

$var'.\omega$	$var.\omega$	$match_{w-unif}(var', var)$	$match_{s-unif}(var', var)$
x	x	$true$	$true$
&	x	$true$, if $x \notin var'.\Phi$	$false$
$\perp$	x	$true$	$false$
x	&	$false$	$false$
&	&'	$true$, if $areConnect(var', var)$	$true$, if $areConnect(var', var)$
$\perp$	&	$true$	$false$
x	$\perp$	$false$	$false$
&	$\perp$	$false$	$false$
$\perp$	$\perp$	$true$	$true$

Table 1. Definition of the strict-unifiable and weak-unifiable variables, where x is a concrete value.

Definition 6.1.14

A **message** msg' is ***weak-unifiable*** (***strict-unifiable***) with a message msg when both messages are sent between the same objects, and relate to a call of the same operation and have *weak-unifiable* (*strict-unifiable*) arguments:

$$match_{q-unif}(msg', msg) \stackrel{\text{def}}{=} \big(src(msg') = src(msg) \land dst(msg') = dst(msg) \land msg'.o = msg.o \land match_{q-unif}(msg'.arg, msg.arg)\big) \quad (6.1.14)$$

where q means '*weak*' or '*strict*'.

Definition 6.1.15

A **communication event** e' is ***weak-unifiable*** (***strict-unifiable***) with a communication event e when both events are of the same type (sending or receiving), and relate to a *weak-unifiable* (*strict-unifiable*) message:

$$match_{q-unif}(e', e) \stackrel{\text{def}}{=} \big(e'.type = e.type \land match_{q-unif}(e'.msg, e.msg)\big) \quad (6.1.15)$$

where q means '*weak*' or '*strict*'.

Let $bSpec: BehaviourSpecification$ means the specification of the system behavior expressed by a set of extended UML sequence diagrams.

Definition 6.1.16

A graph of possible scenarios representing system's interaction with its environment is defined as:

$$G_{bSpec} = \langle V_{bSpec}, A_{bSpec}, guard \rangle \quad (6.1.16)$$

where:

- V_{bSpec} – a set of graph vertices; each vertex is labeled by a configuration which is reachable from the initial configuration,
- A_{bSpec} – a set of graph arcs; each arc is labeled by an event; each arc has the form $\langle u, v, e \rangle \in A_{bSpec}$, where $u, v \in V_{bSpec}$ are vertices labeled by $c_1, c_2{:}\, Configuration$, and $e{:}\, Event$ is the event which causes a transition from c_1 to c_2, noted by $c_1 \xrightarrow{e} c_2$,
- $guard{:}\, A_{bSpec} \longrightarrow Exp \cup \{\perp\}$ – a partial function that assigns a Boolean expression to an arc.

Further, we will use the function, $conf{:}\, V_{bSpec} \longrightarrow Configuration$, which for a given vertex of the graph of possible scenarios returns a configuration labeling the vertex.

6.2 Construction of the graph of possible scenarios

The algorithm of construction of the graph of possible scenarios is presented below. To facilitate presentation of the algorithm a state machine diagram presenting an active copy – a component of a transformed configuration – is shown in Fig. 19. A detailed description of the algorithm is summarized in the form of an activity diagram in Fig. 20, after its textual description.

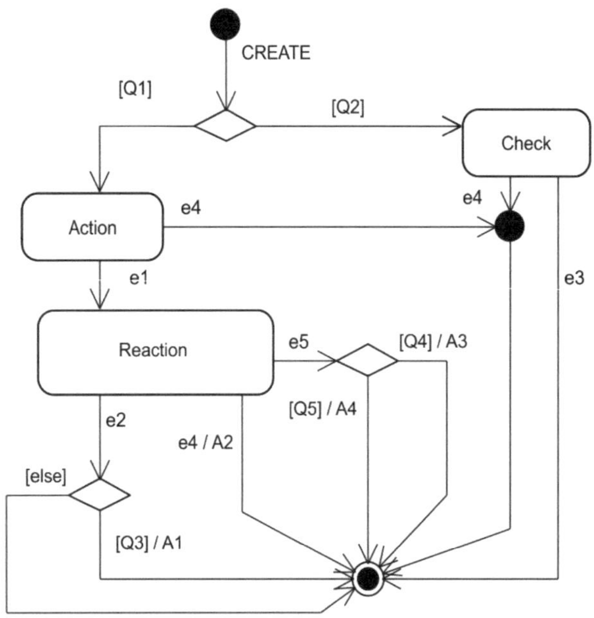

Fig. 19. State machine for an active copy, where:

TRIGGERS:

CREATE - One of the first events of the diagram occurs

- e1 – The SyncEvent - exit from the argument with the stereotype «action» of the diagram occurs
- e2 – The SyncEvent - exit from a combined fragment with the stereotype «action»/«reaction» of the diagram occurs

- e3 – The SyncEvent - exit from a combined fragment with the stereotype «forbidden» or «expected» of the diagram occurs
- e4 – One of the violates events' ordering events of the diagram occurs
- e5 - when(condition), where the condition is defined as: 'The set of events causing transitions for active copies within the configuration is empty'.

GUARDS:

- Q1 - The specification diagram
- Q2 - The monitoring diagram
- Q3 - Active Copy is the last element of the set of active copies of the configuration
- Q4 - The set of events that are accessible at the given configuration contains the event which refers to a variable whose value is not specified
- Q5 - The set of events that are accessible at the given configuration contains the system event which belongs to the scenario representing system activation

ACTIVITIES:

- A1 - Label the configuration as complete final configuration
- A2 - Label the configuration as inconsistent final configuration
- A3 - Label the configuration as unspecified final configuration which represents system's deadlock
- A4 - Label the configuration as incomplete final configuration which represents system's deadlock

The vertices and arcs of graph $G_{bSpec} = \langle V_{bSpec}, A_{bSpec}, guard\rangle$ are constructed iteratively starting from:

- $V_{bSpec} = \{v_0\}$, where v_0 is labeled by the initial configuration: $c_0 = \langle \bot, \emptyset, \emptyset, \emptyset, \emptyset, \emptyset, \emptyset, \emptyset, \emptyset, \bot\rangle$,
- $A_{bSpec} = \emptyset$,
- $guard: A_{bSpec} \longrightarrow Exp \cup \{\bot\}$ – a partial function that assigns a Boolean expression to an arc.

1. The set of events that initiate system's behavior is defined:

$$E_{init} = \left\{e \middle| e \in \bigcup_{sd \in bSpec.Sd_{spec}} sd.E_{init}\right\}.$$

2. The set E_{init} is factorized (elimination of repetitions, marking symbolic variables, setting forbidden values for symbolic variables):

$$factore(c_0, E_{init})$$ /* definition 6.2.1

3. For each initiate event $e \in E_{init}$:
   a. The transition is computed $c_0 \xrightarrow{e}_{com} c$, /* definition 6.2.3
   b. let v be a vertex labeled by the configuration c:

$$V_{bSpec} \leftarrow V_{bSpec} \cup \{v\},$$

   c. let a be an arc of the form $\langle v_0, v, e\rangle$:

$$A_{bSpec} \leftarrow A_{bSpec} \cup \{a\}.$$

4. For each leaf-vertex $v \in V_{bSpec}$, which is not labeled by a final configuration c such that $c = conf(v)$ $(c.type = \perp)$:
   a. If the set of active copies of the configuration is empty $(c.Lc_{spec} = \emptyset)$ return to the initial configuration in which the system awaits for events from its environment:
      i. the configuration is considered as complete final configuration:

$$c.type \leftarrow complete,$$

      ii. let a be an arc of the form $\langle v, v_0, \delta \rangle$:

$$A_{bSpec} \leftarrow A_{bSpec} \cup \{a\},$$

      iii. go to step 4.
   b. The set of events which enable transitions for active copies within the configuration c is defined:

$$E_{advanced} = \left\{ e | e \in \bigcup_{lc \in c.Lc_{spec}} lc.E_{advanced} \right\}.$$

   c. If the set $E_{advanced}$ contains synchronization events, i.e.

$$\left(\exists_{e \in E_{advanced}} : e \in \bigcup_{sd \in bSpec} sd.E_{sync} \right):$$

      i. then for each synchronization event:
      a. define transition $c \xrightarrow{e}_{sync} c'$,
      b. let a be an arc of the form $\langle v, v, e \rangle$: /* definition 6.2.2

$$A_{bSpec} \leftarrow A_{bSpec} \cup \{a\},$$

      ii. go to step 4.
   d. If the set $E_{advanced}$ contains communication events, i.e.

$$\left(\exists_{e \in E_{advanced}} : e \in \bigcup_{sd \in bSpec} sd.E_{com} \right):$$

      i. factorization of the set (elimination of copies, marking the symbolic variables, determining forbidden values of the symbolic variables):

$$factore(c, E_{advanced}).$$ /* definition 6.2.1

      ii. for each communication event:

      a. the transition is calculated $c \xrightarrow{e}_{com} c'$, /* definition 6.2.3
      b. let v' be a vertex labeled by the configuration c':

$$V_{bSpec} \leftarrow V_{bSpec} \cup \{v'\},$$

      c. let a be an arc of the form $\langle v, v', e \rangle$:

$$A_{bSpec} \leftarrow A_{bSpec} \cup \{a\}.$$

      iii. go to step 4.

e. If the set is empty ($E_{advanced} = \emptyset$) then:

i. If the set of events that are accessible at the given configuration contains the event which refers to a variable whose value is not specified, i.e.

$$\left(\exists_{e \in \bigcup_{lc \in c.Lc_{spec}} lc.E_{enabled}}: \left(e \in \bigcup_{sd \in bSpec} sd.E_{com} \wedge e.type = send \wedge e.msg.arg \neq \perp \wedge e.msg.arg.\omega = \perp\right)\right)$$

the configuration is considered as unspecified final configuration which represents system's deadlock:

$$c.type \leftarrow undefined,$$

ii. If the set of events that are accessible at the given configuration contains the system event which belongs to the scenario representing system activation, i.e.

$$\left(\exists_{e \in \bigcup_{lc \in c.Lc_{spec}} lc.E_{enabled}}: \left(e \in \bigcup_{sd \in bSpec} sd.E_{com} \wedge src(e.msg) \notin Environment \wedge action(sd) \in allEnclosing(e)\right)\right)$$

the configuration is considered as incomplete final configuration which represents system's deadlock:

$$c.type \leftarrow incomplete,$$

iii. go to step 4.

Definition 6.2.1

Factorization of the set of the activating events which cause transitions (elimination of copies, marking the symbolic variables, determining forbidden values of the symbolic variables) – $factore(conf: Configuration, E: ComEvent\ [*])$ is defined as follows:

Let the set of events with a fixed valuation of variables is empty, i.e. $E_{out} = \emptyset$:

1. Create a copy of the events:

$$\forall_{e \in E}: E_{out} \leftarrow E_{out} \cup \{\, copy(e)\, \}.$$

2. Remove repetition of the *strict-unifiable* events:

$$\forall_{e,e' \in E_{out}}: e \neq e' \wedge conf.match_{s-unif}(e,e') \Rightarrow E_{out} \leftarrow E_{out} \setminus \{e'\}.$$

3. For each event $e \in E_{out}$, which has a statically undefined variable, extend the set of forbidden values about the statically defined values of variables of the events $e' \in E_{out}$, which are *weak-unifiable* with *e*:

$$\forall_{e,e' \in E_{out}}: e \neq e' \wedge conf.match_{w-unif}(e,e') \wedge var \neq \perp \wedge var.\omega \in \{\perp, \&\} \wedge var'.\omega \notin \{\perp, \&\} \Rightarrow var.\Phi \leftarrow var.\Phi \cup \{var'.\omega\}$$

where:

$$var = e.msg.arg,$$

$$var' = e'.msg.arg.$$

4. Each event sending by system's environment, which refers to a variable with statically undefined value, declare/label its variable as symbolic:

$$\forall e \in E_{out}: e.msg.arg \neq \perp \wedge e.msg.arg.\omega = \perp \wedge src(e.msg) \in Environment \Rightarrow e.msg.arg.\omega \leftarrow \&$$

5. $E_{in} \leftarrow E_{out}$

Definition 6.2.2

The transition relations $c \overset{e}{\rightarrow}_{sync} c'$ is defined by the following rules:

For each active copy of the configuration c $\left(lc \in c.Lc_{spec} \cup c.Lc_{forbidden} \cup c.Lc_{expected}\right)$ for which the event e is reachable ($e \in lc.E_{reachable}$):

1. modify the snapshot of the active copy:

$$lc \longleftarrow advance(lc, e).$$

2. if the event e represents an entry to a combined fragment ($e = \langle cf, entry \rangle$):
   a. which is a strict sequence, negation or assertion combined fragment ($cf.oper \in \{strict, assert, neg\}$) then:

$$lc \longleftarrow advance(lc, \langle cf.cfa_1, entry \rangle),$$

   b. which is a parallel or alternative combined fragment ($cf.oper \in \{par, alt\}$) then:

$$\forall_{cfa \in cf.CfA}: lc \longleftarrow advance(lc, \langle cfa, entry \rangle).$$

3. if the event e represents an exit from an argument of a combined fragment ($e = \langle cf.cfa_i, exit \rangle$):
   a. which is a strict sequence ($cf.opere = strict$):
      i. if there exists a subsequent argument of the combined fragment then entry to the argument:

$$lc \longleftarrow advance(lc, \langle cf.cfa_{i+1}, entry \rangle),$$

      ii. if the event e is an exit from the argument with the stereotype «action» $\left(cf.cfa_i = action(lc.sd)\right)$ then:

$$lc.mode \longleftarrow reaction,$$

   b. which is a parallel ($cf.opere = par$), and all other arguments of this combined fragment reached their end $\left(\forall_{cfa_j \in cf.CfA, j \neq i} \langle cfa_j, exit \rangle \in \downarrow lc.s_{sd}\right)$, then exit the entire combined fragment:

$$lc \leftarrow advance(lc, \langle cf, exit \rangle),$$

c. which is alternative ($cf.opere = alt$) then exit the combined fragment:

$$lc \leftarrow advance(lc, \langle cf, exit \rangle).$$

4. if the event e represents an exit from a combined fragment ($e = \langle cf, exit \rangle$):

   a. which is a strict sequence with «*action*»/«*reaction*» stereotype then remove the active copy from the set of configuration copies.

$$Lc_{spec} \leftarrow Lc_{spec} \setminus \{lc\},$$

   b. which is negation with «*forbidden*» stereotype then remove the active copy from the set of diagram copies representing forbidden behaviors and recording the realized scenario:

$$Lc_{forbidden} \leftarrow Lc_{forbidden} \setminus \{lc\},$$

$$Forbidden \leftarrow Forbidden \cup \{lc.sd\},$$

   c. which is assertion with «*expected*» stereotype then remove the active copy from the set of diagram copies representing expected behaviors and recording the realized scenario:

$$Lc_{expected} \leftarrow Lc_{expected} \setminus \{lc\},$$

$$Expected \leftarrow Expected \cup \{lc.sd\}.$$

Definition 6.2.3

The transition relations $c \overset{e}{\rightarrow}_{com} c'$ is defined recursively by the following rules:

1. $time\_context \leftarrow \emptyset,$
2. $guards \leftarrow \perp,$
3. For each active copy of the configuration c $\left(lc \in c.Lc_{spec} \cup c.Lc_{forbidden} \cup c.Lc_{expected}\right)$, for which there exists an event e' *strict-unifiable* with an event e violating ordering of events

$$\left(\exists_{e' \in lc.E_{violating}} : c.match_{s-unif}(e', e)\right):$$

   a. if $lc.mode \in \{action, check\}$ then remove the active copy form the set of configuration copies:

$$Lc_q \leftarrow Lc_q \setminus \{lc\}, \text{ where: } q \text{ means } spec, forbidden \text{ or } expected.$$

   b. if $lc.mode = reaction$ then label the configuration as inconsistent final configuration:

$$c.type \leftarrow violating.$$

4. For each sequence diagram $sd \in bSpec$, for which its set of first events contains an event e' *weak-unifiable* with the event e $\left(e' \in sd.E_{first} \wedge c.match_{w-unif}(e',e)\right)$, create active copy of the diagram and attach it to a respective set of active configurations:
   a. for $sd \in Sd_{spec}$:

$$Lc_{spec} \leftarrow Lc_{spec} \cup \{lc = \langle sd, initial(sd), action\rangle\},$$

   b. for $sd \in Sd_{forbidden}$:

$$Lc_{forbidden} \leftarrow Lc_{forbidden} \cup \{lc = \langle sd, initial(sd), check\rangle\},$$

   c. for $sd \in Sd_{expected}$:

$$Lc_{expected} \leftarrow Lc_{expected} \cup \{lc = \langle sd, initial(sd), check\rangle\}.$$

5. For each active copy of the configuration c $\left(lc \in c.Lc_{spec} \cup c.Lc_{forbidden} \cup c.Lc_{expected}\right)$, for which the set of reachable events contains an event e′ weak-unifiable with the event e $\left(e' \in lc.E_{reachable} \wedge c.match_{w-unif}(e',e)\right)$ do the following:

   a. for each synchronization event e'' at the diagram which proceeds the event e' and which has not been considered yet $\left(e'' \in lc.sd.E_{sync} \wedge e'' \preccurlyeq_{sd} e' \wedge e'' \notin \downarrow lc.s_{sd}\right)$, determine the transition:

$$c \xrightarrow{e''}_{sync} c',$$

   b. if the event e' is the first event within argument of an alternative combined fragment $(cf \in lc.sd.Cf \wedge cf.oper = alt)$, i.e.

$$\left(\exists_{cfa_q \in cf.CfA}: cfa_q \in allEnclosing(e') \wedge \nexists_{e'' \in lc.sd.E_{com}}: \left(cfa_q \in allEnclosing(e'') \wedge e'' \preccurlyeq_{sd} e'\right)\right)$$

   then exit the second argument of the combined fragment $\left(cfa_p \in cf.CfA \wedge cfa_p \neq cfa_q\right)$:

$$lc \leftarrow advance\left(lc, \langle cfa_p\ exit\rangle\right),$$

$$guards \leftarrow guards \wedge cf.guard$$

   c. modify the active copy of the configuration by including the considered event:

$$lc \leftarrow advance(lc, e'),$$

   d. determine unification of the events e and e':

$$unify(e', e), \qquad \text{/* definition 6.2.4}$$

   e. attach time points to lifelines associated with realization of the event e':

$$time\_context \leftarrow time\_context \cup e'.eventTime,$$

   f. if the event e' represents sending of a message and e'' is the event represents receiving of the message, then modify the lifelines associated with realization of the event e'':

$$lc \longleftarrow advance(lc, e''),$$

$$time\_context \longleftarrow time\_context \cup e''.eventTime,$$

g. for each enabled synchronization event e'' of the monitoring diagram $\left(lc \in c.Lc_{forbidden} \cup c.Lc_{expected} \wedge e'' \in lc.sd.E_{sync} \ \wedge \ e'' \in lc.E_{enabled}\right)$ determine the transition:

$$c \xrightarrow{e''}_{sync} c'.$$

Definition 6.2.4

The procedure of event unification is defined as follows:

$$\begin{aligned} unify(e', e) \quad &\triangleq \quad unify(e'.msg, e.msg) \\ unify(msg', msg) \quad &\triangleq \quad unify(msg'.arg, msg.arg), \\ unify(var', var) \quad &\triangleq \quad 1.\, var'.\omega \leftarrow var.\omega, var'.\Phi \leftarrow var.\Phi, \\ &\quad\;\; 2.\, connect(var', var) \end{aligned}$$ /* definition 6.2.5

Definition 6.2.5

The binding variables procedure is defined as follows:

$$connect(x, y) \triangleq$$

1. $S \longleftarrow \{x, y\}$,
2. If the variable x or y were bounded already then merge the sets:

   a. $\exists_{S_x \in context}: x \in S_x \Rightarrow \quad S \longleftarrow S \cup S_x$
   $\qquad context \longleftarrow context \setminus S_x$

   b. $\exists_{S_y \in context}: y \in S_y \Rightarrow \quad S \longleftarrow S \cup S_y$
   $\qquad context \longleftarrow context \setminus S_y$

3. $context \longleftarrow context \cup S.$

7. Conclusions

UML sequence diagrams allow capturing requirements in a convenient way. Due to their simple, intuitive syntax and semantics, they are a suitable communication medium between analysts, developers, customers and end-users. Due to their focus on inter-object communication they are useful for specification of reactive systems, in particular real-time systems. Of course, they are not the only UML diagrams that may be used for real-time systems specification. For example, in (Roubtsova et al., 2000), system's specification consists of a class and object diagrams representing static, and state diagrams representing behavior aspect of the specification.

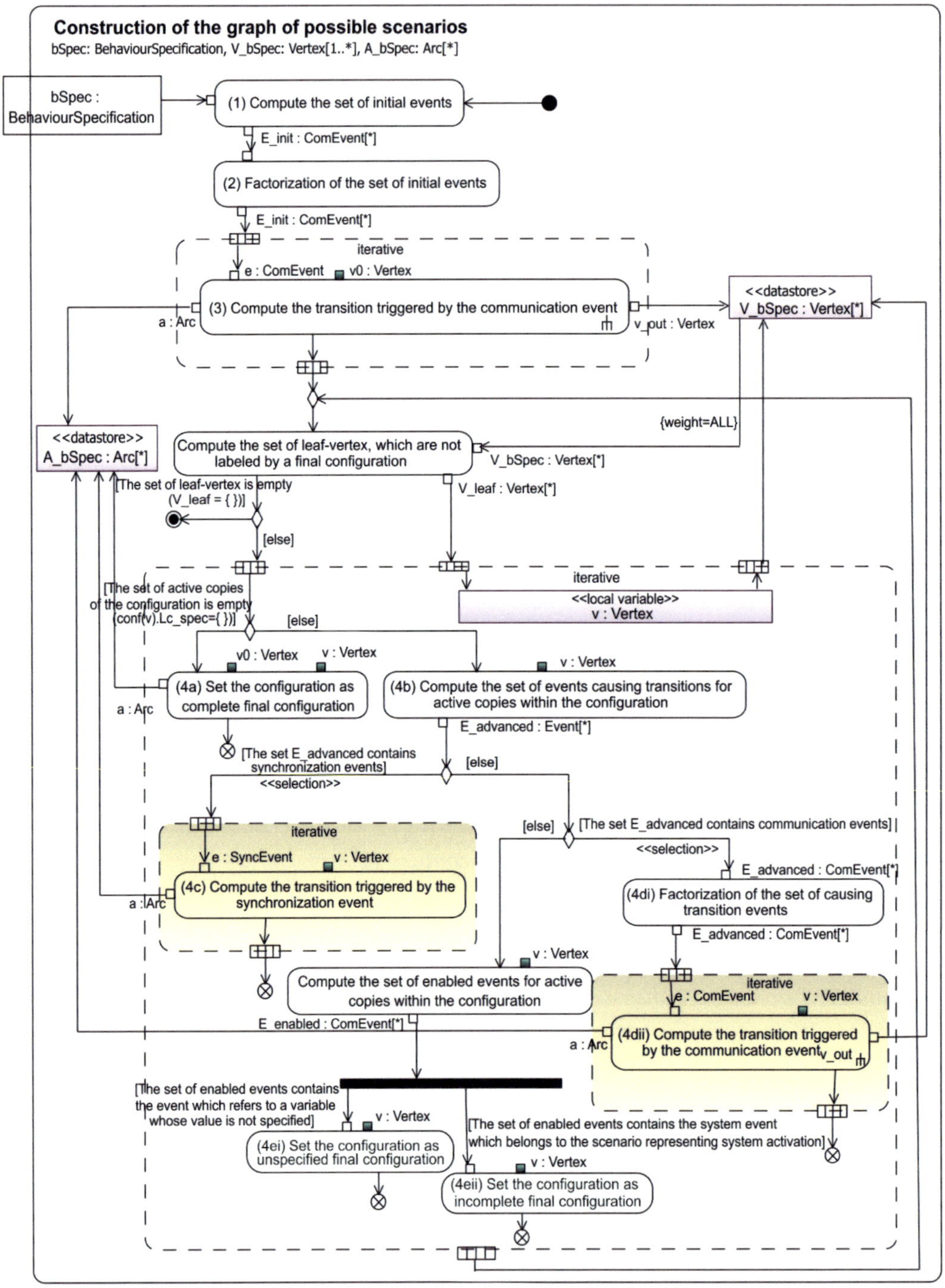

Fig. 20. The activity diagram presenting the construction of the graph of possible scenarios

In the chapter we present a way of effective application of UML sequence diagrams to real-time system specification. Assumption that specification of a system is represented by a set of sequence diagrams is close to the agile software development methodologies: each sequence diagram represents a single user story, and the set of sequence diagrams should represent complete description of the designed system.

In general, the proposed approach to a construction of system specification may be considered as a bottom-up approach - on the base of a set of user stories a complete specification and its semantics is derived. A consequence of the approach is the need to check consistency of the set of user stories. Another bottom-up approach basing on Live Sequence Charts is presented in (Harel & Marelly, 2003). The approach was also inspiration for our works. It is worth to note that application of Live Sequence Charts is further developed in (Maoz & Harel, 2011).

Opposite approaches to system specification are classified as top-down ones. Within these approaches, specification is constructed as a set of hierarchically ordered sequence diagrams. The diagrams at higher level of the hierarchy are composed from diagrams at lower level of the hierarchy, by means of some composition operators. An example of such approach, adopting Message Sequence Charts, is presented in (Cleaveland & Sengupta, 2006).

Lack of precise, formal semantics for UML sequence diagrams brings many interpretation problems. An illustration of this statement is more than a dozen proposals for the semantics of sequence diagrams, which are surveyed in (Micskei & Waeselynck, 2011). However, in contrast to our approach, it should be emphasized that these proposals concern only individual sequence diagrams, but not the set of diagrams.

The proposed approach to semantic definition of a set of UML sequence diagrams is based on transformation of the set into a graph of all possible scenarios. The graph enables system analyst to give answer to practical questions about consistency and completeness of scenarios, and thus about consistency and completeness of specification. Additionally, both consistency and definiteness may be checked automatically on the-fly. The checking algorithm was implemented as a programming tool supporting edition and analysis of specifications (Walkowiak, 2011). This tool has a form of plug-in to Visual Paradigm modeling tool.

8. References

Cleaveland, R. & Sengupta,B. (2006). Triggered Message Sequence Charts. *IEEE Transactions on Software Engineering*, Vol. 32, No. 8, (Aug. 2006), pp. (587 - 607), ISSN 0098-5589

Harel, D. & Marelly, R. (2003). Come, Let's Play: A Scenario-Based Approach to Programming, ISBN 3-540-00787-3, *Springer*

Harel, D. & Maoz, S. (2008). Assert and Negate Revisited: Modal Semantics for UML Sequence Diagrams, *Software and Systems Modeling,* Vol. 7, No. 2, (May 2008), pp. (237-252), ISSN 1619-1366

Huzar, Z. & Walkowiak, A. (2010). Specification of real-time systems using UML sequence diagrams, Przegląd Elektrotechniczny (Electrical Review), R. 86 NR 9/2010, pp. 226-229, ISSN 0033-2097

ITU-T (2004). Z. 120. Message Sequence Charts, available at http://www.itu.int/rec/T-REC-Z.120

Manna, Z. & Pnueli A. (1992). The Temporal Logic of Reactive and Concurrent Systems: Specification, ISBN 0387976647 , *Springer-Verlag*

Manna, Z. & Pnueli A. (1995). Temporal Verification of Reactive Systems: Safety, ISBN 0387944591, *Springer-Verlag*

Maoz, S. & Harel, D. (2011). On tracing reactive systems, Software and Systems Modeling, vol. 10, no. 4., pp. 447-468, ISSN 1619-1366

Micskei, Z. & Waeselynck, H. (2011). The many meanings of UML 2 Sequence diagrams: a survey, Software and Systems Modeling, vol. 10, no. 4., pp. 489-514, , ISSN 1619-1366

Nissanke, N. (1997). Realtime systems, ISBN 978-0136512745, *Prentice Hall*

OMG (2011). Unified Modeling Language, Superstructure, version 2.4.1. Available from: http://www.omg.org/spec/UML/2.4.1/Superstructure/PDF/

Roubtsova, E.E., & van Katwijk, J., & Toetenel, W.J., & Pronk, C., & de Rooij, R.C.M. (2000). Specification of Real-Time Systems in UML, Electronic Notes in Theoretical Computer Science, vol. 39, no. 3.
URL: http//www.elsevier.nl/locate/entcs/volume39.html 13 pages

Störrle, H. (2004). Assert, Negate and Refinement in UML-2 Interactions, *Proceedings of 3rd Int. Workshop on Critical Systems Development with the UML (CSDUML'04)*, Lisbon, October 2004

Walkowiak, A. (2011). Specification of reactive systems, PhD Thesis (in Polish), Wrocław University of Technology, Faculty of Informatics and Management, Institute of Informatics

6

Construction of Real-Time Oracle Using Timed Automata

Seyed Morteza Babamir[1] and Mehdi Borhani Dehkordi[2]

[1]University of Kashan, Kashan,

[2]University of Science and Applied Shar-e-Kord, Shahr-e-Kord,

Iran

1. Introduction

Verification of real time software is facing two problems: (1) how we should manage to produce verification rules and (2) how we should apply the rules to specify the problem. In this chapter we provide a method by which we get down to these two problems. In the first step, we specify real time software using *Timed Automata* and then we state it in RTL, real time logic, propositions. Timed Automata address modeling systems in time (Alure & Dill, 1996). In the second step, we obtain the safety constraints from *reachability graph* of Timed Automata of the problem specification and after that we state it in real time logic propositions. These propositions showing safety constraints are used for verification of the propositions, i.e. the results of the specification obtained in the first step. To show the effectiveness of our method, we set forth it for the RCC (Rail Road Crossing Control) real time system.

Software verification is an important process in constructing software and a main factor for obtaining safety from the quality of software. For verification of software we should deal with its verification against the expected behavior. The expected behavior is safe characteristics or prepositions that the software must always agree with. For this purpose, there are three main approaches: (1) static verification, (2) software testing and (3) run-time verification. Meanwhile one of the important and key approaches, essentially used for mission and safety critical systems, is the run-time verification; the existence of the problems in the first and second approaches is the reason of using run-time verification. For example, we can indicate the disability of the first method in proving the complicated and large specifications. Another instance is rapidly increasing the number of states (called state explosion) in the *model checking* method, which is a static verification one.

Because Timed Automata are methods based on time and event, they are suitable for describing the behavior of real time systems and because Timed Automata are visual methods, their understanding is easy. But they have limitations for specification of some statuses and also they cannot specify some conditions very well. Therefore, we need especial methods for analysis and verification of Timed Automata behavior that increase safety in these systems and decrease the amount of the faults.

There are different ways to verification of Timed Automata behavior. One of these ways is using *reachability graph;* however an especial method should be chosen to cover the weakness of this method. We can use methods that are based on logic for reasoning and timing the Timed Automata. In this chapter, we suggest a framework for setting and executing Timed Automata using *Real Time Logic* (RTL) providing a reasoning framework based on *First Order Logic* (FOL). RTL reflects a different method for timed systems (Paneka et al, 2006).

In this chapter, we show that Timed Automata per se is not able to show constraints of the systems, but if it is used with formal textual language such as RTL, expressing the constraints of the system would by more.

This chapter includes four sections: (1) in the second section, we express a brief explanation about Timed Automata, (2) in the third one we address an explanation about Real Time Logic and (3) in fourth section we express our approach to simulate Timed Automata by means of Real Time logic. In this section, we propose a case study and specify it using Timed Automata and Real Time logic. Then, we discuss the system constraints to supervise unsafe states.

2. Timed automata

Timed Automata (Alur & Dill, 1994) was proposed by Alur and improved by Dill. Timed Automata are finite machines equipped with sorts of clocks. Clocks: (1) are real functions with continuous time that record the times between the events separately and (2) are increased equally. Timed Automata are introduced as a formal specification for modeling the behavior of real time systems. Timed Automata are: (1) general methods for exhibition of timed transition state diagrams that use a number of time variables having real amounts, (2) finite clocked automata to specify the timed systems and (3) suitable for verification of distributed systems, optimization, verification of multi-tasking programs, network analysis, planning and scheduling (Paneka et al, 1998).

In Timed Automat, a safe path from the first state to a final state is a set of states in which actions are performed and timed requirements are satisfied. If such path is found, it is a solution for the problem. Timed Automata are stated in tuple $M=(\sum, S, S_0, X, E)$ in which $\sum$ is a finite set of actions, S is a finite set of states, S_0 is a finite set of initial states ($S_0 \subset S$), X is a finite set of clocks and E is a set of transitions. Every transition consists of $<L, a, g, \lambda, L'>$. A transition from present state L to the next state L' is made when the action a is performed and clock g(x) having true amount is passed. Notation λ is a subset of X during which the transition will be reset. Relation 1 states that clock values or difference of two clock values are real numbers.

$$g::=x\leq c \mid c\leq x \mid x\text{-}y\leq c \mid x<c \mid c<x \mid x\text{-}y<c \mid g\wedge g \mid \text{true that } x,y \in X,\ c\in R \quad (1)$$

2.1 Networks of timed automata

In this section, we define networks of Timed Automata, consisting of several Timed Automata running in parallel and communicating with each other.

Definition. A timed automaton (TA, for short) is a six-element tuple, $\vartheta = (A,L,l^0,E,X,I)$

Where

- A is a finite set of actions, where $A \cap IR_{0+} = \varphi$,
- L is a finite set of locations,
- $l^0 \in L$ is an initial location,
- X is a finite set of clocks,
- $E \subseteq L * A * C_X^{\theta} * 2^X * L$ is a transition relation,
- $I : L \rightarrow C_X^{\theta}$ is a (location) invariant.

Each element *e* of *E* is denoted by $l \xrightarrow{a,cc,X} l'$ represents a transition from the location l to the location l', executes the action a, with the set $X \subseteq \chi$ of the clocks to be reset, and with the clock constraint cc defining an enabling condition. The function I assigns each location $l \in L$ a clock constraint defining the conditions under which ϑ can stay in l.

If the enabling conditions and the values of the location invariant are in the set C_X only, then the automaton is called *diagonal-free*. Given the transition $e : l \xrightarrow{a,cc,X} l'$, we write source(s), action(s), target(s), guard(s) and reset(s) for l, l', a, cc and X, respectively. The clocks in Timed Automata allow expressing the time properties. An enabling condition constrains the execution of a transition. An invariant condition permits an automaton to stay at the location l as long as the clock constraint I(l) is satisfied.

Real-time systems are usually represented by networks (sets) of Timed Automata. A typical example widely considered in the literature, is modeling an automated railroad crossing (known as the Train-Gate-Controller).

A set of timed automata can be composed into a global (product) timed automaton as follows: the transitions of the timed automata that do not correspond to a shared action are interleaved whereas the transitions labeled with a shared action are synchronized. There are many different definitions for a parallel composition. One definition is determining the multi-way synchronization, i.e., each component that contains a communication transition (labeled with a shared action) has to perform this action (Penczek & Polrola, 2006).

Definition. Let $\lambda = \{i_1, ..., i_{n\lambda}\}$ be a finite ordered set of indices, and $\zeta = \{\vartheta_i \mid i \in \lambda\}$ where $\vartheta_i = (A_i, L_i, l_i^0, E_i, X_i, I_i)$, is a set (network) of Timed Automata indexed with λ. The automata in ζ are called components. Let $A(a) = \{i \in \lambda \mid a \in A_i\}$ be a set of the indices of the components containing the action $a \in \bigcup_{i \in \lambda} A_i$. A composition (product) of the Timed Automata $\vartheta_{i_1} \mid \mid ... \mid \mid \vartheta_{i_{n\lambda}}$ is a timed automaton specified as: $\vartheta = (A, L, l^0, E, X, I)$, where

- $A = \bigcup_{i \in \lambda} A_i$,
- $L = \prod_{i \in \lambda} L_i$,
- $l^0 = (l_{i_1}^0, ..., l_{i_n}^0)$,
- $X = \bigcup_{i \in \lambda} X_i$,
- $I((l_{i_1}, ..., l_{i_{n\lambda}})) = \wedge_{i \in \lambda} I_i(l_i)$,

And the *transition relation* is given as Relation 2.

$$\begin{aligned} &(l_{i_1}, ..., l_{i_{n\lambda}}), a, \wedge_{i \in A(a)} cc_i, \bigcup_{i \in A(a)} X_i, (l'_{i_1}, ..., l'_{i_{n\lambda}}) \in E \Leftrightarrow \\ &(\forall i \in A(a))(l_i, a, cc_i, X_i, l'_i) \in E_i \text{and} (\forall i \in \lambda \setminus A(a)) l'_i = l_i. \end{aligned} \tag{2}$$

2.2 Semantics of timed automata

Let $\vartheta = (A, L, l^0, E, X, I)$ be a timed automaton. A concrete state of A is defined as ordered pair (l, v), where $l \in L$ and $v \in IR_{0+}^{n_x}$ is a valuation. The *concrete (dense) state space* ϑ is a *transition system,* $C_c(\vartheta) = (Q, q^0, \xrightarrow[c]{})$ where

- $Q = L * IR_{0+}^{n_x}$ is the set of all the concrete states,
- $q^0 = (l^0, v^0)$ with $v^0(x) = 0$ for all $x \in X$ is the initial state, and
- $\xrightarrow[c]{} \subseteq Q * (E \cup IR_{0+}) * Q$ is the transition relation, defined by an action

A time successor is defined as Relation 3.

$$\text{for } \delta \in IR_{0+}, (l, v) \xrightarrow{\delta}_c (l, v + \delta) \text{iff } v, v + \delta \in \|I(l)\| \text{ (Time successor)}, \tag{3}$$

- For $a \in A, (l, v) \xrightarrow{a}_c (l', v') \text{iff} (\exists cc \in C_x)(\exists X \subseteq x)$ such that
- $l \xrightarrow{a, cc, X} l' \in E$, $v \in [cc]$, $v' = v[X := 0]$, and $v' \in \|I(l')\|$ (action successor).

Intuitively, a time successor does not change the location l of a concrete state, but it increases the clocks, provided that their values still satisfy the invariant l. Since the invariants are zones, if v and v' satisfy $I(l)$, then all the clocks between v and v' satisfy $I(l)$. An action successor corresponding to the action a is executed when the guard cc holds for v and v' obtained after resetting the clocks in X, satisfies the invariant l'.

For $(l, v) \in Q$ and $\delta \in IR_{0+}$, let $(l, v) + \delta$ denotes $(l, v + \delta)$. Concatenation of two time steps $q \xrightarrow{\delta}_c q + \delta$ and $q + \delta \xrightarrow{\delta'}_c q + \delta + \delta'$ is the time step $q \xrightarrow{\delta + \delta'}_c q + \delta + \delta'$. Similarly, if $q \xrightarrow{\delta}_c q + \delta$, then for any δ there exist:

$$\delta_1, \ldots, \delta_k \in IR_{0+} \text{ where, } \delta_1 + \ldots + \delta_k = \delta \;\&\; q \xrightarrow{\delta_1}_c q + \delta_1 \xrightarrow{\delta_2}_c \ldots \xrightarrow{\delta_k}_c q + \delta.$$

The second relation denotes that each time step can be split into an arbitrary number of consecutive times. A (dense) q_0-run ρ of ϑ is a maximal (i.e., non-extendable) sequence,

$$\rho = q_0 \xrightarrow{\delta_0}_c q_0 + \delta_0 \xrightarrow{a_0}_c q_1 \xrightarrow{\delta_1}_c q_1 + \delta_1 \xrightarrow{a1}_c q_2 \xrightarrow{\delta_2}_c \ldots$$

where $a_i \in A$ and $\delta_i \in IR_{0+}$, for each $i \geq N$ (notice that due to the fact that δ can be equal to zero, two consecutive transitions can be executed without any time passing in between, and that consecutive time passages are concatenated). Such runs are called weakly monotonic (Penczek & Polrola, 2006).

3. Real Time Logic

Real Time Logic (RTL) introduced by Jahanian and Mok in 1986, is an FOL having a set of elements for specification of requirements of real time systems (Bellini et al, 2000). The logic is a formal language used for reasoning about time characteristics of the real time systems. RTL deals with ordering of the events (Jahanian-a, 1998). There is a significant difference between event and action in RTL (Jahanian-b et al, 1998).

There are four types of events:

1. External event like pushing a button by the user,
2. The starting event denoting the beginning of an action.
3. The ending event denoting the completion of an action,

Performing an action is shown by starting and ending events [4]. Events have unique name and the capital letters are used for showing them. To show the external events, we use notation Ω before the name of an event. Also notation $\uparrow$ is used before the name of an event to show a starting event (denoted by $\uparrow$A) and notation $\downarrow$ to show an ending event (denoted by $\downarrow$A). Propositions of RTL are the relations between occurrences of the events using orderings $<$, $=$, $>$, $\geq$,$\leq$ (Jahanian-b et al, 1998). The RTL formulas are made of equal/unequal, existential forms, quantifiers $\forall$ and $\exists$ and logical relations, $\wedge,\vee,\rightarrow,\neg$ (Jahanian, 1994). A function is used to show the time of the occurrence of an event and allocation of an amount of time to the occurrence of the event. It is shown by notation "@". Relation "@(e,i)" denotes the ith occurrence of event *e* where *e* can be a starting or external event (Jahanian-a et al, 1998).

Example:

Consider a system specified in a natural language; the system samples and displays data on demand by external stimuli. Upon pressing button #1, action SAMPLE is executed within 30 time units. During each execution of this action, data are sampled and subsequently appeared in the display panel. The computation time of action SAMPLE is 20 time units. The following set of formulas is a partial description of the system in RTL:

$$\forall i \forall t R(\Omega \text{BUTTON1}, i, t) \rightarrow$$
$$[\exists x, y R(\uparrow \text{SAMPLE}, i, x) \wedge R(\downarrow \text{SAMPLE}, i, y) \wedge t \leq x \wedge y \leq t + 30]$$
$$\forall i \forall x, y [R(\uparrow \text{SAMPLE}, i, x) \wedge R(\downarrow \text{SAMPLE}, i, y)] \rightarrow x + 20 \leq y$$

3.1 The RTL Language

In this section, we introduce the RTL language; the following notations are used in RTL formulae:

- true and false
- *A*, set of time variables
- *B*, set of occurrence variables
- C, constants including the natural numerals
- D, set of events
- Function +
- Predicates $\leq,\geq,<,>,=$
- Occurrence relation *R*
- Logical connections: $\wedge$, $\vee$, $\neg$ and $\rightarrow$
- Existential and universal quantifiers: $\forall$, $\exists$.

The *time terms* in RTL consist of constants, variables and if t_1 and t_2 are time terms, then $t_1 + t_2$ is a time term. The *occurrence terms* in RTL are expressions consisting of constants, variables and if *i* and *j* are occurrence terms, then i + j is an occurrence term.

The propositions in RTL consist of truth symbols, *true* and *false* and:

- if t_1 and t_2 are time terms and ρ is an inequality/equality predicate, then $t_1 \rho t_2$ is a proposition
- if *i* and *j* are occurrence terms and ρ is an inequality/equality predicate symbol, then $i \rho j$ is a proposition
- if *i* is an occurrence term, t is a time term and e is an event constant, then R (e, i, t) is a proposition.

The formulas of RTL are constructed from the propositions, logical connections and quantifiers.

Definition: An occurrence relation is a relation on the set E × Z+ × N where E is a set of events, **Z+** is the set of positive integers, and **N** is the set of natural numbers, such that the following axioms hold:

Monotonicity Axioms: For each event *e* in the set D,

$$\forall i \forall t \forall t'[R(e,i,t) \wedge R(e,i,t') \rightarrow t = t'$$
$$\forall i \forall t[R(e,i,t) \wedge i > 1] \rightarrow [\exists t' R(e,i-1,t') \wedge t' < t]$$

The first axiom states that at most onetime value can be associated with each occurrence *i* of an event *e*, i.e., two same occurrences of an event cannot happen at two distinct times. The second axiom expresses that if the ith occurrence of event *e* happens, then the previous occurrences of *e* would happened before. This axiom also states that two distinct occurrences of the same event must happen at different times.

Start/Stop Event Axioms: For each pair of start/stop events in the set **D**, we have:

$$\forall i \forall t R(\downarrow A,i,t) \rightarrow [\exists t' R(\uparrow A,i,t') \wedge t' < t]$$

where ↑A and ↓A denote the events: start and stop of action A, respectively. The axiom states that every occurrence of a stop event would be preceded by a corresponding start event.

Transition Event Axioms: For the transition events in the set *D* corresponding to a state variable *S*, we have the following relations. Proposition 4(a) states that the first occurrence of event (S:=T) is at time zero. This means that initially the system is in state *S*. Proposition 4(b) states that i^{th} occurrence of event (S:=F) is at time *t*. This means that i^{th} time that the system is not in state *S* is at time *t*. The transition from 4(a) to 4(b) shows a *transition event* where the system is initially in state *S* and at future time the system is not in state *S*. The transition from 4(b) to 4(c) shows the entrance of the system to state *S* and the transition from 4(c) to 4(d) shows the exit of the system from state *S*. Transitions in 5(a) to 5(d) is similar to transitions in 4(a) to 4(d) but the system is not initially in state *S*. In fact, Propositions 4(a) to 4(d) and Propositions 5(a) to 5(d) define the order in which two complementary transition events can occur depending on whether S is initially true or false (Jahanian-b et al, 1998).

$$R((S := T),1,0) \rightarrow \tag{4a}$$

$$(\forall i > 1, \forall t > 0, R((S := F),i,t) \rightarrow \tag{4b}$$

$$[\exists t' R((S := T), i, t') \wedge t' < t] \wedge \forall i \forall t R((S := T), i+1, t) \rightarrow \tag{4c}$$

$$[\exists t' R((S := F), i, t') \wedge t' < t] \tag{4d}$$

$$R((S := F), 1, 0) \rightarrow \tag{5a}$$

$$(\forall i \forall t R((S := T), i, t) \rightarrow \tag{5b}$$

$$[\exists t' R((S := F), i, t') \wedge t' < t] \wedge \forall i \forall t R((S := F), i+1, t) \rightarrow \tag{5c}$$

$$[\exists t' R((S := T), i, t') \wedge t' < t] \tag{5d}$$

3.2 State predicates

RTL provides nine different *state predicates* to evaluate the value of S over an interval as follows:

S[x,y], S(x,y), S<x,y>, S[x,y), S[x,y>, S(x,y], S(x,y>, S<x,y], S<x,y)

Each state predicate qualifies the timing of two events, one denotes the transition event that changes the value of the state variable to true and the other denotes the transition event that changes the value of S to false. The arguments, x and y, in the state predicates are used in conjunction with the symbols "[", "]", "(", ")", "<" and ">" to denote an interval over which the state variable remains true (Jahanian, 1994). Suppose E_t and E_f denote the transition events making S true and false, respectively. Informally:

- "[x " denotes that E_t occurs at time x,
- "(x " denotes that E_t occurs before or at time x,
- "<x" denotes that E_t occurs before time x,
- " y]" denotes that E_f occurs at time y,
- " y)" denotes that E_f does not occur before time y,
- " y>" denotes that E_f does not occur before or at time y.

Definition: If state variable S is initially true, i.e., $R((S := T), 1, 0)$, then

$$S[x,y] \equiv \exists i, R((S := T), i, x) \wedge R((S := F), i, y)$$
$$S[x,y) \equiv \exists i, R((S := T), i, x) \wedge [\forall t R((S := F), i, t) \rightarrow y \leq t]$$
$$S[x,y >\equiv \exists i, R((S := T), i, x) \wedge [\forall t R((S := F), i, t) \rightarrow y < t]$$

The other intervals are defined similarly. If state variable S is initially false, i.e., $R((S := F), 1, 0)$, then $S[x,y] \equiv \exists i R((S := T), i, x) \wedge R((S := F), i+1, y)$. The other intervals are defined similarly (Jahanian-b , 1998).

4. The proposed approach

In this section, we propose a method to produce verification rules from Timed Automata. These rules are used for verification of the software behavior that is obtained from the problem specification. Our method has five steps (Fig.1). In the first step, we specify the system behavior in the Timed Automata and then verify the different states of the system. In the second step, we explain specification of the system in RTL. In the third step, based on the model of the Timed Automata, we work out the reachability graph of the system, and show the behavior of the system in safety and risky states. In the fourth step, we use reachability graph obtained in the third step to extract constraints and express them in RTL by which we verify entering the system to unsafe states.

After specifying the system constraints in RTL and specification of the system behavior by the model in the second step, we verify the problem specification (in fact, we show a visual model of the system in Timed Automata and its behavior in RTL. By the rules extracted from the system behavior, we address verification of the system in entering to unsafe states

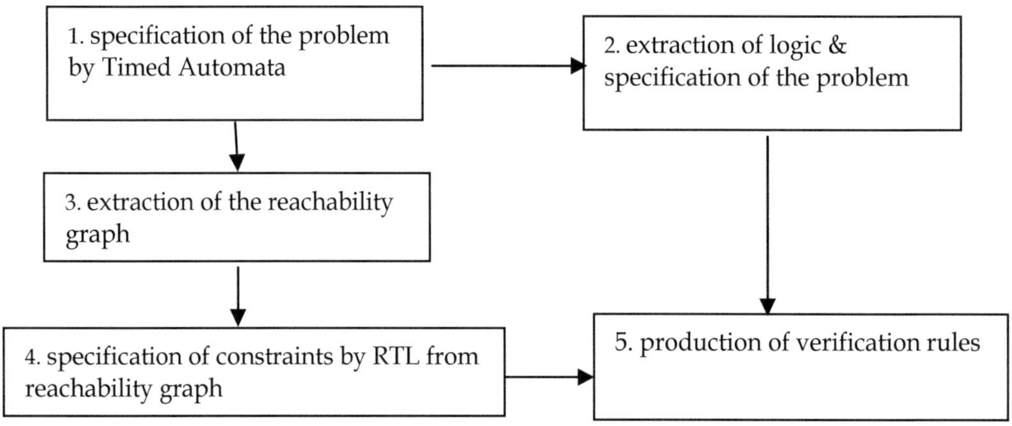

Fig. 1. The proposed approach

4.1 Specifying the problem in timed automata

In this section, we show states of a real time system in the visual and logic forms.

Structure 1: Change of a state due to occurrence of an event. The change of a state in real time systems might be taken place due to occurrence of an event.

Visual definition. When the system is in state p and a guard event takes place, the system makes a transition from state p to state q (Fig. 2).

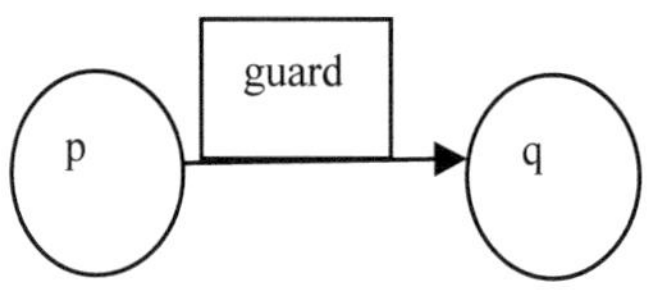

Fig. 2. Change of a state by occurrence of a guard event

Logical definition of structure 1. When the system is in state p at time point t, then by i^{th} occurrence of guard event at time t, the system goes to state q (Relation 6). Considering state predicates in Section 3.2, we define a time point as p(t,t).

$$\forall i\ \forall t[p(t,t)\ \wedge @(GUARD,i)=t\ ] \rightarrow \exists t',d[q(t',t')\wedge t' \geq t+d \wedge d\geq 0] \tag{6}$$

Structure 2. Change of a state by occurrence of an event and the action execution. After occurring the event and the action execution, the state of the system might change.

Visual definition. When the system (Timed Automata) is in state p and a guard event occurs, the action is accomplished and the system holds in state q (Fig. 3).

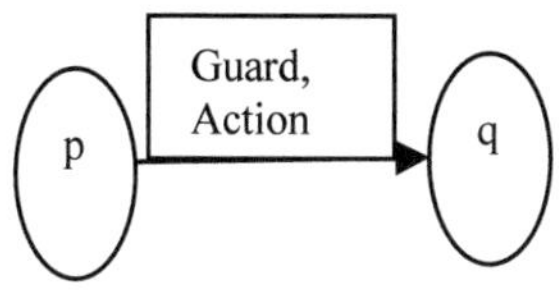

Fig. 3. Change of a state by occurrence of an event and execution of an action

Logical definition of structure 2. If the system is in the state p at time t and a guard event takes place, we have an occurrence of the starting event of the action denoted by ↑ACTION. This causes the start of the action and ending event of action denoted by ↓ACTION. The action is accomplished during the time $\varepsilon>0$ and the state changes (Relation 7).

$$\forall i\ \forall t[p(t,t) \wedge @(GUARD,i)=t\,] \rightarrow \exists j,t',d[@(\uparrow ACTION,j)=t' \wedge t'\geq t+d \wedge d\geq 0] \quad (7)$$

$$\forall i\ \forall t[@(\uparrow ACTION,i)=t] \rightarrow \exists j,t',d[@(\downarrow ACTION,j)=t' \wedge t'\geq t+d \wedge d\geq \varepsilon]$$

$$\forall i\ \forall t[@(\downarrow ACTION,i)=t] \rightarrow \exists t',d[q(t',t') \wedge t'\geq t+d \wedge d\geq 0]$$

Structure 3. Being in one state. In real time systems, a state indicates the system state at a time instant/interval .

Visual definition. According to Fig. 2, when the system is in state p, the state indicates the current state of the system at that specific moment.

Logical definition of structure 3. This structure shows that state p is true at time t. In other words, the system is in state p at time t (Relation 8).

$$\forall i\ \forall t[p(t,t)] \quad (8)$$

Structure 4. Remaining in a state and change of the state. The system should stay in a state for a while and then the state should change.

Visual definition. When the system is in state L_1, it should stay in this state at least for time unit d. After passing of the time and satisfaction of the condition, it would enter to state L_2 (Fig. 4).

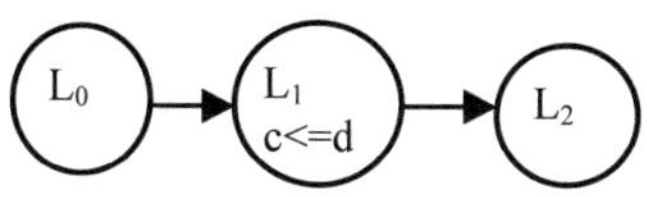

Fig. 4. Change of a state (C indicates clock)

Logical definition of structure 4. If the system is in state L_1 after satisfaction of condition (c<=d) at time t, it would go to a new state (Relation 9).

$$\forall i\ \forall t[L_1(t,t) \wedge @(COND\ (c<=d)\ ,\ i) = t] \rightarrow \exists\ t'\ [L_1(t',t') \wedge t' \geq t+d \wedge d\geq \varepsilon] \quad (9)$$

Structure 5. Transition from one state to several states by different events.

Visual definition. In Timed Automata, some state changes may depend on the condition holds on the transition, i.e., if the condition holds, the state change would happen. Some possible target states may be accessible from one source state when different conditions hold (Fig. 5).

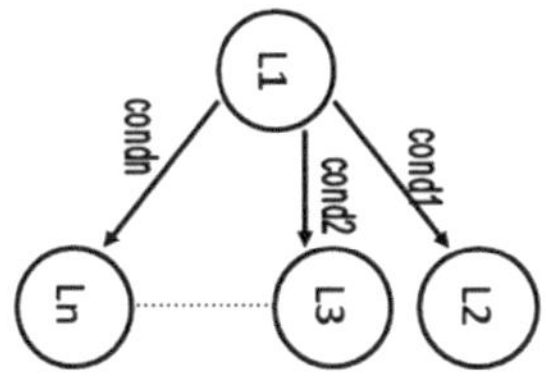

Fig. 5. Change of states by occurrence of event

Logical definition of structure 5. Every time one of the events takes places and according to the occurred event, the system state changes (Relation 10).

$$\forall i, t\,[\,L_0(t,t) \wedge @(COND_1\,, i) = t] \rightarrow \exists\, t',d\,[L_1(t',t') \wedge t' \geq t+d \wedge d \geq 0] \vee \qquad (10)$$

$$\forall i, t\,[\,L_0(t,t) \wedge @(COND_2\,, i) = t] \rightarrow \exists\, t',d\,[L_2(t',t') \wedge t' \geq t+d \wedge d \geq 0] \vee$$

$$\forall i, t\,[\,L_0(t,t) \wedge @(COND_n\,, i) = t] \rightarrow \exists\, t',d\,[L_n(t',t') \wedge t' \geq t+d \wedge d \geq 0]$$

Structure 6. To reach states of a system periodically. When we verify the system behavior, some states may be reached periodically.

Visual definition. In Timed Automata some sets of states and actions might be executed for several times. In such a situation, there will be iterations of some states for several times (Fig. 6).

Logical definition of structure 6. While the system is in state L_n and event $COND_n$ occurs, the system will go to state L_1; this leads to an iteration of states L_1 and L_n. However, if the system is in state L_n and event *condi* take places, the system will go to state L_{n+1} (Relation 11).

$$\forall i\ \forall t\,[L_n(t,t) \wedge @(CONDn\,, i) = t] \rightarrow \exists\, t_1,d\,[L_{n+1}(t_1,t_1) \wedge t_1 \geq t+d \wedge d \geq 0] \vee \qquad (11)$$

$$\forall i\ \forall t\,[L_n(t,t) \wedge @(CONDi\,, i) = t] \rightarrow \exists\, t_2,d\,[L_1(t_2,t_2) \wedge t_2 \geq t+d \wedge d \geq 0]$$

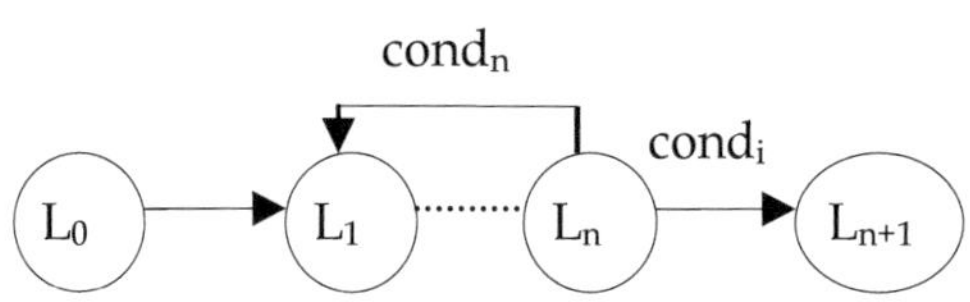

Fig.6. Periodic change of states

4.2 Case study

In this section we propose a critical system and apply the first and second steps (specifying problem in Timed Automata and extracting the logical specification of the problem) of our method. The case study is an example of an automatic controller in which the *railway* gate opens and closes an intersection. The system contains three parts: *train, controller,* and *gate* (Fig.7). The connection between the train and controller is created by two ***exit*** and ***approach*** methods where the former denotes the train exits from the intersection and the latter denotes the train approaches the intersection. It is necessary that the train sends the approach signal less than two minutes before entering the intersection. This has been shown by a *protecting condition* X>2 along with event ***in***. Table 1 shows explanation of states of train, gate and controller.

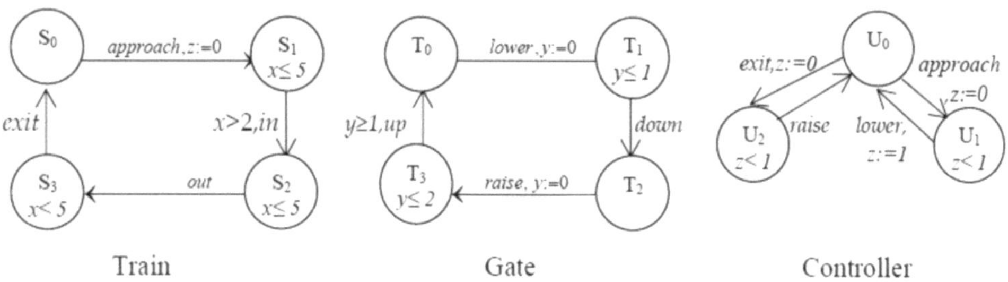

Fig. 7. Train, Gate and Controller states

Train	S_0: the train is far from the intersection S_1:the train is approaching to the intersection S_2: The train is in intersection S_3: The train is leaving the intersection	Controller U_0: the controller is in standby state U_1:The controller is in the lower signal state U_2:The controller is in the raise signal state
Gate	T_0: The gate is in upward state T_1: The gate is coming down T_2: The gate is in down state T_3: The gate is going up	

Table 1. Explanation of Train, Controller and Gate states

In addition, we know that the most delay between *exit* and *approach* signals is five minutes. This has been shown by the conditions X<=5 in transitions between states S_1, S_2 and S3. The gate is opened at T_0 and closed at T_2. The gate answers to ***lower signal*** by the open action in one to two minutes. The system clock is used to show the *constraints*. Initially the controller is in state U_0 (*Idle)*. The controller responses to the gate by sending the *lower signal* when it receives the *approach signal* from the train and the controller responses to the gate by sending the raise signal when it receives the *exit signal* from the train. The response time of the controller for approach and exit signals are one minute and more than one minute respectively; these limitations have been shown by clock ***z***.

The system is in the safe state when the train is in the intersection, and the gate is low. In other words, if the train is in state S_1, the gate should be in state T_2. For example, consider paths originate from nodes S_0, T_0 and U_0 and end with nodes S_1, T_0 and U_1 and paths originate from nodes S_1, T_0 and U_1 and end with nodes S_2, T_0 and U_1 representing the event *approach* followed by event ***in*** immediately. However, this sequence cannot be true if we consider clocks. Now based on the former rules we resemble the previous model with real time logic.

Specification 1 [based on Logical definition 3]. Initially, the train, the gate and the controller are in states S_0, T_0 and U_0 respectively.

$$\forall t\ [S_0(t,t)\ \wedge U_0(t,t)\ \wedge T_0(t,t)]$$

Specification 2 [based on Logical definitions 2 and 3]. When the train is in state S_0 and signal (event) *approach* occurs, after a while event ↑Reset(x) of clock *x* occurs. When event ↓Reset(x) occurs and clock *x* is reset by time *d*, the train is in the *approaching* state.

$$\forall i\ \forall t\ [\ S_0(t,t) \wedge @(\text{SIGNAL(approach)}, i) = t\ ] \rightarrow \exists\ j, t', d\ [@(\uparrow\text{RESET}(x), j)= t' \wedge t' \geq t + d \wedge d \geq 0]$$

$$\forall i\ \forall t\ [@(\uparrow\text{RESET}(x)\ , i)= t] \rightarrow \exists j, t', d\ [@(\downarrow\text{RESET}(x), j) = t' \wedge t' \geq t+d \wedge d \geq \varepsilon]$$

$$\forall i\ \forall t\ [@(\downarrow\text{RESET}(x), i)= t] \rightarrow \exists\ t', d\ [S_1(t', t') \wedge t' \geq t+d \wedge d \geq 0]$$

Specification 3 [based on Logical definitions 2 and 3]. When the train is approaching to the intersection, it is in state S_1.

$$\forall t\ [\ S_1(t,t)\ ] \rightarrow \exists t', d\ [S_1\ (t',t') \wedge t' \geq t+d \wedge d \geq 0 \wedge d \leq 5]$$

Specification 4 [based on Logical definitions 2 and 3]. When the controller is in state *standby* (denoted by state U_0) and signal (event) approach occurs, the clock *z* is reset for making a transition from state U_0 to state U_1.

$$\forall i\ \forall t\ [U_0(t,t) \wedge @(\text{SIGNAL(APPROACH)}, i) = t] \rightarrow$$

$$\exists j, t', d\ [@(\uparrow\text{RESET}(z), j)= t' \wedge t' \geq t + d \wedge d \geq 0]$$

$$\forall i\ \forall t\ [@(\uparrow\text{RESET}(z), i)= t] \rightarrow \exists j, t', d\ [@(\downarrow\text{RESET}(z), j) = t' \wedge t' > t+d \wedge d \geq \varepsilon]$$

$$\forall i\ \forall t\ [@(\downarrow\text{RESET}(z), i)= t] \rightarrow \exists\ t'\ \ [U_1(t',t') \wedge t' \geq t+d \wedge d \geq 0]$$

Specification 5 [based on Logical definitions 1 and 3]. As long as condition *z<=1* holds the controller stays in state U_1.

$$\forall i, t_1, t_2\ [\ U_1(t_1,t_1) \wedge @(\text{COND}(z<=1), i=t_2)\ ] \rightarrow \exists t', d\ [U_1\ (t',t') \wedge t' \geq t+d \wedge d \geq 0 \wedge d \leq 1]$$

Specification 6 [based on Logical definitions 2 and 3]. Assume that: (1) the controller and the gate are in states U_1 and T_0 at time *t* respectively, (2) at this time signal *lower* is generated and (3) event ↑Reset(y) occurs at time *t'*. Accordingly**,** the gate goes to state T_1 and clock *y* is reset. If condition *z=1* holds at time *t*, the controller would enter the state at time *t'*.

$$\forall i,j\ \forall t\ [U_1(t, t \wedge T_0(t, t) \wedge @(\text{SIGNAL(lower)}, i) = t \wedge (\uparrow\text{RESET}(y), j)= t] \rightarrow$$

$$\exists t', q, d\ [T1(t', t') \wedge @(\downarrow\text{RESET}(y), q)= t' \wedge t' \geq t+d \wedge \geq \varepsilon]$$

$$\forall i,j\ \forall t\ [\ U_1(t, t) \wedge T_0(t,t) \wedge @(\ \text{SIGNAL(lower)}, i) = t \wedge @(\uparrow\text{RESET}(y)\ , j)= t \wedge$$

$$@(\text{COND}\ (z=1), i) = t\ ] \rightarrow$$

$$\exists t', q, d\ [T_1(t', t') \wedge U_0(t', t') \wedge @(\downarrow\text{RESET}(y), q)= t' \wedge t' \geq t+d \wedge d \geq \varepsilon].$$

Specification 7 [based on Logical definitions 1, 3 and 4]. Gate stays in state T_1 as long as condition *y<=1* holds. In other words, if the gate is in state T_1 at time *t*, it stays in the same state at time t′ while condition *y<=1* holds.

$$\forall i\ \forall t\ [T_1(t,t) \wedge @(\text{COND}\ (y<=1)\ , i) = t] \rightarrow \exists t',d\ [\ T_1(t',t') \wedge t' \geq t+d \wedge d\leq 1]$$

Specification 8 [based on Logical definitions 1 and 3]. Gate will be in state T_2 at time *t′* if event DOWN occurs at time *t* and after time unit *d* the gate enters state T_2.

$$\forall i\ \forall t\ [T_1(t,t) \wedge @(\text{DOWN}\ , i) = t] \rightarrow \exists t',d\ [\ T_2(t',t') \wedge t' \geq t+d \wedge d\geq 0]$$

Specification 9 [based on Logical definitions 1 and 3]. Train will be in state S_2 at time *t* if at time *t* event *in* occurs and condition *X>2* holds. After that the train goes state S_2 after time unit *d* if condition *X<=5* holds at the same time.

$$\forall i,j\ \forall t,t',d\ S_1(t,t) \wedge @(\ \text{IN}\ , i) = t \wedge @(\text{COND}\ (x>2)\ , i) = t \wedge @(\text{COND}\ (x<=5)\ , i) = t] \rightarrow \\ \exists d,t' [S_2(t',t') \wedge t' \geq t+d \wedge d\geq 0]$$

Specification 10 [based on Logical definitions 1 and 3]. As long as condition *X<=5* holds and train is in state S_2, train stays in this state.

$$\forall i\ \forall t\ [\ S_2(t,t) \wedge @(\text{COND}\ (x<=5)\ , i) = t] \rightarrow \exists t',d\ [S_2(t',t') \wedge t' \geq t+d \wedge d\geq 0]$$

Specification 11 [based on Logical definitions 1 and 3]. Train will be in state S_3 at time *t′* if event OUT have occurred at time *t*. After that, train enters state S_3 after time unit *d* if condition *X<=5* holds.

$$\forall i\ \forall t\ [\ S_2(t,t) \wedge @(\text{COND}\ (x<=5)\ , i) = t \wedge @(\text{OUT}\ , i)=t\ ] \rightarrow \exists t',d\ [S_3(t',t') \wedge t' \geq t+d \wedge d\geq 0]$$

Specification 12 [based on Logical definitions 1 and 3]. Train will be in state S_0 at time *t′* if event *exit* occurs at time *t*. After time unit *d*, train will be in state S_0.

$$\forall i\ \forall t\ [S_3(t,t) \wedge @(\text{SIGNAL}\ (\text{exit})\ , i) = t] \rightarrow \exists t',d\ [S_0(t',t') \wedge t' \geq t+d \wedge d\geq 0]$$

Specification 13 [based on Logical definitions 2 and 3]. Controller will be in state U_2 at time *t′* if it receives event *exit*. The event occurs due to exiting train from intersection at time *t*. Also if at the same time event *reset* of clock *z* occurs, train will enter the state U_2 after time unit *d* and clock *z* is reset to zero at the same time.

$$\forall i,\ j\ \forall t\ [U_0(t,t) \wedge @(\ \text{SIGNAL}\ (\text{exit})\ , i) = t \wedge @(\uparrow\text{RESET}(z),\ j)= t\ ] \rightarrow$$

$$\exists t',\ q,\ d\ [U_2(t',t') \wedge @(\downarrow\text{RESET}(z)\ , q)= t' \wedge t' \geq t+d \wedge d\geq \varepsilon]$$

Specification 14 [based on Logical definitions 1 and 3]. Controller stays in state U_2 as long as condition *Z<=1* holds.

$$\forall i \forall t\ [U_2(t,t) \wedge @(\text{COND}\ (z<=1)\ , i) = t] \rightarrow \exists t',d\ [\ U_2(t',t') \wedge t' \geq t+d \wedge d\leq 1]$$

Specification 15 [based on Logical definitions 1 and 3]. Controller will be in state U_0 after time unit *d* when it receives signal *raise* at time *t*.

$$\forall i\ \forall t\ [\ U_2(t,t) \wedge @(\text{SIGNAL}\ (\text{raise})\ , i) = t] \rightarrow \exists t',d\ [U_0(t',t') \wedge t' \geq t+d \wedge d\geq 0]$$

Specification 16 [based on Logical definitions 2 and 3]. Gate goes upward by receiving signal *raise* at time *t* and event ↑RESET(y) resets clock *y* at the same time. After time unit *d* if condition y<=2 holds, the gate enters state T_3 at time *t′* and at the same time event ↓RESET(y) resets clock *y* to zero.

$$\forall i,j,q\ \forall t,t',d\ [T_2(t,t)\ ) \wedge @(\text{SIGNAL(raise)}, i) = t \wedge @(\uparrow\text{RESET}(y), j) = t \wedge$$

$$@(\text{COND}\ (y<=2), q) = t\ ] \rightarrow$$

$$\exists t', m, d[T_3(t',t') \wedge @(\downarrow\text{RESET}(y), m) = t' \wedge t' \geq t+d \wedge d\geq\varepsilon]$$

Specification 17 [based on Logical definitions 1 and 3]. Gate will be in its first state, T_0, at time *t′* if event *up* occurs at time *t* and at this time, events COND(y<=2) and COND (y>=1) occur. After time unit *d*, the gate enters state T_0.

$$\forall i, j, q\ \forall t\ [\ T_3(t,t) \wedge @(\text{UP}, i) = t \wedge @(\text{COND}\ (y>=1), j) = t \wedge @(\text{COND}\ (y<=2), q) = t] \rightarrow$$

$$\exists t', d\ [T_0(t',t') \wedge t' \geq t+d \wedge d\geq 0]$$

4.3 Extracting reachability graph

In the previous section, we stated textual specification of the Timed Automata of road and railway intersection in RTL. Having extracted reachability graph from Timed Automata, we use RTL to verify those situations in which the system enters *unsafe* states. Fig. 8 shows the reachability graph of road and railway intersection system. The *gray* parts of the graph are *unsafe* states that the system should never enter. To verify the system behavior against the unsafe states, we aim to construct verification rules (constraints). These rules are intended to monitor change of system states against the unsafe states. These rules are based on the structures specified in Section 4.

Verification rule 1. When the train is approaching the intersection, the gate should get lower (state T_1).

$$\forall t\ [S_1(t,t)] \rightarrow \exists t',d\ [T_1(t',t') \wedge t' \geq t+d \wedge d\geq 0]$$

Verification rule 2. When the train is approaching the intersection, the gate should not be up or should not move up (states T_0 and T_1); otherwise it is an unsafe situation (state H_3 in Fig. 8).

$$\forall t\ [S_1(t,t)\ ]\rightarrow \exists t',d\ [\neg T_1(t',t') \wedge \neg T_3(t',t') \wedge t' \geq t+d \wedge d\geq 0]$$

Verification rule 3. When train is in intersection (state S_2), the gate should be down (state T_2); otherwise it is an unsafe situation (state H_4 in Fig. 8).

$$\forall t\ [S_2(t,t)] \rightarrow \exists t',d\ [T_2(t',t') \wedge t' \geq t+d \wedge d\geq 0]$$

Verification rule 4. When train is in intersection (state S_2), the gate should not be up or should not move down; otherwise it is an unsafe situation (states H_4 and H_5 in Fig. 8).

$$\forall t\ [S_2(t,t)\ ]\rightarrow\exists t',d\ [(\neg T_0(t',t') \vee \neg T_1(t',t')\ ) \wedge t' \geq t+d \wedge d\geq 0]$$

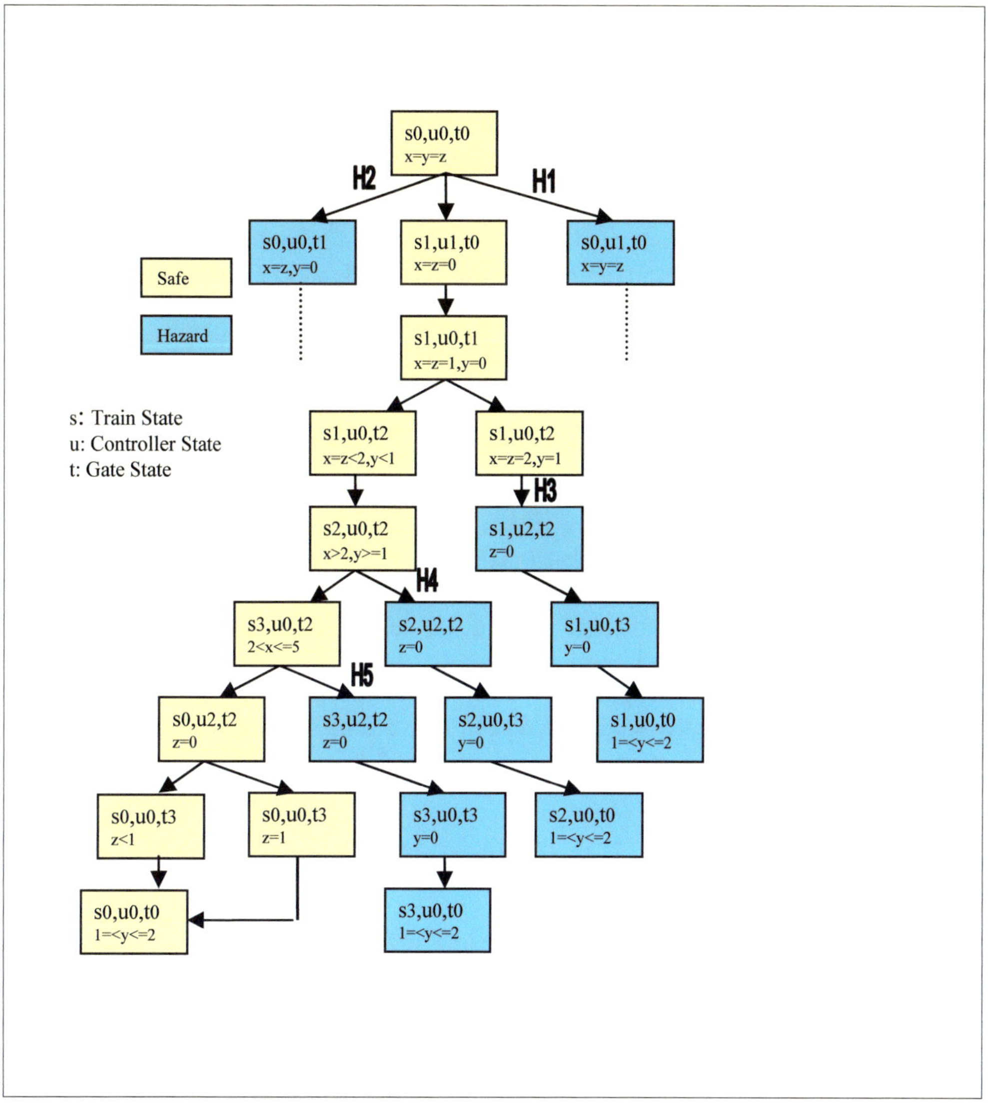

Fig. 8. Reachability graph

Verification rule 5. When train has not left the intersection (state S_3), the gate should be down; otherwise it is an unsafe situation (state H_5 in Fig. 8).

$$\forall t\ [S_3(t,t)] \rightarrow \exists t',d\ [T2(t',t') \wedge t' \geq t+d \wedge d\geq 0]$$

Verification rule 6. When train has not left the intersection (state S_3), the gate should not up or should not move up; otherwise it is an unsafe situation (state H_5 in Fig. 8).

$$\forall t\ [S_3(t,t)\ ] \rightarrow \exists t',d\ [(\neg T_0(t',t') \vee \neg T_1(t',t') \vee \neg T_3(t',t')\ ) \wedge t' \geq t+d \wedge d\geq 0]$$

Verification rule 7. When train is leaving the intersection, the gate should go up; otherwise it is an unsafe situation (state H_2 in Fig. 8).

$$\forall t\ [S_0(t,t) \wedge U_0(t,t)\ ] \rightarrow \exists t',d\ [T_3(t',t') \wedge t' \geq t+d \wedge d\geq 0]$$

Verification rule 8. When train is not in intersection, the gate should not be down or should not move down; otherwise it is an unsafe situation (states H_1 and H_2 in Fig. 8).

$$\forall t\ [S_0(t,t)\ ] \rightarrow \exists t',d[(\neg T_1(t',t') \vee \neg T_2(t',t')) \wedge t' \geq t+d \wedge d\geq 0]$$

5. Conclusions and related work

In this paper, we dealt with producing verification rules for verification of real-time systems systematically. As a matter of fact, our contribution to the rule production had three aspects. The first one was determination and representation of basic constructions of Timed Automata that were susceptible to making basic verification rules. The second one was producing rules systematically, where it was achieved through reachability graph. The reachability graph as a bridge helped us to extract safety rules from visual specifications. The third aspect was mapping the safety properties obtained from the reachability graph into RTL propositions forming the verification rules. Finally, to show effectiveness of our approach we applied it to a real-time system. In the following, we state the related work.

Jahanian and Mok specified high-level requirements by the Modechart visual and specific language and mapped them to a constraint graph (Chen & Rosu, 2005) where the graph was used by a monitor in order to verify software behavior.

Deriving monitors from requirements has been considered by some researchers. The *Eagle* method used the *Eagle logic* to specify requirements and synthesized a rule based monitor (Barringer et al, 2004). It extended Mu Calculus to support past and future time linear logic and real-time one. *Eagle* exploiting a state-based approach (d'Amiron & Havelund, 2005) was extended by the HAWK logic (d'Amiron & Havelund, 2005). To support event-based specifications, the HAWK language, used to specify both high-level specifications and low-level run-time states, has included low-level programming definitions to verify java programs.

(Mok & Liu, 1997, Chen & Rosu, 2005) used real-time logic (RTL) for the requirements specification of real-time system. Li and Dang presented algorithms to combine automata with *black-box testing* in order to verify safety properties (Li, & Dang, 2006). (Mok & Liu,

1997, Douglass, 1999, Jalili & MirzaAghaei, 2007) exploiting event-based approach for real-time systems, used real-time logic (RTL) for high-level specification of system requirements; so, they were capable of specifying real-time requirements, particularly ordering of events.

6. References

Alur R. & Dill D.L. (1994). A theory of timed automata, *Theoretical Computer Science, Elsevier*, Vol. 126, No. 2, pp. 183-235.

Alur R. & Dill D.L. (1996). Automata-theoretic verification of real-time systems, *Formal Methods for Real-Time Computing, Trends in Software Series*, Wiley & Sons, pp. 55-82.

Barringer H. et al. (2004). Rule-Based Runtime Verification, *Proceedings of the 5th International Conference on Verification, Model Checking and Abstract Interpretation (VMCAI'04)*, LNCS2937, Springer, pp. 44-57.

Bellini P. et al (2000). Temporal logics for real-time system specification, *ACM Computing Surveys*, Vol. 32, No. 1, pp. 12-42.

Chen, F. & Rosu, G. (2005). Java-MOP: A Monitoring Oriented Programming Environment for Java, *Proceedings of the 11th International Conference on Tools and Algorithms for the Construction and Analysis of Systems*, pp. 546-550.

d'Amiron, M. & Havelund, K. (2005). Event-Based Runtime Verification of Java Programs, *Proceedings of the 5th Workshop of ICSE (International Conference on Software Engineering) on Dynamic Analysis*, pp. 1-7.

Douglass, B.P. (1999). Doing Hard Time, Developing Real-Time Systems with UML, Objects, Framework and Patterns, Addison-Wesley.

Jahanian-a F. et al (1988). A Graph-theoretic approach for timing analysis in real time logic , *Proceedings of IEEE Real-Time Systems Symposium.*

Jahanian-b F. et al (1988). Formal specification of real-time systems, Technical Report, *University of Texas at Austin Austin, USA.*

Jahanian F. (1994). Modechart: a specification language for real-time systems, *IEEE Trans. on Software Engineering*, Vol. 20 , No.12, pp. 933-947.

Jalili S. & MirzaAghaei, M. (2007). RVERL: Run-time Verification of Real-time and Reactive Programs using Event-based Real-Time Logic Approach, *Proceedings of the 5th International Conference on Software Engineering Research, Management & Applications (SERA 2007)*, IEEE Computer Society, pp. 550-557.

Li, C. & Dang, Z. (2006). Decompositional Algorithms for Safety Verification and Testing of Aspect-Oriented Systems, *Proceedings of Formal Approaches to Software Testing and Runtime Verification, FATES 2006 & RV 2006*, Springer, Vol. 4262.

Mok, A.K. & Liu, G. (1997). Efficient Run-time Monitoring of Timing Constraints, *Proceedings of the IEEE Real-Time Technology and Applications Symposium*, pp. 252-262.

Paneka S. et al (2006). Scheduling and planning with timed automata, *Proceedings of 16th European Symposium on Computer Aided Process Engineering and 9th International Symposium on Process Systems Engineering*, W. Marquardt, C. Pantelides (Editors), Elsevier.

Penczek W. & Polrola A. (2006). Advances in verification of timed petri-nets and timed automata, *Studies in Computational Intelligence,* Springer.

Part 3

Scheduling

7

Handling Overload Conditions in Real-Time Systems

Giorgio C. Buttazzo
Scuola Superiore Sant'Anna
Italy

1. Introduction

This chapter deals with the problem of handling overload conditions, that is, those critical situations in which the computational demand requested by the application exceeds the processor capacity (Buttazzo, 2011). If not properly handled, an overload can cause an abrupt performance degradation, or even a system crash. Therefore, a real-time system should be designed to anticipate and tolerate unexpected overload situations through specific kernel mechanisms.

Overload conditions can occur for different causes, including bad system design, simultaneous arrival of events, operating system exceptions, malfunctioning of input devices, and unpredicted variations of the environmental conditions.

In the following, we consider a set of n periodic or sporadic tasks, $\Gamma = \{\tau_1, \ldots, \tau_n\}$, each characterized by a worst-case execution time (WCET) C_i, a relative deadline D_i, and a period (or minimum inter-arrival time) T_i. Each task τ_i is initially activated at time Φ_i (denoted as the task phase) and generates an infinite sequence of jobs $\tau_{i,k}$ ($k = 1, 2, \ldots$). If a task τ_i is periodic, a generic job $\tau_{i,k}$ is regularly activated at time $r_{i,k} = \Phi_i + (k-1)T_i$. In general, the activation time of job $\tau_{i,k+1}$ is:

$$\begin{cases} r_{i,k+1} = r_{i,k} + T_i & \text{if } \tau_i \text{ is periodic} \\ r_{i,k+1} \geq r_{i,k} + T_i & \text{if } \tau_i \text{ is sporadic} \\ r_{i,k+1} > r_{i,k} & \text{if } \tau_i \text{ is aperiodic.} \end{cases}$$

Also, each job $\tau_{i,k}$ is characterized by an absolute deadline $d_{i,k} = r_{i,k} + D_i$. For a set of periodic tasks, the *hyperperiod* H denotes the minimum interval of time after which the schedule repeats itself. For a set of periodic tasks synchronously activated at time $t = 0$ ($\Phi_i = 0$, for all i), the hyperperiod is equal to the least common multiple of all the periods, that is $H = \text{lcm}(T_1, \ldots, T_n)$.

In a real-time system, the computational load depends on the temporal characteristics of the executing activities. For example, for a set of n periodic tasks, the system load is equivalent to the processor utilization factor (Liu & Layland, 1973):

$$U = \sum_{i=1}^{n} \frac{C_i}{T_i}. \tag{1}$$

A value $U > 1$ means that the total computation time requested by the task set in the *hyperperiod* exceeds the available time on the processor (i.e, the length H); therefore, the task set cannot be scheduled by any algorithm.

For a generic set of real-time jobs that can be dynamically activated, the system load varies at each job activation and it is a function of the current time and the job deadlines. In general, if there are n active jobs at time t, with absolute deadlines $d_1, d_2, \ldots, d_n$, the *instantaneous load* $\rho(t)$ can be defined as follows (Buttazzo & Stankovic, 1995):

$$\rho(t) = \max_i \left\{ \frac{\sum_{d_k \leq d_i} c_k(t)}{d_i - t} \right\}, \tag{2}$$

where $c_k(t)$ denotes the remaining worst-case computation time of the k-th job. Figure 1 shows how the instantaneous load varies as a function of time for a set of three real-time jobs $\{J_1, J_2, J_3\}$ having activation times (r_i: 3, 1, 2), computation times (C_i: 2, 3, 1), and relative deadlines (D_i: 3, 6, 7).

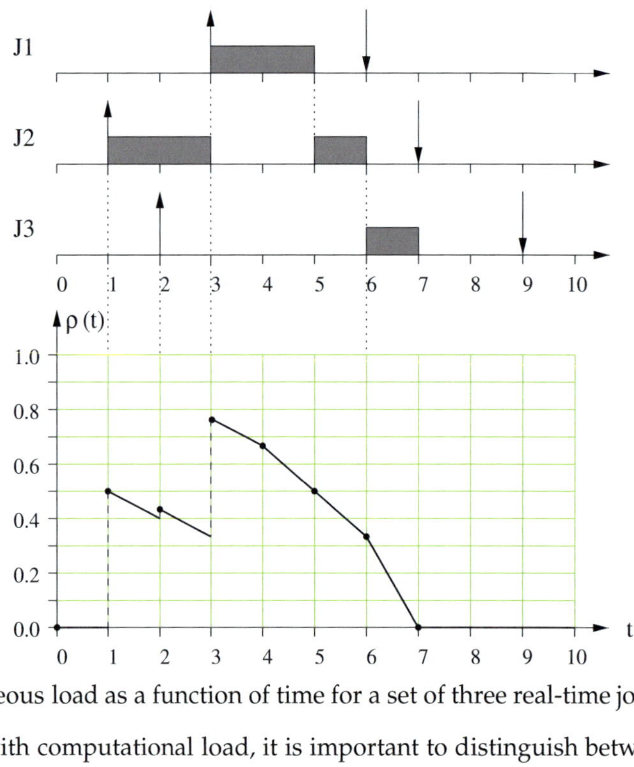

Fig. 1. Instantaneous load as a function of time for a set of three real-time jobs.

When dealing with computational load, it is important to distinguish between overload and overrun:

- A computing system is said to experience an **overload** when the computation time demanded by the task set in a certain interval of time exceeds the available processing time in the same interval.
- A task is said to experience an **overrun** when it exceeds its expected utilization. An overrun may occur either because the next job is activated before its expected arrival

time (*activation overrun*), or because the job computation time exceeds its expected value (*execution overrun*).

Note that, while the overload is a condition related to the processor, the overrun is a condition related to a single job. A job overrun does not necessarily cause an overload. However, a large unexpected overrun or a sequence of overruns on multiple jobs can cause very unpredictable effects on the system, if not properly handled.

In this chapter, two types of overload conditions will be analyzed:

- **Transient overload due to task overruns.** This type of overload is due to periodic or aperiodic tasks that sporadically execute (or are activated) more than expected. Under fixed priority scheduling, an overrun in a task τ_i does not affect tasks with higher priority, but any of the lower priority task could miss its deadline. Under the Earliest Deadline First (EDF) scheduling algorithm (Liu & Layland, 1973), a task overrun can potentially affect all the other tasks in the system. Figure 2 shows an example of an execution overrun under EDF scheduling. In this example, task τ_3 experiences an overrun of 7 units of time (shown in light gray), since its expected execution time was $C_3 = 3$.

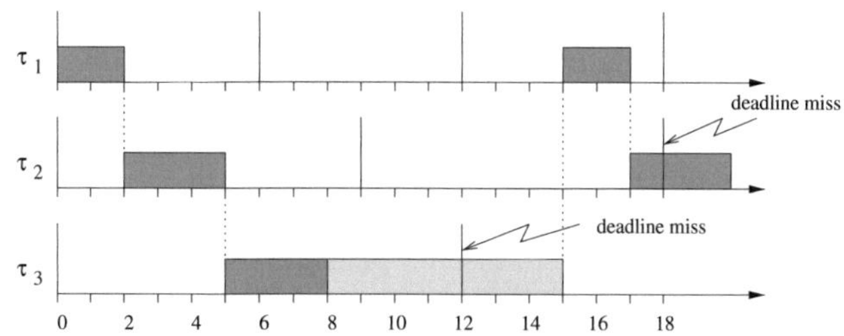

Fig. 2. Effect of an execution overrun in an EDF schedule.

- **Permanent overload in periodic task systems.** This type of overload occurs when the total utilization of the periodic task set is greater than one. This can happen either because the execution requirement of the task set was not correctly estimated, or because of some unexpected activation of new periodic tasks, or because some of the current tasks increased their activation rate to react to some change in the environment. In such a situation, tasks start accumulating in the system's queues (which tend to become longer and longer, if the overload persists), and their response times tend to increase indefinitely. Figure 3 shows the effect of a permanent overload condition in a Rate Monotonic schedule, where computation times are C_i: (2, 3, 2), and periods are T_i: (4, 6, 8). Note that, since $U_p = 1.25$, τ_2 misses its deadline and τ_3 can never execute.

2. Handling transient overloads

If not properly handled, task overruns can cause serious problems in the real-time system, jeopardizing the guarantee performed for the critical tasks and causing an abrupt performance degradation.

To prevent an overrun to introducing unbounded delays on tasks' execution, the system could either decide to abort the current job experiencing the overrun or let it continue with a lower priority. The first solution is not safe, because the job could be in a critical section when aborted, thus leaving a shared resource with inconsistent data (very dangerous). The second solution is much more flexible, since the degree of interference caused by the overrun on the

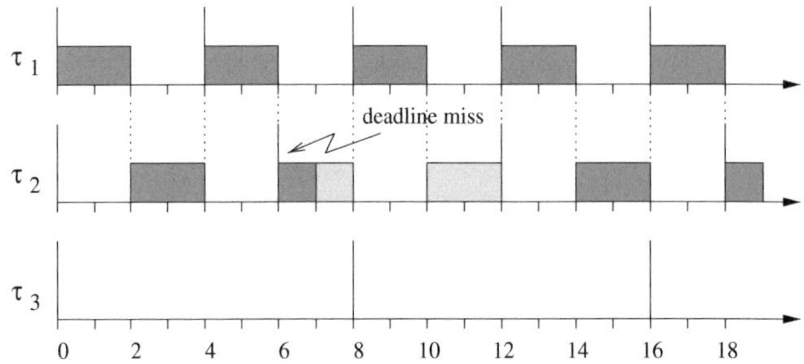

Fig. 3. Example of a permanent overload under Rate Monotonic: τ_2 misses its deadline and τ_3 can never execute.

other tasks can be tuned acting on the priority assigned to the "faulty" task for executing the remaining computation. Such a solution can be efficiently implemented through the resource reservation approach, which is a general kernel technique for limiting the inter-task interference and isolating the temporal behavior of a task subset.

2.1 Resource reservation

Resource reservation is a general technique used in real-time systems for limiting the effects of overruns in tasks with variable computation times. According to this method, each task is assigned a fraction of the processor bandwidth, just enough to satisfy its timing constraints. The kernel, however, must prevent each task to consume more than the requested amount to protect the other tasks in the systems (temporal protection). In this way, a task receiving a fraction U_i of the total processor bandwidth behaves as it were executing alone on a slower processor with a speed equal to U_i times the full speed. The advantage of this method is that each task can be guaranteed in isolation, independently of the behavior of the other tasks.

A resource reservation technique for fixed priority scheduling was first presented by Mercer, Savage and Tokuda (Mercer et al., 1994). According to this method, a task τ_i is handled by a server, which is a kernel mechanism capable of controlling the execution of the task assigned to it through a pair of parameters (Q_s, P_s) (denoted as a CPU *capacity reserve*). The server enables τ_i to execute for Q_s units of time every P_s. In this case, the bandwidth reserved to the task is $U_s = Q_s/P_s$. When the task consumes its reserved quantum Q_s, it is blocked until the next period, if the reservation is hard, or it is scheduled in background as a non real-time task, if the reservation is soft. If the task is not finished, it is assigned another time quantum Q_s at the beginning of the next period and it is scheduled as a real-time task until the budget expires, and so on. In this way, the execution of τ_i is *reshaped* to be more uniform along the timeline, so avoiding long intervals of time in which τ_i prevents other tasks to run.

Under EDF scheduling, resource reservation can be efficiently implemented through the Constant Bandwidth Server (CBS) (Abeni & Buttazzo, 1998; 2004), which is a service mechanism also controlled by two parameters, (Q_s, P_s), where Q_s is the *server maximum budget* and P_s is the *server period*. The ratio $U_s = Q_s/P_s$ is denoted as the *server bandwidth*. At each instant, two state variables are maintained: the server deadline d_s and the actual server budget q_s. Each job handled by a server is scheduled using the current server deadline and whenever the server executes a job, the budget q_s is decreased by the same amount. At the beginning $d_s = q_s = 0$. Since a job is not activated while the previous one is active, the CBS algorithm can be formally defined as follows:

1. When a job $\tau_{i,j}$ arrives, if $q_s \geq (d_s - r_{i,j})U_s$, it is assigned a server deadline $d_s = r_{i,j} + P_s$ and q_s is recharged at the maximum value Q_s, otherwise the job is served with the current deadline using the current budget.
2. When $q_s = 0$, the server budget is recharged at the maximum value Q_s and the server deadline is postponed at $d_s = d_s + P_s$. Note that there are no finite intervals of time in which the budget is equal to zero.

As shown in (Abeni & Buttazzo, 2004), if a task τ_i is handled by a CBS with bandwidth U_s, it will never demand more than U_s, independently of the actual execution time of its jobs. As a consequence, possible overruns occurring in the served task do not create extra interference in the other tasks, but only affect τ_i.

To properly implement temporal protection, however, each task τ_i with variable computation time should be handled by a dedicated CBS with bandwidth U_{s_i}, so that it cannot interfere with the rest of the tasks for more than U_{s_i}. Figure 4 illustrates an example in which two tasks (τ_1 and τ_2) are served by two dedicated CBSs with bandwidth $U_{s_1} = 0.15$ and $U_{s_2} = 0.1$, a group of two tasks (τ_3, τ_4) is handled by a single CBS with bandwidth $U_{s_3} = 0.25$, and three hard periodic tasks (τ_5, τ_6, τ_7) with utilization $U_p = 0.5$ are directly scheduled by EDF, without server intercession, since their execution times are not subject to large variations. In this example, the total processor bandwidth is shared among the tasks as shown in Figure 5.

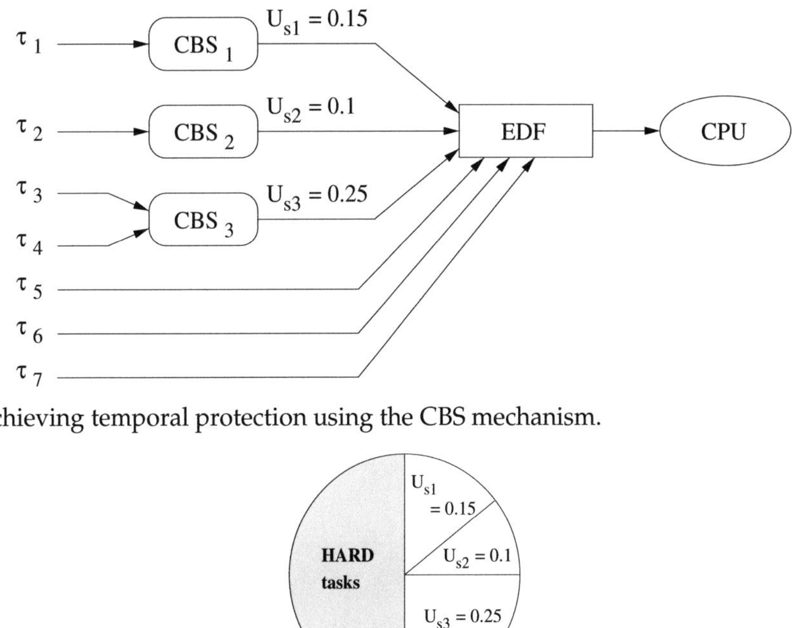

Fig. 4. Achieving temporal protection using the CBS mechanism.

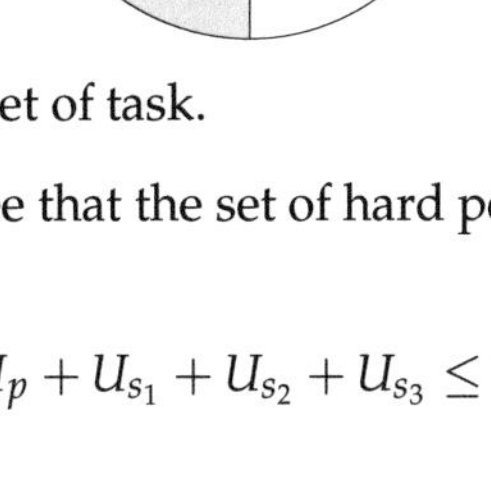

Fig. 5. Bandwidth allocation for a set of task.

The properties of the CBS guarantee that the set of hard periodic tasks (with utilization U_p) is schedulable by EDF if and only if

$$U_p + U_{s_1} + U_{s_2} + U_{s_3} \leq 1. \tag{3}$$

Note that if condition (3) holds, the set of hard periodic tasks is always guaranteed to use 50% of the processor, independently of the execution times of the other tasks. Also observe that τ_3 and τ_4 are not isolated with respect to each other (i.e., one can steals processor time from the other), but they cannot interfere with the other tasks for more than one-fourth of the total processor bandwidth.

The CBS version presented in this book is meant for handling soft reservations. In fact, when the budget is exhausted, it is always replenished at its full value and the server deadline is postponed (i.e., the server is always active). As a consequence, a served task can execute more than Q_s in each period P_s, if there are no other tasks in the system. However, the CBS can be easily modified to enforce hard reservations, just by postponing the budget replenishment to the server deadline.

2.2 Schedulability analysis

Although a reservation R_k is typically implemented using a server characterized by a budget Q_k and a period T_k, there are cases in which temporal isolation can be achieved by executing tasks in a static partition of disjoint time slots.

To characterize a bandwidth reservation independently on the specific implementation, Mok et al. (Mok et al., 2001) introduced the concept of *bounded delay partition* that describes a reservation R_k by two parameters: a bandwidth α_k and a delay Δ_k. The bandwidth α_k measures the fraction of resource that is assigned to the served tasks, whereas the delay Δ_k represents the longest interval of time in which the resource is not available. In general, the minimum service provided by a resource can be precisely described by its *supply function* (Lipari & Bini, 2003; Shin & Lee, 2003), representing the minimum amount of time the resource can provide in a given interval of time.

Definition 1. *Given a reservation, the* supply function $Z_k(t)$ *is the minimum amount of time provided by the reservation in every time interval of length* $t \geq 0$.

The supply function can be defined for many kinds of reservations, as static time partitions (Feng & Mok, 2002; Mok et al., 2001), periodic servers (Lipari & Bini, 2003; Shin & Lee, 2003), or periodic servers with arbitrary deadline (Easwaran et al., 2007). Consider, for example, that processing time is provided only in the intervals [0,3], [6,8], and [9,10], with a period of 12 units. In this case, the minimum service occurs when the resource is requested at the beginning of the longest idle interval; hence, the supply function is the one depicted in Figure 6.

For this example we have $\alpha_k = 0.5$ and $\Delta_k = 3$. Once the bandwidth and the delay are computed, the supply function of a resource reservation can be lower bounded by the following *supply bound function*:

$$\mathsf{sbf}_k(t) \stackrel{\text{def}}{=} \max\{0, \alpha_k(t - \Delta_k)\}. \tag{4}$$

represented by the dashed line in Figure 6. The advantage of using such a lower bound instead of the exact $Z_k(t)$ is that a reservation can be expressed with just two parameters. In general, for a given supply function $Z_k(t)$, the bandwidth α_k and the delay Δ_k can be formally defined as follows:

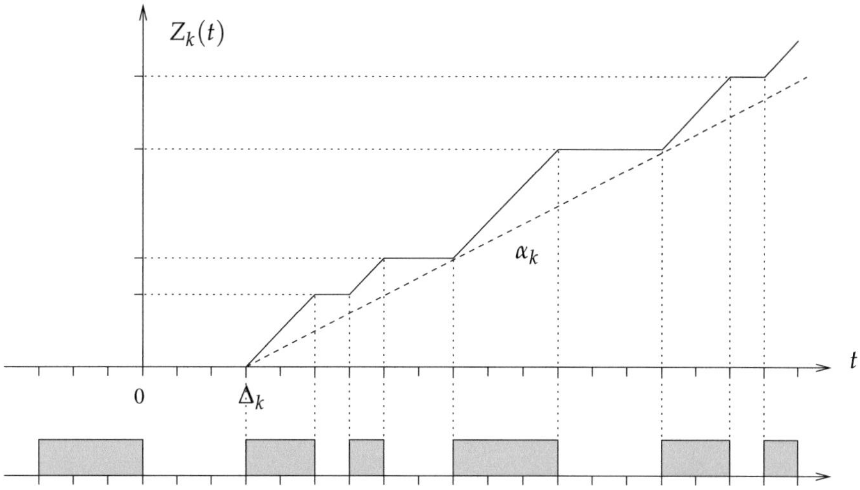

Fig. 6. A reservation implemented by a static partition of intervals.

$$\alpha_k = \lim_{t\to\infty} \frac{Z_k(t)}{t} \tag{5}$$

$$\Delta_k = \sup_{t\geq 0} \left\{ t - \frac{Z_k(t)}{\alpha_k} \right\}. \tag{6}$$

If a reservation is implemented using a periodic server with unspecified priority that allocates a budget Q_k every period T_k, then the supply function is the one illustrated in Figure 7, where

$$\alpha_k = Q_k/T_k \tag{7}$$

$$\Delta_k = 2(T_k - Q_k). \tag{8}$$

It is worth observing that reservations with smaller delays are able to serve tasks with shorter deadlines, providing better responsiveness. However, small delays can only be achieved with servers with a small period, condition for which the context switch overhead cannot be neglected. If σ is the runtime overhead due to a context switch (subtracted from the budget every period), then the effective bandwidth of reservation R_k is

$$\alpha_k^{\text{eff}} = \frac{Q-\sigma}{T_k} = \alpha_k \left(1 - \frac{\sigma}{Q_k}\right).$$

Expressing Q_k and T_k as a function of α_k and Δ_k we have

$$Q_k = \frac{\alpha_k \Delta_k}{2(1-\alpha_k)}$$

$$P_k = \frac{\Delta_k}{2(1-\alpha_k)}.$$

Hence,

$$\alpha_k^{\text{eff}} = \alpha_k + \frac{2\sigma(1-\alpha_k)}{\Delta_k}. \tag{9}$$

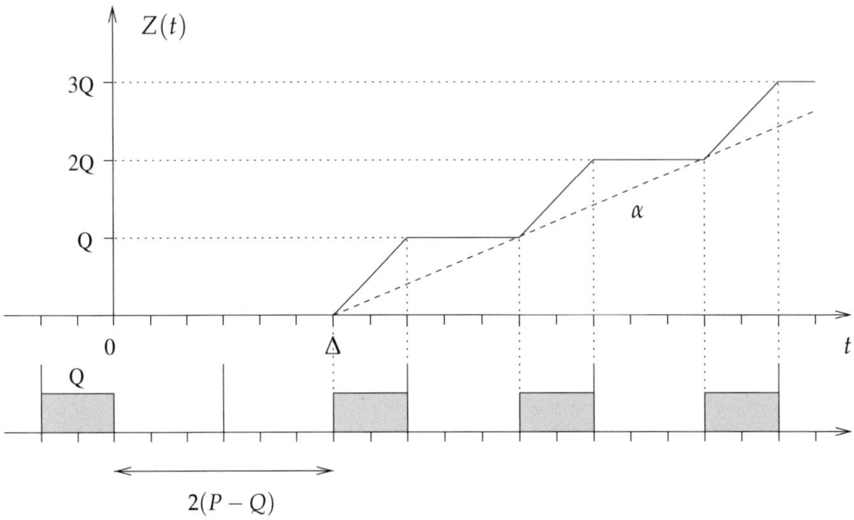

Fig. 7. A reservation implemented by a periodic server.

Within a reservation, the schedulability analysis of a task set under fixed priorities can be performed through the following Theorem (Bini et al., 2009):

Theorem 1 (Bini et al., 2009). *A set of preemptive periodic tasks with relative deadlines less than or equal to periods can be scheduled by a fixed priority algorithm, under a reservation characterized by a supply function $Z_k(t)$, if and only if*

$$\forall i = 1, \dots, n \quad \exists t \in (0, D_i] : W_i(t) \leq Z_k(t). \tag{10}$$

where $W_i(t)$ represents the Level-i workload, computed as follows:

$$W_i(t) = C_i + \sum_{h:P_h > P_i} \left\lceil \frac{t}{T_h} \right\rceil C_h. \tag{11}$$

Similarly, the schedulability analysis of a task set under EDF can be performed using the following theorem (Bini et al., 2009):

Theorem 2 (Bini et al., 2009). *A set of preemptive periodic tasks with utilization U_p and relative deadlines less than or equal to periods can be scheduled by EDF, under a reservation characterized by a supply function $Z_k(t)$, if and only if $U_p < \alpha_k$ and*

$$\forall t > 0 \quad \mathsf{dbf}(t) \leq Z_k(t). \tag{12}$$

where $\mathsf{dbf}(t)$ is the Demand Bound Function (Baruah et al., 1990) defined as

$$\mathsf{dbf}(t) \overset{\text{def}}{=} \sum_{i=1}^{n} \left\lfloor \frac{t + T_i - D_i}{T_i} \right\rfloor C_i. \tag{13}$$

In the specific case in which $Z_k(t)$ is lower bounded by the supply bound function, the test becomes only sufficient and the set of testing points can be better restricted as stated in the following theorem (Bertogna et al., 2009):

Theorem 3 (Bertogna et al., 2009). *A set of preemptive periodic tasks with utilization U_p and relative deadlines less than or equal to periods can be scheduled by EDF, under a reservation characterized by a supply function $Z_k(t) = \max[0, \alpha_k(t - \Delta_k)]$, if $U_p < \alpha_k$ and*

$$\forall t \in \mathcal{D} \quad \mathsf{dbf}(t) \leq \max[0, \alpha_k(t - \Delta_k)]. \tag{14}$$

where

$$\mathcal{D} = \{d_k \mid d_k \leq \min[H, \max(D_{max}, L^*)]\}$$

and

$$L^* = \frac{\alpha_k \Delta_k + \sum_{i=1}^{n}(T_i - D_i)U_i}{\alpha_k - U_p}.$$

2.3 Handling wrong reservations

Although resource reservation is essential for achieving predictability in the presence of tasks with variable execution times, the overall system performance becomes quite dependent on a correct bandwidth allocation. In fact, if the CPU bandwidth allocated to a task is much less than its average requested value, the task may slow down too much, degrading the system's performance. On the other hand, if the allocated bandwidth is much greater than the actual needs, the system will run with low efficiency, wasting the available resources. This problem can be solved by using capacity sharing mechanisms that can transfer unused budgets to the reservations that need more bandwidth.

Capacity sharing algorithms have been developed both under fixed priority servers (Bernat et al., December 5-8, 2004; Bernat & Burns, 2002) and dynamic priority servers (Caccamo et al., 2000). For example, the CASH algorithm (Caccamo et al., 2005) extends CBS to include a slack reclamation. When a server becomes idle with residual budget, the slack is inserted in a queue of spare budgets (CASH queue) ordered by server deadlines. Whenever a new server is scheduled for execution, it first uses any CASH budget whose deadline is less than or equal to its own.

The bandwidth inheritance (BWI) algorithm (Lamastra et al., December 3-6, 2001) applies the idea of priority inheritance to CPU resources in CBS, allowing a blocking low-priority process to steal resources from a blocked higher priority process. IRIS (Marzario et al., 2004) enhances CBS with fairer slack reclaiming, so slack is not reclaimed until all current jobs have been serviced and the processor is idle. BACKSLASH (Lin & Brandt, December 5Ű8, 2005) is another algorithm that enhances the efficiency of the reclaiming mechanism under EDF.

Wrong reservations can also be handled through feedback scheduling. If the operating system is able to monitor the actual execution time $e_{i,k}$ of each task instance, the actual maximum computation time of a task τ_i can be estimated (in a moving window) as

$$\hat{C}_i = \max_k \{e_{i,k}\}$$

and the actual requested bandwidth as $\hat{U}_i = \hat{C}_i / T_i$. Hence, $\hat{U}_i$ can be used as a reference value in a feedback loop to adapt the reservation bandwidth allocated to the task according to the actual needs. If more reservations are adapted online, we must ensure that the overall allocated bandwidth does not exceed the processor utilization; hence, a form of global feedback adaptation is required to prevent an overload condition. Similar approaches to achieve adaptive reservations have been proposed by Abeni and Buttazzo (Abeni & Buttazzo, May 30 - June 1, 2001) and by Palopoli et al. (Palopoli et al., December 3-5, 2002).

3. Handling permanent overloads

This section presents some methodologies for handling permanent overload conditions occurring in periodic task systems when the total processor utilization exceeds one. Basically, there are three methods to reduce the load:

- **Job skipping.** This method reduces the total load by properly skipping (i.e., aborting) some job execution in the periodic tasks, in such a way that a minimum number of jobs per task is guaranteed to execute within their timing constraints.
- **Period adaptation.** According to this approach, the load is reduced by enlarging task periods to suitable values, so that the total workload can be kept below a desired threshold.
- **Service adaptation.** According to this method, the load is reduced by decreasing the computational requirements of the tasks, trading predictability with quality of service.

3.1 Job skipping

The computational load of a set of periodic tasks can be reduced by properly *skipping* a few jobs in the task set, in such a way that the remaining jobs can be scheduled within their deadlines. This approach is suitable for real-time applications characterized by soft or firm deadlines, such as those typically found in multimedia systems, where skipping a video frame once in a while is better than processing it with a long delay. Even in certain control applications, the sporadic skip of some job can be tolerated when the controlled systems is characterized by a high inertia.

To understand how job skipping can make an overloaded system schedulable, consider the following example, consisting of two tasks, with computation times $C_1 = 2$ and $C_2 = 8$ and periods $T_1 = 4$ and $T_2 = 12$. Since the processor utilization factor is $U_p = 14/12 > 1$, the system is under a permanent overload, and the tasks cannot be scheduled within their deadlines. Nevertheless, Figure 8 shows that skipping a job every three in task τ_1 the overload can be resolved and all the remaining jobs can be scheduled within their deadlines.

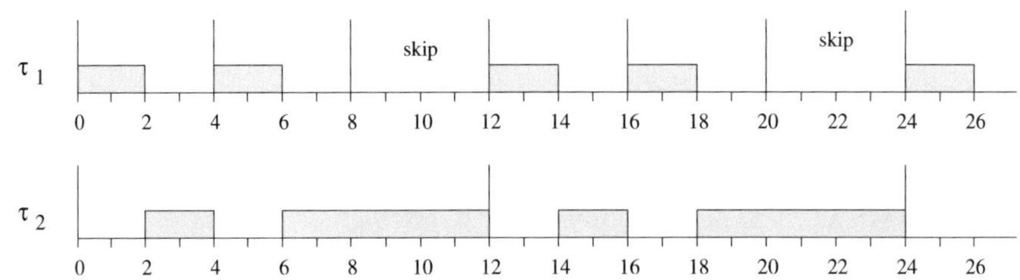

Fig. 8. Overload condition resolved by skipping one job every three in task τ_1.

In order to control the overall system load, it is important to derive the relation between the number of skips (i.e., the number of aborted jobs per task) and the total computational demand. In 1995, Koren and Shasha (Koren & Shasha, 1995) proposed a new task model (known as the *firm* periodic model) suited to be handled by this technique. According to this model, each periodic task τ_i is characterized by the following parameters:

$$\tau_i(C_i, T_i, D_i, S_i)$$

where C_i is the worst-case computation time, T_i its period, D_i its relative deadline (assumed to be equal to the period), and S_i a skip parameter, $2 \leq S_i \leq \infty$, expressing the minimum distance between two consecutive skips. For example, if $S_i = 5$ the task can skip one instance every five. When $S_i = \infty$ no skips are allowed and τ_i is equivalent to a hard periodic task. The skip parameter can be viewed as a *Quality of Service* (QoS) metric (the higher S_i, the better the quality of service).

Using the terminology introduced by Koren and Shasha (Koren & Shasha, 1995), every job of a periodic task can be *red* or *blue*: a red job must be completed within its deadline, whereas a blue job can be aborted at any time. To meet the constraint imposed by the skip parameter S_i, each scheduling algorithm must have the following characteristics:

- if a blue job is skipped, then the next $S_i - 1$ jobs must be red.
- if a blue job completes successfully, the next job is also blue.

The authors showed that making optimal use of skips is NP-hard and presented two algorithms (one working under Rate Monotonic and one under EDF) that exploit skips to schedule slightly overloaded systems. In general, these algorithms are not optimal, but they become optimal under a particular condition, called the *deeply-red* condition.

Definition 2. *A system is* deeply-red *if all tasks are synchronously activated and the first $S_i - 1$ instances of every task τ_i are red.*

Koren and Shasha showed that the worst case for a periodic skippable task set occurs when tasks are deeply-red. For this reason, the feasibility tests are derived under this condition, so that, if a task set is schedulable under the deeply-red condition, it is also schedulable in any other situation.

3.1.1 Schedulability analysis

The feasibility analysis of a set of firm tasks can be performed through the Processor Demand Criterion (Baruah et al., 1990) under the deeply-red condition, assuming that in the worst case all blue jobs are aborted. In such a worst-case scenario, the processor demand of τ_i due to the red jobs in an interval $[0, t]$ can be obtained as the difference between the demand of all the jobs and the demand of the blue jobs:

$$\mathsf{dbf}_i^{skip}(t) = \left(\left\lfloor \frac{t}{T_i} \right\rfloor - \left\lfloor \frac{t}{T_i S_i} \right\rfloor \right) C_i. \tag{15}$$

Hence, the feasibility of the task set can be verified through the following theorem.

Theorem 4 (Koren and Shasha, 1995). *A set of firm periodic tasks is schedulable by EDF if*

$$\forall t \geq 0 \qquad \sum_{i=1}^{n} \left(\left\lfloor \frac{t}{T_i} \right\rfloor - \left\lfloor \frac{t}{T_i S_i} \right\rfloor \right) C_i \leq t. \tag{16}$$

A necessary condition can be easily derived by observing that a schedule is certainly infeasible when the utilization factor due to the red jobs is greater than one.

Theorem 5 (Koren and Shasha, 1995). *Necessary condition for the schedulability of a set of firm periodic tasks is that*

$$\sum_{i=1}^{n} \frac{C_i(S_i - 1)}{T_i S_i} \leq 1. \tag{17}$$

To better clarify the concepts mentioned above, consider the task set shown in Figure 9 and the corresponding feasible schedule, obtained by EDF. Note that the processor utilization factor is greater than 1 ($U_p = 1.25$), but both conditions (16) and (17) are satisfied.

Task	C_i	T_i	D_i	S_i
τ_1	1	3	3	4
τ_2	2	4	4	3
τ_3	5	12	12	∞

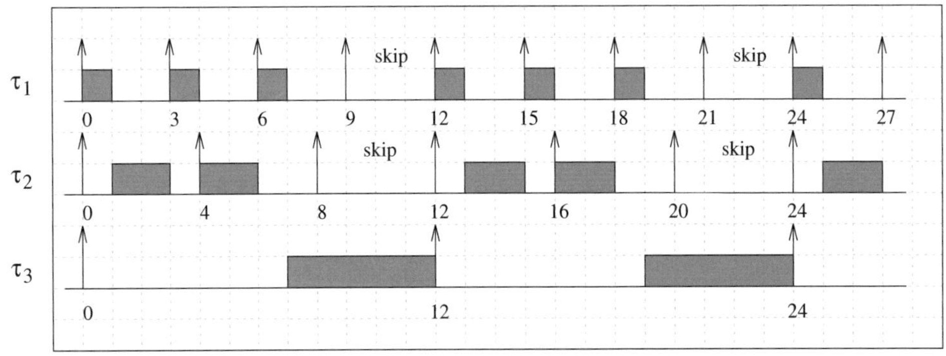

Fig. 9. A set of firm periodic tasks schedulable by EDF.

If skips are permitted in the periodic task set, the spare time saved by rejecting the blue instances can be reallocated for other purposes. For example, for scheduling slightly overloaded systems or for advancing the execution of soft aperiodic requests.

Unfortunately, the spare time has a "granular" distribution and cannot be reclaimed at any time. Nevertheless, it can be shown that skipping blue instances still produces a bandwidth saving in the periodic schedule. Caccamo and Buttazzo (Caccamo & Buttazzo, 1997) identified the amount of bandwidth saved by skips using a simple parameter, the *equivalent utilization factor* U_p^{skip}, which can be defined as

$$U_p^{skip} = \max_{t \geq 0} \left\{ \frac{\sum_i \mathsf{dbf}_i^{skip}(t)}{t} \right\} \tag{18}$$

where $\mathsf{dbf}_i^{skip}(t)$ is given in Equation (15).

Using this definition, the schedulability of a deeply-red skippable task set can be also verified using the following theorem (Caccamo & Buttazzo, 1997):

Theorem 6 (Caccamo and Buttazzo, 1997). *A set Γ of deeply-red skippable periodic tasks is schedulable by EDF if*

$$U_p^{skip} \leq 1.$$

Note that the U_p^{skip} factor represents the net bandwidth really used by periodic tasks, under the deeply-red condition. It is easy to show that $U_p^{skip} \leq U_p$. In fact, according to Equation

(18) (setting $S_i = \infty$), U_p can also be defined as

$$U_p = \max_{t \geq 0} \left\{ \frac{\sum_i \left\lfloor \frac{t}{T_i} \right\rfloor C_i}{t} \right\}.$$

Thus, $U_p^{skip} \leq U_p$ because

$$\left(\left\lfloor \frac{t}{T_i} \right\rfloor - \left\lfloor \frac{t}{T_i S_i} \right\rfloor \right) \leq \left\lfloor \frac{t}{T_i} \right\rfloor.$$

The bandwidth saved by skips can also be exploited by an aperiodic server to advance the execution of aperiodic tasks.

3.2 Period adaptation

There are several real-time applications in which timing constraints are not rigid, but depend on the system state. The possibility of varying tasks' rates increases the flexibility of the system in handling overload conditions, providing a more general admission control mechanism. For example, if the total utilization of the task set is greater than one, the system could reduce the utilizations of some tasks (by increasing their periods in a controlled fashion) to decrease the total load.

The elastic model presented in this section (originally introduced Buttazzo et al. (Buttazzo et al., 1998) and later extended by the same authors to deal with resource constraints (Buttazzo et al., 2002)), provides a novel theoretical framework for flexible workload management in real-time applications.

3.2.1 The elastic model

The basic idea behind the elastic model is to consider each task as flexible as a spring with a given rigidity coefficient and length constraints. In particular, the utilization of a task is treated as an elastic parameter, whose value can be modified by changing the period within a specified range. Each task is characterized by four parameters: a computation time C_i, a minimum period T_i^{min}, a maximum period T_i^{max}, and an elastic coefficient $E_i \geq 0$, which specifies the flexibility of the task to vary its utilization for adapting the system to a new feasible rate configuration. The greater E_i, the more elastic the task. Thus, an elastic task is denoted as

$$\tau_i(C_i, T_i^{min}, T_i^{max}, E_i).$$

In the following, T_i denotes the actual period of task τ_i, which is constrained to be in the range $[T_i^{min}, T_i^{max}]$. Any task can vary its period according to its needs within the specified range. Any variation, however, is subject to an *elastic guarantee* and is accepted only if there is a feasible schedule in which all the other periods are within their range.

It is worth noting that the elastic model is more general than the classical Liu and Layland's task model (Liu & Layland, 1973), so it does not prevent a user from defining hard real-time tasks. In fact, a task having $T_i^{max} = T_i^{min}$ is equivalent to a hard real-time task with fixed period, independently of its elastic coefficient. A task with $E_i = 0$ can arbitrarily vary its period within its specified range, but it cannot be varied by the system during load reconfigurations.

Under the elastic model, given a set of n periodic tasks with utilization $U_p > 1$, the objective of the elastic guarantee is to compress tasks' utilization factors to achieve a new desired utilization $U_d \leq 1$ such that all the periods are within their ranges.

The following definitions are also used in this section:

$$\begin{aligned} U_i^{min} &= C_i/T_i^{max}; \\ U_{min} &= \sum_{i=1}^{n} U_i^{min}; \\ U_i^{max} &= C_i/T_i^{min}; \\ U_{max} &= \sum_{i=1}^{n} U_i^{max}. \end{aligned}$$

Clearly, a solution can always be found if $U_{min} \leq U_d$; hence, this condition has to be verified a priori.

To understand how an elastic guarantee is performed in this model, it is convenient to compare an elastic task τ_i having utilization U_i and elasticity E_i with a linear spring S_i characterized by a length x_i and a rigidity coefficient k_i, equivalent to the inverse of the task's elasticity ($k_i = 1/E_i$). In this comparison, the nominal length x_{i_0} of the spring is equivalent to U_i^{max}, whereas the minimum length x_i^{min} is equivalent to U_i^{min}. Hence, a set of n periodic tasks with total utilization factor $U_p = \sum_{i=1}^{n} U_i$ can be viewed as a sequence of n springs with total length $L = \sum_{i=1}^{n} x_i$.

In the special case in which $U_i^{min} = 0$ for all tasks, the compressed task utilizations can be derived by solving a set of n spring linear equations, under the constraint that $\sum_{i=1}^{n} U_i = U_d$. The resulting expression is:

$$\forall i \quad U_i = U_i^{max} - (U_{max} - U_d)\frac{E_i}{E_s}. \tag{19}$$

where $E_s = \sum_{i=1}^{n} E_i$.

If each spring has a length constraint, in the sense that its length cannot be less than a minimum value x_i^{min}, the problem of finding the values x_i requires an iterative solution. In fact, if during compression one or more springs reach their minimum length, the additional compression force will only deform the remaining springs. Such a situation is depicted in Figure 10.

Thus, at each instant, the set Γ can be divided into two subsets: a set Γ_f of fixed springs having minimum length (equivalent to tasks that reached their minimum utilization with the maximum period), and a set Γ_v of variable springs that can still be compressed. If U_v^{max} is the sum of the maximum utilizations of tasks in Γ_v, and U_f is the total utilization factor of tasks in Γ_f, then, to achieve a desired utilization $U_d \leq 1$, each task has to be compressed up to the following utilization:

$$\forall \tau_i \in \Gamma_v \quad U_i = U_i^{max} - (U_v^{max} - U_d + U_f)\frac{E_i}{E_v} \tag{20}$$

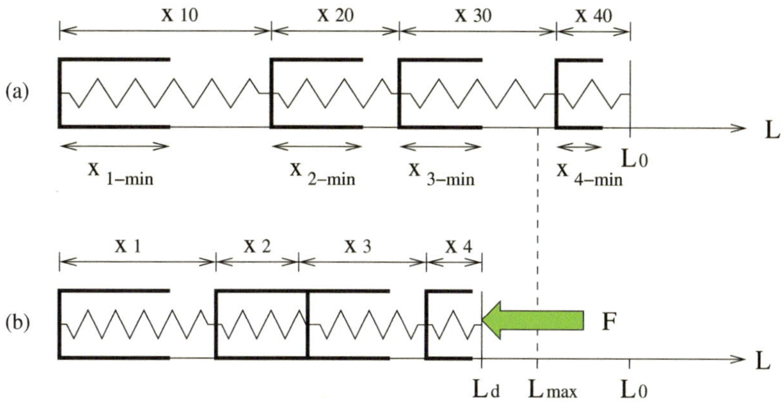

Fig. 10. Springs with minimum length constraints (a); during compression, spring S_2 reaches its minimum length and cannot be compressed any further (b).

where

$$U_v^{max} = \sum_{\tau_i \in \Gamma_v} U_i^{max} \tag{21}$$

$$U_f = \sum_{\tau_i \in \Gamma_f} U_i^{min} \tag{22}$$

$$E_v = \sum_{\tau_i \in \Gamma_v} E_i. \tag{23}$$

If there are tasks for which $U_i < U_i^{min}$, then the period of those tasks has to be fixed at its maximum value T_i^{max} (so that $U_i = U_i^{min}$), sets Γ_f and Γ_v must be updated (hence, U_f and E_v recomputed), and Equation (20) applied again to the tasks in Γ_v. If there is a feasible solution, that is, if $U_{min} \leq U_d$, the iterative process ends when each value U_i computed by Equation (20) is greater than or equal to its corresponding minimum U_i^{min}. The algorithm for compressing a set Γ of n elastic tasks up to a desired utilization U_d is shown in Figure 11.

All tasks' utilizations that have been compressed to cope with an overload situation can return toward their nominal values when the overload is over.

The elastic compression algorithm can be efficiently implemented on top of a real-time kernel as a routine (elastic manager) that is activated every time a new task is created, terminated, or there is a request for a period change. When activated, the elastic manager computes the new periods according to the compression algorithm and modifies them atomically.

To avoid any deadline miss during the transition phase, it is crucial to ensure that all the periods are modified at opportune time instants. In particular, the period of a task τ_i can be increased at any time, but can only be reduced at the next job activation. An earlier instant at which a period can be safely reduced without causing any deadline miss in the transition phase has been computed by Buttazzo et al. (Buttazzo et al., 2002) and later improved by Guangming (Guangming, 2009).

3.2.2 Period rescaling

If the elastic coefficients are set equal to task nominal utilizations, elastic compression has the effect of a simple rescaling, where all the periods are increased by the same percentage. In

Algorithm: Elastic_compression(Γ, U_d)
Input: A task set Γ and a desired utilization $U_d \leq 1$
Output: A task set with modified periods such that $U_p = U_d$

```
begin

    $U_{min} := \sum_{i=1}^{n} C_i / T_i^{max}$;
    if ($U_d < U_{min}$) return(INFEASIBLE);
    for ($i := 1$ to $n$) $U_i^{max} := C_i / T_i^{min}$;

    do
        $U_f := 0$; $U_v^{max} := 0$; $E_v := 0$;
        for ($i := 1$ to $n$) do
            if (($E_i == 0$) or ($T_i == T_i^{max}$)) then
                $U_f := U_f + U_i^{min}$;
            else
                $E_v := E_v + E_i$;
                $U_v^{max} := U_v^{max} + U_i^{max}$;
            end
        end

        $ok := 1$;
        for (each $\tau_i \in \Gamma_v$) do
            if (($E_i > 0$) and ($T_i < T_i^{max}$)) then
                $U_i := U_i^{max} - (U_v^{max} - U_d + U_f) E_i / E_v$;
                $T_i := C_i / U_i$;
                if ($T_i > T_i^{max}$) then
                    $T_i := T_i^{max}$;
                    $ok := 0$;
                end
            end
        end

    while ($ok == 0$);
    return(FEASIBLE);

end
```

Fig. 11. Algorithm for compressing a set of elastic tasks.

order to work correctly, however, period rescaling must be uniformly applied to all the tasks, without restrictions on the maximum period. This means having $U_f = 0$ and $U_v^{max} = U_{max}$. Under this assumption, by setting $E_i = U_i^{max}$, Equation (20) becomes:

$$\forall i \quad U_i = U_i^{max} - (U_{max} - U_d)\frac{U_i^{max}}{U_{max}} = \frac{U_i^{max}}{U_{max}} U_d$$

from which we have

$$T_i = T_i^{min} \frac{U_{max}}{U_d}. \tag{24}$$

This means that in overload situations ($U_{max} > 1$) the compression algorithm causes all task periods to be increased by a common scale factor

$$\eta = \frac{U_{max}}{U_d}.$$

Note that after compression is performed, the total processor utilization becomes

$$U = \sum_{i=1}^{n} \frac{C_i}{T_i} = \sum_{i=1}^{n} \frac{C_i}{\eta T_i^{min}} = \frac{1}{\eta} U_{max} = \frac{U_d}{U_{max}} U_{max} = U_d$$

as desired.

If a maximum period needs to be defined for some task, an online guarantee test can easily be performed before compression to check whether all the new periods are less than or equal to the maximum value. This can be done in $O(n)$ by testing whether

$$\forall i = 1, \ldots, n \quad \eta T_i^{min} \leq T_i^{max}.$$

By deciding to apply period rescaling, we lose the freedom of choosing the elastic coefficients, since they must be set equal to task maximum utilizations ($E_i = U_i^{max}$). However, this technique has the advantage of leaving the task periods ordered as in the nominal configuration, which simplifies the compression algorithm in the presence of resource constraints and enables its usage in fixed priority systems, where priorities are typically assigned based on periods.

3.3 Service adaptation

A third method for coping with a permanent overload condition is to reduce the load by decreasing the task computation times. This can be done only if the tasks have been originally designed to trade performance with computational requirements. When tasks use some incremental algorithm to produce approximated results, the precision of results is related to the number of iterations, and thus with the computation time. In this case, an overload condition can be handled by reducing the quality of results, aborting the remaining computation if the quality of the current results is acceptable.

The concept of imprecise and approximate computation has emerged as a new approach to increasing flexibility in dynamic scheduling by trading computation accuracy with timing requirements. If processing time is not enough to produce high-quality results within the deadlines, there could be enough time for producing approximate results with a lower quality. This concept has been formalized by many authors (Lin et al., 1987; Liu et al., 1987; 1991; 1994;

Natarajan, 1995; Shih et al., 1991) and specific techniques have been developed for designing programs that can produce partial results.

In a real-time system that supports imprecise computation, every task τ_i is decomposed into a *mandatory* subtask M_i and an *optional* subtask O_i. The mandatory subtask is the portion of the computation that must be done in order to produce a result of acceptable quality, whereas the optional subtask refines this result (Shih et al., 1989). Both subtasks have the same activation time r_i and the same deadline d_i as the original task τ_i; however, O_i becomes ready for execution when M_i is completed. If C_i is the worst-case computation time associated with the task, subtasks M_i and O_i have computation times m_i and o_i, such that $m_i + o_i = C_i$. In order to guarantee a minimum level of performance, M_i must be completed within its deadline, whereas O_i can be left incomplete, if necessary, at the expense of the quality of the result produced by the task.

It is worth noting that the task model used in traditional real-time systems is a special case of the one adopted for imprecise computation. In fact, a hard task corresponds to a task with no optional part ($o_i = 0$), whereas a soft task is equivalent to a task with no mandatory part ($m_i = 0$).

In systems that support imprecise computation, the *error* ϵ_i in the result produced by τ_i (or simply the error of τ_i) is defined as the length of the portion of O_i discarded in the schedule. If σ_i is the total processor time assigned to O_i by the scheduler, the error of task τ_i is equal to

$$\epsilon_i = o_i - \sigma_i.$$

The *average error* $\overline{\epsilon}$ on the task set is defined as

$$\overline{\epsilon} = \sum_{i=1}^{n} w_i \epsilon_i,$$

where w_i is the relative importance of τ_i in the task set. An error $\epsilon_i > 0$ means that a portion of subtask O_i has been discarded in the schedule at the expense of the quality of the result produced by task τ_i, but for the benefit of other mandatory subtasks that can complete within their deadlines.

In this model, a schedule is said to be *feasible* if every mandatory subtask M_i is completed within its deadline. A schedule is said to be *precise* if the average error $\overline{\epsilon}$ on the task set is zero. In a precise schedule, all mandatory and optional subtasks are completed within their deadlines.

For a set of periodic tasks, the problem of deciding the best level of quality compatible with a given load condition can be solved by associating each optional part of a task a reward function $R_i(\sigma_i)$, which indicates the reward accrued by the task when it receives σ_i units of service beyond its mandatory portion. This problem has been addressed by Aydin et al. (Aydin et al., 2001), who presented an optimal algorithm that maximizes the weighted average of the rewards over the task set.

Note that in the absence of a reward function, the problem can easily be solved by using a compression algorithm like the elastic approach. In fact, once, the new task utilizations U_i' are computed, the new computation times C_i' that lead to a given desired load can easily be computed from the periods as

$$C_i' = T_i U_i'.$$

Finally, if an algorithm cannot be executed in an incremental fashion or it cannot be aborted at any time, a task can be provided with multiple versions, each characterized by a different quality of performance and execution time. Then, the value C_i' can be used to select the task version having the computation time closer to, but smaller than C_i'.

4. Two case studies

This section describes two real-world applications to illustrate how the presented techniques can be used to prevent the negative effects of the overload. The first example considers a multimedia system and shows how resource reservation can isolate the timing behavior of concurrent applications characterized by highly variable execution times, preventing a performance degradation due to a reciprocal interference. The second example illustrates how to handle a permanent overload in a robot system that activates a new task to cope with obstacle avoidance.

4.1 Resource reservation in multimedia systems

Let us consider a multimedia device, like a cell phone, in which a phone call, a video player, and a web browser can be concurrently executed, so that a user can simultaneously make a phone call while watching a video and downloading a file from the web. These applications are characterized by a highly variable computational demand and share common resources (e.g., processor, memory, touch screen, audio codec, and graphic display). They are briefly described below.

- **Phone call** (A_1). This application consists at least of two periodic activities, executed with a period of 20 ms. A task is in charge of receiving the incoming audio signal, decoding it, and transferring the packets to the speaker buffer for reproduction. The processing time of this task can vary from 1 ms (during silence) up to 3 ms. The second task is responsible for sampling the voice from the microphone, performing data encoding, speech enhancement, and packet transmission through the modem. The processing time of this task can vary from 5 ms (during silence) up to 10 ms. Hence, overall, this application requires a processor bandwidth that can vary from 30% to 65%.
- **Video player** (A_2). The MPEG standard adopted for video compression is characterized by highly variable execution times. For instance, Figure 12 shows the typical distribution of frame decoding times for an MPEG player decoding a specific video on a given platform (Abeni & Buttazzo, 2000; Isovic et al., 2005). Note that the processing time of this task can vary from 6 ms to 30 ms, with an average decoding time of about 12 ms. If using the PAL standard, the frame rate is set to 25 frames per second, meaning that each frame has to be processed every 40 ms. Therefore, running an MPEG player requires an average processor bandwidth of 30%, which can reach 75% in peak load conditions.
- **Web browser** (A_3). This activity is also characterized by high load variations. In fact, when loading a web page, there is a peak processing load to parse the input, taking about one second. Then, a request is submitted to the server for sending a separate content, like images and layout files. At this time, the processing pauses for about another second while waiting for the new input. When full data arrive, there is another peak load, since they should be processed (decoded/parsed and rendered) as quickly as possible (this phase takes a few seconds depending on the content).

Note that, each of the considered applications is typically implemented as a set of tasks with different priorities. Hence, when they are concurrently executed on the same processor,

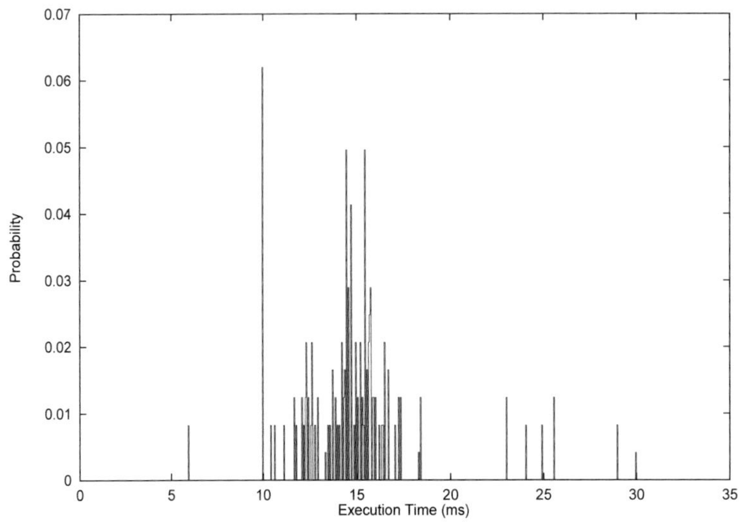

Fig. 12. Distribution of frame decoding times for an MPEG video player.

tasks are subject to reciprocal interference and can experience long blocking delays and jerky behavior. As a consequence, the user could experience a temporary motion stop on the movie, or perceive an annoying jitter in the sound. Although these applications are not safety critical, the unpleasant effects of such interferences on the user perception are taken in a serious consideration by the developers, since they can make a difference with another device produced by a competitor.

Resource reservation can be effectively used in this system to isolate the temporal behavior of the applications and limit their reciprocal interference (Bini et al., 2011). To do that, the processor should be partitioned into three reservations, with bandwidth U_{S_1}, U_{S_2}, and U_{S_3}, each behaving as a slower processor running at speed U_{S_i}. The advantage of this approach is that an overrun occurring in an application does not affect the other applications, but has only the effect of postponing the execution of those tasks in which the overrun is generated. Moreover, an application can be designed and analyzed independently of the others, because its execution behavior only depends on its own computational demand and the allocated bandwidth.

In our system, allocating each bandwidth for satisfying the worst-case processing demand of the application would waste resources and would lead to an infeasible schedule. For instance, the maximum bandwidth requirements of the first two applications already exceed the full processor capacity. To achieve a feasible schedule, the bandwidth can be reserved to satisfy a processing demand slightly higher than the average value, handling sporadic overruns through resource reservation. In the considered example, 40% of the processor can be reserved to the phone call, 50% to the video player, and, the remaining 10% to the web browser, which has less stringent timing constraints.

When the amount of allocated bandwidth results to be quite different from the real application needs, adaptive approaches based on feedback mechanisms can be applied at runtime to adjust the allocated bandwidth to the real resource needs (Abeni & Buttazzo, 1999; Bini et al., 2011).

4.2 Overload handing in robot control systems

Let us consider a mobile robot system whose goal is to explore an unknown environment to localize given targets through a dedicated sensor, while avoiding obstacles along the path using proximity sensing. Note that, by equipping the robot with suitable sensors, the system could be used for very different applications; for instance, to discover electrical sockets in a room, using a video camera, or to localize unexploded mines in a field, using a georadar. For the purpose of this chapter, we consider a robot equipped with two motors to move in two directions on a flat surface, two encoders to measure the angular rotation of the wheels and reconstruct the traveled path, a sensor to detect the target (target sensor), a proximity sensor (e.g., based on ultrasound transducers) to detect the distance from possible obstacles along the path, and an electronic compass to orient the trajectory in desired directions.

From the software point of view, the application consists of the following periodic tasks:

- **Motor Control Task** (MCT or τ_1): it performs the low-level motor control loop to drive the robot in a desired direction (θ) at a given speed (v);
- **Obstacle Detection Task** (ODT or τ_2): it reads the proximity sensor to detect a possible obstacle along the path;
- **Target Detection Task** (TDT or τ_3): it reads the target sensor and stores the target location in a buffer when it is detected;
- **Exploration Task** (EXT or τ_4): it generates the proper set points (exploring direction and speed) for the Motor Control Task;
- **Obstacle Avoidance Task** (OAT or τ_5): it is activated when an obstacle is detected and computes a sequence of set points to be followed to avoid the obstacle and return to the planned path.

To illustrate the use of an overload management technique, we assume that in normal operating conditions (i.e., in the absence of obstacles) the first four tasks ($\tau_1, \ldots, \tau_4$) generate a load equal to $U_{norm} = 0.9$, while the fifth task has a utilization $U_5 = 0.3$. Hence, when τ_5 is activated together with the other tasks, the total system utilization becomes $U_{max} = 1.2$. In this example, the elastic approach is applied to bring the load back to a desired value $U_d = 0.9$ (equal to the normal load condition).

The tasks are organized as shown in Figure 13, where hardware components are represented by rounded boxes, tasks by circles, and shared buffers by rectangles.

To apply the elastic method, each task τ_i must specify a range of valid periods $[T_i^{min}, T_i^{max}]$ and an elastic coefficient E_i. Task parameters are reported in Table 1 and are expressed in milliseconds. Note that, when the OAT task is not active, the utilization of the task set is

Task name	Task ID	C_i	T_i^{min}	T_i^{max}	E_i
MCT	τ_1	3	10	10	0
ODT	τ_2	6	20	30	1
TDT	τ_3	20	100	200	2
EXT	τ_4	20	200	500	1
OAT	τ_5	6	20	40	2

Table 1. Task parameters of the robot application.

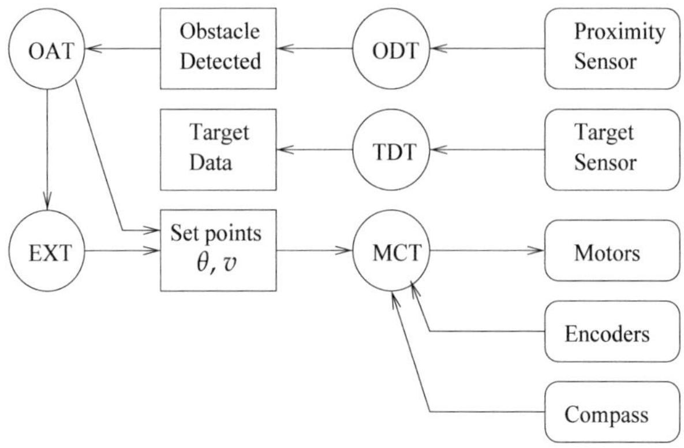

Fig. 13. Task interaction in the robot application.

$$U_{norm} = \sum_{i=1}^{4} \frac{C_i}{T_i} = 0.9$$

whereas, when OAT is active, the system becomes overloaded, being

$$U_{max} = \sum_{i=1}^{5} \frac{C_i}{T_i} = 1.2.$$

By applying the elastic approach, with a desired utilization $U_d = 0.9$ (to keep a safety margin), tasks utilizations are compressed according to Equation (19) and then enforced by re-computing the periods as $T_i = C_i/U_i$. The new tasks utilizations and periods derived by the elastic algorithm are reported in Table 2.

Task name	Task ID	U_i	T_i
MCT	τ_1	3/10	10
ODT	τ_2	1/4	24
TDT	τ_3	1/10	200
EXT	τ_4	1/20	400
OAT	τ_5	1/5	30

Table 2. Task utilizations and periods derived by the elastic compression, with a desired utilization $U_d = 0.9$.

When the obstacle is overcome, task OAT can be suspended and the remaining tasks can return to their original condition, running with their minimum periods.

5. References

Abeni, L. & Buttazzo, G. (1998). Integrating multimedia applications in hard real-time systems, *Proceedings of the 19th IEEE Real-Time Systems Symposium (RTSS'98)*, Madrid, Spain.

Abeni, L. & Buttazzo, G. (1999). Adaptive bandwidth reservation for multimedia computing, *Proceedings of the 6th IEEE International Conference on Real-Time Computing Systems and Applications (RTCSA'99)*, Hong Kong, China, pp. 70–77.

Abeni, L. & Buttazzo, G. (2000). Support for dynamic qos in the hartik kernel, *IEEE Proceedings of the 7th International Conference on Real-Time Computing Systems and Applications (RTCSA'00)*, Cheju Island, South Korea.

Abeni, L. & Buttazzo, G. (2004). Resource reservations in dynamic real-time systems, *Real-Time Systems* 27(2): 123–165.

Abeni, L. & Buttazzo, G. (May 30 - June 1, 2001). Hierarchical qos management for time sensitive applications, *Proceedings of the IEEE Real-Time Technology and Applications Symposium (RTAS'01)*, Taipei, Taiwan.

Aydin, H., Melhem, R., Mossé, D. & Alvarez, P. M. (2001). Optimal reward-based scheduling for periodic real-time tasks, *IEEE Transactions on Computers* 50(2): 111–130.

Baruah, S., Rosier, L. & Howell, R. (1990). Algorithms and complexity concerning the preemptive scheduling of periodic, real-time tasks on one processor, *Journal of Real-Time Systems* 2.

Bernat, G., Broster, I. & Burns, A. (December 5-8, 2004). Rewriting history to exploit gain time, *Proceedings of the 25th IEEE Real-Time Systems Symposium (RTSS'04)*, Lisbon, Portugal.

Bernat, G. & Burns, A. (2002). Multiple servers and capacity sharing for implementing flexible scheduling, *Real-Time Systems* 22: 49–75.

Bertogna, M., Fisher, N. & Baruah, S. (2009). Resource-sharing servers for open environments, *IEEE Transactions on Industrial Informatics* 5(3): 202–220.

Bini, E., Buttazzo, G., Eker, J., Schorr, S., Guerra, R., Fohler, G., Arzen, K.-E., Segovia, V. R. & Scordino, C. (2011). Resource management on multicore systems: The ACTORS approach, *IEEE Micro* 31(3): 72–81.

Bini, E., Buttazzo, G. & Lipari, G. (2009). Minimizing cpu energy in real-time systems with discrete speed management, *ACM Transactions on Embedded Computing Systems* 8(4): 31:1–31:23.

Buttazzo, G. (2011). *Hard Real-Time Computing Systems and Applications - Third Edition*, Springer, pp. 287–292.

Buttazzo, G., Abeni, L. & Lipari, G. (1998). Elastic task model for adaptive rate control, *IEEE Real Time System Symposium*, Madrid, Spain.

Buttazzo, G., Lipari, G., Caccamo, M. & Abeni, L. (2002). Elastic scheduling for flexible workload management, *IEEE Transactions on Computers* 51(3): 289–302.

Buttazzo, G. & Stankovic, J. (1995). Adding robustness in dynamic preemptive scheduling, *in* D. Fussel & M. Malek (eds), *Responsive Computer Systems: Steps Toward Fault-Tolerant Real-Time Systems*, Kluwer Academic Publishers.

Caccamo, M. & Buttazzo, G. (1997). Exploiting skips in periodic tasks for enhancing aperiodic responsiveness, *IEEE Real-Time Systems Symposium*, San Francisco, California, USA, pp. 330–339.

Caccamo, M., Buttazzo, G. & Sha, L. (2000). Capacity sharing for overrun control, *Proceedings of the IEEE Real-Time Systems Symposium*, Orlando, Florida, USA.

Caccamo, M., Buttazzo, G. & Thomas, D. (2005). Efficient reclaiming in reservation-based real-time systems with variable execution times, *IEEE Transactions on Computers* 54(2): 198–213.

Easwaran, A., Anand, M. & Lee, I. (2007). Compositional analysis framework using EDP resource models, *Proceedings of the* 28th *IEEE International Real-Time Systems Symposium*, Tucson, AZ, USA, pp. 129–138.

Feng, X. & Mok, A. K. (2002). A model of hierarchical real-time virtual resources, *Proceedings of the* 23rd *IEEE Real-Time Systems Symposium*, Austin, TX, USA, pp. 26–35.

Guangming, Q. (2009). An earlier time for inserting and/or accelerating tasks, *Real-Time Systems* 41(3): 181–194.

Isovic, D., Fohler, G. & Steffens, L. F. (2005). Real-time issues of mpeg-2 playout in resourse constrained systems, *Journal of Embedded Computing* 1: 239–256.

Koren, G. & Shasha, D. (1995). Skip-over: Algorithms and complexity for overloaded systems that allow skips, *Proceedings of the IEEE Real-Time Systems Symposium*.

Lamastra, G., Lipari, G. & Abeni, L. (December 3-6, 2001). A bandwidth inheritance algorithm for real-time task synchronization in open systems, *IEEE Proceedings of the 22nd Real-Time Systems Symposium (RTSS'01)*, London, UK.

Lin, C. & Brandt, S. A. (December 5Ű8, 2005). Improving soft real-time performance through better slack management, *Proc. of the IEEE Real-Time Systems Symposium (RTSS 2005)*, Miami, Florida, USA.

Lin, K., Natarajan, S. & Liu, J. (1987). Concord: a system of imprecise computation, *Proceedings of the 1987 IEEE Compsac*.

Lipari, G. & Bini, E. (2003). Resource partitioning among real-time applications, *Proceedings of the 15th Euromicro Conference on Real-Time Systems (ECRTS'03)*, Porto, Portugal, pp. 151–158.

Liu, C. & Layland, J. (1973). Scheduling algorithms for multiprogramming in a hard-real-time environment, *Journal of the Association for Computing Machinery* 20(1).

Liu, J., Lin, K. & Natarajan, S. (1987). Scheduling real-time, periodic jobs using imprecise results, *Proceedings of the IEEE Real-Time System Symposium*.

Liu, J., Lin, K., Shih, W., Yu, A., Chung, C., Yao, J. & Zhao, W. (1991). Algorithms for scheduling imprecise computations, *IEEE Computer* 24(5): 58–68.

Liu, J., Shih, W. K., Lin, K. J., Bettati, R. & Chung, J. Y. (1994). Imprecise computations, *Proceedings of the IEEE* 82(1): 83–94.

Marzario, L., Lipari, G., Balbastre, P. & Crespo, A. (2004). Iris: A new reclaiming algorithm for server-based real-time systems, *Proc. of the IEEE Real-Time and Embedded Technology and Applications Symposium*, Toronto, Canada.

Mercer, C. W., Savage, S. & Tokuda, H. (1994). Processor capacity reserves for multimedia operating systems, *Proceedings of IEEE international conference on Multimedia Computing and System*.

Mok, A. K., Feng, X. & Chen, D. (2001). Resource partition for real-time systems, *Proceedings of the 7th IEEE Real-Time Technology and Applications Symposium*, Taipei, Taiwan, pp. 75–84.

Natarajan, S. (ed.) (1995). *Imprecise and Approximate Computation*, Kluwer Academic Publishers.

Palopoli, L., Abeni, L., Lipari, G. & Walpole, J. (December 3-5, 2002). Analysis of a reservation-based feedback scheduler, *Proceedings of the 23rd IEEE Real-Time Systems Symposium (RTSS'02)*, Austin-Texas.

Shih, W., Liu, W. & Chung, J. (1991). Algorithms for scheduling imprecise computations with timing constraints, *SIAM Journal of Computing* 20(3): 537–552.

Shih, W., Liu, W., Chung, J. & Gillies, D. (1989). Scheduling tasks with ready times and deadlines to minimize average error, *Operating System Review* 23(3).

Shin, I. & Lee, I. (2003). Periodic resource model for compositional real-time guarantees, *Proceedings of the 24th Real-Time Systems Symposium*, Cancun, Mexico, pp. 2–13.

8

Real-Time Concurrency Control Protocol Based on Accessing Temporal Data

Qilong Han
College of Computer Science and Technology,
Harbin Engineering University Harbin,
China

1. Introduction

Concurrency control is one of the main issues in the studies of real-time database systems. On the one hand, it is related closely to active real-time database and real-time application. Concurrency control algorithm seriously affect the performance of the system in real-time, may cause unpredictable consequences. On the other hand, updating data in active real-time database may trigger a new transaction and to further increase the difficulty of the concurrency control. How ensures both the consistency of the database and the finish of the transactions before deadline; it is an important problem to the concurrency control research in the active real-time database systems. In the most literature, the existing research more focuses on the transactions deadline and lack of attention the data temporal constraint. This is mainly due to the real-time data is obtained dynamically by sensors in real-time database, and the transactions of real-time databases read the sensor data only, do not write the sensor data. But the real-time data may miss deadline and become invalid before transaction which reads it committed, most concurrency control algorithms are regardless of the sensor data deadline and its invalid effect to systems. This chapter will further discuss the concurrency control method that transactions access real-time sensor data.

Optimism concurrency control method is widely used in real-time database due to no dead-lock and no-block characteristics, but delay conflicts detection brings with great restart overhead. A dynamic adjustment serialization order method is proposed to reduce unnecessary affairs restart number [Haritsa, Lindstrom], according to [Lindstrom, Wang] a method is proposed by control the reading and writing data to reduce the transaction restart number. In [Brad] discussed about the relation between real-time data and the derived data validity, and [Kuo] proposed the concept of real-time data similarity. According to [Brad, Xiong] proposed the concept of data-deadline, and the transaction scheduling strategy by using mandatory waiting method. The [Liu] also discuss on data deadline and transaction scheduling. A real-time transaction scheduling method is proposed based on the combination of [Kuo, Son] improving real-time data similarity mechanism in [Xiong]. But [Xiong, Son] only take account of single transaction scheduling the real data problems, not consider the concurrency control problem that the transactions did not arrive at deadline and its accessed data expired, which will increase the number of transactions restart.

The chapter is organized as follows. Section 2 reviews concurrency control protocols proposed in real-time database systems (RTDBSs) and describes our choice of concurrency control algorithms for accessing temporal data. Section 3 analyzes the validity of active real-time system model and the effects real-time data to the concurrent control. The relevant definition and the effective examination mechanism of transaction reading data were given in Section 4. In Section 5 based on Data temporal characteristics, concurrency control algorithm RTCC-DD (Real-time Concurrency Control Algorithm Based on Data-deadline) is put forward, and proved that the RTCC-DD was the correctness in theory. Section 6 carries on the analysis comparison between our proposed method and the existed method through experiment. Finally, Section 7 gives summary and conclusions of this chapter and future directions for the work.

2. Concurrency control in Real-Time Database Systems

A Real-Time Database Systems (RTDBS) processes transactions with timing constraints such as deadlines [Ramamritham]. Its primary performance criterion is timeliness, not average response time or throughput. The scheduling of transactions is driven by priority order. Given these challenges, considerable research has recently been devoted to designing concurrency control methods for RTDBSs and to evaluating their performance (e. g. [Kuo, Fishwick, Haritsa]). Most of these methods are based on one of the two basic concurrency control mechanisms: locking [Lam] or optimistic concurrency control (OCC) [Kung].

In real-time systems transactions are scheduled according to their priorities. Therefore, high priority transactions are executed before lower priority transactions. This is true only if a high priority transaction has some database operation ready for execution. If no operation from a higher priority transaction is ready for execution, then an operation from a lower priority transaction is allowed to execute its database operation. Therefore, the operation of the higher priority transaction may conflict with the already executed operation of the lower priority transaction. In traditional methods a higher priority transaction must wait for the release of the resource. This is the priority inversion problem presented earlier. Therefore, data conflicts in concurrency control should also be based on transaction priorities or criticalness or both. Hence, numerous traditional concurrency control methods have been extended to the real-time database systems. In the following sections recent and related work in this area is presented.

2.1 Locking-based algorithms

In classical two-phase locking protocol, transactions set read locks on objects that they read, and these locks are later upgraded to write locks for the data objects that are updated. If a lock requested is denied, the requesting transaction is blocked until the lock is released. Read locks Call be shared. while write locks are exclusive.

For real-time database Systems, two-phase locking needs to be augmented with a priority based conflict resolution scheme to ensure that higher priority transactions are not delayed by lower priority transactions. In High Priority scheme, all data conflicts are resolved in favour of the transaction with the higher priority. When a transaction requests a lock on an object held by other transactions in a conflicting lock mode, if the requester's priority is higher than that of all the lock holders, the holders are restarted and the requester is granted the lock; if the requester's priority is lower, it waits for the lock holders to release the lock. In addition, a new read lock requester can join a group of read lock holders only if its priority is higher than that of all waiting write lock operations. This protocol is referred to as 2PL-HP. It is important to note that 2PL-HP loses some of the basic 2PL algorithm's blocking factor due to the partially restart-based nature of the High Priority scheme.

Note that High Priority scheme is similar to Wound-Wait scheme, which is added to two-phase locking for deadlock prevention. The only difference is that High Priority scheme uses priority order decided by transaction timing constraints for conflict resolution decisions, while Wound-Wait employs timestamp order usually decided by transaction arrival time. It is obvious that High Priority serves as a deadlock prevention mechanism, if the priority assignment mechanism assigns unique priority value to a transaction and does not dynamically change the relative priority ordering of concurrent transactions. Also, note that 2PL-HP is free from priority inversion problem, because a higher priority transaction never waits for a lower priority transaction, but restarts it.

In 2PL-WP (2PL Wait Promote) [Huang] the analysis of concurrency control method is enhanced from [Lindstrom]. The mechanism presented uses shared and exclusive locks. Shared locks permit multiple concurrent readers. A new definition is made - the priority of a data object, which is defined to be the highest priority of all the transactions holding a lock on the data object. If the data object is not locked, its priority is undefined.

A transaction can join in the read group of an object only if its priority is higher than the maximum priority of all transactions in the write group of an object. Thus, conflicts arise from incompatibility of locking modes as usual. Particular care is given to conflicts that lead to priority inversions. A priority inversion occurs when a transaction of high priority requests and blocks for an object which has lesser priority. This means that all the lock holders have lesser priority than the requesting transaction. This same method is also called 2PL-PI (2PL Priority Inheritance) [Stankovic].

Sometimes High Priority may be too strict policy. If the lock holding transaction T_h can finish in the time that the lock requesting transaction T_h can afford to wait, that is within the slack time of T_r, and let T_h proceed to execution and T_r B wait for the completion of T_h. This policy is called 2PL-CR (2PL Conditional Restart) or 2PL-CPI (2PL Conditional Priority Inheritance) [Lam, Menasce].

In Priority Ceiling Protocol [Sha] the aim is to minimize the duration of blocking to at most one elementary lower priority task and prevent the formation of deadlocks. A real-time database can often be decomposed into sets of database objects that can be modelled as atomic data sets. For example, two radar stations track an aircraft representing the local view in data objects O_1 and O_2. These objects might include e. g. the current location, velocity, etc. Each of these objects forms an atomic data set, because the consistency constraints can be checked and validated locally. The notion of atomic data sets is especially useful for tracking multiple targets.

A simple locking method for elementary transactions is the two-phase locking method; a transaction cannot release any lock on any atomic data set unless it has obtained all the locks on that atomic data set. Once it has released its locks it cannot obtain new locks on the same atomic data set, however, it can obtain new locks on different data sets. The theory of modular concurrency control permits an elementary transaction to hold locks across atomic data sets. This increases the duration of locking and decreases preemptibility. In this study transactions do not hold locks across atomic data sets.

Priority Ceiling Protocol minimizes the duration of blocking to at most one elementary lower priority task and prevents the formation of deadlocks. The idea is that when a new higher priority transaction preempts a running transaction its priority must exceed the priorities of all preempted transactions, taking the priority inheritance protocol into consideration. If this condition cannot be met, the new transaction is suspended and the blocking transaction inherits the priority of the highest transaction it blocks.

The priority ceiling of a data object is the priority of the highest priority transaction that may lock this object [Sha, Rajkumar, Son]. A new transaction can preempt a lock-holding transaction only if its priority is higher than the priority ceilings of all the data objects locked by the lock-holding transaction. If this condition is not satisfied, the new transaction will wait and the lock-holding transaction inherits the priority of the highest transaction that it blocks. The lock-holder continues its execution, and when it releases the locks, its original priority is resumed. All blocked transactions are alerted, and the one with the highest priority will start its execution.

The fact that the priority of the new lock-requesting transaction must be higher than the priority ceiling of all the data objects that it accesses, prevents the formation of a potential deadlock. The fact that the lock-requesting transaction is blocked only at most the execution time of one lower priority transaction guarantees, the formation of blocking chains is not possible [Sha, Rajkumar, Son].

The Priority Ceiling Protocol is further worked out in [Sha, Rajkumar, Son], where the Read/Write Priority Ceiling Protocol is introduced. It contains two basic ideas. The first idea is the notion of priority inheritance. The second idea is a total priority ordering of active transactions. A transaction is said to be active if it has started but not completed its execution. Thus, a transaction can execute or wait caused by preemption in the middle of its execution. Total priority ordering requires that each active transaction execute at a higher priority level than the active lower priority transaction, taking priority inheritance and read/write semantics into consideration.

A protocol called Real-Time Locking (RTL) that uses locking and dynamic adjustment of serialization order for priority conflict resolution was proposed. The basic idea of serialization order adjustment is to delay the decision of final serialization order among transactions, and to adjust the temporary serialization order dynamically in favour of transactions with high priority. Thus, this scheme can avoid blocking and aborts resulting from a mismatch between serialization order and priority order of transactions. In order to implement the dynamic adjustment of serialization order, in RTL, the execution of a transaction is phase-wise as in OCC. In the first phase called read phase, a transaction reads from database and writes to its local workspace as in OCC. However, unlike OCC where conflicts are resolved only in the validation phase, RTL resolves conflicts in the read phase using transaction priority. In the write phase of RTL, the final serialization order is determined, and updates are made permanent to the database. The use of the phase-dependent control and local workspace for transactions also provides potential for a high degree of concurrency.

2.2 Optimistic Concurrency Control-based algorithms

Optimistic Concurrency Control (OCC), is based on the assumption that conflict is rare, and that it is more efficient to allow transactions to proceed without delays to ensure serializability. When a transaction wishes to commit, a check is performed to determine whether a conflict has occurred. There are three phases to an optimistic concurrency control method:

- Read phase: The transaction reads the values of all data items it needs from the database and stores them in local variables. In some methods updates are applied to a local copy of the data and announced to the database system by an operation named pre-write.
- Validation phase: The validation phase ensures that all the committed transactions have executed in a serializable fashion. For a read-only transaction, this consists of checking that the data values read are still the current values for the corresponding data items. For a transaction that has updates, the validation consists of determining whether the current transaction leaves the database in a consistent state, with serializability maintained.
- Write phase: This follows the successful validation phase for update transactions. During the write phase, all changes made by the transaction are permanently stored into the database.

In optimistic concurrency control, transactions are allowed to execute unhindered until they reach their commit point, at which time they are validated. Thus, the execution of a transaction consists of three phases: read, validation, and write. The key component among these is the validation phase where a transaction's destiny is decided. Validation comes in several flavours, but it can carry out basically in either of two ways: backward validation and forward validation. While in backward scheme, the validation process is done against committed transactions, in forward validation, validating of a transaction is carried out against currently running transactions.

As explained above, in RTDBSs, data conflicts should be resolved in favor of higher priority transactions. In backward validation, however, there is no way to take transaction priority into account in serialization process, since it is carried out against already committed transactions. Thus backward scheme is not applicable to real-time database systems. Forward validation provides flexibility for conflict resolution such that either the validating transaction or the conflicting active transactions may be chosen to restart, so it is preferable for real-time database systems. In addition, forward scheme generally detects and resolves data conflicts earlier than backward validation, and hence it wastes less resources and time.

All the optimistic algorithms used in the previous studies of real-time concurrency control in [Haritsa] are based on the forward validation. The broadcast mechanism in the algorithm, OPT-BC used in [Haritsa] is an implementation variant of the forward validation. We refer to the optimistic algorithm using forward validation as OCC-FV.

A point to note is that unlike 2PL-HP, OCC-FV does not use any transaction priority information in resolving data conflicts. Thus, under OCC-FV, a transaction with a higher priority may need to restart due to a committing transaction with a lower priority. Several methods to incorporate priority information into OCC-FV were proposed and studied in

[Lindstrom] using priority-driven wait or abort mechanism. However, more work is needed to ensure if these methods have any significant impact on improving OCC-FV performance, because the effect of increased waiting time or increased number of aborts in these methods may overshadow the performance gain due to the preferential treatment of transactions.

In the OPT-SACRIFICE [Haritsa] method, when a transaction reaches its validation stage, it checks for conflicts with other concurrently running transactions. If conflicts are detected and at least one of the conflicting transactions has a higher priority, then the validating transaction is restarted, i. e. sacrificed in favour of the higher priority transaction. Although this method prefers high priority transactions, it has two potential problems. First, if a higher priority transaction causes a lower priority transaction to be restarted, but fails in meeting its deadline, the restart was useless. This degrades the performance. Second, if priority fluctuations are allowed, there may be the mutual restarts problem between a pair of transactions. These two drawbacks are analogous to those in the 2PL-HP method [Lee].

When a transaction reaches its validation stage, it checks if any of the concurrently running other transactions have a higher priority. In the OPT-WAIT [Lee] case the validating transaction is made to wait, giving the higher priority transactions a chance to make their deadlines first. While a transaction is waiting, it is possible that it will be restarted due to the commit of one of the higher priority transactions. Note that the waiting transaction does not necessarily have to be restarted. Under the broadcast commit scheme a validating transaction is said to conflict with another transaction, if the intersection of the write set of the validating transaction and the read set of the conflicting transaction is not empty. This result does not imply that the intersection of the write set of the conflicting transaction and the read set of the validating transaction is not empty either [Lee].

The WAIT-50 method is an extension of the OPT-WAIT - it contains the priority wait mechanism from OPT-WAIT method and a wait control mechanism. This mechanism monitors transaction conflict states and dynamically decides when and for how long a low priority transaction should be made to wait for the higher priority transactions. In WAIT-50, a simple 50 percent rule is used - a validating transaction is made to wait while half or more of its conflict set is composed of transactions with higher priority. The aim of the wait control mechanism is to detect when the beneficial effects of waiting are outweighed by its drawbacks [Lee].

We can view OPT-BC, OPT-WAIT and WAIT-50 as being special cases of a general WAITX method, where X is the cut-off percentage of the conflict set composed of higher priority transactions. For these methods X takes the values infinite, 0 and 50 respectively.

In [Lee and Son] a lock based WAIT-50 concurrency control method, OCCL-PW, is presented. The physical implementation of this method uses locks. If the priority of the validating transaction is not highest among the conflicting transactions, the validating transaction waits if at least 50% of the conflicting transactions have higher priority.

The OCC-TI method resolves conflicts using the timestamp intervals of the transactions. Every transaction must be executed within a specific time slot. When an access conflict occurs, it is resolved using the read and write sets of the transaction together with the allocated time slot. Time slots are adjusted when a transaction commits.

In this method, every transaction in the read phase is assigned a timestamp interval (TI). This timestamp interval is used to record a temporary serialization order during the execution of the transaction. At the start of the execution, the timestamp interval of the transaction is initialized as $[0, \infty]$, i. e., the entire range of timestamp space. Whenever the serialization order of the transaction is changed by its data operation or the validation of other transactions, its timestamp interval is adjusted to represent the dependencies.

OCC-DA is based on the Forward Validation scheme. The number of transaction restarts is reduced by using dynamic adjustment of the serialization order. This is supported with the use of a dynamic timestamp assignment scheme. Conflict checking is performed at the validation phase of a transaction. No adjustment of the timestamps is necessary in case of data conflicts in the read phase. In OCC-DA the serialization order of committed transactions may be different from their commit order.

A new optimistic concurrency control method, called OCC-DATI (Optimistic Concurrency Control with Dynamic Adjustment of Serialization Order using Timestamp Intervals), is proposed to reduce the number of transaction restarts in [Lindstrom], which uses information about the criticality of the transactions in the conflict resolution. The main idea behind this method is to offer better chances for critical transactions to complete according to their deadlines. This is achieved restarting transaction with lower criticality if the critical transaction should be restarted because of a data conflict. The proposed method is demonstrated to produce the correct results and the feasibility of the proposed method in practice is tested.

3. System model and real-time data

3.1 System model

Active real-time database consists of a set of objects and ECA (Event-Condition-Action) rule. Each object represents a real world entity; the status of entity is usually monitored by sensors. The entire data object is divided into two categories in database:

1. temporal objects and non-temporal objects

The temporal object is possible to be invalid for expired temporal validity; it can be divided into the absolute validity and the relative validity. Non-temporal object have not temporal validity. Temporal object absolute validity expresses as (value (Xi) , avi (Xi)) , value (Xi) describes the current status of data object X, $avi(Xi)=[avi_b(Xi), avi_e(Xi)]$, $avi_b(Xi) \leq avi_e(Xi)$ is the absolute validity of value (Xi), Xi shows the ith versions of data objects X, $avi_b(Xi)$ denotes the beginning of the absolute validity of Xi , $avi_e(Xi)$ denotes the end of the absolute validity of Xi , after $avi_e(Xi)$, value (Xi) is effective no longer.

Temporal object relative validity denotes rvi(R), R is relatively consistent set, each element is the version temporal data objects. When $t>0$, R is correct status, if and only if

- $Xi \in R$, value(Xi)is logical consistent, satisfying all the integrity constraints
- R is temporal consistent:

i. $Xi \in R$, value(Xi) is absolute consistent, $avi_b(Xi) \leq t \leq avi_e(Xi)$.

ii. R is relatively consistent, Xi, $Yj \in R$, $|avi_b(Xi)-avi_b(Yj)| \leq rvi(R)$.

2. the basic objects and derived objects

The basic objects update the database by the sensor and reflect specific entity in the real environment. Derived objects are composed by the new derived data from basic object and others. In Active real-time database, it can trigger transactions according to ECA rules when basic object is updated by sensor. Triggered transactions may update the status from the basic derived objects. In this chapter, the basic object take need scheduling strategy, until transactions need call, it was called by sensor. Transactions T call temporal data X at time t, absolute validity for the start time is t.

Active real-time database system had sensor transaction, which are used to update basic objects, only writing transaction; triggered updating transaction, which are updated and triggered transaction by the basic objects, and used to update derived object; user transaction, which have user transactions of the deadline. When transaction satisfies only the following conditions in system, it commits successfully:

1. Transaction is consistent logically.
2. Transaction satisfies the deadline.
3. The data that transaction read is temporal consistent, and the data still effective when the transaction read it commits.

3.2 Real-time data

In [Kuo, Mok], relative sensor transaction and trigger who used to update the derived object are discuss in detail, this chapter studies only concurrency control related users transaction, similar with [Liu, Son]. User transactions T have the following attributes:

- $a(T)$: Arrival time of transaction T;
- $s(T)$: Start time of transaction T;
- $d(T)$: Deadline of transaction;
- $dd_t(T)$: Data-deadline of transaction T at time t;
- $L(T)$: The number of data objects which transaction T access;
- $L_t^{to}(T)$: The number of temporal data objects that transaction T will access after time t;
- $L_t^{nto}(T)$: The number of non-temporal data objects that transaction T will access after time t;
- $L_t(T)$: The number of data objects which transaction T will access after time t; $L_t(T) = L_t^{to}(T) + L_t^{nto}(T)$;
- $E_t(T)$: Estimated execution time of transaction T at time t;
- $C_t(T)$: Estimated finished time of transaction T at time t;
- $C_t(T) = t + E_t(T)$;
- $RS_t^{to}(T)$: Temporal data object sets which transaction T access at time t;
- $P_t(T)$: The transaction priority at time t.

In active real-time database, temporal data have lots of features; this section give only related properties which presented algorithm in this chapter. First of all, according to [Son] this article introduces the concept of the data-deadline.

Definition1. Data-deadline of transaction T is the minimum data time validity which transaction T access to the temporal data objects at time t, denote it as $dd_t(T)$,

$$dd_t(T) = \min_{X \in RS_t^{t0}(T)} avi_e(X)$$

The temporal relationship between temporal data and transaction is presented by data-deadline. The data-deadline increased the difficulty of transaction scheduling and concurrent control, because no achieving deadline to the transactions may restart or abort due to the data deadline. Example 1 shows that the data-deadline of transactions influences the concurrent control.

Example 1. Transaction T1: w1(x)r1(y); T2:w2(y)r2(z).

The deadline of transaction T1 is t7, and its estimated time of completion is t6. The deadline of transaction T2 is t8; and its estimated time of completion is t6. The validity of temporal data z is [t4, t6].

As shown in Fig. 1, transaction T2 enter into validation phase at time t5, according to literature [Lindstrom, Wang], WS(Tv)∩RS(Ta)={y}≠Ø, transactions execution sequence is T1→T2, T2 will delay to submit. If transaction T1 submits after t6, transaction T2 will die for the temporal data z exceed deadline.

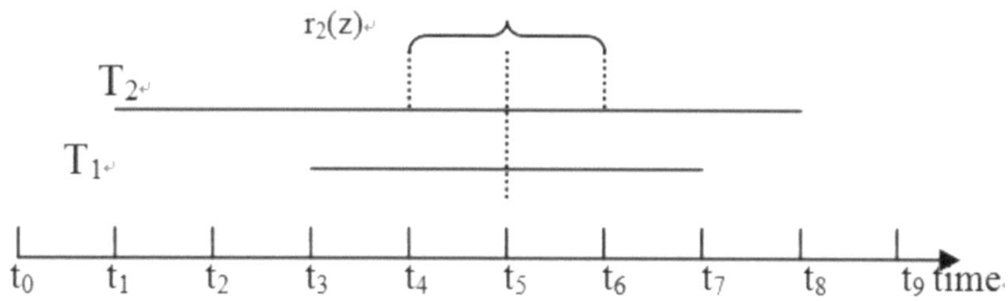

Fig. 1. Execution of Transactions

Do not consider real-time of data, we will succeed scheduling T1, T2 , according to the traditional optimistic method[Lindstrom]; But it increases the real-time nature of data, transaction T2 will die because it can't satisfy data-deadline. Example1 shows the temporal characteristics of the data influence the concurrency control, while the existing concurrency control method is no consideration to the conflict which access temporal data.

In addition to data-deadline, there is another important characteristic is the stability of the data. Real-time data has different rate of change, some change frequently and others not. If $|avi_e(X) - avi_b(X)| < k$, we denoted temporal data as changeful, otherwise stable. According to the different time limit of transactions, the value k dynamic changes along with the transaction access to temporal data, it will be discussed in detail in the next section.

4. Related definition and validation mechanism

As another temporal limit of transaction, data-deadline, if it is less than transaction-deadline, we must consider it; otherwise transactions may read inconsistent temporal data when transactions commit. In order to ensure temporal consistency and the data which transaction read to be effective, we must inspect and estimate the execution time.

Definition2. Transaction-deadline is $d(T)$, estimated time of completion is $C_t(T)$, so delay time is $sd_t(T) = d(T) - C_t(T)$. Because validation transaction has been completed all operation reading and writing, delay time is $sd_t(T) = d(T) - C_t(T)$.

Definition3. If $L_t^{to}(T) = \phi$, we denoted $tsd_t(T)$ as temporal delay time of transaction T.

$$tsd_t(T) = \begin{cases} d(T) - C_t(T), & dd_t(T) \geq d(T) \\ dd_t(T) - C_t(T), & dd_t(T) < d(T) \end{cases}$$

Definition4. At time t, the starting time of transaction T is $s(T)$, the deadline of transaction T is $d(T)$; we denoted $TFD_t(T) = t - s(T)/d(T) - s(T)$ as the completeness of transaction T.

Definition5. Suppose the conflict transaction set of validation transaction Tv is CTS(T), validation factor of Tv shows the ratio between the completeness of Tv and the completeness of CTS(T), denoted $VF_t(T_v) = TFD_t(T_v)/TFD_t(T)$, $T \in CTS(T)$. If $VF_t(T_v) > 1$ at time t, it shows validation transaction is easier to complete t than conflict transaction.

Definition6. Minimum running time of transaction was described from the current time t to the required execution time of transaction.

If the deadline which transaction read temporal data objects is less than minimum running time, transaction can't commit in validity, so the validity is impossibility. Before transaction read data, we use a validation mechanism to check the validity of the data. It is used to prevent transaction from reading invalid data, or the data which has not validity.

Before transaction executing, we declare that transaction access temporal data set $RS_{s(T)}^{to}(T)$ in advance, the number of temporal data is $L_{s(T)}^{to}(T)$. After transaction executing, we access temporal data successively and check the validity of data dynamically in the process. If $dd_t(T) > d(T)$, and $L_t^{to}(T) = \phi$, data-deadline would be longer than transaction-deadline, and transaction can't access other temporal data, so it can't affect the scheduling and concurrency control. If $dd_t(T) > d(T)$, but $L_t^{to}(T) \neq \phi$, transaction will access other temporal data, so we must check whether satisfy $dd_t(T) > d(T)$ or not, when access all the temporal data. CHECKING Algorithm was described as follows.

CHECKING Algorithm ():
INPUT: $RS_{s(T)}^{to}(T) = \{X^1, X^2 ... X^m\}$

OUTPUT: k, $L_t^{to}(T)$

{ $k = \infty$; $N = L_{s(T)}^{to}(T)$; i=1;

While ($RS_t^{to}(T) \neq \varnothing$)

{T accesses Xi from RS(T) ;

$RS_t^{to}(T) = \{X^1, X^2 ... X^m\} - \{X^i\}$;
if(| avie (Xi) −avib (Xi) | <k)
then if $dd_t(T) < C_t(T)$
then Abort(T);
else $k = k\bigcap_{j=1}^{i} | avi_e(X^j) - avi_b(X^j) |$;}
$L_t^{to}(T) = N - 1$;
i=i+1;
}

Before transaction access each temporal data, we call CHECKING Algorithm to ensure the effectiveness of temporal data. At the same time, through dynamically adjusting value k, we make the variable data consistency.

Lemma1. CHECKING Algorithm can ensure the consistency of variable temporal data.

If | avi_e (X) −avi_b (X) | < k , we denoted temporal data as changeful, otherwise stable. Value k denoted the length of absolute validity; it changed dynamically along with the transaction access to temporal data, and the smaller the k value is shows the more unstable temporal data is. If temporal data which transaction access the next is more changeful than the current, | avi_e (Xi) −avi_b (Xi) |<k , we restart to check whether the data can submit before the deadline, if it can satisfy the temporal consistency, value k will be changed the absolute valid length of temporal data. So CHECKING Algorithm check the consistency of each of variable data to ensure transaction to submit correctly.

Theorem1. CHECKING Algorithm can ensure the consistency of transaction scheduling temporal data.

Prove. Induce the number of temporal data n(T) which transaction T need access, When n(T)=1, proposition was established obviously, otherwise transaction will abort. Supposed n(T)=m, proposition was established. When n(T)=m+1, it can be divided into two cases:

1. When | avi_e (Xi) −avi_b (Xi) | ≥ k , it must satisfy the consistency of temporal data. Supposed that transaction T access temporal data Xi at time t, according to the need of the scheduling strategy, avi_b (Xi) = t, so $avi_e(X^i) \geq dd_t(T)$. Supposed n(T)=m, proposition was established, $dd_t(T) \geq C_t(T)$, so $avi_e(X^i) \geq C_t(T)$. So before transactions complete, all the data can satisfy the time limit proposition was established.
2. When | avi_e (Xi) −avi_b (Xi) | <k , the length of the absolute valid which transaction read the next temporal data is less than k. Showing the accessing data is changeful, and compute the value $dd_t(T)$, on the basis of Lemma1, it satisfies temporal consistency of data. Proposition was established. Sum up(1), (2), the proposition is established.

5. Real-Time concurrency control protocol based on accessing temporal data (RTCC-DD)

The concurrency control mechanism in the database must guarantee the consistency of the database; serializability is one correctness standard of concurrency control in the database.

Methods discussed in this chapter are based on the optimistic concurrency control strategy, when the transactions reading stage we use CHECKING Algorithm to guarantee access temporal data consistency. When transactions come into the verify stage, we make the reading and writing adjustment detection, at this stage the changes of the transactions of the database is readable and effective, conflict transactions can read the private cache of transactions to get the change. The transactions submit if all conflicts transactions are serializable. Specific adjustment rules are as follows.

Rule1 At time t, when $Lt(T)=0$, assigned serial number for the transaction T ser(T) and enter the validation phase, the scope of ser (T) is 1, 2 . . .. to n. The number of the first transaction access the validation phase is 1, transactions access later cumulative.

Rule2 At time t, $avi_e(Xi)<C_t(T)$ and the value of the ith version of X is similar with the next version, then adjust the X temporal period to the next version, that temporal object is (value (Xi) , avi (Xi)) , $avi(Xi)=[avi_b(Xi), avi_e(Xi+1)]$.

Rule3 At time t, $VF_t(T)<1$ and $tsd_t(Tv) > tsd_t(Ti)$, $T_i \in CTS(T_v)$ adjust the serialization order of transactions, ser(Ti)=ser(Tv), ser(Tv)=ser(Tv)+1. If $RS(Tv) \cap WS(Ti) \neq \emptyset$, Tv read the data of Ti from private cache.

Rule4 At time t, submit transaction T, if only $\forall T_i \in CTS(T)$, $ser(T) < ser(T_i)$.

Rule1 ensures transactions enter into validation phase and distribute serial number after complete to access data. Rule2 ensures to extend the validity of temporal data valid interval if next version data similar with the current version, and reduces unnecessary transaction to restart. Rule3 ensures to run conflict transaction when the conflict of transaction is more nearer completion than validation transaction, and validation transaction can delay after the conflict transaction committed, and adjust the executive order, when verification transaction is conflict with other transaction, allow validation transaction to read data which conflict transaction update. Rule4 ensures that the submitted transactions are serializability.

To ensure the effectiveness of the temporal data, RTCC-DD method adopts the checking algorithm to check the access data set before transactions executing. And then, using an optimistic approach, adjust the rules of the transaction validation phase. When verify transaction and other transaction are conflict, to judge by the factor of authentication, priority to scheduling the transaction which will be finished; taking consider the state that verify the transaction when the delay time dynamic adjustment of transaction execution in order to ensure the transactions of temporal data scheduling to satisfy the temporal consistency. While it ensured the limit of the data and transaction, minimizing the unnecessary transaction restarts. RTCC-DD concurrency control methods are described below:

if T_v conflicts with T_i, $T_i \in CTS(T_v)$
  if $RS(T_v) \cap WS(T_i) \neq \emptyset$ then
    if $(VF_t(T_v) < 1) \wedge (tsd_t(T_v) > tsd_t(T_i))$
    then adjusts the execute order to T_i, T_v
    else the execute order is T_v, T_i;
  else if $RS(T_i) \cap WS(T_v) \neq \emptyset$ then

if $(VF_t(T_v) \geq 1) \wedge (tsd_t(T_i) > tsd_t(T_v))$

then adjusts the excute order to T_v, T_i

else the execute order is T_i, T_v;

else if $WS(T_i) \cap WS(T_v) \neq \varnothing$ then

if $(VF_t(T_v) < 1) \wedge (tsd_t(T_v) > tsd_t(T_i))$

then adjusts the execute order to T_i, T_v

else the execute order is T_v, T_i;

endif

endif

RTCC-DD method dynamically adjusts the data by checking the value of k, for each variable temporal data are calculated to ensure that the scheduling of variable data; For the next version of similar state cannot meet the time limit to extend the data deadline for its validity; at the same time we using the optimistic concurrency control method, this method won't produce priority inversion and congestion; And it is the first time to solve the problem about temporal data of concurrency control. Improved the problem of which is discussed in the literature about the transaction scheduling problems of access to temporal data.

Example 2. The transaction and implementation in example 2 is the same with example 1, transaction T1: w1(x)r1(y); T2: w2(y) r2(z). The period of validity of T1 is t7, the period of validity of temporal data z is [t4, t6].

At time t5 when T2 access to validation phase, there is WS(Tv)∩RS(Ta)={y}≠Ø, according to the RTCC-DD,

$$VF_t(T_v) = \frac{4}{7} \Big/ \frac{2}{4} = \frac{8}{7} > 1,\ tsd_{t_5}(T_1) = t_7 - t_6,\ tsd_{t_5}(T_2) = t_6 - t_6,$$

thus satisfying the conditions $(VF_t(T_v) \geq 1) \wedge (tsd_t(T_i) > tsd_t(T_v))$, Adjust the order of transaction execution to T2, T1. After the submit of T2, T1 can also meet the constraint of the period of validity, scheduling T2, T1 successfully, so use method RTCC-DD, can avoid transaction unnecessary restarts.

Serializability is one standard of correctness of concurrency control in the database. RTCC-DD can guarantee the concurrency control of temporal data, at the same time satisfy the serializability. We discuss the superiority and accuracy problems of RTCC-DD method as below.

Lemma2 The traditional optimistic concurrency control methods can use RTCC-DD to schedule.

Because the time constraint of access to transaction will influence the scheduling and concurrency control, The traditional optimistic concurrency control methods only consider the case of the transaction deadline, not discuss the deadline for data on the effect to transaction concurrency control. In order to solve the problem, RTCC-DD take the optimistic method; if the scheduling data is not temporal constrain, RTCC-DD will degenerate to the traditional optimistic concurrency control methods, so the traditional optimistic concurrency control methods can use RTCC-DD to scheduling.

Theorem 2 RTCC-DD can guarantee the serializability of the transactions scheduling

Proof, according to the rule 1, if $L_t(T) = 0$, assigned serial number for the transaction T ser(T), guarantee only when the transaction access into the validation phase we assigned serial number, and the serial number is only, according to rule 3 we dynamic adjust the conflict transaction, and guarantee the least serial number first submit. According to the rule 4, only when all the conflict transactions serialize after this transaction, submit this transaction, so submitting the transactions is constrain by serializability number, ensure the serializability.

6. Experiment

A set of experiments have been carried out in order to examine the feasibility of the algorithms in practice. The RTCC-DD method and the OCC-DA, OCC-DATI method are implemented using C++ and compiled with gcc. All tests were performed on a Dell OptiPlex GX270 PC with 2GB of RAM. The database is composed of pages with a number of records and the records meet uniform distribution; the main performance criteria are the transaction miss percentage.

parameter	*value*
Database size	*400*
Transaction execute time	*100ms*
CPU computation time	*10ms*
Disk access time	*20ms*
Page hit rate	*80%*
Operation number per transaction	*5~50*
Restart overhead	*10*
Mean transaction arrive time	*10~200ms*

Table 1. Simulation Parameter

The traditional optimistic concurrency control methods (OCC-DA, OCC-DATI) and the RTCC-DD method are compared in the experiment. The experiment results are shown in Fig. 2. In Fig. 2a, the average temporal data number of transactions accesses changing from 0 to 25, the performance of RTCC-DD is better than OCC-DA and OCC-DATI. The reason is that transactions scheduling considers the deadline of data in RTCC-DD method. If the submitted time exceeds the deadline, the transaction will be restarted. And the methods of OCC-DA and OCC-DATI do not consider the constraint of temporal data. When transaction accesses a little temporal data, the difference of the performance are small, but as shown in Fig. 2b, if there are a lots of temporal data, RTCC-DD method is obvious better than the traditional concurrency control methods. With increasing the temporal data numbers in system, the influence of the time constrain will increase. The more transactions will miss its deadlines because of not satisfy the data deadline.

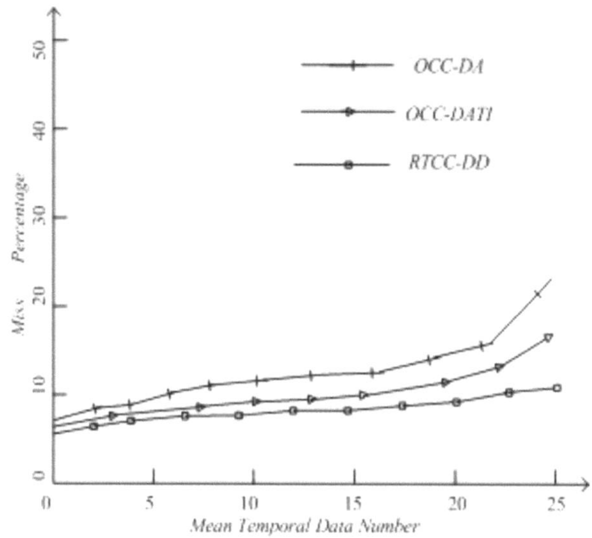

a

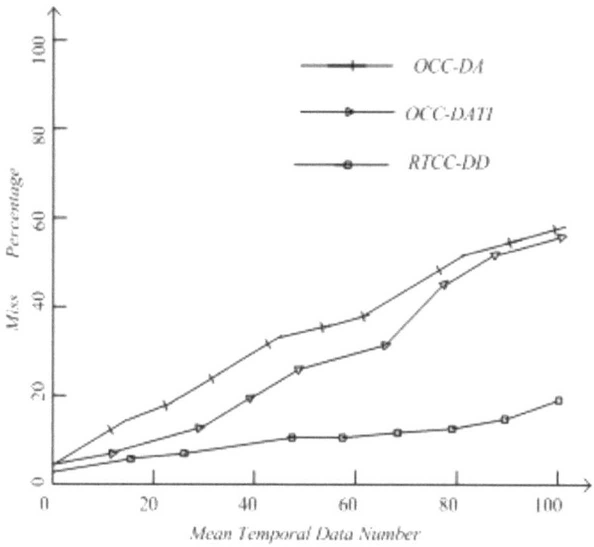

b

a. Little Number of Temporal Data b. Much Number of Temporal Data

Fig. 2. Transactions Miss Percentage

7. Conclusion

The concurrency control method is one of the key problems in the database systems. The optimistic methods are widely used in database system because it is not exists deadlock and block. Unnecessary transactions restarting and nearing completing transactions missing its deadline are the key factor effecting optimistic concurrency control method performances.

Most of the research about the optimism concurrency control method are focus on how reduces unnecessary transactions restarts and the transactions near to completed missing its deadline. The most research is based on dynamic adjustment serialization method. When the transactions access temporal data with time limit, the traditional concurrency control method cannot schedule effectively because it is not consider data-deadline. This chapter improved the validation phase rules and proposed an optimistic concurrency control method based on temporal data (RTCC-DD), which considered the influence between temporal data time limit and the transaction deadline. Theoretical analysis and experimental results demonstrate that the RTCC-DD method can outperform the previous ones for reducing effectively unnecessary restart number of transactions and more suitable for real-time database system.

8. Acknowledgment

The chapter is sponsored by the National Natural Science Foundation of China under Grant No. 41176082, 61073182; Heilongjiang Natural Science Foundation under Grant No. F201024; The Fundamental Research Funds for the Central Universities No. HEUCFZ1010, HEUCF100602.

9. References

A. Brad, K. Ben and G. M. Hector. Database support for efficiently maintaining derived data. Technical Report, Stanford University, 1995: 223~240.

A. Fishwick. SIMPACK: Getting started with simulation programming in C and C++. Department of Computer & Information Science, University of Florida, 1992. IEEE Computer Society Press

D. Menasce and T. Nakanishi. Optimistic versus pessimistic concurrency control mechanisms in database management systems. Information Systems, 7(1):13–27, 1982.

H. T. Kung and J. T. Robinson. On optimistic methods for concurrency control. ACM Transactions on Database Systems, 6(2):213–226, June 1981.

J. Huang, J. A. Stankovic, K. Ramamritham, and D. Towsley. Experimental evaluation of real-time optimistic concurrency control schemes. In Proceedings of the 17th VLDB Conference, pages 35–46, Barcelona, Catalonia, Spain, September 1991. Morgan Kaufmann.

J. Huang, J. A. Stankovic, K. Ramamritham, and D. Towsley. On using priority inheritance in real-time databases. In Proceedings of the 12th IEEE Real-Time Systems Symposium, pages 210–221, San Antonio, Texas, USA, 1991. IEEE Computer Society Press.

J. Lee and S. H. Son. Using dynamic adjustment of serialization order for real-time database systems. In Proceedings of the 14th IEEE Real-Time Systems Symposium, pages 66–75, Raleigh-Durham, NC, USA, 1993. IEEE Computer Society Press.

J. Lee. Concurrency Control Algorithms for Real-Time Database Systems. PhD thesis, Faculty of the School of Engineering and Applied Science, University of Virginia, January 1994.

J. Lindstrom and K. Ratikainen. Dynamic adjustment of serialization order using timestamp intervals in real-time databases. In Proceedings of the 6th International Conference on Real-Time Computing Systems and Applications, pages 13-20, Hong Kong, China, 1999. IEEE Computer Society Press.

J. Lindstrom. Optimistic concurrency control methods for real-time database systems. Ph. D. dissertation. University of Helsinki, FINLAND, 2003.

J. R. Haritsa, M. J. Carey and M. Livny. Dynamic real-time optimistic concurrency control. In Proceedings of the 11th real-time symposium, 1990. 94~103.

J. R. Haritsa, M. J. Carey, and M. Livny. Dynamic real-time optimistic concurrency control. In Proceedings of the 11th IEEE Real-Time Systems Symposium, pages 94–103, Lake Buena Vista, Florida, USA, 1990. IEEE Computer Society Press.

J. R. Haritsa, M. J. Carey, and M. Livny. On being optimistic about real-time constraints. In Proceedings of the 9th ACM Symposium on Principles of Database Systems, pages 331–343, Nashville, Tennessee, 1990. ACM Press.

K. Ramamritham. Real-time databases. Distributed and Parallel Databases, 1:199–226, April 1993.

K. W. Lam, K. Y. Lam, and S. Hung. An efficient real-time optimistic concurrency control protocol. In Proceedings of the First International Workshop on Active and Real-Time Database Systems, pages 209–225, Sk¨ovde, Sweden, 1995. Springer.

K. W. Lam, S. H. Son, and S. Hung. A priority ceiling protocol with dynamic adjustment of serialization order. In Preceedings of the 13th IEEE Conference on Data Engineering, Birmingham, UK, 1997. IEEE Computer Society Press.

L. Sha, R. Rajkumar, and J. P. Lehoczky. Concurrency control for distributed real-time databases. ACM SIGMOD Record, 17(1):82–98, March 1988.

L. Sha, R. Rajkumar, and J. P. Lehoczky. Priority inheritance protocols: An approach to real-time synchronization. IEEE Transactions on Computers, 39(9):1175–1185, September 1990.

L. Sha, R. Rajkumar, S. H. Son, and C. -H. Chang. A real-time locking protocol. IEEE Transactions on Computers, 40(7):793–800, January 1991.

M. Xiong, R. M. Sivasankaran, J. A. Stankovic, K. Ramamritham and D. Towsley. Scheduling transactions with temporal constraints: exploiting data semantics. 17th IEEE Real-time Systems Symposium. 1996.

S. H. Son, K. J. Lin. Real-Time Database Systems: Issues and Applications. Kluwer Academic Publishers, 1997. 167-191

T. Kuo and A. K. Mok. Real-time data semantics and similarity-based concurrency control. IEEE Transactions on Computers. 2000, 49(11): 1241~1254.

T. Kuo, A. K. Mok, SSP: a semantics-based protocol for Real-time data access. 14th IEEE real-time systems symposium. 1993.

Y. S. Liu, G. H. Li. The effect of real-time database data characteristics on transactions. Journal of computer research & development. 1999, 36(3): 364~368.

Y. Y. Wang, Q. Wang, H. A. Wang. Dynamic adjustment of execution order in real-time database. In Proceedings of 18th International Parallel and Distributed Processing Symposium, 2004. 1219~1225.

9

Quality of Service Scheduling in the Firm Real-Time Systems

Audrey Queudet-Marchand and Maryline Chetto
University of Nantes, IRCCyN UMR CNRS 6597
France

1. Introduction

1.1 What does firm real-time mean?

Real-time systems are those in which the time at which the results are produced is important. The correctness of the result of a task is not only related to its logical correctness, but also to when the results occur (Stankovic, 1988). In order to characterize their requirements, real-time systems are traditionaly classified as follows: *hard, soft* and *firm* (Liu, 2000). It is imperative that all time constraints are met in hard real-time systems. In contrast, firm or soft real-time systems do not have as stringent timeliness requirements allowing for some degree of tardiness (soft) or miss ratio (firm). Many researches within the soft and firm real-time area have focused on minimizing tardiness and/or miss ratio but without quantifying acceptable levels. In this chapter, we focus on scheduling firm periodic tasks which have additional requirements. These requirements specify the minimum acceptable completion ratios that should be met in order to maintain system correctness. In a hard real-time system all hard deadline tasks must meet their deadlines to maintain system correctness; otherwise, the system has failed. In contrast, a deadline is considered to be soft if it can be missed occasionally. A task that misses a single soft deadline is not considered a failure. Correctness in a soft real-time system is determined by the degree to which timeliness has been enforced for the entire task set. However, the completion of a tardy firm deadline task is not meaningful since late delivery of the result is considered to be of no value to the real-time system.

Although firm deadlines can occasionally be missed, there is normally an upper limit to the number of misses within a defined interval. The hard real-time paradigm is well established and it has received considerable attention by researchers and practitioners within the academe and the industry alike. Numerous techniques and algorithms – especially in the area of scheduling – have been developed. Most scheduling algorithms developed for soft and firm real-time systems lack the ability to enforce constraints on the upper limit of misses. Unbounded consecutive time constraint violations may occur without such an enforcement. Realistically, if consecutive instances of a task fail to complete before their deadlines, then the system will eventually suffer from a failure. This indicates that there are additional constraints. These constraints express the minimum degree of timeliness that must be enforced for firm real-time tasks. This is the subject of this chapter.

1.2 Quality of Service (QoS) requirements

Quality of Service (QoS) generally refers to a broad collection of networking technologies and techniques. QoS refers to the ability of a network to deliver predictable results. Traditional QoS characteristics include availability, bandwidth, delay or delay jitter (Huston, 2000). However, QoS demands that no task be late (Krings & Azadmanesh, 1999) in hard real-time systems. QoS represents the quantified ratio of tasks that may not be executed – i.e. the total amount of work not contributing to the value of the system – in firm real-time systems. Delay and delay jitter are eliminated from consideration in both cases. Perfect QoS characterization proves to be difficult at the application level. It would be desirable that the scheduling policy adapts to changes in user QoS requirements. Such policy should strive to achieve the desired QoS in an environment with variable resources as well as complex and variable application demands. Consequently, this chapter adresses consideration of the control of the deadline miss ratios as a QoS concern.

1.3 Targeted applications

1.3.1 Typical example: a wireless autonomous surveillance system

Let us consider a real-time monitoring system in charge of sampling key environmental indicators such as ambient temperature, carbon dioxide levels, relative humidity, wind speed/direction or solar radiation. Wireless sensor networks are practical and cost effective solutions for such monitoring. The hardware of a node basically includes various sensors, analog-to-digital converters, data storage, a radio (transceiver) and a microprocessor. Environmental data are collected periodically from the sensors and communicated from the sensor node to a base station as depicted in Figure 1. Note that the sampling rate of sensor data may vary from 5 seconds to 10 minutes according to the nature of the measurement.

A real-time monitoring system must provide updated data within strict time constraints. It is essential to have an efficient real-time scheduling of all the periodic sampling tasks.

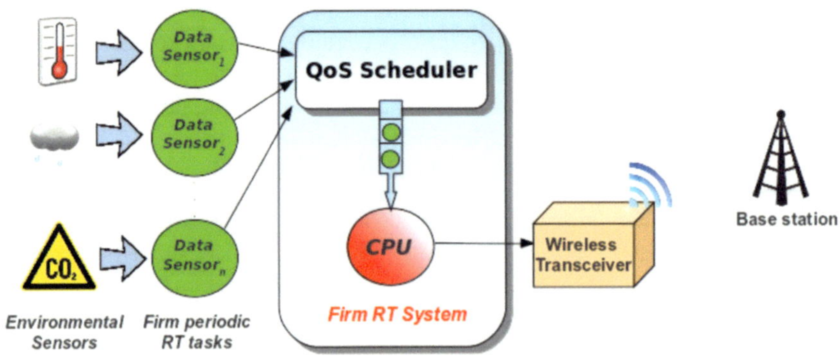

Fig. 1. Simplified architecture of a real-time wireless surveillance application

1.3.2 Scheduling issue

Such a real-time system is often operated in environments that are subject to significant uncertainties. Some parameters such as emergency events, asynchronous demands from external devices (e.g. base station requests for statistical computations on sampled data) or even energy starvation cannot be accurately characterized at design time. The occurrence of such situations will temporarily make the system overloaded (i.e. the processing power required to handle all the tasks will exceed the system capacity). The scheduling will then consist in determining the sequence of execution of sampling tasks in order to provide the best QoS.

The scheduling will play a significant role because of its ability to guarantee an acceptable sampling rate for all the tasks. The scheduler aims to gracefully degrade the QoS (i.e. sampling rate) to a lower but still acceptable level – e.g. a recording at 15 values per minute instead of 30 values per minute for wind speed – in such an overload situation. The execution of some (least important) tasks will be skipped. For instance, it will be less harmful to an air quality surveillance system to skip one wind speed record than to interrupt the transmission of the carbon dioxide level. Given this observation, one gets a better understanding of the real-time CPU scheduling flexibility needed in such applications.

In this chapter, we address the problem of the dynamic scheduling of periodic tasks with firm constraints. The scope of this study concerns maximizing the actual QoS of periodic tasks *i.e.* the ratio of instances which complete before deadline.

2. Scheduling skippable periodic tasks

2.1 Related work

Different approaches have been proposed in order to specify firm real-time systems. In (Hamdaoui & Ramanathan, 1995), the concept of *(m,k)-firm* deadlines permits us to model tasks that have to meet m deadlines every k consecutive instances. The *Distance-Based Priority (DBP)* scheme increases the priority of a job in danger of missing more than m deadlines over a sliding window of k instances for service. In order to specify a task that tolerates x deadlines missed over a finite range or window among y consecutive instances, a *windowed lost rate* is also proposed in (West & Poellabauer, 2000). In (Bernat et al., 2001), the authors describe a more general specification of the distribution of met and lost deadlines. *Virtual Deadline Scheduling (VDS)* (West et al., 2004) and *Dynamic Window-Constrained Scheduling (DWCS)* (Zhang et al., 2004) are other existing schedulers provably superior to *DBP* for a number of specific and non-trivial situations.

The notion of *skip factor* is presented in (Koren & Shasha, 1995). The skip factor of a task equal to s means that the task will have one instance skipped out of s. It is a specific case of the *(m,k)-firm* model with $m = k - 1$. Skipping some task instances then permits us to transform an overload situation into an underload one. Making optimal use of skips has been proved to be an NP-hard problem. (*m*,*k*)-hard schedulers are presented in (Bernat & Burns, 1997). Most of these approaches require off-line feasibility tests to ensure a predictable service.

Scheduling hybrid task sets composed of skippable periodic and soft aperiodic tasks has been studied in (Buttazzo & Caccamo, 1999; Caccamo & Buttazzo, 1997). A scheduling algorithm based on a variant of *Earliest Deadline First (EDF)* exploits skips under the *Total Bandwith Server (TBS)*. In our previous work (Marchand & Silly-Chetto, 2005; 2006), we make use of the same approach with the *Earliest Deadline as Late as possible server (EDL)*. These results led us to propose a raw version of the *Red tasks as Late as Possible (RLP)* algorithm (idle time schedule based on red tasks only) (Marchand, 2006; Marchand & Chetto, 2008).

In contrast, tasks with soft real-time constraints still have a value even when completing after their deadlines. In this case, task overruns can cause overload situations that may be managed by overrun handling mechanisms such as *Overrun Server Method (OSM)* (Tia et al., 1995), *CApacity SHaring (CASH)* (Caccamo et al., 2000) or *Randomized Dropping (RD)* (Bello & Kim, 2007). A more complete survey on overrun handling approaches in soft real-time systems can be found in (Asiaban et al. , 2009).

2.2 The skip-over model

Each periodic task T_i is characterized by a worst-case computation time c_i, a period p_i, a relative deadline equal to its period and a skip factor s_i – which gives the tolerance of this task to missing deadlines – $2 \leq s_i \leq \infty$. Every periodic task instance can be either *red* or *blue* under the terminology introduced in (Koren & Shasha, 1995). A red instance must complete before its deadline; a blue instance can be aborted at any time. The operational specification of a skippable periodic task T_i is composed of four characteristics: (1) the distance between two consecutive skips must be at least s_i periods, (2) if a *blue* instance is skipped, then the next $s_i - 1$ instances are necessarily *red*, (3) if a *blue* instance completes successfully, the next instance is also *blue* and (4) the first $s_i - 1$ instances are *red*. The assumption $s_i \geq 2$ implies that, if a *blue* instance is skipped, then the next one must be *red*. The assumption $s_i = \infty$ signifies that no skip is authorized for task T_i. Skips permit us to schedule systems that might otherwise be overloaded. The system is overloaded since $U_p = \sum_{i=1}^{n} \frac{c_i}{p_i} = \frac{4}{6} + \frac{1}{2} = 1.17$ as shown in Figure 2. Allowing T_2 to skip one instance over three enables us to produce a feasible schedule.

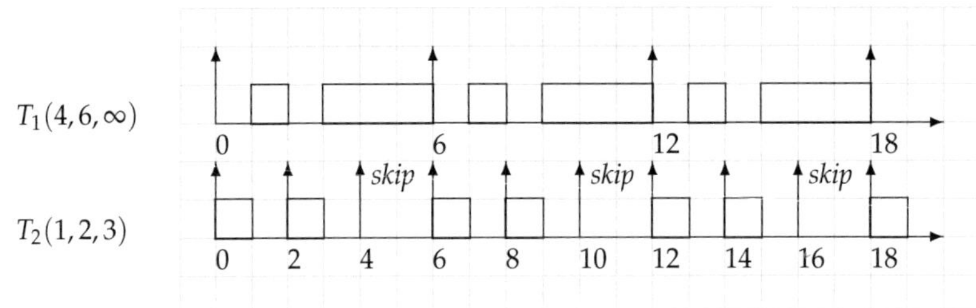

Fig. 2. A schedule with the Skip-Over model

2.3 Feasibility test for skippable periodic task sets

(Liu &Layland, 1973) show that a task set $\{T_i(c_i, p_i); 1 \leq i \leq n\}$ is schedulable if and only if its *cumulative processor utilization* (ignoring skips) is not greater than 1, i.e.,

$$\sum_{i=1}^{n} \frac{c_i}{p_i} \leq 1. \tag{1}$$

(Koren & Shasha, 1995) prove that the problem of determining whether a set of periodic occasionally skippable tasks is schedulable, is NP-hard. However, they prove the following necessary schedulability condition for a given set $\Gamma = \{T_i(p_i, c_i, s_i)\}$ of skippable periodic tasks:

$$\sum_{i=1}^{n} \frac{c_i(s_i - 1)}{p_i s_i} \leq 1. \tag{2}$$

(Caccamo & Buttazzo, 1997) introduce the notion of *equivalent utilization factor* defined as follows.

Definition 1. *Given a set* $\Gamma = \{T_i(p_i, c_i, s_i)\}$ *of n skippable periodic tasks, the equivalent utilization factor is defined as:*

$$U_p^* = \max_{L \geq 0} \frac{\sum_i D(i, [0, L])}{L} \tag{3}$$

where

$$D(i, [0, L]) = (\lfloor \frac{L}{p_i} - \frac{L}{p_i s_i} \rfloor) c_i. \tag{4}$$

They also provide a sufficient condition in (Caccamo & Buttazzo, 1998) for guaranteeing a feasible schedule of a set of skippable tasks:

Theorem 1. *A set* Γ *of skippable periodic tasks is schedulable if*

$$U_p^* \leq 1. \tag{5}$$

2.4 Skip-over scheduling algorithms

2.4.1 RTO (Red Tasks Only)

The first algorithm called Red Task Only (RTO) (Koren & Shasha, 1995) always rejects the blue instances whereas the red ones are scheduled according to EDF. Deadline ties are broken in favor of the task with the earliest release time. Generally speaking, RTO is not optimal. However, it becomes optimal under the particular deeply red task model where all tasks are synchronously activated and the first $s_i - 1$ instances of every task T_i are red. The scheduling decision runs in the worst-case in $O(n^2)$ where all the n tasks are released simultaneously.

Figure 3 depicts a RTO schedule for the task set $\mathcal{T} = \{T_0, T_1, T_2, T_3\}$. Table 1 gives the characteristics of $\mathcal{T}$. Tasks have uniform skip factor $s_i = 2$. The total processor utilization $U_p = \sum \frac{c_i}{p_i}$ is equal to 1.19. The equivalent processor utilization U_p^* is equal to 0.79. This consequently guarantees the feasibility of the task set under minimal QoS.

Task	T_0	T_1	T_2	T_3
c_i	4	6	9	4
p_i	36	24	18	12

Table 1. A basic periodic task set

The schedule produced by RTO exhibits the lowest acceptable QoS level for the task set . All blue instances are systematically rejected every s_i periods for each task.

2.4.2 BWP (Blue When Possible)

The second scheduling algorithm called Blue When Possible (BWP) algorithm (Koren & Shasha, 1995) is an improvement of RTO. Blue instances can execute only if there are no red ready instances. Deadline ties are still broken in favor of the task with the earliest release time. BWP improves RTO in that it offers a higher QoS resulting from the successful completions of blue instances.

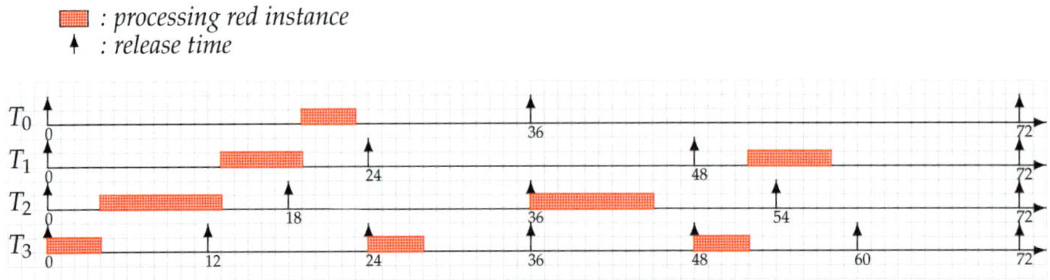

Fig. 3. A schedule produced by the RTO scheduling algorithm ($s_i = 2$)

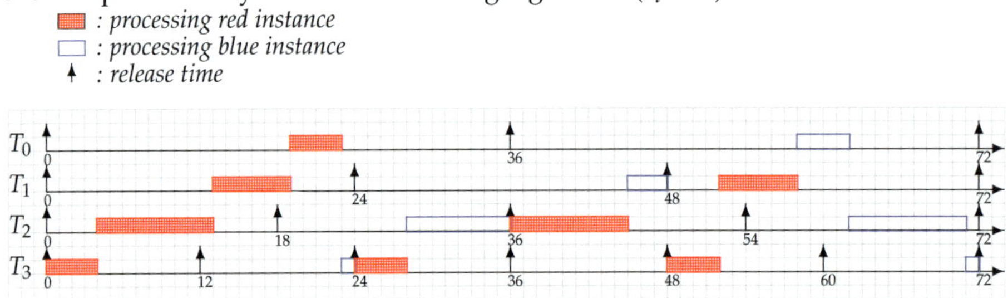

Fig. 4. A schedule produced by the BWP scheduling algorithm ($s_i = 2$)

Figure 4 illustrates a BWP schedule for the task set $\mathcal{T}$ (see Table 1).

As can be seen, BWP increases the total number of task instances that complete successfully. Five deadlines of blue instances are missed at instants $t = 24$ (task T_3), $t = 36$ (task T_2), $t = 48$ (tasks T_1 and T_3) and $t = 72$ (task T_3). In contrast, all deadlines of blue instances are missed under RTO which represents a total of seven instances.

3. Superior skip-over scheduling algorithms

3.1 CPU idle times determination under EDL

The basic foundation of our scheduling approach for enhancing the QoS of skippable periodic tasks relies on the *Earliest Deadline as Late as possible (EDL)* algorithm (Chetto & Chetto, 1989). Thus, we will review the fundamental properties of this algorithm. Such an approach is known as Slack Stealing since it makes any spare processing time available as soon as possible. In doing so, it effectively steals slack from the hard deadline periodic tasks. A means of determining the maximum amount of slack which may be stolen without jeopardizing the hard timing constraints is thus key to the operation of the EDL algorithm. We described in Chetto & Chetto (1989) how the slack available at any current time can be found. This is done by mapping out the processor schedule produced by EDL for the periodic tasks from the current time up to the end of the current hyperperiod (the least common multiple of task periods). This schedule is constructed dynamically whenever necessary. It is computed from a static EDL schedule constructed off-line and memorized by means of the following two vectors:

- K, called static deadline vector. K represents the instants from 0 to the end of the first hyperperiod – at which idle times occur – and is constructed from the distinct deadlines of periodic tasks.

- D, called static idle time vector. D represents the lengths of the idle times which start at instants of K.

The dynamic EDL schedule is updated at run-time from the static one. It takes into account the execution of the current ready tasks. It is described by means of the following two vectors:

- K_t, called dynamic deadline vector. K_t represents the instants k_i from t in the current hyperperiod at which idle times occur.
- D_t, called dynamic idle time vector. D_t represents the lengths of the idle times that start at instants k_i given by K_t.

Assume now that, given the task set $\mathcal{T} = \{T_1(3,10,10); T_2(3,6,6)\}$, we want to compute idle times from instant $t = 5$ while tasks have been processed by EDF from 0 to t. The resulting schedule is depicted in Figure 5. Note that $f^{EDL} = 1$ if the processor is idle at t, 0 otherwise.

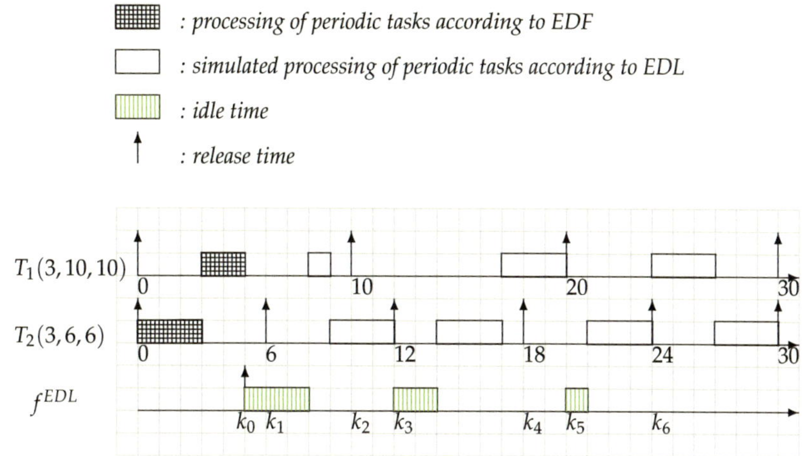

Fig. 5. EDL computation of dynamic idle times at time $t = 5$

Next, tasks are scheduled as late as possible according to EDL from time $t = 5$ to the end of the hyperperiod. Nonzero idle times resulting from the computation of vectors K_t and D_t appear at times $t = 5$, $t = 6$, $t = 12$ and $t = 20$.

Chetto & Chetto (1989) showed that the EDL schedule computation can be efficiently used for improving the service of aperiodic tasks. By definition, soft aperiodic requests must not compromise the guarantees given for periodic tasks and should be completed as soon as possible. No acceptance test is performed for soft aperiodic requests; they are served on a best-effort basis within the computed idle times, the goal being to minimize their response times. Concerning hard aperiodic tasks, each task is subject to an acceptance-rejection test upon arrival. Hard aperiodic tasks can indeed easily be admitted or rejected on the basis of the knowledge of idle times localization.

In the next sections, we are first interested in using EDL to build a schedule on the red instances only so as to execute the blue instances as soon as possible in the remaining EDL idle times (see section 3.2 The RLP algorithm). In a second phase, EDL will allow us to derive a test for deciding on-line whether a blue instance can be accepted for execution or not (see section 3.3 The RLP/T algorithm).

3.2 The RLP algorithm

BWP executes blue instances in background beside red ones. Processor time is often wasted due to the abortion of uncompleted blue instances that have reached their deadlines. Figure 4 shows that task T_2 is aborted at time $t = 36$. This leads to 8 units of wasted processor time.

3.2.1 Algorithm description

The *Red tasks as Late as Possible (RLP)* algorithm (Marchand & Chetto, 2008) brings forward the execution of blue instances so as to enhance the actual QoS (*i.e.*, the total number of successful executions). From this perspective, RLP runs as follows:

- if no blue instance waits for execution, red instances execute as soon as possible according to the EDF scheduling rule.
- else (i.e. at least one blue instance is ready for execution), blue instances execute as soon as possible according to EDF scheduling (note that it could be according to any other scheduling heuristic), and red instances are processed as late as possible according to EDL.

Figure 6 gives the pseudo-code of the RLP algorithm. RLP maintains three task lists which are sorted in increasing order of deadline: *waiting list*, *red ready list* and *blue ready list*.

- *waiting list*: list of instances waiting for their next release,
- *red ready list*: list of red instances ready for execution,
- *blue ready list* : list of blue instances ready for execution.

At every instant t, the scheduler performs the following actions:

1. it updates all the three lists: instances may be released or aborted according to their current state (i.e. waiting or ready red/blue instances),
2. if t belongs to an EDL idle time, it selects the first instance in the blue ready list for execution. Otherwise it selects the first instance in the red ready list.

The main idea of this approach is to take advantage of the slack of red instances. The determination of the latest start time for every red instance requires preliminary construction of the schedule by a variant of the EDL algorithm taking skips into account (Marchand & Silly-Chetto, 2006). We assume in the EDL schedule established at time τ that the instance following immediately a blue one - which is part of the current periodic instance set at time τ - is red. Indeed, none of the blue instances is guaranteed to complete within its deadline.

We proved in (Silly, 1999) that the online computation of the slack time is required only at instants which corresponds to the arrival of a request while no other is already present on the machine. The EDL sequence is constructed here not only when a blue instance is released - and no other one was already present - but also after a blue task completion, if blue tasks remain in the system. The next task instance of the completed blue task has then to be considered as a blue one. Note that blue instances are executed in the EDL idle times with the same importance as red instances, contrary to BWP which always assigns higher priority to red instances.

```
Algorithm RLP(t : current time)
begin
  /*checking blue ready list in order to abort tasks*/
  while (task=next(blue ready list)=not(∅))
      if (task→release time+task→critical delay<t)
        break
      endif
      Pull task from blue ready list
      task→release time+= task→period
      task→current skip value=1
      Put task into waiting list
  endwhile
  /*checking waiting list in order to release tasks*/
  while (task=next(waiting list)=not(∅))
      if (task→release time>t)
        break
      endif
      if ((task→current skip value < task→max skip value)
      and (f_EDL(t)=0))
        /*red task release*/
        Pull task from waiting list
        Put task into red ready list
      else
        if (blue ready list=∅)
          Compute EDL_schedule
        endif
        if (f_EDL(t)!=0)
          /*blue task release*/
          Pull task from waiting list
          Put task into blue ready list
        endif
      endif
      task→current skip value+=1
  endwhile
  if ((blue ready list=not(∅)) and (f_EDL(t)!=0))
      /*checking red ready list in order to suspend task*/
      while (task=next(red ready list)=not(∅))
        Pull task from red ready list
        Put task into waiting list
      endwhile
  endif
end
```

Fig. 6. RLP scheduling algorithm

3.2.2 Illustrative example

Consider the periodic task set $\mathcal{T}$ defined in Table 1. The relating RLP scheduling is illustrated in Figure 7. The number of deadline misses has been reduced to four. Missed deadlines occur at instants $t = 36$ (task T_3), $t = 54$ (task T_2) and $t = 72$ (tasks T_1 and T_3). Observe that the first blue instance T_2 which failed to complete within its deadline under BWP scheduling (see Figure 4) has enough time to succeed under RLP scheduling. The execution of the first red instances of T_1 and T_0 is postponed. Red instances are scheduled as soon as possible until time $t = 12$ and execute as late as possible in the presence of blue instances from time $t = 12$ up to the end of the hyperperiod. This enhances the actual QoS of periodic tasks.

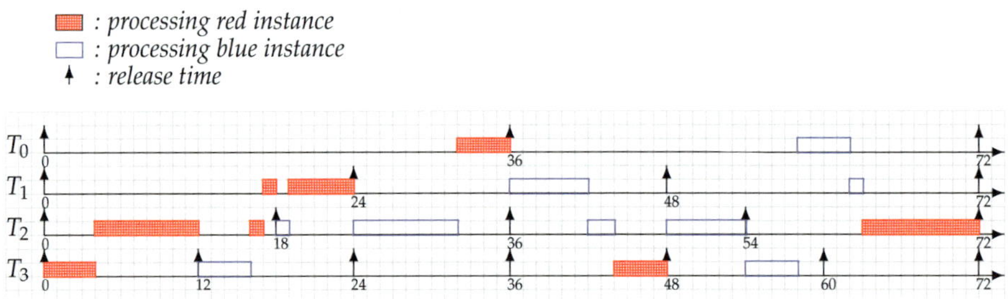

Fig. 7. A schedule produced by the RLP scheduling algorithm ($s_i = 2$)

3.3 The RLP/T algorithm

3.3.1 Algorithm description

The *Red tasks as Late as Possible with blue acceptance Test (RLP/T)* algorithm (Marchand & Chetto, 2008) is an improvement of RLP designed to maximize even more the actual QoS.

RLP/T runs as follows: red instances enter the system directly at their arrival time whereas blue instances integrate the system upon acceptance. A blue instance is scheduled as soon as possible together with red ones once accepted. All the ready instances are of the same importance. Deadline ties are broken in favor of the task with the earliest release time.

Processor idle times are computed according to the EDL strategy once a new blue instance is released. We assume that the instance immediately following a blue instance is also blue in the EDL schedule established at time τ. All blue instances previously accepted at τ are guaranteed by the schedulability test. It ensures there are enough idle times to accommodate the new blue instance within its deadline, as described hereafter.

3.3.2 Acceptance test of blue instances under RLP/T

The question we ask now can be formulated as follows: "Given any occurring blue instance B, can B be accepted?". B will be accepted provided a valid schedule exists, i.e. a schedule in which B will complete within its deadline while all periodic instances previously accepted will still meet their deadlines. Let τ be the current time which coincides with the release of a blue instance B. $B(r, c, d)$ is characterized by its release time r, its execution time c and its deadline d, with $r + c \leq d$. We assume that the system supports several uncompleted blue instances at time τ previously accepted. Let's denote by $\mathcal{B}(\tau) = \{B_i(c_i(\tau), d_i), i\text{=1 to } blue(\tau)\}$, the blue instance set at time τ. The value $c_i(\tau)$ is called *dynamic execution time* and represents the remaining execution time of B_i at τ. $\mathcal{B}(\tau)$ is ordered such that $i < j$ implies $d_i \leq d_j$.

Theorem 2 presents the acceptance test of blue instances within a system involving RLP skippable tasks. This test is based on theoretical results established in (Silly-Chetto et al., 1990) for the acceptance of sporadic requests that occur in a system composed of non-skippable periodic tasks.

THEOREM 2. *Instance B is accepted if and only if, for every instance $B_i \in \mathcal{B}(\tau) \cup \{B\}$ such that $d_i \geq d$, we have $\delta_i(\tau) \geq 0$, with $\delta_i(\tau)$ defined as:*

$$\delta_i(\tau) = \Omega^{EDL}_{\mathcal{T}(\tau)}(\tau, d_i) - \sum_{j=1}^{i} c_j(\tau) \tag{6}$$

$\delta_i(\tau)$ is called *slack of instance B_i at time τ*. It defines the maximum units of time during which B_i could be delayed without violating its deadline. $\Omega^{EDL}_{\mathcal{T}(\tau)}(\tau, d_i)$ denotes the total units of time that the processor is idle in the time interval $[\tau, d_i]$. The total computation time required by blue instances within $[\tau, d_i]$ is given by $\sum_{j=1}^{i} c_j(\tau)$.

The acceptance test is based on the computation of EDL idle times which gives the slack of any blue instances. Then, this slack is compared to zero. The acceptance test runs in $O(\lfloor \frac{R}{p} \rfloor n + blue(\tau))$ in the worst-case, where n is the number of periodic tasks, R is the longest deadline and p is the shortest period. $blue(\tau)$ denotes the number of blue instances at time τ whose deadline is greater or equal to the deadline of B_i. A specific updating of additional data structures with slack tables may reduce the complexity to $O(n + blue(\tau))$ as proved in (Tia et al., 1994).

3.3.3 Illustrative example

Figure 8 gives an illustration of RLP/T scheduling for the periodic task set $\mathcal{T}$ defined in Table 1. Clearly, RLP/T improves on both RLP and BWP. Only three deadline violations relative to blue instances are observed: at instants $t = 36$ (task T_3), $t = 54$ (task T_2) and $t = 72$ (task T_3). The acceptance test contributes to compensating for the time wasted in starting the execution of blue instances which are not able to complete before deadline. The blue instance T_2 released at time $t = 36$ is aborted at time $t = 54$ – 8 units of time were indeed wasted – in the RLP case (see Figure 7). This rejection performed with RLP/T permits us to save time recovered for the successful completion of the blue instance T_1 released at time $t = 48$.

4. Performance analysis

4.1 Simulation details

We report part of a performance analysis composed of three simulation experiments in order to evaluate RLP/T with respect to RTO, BWP and RLP.

We successively measure:

- *the QoS* (i.e. the ratio of instances that complete within their deadline),
- *the CPU wasted time ratio* (i.e. the percentage of useless processing time),

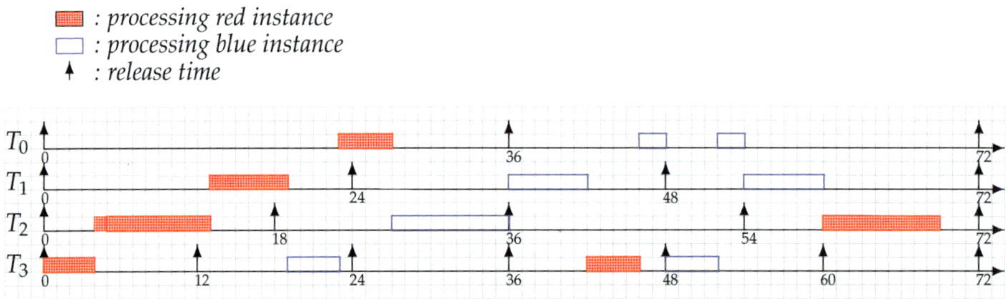

Fig. 8. A schedule produced by the RLP/T scheduling algorithm ($s_i = 2$)

- *the CPU idle time ratio* (i.e. the percentage of time during which the processor is not processing any task).

We make the processor utilization U_p vary. The simulator generates 50 sets of periodic tasks. Each set contains 10 tasks with a least common multiple of periods equal to 3360 time units. The tasks have a uniform skip factor s_i. Worst-case computation times depend on U_p. Deadlines are equal to periods and greater than or equal to computation times. Simulations have been processed over 10 hyperperiods.

4.1.1 Experiment 1

Figure 9 depicts the simulation results for s_i=2. The results are given for an actual computation time (ACET) equal to 100% and 75% of the worst-case computation time (WCET) respectively. Let us recall that the tasks have variable actual computation times assumed to be less than an estimated worst-case computation time. The assumption that a task consumes its WCET in every activation is not necessarily true. This implies that the actual CPU utilization never exceeds the estimated one used in the schedulability test.

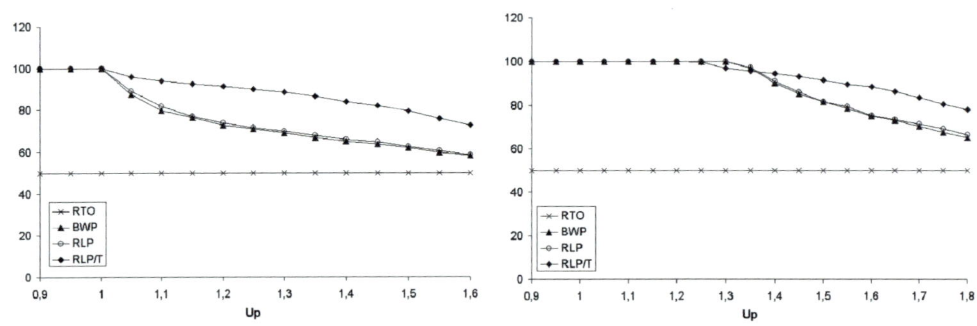

(a) ACET=WCET (b) ACET=0.75*WCET

Fig. 9. QoS for s_i=2

BWP and RLP outperform RTO – for which the QoS is constant and minimal – for any processor workload. Both BWP and RLP succeed in completing all blue instances that respectively execute after and before red instances for $Up \leq 1$. RLP and BWP give almost the same performances under overload. Nevertheless, RLP/T provides a significant improvement in performance compared with RLP.

The QoS observed for BWP, RLP and RLP/T is higher for a given processor utilization when the task's computation time is less than the task's worst-case execution time. As the amount of time given by $WCET - ACET$ is not used by each instance, additional CPU time permits us to successfully complete a higher number of instances.

Moreover, note that BWP and RLP outperform RLP/T for low overloads with ACET=0.75* WCET. This comes from the admission test in RLP/T which uses WCET values and not ACET ones. Consequently, RLP/T rejects instances that after all could have been accepted on the basis of their ACET. This is exactly what we observe for U_p equal to 130%: RLP/T temporarily offers lower performances than BWP and RLP. Note that this phenomenon is no longer observable once the skip factors are higher (e.g. $s_i = 6$).

Finally, other tests (Marchand, 2006) – not reported here – show that the higher the skip factor is, the more significant the advantage of RLP/T over the other scheduling algorithms.

4.1.2 Experiment 2

We study here the CPU time wasted in incomplete executions of blue instances. The simulation results for $s_i = 2$ and $s_i = 6$ are depicted in Figure 10.

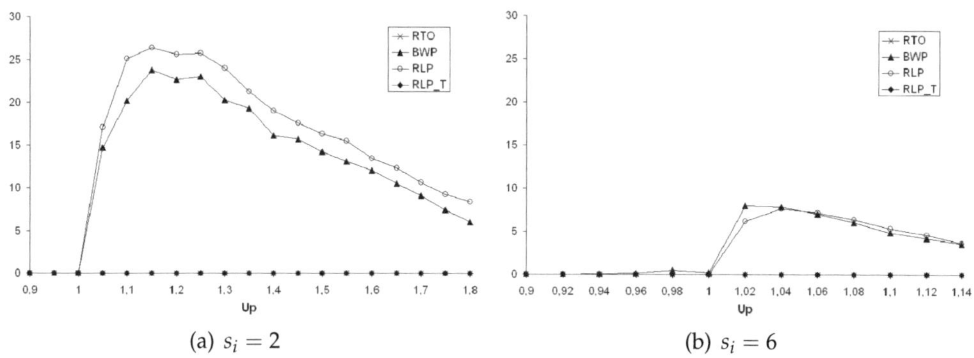

Fig. 10. Wasted CPU time for low and high skips

The wasted CPU time is equal to zero for RTO since all red instances execute successfully. It is also equal to zero under RLP/T for any CPU utilization. This is due to the admission test that prevents from the abortion of blue instances. A blue instance is accepted if and only if it can complete before deadline.

The wasted CPU time is always positive under BWP and RLP once the system is overloaded ($U_p > 1$). BWP and RLP involve the largest wasted CPU time – 24% et 26% respectively – for $U_p = 115\%$ and $s_i = 2$. The BWP and RLP curves present a decline beyond that load. More red instances have to be executed under high overload. Less available CPU time is consequently available for the execution of blue instances.

Additional results reported in (Marchand, 2006) show that wasted CPU time is all the less significant as skip factors grow.

4.1.3 Experiment 3

Finally, we study the CPU idle time ratio given by the percentage of time during which the processor is not processing any task. This measure quantifies the ability to face a dynamic processing surplus (e.g. the arrival of an aperiodic task). Simulation results for $s_i = 2$ and $s_i = 6$ are presented in Figure 11.

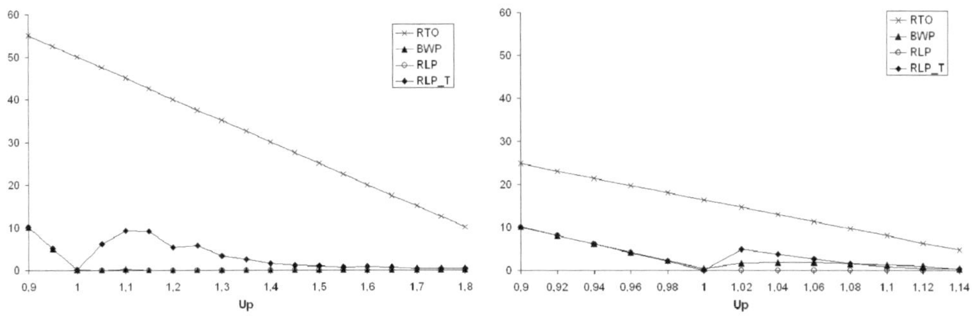

(a) $s_i = 2$ (b) $s_i = 6$

Fig. 11. CPU idle time for low and high skips

We note that the CPU idle time ratio under RTO is the highest one compared with all strategies. This ratio declines in a linear fashion according to U_p. It varies from 55% for $U_p = 90\%$ to 10% for $U_p = 180\%$ and $s_i = 2$. Note the singular points of the curves $s_i = 2$ and $s_i = 6$: when $U_p = 100\%$ idle time ratios are respectively equal to $\frac{1}{2} = 50\%$ and $\frac{1}{6} = 16.7\%$ which correspond exactly to the skip factors.

Idle time ratios are identical and positive – e.g. idle time $= 10\%$ for $U_p = 90\%$ – when $U_p < 100\%$ under BWP, RLP and RLP/T. They decline in a linear fashion until reaching a zero value for $U_p = 100\%$.

Results differ for overloaded systems ($U_p > 100\%$). RLP involves no CPU idle time whatever the skip factors are. We observe that BWP involves a low idle time ratio only under low skip ratios. RLP/T clearly appears as the most efficient strategy, still offering idle time under light overloads. For example, the idle time ratio under RLP/T for $s_i = 2$ and $U_p = 115\%$ is equal to 9%. RLP/T gives a low and still positive idle time ratio even when the system is highly overloaded.

In summary, RLP/T proves to be the most suitable scheduling strategy to cope with transient overloads while providing the highest Quality of Service.

4.2 Integration into an open-source operating system

4.2.1 The CLEOPATRE Library

From 2002 until 2006, we developed a library of free software components within the French National project *CLEOPATRE (Software Open Components on the Shelf for Embedded Real-Time Applications)*. This project aims to provide efficient services to real-time applications (Silly et al., 2007). It enriches real-time Linux variants with enhanced real-time facilities.

CLEOPATRE components have been prototyped under *Linux/RTAI (Real-Time Application Interface)* (Racciu & Mantegazza, 2006) and distributed under the LGPL license. The LGPL allows proprietary code to be linked to the GNU C library, glibc. When a program is linked with a library – whether statically or using a shared library – the combination of the two is legally speaking a combined work, a derivative of the original library. Companies do not have to release the source to code that which has been dynamically linked to an LGPLed library. This makes the use of such codes much more attractive.

The CLEOPATRE library offers selectable COTS (Commercial-Off-The-Shelf) components dedicated to dynamic scheduling, aperiodic task servicing, resource control access, fault-tolerance and QoS scheduling. An additional task named *TCL (Task Control Logic)* interfaces all the CLEOPATRE components and has the highest priority. It has been added as a dynamic module in *$RTAIDIR/modules/TCL.o* and interfaces with the legacy RTAI scheduler defined in *$RTAIDIR/modules/rtai_sched.o*, as depicted in Figure 12.

The CLEOPATRE interface is totally independent from the RTAI core layer. It can be directly used with Xenomai – which supports the RTAI API – and easily adapted to any other real-time Linux extension.

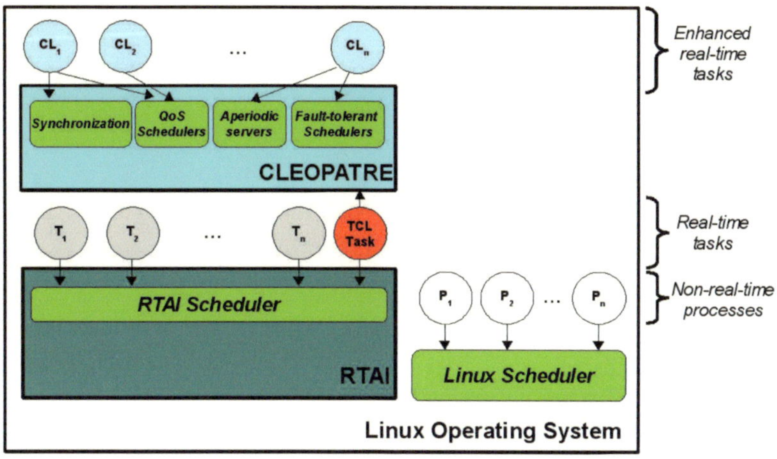

Fig. 12. Cleopatre Library within Linux/RTAI

CLEOPATRE applications are highly portable to any new CPU architecture thanks to this OS abstraction layer which makes the library of services generic (Silly et al., 2007). The CLEOPATRE Off-the-Shelf components are optional except for the OS abstraction layer (TCL) and the scheduler. At most one component per shelf can be selected. Since all components of a given shelf have the same programming interface, they become interchangeable. Everything needed to use or extend CLEOPATRE can be downloaded from the project web site *http://cleopatre.rts-software.org*.

4.2.2 Overheads and footprints

The memory and disk footprints of the operating system turn out to be key issues for embedded real-time applications as well as the time overhead incurred by the operating system itself. Table 2 gives the footprints for the schedulers provided by CLEOPATRE.

QoS components	Hard disk size (KB)	Memory size (KB)
RTO	3.2	2.3
BWP	4.1	3.2
RLP	9.7	7.6
RLP/T	13.3	10.8

Table 2. Footprints of QoS components

The smallest footprint of an application using a QoS scheduler comes to 52.4 KB in memory (65.2 KB on hard disk). This corresponds to the total load due to RTAI, the TCL task and the RTO scheduler. On the contrary, the greatest footprint corresponds to the RLP/T scheduler (i.e. 60.9 KB in memory and 75.3 KB on hard disk). Any QoS scheduler, including RLP/T scheduler, easily fits into the flash memory of an embedded system.

We conducted experiments to obtain a quantitative evaluation of the overhead led by the QoS schedulers. We measured the overhead for various numbers of tasks (5, 10, 15, 20,...) with all periods equal to 10 milliseconds. Periods are harmonic with a hyperperiod equal to 3360 timer ticks. The measurements were performed over a period of 1000 seconds on a computer system with a 400 MHz Pentium II processor with 384 Mo RAM. Figure 13 shows the resulting overhead.

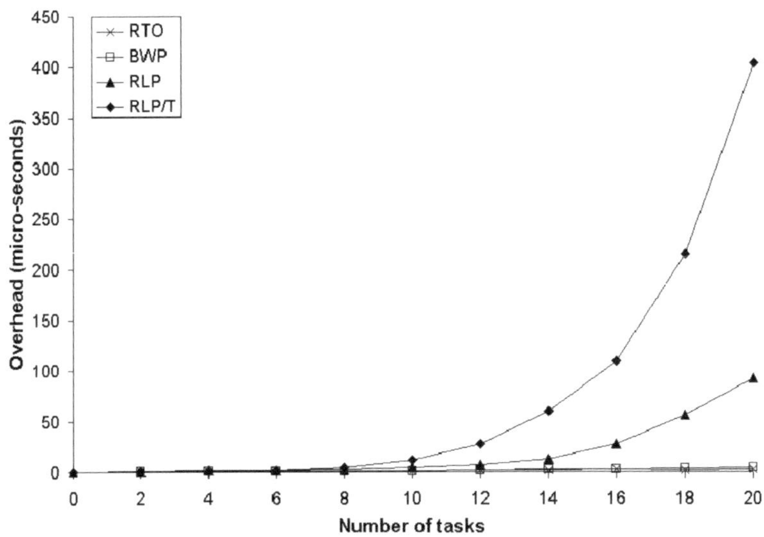

Fig. 13. Dynamic overhead of the QoS schedulers

The average overhead led by the QoS schedulers scales with the number of installed tasks. BWP exhibits an average execution time that is substantially higher than the RTO. This comes from the management of blue instances under BWP. The curve obtained for RLP and RLP/T mainly comes from the amount of time spent on the EDL schedule (performed only when a blue instance is released or completed). As a matter of fact, we observe that overhead is closely related to efficiency. An interesting feature of the component approach lies in that the selected scheduler can be tuned to balance performance versus complexity, and thus easily conforms to implementation requirements.

5. Conclusion

5.1 Summary

While it is imperative that all time constraints – generally expressed in terms of deadlines – are met in hard real-time systems, firm real-time systems do not have as stringent timeliness requirements since they allow for some degree of miss ratio. Video reception and multimedia-oriented mobile applications are typical firm real-time applications that require the need for a suitable real-time scheduler which represents the central key service in any operating system. The proliferation of these applications has motivated many research efforts over the last twenty years in order to produce a scheduling framework that explicitly addresses their specific requirements and improves the global Quality of Service.

A firm real-time system is typically characterized by dynamic changes in workloads (tasks have variable actual execution times). It consequently needs a scheduler able to handle possible overload situations and to allow the system to achieve graceful degradation by skipping some tasks. The scheduler has to supply a dynamic mechanism that determines on-line the task to be shed from the system. Multimedia systems are typically systems in which performance is sensitive to the distribution of skips: if skips occur for several consecutive instances of the same task, then the system performance may be totally unacceptable leading to some form of instability. To overcome the shortcoming of the Quality of Service metrics only based on the average rate of dropped tasks, Koren and Shasha proposed the skip-over model in which a periodic task with a skip factor of s is allowed to have one instance skipped out of s consecutive instances (Koren & Shasha, 1995).

In this chapter, we have considered the skip-over model where independant tasks run periodically on a uni-processor architecture and can be preempted at any time. Additionally, they have a skip factor. We described two on-line scheduling algorithms respectively named RLP and RLP/T, the latter being based on an admission control mechanism. The results of an experimental study indicate that improvements with both RLP and RLP/T are quite significant compared with the two basic algorithms introduced by Koren and Shasha. We have integrated all the QoS schedulers presented in this chapter as software components which are part of the CLEOPATRE open-source library. We have performed their evaluation under a real-time Linux-based operating system, namely Linux/RTAI. The observed overheads and footprints enabled us to state their ability to be used even for embedded applications with severe memory and timeliness requirements.

5.2 Future work

5.2.1 QoS and energy harvesting

Many embedded systems work in insecure or remote sites (e.g. wireless intelligent sensors). The new generation of these systems will be smaller and more energy efficient while still offering sufficient performance. A typical example is data farming where sensors are spread over an area to supervise the environment and send collected data for further processing to a base station. Sensors are deployed and then must stay operational for a long period of time, in the range of months or even years.

One way to prolong the lifetime of such autonomous systems is to harvest the required energy from the environment. Energy Harvesting is defined as the process of capturing energy from one or more natural energy sources accumulating it and storing it for later use (Priya & Inman,

2009). Energy harvesting from a natural source where a remote application is deployed and where energy is inexhaustible appears as an attractive alternative to inconvenient traditional batteries. Energy harvesting with solar panels is one of the most popular technologies. Nowadays, many real life applications using energy harvesting are operational. Wireless sensor network systems, including ZigBee systems, benefit from this technology.

A wireless sensor has timing constraints that must be satisfied and consume only as much energy as the energy harvester can collect from the environment. But the harvested energy is highly dependent on the environment and the power drained from most environmental energy sources is not constant over time. Consequently, energy consumption coming from the execution of tasks should be continuously adjusted in order to maximize the Quality of Service and not only to minimize the energy consumption. The main challenge of research is to provide an energy-aware scheduling algorithm that will schedule tasks so as to consider jointly two kinds of constraints: time (i.e. deadlines) and energy availability.

To address the above problem, we proposed in a recent paper (El Ghor et al., 2011) an efficient scheduling algorithm called EDeg which is based on both the energy stored and the energy estimated to be harvested in the future. We performed a series of experiments based on the rate of missed deadlines in order to compare EDeg with other scheduling methods. Experimental results show that EDeg significantly outperforms the classical greedy schedulers, including EDF.

We are now extending this scheduling strategy to the skip-over model. The objective is to reduce the rate of missed deadlines when the system lacks either time or energy, by taking into account skip factors. To summarize, our current work focuses on the same problem studied in this chapter but considers the specific issue of real-time energy harvesting systems.

5.2.2 QoS and multicore systems

While real-time applications are becoming more and more concurrent and complex, the drive toward multicore systems seems inevitable. Multicore processors solve the problem of heat that has been slowing processor growth in the past while providing increased performance. We propose in a recent paper (Abdallah et al., 2011) to tackle the problem of distributing skippable periodic tasks over such platforms. Our contribution is twofold. First, we design a schedulability test for multicore task sets under QoS constraints. Second, based on this test, we propose new partitioned scheduling heuristics to assign tasks with QoS constraints to processors so as to minimize the number of processors used. In conclusion, this new line of investigation extends the work presented in this chapter to multicore platforms.

6. References

Abdallah, N., Queudet, A., Chetto, M. & Chehade, R.-H. (2011). Partitioned EDF Scheduling in Multicore systems with Quality of Service constraints. *Proceedings of IEEE International Conference on Electronics, Circuits, and Systems*, December 2011, Beirut (Lebanon).

Asiaban, S., Moghaddam, M.-E. & Abbaspour, M. (2009). A Real-Time Scheduling Algorithm for Soft Periodic Tasks. *International Journal of Digital Content Technology and its Applications*, 3(4):100–111.

Bernat, G. & Burns, A. (1997). Combining (n/m)-hard deadlines and dual priority scheduling, *Proceedings of the 18th IEEE Real-Time Systems Symposium*, pp 46-57, December 1997, San Francisco (USA).

Bernat, G., Burns, A. & Llamosi, A. (2001). Weakly-hard real-time systems, *IEEE Transactions on Computers*, 50(4):308-321.

Bello, L.-L. & Kim, K. (2007). Overrun handling approaches for overload-prone soft real-time systems. *Advances in Engineering Software*, 38(11-12):780–794.

Buttazzo, G.-C. & Caccamo, M. (1999). Minimizing Aperiodic Response Times in a Firm Real-Time Environment, *IEEE Transaction on Software Engineering*, 25(1):22–32.

Caccamo, M. & Buttazzo, G.-C. (1997). Exploiting skips in periodic tasks for enhancing aperiodic responsivess, *Proceedings of the 18th IEEE Real-Time Systems Symposium*, December 1997, San Francisco (USA).

Caccamo, M., & Buttazzo, G.-C. (1998). Optimal Scheduling for Fault-Tolerant and Firm Real-Time Systems. *Proceedings of the IEEE Real-Time Computing Systems and Applications*, October 1998, Hiroshima (Japan).

Caccamo, M., Buttazzo, G. & Sha, L. (2000). Capacity sharing for overrun control. *Proceedings of the 21st IEEE Real-Time Systems Symposium*, November 2000, Orlando (USA).

Chetto, H. & Chetto, M. (1989). Some Results of the Earliest Deadline Scheduling Algorithm. *IEEE Transactions on Software Engineering*, 15(10):1261–1269.

El Ghor, H., Chetto, M. & Chehade, R.-H. (2011). A real-time scheduling framework for embedded systems with environmental energy harvesting. *Computers & Electrical Engineering Journal*, 37(4):498–510.

Hamdaoui, M. & Ramanathan, P. (1995). A Dynamic Priority Assignment Technique for Streams with (m,k)-firm deadlines. *IEEE Transactions on Computers*, 44(4):1443–1451.

Huston, G. (2000). Quality of Service - Fact or Fiction? *The Internet Protocol Journal*, 3(1):1–40.

Krings, A.W. & Azadmanesh, M.H. (1999). QoS Considerations In Real-Time Scheduling, *Proceedings of the 2nd International Conference on Parallel Computing Systems*, August 1999, Ensenada (Mexico).

Koren, G. & Shasha, D. (1995). Skip-Over Algorithms and Complexity for Overloaded Systems that Allow Skips. *Proceedings of the 16th IEEE Real-Time Systems Symposium*, December 1995, Pisa (Italy).

Liestman, A-L. & Campbell, R-H. (1986). A fault tolerant scheduling problem. *Proceedings of the IEEE Transaction on Software Engineering*, 12(10):1089–1095.

Liu, J.-W.-S. (2000). *Real-Time Systems*, Prentice-Hall.

Liu, C-L. & Layland, J-W. (1973). Scheduling Algorithms for Multiprogramming in a Hard Real-Time Environment. *Journal of the Association for Computing Machinery*, 20(1):46–61.

Marchand, A. (2006). Ordonnancement Temps Réel avec Contraintes de Qualité de Service - De la théorie à l'intégration. *PhD Thesis*, University of Nantes (France), October 2006.

Marchand, A. & Chetto, M. (2008). Quality of Service Sccheduling in Real-Time Systems. *International Journal on Computers, Communications & Control*, 3(4):354–366.

Marchand, A. & Silly-Chetto, M. (2005). QoS Scheduling Components based on Firm Real-Time Requirements, *Proceedings of the ACS/IEEE International Conference on Computer Systems and Applications*, January 2005, Le Caire (Egypt).

Marchand, A. & Silly-Chetto, M. (2006). Dynamic Real-Time Scheduling of Firm Periodic Tasks with Hard and Soft Aperiodic Tasks. *Journal of Real-Time Systems*, 32(1-2):21–47.

Priya, S., Inman, D.-J. (2009). *Energy Harvesting Technologies*, Springer.

Racciu, G. & Mantegazza, P. (2006). RTAI User Manual 3.4 rev 0.3. URL:www.rtai.org

Silly, M. (1999). The EDL Server for Scheduling Periodic and Soft Aperiodic Tasks with Resource Constraints. *The Journal of Real-Time Systems*, 17(1): 87-111.

Silly-Chetto, M., Chetto, H. & Elyounsi, N (1990). An Optimal Algorithm for Guranteeing Sporadic Tasks in Hard Real-Time Systems. *IEEE Symposium on Parallel and Distributed Processing*, December 1990, Dallas (USA).

Silly-Chetto, M., Garcia-Fernandez T. & Marchand-Queudet, A. (2007). CLEOPATRE: Open-source Operating System Facilities for Real-Time Embedded Applications. *The Journal of Computing and Information Technology*, 15(2): 131-142.

Stankovic, J.-A. (1988). Misconceptions about real-time computing: a serious problem for next-generation systems. *IEEE Computer*, 21(10):10–19.

Tia, T., Liu, J., Sun, J. & Ha, R. (1994). A Linear-Time Optimal Acceptance Test for Scheduling of Hard Real-Time Tasks, *Tech. report*, University of Illinois, Urbana-Champaign (USA).

Tia, T.-S., Deng, Z., Shankar, M., Storch, M., Sun, J., Wu, L.-C. & Liu, J.-W.-S. (1995). Probabilistic performance guarantee for real-time tasks with varying computation times, *Proceedings of the IEEE Real-Time Technology and Applications Symposium*, May 1995, Chicago (USA).

West, R. & Poellabauer, C. (2000). Analysis of a Window-constrained scheduler for real-time and best-effort packet streams, *Proceedings of the 21st IEEE Real-Time Systems Symposium*, December 2000, Orlando (USA).

West, R., Zhang, Y., Schwan, K. & Poellabauer, C. (2004). Dynamic window-constrained scheduling of real-time streams in media servers, *IEEE Transactions on Computers*, 53(6):744–759.

Zhang, Y., West, R. & Qi, X. (2004). A virtual deadline scheduler for window-constrained service guarantees, *Technical Report*, No. 2004-013, Boston University (USA).

Part 4

Real World Applications

10

Linearly Time Efficiency in Unattended Wireless Sensor Networks

Faezeh Sadat Babamir and Fattaneh Bayat Babolghani
Shahid Beheshti University of Tehran
Iran

1. Introduction

In the past decades, wireless Sensor Networks (WSNs) attracted many researchers. A lot of them considered important issues such as: routing, security, power awareness and data abstraction, But security is prior common assumption in the most of works. On the other hand, WSNs should collect small size and especially secure data in real-time manner. This problem is considered because sensor nodes are small, low power with low storage. Therefore, classical algorithms maybe inapplicable, i.e. considering constrained sensor, these algorithms cannot guarantee the security of data. The aforementioned problem is very critical in the new generation of WSNs referred to as Unattended or disconnected wireless sensor networks.

The disconnected networks are established in critical or military environments. Hence, sink or collector is unable to gather data in real-time manner. Moreover, the network will be leaved unattended and will be periodically visited. This property provides some threats such as discovering and compromising sensor nodes by adversary without detection. Moreover, adversary invisibly performs to be intractable and unpredictable. Also, some adversary is curious and aims just to disclose data, while some aims search data to replace them with forged. The third kind of network adversary whiles to inject invalid data to corrupt network called DoS attack or mislead sink. In such setting, the main challenge is assurance about data survival for long time.

In this research, we propose scheme that firstly shares generated data and encodes them to provide confidentiality and integrity. Moreover, utilizing efficient mathematical solution, every sensor with unique identification encodes shares, in which encoding process is one-way with initial boundary conditions. Then a linear signing algorithm applies to provide authentication and prevent DoS attack. In addition, in order to defend curious adversary, the signed generated data will be broadcasted to the neighbour sensors. Every neighbour uses network-encoding for received shares and homomorphic signs to remove previous signature and generate unique signature. This process decrease size of total received shares.

Organization: Section 2 reviews the related work of UWSNs. Section 3 sketches our proposed algorithm including applied network coding, homomorphic and mathematical solution. In section 4 we have demonstrated our scheme efficiency implemented by Maple. We have ended this chapter with conclusion section.

2. Related works

In this setting, the adversary may have different goals. Reactive adversary is the adversary who starts compromising sensors after he identifies the target. More exactly, such an adversary is inactive until it gets a signal that certain data must be erased, then it wakes up and starts compromising up to l sensors per round unlike the proactive adversary who can compromise sensors before identifying the target i.e. he essentially starts compromising sensors at round 1, *before* receiving any information about the target sensor and the target data collection round. He would choose and compromise different sensors in a geographic area even before such signal is received. This powerful adversary who usually referred to as mobile adversary can even roam around the network and change from one set of compromised nodes to another, making such attacks more difficult to delete and prevent.

Di Pietro et al. in [1] investigated the data survival for the first time. They proposed a straight-forward non-cryptographic technique to hide the sensed data from the adversary. In [1], the adversary was actively hunting data and was not afraid to delete/erase any data he found. They claimed that they could achieve surprising degree of data survival with respect to the time between successive sink visits but they considered small number of compromised sensors including k=2, 3, 5, 10 which make it non-realistic. So when l increases, the benefits of replication attack are magnified. Observing that the simple technique has certain basic limitations, they proposed a more advanced approach based on standard cryptographic tools. They discussed the effects of encryption and claimed that regardless of the encryption type, the adversary has equally diminished capacity to detect and erase target data as it inspects the memory of compromised nodes.

To defend reactive adversary, many papers have been proposed encryption based schemes. Encryption can be employed to hide the collected information as well as the identity of the sensors that collect it. If the key of compromised node is not available, the reactive adversary is unable to distinguish the specific piece of collected data but proactive adversary can restore the keys of the other earlier compromised nodes to memorize encrypted data. These keys help adversary to encrypt some forged data and place them with the target data. Therefore encryption is not enough to defend proactive adversary.

Mateus et al. in [2] evaluated proposed cryptographic based schemes on a real sensor platform. They measured some basic operation usage and presented results for encryption, super-encryption and key evolution which are feasible for protecting UWSNs against mobile adversary. Encryption is the central tool in the design of any symmetric scheme and is usually implemented by means of a block-cipher. Therefore, it becomes necessary to choose a suitable block-cipher for the development of secure and efficient schemes for super encryption.

Finally they calculated that if super-encryption is applied many rounds by different nodes, an adversary would have to make a great effort in order to find and destroy the targeted data. However the number of rounds and the payload size in super-encryption have significant impact over the performance of this technique. These disadvantages presented in figure 1 and table 1 in terms of time and energy consumption.

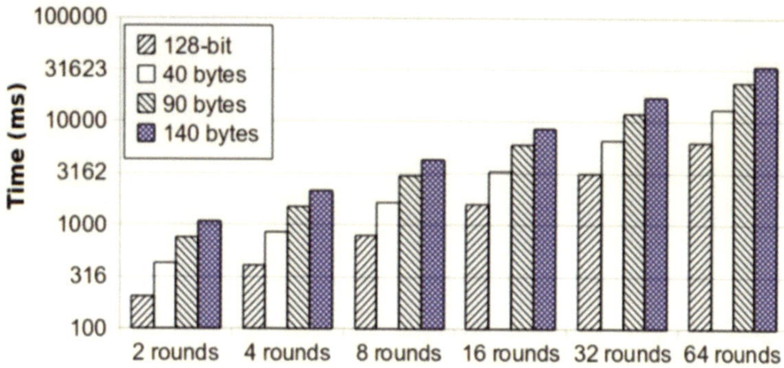

Fig. 1. Time costs for super-encryption (100 executions)

	Energy (mJ)
2 rounds	1.09 ± 0.04
4 rounds	2.21 ± 0.01
8rounds	4.45 ± 0.02

Table 1. Super-encryption energy consumption (100 executions)

[2] In order to implement and evaluate some key operations for re-encryption process, the code of the MIRACL library [3] is adapted. They measure inversion and exponentiation operations through the polynomial arithmetic which depend on the field chosen. The algorithm used for inversion is a polynomial version of the Extended Euclidian algorithm from Lim and Hwang [4]. They have chosen a general algorithm for exponentiation. Although the symmetric algorithms are not expensive, the re-encryption strategy is still the main alternative against proactive adversaries. Moreover, according to [2], the Elliptic Curve Cryptography (ECC) schemes show an important drawback of the re-encryption solutions,since the exponentiation is not as suitable as polynomial operations. Hence Public Key Cryptography (PKC) should be considered.

3. Proposed scheme

Ren et al. [5] prove that in order to achieve perfect security, data sharing between neighbours is suitable way. Therefore, in our scheme, sensor node collects data *data* and breaks it to equal shares $d_1, d_2..., d_n$. Using following process, the sensor sends signed encoded Y_i to the randomly selected neighbours.

3.1 Share generation, encoding, signing and broadcasting processes

After sensor v_i collects data *data*, it proceeds following steps to achieve data integrity, confidentiality and also authenticity.

1. Shares *data* into equal $d_1,d_2,...,d_n$.
2. Using our mathematical encoding solution (refer to section 3.5), the sensor encodes every d_i to Y_i.
3. Every Y_i will be signed by sensor $v_i(\delta_i)$.
4. Lastly, sensor v_i broadcasts every δ_i to the each neighbour.

Below we describe mathematically this algorithm. Set_i is the set of all neighbours of sensor i.

Alg. 1: Collecting and sending data(*data, set_i*)

{

Shares data into $d_1,d_2,..,d_n$.

Encode d_i by $Y_i=f(d_i)$.

Sign e_i by $\delta_i=Sig\ (Y_i)$

Obtain $pk_i=\{Y_i \,||\, \delta_i \,||\, t \,||\, TS \,||\, CNT\}$

Broadcast every pk_i to every neighbour sensor belong to set_i.

}

3.2 β-bounded moving(adapted [5])

Every signed Y_i should disperse enough to defend against mobile adversary. To determine β value, *DLE* variable is defined to determine the entropy of data d_i location entropy. This concept makes trade-off between hops steps and energy communication. Moreover, more β consumes much energy communication but makes higher security against mobile adversary. *DLE* helps us to determine suitable value.

Finally, $pk_i = \{Y_i \,||\, \delta_i \,||\, t \,||\, TS \,||\, CNT\}$ is output of sensor v_i to another neighbour, e.g. v_j in which Y_i, δ_i, t, CNT are encoding vector of data share, signature of Y_i, sequence order of d_t and $CNT=\beta$ respectively. Also, TS is time stamp of producing time. We define tuple $UID=\{TS \,||\, t\}$, that can uniquely identify a share.

3.3 Network coding

In this paper, we use two kinds of sensors that were called source sensor and forwarder sensor; source sensor should collect data and broadcast them, while forwarder sensor receives the data packets from other sensors and then transforms theses data packets into one packet; Moreover, since communications consume more energy than computation, forwarding nodes probability encode received packets into one using network coding solution. Clearly, network coding technique increases overall computation energy instead it significantly decreases communication consumption. Finally the forwarding sensor signs the packet through homomorphic signature (refer to section 3.4).

3.3.1 Basic setting

In this setting, we show the network with $G=(V,E)$. Source nodes and forwarding nodes are $S = \{s_1, s_2, \dots, s_N\} \subseteq V$ and $f = \{f_1, f_2, \dots, f_L\} \subseteq V$ respectively. The inputs of forwarding nodes are $Y_i, i \epsilon [1,p]$ of pk_i and output packets are Z_j, $j \epsilon [1,q]$. Source nodes (s_i) propagate packets pk_i to the forwarding nodes. Each forwarding sensor, after receiving Y_i of pk_i from p incoming channels, computes following linear combination Y_j to transmit it to the j-the channel. The linear combination formula is:

$$Z_j = \sum_{i=1}^{p} (\alpha_i)(Y_i) \tag{1}$$

In formula (1), $\alpha = (\alpha_1, \alpha_2, \dots, \alpha_p)$ is encoding vector. The node randomly generates α or α is pre-deployed, (depend on static network topology). It is proven that random coefficient optimises network performance with high probability because of independency of network topology.

3.3.2 Random linear network coding algorithm

In proposed scheme, every forwarding node receives some Y_is $i\epsilon[1,p]$and encodes them via network coding with probability p_{nc}. Finally, it sends one packet contained p encoded vectors. For simplicity, we let pre-deployed encoding vector (α). Consider, Alg. 1, for encoding p packets. The final outputs are encoded vectors Z_j and the same inputs.

$$\begin{pmatrix} \alpha_{11} & \alpha_{12} & \cdots & \alpha_{1p} \\ \vdots & \cdots & \cdots & \vdots \\ \alpha_{i1} & \alpha_{i2} & \cdots & \alpha_{ip} \\ \vdots & \cdots & \cdots & \vdots \\ \alpha_{j1} & \alpha_{j2} & \cdots & \alpha_{jp} \end{pmatrix} \begin{pmatrix} Y_1 \\ \vdots \\ Y_i \\ \vdots \\ Y_p \end{pmatrix} = \begin{pmatrix} Z_1 \\ Y_2 \\ \vdots \\ Y_{p-1} \\ Z_j \end{pmatrix}$$

Fig. 2. Encoder Matrix

Our scheme is able to reconstruct thoroughly the primary data from all received packets. Moreover, by using aforementioned equation $data_i$ will be recovered in polynomial time (adapted [5]). In section 3.5, we propose a new algebraic algorithm to easily encoding shares with *time efficiency*. This innovation solution is considerable either for sink or forwarding nodes, i.e. our scheme either in node side or in sink side is efficiently ran.

3.4 Applied linear homomorphic signature over $\mathcal{F}_2$

In this paper, we utilize Boneh et al. scheme which is inspired by Gentry, Peikert and Vaikuntanathan [6] defined linearly over binary field [7]. This signature is a short vector $\delta\epsilon Z^m$in $\Lambda_{2q}^{q.v}(\Delta)$, i.e. δ is in both $\Lambda_q^{\perp}(\Delta)$ and $\Lambda_2^{v}(\Delta)$ simoltaneusly. Mod 2 relates the signature to the message while mod q is designed to prove unforgeability of the scheme. This Δ is different for signing every packet.

The source sensor signs every Y_i using its identity based private key and then sends (Y_i, δ_i) to the forwarding neighbour node. Forwarding node receives Y_is along with their signatures.

Firstly, it checks the validity of signature. If it is not valid, forwarding sensor removes it as bogus data. Receiving enough valid data, forwarding sensor re-encodes them to the e' and generates a homomorphic signature from share signatures without knowing the original messages (d_i) or the private key of source nodes. The detail of scheme is as follow:

3.4.1 Parameter setup phase

Following, we define parameters that used in [7] to describe applied signature. Λ is an m-dimensional lattice whose points are defined on $\mathbb{Z}^m$. Also, Λ is a full-rank discrete subgroup of $\mathbb{R}^m$ and consist of vectors either generated by or orthogonal to a certain "parity check matrix" $\Delta \epsilon \mathbb{Z}_q^{m\times n}$ modular integer q. The utilized lattices are defined:

$$\Lambda_q^{\perp}(\Delta) = \{e\epsilon\mathbb{Z}^m : \Delta.e = 0 \; mod \; q\} \quad (2)$$

$$\Lambda_q^{u}(\Delta) = \{e\epsilon\mathbb{Z}^m : \Delta.e = u \; mod \; q\} \quad (3)$$

$$\Lambda_q(\Delta) = \{e\epsilon\mathbb{Z}^m \; : \; \exists s\epsilon\mathbb{Z}_q^n \; with \; \Delta^t.s = e \; mod \; q\}$$

In formula (3), $\Lambda_q^u(\Delta)$is a coset of lattice $\Lambda_q^\perp(\Delta)$ of formula (2) such that $\Lambda_q^u(\Delta) = \Lambda_q^\perp(\Delta) + t$ in which t holds in $\Delta . t = u \bmod q$.

3.4.2 Signature scheme

Firstly, we describe following functions that used in the Boneh et al. scheme:

TrapGen(q, n): this algorithm receives an integer q and n holds in $m = [6nlgq]$. Also this algorithm outputs $(\Delta \epsilon \mathbb{Z}_q^{n\times m}, S \epsilon \mathbb{Z}^{m\times m})$, where Δ is statistically close to a uniform matrix in $\mathbb{Z}_q^{n\times m}$ and S is a basis for $\Lambda_q^\perp$.

ExtBasis(S, B): let m' be an arbitrary dimension. This algorithm gets $(S, B = \Delta \| \Delta')$ where $\Delta' \epsilon \mathbb{Z}_q^{n\times m'}$and $S \epsilon \mathbb{Z}^{m\times m}$be an arbitrary basis of $\Lambda^\perp(\Delta)$ for a rank n matrix $\Delta \epsilon \mathbb{Z}_q^{n\times m}$that outputs a basis T of $\Lambda^\perp(B) \subset \mathbb{Z}^{(m+m')\times(m+m')}$.

SamplePre(Δ, T, u, δ): this algorithm inputs matrix $\Delta \epsilon \mathbb{Z}_q^{n\times m}$, a basis T of $\Lambda_q^\perp(\Delta)$, a parameter δ and a vector $u \epsilon \mathbb{Z}^n$. Then outputs a sample which is statistically close to the distribution of $\mathfrak{D}_{\Lambda_q^u, \delta}$.

- Signing algorithm

1- Choose a $id \overset{R}{\leftarrow} \{0,1\}^n$ randomly. If id has already been queried to the hash function H, then abort. (The simulation has failed).

a. Setup(1^n; k)

On input of a security parameter n and a maximum data set size k, do the following:

1. Choose two primes p, q = poly(n)with q ≥ $(nkp)^2$. Define l :=[n/6 log q].
2. Set $\Lambda_1 := pZ^n$.
3. Use TrapGen(q;l; n) to generate a matrix $\Delta \epsilon F_q^{l\times n}$along with a short basis T_q of $\Lambda_q^\perp(\Delta)$. Define$\Lambda_2 = \Lambda_q^\perp(\Delta)$and $T := p.T_q$. Note that T is a basis of $\Lambda_1 \cap \Lambda_2 = p\Lambda_2$.
4. Set $v := p.\sqrt{n.logq}.logn$.
5. Let $H: \{0,1\}^* \rightarrow F_q^l$be a hash function (modeled as a random oracle).
6. Output the public key $pkey = (\Lambda_1, \Lambda_2, v, k, H)$and the secret key $skey$= T.

The public key $pkey$ defines the following system parameters:

- The message space is $F_p^n$and signatures are short vectors in Z^n.
- The set of admissible functions F is all F_p-linear functions on k-tuples of messages inF_p^n.
- For a function $f \epsilon F$defined by $f(m_1, \ldots, m_k) = \sum_{i=1}^k c_i m_i$, we encode f by interpreting the c_i as integers in (-p/2, p/2].

b. Sign($\boldsymbol{skey}, \boldsymbol{\tau}, \boldsymbol{m}, \boldsymbol{i}$)

On input of a secret key $skey$, a tag$\tau \epsilon \{0,1\}^n$, a packet$pkey \epsilon F_p^n$and an index i, do:

1. Compute $\alpha_i = H(\tau || i) \in F_q^l$.
2. Compute $t \in Z^n$such that $t$mod p = $pkey$and $\Delta . t$ mod q $= \alpha_i$.
3. Output $\sigma \leftarrow \mathrm{SamplePre}(\Lambda_1 \Lambda_2, \mathrm{T}, \mathrm{t}, \mathrm{v}) \in (\Lambda_1 \Lambda_2) + \mathrm{t}$.

c. Verify$(\boldsymbol{pk}, \boldsymbol{\tau}, \boldsymbol{pk}, \boldsymbol{\sigma}, \boldsymbol{f})$

On input of a public key *pkey*, a tag$\tau \in \{0,1\}^*$,a message $m \in F_p^n$, a signature$\sigma \in Z^n$and a function$f \in F$, do:

1. If all of the following conditions hold, output 1 (accept); otherwise output 0 (reject):

a. $||\sigma|| \leq k.\frac{p}{2}.v\sqrt{n}$
b. σ mod p = pkey.

Evaluate($pkey, \tau, f, \vec{\sigma}$). On input a public key *pkey*, a tag $\tau \in \{0,1\}^*$, a function $f \in F$ encoded as< f >= $(c_1, \dots, c_k) \in Z^k$and a tuple of signatures$(\sigma_1, \dots, \sigma_k) \in Z^k$, output $\sigma = \sum_{i=1}^{k} c_i\, \sigma_i$.

After sink receives all signed encoded shares, it verifies the homographic signature and decodes them to reconstruct *data*.

In this signing algorithm, we apply linear signing and efficient encoding algorithms. More exactly, we firstly encode d_i into Y_i included in pk_i= $\{Y_i || \delta_i || t || TS || CNT\}$by proposed mathematic function. This encoding solution prevents adversary to read data because our mathematical encoding solution (equation 4) is a differential equation and insolvable without knowing boundary conditions. Boundary conditions are initial values of the equation 4 which is available for either sender or receiver. We discuss about our mathematical technique in following section.

3.5 Mathematical encoding solution

In this section, we used the Ordinary Differential Equation(denoted as ODE) for encoding the data shares. This ODE is solvable (or received data is decodable) just with presence of boundry conditions. Moreover, we solve this equation by modified generalized Laguerre which is orthogonal function. The utilization of colocation method reduces the solution of our problem to the solution of algebratic equation. Applying our technique, we show that the encoding process is time efficient, more accurate and converges faster.

We basicallywork on an equation of flow and diffusion of chemical reactive species over a nonlinearly stretching sheet problem. this non-linear ordinary differential equation is [8-23, 35]:

$$f'''(d_i) + f(d_i)f''(d_i) - \left(f'(d_i)\right)^2 - idf'(d_i) = 0 \tag{4}$$

Subject to boundary conditions,

$$f(0) = 0, f'(0) = 1, f'(\infty) = 0, \tag{5}$$

Where *id* is identification of every sensor and $d_1, d_2, .., d_n$ are data shares. Considering unique *id* for every sensor, the equation 4 releases new equation which is unique for every sensor. Moreover, all of equation replaced in sensors, are different as well as the whole equations are hard to invert. These issues gurantee the security against curious adversary.

Different techniques have been used to obtain analytical and numerical solutions for this problem. Raptis and Perdikis [13] used the shooting method for this problem. Kechil and

Hashim [15] obtained approximate analytical solution via Adomian decomposition method. Recently, in [16] and [14] the homotopy analysis method was also applied for solving the above equation [14].

3.5.1 Modified generalized Laguerre functions

This section is devoted to the introduction of the basic notions and working tools concerning orthogonal modified generalized Laguerre. It has been widely used for numerical solutions of differential equations on infinite intervals. $L_n^a(x)$

$L_n^a(x)$ (generalized Laguerre polynomial) is the n-th eigenfunction of the Sturm-Liouville problem [24-27]:

$$x\frac{d^2}{dx^2}L_n^a(x) + (\alpha + 1 - x)\frac{d}{dx}L_n^a(x) + nL_n^a(x) = 0,$$

$$x \in I = [0, \infty), n = 0, 1, 2, \ldots. \tag{6}$$

The generalized Laguerre in polynomial manner are defined with the following recurrence formula:

$$L_0^a(x) = 1, \tag{7}$$

$$L_1^a(x) = 1 + \alpha - x,$$

$$nL_n^a(x) = (2n - 1 + \alpha - x)L_{n-1}^a(x) - (n + \alpha - 1)L_{n-2}^a(x),$$

These are orthogonal polynomials for the weight function $w_\alpha = x^\alpha e^{-x}$. We define Modified generalized Laguerre functions (which we denote MGLF) ϕ_j as follows [24]:

$$\phi_j(x) = \exp\left(\frac{-x}{2L}\right) L_j^1\left(\frac{x}{L}\right), L > 0. \tag{8}$$

This system is an orthogonal basis [35, 36] with weight function $w(x) = \frac{x}{L}$and orthogonality property [24]:

$$\langle\phi_m, \phi_n\rangle_{w_L} = \left(\frac{\Gamma(n+2)}{L^2 n!}\right)\delta_{nm}, \tag{9}$$

where δ_{nm} is the Kronecker function.

3.5.2 Function approximation with Laguerre functions

A function $f(x)$ defined over the interval $I = [0, \infty)$ can be expanded as:

$$f(x) = \sum_{i=0}^{+\infty} a_i\phi_i(x), \tag{10}$$

Where

$$a_i = \frac{\langle f, \phi_i\rangle_w}{\langle\phi_i, \phi_i\rangle_w}. \tag{11}$$

If the infinite series in Eq. (10) is truncated with N terms, then it can be written as [24].

$$f(x) \simeq \sum_{i=0}^{N-1} a_i \phi_i(x) = A^T \phi(x), \tag{12}$$

with

$$A = [a_0, a_1, a_2, \ldots, a_{N-1}]^T, \tag{13}$$

$$\phi(x) = [\phi_0(x), \phi_1(x), \ldots, \phi_{N-1}(x)]^T. \tag{14}$$

3.5.3 Modified generalized Laguerre functions collocation method

Laguerre-Gauss-Radau points and generalized Laguerre-Gauss-type interpolation were introduced by [24, 28-30].

Let:

$$\Re_N = Span\{1, x, \ldots\ldots, x^{2N-1}\} \tag{15}$$

we choose the collocation points relative to the zeroes of the functions [24].

$$p_j(x) = \phi_j(x) - (\tfrac{j+1}{j})\phi_{j-1}(x). \tag{16}$$

Let$w(x) = \frac{x}{L}$ and $x_j, j = 0, 1, \ldots, N-1$, be the N MGLF-Radau points. The relation between MGLF orthogonal systems and MGLF integrations is as follows [24, 31]:

$$\int_0^{+\infty} f(x)w(x)dx = \sum_{j=0}^{N-1} f_j(x)w_j + \left(\frac{\Gamma(N+2)}{(N)!(2N)!}\right) f^{2N}(\xi)e^{\xi}, \tag{17}$$

where $0 < \xi < \infty$ and

$$w_j = x_j \frac{\Gamma(N+2)}{(L(N+1)!\,[(N+1)\phi_{N+1}(x_j)]^2)}, j = 0, 1, 2, \ldots, N-1.$$

In particular, the second term on the right-hand side vanishes when $f(x)$ is a polynomial of degree at most $2N-1$ [24]. We define:

$$I_N u(x) = \sum_{j=0}^{N-1} a_j \phi_j(x), \tag{18}$$

Such that:

$$I_N u(x_j) = u(x_j), j = 0, 1, 2, \ldots, N-1.$$

$I_N u$ is the orthogonal projection of u upon $\Re_N$ with respect to the discrete inner product and discrete norm as [24]:

$$< u, v >_{w,N} = \sum_{j=0}^{N-1} u(x_j)v(x_j)w_j, \tag{19}$$

$$||u||_{w,N} = < u, v >_{w,N}^{1/2} \tag{20}$$

thus for the MGLF Gauss-Radau interpolation we have:

$$< I_N u, v >_{w,N} = < u, v >_{w,N} \ \forall u.v \epsilon \Re_N$$

$$< I_N u, v >_{w,N} = < u, v > \tag{21}$$

3.5.4 Solving the problem with modified generalized Laguerre functions

To apply modified generalized Laguerre collocation method to Eq. (24) with boundary conditions Eq. (5), at first we expand$f(d_i)$ as follows:

$$I_N f(d_i) = \sum_{j=0}^{N-1} a_j \phi_j, \tag{22}$$

To find the unknown coefficients a_j's, we substitute the truncated series $f(d_i)$ into Eq. (24) and boundary conditions in Eq. (5). Also, we define Residual function of the form:

$$Res(d_i) = \sum_{j=0}^{N-1} a_j \phi_j'''(d_i) + \sum_{j=0}^{N-1} a_j \phi_j(d_i) \sum_{j=0}^{N-1} a_j \phi_j''(d_i) - \left(\sum_{j=0}^{N-1} a_j \phi_j'(d_i)\right)^2 - id \sum_{j=0}^{N-1} a_j \phi_j'(d_i) \tag{23}$$

$$\sum_{j=0}^{N-1} a_j \phi_j(0) = 0, \tag{24}$$

$$\sum_{j=0}^{N-1} a_j \phi_j'(0) = 1, \tag{25}$$

$$\sum_{j=0}^{N-1} a_j \phi_j(\infty) = 0. \tag{26}$$

Applying d_i in Eq. (23) with the N collocation points which are roots of functions L_n^a , we have N equations that generate a set of N non-linear equations; also, we have one boundary equation in Eq. (24-25). Now, all of these equations can be solved by Newton method for the unknown coefficients. We must mention Eq. (26) is always true; therefore, we do not need to apply this boundary condition.

Here we note that the Eq.(24) subject to boundary conditions Eq.(5) has an exact solution [35] as:

$$f(d_i) = \frac{1}{\sqrt{1+id}}(1 - e^{-\sqrt{1+(id)d_i}}) \tag{27}$$

While in the absence of the magnetic field where *id =0* , the exact solution first obtained by Crane [16] is

$$f(d_i) = 1 - e^{-d_i}. \tag{28}$$

The absolute error between MGLFMs solution and exact solution of the velocity profile $f(d_i)$ for $id = 0.6$ is shown in Figure 2.

4. Performance analysis

This approach is based on the modified generalized Laguerre which is an orthogonal function that solves the non-linear differential equation governing the problem on the semi-infinite domain without truncating it to a finite domain. Modified generalized Laguerre function was proposed to provide simple way to improve the convergence of the solution through collocation method by $N = 20$, $\alpha = 1$and $L = 0.99$. The absolute error between MGLFMs solution and exact solution of the velocity profile $f(d_i)$for $id = 0.6$ is shown in Figure 2. This Figure shows more accurate manner and convergencesfaster.

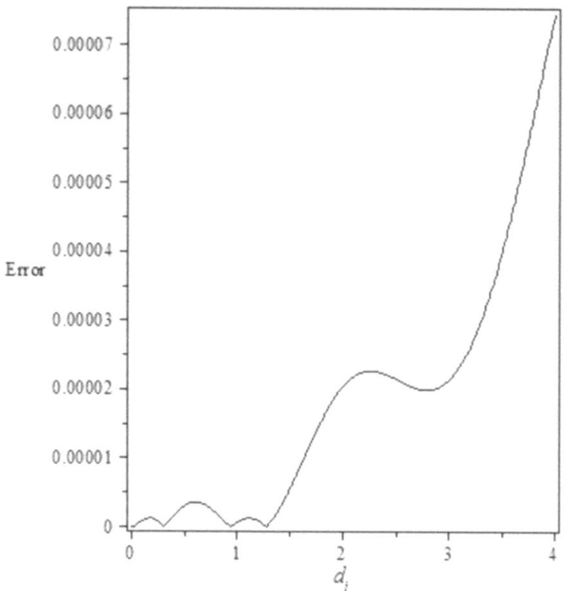

Fig. 2. Graph of Error by MGLFMs solution for id=0.6

In addition, The codes of MAPLE software of this implementation are mentioned in Appendix A. This implementation was executing in a computer whose information was:

- Windows Seven
- Proccesor: Intel(R) Core(TM) i3 CPU 2.53 GHz
- RAM: 4.00 GB
- System type: 32-bit Operating System

In this condition, the time of solution was reported 3.96s which is more efficient than other solutions. Also, solving this problem is not possible without boundary conditions; therefore, only the owner of these boundary conditions can solve this in efficient time.

5. Conclusion

In this paper, we proposed an efficient scheme including special technique to defend adversary against curious, search-replace and injection attacks. Actually, we shared data (defence against curious attack) and code them using a mathematical function (defence against search and replace), and efficiently sign every unit of data to prevent injection attack. Mathematical function is designed for initializing with the sensor properties such as id. Therefore, we use one-to-one function that hold in equation 4.

Moreover, based on this equation and boundary conditions, a new function for every sensor is released. This equation is general as well as the adversary knows this equation but the calculated function is hard to obtain without knowing boundary condition. Hence, variable encoded packet of every function detects no information about the original data. This technique is firm against injection attack which is the most rampant attack in general unattended wireless sensor network. Totally, we can claim that, our work is applicable and secure against various attacks.

6. Appendix A

```
>restart :
>with(orthopoly) : with(LinearAlgebra) :
>with(student) :
>with(plots) :
>n := scanf(`%d`)[1] :
>id := 0.6 : l := 0.99 :
>y := [evalf(solve(L(n, 1, x/l), x))] :
>
 E := 0 :
 for i from 0 to n - 1do
    E := E + a[i]*(exp(-x/(2·l))·L(i, 1, x/l)) :
 end do:
 E :
>dE := diff(E, x) :
>ddE := diff(E, x, x) :
>dddE := diff(E, x, x, x) :
>Eq := dddE + E·ddE - (dE)^2 - id·(dE) :
>for i from 1 to n do A[i] := eval(Eq, x = y[i]) = 0;  end do:
>A[n - 1] := eval(E, x = 0) = 0 :
>A[n] := eval(dE, x = 0) = 1 :
>X := fsolve({seq(A[m], m = 1 .. n)}, {seq(a[i] = 0, i = 0 .. n - 1)}) :
>c1 := array(0 ..n - 1) :
>for i from 0 to n - 1 do c1[i] := subs(X, a[i]); od:
>fu := sum(c1[u]*exp(-x/(2·l))·L(u, 1, x/l), u = 0 .. n - 1) :
>dfu := diff(fu, x) :
>ddfu := diff(fu, x, x) :
>subs(x = 0, ddfu); dddfu := diff(fu, x, x, x) :
>plot(fu, x = 0 .. 5)
>plot(ddfu, x = 0 .. 5)  :
>evalf(eval(ddfu, x = 0)) :
>m := abs(fu - 1/sqrt(1 + id)·(1 - e^(-sqrt(1 + id)·x))) :
>plot(m, x = 0 ..4) ;
>fu :
>Eq1 := (dddfu) + (fu)·(ddfu) - (dfu)^2 - id·(dfu) :
> evalf(int((Eq1)^2, x = 0 ..10)) :
>∫_0^10 (Eq1)^2 dx :
```

7. References

[1] Pietro, R.D. Mancini, L.V. Spognardi, A. Soriente, C. Tsudik, G.: Catch me (if you can): Data survival in unattended sensor networks. IEEE international conference on pervasive computing and communications (PerCom). China. 185-194 (2008)

[2] Mateus, A. S. S. Margi, C. B. Simplicio, M. A. Geovandro, C. C. F. P. de Oliveira, B. T. : Implementation of data survival in unattended wireless sensor network using cryptography. IEEE conference on Local Computer Networks (LCN). USA. 961-967 (2010)

[3] MIRACL Big Integer Library, http://www.shamus.ie/(2009)

[4] Lim, C. H. Hwang, H. S.: Fast implementation of elliptic curve algorithm in GF(p^n). in public key cryptography series, lecture notes in computer science. springer. 1751. 405-421 (2000)

[5] Ren, W., Zhao, J., Ren, Y.: network coding based dependable and efficient data survival in unattended wireless sensor networks. Journal of Communications. 4, NO. 11,894-901 (2009)

[6] Gentry, C., Peikert, C., Vaikuntanathan, V.: trapdoors for hard lattices and new cryptography constructions: In STOC, ed. R. E. Ladner and C. Dwork, ACM, 197-206(2008)

[7] Boneh, D., Freeman, D. M.: linearly homomorphic signature over binary fields and new tools for lattice-based signatures. In Proceeding of PKC'11, LNCS 6571. 1-16

[8] Sakiadis, B. C.: Boundary-layer behaviour on continuous solid surfaces: I. boundary-layer equations for two-dimensional and axisymmetric Flow. AIChE J. 7, 26-28 (1961)

[9] Sakiadis, B. C.: Boundary-layer behaviour on continuous solid surfaces: II. boundary-layer equations for two-dimensional and axisymmetric flow. AIChE J. 7, 221-225 (1961)

[10] Crane, L. J.: Flow past a stretching plate. Z. Angew. Math. Phys. 21, 645-647 (1970)

[11] Andersson, H. I., Hansen, O. R., Holmedal, B.: Diffusion of a chemically reactive species from a stretching sheet. Int. J. Heat Mass Trans. 37, 659-664 (1994)

[12] Thakar, H. S., Chamkha, A. J., Nath, G.: Flow and mass transfer on a stretching sheet with a magnetic filed and chemically reactive species. Int. J. Eng. Sci. 38, 1303-1314 (2000)

[13] Raptis, A., Perdikis, C.: Viscous flow over a non-linearly stretching sheet in the presence of a chemical reaction and magnetic field. Int. J. Nonlinear. Mech. 41, 527-529 (2006)

[14] Rajagopal, K., Veena, P. H., Pravin, V. K.: Nonsimilar solutions for heat and mass transfer flow in an electrically conducting viscoelastic fluid over a stretching sheet saturated in a porous medium with suction/blowing. J. Porous Media. 11, 219-230 (2008)

[15] Bejan, A.: Convection heat transfer. Wiley-Interscience, New York, USA (1984)

[16] Akyildiz, F. T., Bellout, H., Vajravelu, K.: Diffusion of chemically reactive species in a porous medium over a stretching sheet. J. Math. Anal. Appl. 320, 322-339 (2006)

[17] Cortell, R.: MHD flow and mass transfer of an electrically conducting fluid of second grade in a porous medium over a stretching sheet with chemically reactive species. Chem. Eng. Process. 46, 721-728 (2007)

[18] Cortell, R.: Toward an understanding of the motion and mass transfer with chemically reactive species for two classes of viscoelastic fluid over a porous stretching sheet. Chim. Eng. Process. 46, 982-989 (2007)

[19] Prasad, K. V., Abel, M. S., Khan, S. K., Datti, P. S.: Non-darcy forced convective heat transfer in a viscoelastic fluid flow over a non-isothermal stretching sheet. J. Porous Media. 5, 41-47 (2002)
[20] Prasad, K. V., Abel, M. S., Datti, P. S.: Diffusion of chemically reactive species of a non-newtonian fluid immersed in a porous medium over a stretching sheet. Int. J. Non-Linear Mech. 38, 651-657 (2003)
[21] Ziabakhsh, Z., Domairry, G., Bararnia, H., Babazadeh, H.: Analytical solution of flow and diffusion of chemically reactive species over a nonlinearly stretching sheet immersed in a porous medium. J. Taiwan Inst. Chem. Eng. 41, 22-28 (2010)
[22] Kechil, S. A., Hashim, I.: Series solution of flow over nonlinearly stretching sheet with chemical reaction and magnetic fleld. Phy. Lett. A 372, 2258-2263 (2008)
[23] Dinarvand, S.: A reliable treatment of the homotopy analysis method for viscous flow over a non-linearly stretching sheet in presence of a chemical reaction and under influence of a magnetic fleld. Cent. Eur. J. Phys. 7, 114-122 (2009)
[24] Parand, K., Taghavi, A.: Rational scaled generalized Laguerre function collocation method for solving the Blasius equation. J. Comput. Appl. Math. 233, 980-989 (2009)
[25] Parand, K., Taghavi, A., Shahini, M.: Comparison between rational Chebyshev and modified generalized Laguerre functions Pseudospectral methods for solving Lane-emden and unsteady gas equentions. Acta Physica Polonica B. 40, 1749-1763 (2009)
[26] Coulaud, O., Funaro, D., Kavian, O.: Laguerre spectral approximation of elliptic problems in exterior domains. Comput. Method. Appl. Mech. Eng. 80, 451-458 (1990)
[27] Guo, B. Y., Shen, J., Xu, C. L.: Generalized Laguerre approximation and its applications to exterior problems. J. Comput. Math. 23, 113-130 (2005)
[28] Zhang, R., Wang, Z. Q., Guo, B. Y.: Mixed Fourier-Laguerre spectral and Pseudospectral methods for exterior problems using generalized Laguerre functions. J. Sci. Comput. 36, 263-283 (2008)
[29] Wang, Z. Q., Guo, B. Y., Wu, Y. N.: Pseudospectral method using generalized Laguerre functions for singular problems on unbounded domains. discret. contin. dyn. s. 11, 1019-1038 (2009)
[30] Iranzo, V., Falqus, A.: Some spectral approximations for differential equations in unbounded domains. Comput. Methods Appl. Mech. Engrg. 98, 105-126 (1992)
[31] Szeg, G.: Orthogonal polynomils. AMS, New York, (1939)
[32] Parand, K., Dehghan, M., Taghavi, A.: Modified generalized Laguerre function Tau method for solving laminar viscous flow: The Blasius equation. Int. J. Numer. Meth. Heat Fluid Flow. 20, 728-743 (2010)
[33] Parand, K., Shahini, M., Dehghan, M.: Rational Legendre Pseudospectral approach for solving nonlinear difierential equations of Lane-Emden type. J. Comput. Phys. 228, 8830-8840 (2009)
[34] Rajagopal, K., Tao, L.: Mechanics of mixture. World Scientific, Singapore, (1995)
[35] Gasper, G. Stempak, K., Trembels, W.: Fractional integration for Laguerre expansions. J. Math. Appl. Anal. 67, 67-75 (1995)
[36] Taseli, H.: On the exact solution of the Schrodinger equation with quartic anharmonicity. Int. J. Quantom. Chem. 63, 63-71 (1996)

11

Real-Time Algorithms of Object Detection Using Classifiers

Roman Juránek, Pavel Zemčík and Michal Hradiš
Graph@FIT
Faculty of Information Technology, Brno University of Technology
Czech Republic

1. Introduction

Object detection, or more generally pattern detection and recognition, can be based on many different principles. The objects can be described through their structure, shape, color, texture, etc. [Blaschko & Lampert (2009); Chen et al. (2004); Fidler & Leonardis (2007); Leibe et al. (2008); Lowe (1999); Serre et al. (2005); Viola & Jones (2001)]; therefore, a variety of object detection mechanisms was developed over time. One of the modern approaches to object detection is similarity-based detection where the objects of interest are defined through a set of examples and typically also through a set of counter-examples and the decision whether an object is an object of interest is done through machine learning-based functional block – classifier. The object detection in an image is performed by the application of the classifier on sub-windows of the image.

The focus in this chapter is on statistical binary classifiers whose function is to make a binary decision on whether an image region is or is not an object of interest. The methods of interest include mainly AdaBoost [Freund (1995); Schapire et al. (1998)] whose original purpose was to fuse a small number of relatively well working so-called *weak hypotheses* into one, better working, *strong classifier*. This approach was further developed into an approach, which instead of a small number of weak classifiers, took into account a large number of simple functions and selected suitable weak classifiers automatically from these functions. This method has been demonstrated in the pioneer work of Viola and Jones [Viola & Jones (2001)].

The AdaBoost approach has been further refined and modified [Bourdev & Brandt (2005); Li et al. (2002); Sochman & Matas (2004; 2005)]. Perhaps the most important modification was by Sochman & Matas (2005), called WaldBoost which was based on Wald's sequential decision making [Wald (1947)] combined with AdaBoost. The main advantage of WaldBoost is its significant performance gain comparing it to the AdaBoost classifiers with virtually no change in classification quality.

The detection through classification involves the application of the classifier on a selection of sub-images of the analyzed image. As the classification results of neighboring sub-images may be statistically significantly interdependent, it is worth studying whether the inter-dependencies can be exploited to reduce the computational effort through the prediction of classifier results in certain sub-images, through suppression of unwanted object detection

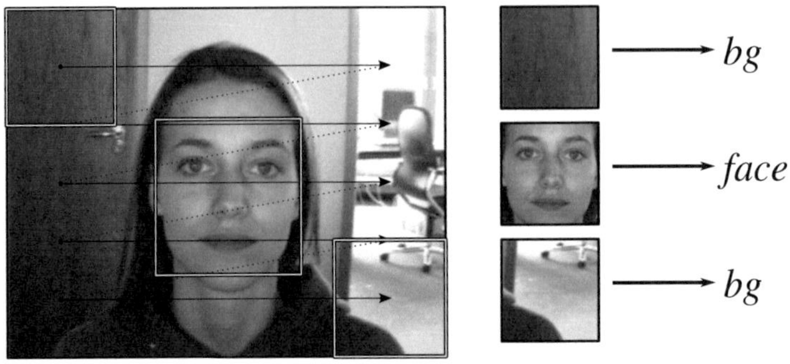

Fig. 1. Scanning the image with a classifier. Individual sub-images of the image are classified by a classifier (Image source: BioID dataset).

(e.g. multiple detections in very close image locations), or simply through the sharing of intermediate results of the calculations. These aspects of object detection are addressed in this chapter as well.

The structure of the chapter is as follows. The next section gives a brief introduction to object detection with classifiers. Section 3 discusses properties of features extracted from image and describes feature types often used for rapid object detection. Section 4 describes the ideas behind AdaBoost and WaldBoost learning procedures. Acceleration methods for WaldBoost-based detection are introduced in Section 5. Implementation of the detection runtime on different platforms is discussed in Section 6. Some results of the detection acceleration are presented in Section 7, and finally we conclude in Section 8 with some ideas for future research.

2. Object detection with classifiers

Classifiers are suitable for making the decision, whether some sub-images are images of object of interest or not. Such functionality is obviously of interest for object detection but it is not sufficient on its own. The reason is that for reliable classification, variability of objects of interest has to be minimized - the classifiers are trained to detect well-aligned, centered and size-normalized objects in the classified sub-image. Therefore, the actual detection of objects is performed through a classification of contents of all the sub-windows that can contain the object of interest, or simply through classification of all the possible sub-windows. This is usually performed by *scanning* the image with a moving window of a fixed size where the content of the window is classified for each location and, if the object of interest is found, the location is considered the output of the detection process.

The above described approach involves, in fact, an exhaustive search for an object of interest in the image, where all the sub-images are classified in order to understand whether they contain an object of interest or not. While the classification process is in general quite simple (as shown in more detail below), sometimes it might be feasible to pre-process the analyzed image in order to identify the image parts where the object(s) of interest cannot be present; such parts of the image can be excluded from the classification process and the computational effort can be reduced. Good examples of such approach are color-based pre-processing, where e.g. a flower cannot be present in a part of the image that contains "completely blue sky"; or a human face cannot be found in a part of an image that does not contain "skin color"; or geometry-based approaches where it cannot be expected that an airplane would be detected below walking people in the image.

As it is obvious from the above description, detection of objects through AdaBoost/WaldBoost methods is dependent on object orientation and size; however, in many applications it is desirable to detect objects regardless of their size or orientation. While this requirement is difficult or often impossible to handle directly in the AdaBoost/WaldBoost machine learning process, the feasible approach is to handle it indirectly through repeating the detection process for different scales and/or orientations. The main reason is that in general, the feature extraction methods (weak classifiers) are not rotation, scale or shift invariant. Therefore, the detection process should be applied repeatedly to *sample* the rotation, scale, etc. in the needed range. The density of image sampling is dependent on the tolerance of the classifier to rotation, scale, etc. The tolerance is in general not predictable and depends on the dataset.

3. Efficient feature extraction

The performance of the object detection is for the large part influenced by underlying feature extraction methods. Two main properties of features extracted from an image exist: *a)* descriptive power and *b)* computational complexity. The goal in rapid object detection is to use computationally simple and, at the same time, descriptive features. In the vast majority of cases, these two properties are mutually exclusive and thus there are computationally simple features with low descriptive power (e.g. isolated pixels, sums of area intensity) or complex and hard to compute features with high descriptive power (Gabor wavelets [Lee (1996)], HoG [Dalal & Triggs (2005)], SIFT and SURF [Bay et al. (2008); Lowe (2004)], etc.). A close to ideal approach is Viola and Jones [Viola & Jones (2001)] with their Haar features calculated in constant time from an integral representation of image. The features used in this chapter are Local Binary Patterns (LBP) [Zhang et al. (2007)], Local Rank Patterns (LRP) [Hradiš et al. (2008)] and Local Rank Differences (LRD) [Zemcik et al. (2007)]. Their main properties are as follows.

- *Strict locality* – Evaluation is based strictly on local data (i.e. no normalization is needed).
- *Simple evaluation* – The input is coefficients extracted from an image by convolution with a rectangular kernel. The coefficients are processed by a simple formula.

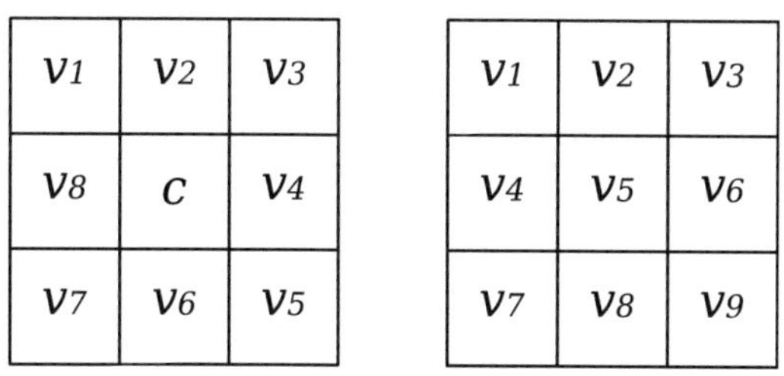

Fig. 2. Feature samples for LBP (left), LRD and LRP (right)

All presented features are based on the same model. The only difference is their evaluation function. First, coefficients v_i from regular 3×3 grid (see Fig. 2) are extracted by convolution. The coefficients are processed by an evaluation function producing the response.

$$LBP(\mathbf{v}, c) = \Sigma_{i=0}^{N} (v_i > c) 2^i \tag{1}$$

$$LRD(\mathbf{v}, a, b) = r(v_a, \mathbf{v}) - r(v_b, \mathbf{v}) \tag{2}$$

$$LRP(\mathbf{v}, a, b) = 10 r(v_a, \mathbf{v}) + r(v_b, \mathbf{v}) \tag{3}$$

The evaluation of LBP works such that all samples are compared to the central one. The result of each comparison is treated as a single bit in the 8 bit code (1). The LRD and LRP features are parametrized by indices of two samples whose ranks are calculated (4). The ranks are subtracted in the case of LRD or combined together in LRP (2,3).

$$r(v, \mathbf{v}) = \sum_{i=1}^{9} \begin{cases} 1, \text{when } v > v_i \\ 0, \text{otherwise} \end{cases} \tag{4}$$

The response range of the features is $\langle 0, 255 \rangle$ for LBP, $\langle -8, 8 \rangle$ for LRD and $\langle 0, 99 \rangle$ for LRP. The response is used as an input to a weak classifier which is essentially a look-up table assigning a weak classifier response to a feature response.

4. AdaBoost and WaldBoost

AdaBoost [Freund (1995)] and other boosting algorithms [Friedman et al. (2000); Grove & Schuurmans (1998); Ratsch (2001); Rudin et al. (2004); Schapire et al. (1998)] all combine *weak hypotheses* $h_t : \chi \rightarrow \mathbb{R}$ into a *strong classifier* H_t. The combination is a weighted average where responses of the weak hypotheses are multiplied by weights α determining their importance:

$$H_T(\mathbf{x}) = \sum_{t=1}^{T} (h_t(\mathbf{x})) \tag{5}$$

The weak hypotheses often internally partition the object space **Ø** into a set of disjoint areas based on a single feature response. Such weak hypotheses are called space partitioning weak hypotheses [Schapire & Singer (1999)] and the partition functions $f : \chi \rightarrow \mathbb{N}$ are referred to in the following text simply as *features*. The weak space partitioning hypotheses are combinations of such features and a *look-up table function* $l : \mathbb{N} \rightarrow \mathbb{R}$

$$h_t(\mathbf{x}) = l_t(f_t(\mathbf{x})). \tag{6}$$

The real value assigned by l_t to output j of f_t is denoted as $c_t^{(j)}$ in the text.

Most of the boosting algorithms order the weak classifiers starting with the most informative one and thus it is reasonable to evaluate them in this order and stop when the classification decision is certain enough. Such classifiers are called *soft cascades* [Bourdev & Brandt (2005)] and can be formalized as a *sequential decision strategy* [Sochman & Matas (2005)] S which is a sequence of decision functions $S = S_1, S_2, \ldots, S_T$, where $S_t : \mathbb{R} \rightarrow \sharp, -1$. The evaluation of the strategy is terminated with a negative result when a decision function outputs -1. The decision functions S_t decide based on a tentative sum of the weak hypotheses H_t, $t < T$ which is compared to a threshold θ_t:

$$S_t(\mathbf{x}) = \begin{cases} \sharp, & \text{if } H_t(\mathbf{x}) > \theta_t \\ -1, & \text{if } H_t(\mathbf{x}) \leq \theta_t \end{cases}. \tag{7}$$

WaldBoost [Sochman & Matas (2005)] is a method which produces an optimal decision strategy for a target false negative rate. The algorithm combines real AdaBoost Schapire & Singer (1999) and Wald's *sequential probability ratio test* Wald (1947).

Given a weak learner algorithm, training data $\{(x_1, y_1) \ldots, (x_m, y_m)\}, x \in \chi, y \in \{-1, +1\}$ and a target false negative rate α, the WaldBoost algorithm finds a decision strategy S^* with a miss rate α_S which is lower than α and the average evaluation time $\bar{T}_S = E(\arg\min_i (S_i \neq \sharp))$ is minimal:

$$S^* = \arg\min_S \bar{T}_S, \text{ s.t. } \alpha_S < \alpha.$$

WaldBoost uses real AdaBoost to iteratively select the most informative weak hypotheses h_t. The threshold θ_t is then selected in each iteration so that as many negative training samples are rejected as possible while asserting that the likelihood ratio that is estimated on training data

$$\hat{R}_t = \frac{p(H_t(\mathbf{x}) < \theta_t | y = -1)}{p(H_t(\mathbf{x}) < \theta_t | y = +1)}$$

satisfies $\hat{R}_t \geq \frac{1}{\alpha}$.

5. Acceleration of WaldBoost based object detection

Acceleration of object detection can be in general based on several principles, the key ones being:

- Implementation on a (more) powerful computational platform – simple general improvement of computational platforms
- exploitation of a structurally different platform compared to the traditional processor platform
- improvement of the AdaBoost/WaldBoost machine learning and/or feature extraction algorithms
- exploitation of redundancy and coherence in results of classification in different (adjacent or close) areas of the image.

The case of general improvement of computational platforms is not of interest here in this publication. On the other hand, structurally novel computational platforms are interesting in general due to their rapid growth in computer technology and specifically in the object detection, where the structure of exploitation of the computational resources suggests that the traditional platforms are not ideal and that the massive parallel platforms are also not completely suitable.

The general improvements of the AdaBoost/WaldBoost machine learning methods are outside the scope of this publication. However, the algorithmic improvements not connected with the classification itself, but rather with the redundancy due to correlation of the classification results in different sub-images of the same image, are quite important to investigate. Their exploitation can significantly reduce the computational effort needed for object detection.

5.1 Classification cost and its minimization

The relative cost of classifier evaluation can be measured and used for the reduction of the computational effort by combining two or more different approaches of classifier implementation; for example, a hardware pre-processing unit connected to post-processing unit on traditional CPU. The minimization method can be applied to various types of relative cost (computations, memory, hardware price, etc.) as its formulation is general. In this chapter, the interest is in the minimization of the use of computational resources and the relative cost thus roughly corresponds to computational time (except when otherwise noted).

5.1.1 Classifier statistics

The main property of a classifier is the probability of the evaluation of a weak hypothesis, reflecting on how often a weak hypothesis is executed during the detection. This value p can be calculated for every stage i from statistics obtained on a dataset of images. Due to the rejection nature of WaldBoost classifiers, the sequence of p_i decreases and the first stage is always evaluated (i.e. the $p_1 = 1$). Example of such statistics is shown on the left in Fig. 3. The p_i captures computational the complexity of the classifier.

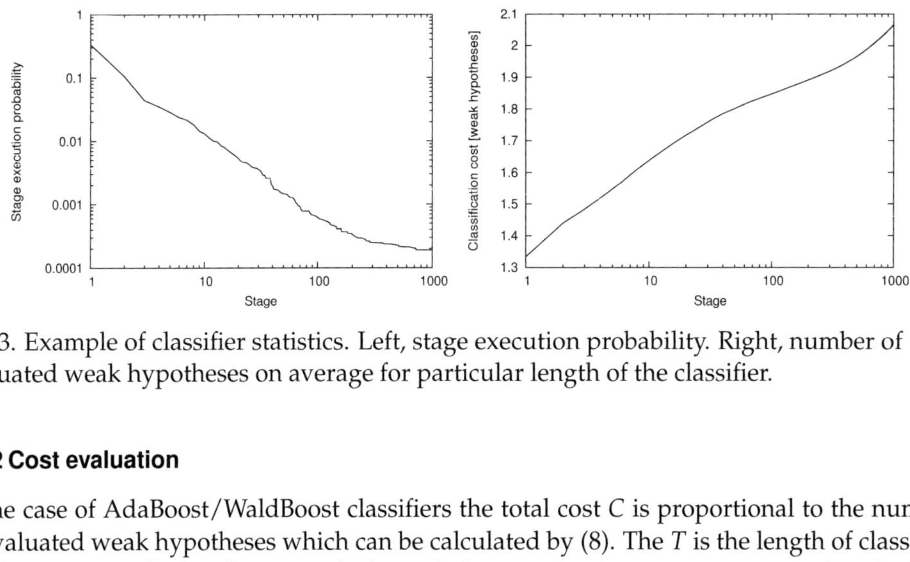

Fig. 3. Example of classifier statistics. Left, stage execution probability. Right, number of evaluated weak hypotheses on average for particular length of the classifier.

5.1.2 Cost evaluation

In the case of AdaBoost/WaldBoost classifiers the total cost C is proportional to the number of evaluated weak hypotheses which can be calculated by (8). The T is the length of classifier. The k is the overall classifier cost which symbolizes evaluation cost on a particular platform on which the classification is implemented. The p is the probability of the execution of a particular weak hypothesis (see Section 5.1.1). The c is the relative cost of the weak hypothesis evaluation which addresses the possibility that the hypotheses have a different cost (due to the use of different features, for example).

$$C = k \sum_{i=1}^{T} p_i c_i \tag{8}$$

When analyzing real classifiers, p can be obtained from the statistics on input images and c by time measurement or other cost estimation and k can be set to a constant value. In Fig 3, the left plot shows the value of p_i and the right plot the area under the p_i curve which is proportional to the amount of computational resources needed for the evaluation of the classifier.

In object detection, the most common are homogeneous classifiers (i.e. those with all weak classifiers and features of the same type). In such cases, the cost of hypothesis evaluation is constant $c_i = c$. Additionally in AdaBoost, all weak hypotheses are executed every time and the probability of executing all hypotheses is equal to $p_i = 1$. The C from (8) can thus be simplified to $C^{(AB)}$ (for AdaBoost) and $C^{(WB)}$ (for WaldBoost) in (9).

$$C^{(AB)} = knc \qquad C^{(WB)} = kc \sum_{i=1}^{n} p_i \tag{9}$$

5.1.3 Cost minimization

The cost of classification is not the only property of the classifier, but it is also the property of implementation of the run-time in which the classifier is executed – feature extraction and classifier evaluation. Different implementations with different properties exist. Imagine, for example, an implementation A which can evaluate very efficiently $K > 1$ weak hypotheses in a row, but it always evaluates *all* of them no matter how many weak hypotheses is actually needed for the evaluation. It could be a pre-processing unit implemented in a hardware which rejects areas without an occurrence of the target object. Then, there is implementation B in software which can evaluate the classifier in standard way. The computational cost for one feature in A is much less than in B but implementing the whole classifier in the hardware is hard to achieve due to limited resources.

$$C = \arg\min_{0 \le u \le T} \left(k_1 \sum_{i=0}^{u-1} p_{1,i} c_{1,i} + k_2 \sum_{i=u}^{T-1} p_{2,i} c_{2,i} \right) \tag{10}$$

Both implementations can be put together, but the problem is how many weak hypotheses have to be put in a hardware unit and how many are left in the software. The precise position of division of the evaluation is subject to minimization of classification cost (10) in order to find a composition with minimal cost.

The two-phase classifier can be fine tuned by one parameter. Equation 10 shows the minimization problem and Fig. 4 shows values of C for different settings of u. The C is the total minimal cost of the evaluation; u is the point of classifier division; and k, c and p correspond to the parameters of the cost computation from Equation 8. It should be noted, that although the properties p of the classifier are the same for both parts, the p can be in general different for each part. This is due to the structure of the evaluation in particular implementation which can *force* different probabilities of feature evaluation (e.g. by evaluating more features in one step; see Section 5.1.1).

When going beyond the example given above, more than two phases of evaluation can be used. And minimization problem is thus multi-dimensional. In the general case, described by (11), the classifier division is vector $\mathbf{u}$ whose values are searched for in order to find the best composition of parts with different properties. Note that u_i can be equal to u_{i+1} and some

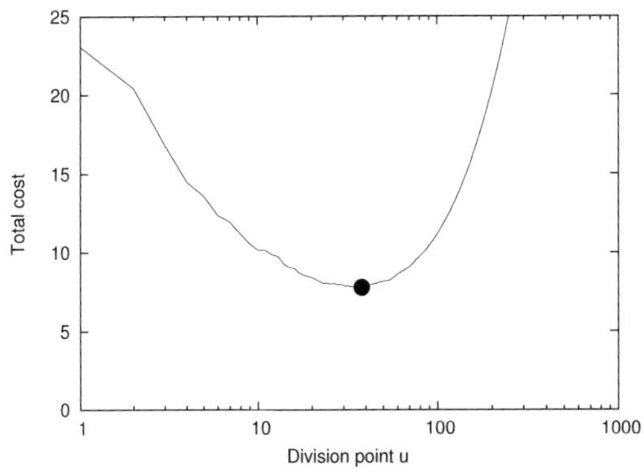

Fig. 4. Example of minimization of classification cost for two-phase classifier. The first phase always evaluates all weak hypotheses but the cost for a weak hypothesis is 0.1 of the second phase. The second phase evaluates weak hypotheses one by one. The black dot marks the division between the parts that lead into the minimum cost.

parts could be in fact skipped when they are evaluated as useless in the optimization.

$$\begin{aligned} &C = \arg\min_{\mathbf{u}} \left(\sum_{m=1}^{M} \left(k_m \sum_{i=u_{m-1}}^{u_m - 1} p_{m,i} c_{m,i} \right) \right) \\ &s.t. \\ &u_0 = 0 \\ &u_m = T \\ &u_{i-1} \leq u_i, \;\; 0 \leq i \leq M \end{aligned} \tag{11}$$

In practical applications, it is easy to get classifier statistics – it reflects classifier behavior on images. On the other hand, it is tricky to identify values of c and k. It has to be done by careful examination of performance of the particular implementation of the detection (e.g. by the precise measurement of time needed for the execution of weak hypotheses).

5.2 Exploiting neighbors

In scanning window object detection using a soft cascade detector, each image position is processed independently. However, much information is shared between neighboring positions and utilizing this information has a potential for increasing the speed of detection.

One way to utilize the shared information is to learn *suppression classifiers* [Zemčík et al. (2010)] to predict the responses of the original detection classifier at neighboring positions. Computation of the original detector can then be suppressed at positions for which this prediction is negative and with enough confidence.

In the case of *space partitioning weak hypotheses* (see Section 4), the suppression classifiers can be made computationally very efficient by re-using the features h_t computed by the original classifier. In that case, adding the suppression classifiers just increases the size of the look-up table $l : \mathbb{N} \rightarrow \mathbb{R}$.

The task of learning the suppression classifiers can be formulated as detector emulation [Šochman & Matas (2007); Sochman & Matas (2009)] which allows usage of

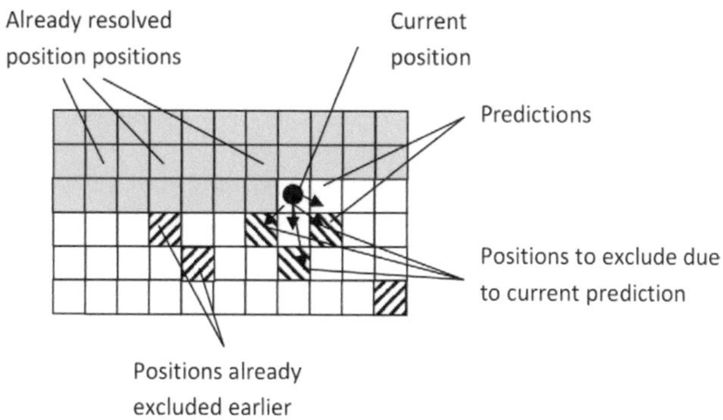

Fig. 5. Neighborhood suppression - during scanning, positions surrounding the currently evaluated position can be suppressed. On such positions the classifier will not be computed.

unlabeled data for training and does not require any modifications in learning the original detection classifier. Moreover, previously created detectors can be used as well.

In the classifier emulation [Šochman & Matas (2007); Sochman & Matas (2009)] approach, an existing detector is considered a black box and its decisions are used as labels for a new WaldBoost learning problem. The algorithm for learning the suppression classifiers differs from this basic scenario in three distinct aspects discussed below. The whole algorithm for learning suppression classifier is summarized in Algorithm 1.

The first change, as mentioned earlier, is that the weak hypotheses h'_t of a suppression classifier, reused features f_t of the original detector and only new look-up table functions l'_t are learned. By restricting the features, the learning process is very fast as the selection of an optimal weak hypothesis is generally the most time consuming step.

The second difference is that the labels for training the suppression classifier are obtained from a different image position than where the classifier gets information from (the position containing the original features l_t). This is consistent with the fact that we want to predict responses in the neighborhood of the currently evaluated position.

Finally, the set of training samples is pruned twice in each iteration of the learning algorithm instead of only once as in WaldBoost. The samples rejected by the new suppression classifier are removed from the training set, as well as, the samples rejected by the original classifier. This reflects the behavior during scanning when only those features which are needed by the detector to make a decision are computed and, consequently, the suppression classifiers can only use these computed features to make their own decision.

5.3 Early non-maxima suppression

Detection of objects by a scanning window technique usually employs some kind of *non-maxima suppression* to select a position with the highest classifier response from a small neighborhood in position, scale and other possible degrees of freedom. The suppressed detections have no influence on the resulting detection and it may not be necessary to compute the detectors completely in these positions. In other applications only the highest response on a number of samples is of interest as well. Examples of such applications are speaker

Algorithm 1 WaldBoost for learning suppression classifiers

Input: original soft cascade $H_T(x) = \sum_{t=1}^{T} h_t(x)$, its early termination thresholds $\theta'^{(t)}$ and its features f_t; desired miss rate α; training set $\{(x_1, y_1) \ldots, (x_m, y_m)\}, x \in \chi, y \in \{-1, +1\}$, where the labels y_i are obtained by evaluating the original detector H_T at an image position with a particular displacement with respect to the position of corresponding x_i

Output: look-up table functions l'_t and early termination thresholds $\theta'^{(t)}$ of the new suppression classifier

Initialize sample weight distribution $D_1(i) = \frac{1}{m}$

for $t = 1, \ldots, T$

1. estimate new l'_t such that its

$$c_t^{(j)} = -\frac{1}{2} \ln \left(\frac{Pr_{i \sim D}(f_t(x_i) = j | y_i = +1)}{Pr_{i \sim D}(f_t(x_i) = j | y_i = -1)} \right)$$

2. add l'_t to the suppression classifier

$$H'_t(x) = \sum_{r=1}^{t} l'_r(f_r(x))$$

3. find optimal threshold $\theta'^{(t)}$
4. remove from the training set samples for which $H_t(x) \leq \theta^{(t)}$
5. remove from the training set samples for which $H'_t(x) \leq \theta'^{(t)}$
6. update the sample weight distribution

$$D_{t+1}(i) \propto \exp(-y_i H'_t(x_i))$$

and person recognition where a short utterance or face image is matched by a classifier to templates from a database.

The main idea of *Early non-Maxima Suppression* [Herout et al. (2011)] (EnMS) is to perform non-maxima suppression already during computation of classifiers and to stop computing classifiers for objects having very low probability to reach the best score in the set of the competing objects.

In the context of soft cascades, EnMS can be formalized as the *Conditioned Sequential Probability Ratio Test* (CSPRT) which allows the decision functions S_t (see Equation 7 for the original formulation) to be conditioned by some additional data $z_t \in \mathcal{Z}$:

$$S_t(x, z_t) = \begin{cases} -1, & \text{if } H_t(x) < \theta_t(z_t) \\ \sharp, & \text{if } \theta_t(z_t) \leq H_t(x) \end{cases} \tag{12}$$

Here the threshold becomes a function of the conditioning data.

In order to create an optimal CSPRT strategy, the threshold functions $\theta_t(z_t)$ should be optimized for the same objectives as the thresholds θ_t in WaldBoost (see Equation 13). Parameters of $\theta_t(z_t)$ should be set so that as many negative training samples are rejected as possible while asserting that the likelihood ratio is estimated on the training data

$$\hat{R}_t = \frac{p(H_t(\mathbf{x}) < \theta_t(z_t)|y = -1)}{p(H_t(\mathbf{x}) < \theta_t(z_t)|y = +1)} \tag{13}$$

satisfies $\hat{R}_t \geq \frac{1}{\alpha}$.

For the EnMS approach to be effective, the conditioning information z_t has to encode how well the other competing samples are classified and the function form of the threshold function $\theta_t(z_t)$ has to be simple enough to allow reliable estimation of its optimal parameters.

In our approach, the weak hypothesis h_t is evaluated for the whole set of competing samples $\mathcal{X}$ at a time, and the conditioning information is the maximum tentative classifier response on the competing samples

$$z_t = \max_{x \in \mathcal{X}}(H_t(x)). \tag{14}$$

We choose $\theta_t(z_t)$ as

$$\theta_t(z_t) = z_t - \lambda_t. \tag{15}$$

With this choice of $\theta_t(z_t)$, the EnMS condition for rejecting samples in Equation 12 becomes

$$H_t(x) < z_t - \lambda_t. \tag{16}$$

With these choices, EnMS introduces only a very small computational overhead. When computed sequentially, a weak hypothesis h_t can be computed on all active positions; then the maximal responses can be gathered and the samples fulfilling $H_t(x) < z_t - \lambda_t$ can be suppressed. When computing positions in parallel, the process has to be synchronized before the suppression step and gathering the maximal value may require synchronization, atomic instructions or a special value reduction method. However, even in highly parallel environments, the possible issues are not that significant as the potential serial operations are simple. Furthermore, suppression does not have to be performed after each weak hypothesis and the computation does not have to be strictly enforced without any significant performance drawbacks.

6. Runtime design

6.1 Exploiting SIMD architectures

The SIMD (Single Instruction Multiple Data) architectures exploit data level parallelism to accelerate certain operations. Contrary to instruction parallelism, the data parallelism is works so that the CPU performs the same instruction with vectors of data. This approach is very efficient in tasks where a simple computation is performed on large amount of data (e.g. stream processing).

Typically, CPUs contain a standard instruction set which processes integers and floats. This set is extended with a set of vector instructions which work over vectors of data stored in the memory. Vector instructions typically include standard arithmetic and logic instructions, instructions for data access and other data manipulation instructions (packing, unpacking, etc.). This is the case of general purpose CPUs like Intel, AMD or PowerPC. Beside the general purpose CPUs, there are GPGPU (General Purpose Graphics Processing Units), successors of traditional GPUs (purposed to process graphics primitives) that can execute parallel kernels over data, and that can be viewed as advanced SIMD processors.

The SIMD architecture can be used especially to accelerate the following parts of detection.

- *Weak classifier evaluation* - the instructions can be used to evaluate multiple weak classifiers.
- *Feature evaluation* - the features like LRD, LRP and LBP can be evaluated in a data-parallel fashion.

When evaluating the weak hypotheses in a one-by-one manner, the evaluation of a feature can be transformed to SIMD processing so that all feature samples are loaded to registers and the response is evaluated by using SIMD instructions instead of a typical implementation by a loop [Herout et al. (2009); Juránek et al. (2010)]. This necessarily needs a pre-processing stage that transforms an image to a SIMD-friendly form and which allows for simple access to the data belonging to a feature - convolution of image. Speed up of this method compared to a naive implementation is very high, around 3 to 5, depending on the particular architecture on which it is implemented.

When evaluating multiple hypotheses, the implementations is pretty much the same as for one weak hypothesis without SIMD instructions. The difference is that the SIMD registers can hold information for more weak hypotheses (16 in the case of Intel SSE). This leads into efficient implementation of AdaBoost classifiers. WaldBoost classifiers, on the other hand, can be inefficient using this implementation as many weak hypotheses are calculated even when they are not necessarily needed for the classifier evaluation. Pre-processing is needed again to simplify the data access and feature evaluation. Speed-up achieved by this method is very high. In fact, when implementing WaldBoost evaluation, it is comparable to the method in the previous paragraph, even though many weak hypotheses are calculated unnecessarily.

In some cases, the feature response can be pre-calculated for all positions in the image and during detection, the feature is extracted by only one access to a pre-calculated image. In this case, for each version of a feature, an image with a pre-calculated result must be created. This is only possible when a small number of feature variant exist. For example, LBP with restricted size to 2×2 pixels ber block has four variants. On the other hand, LRD with the same restriction has 144 variants (as it is additionally parametrized by A and B indices) and calculation of such a high amount of images would be computationally expensive.

To summarize, benefits brought up by SIMD processing are the following: SIMD allows for features to be extracted very efficiently and the performance of a classifier evaluation can evan be increased by multiple number of times. On the other hand, the SIMD comes with the need of pre-processing which, when implemented without care, can reduce performance.

6.2 GPU implementation of the detection

Implementation of object detection in GPU was historically detected using programmable shaders [Polok et al. (2008)]; however, contemporary state of the art is in GP-GPU programming languages, such as CUDA or OpenCL [Herout et al. (2011)]. GP-GPUs programmed using one of these languages present one of the most powerful and efficient computational devices. When used for object detection, GP-GPUs can be seen as a SIMD device with a high level of parallelism.

Unfortunately, the high level of parallelism is difficult to employ in WaldBoost detection as the amount of computation in adjacent positions in the image is not correlated and in general is quite unpredictable, which fact heavily complicates usage of the ALUs in the SIMD device.

The efficient implementation of object detection using CUDA [Herout et al. (2011)] solves the problems of two main domains: the classifier operating on one fixed-size window, and parallel execution of this classifier on different locations of the input image. The problem of object detection by statistical classifiers can be divided into the following steps:

- loading and representing the classifier data
- image pre-processing
- classifier evaluation
- retrieving results.

The constant data containing the classifier (image features' parameters, prediction values of the weak hypotheses summed by the algorithm and WaldBoost thresholds) could be accommodated in the texture memory or constant memory of the CUDA architecture. These data are accessed in the evaluation of each feature at each position, so the demands for access speed are critical. Programs that are run on the graphics hardware using CUDA are executed as *kernels*; each kernel has a number of blocks and each block is further organized into threads. The code of the threads consumes hardware resources: registers and shared memory; this limits the number of threads that can be efficiently executed in a block (both the maximal and minimal number of threads).

One thread computes one or more locations of the scanning window in the image. The image pixels (or more precisely, window locations) are therefore divided into rectangular tiles, which are solved by different thread blocks. Experiments showed that the suitable number of threads per block was around 128. Executing blocks for only 128 pixels of the image would not be efficient, so we chose that one thread calculated more than one position of the window – a whole column of pixels in a rectangular tile. A good consequence of this layout is easy control of the resources used by one block: the number of threads is determined by the width of the tile, and the height controls the whole number of processed window positions by the block. The tile can extend over the whole height of the image or just a part of it. In order to avoid collisions of concurrently running threads and blocks, atomic increment (`atomicInc` function) of one shared word in the global memory is used for synchronization. This operation is rather costly, but the positive detections are so rare that this means of output can be afforded. As a consequence, the results of the whole process are at the end available in one spot of the global memory, which can be easily made available on the host computer.

The main property of the CUDA implementation is that the CUDA outperforms the CPU implementation mainly for high resolution videos. This can be explained by extra overhead connected with transferring the image to the GPU, starting the kernel programs, retrieving the results, etc. These overhead operations typically consume constant time independent of the problem size, so they are better amortized in high-resolution videos.

6.3 Programmable hardware

The runtime for object detection does not necessarily need to be implemented only in software; programmable hardware is one of the options as well, namely field programmable gate arrays

[Jin et al. (2009); Lai et al. (2007); Theocharides et al. (2006); Wei et al. (2004); Zemčík & Žádník (2007)]. While the algorithms of the object detection are in principle the same for software and hardware implementation, the hardware platform offers features largely different from the software and thus the optimal methods need to implement detection in programmable hardware are often different from the ones used in software and, in many cases, the hardware implementation may be very efficient.

The key features that are important for object detection are very different in hardware and software, and which are beneficial for hardware implementation, include:

- massive parallelism achievable with good performance/electrical power ratio
- variable data path width in hardware adjustable to exact algorithmic needs
- simple implementation of bit manipulation and logical functions
- nearly seamless complex control and data flow implementation

Of course, the hardware implementation also has severe limitations, the most important being:

- limited complexity of the hardware circuits
- computational resources for complex mathematical functions expensive
- memory structures relatively limited
- in most cases lower clock speed comparing to the processors

Taking into account the above advantages and limitations of programmable hardware, it can be considered for object detection designed specifically for the following cases:

- low end computational power embedded system with programmable hardware with programmable hardware as a co-processor; in this setup, it is expected that the programmable hardware performs more or less a complete detection task;
- high end computational system with programmable hardware as a pre-processing unit; this setup is different from the above one with respect to the detection which does not have to be done completely in programmable hardware, but rather the hardware is considered a resource to relieve the processor of the host system from as much computation as possible, and so it is feasible to implement perhaps incomplete but high performance pre-processor that reduces the need for computations;
- a complete object detection system in programmable hardware that can be combined with image pre-processing and where the complete detection task along with some image data flow considerations should be implemented.

Based on the above methods of exploitation, the methods of implementation of object detection in programmable hardware can be subdivided into a complete detection and pre-processing.

The typical methods of complete object detection in programmable hardware is feasible to implement using a sequential engine, possibly microprogrammable, which performs detection location by location, weak classifier by weak classifier until a decision is reached. As the evaluation of each weak classifier is relatively complex, the operation of the sequential unit is pipelined, so that several instances can be running in parallel. At the same time, different locations, in general, require a different number of weak classifiers to be evaluated. These

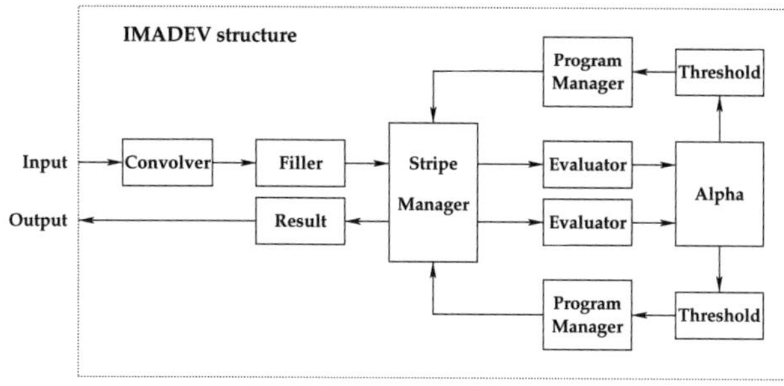

Fig. 6. Block structure of the object detector in programmable hardware (source Zemčík & Žádník (2007)).

facts lead into relatively complex timing and synchronization of processing; however, very good performance can be achieved [Zemčík & Žádník (2007)].

In a situation, where a complete evaluation of the detection is not required (e.g. in cases where a powerful CPU is available) and programmable hardware can be exploited for pre-processing, the best approach is probably a synthesis of fixed-function circuits synthesized based on results of the machine learning process "on demand" for each classifier. Such a synthesized circuit is most efficient when processing a (small) fixed number of weak classifiers for every evaluated position. While some of the weak classifiers are in such cases evaluated unnecessarily (assuming WaldBoost algorithm), the average price of weak classifier implementation is still often much lower than in the sequential machine described above. The main advantage of this approach is that all weak classifiers can be evaluated in a parallel way. However, as each weak classifier consumes chip resources, only a very small number of weak classifiers can be implemented in this way.

7. Results

7.1 Classifier cost minimization

This section gives an example of optimization of classifier performance by the balancing amount of computation between a fast hardware pre-processing unit and software post-processing unit. The classifiers used in this experiment were face detectors composed from 1000 weak hypotheses with LBP features and different false negative error rates (in a range from 0.02 to 0.2).

As a baseline, software implementation working on an integral image was selected, as it is the standard way of implementation of the detection. The other implementations ised in the experiments were SSE implementation that evaluate features one by one (SSE-A), and the SSE implementation that evaluates 16 weak hypotheses in a row (SSE-B).

The cost of the hardware unit was selected according to the area on the chip taken by the design. We set the cost constantly to $c_i = \frac{1}{m}$ where m is the maximal number of hypotheses that can be fit in the circuit. In this experiment, we use $m = 50$. In general, setting the cost to a low value, we simply say that the cost of the hardware unit is not of much interest to us, and conversely, setting the cost to a large value, we say that the cost of the hardware is very important. The cost of the post-processing unit was calculated from the measurement of

	Cost per weak hyp.
INTEGRAL (ref.)	0.215
SSE-A	0.110
SSE-B	0.070
FPGA	0.002

Table 1. Costs of weak hypotheses evaluation in different implementations of detection runtime used in the experiment.

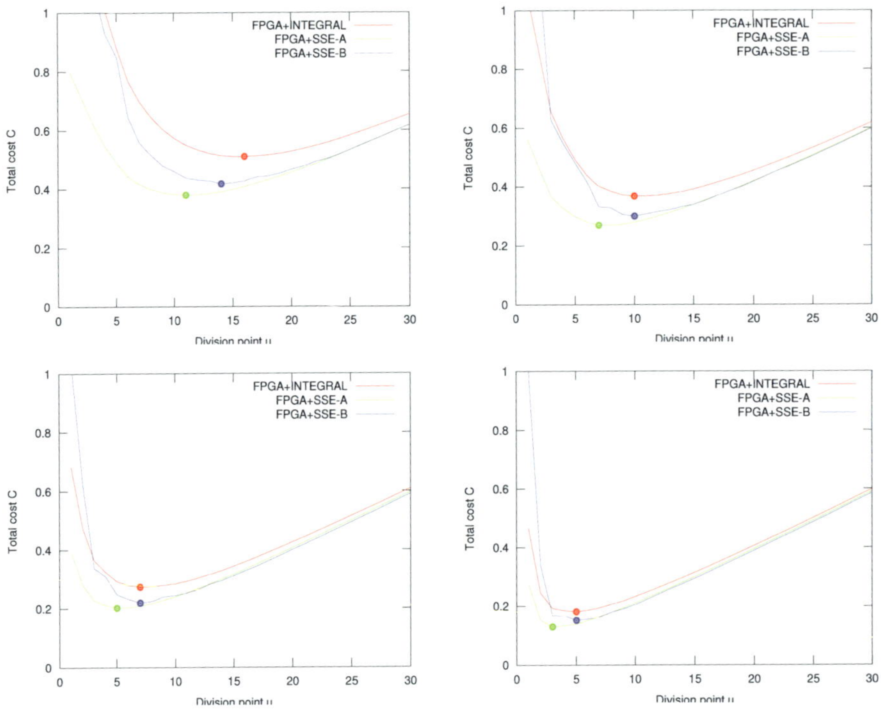

Fig. 7. Optimization results for classifiers with different false negative rates. Each plot shows the total cost of composition of FPGA with a software implementation. The division point is on the horizontal axis and the cost on the vertical axis.

processing time of the implementations of a standard PC, and it corresponds to microseconds per weak hypothesis. The cost values are summarized in Table 1. According to selected costs, the optimization minimize circuit area and, at the same time, the amount of computations in the software. By the combination of such diverse cost measures the result given by the optimization can be viewed as a "relative cost", but the interpretation of the value might be somewhat problematical. This does not, however, matter too much as we do not care about the absolute value of the cost, but about the position of the minima.

Figure 7 shows four plots of total cost for different classifiers. Each plot shows the value of total cost for different settings of the classifier division point and each curve corresponds to a particular combination of FPGA and software implementation. The results of optimization for a classifier with $\alpha = 0.02$ are summarized in Table 2. The *Division* column shows the division

	Division	Best cost	Computations
Integral	0/1000	1.56	0/1
SSE-A	0/1000	0.80	0/1
SSE-B	0/1000	1.24	0/1
FPGA+Integral	16/977	0.51	0.87/0.13
FPGA+SSE-A	11/988	0.38	0.78/0.22
FPGA+SSE-B	14/984	0.41	0.85/0.15

Table 2. Summary of results for classifier with LBP features and $\alpha = 0.02$.

of the classifier between hardware and software units; the *Best cost* column reflects the relative cost of the best solution and the *Computations* column shows the fraction of computations performed in hardware and software units.

This example shows that it can be beneficial to use a combination of more implementations of detection instead of one. It turns out that using a hardware pre-processing unit improves the detection performance (in terms of computational effort). Additionally, improving the performance of the software part allows for using shorter classifiers in hardware. This is an important fact as the FPGAs (and especially the cheaper ones) have typically limited resources and it could be impossible to put longer classifiers in them. Even higher performance could be achieved by using a neighborhood suppression method which would affect stage execution probability p in the optimization. This would result in shorter pre-processing units and lower total cost.

The application of such classifier optimization is, for example, in the field of smart camera design. The pre-processing module can be placed directly in the camera which then outputs, beside the normal image, the image with potential occurrence of target objects. Such information, as the above example has shown, dramatically decreases the required computation time in the post-processing module.

7.2 Neighborhood suppression results

The suppression of neighboring positions was tested on the standard frontal face MIT+CMU dataset. Three WaldBoost classifiers with target false positive rates of 0.01, 0.05 and 0.2 were trained for four types of image features: LRD, LRP, LBP and Haar. For each classifier, three neighborhood suppression strategies were trained with target false positive rates of 0.01, 0.05 and 0.2. Comparing results of the combinations allows us to evaluate if it is more effective to use neighborhood suppression than just by using a WaldBoost classifier with a higher false positive rate. The results of this experiment in Fig. 8 clearly show that neighborhood suppression is indeed effective and on average it evaluates less weak hypotheses per image position for the same accuracy.

7.3 EnMS results

EnMS was evaluated on a face localization task. The dataset was downloaded from Flicker groups *portraits* (training) and *just_faces* (testing). The dataset contains 84,251 training and 6,704 near-frontal faces. The images were rescaled to a 100×100 pixel resolution with the face approximately 50×50 pixels large and positioned in the middle. Both WaldBoost and

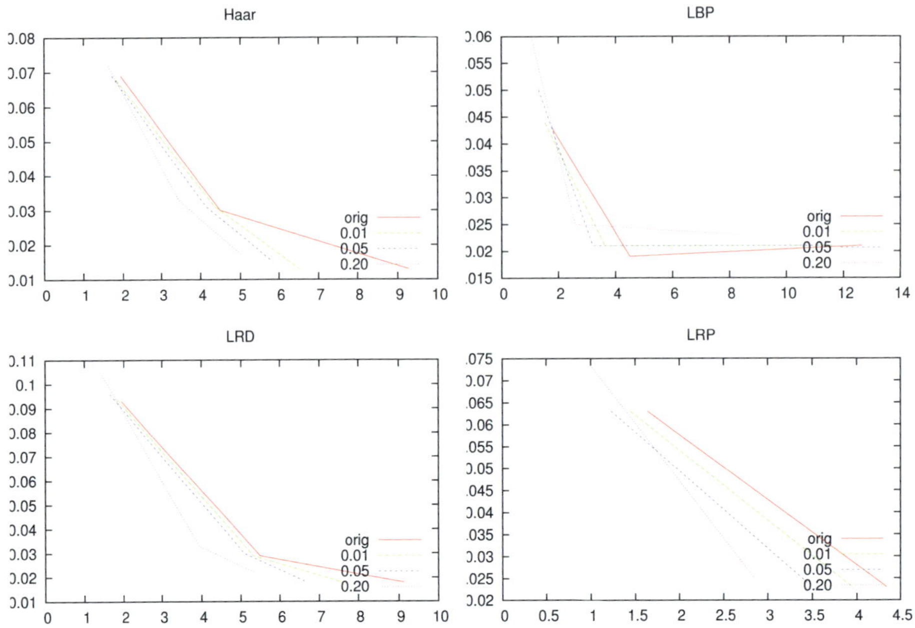

Fig. 8. The graphs show AUC on y-axis (Area Under ROC) versus the average number of weak classifiers evaluated per image position as measured on the MIT+CMU frontal face dataset. The individual lines are for original WaldBoost detectors without neighborhood suppression (full line) and the other lines are with added neighborhood suppression with different target false negative rates. Good results should be in the left (fast) bottom (accurate) corner.

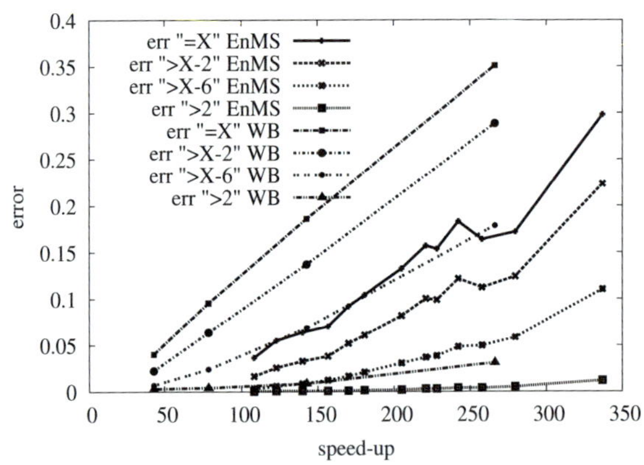

Fig. 9. The graphs show frontal face localization error (y-axis) for different speed-ups achieved by WaldBoost and EnMS. The speed-up is measured as reduction of the number of weak hypotheses evaluated on average per image position relative to the full length of the classifier (length is the same for WaldBoost and EnMS). The lines represent differently computed errors (see text) of WaldBoost and EnMS.

EnMS were evaluated on this data for several target false negative rates. The localization accuracy was measured as the number of images where the detector returned a position with the highest response of a classifier which always evaluated all weak hypotheses. In order to allow for some tolerance, errors were also counted as failure to detect position with the reference classifier response lower by 2 and 6 than the best response and failure to detect position with the reference response higher than 2 which is an operating point that still gives reasonably low false alarms in the detection task. The results in Fig. 9 show that EnMS provides approximately two times better speed for the same error rates than WaldBoost.

8. Conclusions

This chapter focused on methods of real-time object detection with classifiers. It has been demonstrated that the object detection methods working in real-time are feasible and can be implemented on a variety of platforms, such as personal computer processors, GP-GPU platforms, or even in programmable hardware.

In order to achieve real-time performance, an efficient implementation platform and efficient implementation itself is necessary, but further enhancement through algorithmic acceleration is needed as well. Two examples of such acceleration are presented in the chapter: exploitation of information about neighborhoods of the already classified positions in the image and early suppression of non-maxima of the classifier responses. The approach of exploitation of the neighborhoods in the image is based on the idea that classification of the overlapping sub-images in the image - the neighborhoods - may share some properties and information. One of the possible ways to share such information is through re-using the weak classifiers used during classification of one location through WaldBoost for predicting results in the other neighboring locations. This prediction is done through a machine learning process similar to WaldBoost where the difference to WaldBoost is that the training process actually reuses the already selected weak classifiers that were used at the original location. While this process works well only in close neighborhoods, it brings a significant speed-up.

Pre-processing that rules out some parts of the image from the detection process can significantly speed up the detection process. Important future research certainly includes machine-learning based pre-processing methods and research of under-sampling in scanning methods that can also improve detection performance possibly without any adverse effects on precision. Future research also includes algorithmic improvements of acceleration methods, such as improvement in the processor assignment in GP-GPU, improved scanning trajectories in neighborhood exploitation, or further improvements in feature extraction.

9. Acknowledgement

This work has been supported by the FIT VUT Brno project "Advanced recognition and presentation of multimedia data", FIT VUT, FIT-S-11-2, Centre of excellence in computer science "The IT4Innovations Centre of Excellence", EU, CZ 1.05/1.1.00/02.0070, "Reduced Certification Costs Using Trusted Multi-core Platforms", Artemis JU, RECOMP #100202, "Smart Multicore Embedded Systems", Artemis JU, SMECY #100230, and the Czech Ministry of Education, Youth and Sports, "Security-Oriented Research in Information Technology", CEZ MŠMT, MSM0021630528 and “Centre of Computer Graphics", MŠMT, LC06008.

10. References

Bay, H., Ess, A., Tuytelaars, T. & Van Gool, L. (2008). Speeded-up robust features (surf), *Comput. Vis. Image Underst.* 110(3): 346–359.

Blaschko, M. B. & Lampert, C. H. (2009). Object localization with global and local context kernels, *British Machine Vision Conference*.

Bourdev, L. & Brandt, J. (2005). Robust object detection via soft cascade, *CVPR*.

Chen, J., Shan, S., Yang, P., Yan, S., Chen, X. & Gao, W. (2004). Novel face detection method based on gabor features, *Sinobiometrics 2004*, Lecture Notes in Computer Science, Springer Berlin / Heidelberg, pp. 90–99.

Dalal, N. & Triggs, B. (2005). Histograms of oriented gradients for human detection, *CVPR '05: Proceedings of the 2005 IEEE Computer Society Conference on Computer Vision and Pattern Recognition (CVPR'05) – Volume 1*, IEEE Computer Society, Washington, DC, USA, pp. 886–893.

Fidler, S. & Leonardis, A. (2007). Towards scalable representations of object categories: Learning a hierarchy of parts, *Computer Vision and Pattern Recognition, IEEE Computer Society Conference on* 0: 1–8.

Freund, Y. (1995). Boosting a weak learning algorithm by majority, *Inf. Comput.* 121(2): 256–285.

Friedman, J., Hastie, T. & Tibshirani, R. (2000). Additive logistic regression: a statistical view of boosting, *Annals of Statistics* 28: 2000.

Grove, A. J. & Schuurmans, D. (1998). Boosting in the limit: Maximizing the margin of learned ensembles, *In Proceedings of the Fifteenth National Conference on Artificial Intelligence*, pp. 692–699.

Herout, A., Hradiš, M. & Zemčík, P. (2011). Enms: Early non-maxima suppression, *Pattern Analysis and Applications* 2011(1111): 10.

Herout, A., Zemčík, P., Hradiš, M., Juránek, R., Havel, J., Jošth, R. & Žádník, M. (2009). *Low-Level Image Features for Real-Time Object Detection*, IN-TECH Education and Publishing, p. 25.

Hradiš, M., Herout, A. & Zemčík, P. (2008). Local rank patterns - novel features for rapid object detection, *Proceedings of International Conference on Computer Vision and Graphics 2008*, Lecture Notes in Computer Science, pp. 1–2.

Jin, S., Kim, D., Nguyen, T. T., Jun, B., Kim, D. & Jeon, J. W. (2009). An fpga-based parallel hardware architecture for real-time face detection using a face certainty map, *Application-Specific Systems, Architectures and Processors, IEEE International Conference on* 0: 61–66.

Juránek, R., Herout, A. & Zemčík, P. (2010). Implementing local binary patterns with simd instructions of cpu, *Proceedings of Winter Seminar on Computer Graphics*, West Bohemian University, p. 5.

Lai, H.-C., Savvides, M. & Chen, T. (2007). Proposed fpga hardware architecture for high frame rate face detection using feature cascade classifiers, *First IEEE International Conference on Biometrics: Theory, Applications, and Systems, 2007. BTAS 2007.*, pp. 1 –6.

Lee, T. S. (1996). Image representation using 2d gabor wavelets, *IEEE Transactions on Pattern Analysis and Machine Intelligence* 18(10): 959–971.

Leibe, B., Leonardis, A. & Schiele, B. (2008). Robust object detection with interleaved categorization and segmentation, *Int. J. Comput. Vision* 77(1-3): 259–289.

Li, S., Zhang, Z., Shum, H. & Zhang, H. (2002). Floatboost learning for classification, *The Conference on Advances in Neural Information Processing Systems (NIPS)*.

Lowe, D. G. (1999). Object recognition from local scale-invariant features, *ICCV '99: Proceedings of the International Conference on Computer Vision-Volume 2*, IEEE Computer Society, Washington, DC, USA, p. 1150.

Lowe, D. G. (2004). Distinctive image features from scale-invariant keypoints, *International Journal of Computer Vision* 60(2): 91–110.

Polok, L., Herout, A., Zemčík, P., Hradiš, M., Juránek, R. & Jošth, R. (2008). "local rank differences" image feature implemented on gpu, *Proceedings of the 10th International Conference on Advanced Concepts for Intelligent Vision Systems*, Lecture Notes In Computer Science; Vol. 5259, Springer Verlag, pp. 170–181.

Ratsch, G. (2001). *Robust Boosting via Convex Optimization: Theory and Applications*, PhD thesis, Mathematisch-Naturwissenschaftichen Fakultat der Universitat Potsdam.

Rudin, C., Schapire, R. E. & Daubechies, I. (2004). Boosting based on a smooth margin, *Learning Theory*, Vol. 3120/2004 of *Lecture Notes in Computer Science*, Springer, pp. 502–517.

Schapire, R. E., Freund, Y., Bartlett, P. & Lee, W. S. (1998). Boosting the margin: A new explanation for the effectiveness of voting methods, *The Annals of Statistics* 26(5): 1651–1686.

Schapire, R. E. & Singer, Y. (1999). Improved boosting algorithms using confidence-rated predictions, *Mach. Learn.* 37(3): 297–336.

Serre, T., Wolf, L. & Poggio, T. (2005). Object recognition with features inspired by visual cortex, *CVPR '05: Proceedings of the 2005 IEEE Computer Society Conference on Computer Vision and Pattern Recognition (CVPR'05) - Volume 2*, IEEE Computer Society, Washington, DC, USA, pp. 994–1000.

Sochman, J. & Matas, J. (2004). Adaboost with totally corrective updates for fast face detection, *FGR*, pp. 445–450.

Sochman, J. & Matas, J. (2005). Waldboost - learning for time constrained sequential detection, *CVPR '05: Proceedings of the 2005 IEEE Computer Society Conference on Computer Vision and Pattern Recognition (CVPR'05) - Volume 2*, IEEE Computer Society, Washington, DC, USA, pp. 150–156.

Šochman, J. & Matas, J. (2007). Learning a fast emulator of a binary decision process, *in* Y. Yagi, S. B. Kang, I. S. Kweon & H. Zha (eds), *ACCV*, Vol. II of *LNSC*, Springer, Berlin Heidelberg, pp. 236–245.

Sochman, J. & Matas, J. (2009). Learning fast emulators of binary decision processes, *International Journal of Computer Vision* 83(2): 149–163.

Theocharides, T., Vijaykrishnan, N. & Irwin, M. (2006). A parallel architecture for hardware face detection, *IEEE Computer Society Annual Symposium on Emerging VLSI Technologies and Architectures*.

Viola, P. & Jones, M. (2001). Rapid object detection using a boosted cascade of simple features, *IEEE Computer Society Conference on Computer Vision and Pattern Recognition* 1: 511–518.

Wald, A. (1947). *Sequential Analysis*, John Wiley and Sons, Inc.

Wei, Y., Bing, X. & Chareonsak, C. (2004). Fpga implementation of adaboost algorithm for detection of face biometrics, *IEEE International Workshop on Biomedical Circuits and Systems*, pp. S1/6–17–20.

Zemcik, P., Hradis, M. & Herout, A. (2007). Local rank differences - novel features for image, *Proceedings of SCCG 2007*, pp. 1–12.

Zemčík, P. & Žádník, M. (2007). Adaboost engine, *Proceedings of FPL 2007*, IEEE Computer Society, p. 5.

Zemčík, P., Hradiš, M. & Herout, A. (2010). Exploiting neighbors for faster scanning window detection in images, *ACIVS 2010*, LNCS 6475, Springer Verlag, p. 12.

Zhang, L., Chu, R., Xiang, S., Liao, S. & Li, S. Z. (2007). Face detection based on multi-block lbp representation, *ICB*, pp. 11–18.

12

Energy Consumption Analysis of Routing Protocols in Mobile Ad Hoc Networks

Ali Norouzi and A. Halim Zaim
Department of Computer Engineering, Istanbul University,
Avcilar, Istanbul,
Turkey

1. Introduction

Wireless networks are divided into two types: cellular [Swaroop et al, 2009] and mobile [Fapojuwo et al, 2004]. Cellular networks have been comprised of a fixed spinal column and radio base station so that the last hop that the user uses is wireless in form; however, many things are dependent on space and time [Dixit et al, 2005]. Figure 1 shows an example of cellular networks.

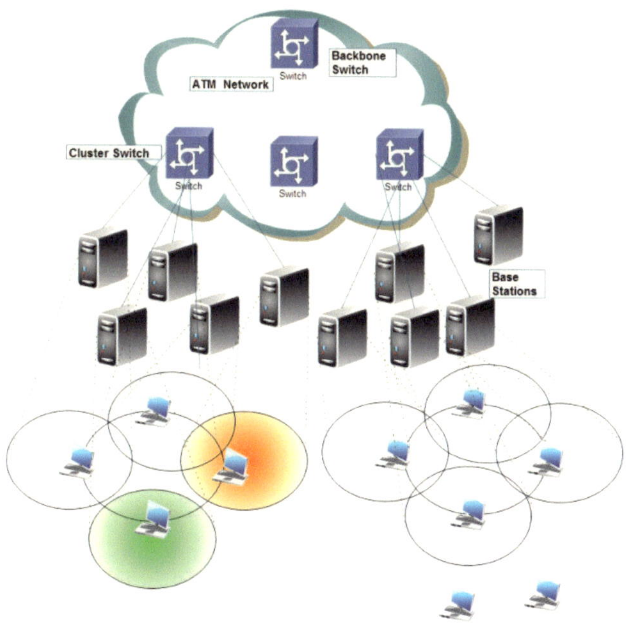

Fig. 1. An example of cellular networks

1.2 Basis of mobile ad hoc networks

A MANET is one that does not have any base station and fixed substructure that can freely and dynamically self-organize into temporary network topologies. An ad hoc mobile network is an unstable network formed dynamically by a collection of wireless mobile nodes without the use of an existing network substructure [Chlamtac et al, 2003]. Such networks back up calculations at any time and in any place, and their structures can change automatically [Norouzi. A and Ustundag B. B, 2011]. In such networks, each mobile host acts as a router. For this reason, peer-to-peer communication as well as peer-to-remote communication is possible in this kind of network [Camp et al, 2002].

Fig. 2. An example of a Mobile Ad hoc Network (MANET)

Figure 2 shows an example of a MANET. This type of network has been comprised of different kinds of mobile devices such as PDAs, smart signals and mobile hosts. In MANETs, routing is a complex problem and the reason for this is mobility of routes. However, links may change frequently and this subject refers to the fact that communication links should be updated continually and their messages should be sent frequently; hence this control creates traffic [Perkins E, 2008].

There are special devices in different forms, but one of their common specifications is that they use battery energy, and this energy is limited. Wireless transmission, collision, resubmission and conductive radio waves are all effective in energy consumption. As a result, there is strong need for the presence of protocols which use energy efficiently and effectively as well as technology for better management of energy [Norouzi. A and Ustundag B. B, 2011].

2. Related work

In the energy consumption and performance evaluation of protocols for an ad hoc network, the protocols should be tested under realistic conditions. This chapter is a research in which mobile ad hoc networks are described and some routing protocols explained. During simulation, different results were given by changing the selected parameters. Firstly we have a technical look at these types of protocols and their specifications [Jayakumar. G and Gopinath. G, 2007].

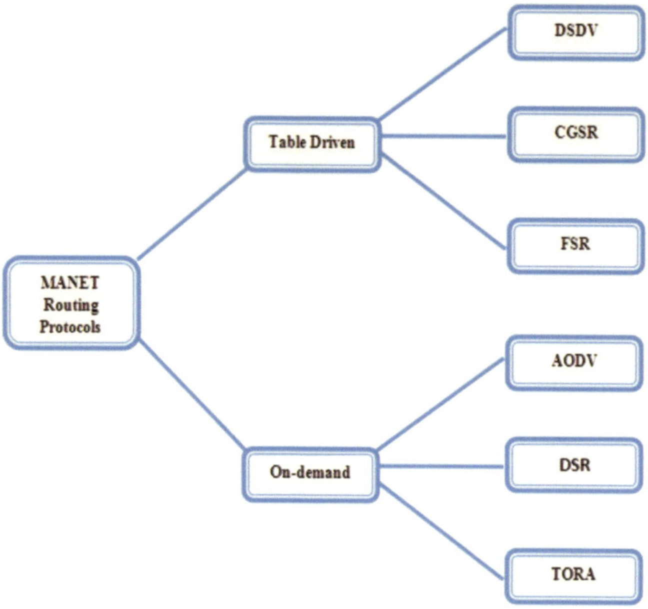

Fig. 3. Categorization of MANET routing protocols

2.1 Mobile ad hoc network routing protocols

As shown in Figure 3, routing protocols in mobile ad hoc networks are classified into two classes: table-driven and on-demand [Misra S et al, 2008]. The table-driven d, or proactive, method is used for alternate updating links and can use both the distance vectors and link statuses used in fixed networks. The word "proactive" means that this method is always active and will also react to a change in the linkage [Norouzi. A and Ustundag B. B, 2011]. A problem arises for this method when movement is low because additional work is done and the network tends toward instability [Bai F et al, 2004].

In the on-demand method with reactions, other nodes do not update the route and the routes are determined at the origin of the request. Therefore, there is the possibility of using a caching mechanism. The advantage of this method is that both energy and bandwidth are used effectively. In this chapter, the table-driven and the on-demand protocols are explained and then compared with different parameters [Dixit et al, 2005].

2.2 Table-driven protocols

In this group of protocols, each node maintains one or more tables that include routing information to other nodes of the network. All nodes update their tables to preserve compatibility and to give upgraded viewpoints of the network. When the topology of the network changes, the nodes distribute update messages across the network [Misra S et al, 2008]. Some identifying aspects of this class of routing protocols include the ways in which information is distributed, the ways the topology is changed and the number of tables necessary for routing. The following sections explain some of these routing protocols [Boukerche. A et al, 2011].

2.2.1 DSDV (Dynamic Destination-Sequence Distance – Vector routing protocol)

This protocol is based on the BELLMANFORD routing idea, with a series of improvements [Bagad V. S and Dhotre, 2009]. Each mobile base maintains a routing table that includes all accessible destinations, the number of hops necessary for reaching that destination and the sequence of the digits appropriate to that destination. This sequence of digits is used to distinguish new routes from old routes and to determine the creation of a ring. In DSDV, stations send their routing tables alternatively to their direct neighbors [Maan. F and Mazhar. N., 2011]. Tables are updated generally in two perfect updating and incremental updating methods. Any route updating package increases information about routing. This protocol performs periodic updates, but also generates a supplementary traffic that adds to the real data traffic. [Bamis. A et al, 2007].

2.2.2 CGSR Protocol (Cluster head Gateway Switch Routing protocol)

This protocol is based on the DSDV routing algorithm. Mobile nodes are collected inside packets, and a cluster head is selected. A gateway node is a node in a communication interval between two or more cluster heads. In a dynamic network, the idea of a cluster head can decrease the efficiency resulting from the frequency of selecting cluster heads. Thus, CGSR uses an algorithm to change the last cluster or LCC. [Murthy S and Aceves J. J, 1996].

In LCC, a change in cluster head is made when changes are made in the network. In this state, the origin sends the packet to its cluster head; the cluster head sends this packet to the gateway node to which it and the node which is located in the route of destination are connected. The gateway sends the packet to another cluster head and this action continues until the cluster head receives the destination node of packet. Finally, the destination cluster head sends the packet to the destination node [Boukerche. A et al, 2011]. Figure 4 indicates an example of a CGSR routing plan.

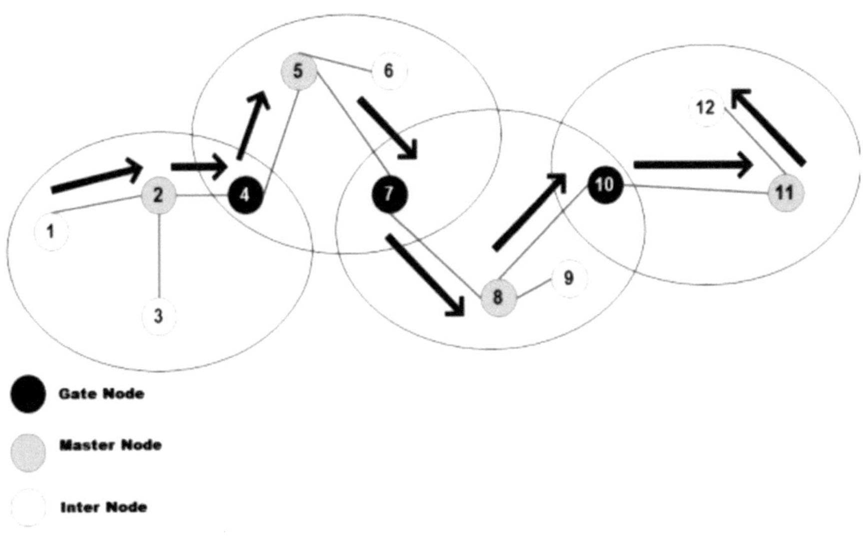

Fig. 4. Example of CGSR routing from node 1 to node 12

2.2.3 FSR protocol (Fisheye State Routing)

In an FSR, an updating message does not include information about all of the nodes. Instead, it exchanges information with the adjacent nodes with a higher frequency more than it does with farther nodes, leading to a decrease in the size of the updating message [Pei. G et al, 2000]. Thus, each node has accurate information about its neighbours, and the details and accuracy of the information decrease when the distance between two nodes increases. Figure 5 defines the area of a fisheye for a central node that has been indicated in red [Boukerche. A et al, 2011].

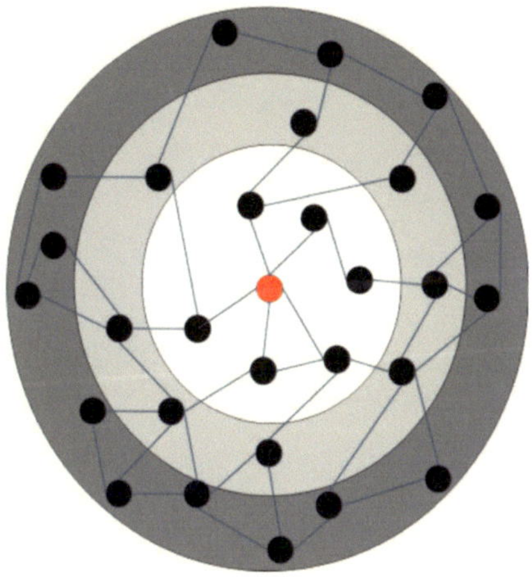

Fig. 5. Accuracy of information in FSR protocol

The central node should know more detail about the nodes that are located inside the white circle. FSR is suitable for massive networks, because in this method, overload is controlled [Liu. Y et al, 2004].

2.3 On-demand protocols

In comparison with table-driven routing protocols, all updated routes are not maintained in each node in this group of protocols; instead, routes are constructed only when it is necessary. When an origin node wants to send something to a destination, it makes a request to the destination for the route detection mechanisms. For this reason, this type of protocol is known as a reactive protocol. This route remains valid until the destination is accessible. This section explains some of the on-demand routing protocols [Boukerche. A et al, 2011].

2.3.1 AODV (Ad-Hoc On-demand Distance Vector routing)

This protocol can be regarded as an improvement of DSDV. AODV minimises the number of distributions by creating routes on-demand [Esmaili. H et al, 2011]. In contrast, DSDV maintained a list of all routes to find a route to the destination whenever the origin broadcasts a route request packet to all nodes. The neighbours distribute the packets among their neighbours until the packet reaches an intermediate node with a new route to the destination [Song J. H et al, 2004].

Figure 6 (a) indicates a distribution packet among neighbors. If a node saw the packet previously, it will discard it and will not pay attention to it. Route demand packet uses sequence numbers in order to ensure that a ring is not formed in the route [Bai F et al, 2004]. This mechanism also guarantees that if intermediate nodes reply to this request, it will be based on their latest information. AODV uses only symmetric and two-sided links because routing the reply packet is achieved by simply reversing the packet route. Figure 2. 3 (b) shows the process of reply to demand [Bamis. A et al, 2008].

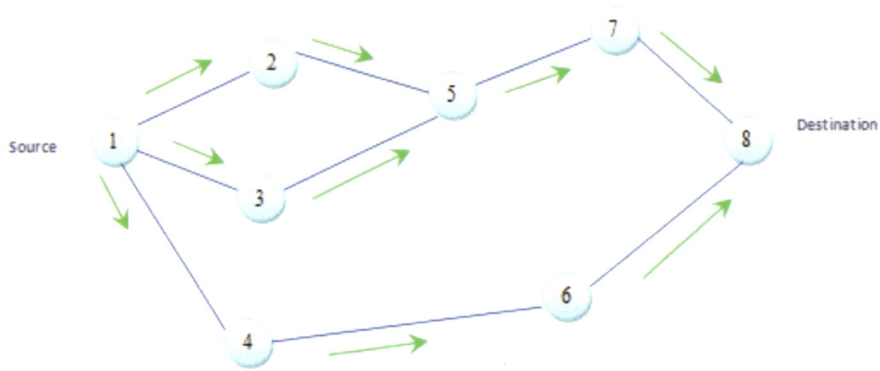

(a)Distribution packet among neighbors

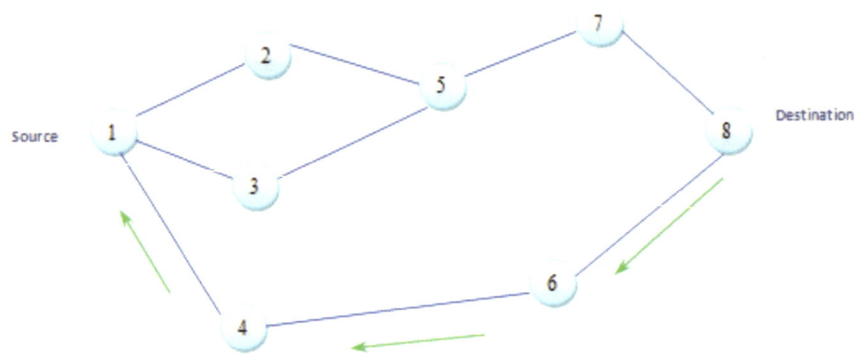

(b) Reply to demand

Fig. 6. Detection of route in AODV

2.3.2 DSR (Dynamic Source Routing protocol)

The Dynamic Source Routing protocol (DSR) is a simple and efficient routing protocol designed specifically for use in multi-hop wireless ad hoc networks of mobile nodes. DSR allows the network to be completely self-organising and self-configuring, without the need for any existing network infrastructure or administration. The protocol is composed of two main mechanisms - "route discovery" and "route maintenance" - that work together to allow nodes to discover and maintain routes to arbitrary destinations in the ad hoc network [Suresh A. et al, 2011].

Figure 7 (a) shows how the route demand packet is distributed in the network and indicates its route record section [Perkins E, 2008]. If the destination node produces a reply on each route, this node places the route record section of the route demand packet in the route reply [Suresh A et al 2011]. In another state, if an intermediate node wants to produce a route reply, it will place its cached route to the destination in the route record section of the route demand packet. Figure 7 (b) indicates the state in which the destination node itself has sent a route reply [Qun Z. A et al 2011].

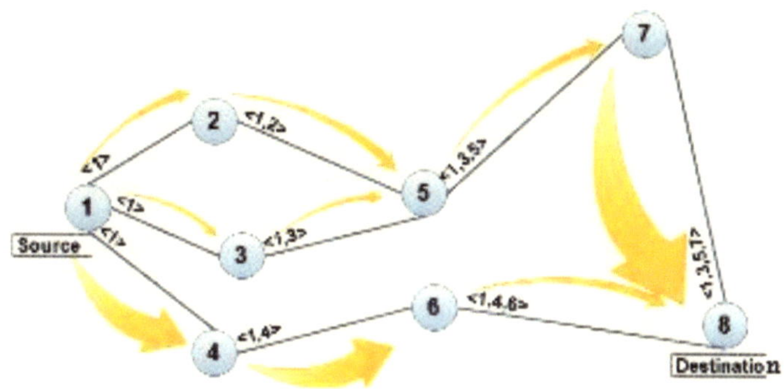

(a)Distribution of demand packets

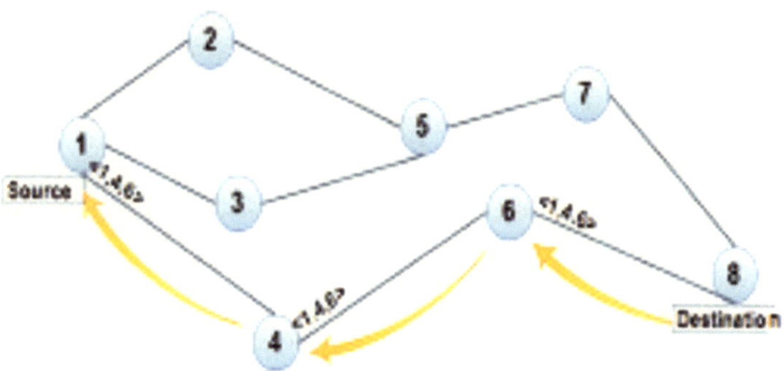

(b)Reply packets

Fig. 7. An instance of route detection in DSR

2.3.3 TORA protocol (Temporally-Ordered Routing Algorithm)

The main characteristic of TORA is the centralization of control messages in a very small set of near local nodes in which topological changes have been made. To achieve this property, nodes maintain routing information for the adjacent nodes for some interval. This protocol has three duties: route formation, route renovation and route cleaning. Route formation is performed with QRY* and UPD† [Park. V et al 2001]. A route formation algorithm starts by determining a zero set for height of destination node and empty set for height of other nodes.

---

*Query protocol

†User Datagram Protocol

The origin distributes a QRY packet in which destination node identifier is located. In this method, a non-circular graph is created from origin to destination. Figure 8 indicates a process of route formation in TORA. As shown in Figure 8 (a), node 5 receives the QRY packet from node 3 but it doesn’t publish it because this packet has reached this node through node 2 previously. In Figure 8 (b), the origin, i. e. , node 1 can receive the UPD packet from node 2 or node 3 but it doesn't receive it from node 4 of which the height is lower.

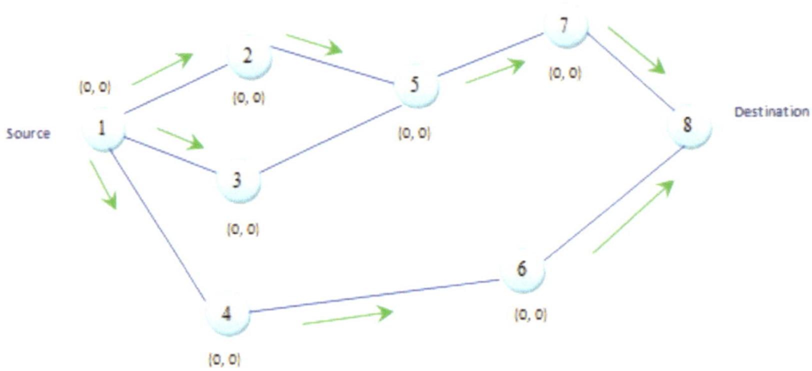

a)Broadcast QRY

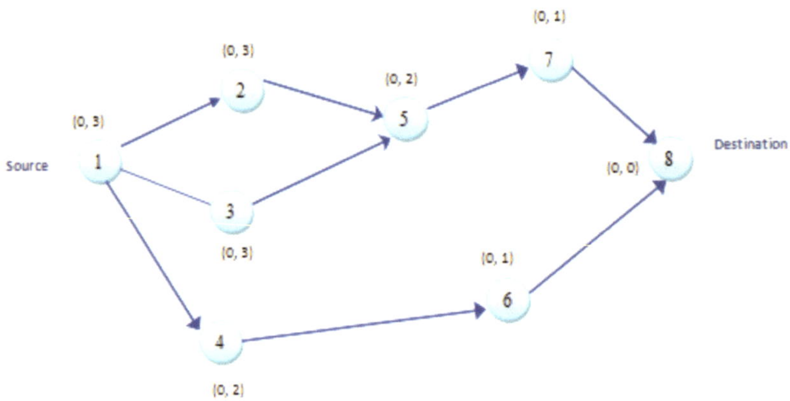

b) Distribute UDP packet

Fig. 8. Detection of route in TORA

2.3.4 CBRP (Cluster based Routing Protocols)

In these protocols, clusters are formed by dividing the whole network into self-managed groups of nodes. These groups are dynamically rearranged when the topology of the network is changed. To form these clusters, the following algorithm is used. When a node enters the network, it enters an indefinite state. In this state, it adjusts a timer and distributes a Hello message for all other nodes. When a cluster head receives this Hello message, it replies with a Hello message immediately. When the unknown node receives this message, it changes its state to member. If the indefinite node does not receive a reply after the defined time, it introduces itself as a cluster head in the case that it has a two-sided conductive linkage with a node or nodes that are its neighbours. Otherwise, it remains in the indefinite state and repeats the procedure [Jiang M et al 1999].

3. Simulation and comparison

Since energy consumption during communication is a major energy depletion parameter, the number of transmissions must be reduced as much as possible to achieve extended battery life. As a result, there is a strong need for the presence of protocols which use energy efficiently and effectively as well as technology for better management of energy. Unfortunately, battery technology doesn't grow as rapidly as CPU or memory does [Akkaya. K et al 2005]. In this section we would like to analyse comprehensively the results of the simulation for mobile ad hoc routing protocols in some aspects and different scenarios of energy consumption such as movement model, traffic model, data-sending model, environment and amount of nodes. To compare the protocols [Qasim. N et al 2009], a simulation of a MANET is required to be performed in a Network Simulator [Qun Z. A et al 2011] environment. The simulation includes motion models, a physical layer with a radio broadcast, radio network communications and the IEEE 802. 11 (MAC) protocol [Chowdhury et al 2010] with a distributed coordination equation or DCE. This model includes collisions, broadcast delays and signal damping with a bandwidth of 2 Mbps and a transmission range of 250 m. There are some protocols that have been selected for comparison, such as DSR, AODV, DSDV, TORA, FSR, CBRP and CGSR. The first four protocols have been completely simulated by NS2 [26], and the code of other protocols has been added to NS2. [Stemm. M and Katz. R 1997].

The basic model parameters that have been used in the following experiments are summarised in Table 1.

Parameter	*Value*
Simulator	NS-2
Protocols studied	DSR, AODV, DSDV, TORA, FSR, CBRP and CGSR
Simulation time	900 sec
Simulation area	500 x 500
Transmission range	250 m
Node movement	Random waypoint
Traffic type	CBR (UDP)
Data payload	Bytes/packet
Bandwidth	2 Mbps

Table 1. Simulation parameters

3.1 Energy consumption model

The following equations show the energy consumed in the transfer of a packet (equation 1) and receipt of a packet (equation 2), in which packet size is based on bits:

$$Energy_{tx}=(330*5*PacketSize)/2*10^6 \quad (1)$$

$$Energy_{rx}=(230*5*PacketSize)/2*10^6 \quad (2)$$

Energy consumption in actual equipment occurs not only during sending and receiving data but also during the hearing process; however, in this simulation, it has been assumed that hearing needs no energy and that the nodes have no energy consumption at any idle time. In fact, energy consumption has been considered only at times of packet sending and receiving.

An important point considered in this simulation is that when a packet is sent, a percentage of the consumed energy is the energy of the radio frequency. In this simulation, the value of RF has been maintained at 281. 1 mw, which is equivalent to the RF energy needed for a model with a 250 metre transmission range.

3.2 Work methodology

The final aim of this work is to measure and compare the energy consumption in seven DSR, AODV, DSDV, TORA, FSR, CBRP and CGSR protocols.

The five parameters selected for this simulation are as follows:

- Number of moving nodes
- Size of nodes movement zone
- Nodes movement model
- Traffic of origin nodes
- Data traffic model

In this simulation, nodes move according to the RWP‡ Model, and this movement is specified with two factors: maximum speed and stop time. The Random Waypoint (RWP) model is a commonly used synthetic model for mobility, e. g. , in ad hoc networks. It is an elementary model which describes the movement pattern of independent nodes by simple terms. During simulation, each node starts moving from its primary position to a random target point inside the simulation area, and the movement speed of each node is an unsteady value between zero and its maximum speed. When a node reaches its target point, it waits for its stop time and starts moving by selecting another random target point. All traffic origins used in the simulation produce a fixed data traffic rate CBR (continuous bit-rate). The traffic structure changes with two factors: the rate of sending and the packet size.

In a basic scenario, a MANET has been considered with 25 moving nodes distributed randomly in an environment with an area of 500×500 m^2. Nodes move with a maximum speed of 500 m/s and have a stop time of 0 seconds. Twenty traffic origins produce CBR data traffic sending four packets per second and with a packet size of 512 bites. Each simulation has been performed for 900 seconds. In this simulation, working indices of total energy consumption, energy consumption based on the sending operation (TX) and receiving (RX) and energy consumption based on the type of packets (MAC, CBR and routing) have been assessed.

---

‡Random Waypoint

3.3 Results of simulation

In this section, seven selected routing protocols are compared with the basic scenario and with different scenarios by changing five selected parameters. Figure 9 (a) shows the total percentage of energy consumed in the sending and receiving operations at the MAC level. It is observed that energy consumption is higher during the receiving process. The receiving process includes two kinds of activity: actual receipt of data and overhearing data from neighbourhood nodes. Figure 9 (b) shows the percentage of energy consumed based on all kinds of packets. It is observed that MAC packets have a major effect on energy consumption.

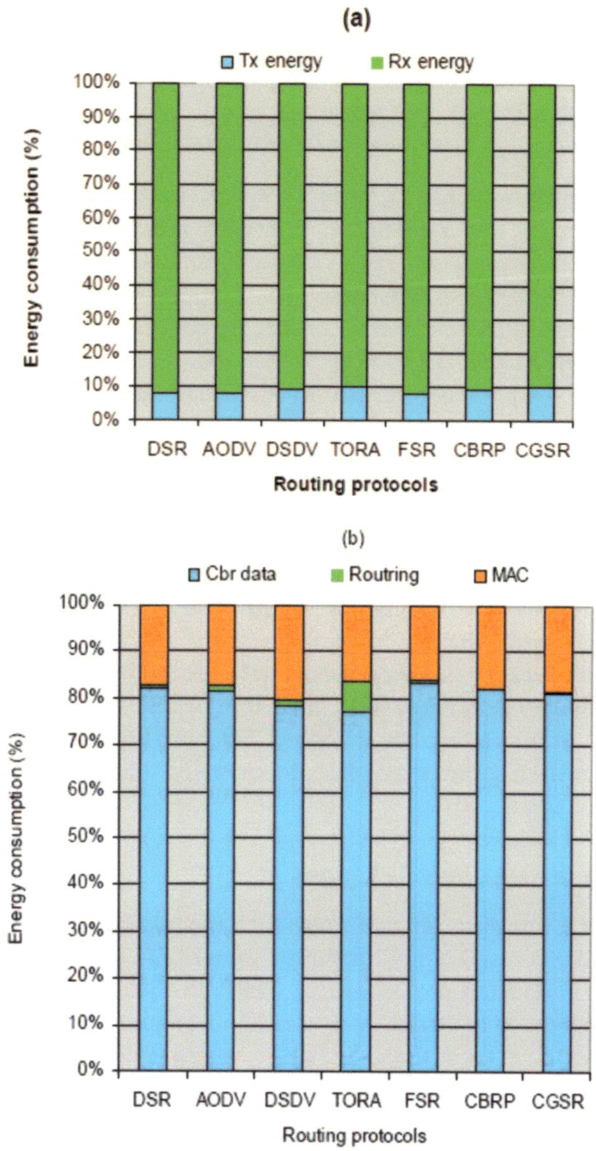

Fig. 9. Energy consumption for (a) RX and TX operations, (b) for different kinds of MAC, CBR and routing packets

These comparisons show that the efficiency of DSR is better than that of AODV and DSDV. Although DSR uses origin routing and AODV uses hop-to-hop routing, it is seen that DSR is more efficient than AODV. This result may come about from the caching mechanism. It can help to save energy, time, and bandwidth. FSR falls between DSR and AODV protocols. CBRP and CGSR have shown higher energy consumption than DSR. TORA has the highest energy consumption due to the assembly of route detection packets and packet maintenance [Tuteja. A et al 2010].

3.4 Results obtained from movement model changes

In this section, a movement model is presented in the basic scenario changes, and the simulation is implemented for stop times of 30, 120, 600 and 900 s. These implementations provide an interval between discrete simulation (no stop time) and static simulation (stop time of 900).

Figure 10 shows energy consumption with seven protocols. DSR shows the best result and TORA shows the worst result. For on-demand protocols, i. e., TORA, AODV, DSR and CBRP, we see considerable changes in energy consumption in the change in movement model [Cano. J. C et al 2000]; however, the energy consumption of table-driven protocols is not related to the movement model and keeps its state, in contrast to on-demand protocols [Sargolzaey. H et al 2009]. In this simulation, TORA shows the worst result due to its assembly of IMEP[§] and TORA packets [Prakash. Sh et al 2011]. According to this scenario, it is observed that DSR and AODV have shown relatively similar behaviour in static networks, but when the movement of nodes is stable (low stop time), their behaviour will be different. In this movement model, DSR (using a caching mechanism as well as irregular nodes technique) and AODV (due to having low parasite during sending route detection packets) could have shown the best result [Gupta. A. K et al 2010].

Figure 11 shows results obtained by varying the maximum speed of nodes between 0, 1, 15 and 25 m/s. These values have been considered, respectively, as simulating a fixed network, a network for pedestrians, a network for cyclists, a network for drivers and a network for train travellers. The obtained results show fixed behaviour of DSDV even in movement with high speed but energy consumption has increased for four on-demand protocols with regard to increase in maximum speed of movement. Generally, when speed is added, DSDV is better than AODV [Liu. Y et al 2004].

3.5 Results obtained from traffic model changes

Figure 12 shows the behaviour of seven protocols when the number of origin nodes varies between 10, 20 and 30. In this case, energy consumption in DSDV is fixed without regard to traffic load, and in four on-demand protocols, i. e., CBRP, DSR, DSDV and TORA, changes in energy consumption are made more slowly than traffic changes.

When the number of origins changes from 10 to 20, routing energy increases to 7. 31% in DSR, 88. 97% in AODV and 4. 71% in TORA. During traffic increase from 20 to 30, this routing increases to 41. 73%, 15. 88% and 13. 37% for DSR, AODV and TORA, respectively.

[§] IMEP

The main reason for this behaviour is that in on-demand routing protocols, nodes use the previous packets for receiving new route information and when traffic increases, so too does the activity of nodes [Sargolzaey. H et al 2009].

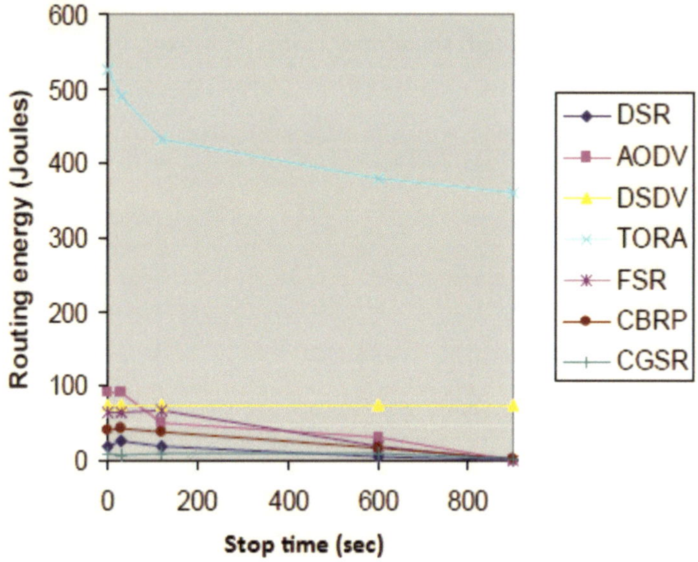

Fig. 10. Energy consumption as a function of stop time for seven protocols

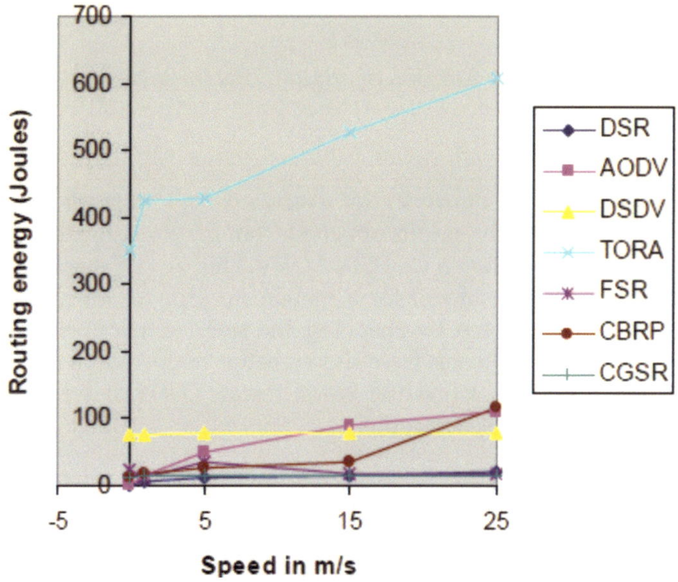

Fig. 11. Energy consumption as a function of maximum speed for seven protocols

4. Experimental results and analysis

We can summarise our final conclusion from our experimental results as follows:

Increasing the number of nodes with constant origin makes TORA unstable, and its energy consumption increases by 518% when the number of nodes increases from 25 to 50. DSDV has shown fixed behaviour in all scenarios due to its table driven specification. DSR has acted better than AODV and CBRP in similar situations, and FSR has mostly had values between those of DSR and AODV. CGSR has had no constant behaviour and sometimes performs better than DSR, although sometimes worse. However, its overall performance is similar to that of DSR.

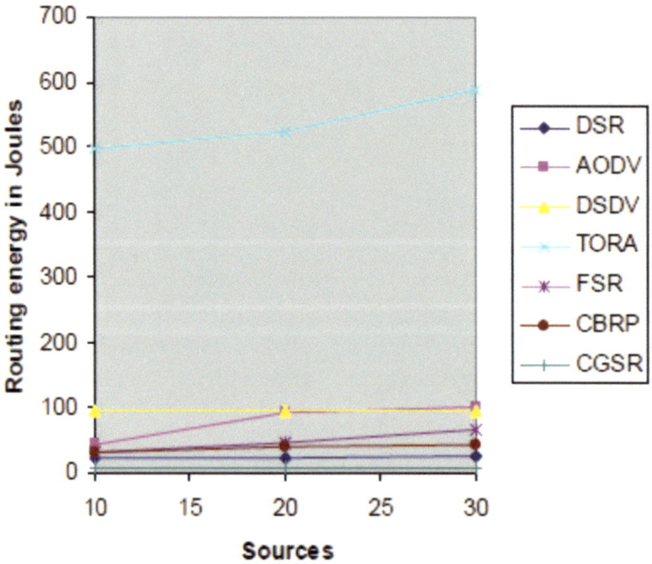

Fig. 12. Energy consumption as a function of origin traffic for seven protocols

5. Conclusion

In this article, Mobile Ad Hoc networks are described, and some of the most important routing protocols are studied. The results obtained from the assessment and comparisons of the energy consumption were shown for DSR, AODV, DSDV, TORA, FSR, CBRP and CGSR protocols. Parameters were considered for a mobile Ad Hoc networks, as well as a basic state. Different results were given by changing the selected parameters. Based on these results, the DSR and AODV protocols have shown better performance than other protocols, and for all scenarios, TORA has had the worst result. DSDV has fixed behavior in all scenarios due to its table driven specification.

6. References

Akkaya. K and Younis. M, "A Survey of Routing Protocols in Wireless Sensor Networks, " in the Elsevier Ad Hoc Network Journal, Vol. 3/3, pp. 325349, 2005.

Bagad V. S, Dhotre A, Computer Networks – II, Chapter 8, ISBN 818431616X, 9788184316162, Technical Publications, 2009

Bai F, Sadagopan N, Krishnamachari B, Helmy A, Modeling Path Duration Distributions in MANETs and Their Impact on Reactive Routing Protocols, IEEE Journal On Selected Areas In Communications, VOL. 22, NO. 7, Pages 1357-1373, September 2004

Bamis. A, Boukerche. A, Chatzigiannakis. I, Nikoletseas. S, "A mobility aware protocol synthesis for efficient routing in ad hoc mobile networks", Elsevier Computer Networks, doi:10. 1016/j. comnet. 2007. 09. 023, Vol 52, 2008 p130- 154.

Boukerche. A, Turgut. B, Aydin. N, Ahmad. M. Z, Bölöni. L and Turgut. D, Routing protocols in ad hoc networks: A survey, Elsevier Computer Networks, doi:10. 1016/j. comnet. 2011. 05. 010, Volume 55, Issue 13, 15 September 2011, Pages 3032-3080

Camp. T, Boleng. J, and Davies. V "A survey of mobility models for ad hoc network research", Wireless Communications & Mobile Computing (WCMC): Special issue on Mobile Ad Hoc Networking: Research, Trends and Applications, vol. 2, no. 5, pp. 483-502, August 2002

Cano. J. C, Manzoni. P, "A Performance Comparison of Energy Consumption for Mobile Ad Hoc Networks Routing Protocols", IEEE/ACM MASCOTS 2000: Eighth International Symposium on Modeling, Analysis and Simulation of Computer and Telecommunication Systems, San Francisco (USA), August 2000.

Cheng. Z, Heinzelman W. B, "Discovering long lifetime routes in mobile ad hoc networks", Elsevier Ad Hoc Networks, doi:10. 1016/j. adhoc. 2007. 06. 001, Vol 6, 2008, p661-674.

Chlamtac I, Conti M, Liu J. N, Mobile ad hoc networking: imperatives and challenges, Ad Hoc Networks, doi: 10. 1016/S1570-8705(03)00013-1, pages: 13-64, Elsevier 2003

Chowdhury, S. A. Islam, M. T. Jaigirdar, F. T. Faruqui, M. R. U. Al Noor, S.; Performance study and simulation analysis of CSMA and IEEE 802. 11 in Wireless Sensor Networks and limitations of IEEE 802. 11 in Proc. IEEE ICCIT 2009. Conf. , Pages: 431 - 436, DOI: 10. 1109/ICCIT. 2009. 5407277, Feb 2010

Dixit. S.; Yanmaz, E.; Tonguz, O. K.; On the Design of Self-Organized Cellular Wireless Networks, DOI: 10. 1109/MCOM. 2005. 1470827, July 2005, IEEE

Du. Y, Gupta S. K. S, Varsamopoulos G, Improving on-demand data access efficiency in MANETs with cooperative caching, Ad Hoc Networks, Vol 7, Pages 579-598, doi:10. 1016/j. adhoc. 2008. 07. 007, Elsevier 2009

Esmaili. H. A. , Khalili Shoja. M. R, Gharaee. H, Performance Analysis of AODV under Black Hole Attack through Use of OPNET Simulator in Proc. IEEE WCSIT 2011. Conf. , Vol. 1, No. 2, Pages 49-52, ISSN: 2221-0741

Fall. K and Varadhan. K "ns Notes and Documents", The VINT Project. UC Berkeley, LBL, USC/ISI, and Xerox PARC, February 25, 2000. Available from

Fapojuwo, Salazar. A. O, Sesay O., Performance of a QoS-based multiple-route ad hoc on-demand distance vector protocol for mobile ad hoc networks in proceeding of IEEE Conf. CJECE. 2004 PP 149-155

Gupta. A. K. , Sadawarti. H, Verma. A. K, Performance analysis of AODV, DSR & TORA Routing Protocols, IJET Vol. 2, No. 2, April 2010, Pages 226-231 http://www. isi. edu/~salehi/ns_doc/.

Jayakumar G, Gopinath. G, Ad Hoc Mobile Wireless Networks Routing Protocols - A Review, Journal of Computer Science Vol 3 No8: 574-582, 2007

Jiang M, Li J, Tay Y. C, "Cluster Based Routing Protocol (CBRP)", draft -ietfmant-cbrp-spec-01. txt, work in progress, July 1999.

Jung. S, Hundewale. N, Zelikovsky. A, Energy Efficiency of Load Balancing in MANET Routing Protocols in Proceeding of IEEE Conf. SNPD/SAWN'05, DOI: 0-7695-2294-7/05, 2005

Liu. Y, Lau. J, A novel link state routing protocol and TCP performance investigation in ad hoc networks, , DOI: 10. 1016/S0140-3664(03)00214-7, Computer Communications 27 (2004) Pages 187-196, Elsevier 2004

Maan F, Mazhar N, "MANET Routing Protocols vs Mobility Models: A Performance Evaluation in Proc.", IEEE ICUFN 2011. Conf. , pp. 179–184. DOI 978-1-4577-1177-0/11

Misra S, Sanjay K. Dhurandher, Obaidat M. S, Nangia A, Bhardwaj N, Goyal P, and Sumit Aggarwal, Node Stability-Based Location Updating in Mobile Ad-Hoc Networks, IEEE Systems Journal, Vol. 2, No. 2, pages 237-247, June 2008

Murthy S and Aceves J. J, "An Efficient Routing Protocol for Wireless Networks", ACM Mobile Networks and App. J. , Special Issue on Routing in Mobile Communication Networks, Oct. 1996, pp. 183-97.

Norouzi. A, Ustundag B. B, A Novel Routing Protocol with High Energy Performance in Mobile Special Networks, Journal of Computer Science, PP 108-113, VOL. 7 No. 1, DOI:10. 3844/jcssp. 2011. 108. 113, June 2011

Park. V, Corson. S, Tora (Temporally-Ordered Routing Algorithm routing protocol) - Temporally-Ordered Routing Algorithm (TORA) Version 1 Internet Draft, draft-ietf-manet-tora-spec- 03. txt, work in progress, June 2001.

Park. V. D and M. Scott Corson. A performance comparison of TORA and Ideal Link State routing. In Proceedings of IEEE Symposium on Computers and Communication '98, June 1998.

Pei. G, Gerla Mand, Chen T. -W, "Fisheye State Routing in Mobile Ad Hoc Networks", In Proceedings of the Workshops ICDCS 2000, Taipei, Taiwan, Apr. 2000, pp. D71- D78.

Perkins E, Ad Hoc Networking, ISBN: 0321579070, Addison-Wesley Pub Co Inc, 2008

Prakash. Sh, Saini. J. P. , Gupta. S. C., A survey of multipath routing in Mobile Ad Hoc Networks, International journal GJCAT, Vol 1, 2011 Page 11-23

Qasim. N, Said. F, Aghvami. H, Mobile Ad Hoc Networking Protocols' Evaluation through Simulation for Quality of Service, International Journal of Computer Science, 36:1, IJCS_36_1_10, 2009

Qun Z. A., Jun W, "Application of NS2 in Education of Computer Networks in Proceeding of ICACTE 2008, Pages 368-372, DOI 10. 1109, 2008 IEEE

Sargolzaey. H, Akbari Moghanjoughi. A, Khatun. S, A Review and Comparison of Reliable Unicast Routing Protocols For Mobile Ad Hoc Networks, IJCSNS Vol 9 No 1 Jan 2009 Pages:189-196

Song J. H, Wong V. W. S, Victor C. M, Leung, Efficient On-Demand Routing for Mobile Ad Hoc Wireless Access Networks, IEEE Journal On Selected Areas In Communications, Vol. 22, No. 7, PP 1374-1383, September 2004

Stemm. M and Katz. R, "Measuring and Reducing Energy Consumption of Network Interfaces in Hand-held devices", IEICE Transactions on Communications, Special Issue on Mobile Computing, Invited paper, E80-B(8): p1125-1131, August 1997

Suresh A, Duraiswamy K, Mobile Ad Hoc Network Security for Reactive Routing Protocol with Node Reputation Scheme, Journal of Computer Science Vol 7 No 2 PP: 242-249, 2011

Swaroop. A, Singh A. K, A Token-Based Group Mutual Exclusion Algorithm for Cellular Wireless Networks in proceeding of IEEE Indicon 2009 Conf. PP:1-4

Tuteja. A, Gujral. R, Thalia. S, Comparative Performance Analysis of DSDV, AODV and DSR Routing Protocols in MANET using NS2, in Conf. proceeding ACE 2010 IEEE, DOI 10. 1109/ACE. 2010. 16

Vadde K. K, Syrotiuk V. R, Factor Interaction on Service Delivery in Mobile Ad Hoc Networks, IEEE Journal On Selected Areas In Communications, Vol. 22, NO. 7, Pages 1335-1346, September 2004,

13

Real-Time Motion Processing Estimation Methods in Embedded Systems

Guillermo Botella and Diego González
Complutense University of Madrid,
Department of Computer Architecture and Automation
Spain

1. Introduction

Motion estimation is a low-level vision task which manages a high number of applications as sport tracking, surveillance, security, industrial inspection, robotics, navigation, optics, medicine and so on. Unfortunately, many times it is unaffordable to implement a fully functional embedded system for real-time operation which works in a while with enough accuracy due the nature and complexity of the signal processing operations involved.

In this chapter, we will introduce different motion estimation systems and their implementation when real-time is required. For the sake of clarity, it will be previously shown a general description of the motion estimation paradigm. Subsequently, three systems regarding low-level and mid-level vision domain will be explained.

The present chapter is thus organized as follows, after an introductory part, the second section is regarding the motion estimation and optical flow paradigms, the similarities and differences to understand the real-time methods and algorithms. Later will be performed a classification of motion estimation systems according different families and enhancements for further approaches. This second section is finished with a plethora of real-time implementations of the systems explained previously.

The third section focuses on three different case studies of real-time optical flow systems developed by the authors, where also are presented the throughput and resource consuming data from a reconfigurable platform (FPGA-based) used in the implementation.

The fourth section analyses the performance and the resources consumed by each one of this three specific real-time implementations. The rest of the sections, fifth to seventh, approaches the conclusion, the acknowledgements and the bibliography, respectively.

2. Motion estimation

The term "optic flow" was named by James Gibson after the Second World War, when he was working on the development of tests for pilots in the U.S. Air Force (Gibson, 1947). His basic principles provided the basis for much of the work of computer vision 30 years later (Mar, 1982). In later publications, Gibson defines the deformation gradient image along the motion of the observer, a concept that was dubbed "flow".

When an object moves on, for example, a camera, the two-dimensional projection image moves with the project as shown in Figure 1. The projection of three-dimensional motion vectors on the two-dimensional detector is called the apparent field of flow velocities or image. The observer does not have access to the velocity field directly, since the optical sensors provide luminance distributions, not speed, and motion vectors may be decidedly different from this luminance distribution.

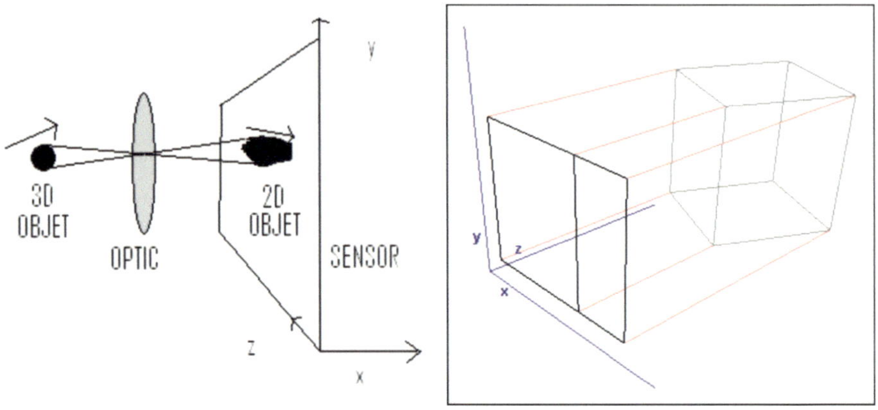

Fig. 1. Projection from 3D world to 2D detector surface.

The term "apparent" refers to one of the capital problems in computer vision, in the absence of speed never real, but a two dimensional field called motion field. However, it is possible calculate the movement of local regions of the luminance distribution, being known as the field of optical flow motion, providing only an approximation to the actual field of speeds (Verri & Poggio, 1989).

As an example, it is easy to see that the optical flow is different from the velocity field. As shown in Figure 2, there is a sphere rotating with constant brightness, which produces no change in the luminance of the image. The optical flow is zero everywhere in contradiction with the velocity field. The reverse situation yields with a static scene with a moving light in which the velocity field is zero everywhere, even though the luminance contrast induces no zero optical flow. One additional example can be appreciated with the rotational poles announcing the barbershops of yesteryears, with the velocity field perpendicular to the flow.

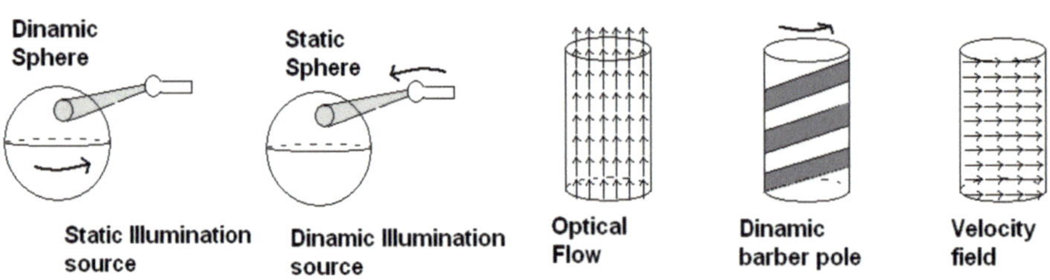

Fig. 2. Difference between velocity field and optical flow.

Among these atypical situations, under certain limits it is possible to recover motion estimation. Motion algorithms described in this chapter recover the flow as an approximation of the velocity field projected flow information. They deliver two dimensional array of vectors that may be subject to several high-level performances. In the literature appears several applications in this regard (Nakayama, 1985; Mitiche, 1996).

Optical flow is an ill-conditioned problem since it is based on imaging three dimensions on a two-dimensional detector. The process removes information, and its recovery is not trivial. Therefore, the flow is a measure of the ill-posed problem, since there are infinite velocity fields that may cause the observed changes in the luminance distribution, in addition, there are infinite three-dimensional movements that can generate a given field of velocities.

Thus, it is necessary to consider a number of clues or signals to restore the flow. The so-called problem of aperture (Wallach, 1976; Horn & Schunck, 1981; Adelson & Bergen, 1985) appears when measuring the two-dimensional velocity components using only local measurements. It is possible recovering the component of the velocity gradient perpendicular to the edge, forcing adding external conditions that usually require obtaining information from a finite neighbourhood area, see Figure 3a. The region must be large enough to get a solution as the search for a corner to resolve this problem, for example. However, the collection of information across a region increases the probability of also taking on different motion contours and hence, to truncate the results, needing a trade-off solution, this last question is named as the aperture general problem (Ong & Spann, 1999).

2.1 State of art estimating real-time motion

There are many algorithms and architectures frequently used for real-time optical flow estimation, emanating from artificial intelligence, signal theory, robotics, psychology and biology. There is an extensive literature, and it is not the purpose of this section to explain all the algorithms. It will be reviewed the state of the art as descriptive as possible, for the sake of clarity, in order to justify the real-time implementations presented specifically at the end of this chapter.

We can classify motion estimation models in three different categories:

- Correlation based methods. They work comparing positions from image structure between adjacent frames and inferring the speed of the change in each location. They are probably the most intuitive methods (Oh, 2000).
- Differential or gradient methods. They are derived from work using the image intensity in space and time. The speed is obtained as a ratio from the above measures (Baker and Matthews, 2004; Lucas & Kanade, 2001).
- Energy methods. They are represented by filters constructed with a response oriented in space and time to work at certain speeds. The structures used in this processing are parallel filter banks that are activated for a range of values (Huang, 1995).

The different approaches to motion estimation are appropriate under each application. According to the sampling theorem (Nyquist, 2006), a signal must be sampled at a sampling rate that is at least twice the highest frequency that has such this signal. Therefore, it ensures us the motion between two frames is small compared to the scale of the input pattern.

When this theorem is no longer fulfilled, it appears the phenomenon of sub-sampling or aliasing. In space-time images, this phenomenon produces incorrect inclinations or structures unrelated to each other, as an example of temporal aliasing, we can observe a rotation of the propeller of the planes in the opposite direction to true as shown in Figure 3b. In short, no long displacements can be estimated from input patterns with small scales. In addition to this problem, we have the problem of aperture, discussed previously. These two problems (aliasing and aperture) fulfill the general problem of correspondence as shown in Figure 3.

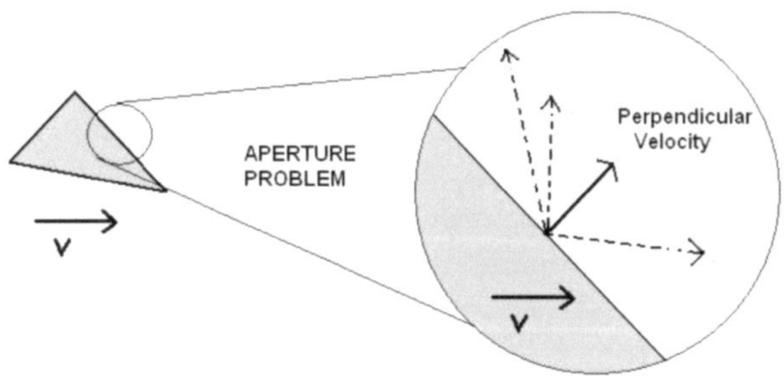

Fig. 3. (3a. left). So-called "Aperture problem". (3b. right) "Aliasing problem". The two problems conform the "correspondence problem" for motion estimation.

Therefore, the movement of the input patterns does not always corresponds to features of consecutive frames in an unambiguous manner. The physical correspondence may be undetectable due to the problem of aperture, the lack of texture (example of Figure 2), the long displacements which commute between frames, etc. Similarly, the apparent motion can lead to a false correspondence. For such situations, it is possible using matching algorithms (tracking and correlation), although currently there is much debate about the advantages and disadvantages of using these techniques rather than those based on gradient and energy of motion.

The correlation methods are less sensitive to changes in lighting, they are able to estimate long displacements that do not meet the sampling theorem (Yacoob & Davis, 1999). However, they are extremely sensitive to cyclical structures providing various local minima and when the aperture problem arises, the responses obtained are unpredictable.

Alternatively, the other methods are better in efficiency and accuracy; they are able to estimate the perpendicular optical flow (in the presence of the aperture problem).

Typically in machine vision CCD cameras are used with a discrete ratio, where varying this modifies the displacement between frames, if these shifts are too large, so gradient methods fail (since it fractures the continuity of space-time volume). Although it is possible using an anti-aliasing spatial smoothing to avoid temporal aliasing (Christmas, 1998; Zhang & Wu, 2001), this is the counterpart to degrade spatial information. Therefore, for a given spatial resolution, one has to sample at a high temporal frequency (Yacoob & Davis, 1999).

On the other hand, it is quite common, for real-time optical flow algorithms remain a functional architecture, as shown in Figure 4, via a hierarchical process.

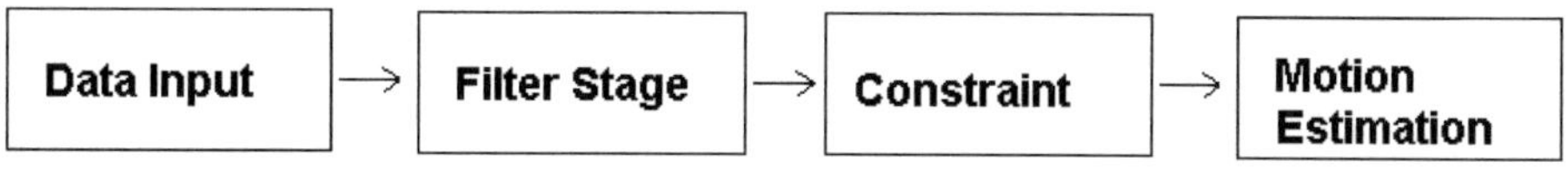

Fig. 4. Functional real-time architecture found in most optical flow algorithms

Previously, it filters the sequence of images or the temporary buffer to obtain basic measures through convolutions, Fast Fourier Transform (FFT), extraction of patterns, arithmetic, and so on.

The measures are then recombined by through various methods to reach a basic evaluation of speed (usually incomplete and deficient in these early stages). Subsequently, the final flow estimation is done by imposing a set of constraints on action and results. These are generated by assumptions about the nature of the flow or change (such as restrictions of a rigid body), but even with these restrictions, the retrieved information is often not robust enough to get a unique solution for optical flow field.

At the beginning of this section, was explained that the optical flow motion is estimated from the observable changes in the pattern of luminance over time. In the case of a no detectable movement, situation such as a sphere rotating with the same brightness (Figure 2), the estimated optical flow is zero everywhere, even if current speeds are not zero. Another attention is given by the non-existence of a unique movement of the image, in order to justify a change in the observed brightness, therefore, the visual motion measurement is often awkward and always have to be associated with a number of physical interpretations.

2.2 Basic movement patterns

Despite the difficulties in the recovery of flow, the biological systems work surprisingly well in real-time. In the same way that these systems have specialized mechanisms to detect color and stereopsis, are also devoted to visual motion mechanisms (Albright, 1993). As in other areas of research in computer vision, they are formed models of such natural systems to formalize bio-inspired solutions.

Thanks to psychophysical and neurophysiological studies, it has been possible to build models that extract the motion from a sequence of images, usually characterized these biological models to be complex and designed to operate poorly at high speed in real-time.

One of the first models based on real-time bio-inspired visual sensor was proposed by Reichardt (Reichardt, 1961). The detector consists of a couple of receptive fields as shown in Figure 5, where the first signal is delayed with respect to the second before nonlinearly combined by multiplication.

Receptors 1 and 2 (shown as edge detectors) are spaced a distance ΔS, imposing a delay on each signal, after the signal C1 and C2 are operated via multiplication. In the final stage, the result of the first half of the detector is subtracted from the next, and then estimated what each contributes to increased directional selectivity. The sensors shown in Figure 5 are Laplacian detectors, although it is possible using any spatial filter or feature detector.

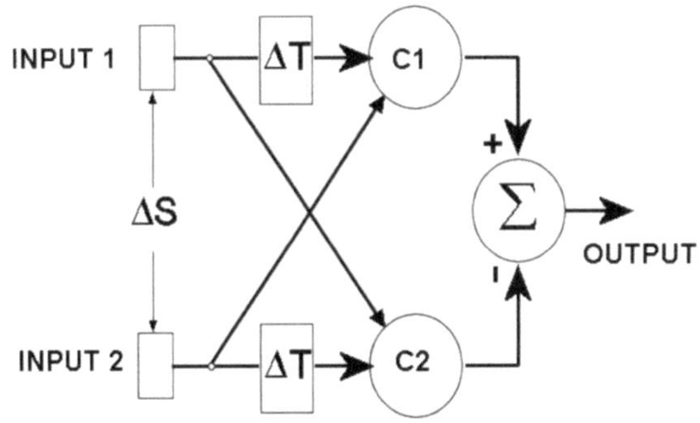

Fig. 5. Reichardt real-time correlation model.

One of the main disadvantages of this detector, is that the correlation is dependent on the contrast, in addition, no speed can be retrieved directly. It requires banks of detectors calibrated at various speeds and directions, and its interpretation at least ambiguous. However, despite these drawbacks, the Reichardt detector can be easily applied by biological systems and is used successfully to explain the visual system of insects. The detector continues to be used as a starting point for more sophisticated models of vision (Beare & Bouzerdoum, 1999; Zanker, 1996), detectors can be implemented in real-time CCD sensor using VLSI technology (Arias-Estrada *et al.*, 1996).

2.2.1 Change detection and correlation methods

Considering the basic case of a segmented region with motion in static regions, it comes up as result a binary image which shows regions of motion. The process may seem easy, so they are simply looking for changes in image intensity over a threshold, which is supposed to cause the movement of an object in the visual field. However, the number of false positives that stem from sources such as noise sensors, camera movement, shadows, environmental effects (rain, reflections, etc.), occlusions and lighting changes make extraordinarily difficult to detect robust movement.

Biological systems again despite being highly sensitive to movement are also robust to noise and visual effects uninteresting. This technique is used in situations where motion detection is an event that should be taken into account for future use. Currently, the requirements of estimation for these algorithms are minimal reaching a satisfactory result with little more than an input buffer, arithmetic signs and some robust statistics, as the supervisory systems have to be particularly sensitive and not normally available in large computing power (Rosin, 1998; Pajares, 2007).

When the differential approaches are subject to errors due to noncompliance with the sampling theorem (Nyquist, 2006) or inconvenience lighting changes, it is necessary to apply other strategies. The methods of correlation or pattern matching are the most intuitive to regain speed and direction of movement, work characteristics in selecting a frame in the sequence of images and then looking for these same characteristics in the next as shown in Figure 6. Changes in the position indicate movement in time, i.e speed.

These algorithms are characterized by a poor performance due to its exhaustive search and iterative operations, usually requiring a prohibitive amount of resources. If the image is of size M^2, the search template is size N^2, and the search window size is L^2, then the whole estimate of computational complexity required would be around $M^2N^2L^2$. By way of example, with an typical image of 640x480 points, a template window size 50x50 and search one of 100x100, would be required to compute 0.8 billion (long scale) operations. The current trend is to try to reduce the search domain (Oh & Lee, 2000; Anandan *et al.*, 1993; Accame *et al.*, 1998), although still the need for resources is too high. One of the most common application models used is the encoding of video in real time (Accame *et al.*, 1998; Defaux & Moscheni, 1995) increasing the amount of effort devoted to research in these algorithms.

Fig. 6. Block-Matching technique.

A key in video compression is the similarity between adjacent images temporarily in a sequence. This technique, demand less bandwidth to transfer the differences between frames than to transfer the entire sequence. It is possible even further reduce the data amount transmitted if known a priori the movement and deformation needed to move from one frame to the next.

This family of algorithms can be classified deeply, and there are two prominent approaches:

- Correlation as a function of 4 variables, depending on the position of the window and displacement, with output normalized between 0 and 1, independent of changes in lighting.
- Minimizing the distance, quantifying the dissimilarity between regions. Many optimizations have been on the line to reduce the search space (Oh & Lee, 2000) and increase their speed (Accame *et al.*, 1998).

Adelson and Bergen (Adelson & Bergen, 1985) advocate no biological evidence of such models, since they are not able to make predictions about complex stimuli (as example randomly positioned vertical bars), for which, experimental observers perceive different moves in different positions. These techniques are straightforward, have spent many years researching and dominate in industrial inspection and quality control.

The ability to work in environments where the displacements between frames are longer than a few points is one of the main advantages. Though this requires extensive processing search spaces.

2.2.2 Space-time methods: Gradient and energy

The movement can be considered as an orientation in the space-time diagram. For example, Figure 7a presents a vertical bar moving continuously from left to right, sampled four times over time. Examining the space-time volume, we can observe the progress of the bar about the time axis thus a stationary angle oriented which shows the extent of movement.

The orientation of the space-time structure can be retrieved through low-level filters. There are currently two dominant strategies: the gradient model and the model of energy as shown in Figure 7b, where the ellipsis represents the negative and positive lobes.

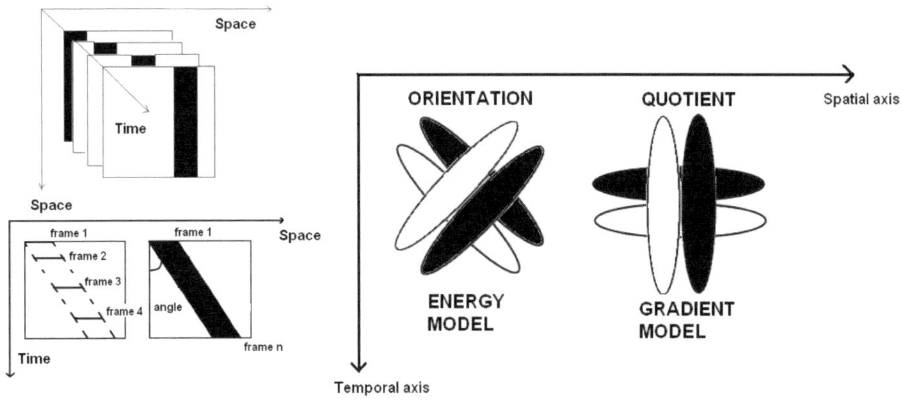

Fig. 7. (7a.left). Motion as orientation in the space-time (*x-t* plane) where the angle increases with the velocity. (7b.right). Space-time filtering models.

The gradient model applies the ratio of a spatial and a temporal filter as a measure of speed, however, the energy model uses a set of filter banks oriented in space-time. Both models use a bio-inspired tightly filters (Adelson & Bergen, 1985; Young & Lesperance, 1993). The debate about which is the scheme adopted by the human visual system remains open, and there are even gateways to go from one model to another because it is possible to synthesize the filters oriented in the pattern of energy through space-time separable filters (Fleet & Jepson, 1989; Huang & Chen, 1995). It is also interesting to note that independent component analysis (ICA) notices these spatial filters are those that cover the majority of components of the structure of the image (Hateren & Ruderman, 1998). In the gradient model, the main working hypothesis is the conservation of intensity over time (Horn & Schunk, 1981). Assuming this, over short periods of time, the intensity variations are due only to translation and not to lighting change, reflectance, etc. The total derivative of image intensity with respect to time is zero at every point in space-time, therefore, defining the image intensity as I (x, y, t), we have:

$$dI(x, y, t) / dt = 0 \tag{1}$$

Differentiating by parts, we obtain the so-called motion constraint equation:

$$\frac{\partial I}{\partial x}\frac{dx}{dt}+\frac{\partial I}{\partial y}\frac{dy}{dt}+\frac{\partial I}{\partial t}\frac{dt}{dt}=0 \tag{2}$$

$$\frac{\partial I}{\partial x}u+\frac{\partial I}{\partial y}v+\frac{\partial I}{\partial t}=0 \tag{3}$$

where u=dx/dt and v=dy/dt. The parameters (x, y, t) are omitted for the sake of clarity. Since there is only one equation with two unknowns, (two unknown velocity components), it is possible to recover only the velocity component v_n, which lies in the direction of the gradient of luminance.

$$v_n=\frac{-\partial I/\partial t}{\sqrt{\left(\partial I/\partial x\right)^2+\left(\partial I/\partial y\right)^2}} \tag{4}$$

There are several problems associated with the motion constraint equation, because it is an equation with two unknowns, therefore, insufficient for estimating the optical flow. Using just only equation (3), is possible only to obtain a linear combination of velocity components, this effect, moreover, is fully consistent with the aperture problem mentioned before in the present section. A second problem arises if I_x or I_y spatial gradients become very small or zero, in which case, the equation becomes ill-conditioned and estimated speed tends asymptotically to infinity. Furthermore, the stable realization of the spatial derivatives is something problematic by itself, applying a differential filter convolution, as operators of Sobel, Prewitt or difference of Gaussians.

As they are using numerical derivatives of a function sampled, they are best suited for space-time intervals small, the problem of aliasing will appear every time the sample in the space-time is not enough, especially in the time domain, as commented before. There are several filtering techniques to solve this problem, such as a spatiotemporal low-pass filtering as noted by Zhang (Zhang & Jonathan, 2003).

Ideally, the sampling rate should be high enough to reduce all movements within one pixel/frame, so the temporal derivative is well-conditioned (Nyquist, 2006). Moreover, the differential space-time filters that are used to implement gradient algorithms seem reasonably to those found in the visual cortex, although there is no consensus on the optimal from the point of view of functionality (Young and Lesperance, 2001). One advantage of models on the energy gradient, is that they provide a speed from a combination of filters, however energy models provide a population of solutions.

2.3 Improving optical flow measures

We have seen that the equation of motion constraint (MCE) has some anomalies have to be addressed properly to estimate optical flow. There is a wide range of methods to improve it. Many restrictions apply to resolve the two velocity components u and v, collecting more information (through the acquisition of more images or getting more information for each image) otherwise, applying physical restraints to generate additional MCEs:

- Applying multiple filters (Mitiche, 1987; Sobey & Srinivasan, 1991; Arnspang, 1993; Ghosal & Mehrotra, 1997).
- Using a neighborhood integration (Lucas & Kanade, 1981; Uras *et al.*, 1988; Simoncelli & Heeger, 1991).

- Using multispectral images (Golland & Bruckstein, 1997).

There are different general methods for restricting MCE and improve optical flow measures:

- Conducting global optimizations, such as smoothing (Horn & Schunck, 1981; Nagel, 1983; Heitz & Bouthemy, 1993).
- Restricting the optical flow to a model known, for example, the affine model (Liu *et al.*, 1997; Ong & Span, 1997; Fleet & Jepson, 2000).
- Using multi-scale methods in a space and time domain (Anandan, 1989; Webber, 1994; Yacoob & Davis, 1999).
- Exploiting temporal consistency (Giaccone & Jones, 1997, 1998).

2.3.1 Applying physical restraints to generate additional MCEs

A motion constraint equation alone is not sufficient to determine the optical flow, as indicated previously. It is proposed an refinement of the same given that its partial derivatives provide additional solutions to the flow working as multiple filters. Nagel (Nagel, 1983) was the pioneer in applying this method uses second-order differentiates, in fact, the differential operator is one of many that could be used to generate multiple MCES. Usually these operators are used numerically by convolutions as linear operators.

This process works because the convolution does not change the orientation of the space-time structure. On the other hand, it is important to use filters that are linearly independent otherwise the produced MCES will degenerate and will not have won anything. The filters and their differentials can be estimated previously to achieve efficiency and, due to the locality of the operators, a massively parallel implementation of these structures.

It is possible also using neighborhood information from local regions to generate motion constraint equations extras (Lucas & Kanade, 1981; Simoncelli & Heeger, 1991). It is assumed, therefore, that the movement is a pure translation in a local region, where these constraints are modeled using a weight matrix so that the results are placed centered within a local region as for example, following a Gaussian distribution. It is rewritten then, the MCE as a minimization problem. The error term is minimized, or solved the set of equations generated by numerical methods.

Working with multicolored images, can be generated different functions of brightness. For example, the planes of red, green and blue of a standard camera can be treated as three separate images, producing three MCES to solve. As a counterpart to this multispectral method, it should be noted that the color planes are usually correlated, a fact, moreover, that is exploited by most compression algorithms. In these situations, the linear system of equations can be degenerate, so that ultimately there is no guarantee that the extra cost in computing lead to an improvement in the quality of flow.

A variation of this method is using additional invariance with respect small displacements and lighting changes, basing these measures in the proportion of different planes of color (spectral sensitivity functions) such as RGB or HSV commonly used. Using this last variant is obtained significant improvements over the use of a single plane RGB (Golland & Bruckstein, 1997).

2.3.2 Different general methods for restricting MCE and improve optical flow measures

Due to the lack of information and spatial structure of the image, is not easy to estimate a sufficiently dense velocity field.

To correct this problem, several restrictions are applied, as for example, that the points move closer together in a similar way. The general philosophy is that the original flow field, once estimated, is iteratively regularized with respect to the smoothing restriction.

The first constraint was proposed by Horn and Schunk (Horn & Schunk, 1981). Optic flow resulting from the global constraints, is quite robust due to the combination of results, and is also flattering to the human eye. Two of the biggest drawbacks are its iterative nature, requiring large amounts of time and computing resources, and motion discontinuities are not handled properly, so that erroneous results are produced in the regions surrounding the motion edges. To address these latter gaps are proposed other techniques that use global statistics such as random Markov chains (Heitz & Bouthemy, 1993).

In all MCE estimation techniques, appear significant restrictions on a neighborhood where it is assumed constant flux. To meet this requirement when there are movement patterns, this neighborhood has to be as small as possible, but at the same time it must be large enough to obtain information and to avoid the aperture problem. Therefore, we need a trade-off compromise.

A variety of models uses estimations related to this neighborhood, such as least squares. If using a quadratic objective function, is assumed a Gaussian residual error rate, but if having multiple movements in the neighborhood, these errors can no longer be considered Gaussian. Even if these errors were independent (very usual situation) the error distribution can be modeled as a bimodal.

There are approximate models can be incorporated into the flow range of techniques that are being exposed. These approaches also model spatial variations of multiple movements. The neighborhood integration techniques, as mentioned, assume that the image motion is purely translational in local regions. Thus, more elaborate models (such as the affine model) can extend the range of motion, and provides additional restrictions. These methods recast the MCE with an error function that will resolve or minimize least squares (Campani & Verri, 1992; Bergen & Bart, 1992; Gupta & Kanal, 1995, 1997; Giaccone & Jones, 1997, 1998).

Large displacements between frames that originate gradient methods, behave inappropriately, since the image sequences are insufficient or that the time derivative measures are inaccurate. As a workaround it is possible using larger spatial filters than early model (Christmas, 1998).

The use of multi-scale Gaussian pyramid can handle high movements between frames and fill the gaps in large regions where the texture is uniform, so that estimates of coarse-scale motion are used as sources for a finer scale (Zhang, 2001).

The use of temporal multi-scale (Yacoob & Davis, 1999) also allows the accurate estimation of a range of different movements, but this method requires using a high enough sampling rate to reduce movements about a pixel/frame.

The schemes discussed so far, consider the calculation of optical flow as a separate problem for each frame, without any feedback (the results of motion of a frame does not cover the analysis of the following). Giaccone and Jones (Giaccone & Jones; 1998, 1999) have designed an architecture capable of dealing with multiple motions (keeping the temporal consistency) which segments moving regions by using a method of least squares.

This algorithm has proven to be robust for a given speed limits, also works well when compared to similar models. The cost calculation is overwhelmed by the generation of a projected image, PAL sizes needed for about 40 seconds/image, with SPARC 4/670MP.

However, this time consistency constraint is only used sporadically today. The objects in the real world must obey physical laws of motion and the inertia and gravity, so that there is predictability in their behavior, and at least surprising, that most real-time algorithms do not implement a flow based feedback.

For this purpose, it is used the fact that it is possible to create an additional constraint equation from the velocity field for use in the next iteration, managing the problem as an evolutionary phenomenon. The use of probabilistic models or Bayesian (Simoncelli & Heeger, 1991) may be an alternative to using real world information and update results of previous estimates integrating temporal information.

We have seen that the perception of motion can be modeled as an orientation in space-time, where the methods of extracting this orientation gradient across the filter ratio oriented. The so-called motion energy models are often based or similar in many respects to models of gradient, since both systems use filter banks to obtain this time-space orientation, and therefore the motion. The main difference is that the filters used in energy models, are designed to meet time-space directions, rather than a ratio of filters. The design of space-time oriented filters is usually performed in the frequency domain.

The methods of energy of motion are biologically plausible, but the implementations have an extra computer associated high due to the large number of filtering required being difficult its implementation in real-time. The resultant velocity of energy methods is not obtained explicitly, unlike gradient methods, only using a solution population, being these last Bayesian models.

One advantage, is that the bimodal velocity measurements as invisible movements, can be treated by these structures (Simoncelli & Heeger, 1991). The correct interpretation of the processed results is not an easy task when dealing with models of probabilistic nature. Interesting optimizations have been developed to increase the speed of these methods, combined with Reichardt detectors (Franceschini *et al*, 1992) as support.

2.4 Configurable hardware algorithms implemented for optical flow

There are several real-time hardware systems founded on the algorithms mentioned herein, proceeding to do a quick review.

- Some algorithms used are of matching or gradient, such as Horn and Schunck algorithm (Horn & Schunk, 1981) that has been carried out using a FPGA (Zuloaga *et al.*, 1998; Martin *et al.*, 2005). The model used is straightforward, is not robust and does not provide optimal overall results in software, but the implementation is efficient and the model is capable of operating in real time. The design uses a recursive implementation of the constriction of applying a smoothing iteration in each frame.

- There is also an implementation of Horn and Schunck algorithm (Horn & Schunk, 1981) by Cobos (Cobos *et al.*, 1998) on a FPGA platform, but with the same counterparty recorded earlier on the reliability of the model used and grazing real time.
- ASSET-2 algorithm is based on features and has been implemented to run in real time using custom hardware (Smith, 1995). The algorithm is easy and determines the position of the axes and corners trying to solve the problem of the correspondence between neighboring frames in time. The system was implemented using a PowerPC with custom hardware to extract features in real time. This system does not provide continuous outcomes, these being scarce, but cluster groups of similar speeds to segment objects according to their movement.
- Niitsuma *et al.* (Niitsuma & Maruyama, 2004) apply a model-based optical flow correlation, with a joint operation of a stereoscopic system also measures the distance of moving objects. This system is based on a Virtex 2 XC2V6000 scheduled at 68 MHz and delivers results in real time resolution of 640x480 points.
- Tomasi & Diaz (Díaz *et al.*, 2006) implemented a real-time system based on Lucas and Kanade algorithm (Lucas & Kanade, 1981; Díaz *et al.*, 2006) with satisfactory results in terms of performance. This is an algorithm within the so-called gradient that is used as a didactic introduction to optical flow in most colleges. It has shown a significant relationship between performance and implementation effort. The problem with this implementation is given by abrupt changes in light and heavy dependence on the aperture problem. Its advantage is the extensive documentation and the experience gathered with this algorithm (more than 25 years) from the scientific community. After that, Tomasi has implemented in 2010 and 2011 a fully real-time multimodal system mixing motion estimation and binocular disparity (Tomassi *et al.*, 2010, 2011) combining low-level and mid-level vision primitives.
- Botella *et al.* implemented a robust gradient based optical flow real-time system and its extension to mid-level vision combining orthogonal variant moments (Botella *et al.*, 2009, 2010, 2011). Also the block matching acceleration motion estimation has been implemented in real-time by Gonzalez and Botella (González *et al.*, 2011). All these models will be analyzed thoroughly in this chapter.

3. Case studies of real-time implementation performed

They are presented several case studies of the real-time implementation performed in these last years by the author of the present chapter and other authors.

3.1 Multichannel gradient Model

Multichannel gradient Model (McGM), developed by Johnston (Johnston *et al.*, 1995, 1996), has been recently implemented and selected due its robustness and bio-inspiration. This model deals with many goals, such as illumination, static patterns, contrast invariance, noisy environments. Additionally it is robust against fails, justifies some optical illusions (Anderson *et al.*, 2003), and detects second order motion (Johnston, 1994) that is particularly useful in camouflage tasks, etc. At the same time, it avoids operations such as matrix inversion or iterative methods that are not biologically justified (Baker & Matthews, 2004; Lucas & Kanade, 1981). The main drawback of this system is its huge computational complexity. It is able to handle complex situations in real environments better than others algorithms (Johnston *et al.*, 1994), with its physical architecture and design principles being based on the biological neural systems of mammalians (Bruce *et al.*, 1996). Experimental results are provided using a Celoxica RC1000 platform (Alphadata, 2007).

This approach is based on the gradient one commented previously, the starting point is the motion constraint equation (MCE) shown in the expression 2. The luminance variation is assumed negligible over time. In this approach, velocity is calculated dividing the temporal derivative by the spatial derivative of image brightness, thus a gradient model can be obtained applying couples of filters, one of them being the spatial derivative and the other one a temporal derivative. If for the sake of clarity we only consider x variable in expression 2 and we get the velocity taking the quotient of the output filters:

$$v = \frac{dx}{dt} = -\frac{\partial I}{\partial t} \Big/ \frac{\partial I}{\partial x} \tag{5}$$

Since velocity is given directly via the ratio of luminance derivatives, one potential problem appears when the output of the spatial filter is null, being the velocity undefined. This can be solved applying a threshold to the calculation or restricting the evaluation value (Baker & Matthews, 2004). Our approach is based on the fact that the human visual system measures at least three orders of the spatial derivative (Johnston *et al.*, 1999; Koenderick & Van Doorn, 1988) and three orders of temporal differentiation (Baker & Matthews, 2004; Hess & Snowden, 1992). Therefore, it is possible to build low level filters for calculating the speed with additional derivatives, although it may be still ill-conditioned:

$$\mathrm{v} = -\frac{\partial^n \mathrm{I}}{\partial \mathrm{x}^{n-1}\mathrm{t}} \Big/ \frac{\partial^n \mathrm{I}}{\partial \mathrm{x}^n} \tag{6}$$

Two vectors X and T, containing the results of applying the derivative operators to the image brightness, can be built:

$$\mathrm{X} = \left(\frac{\partial \mathrm{I}}{\partial \mathrm{x}}, \frac{\partial^2 \mathrm{I}}{\partial \mathrm{x}^2}, \ldots, \frac{\partial^n \mathrm{I}}{\partial \mathrm{x}^n} \right) \quad \mathrm{T} = \left(\frac{\partial \mathrm{I}}{\partial \mathrm{t}}, \frac{\partial^2 \mathrm{I}}{\partial \mathrm{x} \partial \mathrm{t}}, \ldots, \frac{\partial^n \mathrm{I}}{\partial \mathrm{x}^{n-1} \partial \mathrm{t}} \right) \tag{7}$$

For extracting the best approximation to the speed from each of the measurements, a Least Squares Formulation is applied, thus recovering a value v′. The denominator is a sum of squares and therefore it is never null, so a spatial structure is provided:

$$\mathrm{v}' = \frac{\sum_n \frac{\partial^n \mathrm{I}}{\partial \mathrm{x}^n} \frac{\partial^n \mathrm{I}}{\partial \mathrm{x}^{n-1} \partial \mathrm{t}}}{\sum_n \frac{\partial^n \mathrm{I}}{\partial \mathrm{x}^n} \frac{\partial^n \mathrm{I}}{\partial \mathrm{x}^n}} \tag{8}$$

In this framework, we represent the local image structure in the primary visual cortex as a spatial-temporal truncated Taylor expansion (Johnston *et al.*, 1996, 1999; Koenderick & Van

Doorn, 1988), in order to represent a local region by the weighted outputs of a set of filters applied at a location in the image as shown in the next expression (9). The weights attached depend on the direction and length of the vector joining the point where the measurements are taken and the point where we wish to estimate image brightness:

$$\begin{aligned} I(x+p,y+q,t+r) &= [I(x,y,t)] + [I_x(x,y,t) + I_y(x,y,t) + I_t(x,y,t)] \\ &+ \frac{1}{2}[I_{2x}(x,y,t)p^2 + I_{xy}(x,y,t)2pq + I_{xt}(x,y,t)2pr + I_{yt}(x,y,t)2qr] + \ldots \end{aligned} \tag{9}$$

These filters are generated by progressively increasing the order of the spatial and temporal differential operators applied to the following kernel filter:

$$K(r,t) = \frac{1}{4\pi\sigma} e^{-\frac{r^2}{4\sigma}} \frac{1}{\sqrt{\pi\tau\alpha}\, e^{r^2/4}} e^{-\left(\frac{\ln(t/\alpha)}{\tau}\right)_2} \tag{10}$$

with σ=1.5, α=10 and τ=0.2. This expression is originally scaled so that the integral over its spatial-temporal scope is equal to 1.0. Also, it is tuned assuming a spatial frequency limit of 60 cycles/deg and a critical flicker fusion limit of 60 Hz, following evidences from the human visual system (Johnston *et al.*, 1994).

The Taylor representation requires a bank of linear filters, taking derivatives in time, t, and two spatial directions, x and y, with the derivatives lobes in theirs receptive fields tuned to different frequencies. There are neurophysiological and psychophysical evidences that support this (Johnston *et al.*, 1994; Bruce *et al.*, 1996). This algorithm can be built by neural systems in the visual cortex since all operations involved in the model can be achieved by combining the output of linear space-temporal orientated filters through addition, multiplication and division.

A truncated Taylor expansion is built eliminating terms above first order in time and orthogonal direction for ensuring that there are no more than three temporal filters and no greater spatial complexity in filters (Hess & Snowden, 1992).

The reference frame is rotated through a number of orientations with respect to the input image. Several orientations (24 in the original model spaced over 360º) are employed. For each orientation, three vectors of filters are created by differentiating the vector of filter kernels with respect to *x*, *y* and *t*. From these last measurements, speed, orthogonal speed, inverse speed and orthogonal inverse speed are calculated with the local speed by rotating the reference frame:

$$\hat{s}_{II} = \text{speed} = \frac{X \cdot T}{X \cdot X}\cos^2\theta = \frac{X \cdot T}{X \cdot X}\left(1 + \left(\frac{X \cdot Y}{X \cdot X}\right)^2\right)^{-1} \tag{11}$$

$$\hat{s}_{\perp} = \text{orthog. speed} = \frac{Y \cdot T}{Y \cdot Y}\sin^2\theta = \frac{Y \cdot T}{Y \cdot Y}\left(1 + \left(\frac{X \cdot Y}{Y \cdot Y}\right)^2\right)^{-1} \tag{12}$$

$$\breve{s}_{II} = \text{inverse speed} = \frac{X \cdot T}{T \cdot T} \tag{13}$$

$$\breve{s}_{\perp} = \text{inverse orthog. speed} = \frac{Y \cdot T}{T \cdot T} \tag{14}$$

Where *X, Y, T* are the vector of outputs from the x, y, t differentiated filters. Raw speed (*X·T / X·X*) and orthogonal speed (*Y·T / Y·Y*) measurements are ill-conditioned if there is no change over x and y, respectively.

To avoid degrading the final velocity estimation, they are conditioned by measurements of the angle of image structure relative to the reference frame (θ). If the speed is large, (and inverse speed is small) direction is led by the speed measurements. However, if the speed is small (and inverse speed is large) the measurement is led by inverse speed.

The use of these antagonistic and complementary measurements provides advantages in any system susceptible of having small signals affected by noise (Anderson *et al.*, 2003). There is evidence of the neurons that built inverse speed (Lagae *et al.*, 1983), also it provides an explanation to sensitivity to static noise for motion blind patients.

The calculus of additional image measurements in order to increase robustness is one of the core design criteria that enhances the model. Finally, the motion modulus is calculated through a quotient of determinants:

$$\text{Modulus}^2 = \left[\frac{\begin{matrix} \hat{s}_{II}\cos\theta & \hat{s}_{II}\sin\theta \\ \hat{s}_{\perp}\cos\theta & \hat{s}_{\perp}\sin\theta \end{matrix}}{\begin{matrix} \hat{s}_{II}\breve{s}_{II} & \hat{s}_{II}\breve{s}_{II} \\ \hat{s}_{\perp}\breve{s}_{\perp} & \hat{s}_{\perp}\breve{s}_{\perp} \end{matrix}} \right] \tag{15}$$

Speed and orthogonal speed vary with the angle of reference frame. The numerator of (12) takes a measure of the amplitude of the distribution of speed measurements that are combined across both speed and orthogonal speed. The denominator is included to stabilize the final speed estimation. Direction of motion is extracted by calculating a measurement of phase that is combined across all speed related measures, since they are in phase:

$$\text{Phase} = \tan^{-1}\left(\frac{(\breve{s}_{II} + \hat{s}_{II})\sin\theta + (\breve{s}_{\perp} + \hat{s}_{\perp})\cos\theta}{(\breve{s}_{II} + \hat{s}_{II})\cos\theta - (\breve{s}_{\perp} + \hat{s}_{\perp})\sin\theta} \right) \tag{16}$$

The model can be degraded to an ordinary Gradient (Baker & Matthews, 2004; Lucas & Kanade, 1981) by suppressing the number of orientations of the reference frame, taking only one temporal derivative and two spatial derivatives, not considering the inverse velocity measures, etc. The computations of speed and direction are based directly on the output of filters applied to the input image, providing a dense final map of information.

The general structure of the implementation is summarized in Figure 8, where operations are divided in conceptual stages with several variations to improve the viability of the hardware implementation.

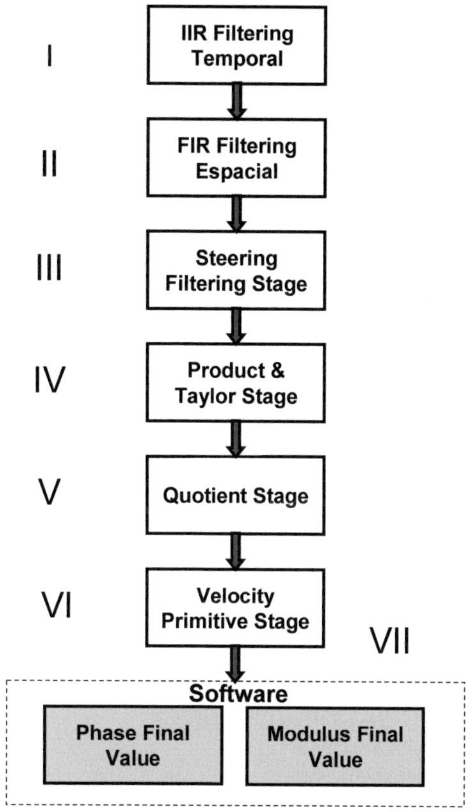

Fig. 8. General structure of the model implemented.

Stage I contains temporal differentiation through IIR filtering, being the output of this stage the three first derivatives of the input. Stage II performs the spatial differentiation building a pyramidal structure of each temporal derivative. Figure 9 represents what the authors (Botella *et al.*, 2010) call as "Convolutive Unit Cell" which implements the separable convolution organized in rows and columns. Each part of this cell will be replicated sufficiently to perform a pyramidal structure.

Stage III steers each one of space-time functions calculated previously. Stage IV performs a Taylor expansion and its derivatives over x, y and t delivering at the output a sextet which contains the product of those. Stage V forms a quotient of this sextet. Stage VI forms four different measurements corresponding to the direct and inverse speeds (8-11), which act as primitives for the final velocity estimation. Finally, Stage VII computes the modulus and phase values (12-13) on software.

Stage VI does not calculate the final velocity estimation due to the bioinspired nature of the model (combining multiple speed measurements, so if direct speed does not provide an accurate value, inverse speed will do that, and *vice versa*). However, every measurement of the speed has entity of velocity, so it could be used as final velocity estimation, even though it would degrade the robustness of the mode

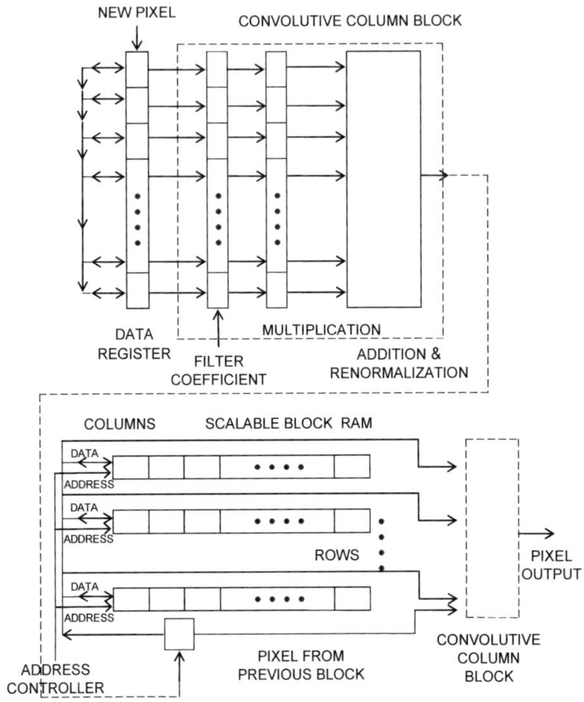

Fig. 9. Unit cell to perform the convolution operation.

3.2 Low and mid-level vision platform. Orthogonal variant models

One of the most well established approaches in computer-vision and image analysis is the use of Moment invariants. Moment invariants, surveyed extensively by Prokop and Reeves (Prokop & Reeves, 1992) and more recently by Flusser (Flusser, 2006), were first introduced to the pattern recognition community by Hu (Hu, 1961), who employed the results of the theory of algebraic invariants and derived a set of seven moment invariants (the well-known Hu invariant set). The Hu invariant set is now a classical reference in any work that makes use of moments. Since the introduction of the Hu invariant set, numerous works have been devoted to various improvements, generalizations and their application in different areas, e.g., various types of moments such as Zernike moments, pseudo-Zernike moments, rotational moments, and complex moments have been used to recognize image patterns in a number of applications (The & Chin, 1986).

The problem of the influence of discretization and noise on moment accuracy as object descriptors has been previously addressed. There are proposed several techniques to increase the accuracy and efficiency of moment descriptors. (Zhang, 2000), (Papakostas *et al.*, 2007, 2009). (Sookhanaphibarn & Lursinsap, 2006).

In short, moment invariants are measures of an image or signal that remain constant under some transformations, e.g., rotation, scaling, translation or illumination. Moments are applicable to different aspects of image processing, ranging from invariant pattern recognition and image encoding to pose estimation. Such Moments can produce image descriptors invariant under rotation, scale, translation, orientation, etc.

The implementation of these systems combines the low-level vision optical flow model (Botella *et al.*, 20010) with the orthogonal variant moments (Martín.H *et al.*, 2010) as Area, Length and Phase for the two cartesian components (A, L_X, L_Y, P_X, P_Y) to built a real-time mid-level vision platform which is able to deliver output task as tracking, segmentation and so on (Botella *et al.*, 2011).

The architecture of the system can be seen in the Figure 10. Several external banks have been used for different implementations, accessing to them from both the FPGA and the PCI bus. Low-level optical flow vision is designed and built through an asynchronous pipeline (micropipeline), where a token is passed to the next core each time one core finish its processing. The high level description tool Handel-C is chosen to implement this core with the DK environment. The board used is the well-known AlphaData RC1000 (Alphadata, 2007) which includes a Virtex 2000E-BG560 chip and 4 SRAM banks of 2MBytes each one as shown in the Figures 11a and 12a. Nevertheless Low-level moment vision platform is implemented in a parallel way, being independent the wielding of single one. Each orthogonal variant moment and the optical flow scheme advances the final Mid-Level Vision estimation. The Multimodal sensor core integrates information from different abstraction layers (six modules for optical flow, five modules for the orthogonal moments and one module for the Mid-Level vision tasks). Mid-Level vision core is arranged in this work for segmentation and tracking estimation with also an efficient implementation of the clustering algorithm, although additional functionality to this last module can be added using this general architecture.

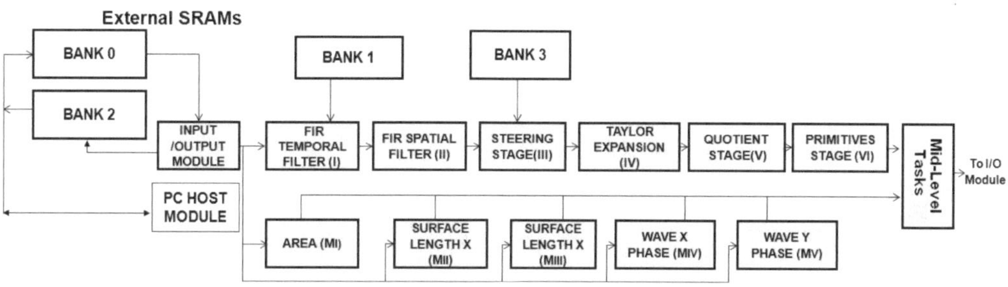

Fig. 10. Scheme of the real-time architecture of low-level and mid-level vision.

Fig. 11. (11a.left)Xilinx Virtex 2000E. (11b.right) Altera Cyclone II.

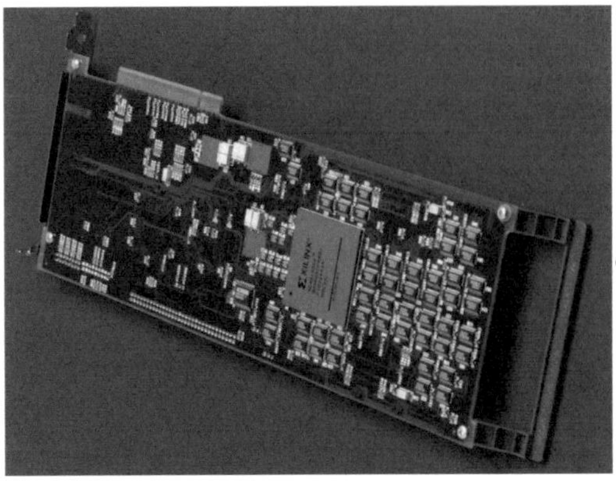

Fig. 12. (12a.left) ALPHADATA RC1000 branded by Celoxica. (12b.right) DE2 branded by Altera.

3.3 Block Matching models

The full search technique (FST) is the most straightforward Block Matching Method (BMM) and also the most accurate one. FST (Figure 13a) matches all possible blocks within a search window in the reference frame to find the block with the minimum Summation of absolute differences (SAD), which is defined as:

$$SAD(x,y;u,v) = \sum_{x=0}^{31}\sum_{y=0}^{31}\left|I_t(x,y) - I_{t-1}(x+u,y+v)\right|, \quad (17)$$

Where It(x, y) represents the pixel value at the coordinate (x, y) in the frame t and the (u, v) is the displacement of the possible Macro Block (MB). For example, for a block with size 32×32, the FST algorithm requires 1024 subtractions and 1023 additions to calculate a SAD. The required number of checking blocks is $(1+2d)^2$ while the search window is limited within ± d pixels, currently is used for it a power of two. Three Steps Search Technique (TSST) is not an exhaustive search.

The step size of the search window is chosen to be half of the search area (Figure 13b). Nine candidate points, including the centre point and eight checking points on the boundary of the search are selected in each step. Second step, will move the search centre forwarding to the matching point with the minimum SAD of the previous step, and the step size of the second step is reduced by half. Last step stops the search process with the step size of one pixel; and the optimal MV with the minimum SAD can be obtained.

The hierarchical methods as Multi-scale Search Technique are based on building a pyramidal representation for each frame. This representation calculates an image where each pixel's value is a mean of itself with its neighbourhood; after that, the image is under sampled to the half, as shown in Figure 13c. This model is implemented using the Altera DE2 board and the Cyclone II FPGA as shown in the Figures 11b and 12b (González *et al.*, 2011), balancing the code between the microprocessor implemented and the acceleration system which uses Avalon Bus thanks to so-called "C to hardware compiler" from Altera (Altera, 2011).

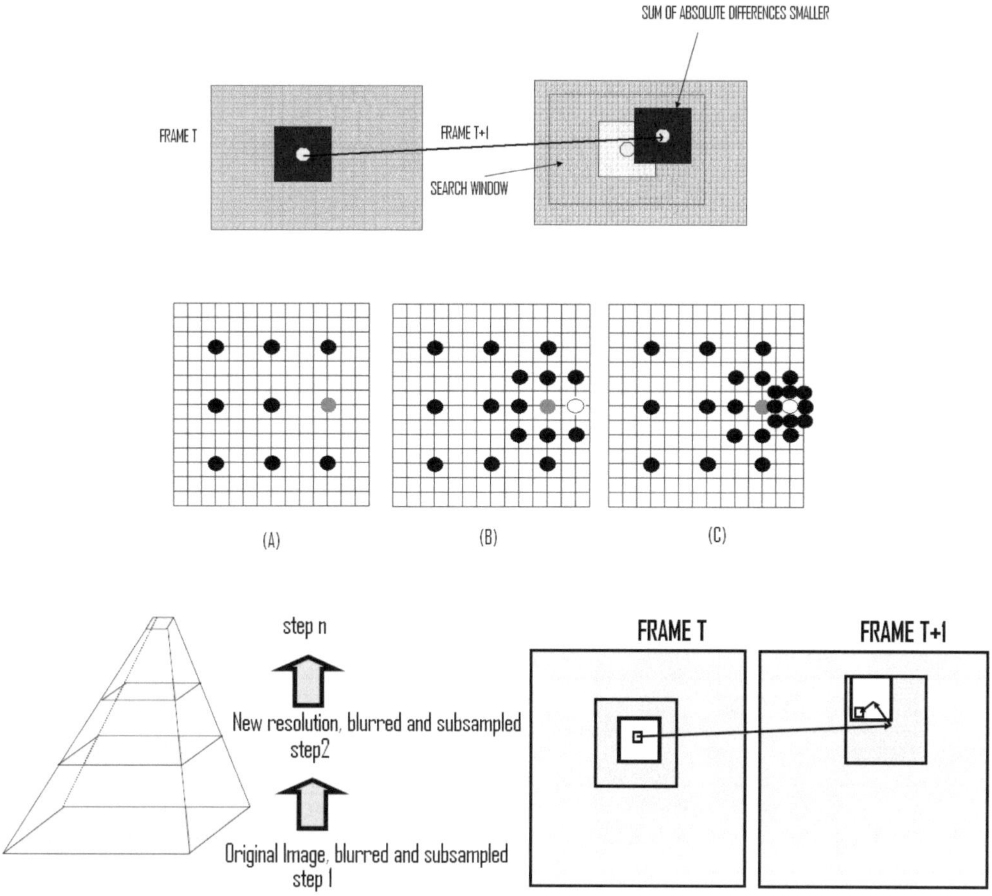

Fig. 13. (13a. Upper row) Full Search Technique. (13b. medium row) Three Steps Search Technique. (13c. lower row) Multiscale Search Technique.

4. Computational resources and throughput of the real-time systems

In this section, we analyse each of these real-time motion estimation systems regarding the computational resources needed and the throughput obtained. The resources used in the implementations described in 3.1 and 3.2 are shown in the Tables 1-3 as Slices and Block Ram percentage accounting. MC is the maximum delay in terms of the number of clock cycles needed for each modulus implemented. Finally, the Throughput provides the Kilo pixels per second (Kpps) of the implementations.

Table 1 shows a set of these parameters just for the McGM optical flow implementation, (see case 3.1) but Table 2 manages the multimodal sensor treated in 3.2. For this last case, has been separated the implementation of each one of the orthogonal variant moments (Table 2) and just the whole implementation (all modules working together as shown in Table 3).

Tables 4 is regarding the implementation explained in 3.3. The FPGA used is Altera Cyclone II EP2C35F672C6 with a core NIOS II processor embedded in a DE2 platform.

Low-level Vision Stage (Optical flow)	FIR Temporal Filtering(I)	FIR Spatial Filtering(II)	Steering (III)	Product & Taylor (IV)	Quotient (V)	Primitives (VI)
Slices (%)	190 (1%)	1307 (7%)	1206(6%)	3139(19%)	3646(20%)	2354(12%)
Block RAM (%)	1%	31%	2%	13%	16%	19%
MC	13	17	19	23	21	19
Throughput (Kpixels/s)/Freq.(Mhz)	4846/ 63	3235/55	2526/48	1782/41	1695/39	2000/38

Table 1. Slices, memory, number of cycles and performance for Low-level Optical flow scheme.

Low-level Vision Stage (Orthogonal Variant Moments)	Area (M_I)	L_X (M_{II})	L_Y (M_{III})	P_X (M_{IV})	P_Y (M_V)
Slices (%)	321(2%)	1245(7%)	1245(7%)	658(4%)	658(4%)
Block RAM (%)	1%	4%	4%	3%	3%
MC	7	11	11	5	5
Throughput (Kpixels/sec)/ Frecuency (MHz)	4546/49				

Table 2. Slices, memory, number of cycles and performance for Orthogonal Moment scheme.

COMPLETE Mid-level and Low level Vision	Motion Estimation (Low-Level)	Orthogonal Variant Moments (Low-Level)l	Tracking & Segmentation Unit (Mid-Level)	Multimodal Bioinspired Sensor. (Mid & Low Level)
Slices (%)	4127 (24%)	11842 (65%)	1304 (6%)	17710 (97%)
Block RAM (%)	15%	80%	4%	(99%)
MC (limiting)	29	11	18	29
Throughput (Kpixels/s)/Freq.(Mhz)	4546/49	2000/38	2000/38	2000/38

Table 3. Resources needed and performance for Low and Mid-Level vision. Multimodal system.

Method, Processor / Quality	Logic Cells	Embedded DSPs (9 × 9)	Total memory bits
FST, e / Quality I	4925 (15%)	0 (0%)	62720 (13%)
FST, e / Quality II	7708 (23%)	28 (40%)	
FST, e / Quality III	14267 (43%)	39 (56%)	
FST, s / Quality I	5808 (18%	0 (0%)	99200 (20%)
FST, s/ Quality II	8501 (26%)	20 (28%)	
FST, s / Quality III	15627 (47%)	32 (48%)	
FST, f / Quality I	6488 (20%)	0 (0%)	134656 (28%)
FST, f / Quality II	9225 (30%)	32 (48%)	
FST, f / Quality III	16396 (50%)	43 (61%)	

Table 4. Resources needed and performance for Low level vision Block matching system.

The parameters for measuring the resources for this technology are Logic Cell and Embedded DSPs. For this implementation, we have used different embedded NIOS II microprocessors (E, S, F from "economic", "standard", and "full" with different characteristics (González *et al.*, 2011) and for each one of these microprocessors we have applied different parts of the code, distinguishing between "Quality I, II or III" depending of the piece of the code running just into the microprocessor and the part that is accelerated using C2H compiler. (Altera, 2011).

For the multimodal system, it is possible reach up a real-time performance (see Section 3.2 and Table 5). This throughput is between 12 Mega pixels per seconds (Mpps) with basic quality (most of the source code running in Nios II microprocessor) and 30 Mpps (most of the source code being accelerated with C to hardware compiler) which means between 40 and 98 fps at 640x480 resolution.

COMPLETE Mid-level and Low-level Vision	Orthogonal Variant Moments (Low-Level)	Motion Estimation (Low-Level)	Multimodal Bioinspired Sensor. (Mid & Low-Level)
resolution 120x96	395 frames/sec	174 frames/sec	174 frames/sec
resolution 320x240	59 frames/sec	26 frames/sec	26 frames/sec
resolution 640x480	28 frames/sec	14 frames/sec	14 frames/sec
Throughput	4546 Kpixels/sec	2000 Kpixels/sec	2000 Kpixels/sec

Table 5. Throughput in terms of Kpps and fps for the embedded sensor.

COMPLETE Mid-level and Low-level Vision	Quality I	Quality II	Quality III
Throughput	12 Mpixels/sec	20 Mpixels/sec	30 Mpixels/sec

Table 6. Throughput in terms of Kpps and fps for the block matching technique.

5. Conclusion

This chapter has approached the problem of the real-time implementation of motion estimation in embedded systems. It has been descripted representative techniques and systems belonging to different families that contribute with solutions and approximations to a question that remains still open, due the ill-posed nature of the motion constraint equation.

It has been also proposed an overview of different implementations capable of computing real-time motion estimation in embedded systems delivering just low primitives: (gradient model and block matching respectively) and delivering the mid-level vision primitives (combination optical flow with orthogonal variant moments). In the Table 7 are shown the different methods implemented regarding the machine vision domain, the final performance obtained, the robustness implementation and the complexity of the final system.

These systems designed are scalable and modular, also being possible choice the visual primitives involved -number of moments- as well as the bit-width of the filters and computations in the low-level vision -optical flow-. This architecture can process concurrently different visual processing channels, so the system described opens the door to the implementation of complex bioinspired algorithms on-chip.

The implementation of these systems shown offers robustness and real-time performance to applications in which the luminance varies significantly and noisy environments, as industrial environments, sport complex, animal and robotic tracking among others.

Method Implemented	Vision Domain	Throughput FPS (320x200)	Robustness	Complexity of the Implementation (FPGA board)
Orthogonal Variant Moments	Low&Mid	59 fps	Low	Easy
Motion Estimation (McGM)	Low	26 fps	Very High	High
Multimodal Bioinspired Sensor.	Low&Mid	26 fps	Very High	Very High
Block Matching (Full Search Tecnique)	Low	120 fps	Medium	Easy

Table 7. Comparison of the different methods implemented.

6. Acknowledgment

This work is partially supported by Spanish Project project TIN 2008-00508/MIC. The authors want to thank to Prof. Alan Johnston and Dr. Jason Dale from University College London, (UK) for their great help with Multichannel Gradient Model (McGM), explained partially in this chapter.

7. References

A. Anderson, P. W. McOwan. (2003). Humans deceived by predatory stealth strategy camouflaging motion, *Proceedings of the Royal Society*, B 720, 18-20.

A. Johnston, C. W Clifford. (1995). Perceived Motion of Contrast modulated Gratings: Prediction of the McGM and the role of Full-Wave rectification, *Vision Research*, 35, pp. 1771-1783.

A. Johnston, C. W. Clifford. (1994). A Unified Account of Three Apparent Motion Illusions, Vision Research, vol. 35, pp. 1109-1123.

A. Johnston, P.W. McOwan, C.P. Benton. (2003). Biological computation of image motion from flows over boundaries, *Journal of Physiology*. Paris, vol. 97, pp. 325-334.

A. Mikami, W.T Newsome, R.H Wurtz. (1986). Motion selectivity in macaque visual cortex. I. Mechanisms of direction and speed selectivity in extrastriate area MT. *J. Neurophysiol*, vol. 55, pp. 1308-1327.

Accame M., De Natale F. G. B., Giusto D. (1998). High Performance Hierachical Block-based Motion Estimation for Real-Time Video Coding, *Real-Time Imaging*, 4, pp. 67-79.

Adelson E. H., Bergen J. R. (1985). Spatiotemporal Energy Models for the Perception of Motion. *Journal of the Optical Society of America A*, 2 (2), pp. 284-299.

Albright T. D. (1993). *Cortical Processing of Visual Motion*, In Miles & Wallman. Visual Motion and its Role in the Stabilisation of Gaze, pp. 177-201.

AlphaData RC1000 product (2006). , http://www.alpha-data.com/adc-rc1000.html.

Altera (2011). *C to Hardware.*

Anandan P., Bergen J. R., Hanna K. J., Hingorani R. (1993). *Hierarchical Model-based Motion Estimation.* In M.I.Sean and R.L.Lagendijk, editors, Motion Analysis and Image Sequence Processing. Kluwer Academic Publishers.

Arias-Estrada M., Tremblay M., Poussart D. (1996). A Focal Plane Architecture for Motion Computation, *Real-Time Imaging*, 2, pp. 351- 360.

Arnspang J. (1993). Motion Constraint Equations Based on Constant Image Irradiance, *Image and Vision Computing*, 11 (9), pp. 577-587.

Baker, S., Matthews, I. (2004). Lucas-Kanade 20 Years On: A Unifying Framework. *International Journal of Computer Vision*, Vol.56, N° 3, pp. 221-255.

Beare R., Bouzerdoum A. (1999). Biologically inspired Local Motion Detector Architecture, *Journal of the Optical Society of America A*, 16 (9), pp. 2059-2068.

Bergen J. R., Burt P. J. (1992). A Three-Frame Algorithm for Estimating Two-Component Image Motion, *IEEE T. On Pattern Analysis and Machine Intellig.*, 14 (9), pp. 886-895.

C.-H. Teh, R.T. Chin. (1988). On image analysis by the methods of moments, *IEEE Trans. Pattern Anal. Mach. Intell*igence. vol.10 (4), pp. 496–513.

C.-Y. Wee, R. Paramesran, F. Takeda. (2004). New computational methods for full and subset zernike moments, *Inform. Sci.* vol. 159 (3–4), pp. 203–220.

Campani M., Verri A. (1992). Motion Analysis from First-Order Properties of Optical Flow. CVGIP: Image Understanding 56 (1), pp. 90-107.

Christmas W. J. (1998). Spatial Filtering Requirements for Gradient- Base Optical Flow Measurements, *Proceedings of the British Machine Vision Conference*, pp.185-194.

D. González, G. Botella, S. Mookherjee, U. Meyer-Baese. (2011). NIOS II processor-based acceleration of motion compensation techniques. *SPIE'11*,. Orlando, FL.

Defaux F., Moscheni F. (1995). Motion Estimation Techniques for Digital TV: A Review and a New Contribution, *Proceedings of the IEEE*, 83 (6), pp. 858-876.

Fleet D. J., Black M. J., Yacoob Y., Jepson A. D. (2000). Design and Use of Linear Models for Image Motion Analysis, *Int. Journal of Computer Vision*, 36 (3), pp. 171-193.

Fleet D. J., Jepson A. D. (1989). Hierarchical Construction of Orientation and Velocity Selective Filters, *IEEE Transactions on Pattern Analysis and Machine Intelligence*, 11 (3), pp. 315-325.

Franceschini N., Pichon J. M., Blanes C. (1992). From Insect Vision to Robot Vision, *Philosophical Transactions of the Royal Society of London B*, 337, pp. 283-294.

G. Botella, A. García, M. Rodríguez, E. Ros, U. Meyer-Baese, M.C. Molina. (2010). Robust Bioinspired Architecture for Optical Flow Computation, *IEEE Transactions on Very Large Scale Integration (VLSI) System*, 18(4), pp. 616-629.

G. Botella, J.A. Martín-H, M. Santos, U. Meyer-Baese. (2011). FPGA-Based Multimodal Embedded Sensor System Integrating Low- and Mid-Level Vision, *Sensors*, 11(8), pp. 8164-8179.

G. Botella, U. Meyer-Baese, A. García. (2009). Bioinspired Robust Optical Flow Processor System for VLSI Implementation, *IEEE Electronic Letters*, 45(25), pp. 1304-1306.

G.A. Papakostas, D.E. Koulouriotis. (2009). A unified methodology for the efficient computation of discrete orthogonal image moments, *Inform.Sci.* 176, pp. 3619–3633.

G.A. Papakostas, Y.S. Boutalis, D.A. Karras, B.G. Mertzios (2007). A new class of zernike moments for computer vision applications, *I. Science*, vol. 177 (13), pp. 2802–2819.

Ghosal S., Mehrotra R. (1997). Robust Optical Flow Estimation Using Semi-Invariant Local Features. Pattern Recognition, 30 (2), pp. 229- 237.

Giaccone P. R., Jones G. A. (1997). Feed-Forward Estimation of Optical Flow, *Proceedings of the IEE International Conference on Image Processing and its Applications*, pp. 204-208.

Giaccone P. R., Jones G. A. (1998). Segmentation of Global Motion using Temporal Probabilistic Classification, *Proc. of the British Machine Vision Conference*, pp. 619-628.

Gibson, J. J. (1950). Perception of the Visual World *(Houghton Mifflin, Boston)*.

Golland. P., Bruckstein A. M. (1997). Motion from Color, *Computer Vision and Image Understanding*, 68 (3), pp. 346-362.

Gupta N. C., Kanal L. N. (1995).3-D Motion estimation from Motion Field, *Artificial Intelligence*, 78, pp. 45-86.

Gupta N. C., Kanal L. N. (1997). Gradient Based Image Motion Estimation without Computing Gradients. International Journal of Computer Vision, 22 (1), pp. 81-101.

Heitz F., Bouthemy P. (1993). Multimodal Estimation of Discontinuous Optical Flow Using Markov Random Fields, *IEEE Transactions on Patterns Analysis and Machine Intelligence*, 15 (12), pp. 1217-1232.

Horn B. K. P., Schunck B. G. (1981). Determining Optical Flow. *Artificial Intelligence*, 17, pp. 185-203.

http://www.altera.com/devices/processor/nios2/tools/c2h/ni2-c2h.html.

Huang C. and Chen, Y. (1995). Motion Estimation Method Using a 3D Steerable Filter, *Image and Vision Computing*, 13(1), pp.21-32.

J. Díaz, E. Ros, F. Pelayo, E. M. Ortigosa, S. Mota. (2006). FPGA-based real-time optical-flow system, *IEEE Trans.Circuits and Systems for Video Technology*, 16(2), pp.274-279.

J. Díaz, E. Ros, R. Agís, J.L. Bernier. (2008). Superpipelined high-performance optical flow computation architecture., *Comp. Vision and Image Understanding* ,112, pp. 262–273.

J. Flusser, (2006). Moment invariants in image analysis, in: *Proceedings of the World Academy of Science, Engineering and Technology*, vol. 11, pp. 196–201.

J.J. Koenderink, A.J. Van Doorn. (1987). Representation of local geometry in the Visual System, *Biological Cybernetics*, 55, pp. 367-375.

Johnston A., McOwen P. W., Benton C. (1999). Robust Velocity Computation from a Biologically Motivated Model of Motion Perception, *Proceedings of the Royal Society of London B*, 266, pp. 509-518.

José Antonio Martin H., Matilde Santos, Javier de Lope. (2010). Orthogonal Variant Moments Features in Image Analysis, *Information Sciences*, vol. 180, pp. 846 - 860.

K. Sookhanaphibarn, C. Lursinsap. (2006). A new feature extractor invariant to intensity, rotation, and scaling of color images, *Inform. Sci.* vol. 176 (14), pp. 2097–2119.

L. Lagae, S. Raiguel, G.A Orban. (1993). Speed and direction selectivity of macaque Middle temporal neurones, *J. Neurophysiol*, vol. 69, pp. 19-39.

Liu H., Hong T., Herman M. (1997). A General Motion Model and Spatio-Temporal Filters for Computing Optical Flow, *Int.Journal of Computer Vision*, 22 (2), pp. 141-172.

Lucas B. D., Kanade T. (1981). An Iterative Image Registration Technique with an Application to Stereo Vision. *Proceedings of the Seventh International Joint Conference on Artificial Intelligence*, pp. 674-679.

M. Tomasi, F. Barranco, M. Vanegas, J. Díaz, E. Ros. (2010). Fine grain pipeline architecture for high performance phase-based optical flow computation, *Journal of Systems Architecture*, vol. 56, pp. 577–587.

M.-K. Hu. (1961). Pattern recognition by moment invariants, in: *Proceedings of IRE (Correspondence) Trans. Inform. Theory*, vol. 49, pp. 14–28.

Marr, D. (1982) *Vision*. Edit. W.H.Freeman. (1982).

Martín J.L., Zuloaga A., Cuadrado C., Lázaro J., and Bidarte U. (2005), *Hardware implementation of optical flow constraint equation using FPGAs*, ComputerVision and Image Understanding, 98, no. 3, pp. 462-490.

Mitiche A. (1987). Experiments in Computing Optical Flow with the Gradient-Based, Multiconstraint Method, *Pattern Recognition*, 20(2), pp. 173-179.

Mitiche A., Bouthemy P. (1996). Computation and Analysis of Image Motion: A Synopsis of Current Problems and Methods, *International Journal of Computer Vision*, 19 (1), pp. 29-55.

Nagel H. (1983). Displacement Vectors Derived from Second-Order Intensity Variations in Image Sequences, *Computer Vision, Graphics and Image Processing*, 21, pp. 85-117.

Nakayama K. (1985). Biological Image Motion Processing: A Review. *Vision Research*, 25, pp. 625-660.

Niitsuma, H. and Maruyama T. (2004). Real-Time Detection of Moving Objects, *Lecture Notes in Computer Science*, FPL 2004, vol. 3203, pp. 1153-1157.

Nyquist. (2007). http://en.wikipedia.org/wiki/Nyquist%E2%80%

Oh H., Lee H. (2000). Block-matching algorithm based on an adaptive reduction of the search area for motion estimation, *Real-Time Imaging*, 6, pp.407-414 (2000)

Ong E. P., Spann M. (1999). Robust Optical Flow Computation Based on Least-Median-of-Squares Regression, *International Journal of Computer Vision*, 31(1), pp. 51-82.

Pajares, G. De la Cruz, Jesús. (2003), *Visión por Computador (imágenes digitales y aplicaciones)*. ISBN 84-7897-472-5. RA-MA.

R. F. Hess, R. J Snowden. (1992). Temporal frequency filters in the human peripheral visual field, *Vision Research*, vol. 32, pp. 61-72.

R.J. Prokop, A.P. Reeves. (1992). A survey of moment-based techniques for unoccluded object representation and recognition. *Models Image Process*, vol. 54, pp. 438-460.

Reinery L. (2000). Simulink-based Hw/Sw codesign of embedded neuron-fuzzy systems. *International Journal of Neural Systems*, Vol. 10, No. 3, pp. 211-226.

Rosin P.L. (1998). Thresholding for Change Detection, *Proceedings of the International Conference of Computer Vision*, pp. 274-279.

Simoncelli E. P., Adelson E. H., Heeger D. J. (1991). Probability Distributions of Optical Flow, *Proceedings of the IEEE Conference on Computer Vision and Pattern Recognition*.

Simoncelli E. P., Heeger D. J. (1998). A Model of Neuronal Responses in Visual Area MT, *Vision Research*, 38 (5), pp. 743-761.

Smith S. M. (1995). ASSET-2: Real-Time Motion Segmentation and Object Tracking. Technical Report TR95SMS2b available from www.fmrib.ox.ac.uk/~steve.

Sobey P. and Srinivasan M. V. (1991). Measurement of Optical Flow by a Generalized Gradient Scheme, *Journal of the Optical Society of America A*, 8(9), pp. 1488-1498.

Uras S., Girosi F., Verri A., and Torre V. (1998). A Computational Approach to Motion Perception, *Biological Cybernetics*, 60, pp. 79-87.

V. Bruce, P.R. Green, M.A. Georgeson. (1996). *Visual Perception: Physiology, Psychology & Ecology*. third ed., Laurence Erlbaum Associates, Hove.

Van Hateren J. H., Ruderman D. L. (1998). Independent Component Analysis of Natural Image Sequences Yield Spatio-Temporal Filters Similar to Simple Cells in Primary Visual Cortex. *Proceedings of the Royal Society of London B 265*, pp. 2315- 2320.

Verri A., Poggio T. (1989). Motion Field and Optical Flow: Qualitative Properties. *IEEE Transactions on Pattern Analysis and Machine Intelligence*, 11, pp. 490-498.

Wallach H. (1976). *On Perceived Identity: 1. The Direction of Motion of Straight Lines*. In On Perception, New York: Quadrangle.

Weber K., Venkatesh S., Kieronska D. (1994). Insect Based Navigation and its Application to the Autonomous Control of Mobile Robots, *Proceedings of the International Conference on Automation, Robotics and Computer Vision*.

Y.N. Zhang, Y. Zhang, C.Y. Wen. (2000). A new focus measure method using moments, *Image Vision Comput*. vol. 18, 959–965.

Yacoob. Y. and Davis. L. S. (1999). Temporal Multi-scale Models for Flow and Acceleration. *International Journal of Computer Vision*, 32 (2), pp.1-17.

Yacoob. Y. and Davis. L. S. (1999). Temporal Multi-scale Models for Flow and Acceleration, *International Journal of Computer Vision*, 32 (2), pp.1-17.

Young R. A., Lesperance R. M. (1993). A Physiological Model of Motion Analysis for Machine Vision. *Technical Report GMR 7878*, Warren, MI: General Motors Res. Lab.

Zanker J. M. (1996). On the Elementary Mechanism Underlying Secondary Motion Processing, *Phil. Transactions of the Royal Society of London*, B 351, pp. 1725-1736.

Zhang J. Z., Jonathan Wu. Q. M. (2001). A Pyramid Approach to Motion Tracking, *Real-Time Imaging*, 7, pp. 529-544.

Zuloaga A., Bidarte U., Martin J., Ezquerra J. (1998). Optical Flow Estimator Using VHDL for Implementation in FPGA, *Proc. of the Int. Conf. on Image processing*, pp. 972-976.

14

Real Time Radio Frequency Exposure for Bio-Physical Data Acquisition

Alessandra Paffi[1], Francesca Apollonio[1], Guglielmo d'Inzeo[1], Giorgio A. Lovisolo[2] and Micaela Liberti[1]

[1]Sapienza University of Rome
[2]RC Casaccia, ENEA
Italy

1. Introduction

Focus of this chapter is the description of the exposure systems used for data acquisition during the exposure to radiofrequency (RF) electromagnetic (EM) fields in bioelectromagnetic investigations. Such a kind of system will be referred to as real-time and can be defined as an EM structure (waveguide or antenna) able to generate and control a known and reproducible EM field and suitable to be used in experiments where data acquisition has to be carried out simultaneously with the exposure (Paffi et al., 2010).

Common real-time applications are usually based on programs that function within a time frame that the user senses as immediate and which require what is called real-time computing (RTC). In biomedicine the real-time concept is applied to both fast calculation of some parameters of biomedical significance (Seong et al., 2011; Wang et al., 2011) and the experimental acquisition of physiological data simultaneously with a correlated event (Li et al., 2010; Voyvodic et al., 2011).

In this context, real-time exposure systems are used to acquire fast biological responses, typically in the order of milliseconds, simultaneously with the exposure to EM fields, in order to study possible health effects due to EM exposure. Usually the responses to be recorded are electrophysiological signals as cellular currents (mA) or membrane potentials (mV); they need to be acquired through a sophisticated instrumentation made of microscopes, patch-clamp recording electrodes, temperature sensors, which fix strict and defined requirements to the design and optimization of the exposure system.

The introduction of this kind of systems has been made necessary due to the need to better investigate the coupling of RF EM fields with learning and memory in both animal models and humans. Neurons, which are at the basis of brain functioning, are electrically active cells. Their electric fields are maintained and controlled by a wide variety of biochemical and metabolic processes. In neurons, fundamental functions such as neurotransmitter release, enzyme activation, intracellular signal transduction, and gene expression are critically dependent on electrical signals. Therefore it has been postulated several times a possible coupling of their electrical activity with a RF EM field.

In the past, several studies were carried out suggesting a possible interference of the EM fields with neurons, but with controversial results and unable to clearly state the molecular basis of this interaction (Sienkiewicz et al., 2000; Wang and Lai, 2000; Dubreuil et al., 2003; Preece et al., 2005). For a review on EM field effects on cognitive functions see (D'Andrea et al., 2003). This is not surprising: experimental investigation of the EM coupling with neurons, in fact, is rather complicated since it involves measurements of the electrical activity of neurons, i.e. the acquisition of electrophysiological recordings of the transmembrane voltage and of the ionic currents. Therefore, a prerequisite of well-posed experiments involving neuronal activity is the possibility to acquire the useful signals simultaneously with the exposure to the RF EM field. Hence, in the last years, there has been a pressing need to design real-time exposure systems.

Some of the most recent results achieved with the aid of ad hoc designed real-time systems state that there is no significant coupling between low intensity RF EM fields and specific membrane channels, i.e. biological membrane proteins which allow the passive movement of ions from the external to the internal of the cell and vice-versa (Marchionni et al., 2006; Platano et al., 2007). Other studies, investigating the effects of low intensity RF EM fields on electrical activity in rat hippocampus, one of the major component of brain, (Tattersall et al., 2001) described an effect on synaptic transmission; however the effect reported has been later explained by localised heating produced by interaction of the RF fields with the recording and stimulating electrodes. This contradiction emphasizes the fundamental issue related to the proper design of real-time systems.

Although real-time investigations have been gaining increasing interest in the last ten years, a complete and systematic framework on specific requirements of RF exposure systems when applied to real-time data acquisition is still lacking.

Aim of this chapter is to merge the well-assessed design procedure of RF exposure systems (Kuster and Schönborn, 2000; Paffi et al., 2010) with the requirements emerging from real-time investigations, thus providing a reference work on this segment of knowledge.

In the chapter, at first a description of what is an exposure system and which are the guidelines to optimally design it are given. Then, it is provided how to adapt the general rules for exposure system design to real-time systems ones, which, of course, have very specific requirements. Finally, a complete and updated review of the real-time systems available in literature is provided.

2. Basic requirements for the exposure systems

Since the early development of mobile telephony, concern aroused on the possibility of the exposure to EM signals in the RF range inducing hazardous effects on population health. Consequently, a number of experiments were carried out (Lin, 2004; Valberg et al., 2007) aiming at the evaluation of possible biological effects of RF EM fields. The obtained results were often conflicting and difficult to replicate, mostly due to inaccurate dosimetry and to a lack of well-characterized exposure conditions.

Since the 90s, the need of a common approach to the bioelectromagnetic research became evident, as pointed out by a number of workshops and publications yielded by the scientific community. In 1994, the Wireless Technology Research (WTR) held a workshop to highlight the appropriate directions for the development of exposure systems (Carlo, 1998). In 1996, the EMF Project of the World Health Organization (WHO) fixed these concepts and emphasized the importance of an accurate dosimetry in all scientific studies (WHO, 1996). Such items, together with a deep discussion on quality assurance, were the main arguments of two European Cooperation in Science and Technology (COST) workshops: "Exposure systems and their dosimetry", in Zurich, in February 1999 (Schönborn et al., 1999; Bitz et al., 1999) and "Forum on future European research on mobile communication and health", in Bordeaux, in April 1999 (Kuster and Schönborn, 1999).

In 2000, recommended minimal requirements for exposure systems, in order to obtain reproducible and scientifically valuable results, were synthesized in (Kuster and Schönborn, 2000). Basically, two classes of requirements can be identified: biological and EM ones. Biological requirements are dictated by the laboratory equipment, the experimental procedures, and the environment; the EM ones define the exposure parameters (frequency, amplitude, modulation scheme of the signal), the characteristics of the induced EM field (polarization, intensity and homogeneity), and the "dose" at the location of the biological sample.

More in detail, to meet the biological requirements, the exposure system must allow for the exposure of the required number of samples or animals; in the meantime, the environmental conditions required by the specific experiment must be guaranteed (Kuster and Schönborn, 2000). As for the EM requirements, (i) the delivered signal must be precisely defined in terms of frequency, amplitude, and modulation scheme; (ii) the electric and magnetic field strength and polarization must be known at the location of the exposed biological target; (iii) the fields inside the sample should be homogeneous; (iv) any electromagnetic interference (EMI) and/or electromagnetic compatibility (EMC) issue must be avoided (Kuster and Schönborn, 2000). Moreover, the system should guarantee the monitoring of relevant parameters, such as the temperature and the delivered power, during the experiment and the possibility of carrying out sham exposures and blind experiments. In the sham exposure, a number of cell cultures or animals are subjected to environmental conditions identical to those of the group of the exposed subjects, except for the exposure. Data collected by the sham group are thus used as negative control. This is an unavoidable procedure to prevent the incorrect attribution to the RF exposure of an observed effect, which might be due to other factors, e.g. to the stress of the animals (Samaras et al., 2005). In blind experiments the exposure setup provides an automated procedure to assign the real and the sham exposure to two different groups of samples. In this way, experimenter polarization errors are removed, since he/she does not know which samples are really exposed.

Finally, the exposure system should be easy to be handled even by non-engineering personnel and its cost should be reasonable (Kuster and Schönborn, 2000). To maintain low the cost of the whole exposure setup, in particular of the signal amplifier of the generation chain, the EM structure should be designed to have the power efficiency as high as possible. The power efficiency is defined as the mean EM power absorbed by the unitary mass of sample per unitary input power feeding the EM structure.

Biological requirements are usually the most limiting ones on the exposure setups. As example, the kind of experiment may dictate the equipment needed and the environment; the overall duration of the experiment and the number of samples or animals necessary for statistical significance may strongly influence the choice of the EM structure employed as exposure system. For this reason, a lot of different exposure systems have been published during the past ten years (Lovisolo et al., 2009; Paffi et al., 2010, 2011), according to the great variety of experimental endpoints and protocols.

Moreover, during the past years, several cooperative research programmes, e.g. the European projects: PERFORM A, PERFORM B, and RAMP2001 have been carried out. The necessity of conducting a coordinate research activity in laboratories of different countries has arisen the issue of whether standardized exposure systems and protocols should be used. This was one of the topics of the Workshop: "EMF health risk research lessons learned and recommendations for the future" held in Monte Verita in November 2005. The outcome of the work stated that, due to different endpoints and protocols used in bioelectromagnetic investigations, exposure setups could not be standardized. In the same time, strong quality control on dosimetry is mandatory to assure the repeatability and reproducibility of results even when different exposure systems are used (Samaras et al., 2005; Lovisolo et al., 2009). Although the concept of using a standardized exposure system for all types of studies is not possible, the choice, design, and characterization of the system can be standardized to obtain repeatable and reproducible results from biological experiments (Paffi et al., 2010).

3. Exposure systems for experimental investigations

Well-defined and characterized exposure conditions are necessary for health-risk assessments (WHO, 1996). Unless the "dose" is accurately known, the results of bioelectromagnetics studies will have little value for determining exposure thresholds for health risk or for developing exposure limits in standards; therefore, great research effort has been devoted to reproduce well-defined exposure conditions in the last twenty years.

For the EM exposure in the RF range, the "dose" is considered the incremental absorbed EM energy per unit mass (ICNIRP, 1998), given in terms of Specific Absorption Rate (SAR), which is defined as follows:

$$\mathrm{SAR} = \frac{\mathrm{d}}{\mathrm{dt}}\left(\frac{\mathrm{dW}}{\mathrm{dm}}\right) = \frac{\mathrm{d}}{\mathrm{dt}}\left(\frac{\mathrm{dW}}{\rho \mathrm{dV}}\right) \tag{1}$$

where dW is the incremental energy dissipated in an incremental mass dm included in an incremental volume dV and ρ is the mass density. SAR (measured in W/kg) can be calculated directly from the electrical loss, which is proportional, through the conductivity σ, to the mean square of the electric field strength E locally induced in the tissue (ICNIRP, 1998), as follows:

$$\mathrm{SAR} = \frac{\sigma \mathrm{E}^2}{\rho} \tag{2}$$

To have a precise and accurate knowledge of the SAR distribution inside the exposed sample during the experiments, exposure systems have to be designed, fabricated, and characterized, in order to meet all the requirements discussed in Section 2. In fact one cannot employ commonly used EM sources, such as phone cells or microwave ovens, as done in several cases, especially in studies published prior to 1990s, since in these cases the dose absorbed by the target will be completely unpredictable.

The aim of an exposure system is to expose a biological target to a well-controlled and reproducible SAR, while maintaining appropriate environmental conditions and allowing the monitoring of some parameters during the exposure, such as temperature (Lin et al., 2009).

An exposure system is a complex structure used for allocating the biological samples during the exposure phase in a biological experiment. It encompasses:

1. the EM structure emitting the EM field;
2. the chain for the generation and control of the EM signal;
3. the system for maintaining the environmental parameters needed for the well-being of the exposed samples;
4. the software for the system management.

Although the exposure system is the complex structure, consisting of several parts, guaranteeing the desired exposure conditions of the sample, in the following, with the term exposure system, we will refer to its main part: the EM structure emitting the field, which can be an antenna, a waveguide, a resonator, as described in detail in Section 6.

Essentially it is possible to find exposure systems for *in vitro* and for *in vivo* biological experiments. In the first case, the biological target is constituted by cultured tissues or cells contained in sample holders such as flasks, tubes, Petri dishes, multiwells, and cuvettes. In the second case, the target is a specific animal or part of it, e.g. head, eyes, and ears.

In vitro experiments are an accepted method for determining, at cellular level, the SAR threshold for the onset of biological effects and damage (Guy et al., 1999). One of the main limitations of *in vitro* experiments is that the effects observed in cell cultures do not necessary imply any impairment at physiological level. For this reason, *in vivo* experiments, carried out on living animals, such as mice, rats, and rabbits, are of great scientific interest.

In vivo exposure systems could be rather different from the *in vitro* ones (Lin et al., 2009). This is mainly due to the larger dimensions of animals with respect to the *in vitro* sample holders. Moreover, animals tend to move inside the exposure system, unless they are restrained inside special containers, as required in some experiments. Finally, requirements for the maintenance of the environment conditions depend on whether cells or animals have to be exposed. In the first case, generally an incubator is needed; in the second case, ventilation, food and water should be provided, especially for long-term exposures.

4. The concept of real-time acquisitions in bioelectromagnetic investigations

Real-time data acquisition in biomedicine is employed in a lot of different applications, both *in vitro* and *in vivo*. Real-time monitoring of chemical reactions (Shutes and Der, 2005), gene expression (Gubern et al., 2009), drug release from nanoparticles (Chouhan and Bajpai, 2009) are significant examples of *in vitro* applications. As for *in vivo* investigations, the real-time acquisition is usually based on non-invasive imaging techniques (Ohtani et al., 2010; Li et al., 2010; Voyvodic et al., 2011) suitable to be applied to living animals.

The common issue in both *in vitro* and *in vivo* real-time experiments for biomedicine is that the experimental acquisition of physiological data is performed simultaneously with the correlated event.

In bioelectromagnetic investigation the concept of real-time is applied to experimental acquisition of data, which have to be collected simultaneously with the EM exposure, as schematically reported in Fig. 1.

In real-time experiments, the time slot of data acquisition often starts before and ends after the exposure period. The data acquired before and after the exposure are compared with those collected during the exposure. The pre-exposure data are used as a negative control; the post-exposure ones are used to identify possible long term or permanent modifications induced by the RF field on the observed parameter. Conversely, in off-line experiments data acquisition is carried out at the end of the exposure (Fig. 1) and the negative control is obtained from a parallel session (sham exposure) where biological samples are subjected to environmental conditions identical to those of the group of the exposed ones, except for the exposure. On the contrary, in real-time experiments, the same sample, observed in different time slots, is used as its own control. This concept is better explained in Fig. 2, showing the current through an ionic channel recorded before (black trace on the left), during (red trace on the center) and after (black trace on the right) the exposure.

From Fig. 2, a clear effect of the RF field is observable only comparing the three segments of the recorded current. Being reversible, such an effect would not be detected in off-line experiments.

Therefore, the main advantage of real-time acquisition is that it enables the experimenter to identify possible reversible or cumulative effects, otherwise difficult or even impossible to be detected. Moreover real-time experiments permit time saving, since one does not have to wait for the end of the experiment before collecting and analyzing the biological data.

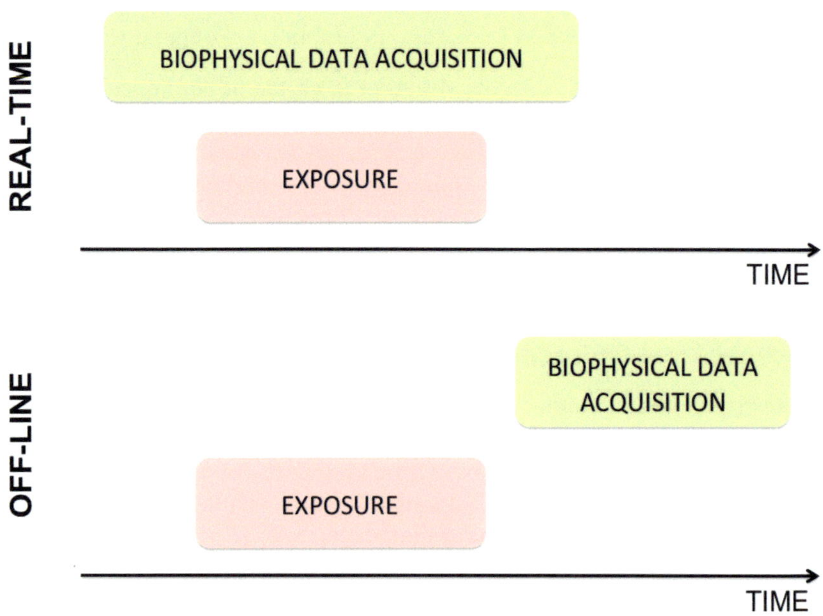

Fig. 1. Schematic representation of the time scheduling of exposure and data acquisition in real-time and off-line experiments

Fig. 2. Single channel current recorded before, during, and after the exposure to RF field

Real-time experiments have revealed a powerful tool especially in the investigation on possible modifications of the activity of neuronal cells or cell networks during the exposure, through electrophysiological recordings, as evident from Table 1, where information on published *in vitro* real-time experiments is summarized.

SAMPLE	OBSERVABLE	EXPOSURE	TECHNIQUE/ INSTRUMENT
Neuronal cells	Ionic current; Membrane voltage	CW 900; 1800 MHz; GSM900	Patch-clamp recording
Organ of Corti	Ionic current	GSM900; GSM1800; UMTS	Patch-clamp recording
Brain slices	Field potential	CW 700 MHz; Pulsed 9.2 GHz; CW 1.8 GHz	Extracellular recording
Heart slices	Field potential	Pulsed 9.2 GHz	Extracellular recording
Skeletal muscle	Muscle contraction	CW 0.75-1.12 GHz	Force transducer
Chromaffin cells	Catecholamine release	CW 0.75-1.12 GHz; CW 1-6 GHz	Electrochemical detector
Liposomes	Enzymatic activity	CW 2.45 GHz	Spectrophotometer

Table 1. Schematic description of the *in vitro* real-time experiments in the literature, in terms of samples, observables, RF signals and techniques used for the experimental activity

The most used experimental samples are excitable cells and tissues since they are likely to be sensitive to EM stimulation and to display reversible effects. They include single neuronal cells (Liberti et al., 2004; Platano et al., 2006; Marchionni et el., 2005; Paffi et al., 2007), neuronal networks (Tattersall et al., 2001; Pakhomov et al., 2003; Koester et al., 2007; Merla et al., 2011), inner ear hair cells of the organ of Corti (El Ouardi et al., 2011), and muscles, both skeletal (Lambrecht et al., 2006) and cardiac (Pakhomov et al., 2000). The observables are mostly electrophysiological parameters, such as the ionic current and the membrane voltage at the level of single cell, or the field potential generated by a group of interconnected neuronal cells. This latter observable is largely used in the studies on synaptic plasticity, the basic mechanism underlying high cognitive functions, such as memory and learning. However, even chemical parameters can be analyzed, such as the enzymatic activity, through a spectrophotometer (Ramundo-Orlando et al., 2004), or the neurotransmitter release, through an electrochemical detector (Hagan et al., 2004; Yoon et al., 2006). The techniques employed for the acquisition of the electrophysiological traces are patch-clamp (Neher and Sakmann, 1998) and extracellular recordings. Both of them require the use of microelectrodes near the membrane cell (extracellular recordings) or in close contact with it (patch-clamp). The EM signals mostly used in the experiments are continuous waves (CW) or modulated signals, especially at the frequencies typical of mobile communication. In one case (Pakhomov et al., 2003), the effects of a pulsed signal at 9 GHz on brain slices were investigated.

Due to the complexity of the experimental procedure, generally exposure systems for real-time experiments are more difficult to design since, beside the requirements typical of any exposure system (see Section 2), they have to meet additional and demanding requirements (see Section 5).

In particular, for *in vivo* experiments, only two real-time systems are present in the literature from 1999 until now (Testilier et al., 2002; Arima et al., 2011). Both of them are based on a simple EM structure (i.e. an antenna), while the real-time monitoring of the biological parameter is obtained through highly invasive techniques. In Testilier et al. (2002) neurotransmitter levels in a rat brain were monitored during the exposure through an invasive microdialysis technique; in Arima et al. (2011) the microcirculation of the rat brain during the exposure is observed through a cranial window on the skull.

The reason of such a reduced number of *in vivo* studies can be found in bioassays typically used to measure the effects of EM fields that require the employment of complex procedures and instrumentation. Biological data are often collected after the animal sacrifice and the subsequent removal of organs and tissues for the analysis.

5. Design procedure

In (Paffi et al., 2010) a standardized procedure was proposed for reaching the optimum exposure design. It consists of seven main steps, as schematically shown in Fig. 3.

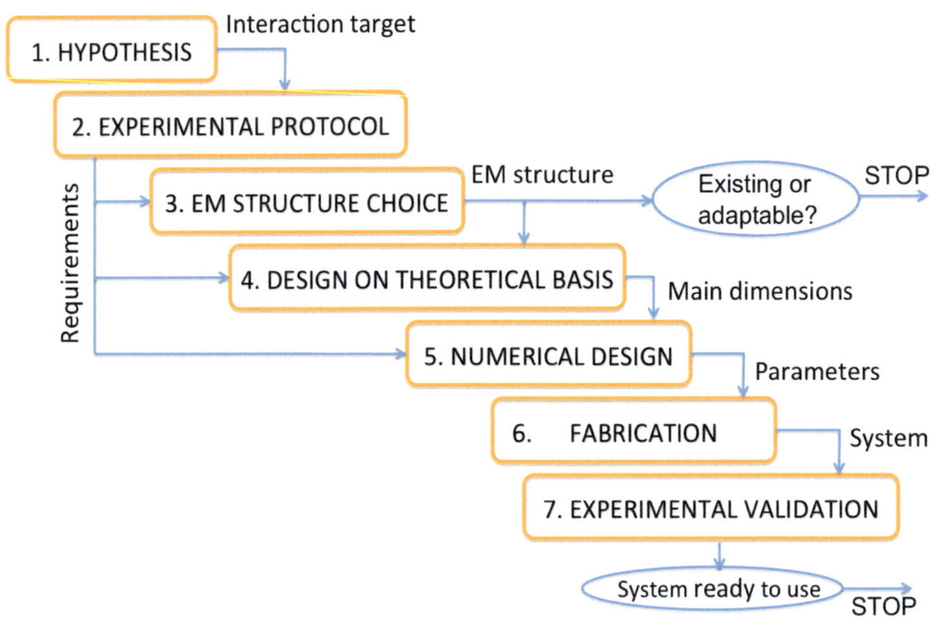

Fig. 3. Flow chart of the standardized procedure for the design and characterization of exposure systems

Before carrying out the experimental activity, a hypothesis is formulated (step 1), leading to the choice of an appropriate biological system to be exposed. It can be a particular kind of cell, a tissue, an organ, or a whole organism, as an animal. The experiment to test the hypothesis is then defined (step 2), including biological models, endpoints, techniques, and exposure parameters. The outcome of the analyses carried out during this step determines all the requirements, both biological and EM, of the exposure system. Moving from biological protocol and requirements on exposure parameters, the most suitable EM basic structure is chosen (step 3). If a system meeting all the requirements for the planned experiment is already present in the literature, one may decide to use that system as it is or to adapt it to new constrains; otherwise, the chosen EM structure must be first dimensioned on theoretical bases (step 4). Generally, the basic structure must be modified in order to meet all the biological and EM requirements. Thus, an iterative process of adaptation and optimization of the system (step 5) takes place using numerical tools, leading to the final design parameters (dimensions, materials, sample position, etc.). The next two steps are the manufacture (step 6) and the experimental validation (step 7) of the exposure system. Measurements should be conducted firstly with the empty structure; then it has to be loaded with the biological sample to validate the behavior of the system and to experimentally evaluate the dosimetry, i.e. the SAR distribution in the sample. If acceptable agreement between measurement and simulation is not achieved, one must return to steps 5, 6, or 7 depending on the hypothesized cause of mismatch.

As already noted, biological requirements represent a crucial point for the design of an exposure system since they could be the most limiting ones, especially when a particular equipment and protocol procedures are needed, e.g. in real-time experiments.

5.1 Special requirements for the design of real-time systems

Although the procedure (Paffi et al., 2010) for the design and characterization of the exposure system is the same regardless of the particular kind of analysis (real-time or off-line), real-time acquisitions impose additional biological requirements to the system. In particular, when dealing with the electrophysiological recordings, they can be summarized in the easy access to the sample (i.e. through the microscope, the electrodes, and the perfusion apparatus) and the minimum coupling between the EM field and the acquisition equipment, in order to avoid artifacts.

For the correct placement of the electrodes, the sample must be illuminated and observed through a microscope. Moreover, in some experiments, the biological sample, e.g. brain slices, has to be perfused to preserve its structure and function. For these reasons, in order to easily reach the sample, the exposure system must be either an open structure or a closed one modified with holes.

The microelectrodes for electrophysiological recordings are usually made of glass filled with a saline solution with a metallic wire inside. Being the biological cultures exposed to CW or modulated signals, especially at the frequencies typical of mobile communication, the real-time acquisition implies the possibility of EM coupling between the electrodes and the electric field, with consequent artifacts on the recorded trace. Another possible source of artifacts is the interference between the EM field generated by the system and the whole acquisition setup. To minimize the coupling between the field and the electrode, the direction of the electric field must be almost orthogonal to the electrode. Moreover, to avoid interference of the field with the laboratory equipment, in principle, the EM field should be confined in a closed structure. However, even open structures can be used, provided that the electric and magnetic fields sharply decay with the distance from the system.

Finally, the presence of metallic and/or dielectric objects (microscope objective, lamp, electrodes, perfusion apparatus), placed very close to the region where the sample is exposed (see Figure 4), may modify the field distribution and thus the whole behavior of the system. This kind of coupling must be carefully taken into account during the numerical optimization of the system in order to minimize it.

The different solutions adopted to meet such demanding requirements will be described in Section 6.

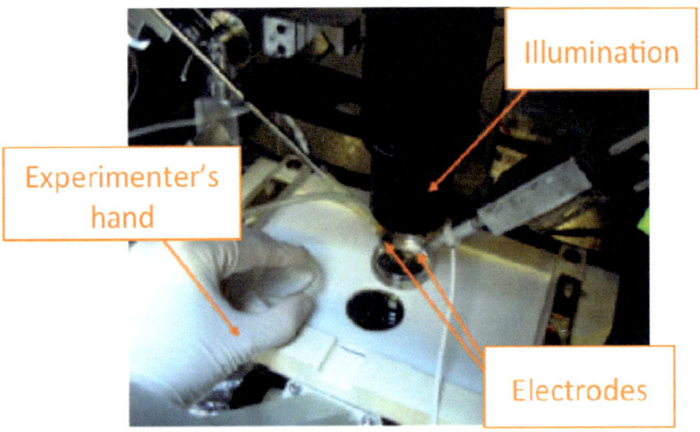

Fig. 4. Picture of a planar exposure system used for electrophysiological recordings from brain slices (Paffi et al., 2007). Arrows highlight the presence of different objects placed very close to the system surface during the experiments.

6. Classification of the exposure systems

6.1 General classification

Due to the great variety of biological targets and protocols, a number of different exposure systems have been adopted in the experimental investigation, both *in vivo* and *in vitro*.

Despite their peculiarities, the exposure systems can be classified on the basis of the employed EM structure into three main groups: radiating, propagating and resonant systems, as proposed in (Lovisolo et al., 2009; Paffi et al., 2010).

Conversely, for what concerns the biological experiment, the main classification is between the *in vitro* and *in vivo* setups, as already discussed in Section 3.

In turn, with respect to the experimental protocol, *in vivo* systems have been classified in two main classes, depending on whether the exposure involves the whole body or is focalized into a specific organ (Paffi et al., 2011). An additional criterion of organization is the possibility for the animals to freely move during the exposure (Paffi et al., 2011). In this case, animals are generally housed in their own cages, provided with food and water.

Otherwise animals are restrained inside plastic holders, to guarantee their relative position and orientation with respect to the electric and magnetic fields.

Conversely, *in vitro* exposure systems have been classified (Paffi et al., 2010) in two different groups: off-line and real-time, depending on the kind of data acquisition they have been designed for. This latter classification has not been adopted for the *in vivo* setups, since real-time acquisitions are very uncommon for *in vivo* experiments, as pointed out in Section 4.

Proposed classification is reported in Figure 5, together with the number of systems belonging to each category and published in international journals since 1999.

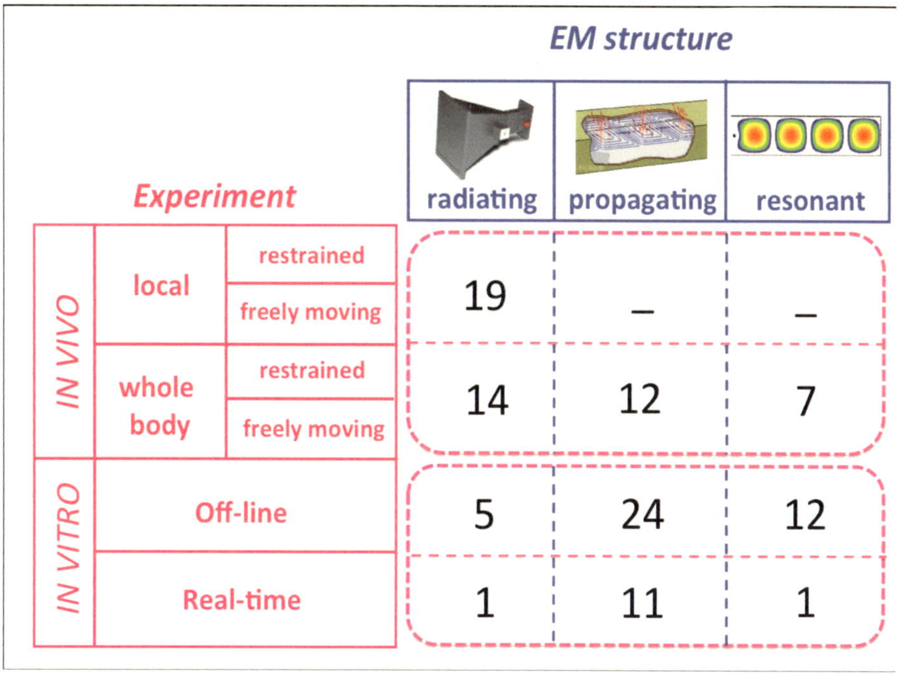

Fig. 5. Classification of the exposure systems. For each category the number of systems published from 1999 is reported

Among the 52 *in vivo* systems, those used for local exposure (19) are exclusively based on radiating structures. In particular, they are small antennas placed close to the target organ (brain, ear, eye) to induce significant and localized power absorption (Paffi et al., 2011). To reduce the cost of the experiment, a single antenna can be used to simultaneously expose several animals, if they are arranged in a sort of carousel around it (Schönborn et al., 2004). Generally, animals locally exposed are restrained within plastic holders to obtain a more accurate and precise SAR distribution, even though body-mounted antennas (Bahr et al., 2007) become necessary for the well being of animals when the exposure is prolonged.

For the 33 whole body exposure setups, the uniformity of SAR absorbed by animals of the same group and within each animal was a critical requirement (Paffi et al., 2011). This is particularly difficult to achieve especially for large-scale experiments. In this case, radiating structures (14 systems found in the literature) could be particularly suitable since a lot of bodies can be simultaneously exposed to a plane-wave equivalent field (Paffi et al., 2011).

However, the power efficiency is quite low (Paffi et al., 2011). Propagating systems are mainly based on rectangular or radial waveguides (Hansen et al., 1999), whereas resonant cavities are mainly obtained by shorting radial waveguides through metallic rods (Balzano et al., 2000). These structures are characterized by high volume efficiency, i.e. a lot of bodies (up to 65 animals) can be simultaneously exposed in a limited space. However, due to the importance of a correct body positioning, animals are restrained within plastic cylinders. Therefore, resonant cavities are suitable for chronic long-term (days or moths) exposures only if the exposure is limited to a few hours per day, as done in some two years bioassay experiments (e.g. PERFORM A).

A separated mention must be made of reverberating chambers (Corona et al., 2001). Inside those systems a statistically uniform field can be obtained and a large number of animals can be simultaneously exposed in a habitat simulating the usual one of animals (Wu et al., 2010). These are the reasons why they are suitable for large-scale, long-term experiments.

Moving to the *in vitro* systems, among the 54 off-line setups found in the literature, the most used (24) are propagating structures (Paffi et al., 2010), such as Transverse Electromagnetic (TEM) cells and rectangular waveguides. The main advantages of propagating structures are the EM field uniformity inside the biological sample and versatility. With a proper dosimetric characterization, propagating systems have been used to expose different volumes of various kinds of cells inside sample holders, such as multiwells, Petri dishes, and flasks (Paffi et al., 2010). Also resonant systems have been largely used (12) in off-line *in vitro* experiments (Paffi et al., 2010). They are closed and compact structures, such as short-circuited waveguides; thus both the active and the sham systems easily fit inside a commercial incubator, often needed for maintaining the optimal environmental conditions (Schuderer et al., 2004). Due to the onset of a standing wave inside resonant systems, the power efficiency is generally high, but the positioning of the sample is critical, because of the extremely localized regions of field uniformity (Paffi et al., 2010). On the contrary, radiating systems, usually consisting of commercial or ad hoc fabricated antennas, present low power efficiency, but generally allow for the simultaneous exposure of a lot of samples. However, they need EM compatible arrangements due to the lack of enclosures confining the emitted field (Paffi et al., 2010).

Regarding the 13 real-time *in vitro* systems, they are mostly based on propagating structures, with the only exception of one resonant (Hagan et al., 2004) and one radiating system (Yoon et al., 2006). Indeed, propagating structures are generally the most versatile and adaptable to the additional constrains imposed by real-time acquisition.

To meet such requirements, two main solutions have been proposed in the literature (Paffi et al., 2010): closed structures modified with holes for sample observation and data recording and open systems specially designed to have the field confined in a small volume around the surface. This latter solution also implies high values of power efficiency (Liberti et al., 2004; Paffi et al., 2007).

A detailed description of different kinds of real-time systems, together with their main features, will be given in Section 6.2.

6.2 Real time systems in the literature

According to the classification described above, real-time *in vitro* systems published in international journals from 1999 up to now, have been organized in a schematic view in Table 2.

<table>
<tr><th colspan="3">EXPOSURE SYSTEM</th><th>REFERENCE</th></tr>
<tr><td rowspan="8">REAL-TIME</td><td rowspan="6">PROPAGATING</td><td>Modified TEM cell</td><td>(Linz et al., 1999);
(Merla et al., 2011).</td></tr>
<tr><td>Modified rectangular waveguide</td><td>(Linz et al., 1999);
(Pakhomov et al., 2000);
(Lambrecht et al., 2006);
(Koester et al., 2007).</td></tr>
<tr><td>Parallel plates</td><td>(Tattersall et al., 2001).</td></tr>
<tr><td>Coplanar waveguide</td><td>(Liberti et al., 2004);
(Paffi et al., 2007).</td></tr>
<tr><td>Modified stripline</td><td>(Ramundo-Orlando et al., 2004).</td></tr>
<tr><td>Fin-line</td><td>(El Ouardi et al., 2011).</td></tr>
<tr><td>RESONANT</td><td>Modified rectangular waveguide</td><td>(Hagan et al., 2004).</td></tr>
<tr><td>RADIATING</td><td>Horn antenna</td><td>(Yoon et al., 2006).</td></tr>
</table>

Table 2. Classification of the real-time *in vitro* systems published from 1999

6.2.1 Propagating structures

Propagating systems for real-time studies are generally closed structures modified with holes for sample observation and perfusion, and for online monitoring of biochemical or biophysical parameters.

They are mostly TEM cells and rectangular waveguides as described in (Linz et al., 1999), where the electrophysiological activity of myocyte cells was recorded, through the patch-clamp technique, during the exposure to 900 MHz and 1800 MHz CW. The systems were equipped with two holes: one in the top wall to insert the recording electrode and the other in the bottom to observe the sample with a microscope. The solution adopted to avoid interference between the electric field inside the guide and the metallic wire of the patch-clamp electrode was the elongation of the glass microelectrodes used for sealing the cell in order to place the wire outside the exposure device. The power efficiency was not bad: 1.66 (W/kg)/W at 900 MHz and 3.16 (W/kg)/W at 1800 MHz.

A rectangular waveguide (Lambrecht et al., 2006), operating between 0.75-1.12 GHz, was also used to measure, through a force transducer, the effects of the RF field on skeletal muscle inserted in a bath placed in the center of the waveguide. The waveguide was modified with slots in the walls to allow connection with measurement, control, and stimulating devices outside the system. The power efficiency was good (> 3 (W/kg)/W) and SAR homogeneity, around 79 %, was in line with minimal requirements for *in vitro* experiments (homogeneity > 70 %). A modified rectangular waveguide was used for delivering CW or Universal Mobile Telecommunications System (UMTS) signals to neuronal networks during electrophysiological recordings from multiple electrodes (Koester et al.,

2007). The neuronal network was cultivated on a microsensor chip fitted into a recess in the guide to avoid short circuiting the measuring probes while exposing the neuronal cells.

For a similar experiment at 1800 MHz, a different solution was proposed in (Merla et al., 2011). The exposure system consisted of a TEM cell open in correspondence of the lateral walls. The multiple electrode array used for the electrophysiological recordings was inserted in a circular hole in the TEM cell bottom plate. The power efficiency of 3.2 (W/kg)/W was comparable to that of the closed systems described above.

A waveguide terminated with an exposure cell containing the sample was used to expose heart slices (Pakhomov et al., 2000) and brain slices (Pakhomov et al., 2003) to high-power microwave pulses (repetition frequency 9.2 GHz). The system had an extremely high efficiency of 3.3 (kW/kg)/W which decreased about twofold per millimeter with distance from the waveguide aperture. In this case, the sample was used as the load of the guide; the impedance matching was achieved through a sapphire matching plate to maximize the power absorbed by the slices.

To record brain slices electrophysiological activity simultaneously with the exposure to a 700 MHz field, Tattersall *et al.* (Tattersall et al., 2001) utilized a waveguide made of two parallel plates. In this case, as in (Linz et al., 1999), the top and bottom plates of the guide had holes to observe the sample and insert both stimulating and recording electrodes. The coupling between the electric field and the electrodes was not avoided since the electrodes were placed at an angle of about 45° to the electric field (Misfud et al., 2007). The estimated efficiency value was lower than 0.03 (W/kg)/W.

A completely different solution, based on an open coplanar waveguide was adopted in studies involving patch-clamp recordings from neuronal cells (Liberti et al., 2004) and field potential recordings from brain slices (Paffi et al., 2007). Both systems operate in the 800–2000-MHz frequency band and differ from each other by the distance between the central and lateral conductors because of the different size of biological samples to be exposed to the EM fields. The open planar geometry and the transparent glass substrate allowed easy access to the samples through the microscope and the electrodes; the electric and magnetic fields were confined in a small volume around the surface that guaranteed the avoidance of interference with the data acquisition setup and high efficiency values (> 17 (W/kg)/W) at all frequencies.

To perform patch-clamp recordings from the ear hair cells of Corti organ, three exposure systems were described in (El Ouardi et al., 2011), operating at 900 MHz, 1.8 GHz and 2 GHz, respectively. All of them are based on the concept of the fin-line: a quasi-planar transmission line structure embedded in a metallic rectangular waveguide. In this case, the two fins were placed in the magnetic field plane of the waveguide. The chamber containing the samples was placed onto the two fins with a slot in between, where the exposure field concentrates, and inserted inside the guide through a circular opening in the top plate. This opening was also used to insert the electrodes and the microscope objective during the experiments. The efficiency was very high (> 40 (W/kg)/W for all systems), with a good homogeneity of 90 %. The drawback was the narrow band that imposed the fabrication of three different systems, one for each frequency band of interest (El Ouardi et al., 2011).

A modified stripline, where the sample holder (a cuvette) and the temperature regulating chamber were part of the dielectric substrate, was described in (Ramundo-Orlando et al., 2004). The system was placed inside a spectrophotometer for monitoring the enzymatic activity of ascorbate oxidase trapped in liposomes during the exposure to a CW at 2.45 GHz.

6.2.2 Resonant structures

Only one example of resonant structure used for real-time acquisition is presented in literature. The resonant system proposed by Hagan *et al.* (Hagan et al., 2004) was a short circuited rectangular waveguide designed to expose neural cells in the frequency range of 0.75–1.12 GHz while monitoring catecholamine release. The guide had slots on the plates to allow the communication between the cell perfusion apparatus, placed inside the waveguide, and the exterior.

6.2.3 Radiating structures

Even for radiating structures only one system has been published. A radiating system, based on a horn antenna, with the perfusion chamber placed in the far-field region, was used in (Yoon et al., 2006). The biological protocol was the same described in (Hagan et al., 2004), but the exposure frequencies were higher (1-6 GHz). For this higher frequency range, a standard waveguide is too small to accommodate the sample and the cell-perfusion apparatus and a radiating system is necessary. However, this solution required a special arrangement to avoid interference with the experimental equipment that was shielded in a conducting box behind the perfusion chamber and a layer of absorber material was used to prevent electric field reflection. The whole system was placed within an anechoic chamber.

7. Conclusion

Real-time data acquisition in biomedicine is employed in a lot of different applications, both *in vitro* and *in vivo*. Examples are given in monitoring of chemical reactions (Shutes and Der, 2005), gene expression (Gubern et al., 2009), and drug release (Chouhan and Bajpai, 2009). Concerning living animals, the real-time acquisition is usually based on non-invasive imaging techniques (Ohtani et al., 2010; Li et al., 2010; Voyvodic et al., 2011).

The common issue in both real-time *in vitro* and *in vivo* investigations for biomedicine is that the experimental acquisition of physiological data is performed simultaneously with the correlated event. This is also the case of bioelectromagnetic investigations.

Focus of this chapter was a review of the exposure systems used in real-time biological experiments, i.e. in those investigations where bio-chemical or bio-physical data are acquired from the sample simultaneously with the exposure to the EM field. Real-time investigation is widely spreading, especially in the study of the interaction between nervous system and RF EM fields through *in vitro* electrophysiological techniques.

Although real-time investigations have been gaining increasing interest in the last ten years, a complete and systematic framework on specific requirements of RF exposure systems when applied to real-time data acquisition is still lacking.

Aim of this chapter was to merge the well-assessed design procedure of RF exposure systems (Kuster & Schönborn, 2000; Paffi et al., 2010) with the requirements emerging from real-time investigations, thus providing a reference work on this segment of knowledge.

The exposure system, defined as the complex structure used for allocating the biological samples (cell cultures for the *in vitro* experiments, animals for the *in vivo* ones) during the exposure phase of a biological experiment, is a fundamental device in the whole experimental setup. Indeed, a well-designed and characterized exposure system is a prerequisite for obtaining reproducible and scientifically meaningful results useful in the process of health risk assessment. Therefore, moving from the analysis of both biological and EM requirements (Kuster et al., 2000), a standardized procedure for the design of the system should be used, as proposed in (Paffi et al., 2010).

Due to the great variety of biological protocols and exposure parameters (dose, duration, frequency and waveform of the EM signal), different exposure systems can be found in the literature, based on radiating (antennas), propagating (waveguides), and resonant (resonant cavities) structures. From an accurate review of them, it emerges that real-time systems, in almost all cases, were designed for *in vitro* investigations on the electrophysiological activity of excitable cells. Such systems generally require modifications of standard RF structures to allow the continuous monitoring of the sample while avoiding RF coupling and interference with the recording apparatus (Paffi et al., 2010). Different solutions can be found in the literature, almost all based on propagating structures. They are mostly open planar structures or semi-open and closed structures modified with holes to allow the access to the sample for the data acquisition. The proposed systems, tailored for the particular biological endpoint and protocol, often result from the trade-off between the two conflicting requirements: the easy access to the sample and the avoidance of interference with the laboratory equipment. Therefore, in these cases, guidelines to design the optimal and most efficient system are particularly significant.

8. References

Arima, T.; Watanabe, H.; Wake, K.; Masuda, H.; Watanabe, S.; Taki, M.; Uno, T. (2011). Local exposure system for rat head using figure-8 loop antenna in 1500 MHz band. *IEEE Transaction on Biomedical Engineering*, Vol. 58, No. 10, pp. 2740-2747, ISSN 0018-9294

Bahr, A.; Adami, C.; Bolz, T.; Rennings, A.; Dorn, H.; Ruttiger, L. (2007). Exposure Setups for Laboratory Animals and Volunteer Studies Using Body-Mounted Antennas. *Radiation Protection Dosimetry*, Vol. 124, No. 1, pp. 31–34, ISSN 0144-8420

Balzano, Q.; Chou, C.; Cicchetti, R.; Faraone, A.; Tay, R. Y. (2000). An Efficient RF Exposure System with Precise Whole-Body Average SAR Determination for in vivo Animal Studies at 900 MHz. *IEEE Trans. on Microw. Theory and Tech.*, Vol. 48, No. 11, pp. 2040-2049, ISSN 0018–9480

Bitz, A.; Steckert, J.; & Hansen, V. (1999). Exposure setups for a large number of samples: In vitro setups for HF exposure. in *Proc. 6th COST 244bis Exposure Syst. and Their Dosimetry Workshop*, pp. 24–30, Zurich, Switzerland, Feb. 14–15, 1999

Carlo, G.L., (1998). *Wireless phones and health: scientific progress*, Kluwer Academic Publishers, ISBN 0792383478, Boston, USA

Chouhan, R.; Bajpai, A.K. (2009). Real time *in vitro* studies of doxorubicin release from PHEMA nanoparticles. *Journal of Nanobiotechnology*, Vol. 7, No. 5, ISSN 1477-3155

Corona, P.; Ladbury, J.; Latmiral, G. (2002). Reverberation-Chamber Research—Then and Now: A Review of Early Work and Comparison With Current Understanding. *IEEE Transactions on Electromagnetic Compatibility*, Vol. 44, No. 1, (February 2002), pp. 87-94, ISSN 0018-9375

D'Andrea, J.A.; Chou, C.K.; Johnston, S.A., Adair, E.R. (2003). Microwave effects on the nervous system. *Bioelectromagnetics*, Suppl 6, pp. S107 - S147, ISSN 0197-8462

Dubreuil, D.; Jay, T.; Edeline, J.M. (2003). Head-only exposure to GSM 900-MHz electromagnetic fields does not alter rat's memory in spatial and non-spatial tasks. *Behav Brain Res*, Vol. 145, N° (1 - 2), pp. 51 - 61, ISSN 0166-4328

El Ouardi, A.; Streckert, J.; Bitz, A.; Munkner, S.; Engel, J.; Hansen V. (2011). New Fin-Line Devices for Radiofrequency Exposure of Small Biological Samples In Vitro Allowing Whole-Cell Patch Clamp Recordings. *Bioelectromagnetics*, Vol. 32, pp. 102-112, ISSN 0197-8462

Gubern, C.; Hurtado, O.; Rodríguez, R.; Morales, J.R.; Romera, V.G.; Moro, M.A.; Lizasoain, I.; Serena, J.; Mallolas, J. (2009). Validation of housekeeping genes for quantitative real-time PCR in in-vivo and in-vitro models of cerebral ischaemia. *BMC Molecular Biology*, Vol. 10, No. 57, ISSN 14712199

Guy, A.W.; Chou, C.K. & McDougall, J.A. (1999). A quarter century of in vitro research: A new look at exposure methods. *Bioelectromagnetics*, Vol. 20, Suppl. 4, (December 1999), pp. 21–39, ISSN 0197-8462

Hagan, T.; Chatterjee, I.; McPherson, D. & Craviso, G. L. (2004). A novel waveguide-based radiofrequency/ microwave exposure system for studying nonthermal effects on neurotransmitter release-finite difference time domain modeling. *IEEE Transactions Plasma Science*, Vol. 32, No. 4, (August 2004), pp. 1668–1676, ISSN 0093-3813

Hansen, V. W.; Bitz, A. K.; Streckert, J. R. (1999). RF Exposure of Biological Systems in Radial Waveguides. *IEEE Trans. on Electrom. Compat.*, Vol. 41, No. 4, pp. 487-493, ISSN 0018-9375

International Commission on Non-Ionising Radiation Protection (ICNIRP), (1998). Guidelines for Limiting Exposure to Time-Varying Electric, Magnetic, and Electromagnetic Fields (up to 300 GHz). *Health Physics*, Vol. 74, No. 4, (April 1998), pp. 494-522, ISSN 0017-9078

Koester, P.; Sakowski, J.; Baumann, W.; Glock, H. & Gimsaa, J. (2007). A new exposure system for the in vitro detection of GHz field effects on neuronal networks. *Bioelectrochemistry*, Vol. 70, (January 2007), pp. 104–114, ISSN 1567-5394

Kuster, N. & Schönborn, F. (1999). Requirements for exposure systems. in *Proc. COST 244bis Forum on Future Eur. Res. on Mobile Commun. and Health Workshop*, pp. 53–59, Bordeaux, France, Apr. 19–20, 1999

Kuster, N. & Schönborn, F. (2000). Recommended minimal requirements and development guidelines for exposure setups of bio-experiments addressing the health risk concern of wireless communications. *Bioelectromagnetics*, Vol. 21, (October 2000), pp. 508–514, ISSN 0197-8462

Lambrecht, M. R.; Chatterjee, I.; McPherson, D.; Quinn, J.; Hagan, T.; & Craviso, G. L. (2006). Design, characterization, and optimization of a waveguide-based RF/MW exposure system for studying nonthermal effects on skeletal muscle contraction. *IEEE Transactions Plasma Science*, Vol. 34, No. 4, (August 2006), pp. 1470–1479, ISSN 0093-3813

Li, C.; Aguirre, A.; Gamelin, J.; Maurudis, A.; Zhu, Q.; Wang, L.V. (2010). Real-time photoacoustic tomography of cortical hemodynamics in small animals. *Journal of Biomedical Optics*, Vol. 15, No. 1, ISSN 1083-3668

Liberti, M.; Apollonio, F.; Paffi, A.; Pellegrino, M. & d'Inzeo, G. (2004). A coplanar waveguide system for cells exposure during electrophysiological recordings. *IEEE Transactions Microwave Theory Techique*, Vol. 54, No. 11, (November 2004), pp. 2521–2528, ISSN 0018–9480

Lin, J.C. (2004). Studies on microwaves in medicine and biology: From snails to humans. *Bioelectromagnetics*, Vol. 25, pp. 146-159, ISSN 0197-8462

Lin, J. C.; Bernardi, P.; Pisa, S.; Cavagnaro, M., Piuzzi, E. (2009). Antennas for Biological Experiments, In: *Modern Antenna Handbook,* C. Balanis, (Ed.), 1429-1463, Wiley & Sons, ISBN 978-0-470-03634-1, USA

Linz, K.W.; von Westphalen, C.; Streckert, J.; Hansen, V. & Meyer, R. (1999). Membrane potential and currents of isolated heart muscle cells exposed to pulsed radio frequency fields. *Bioelectromagnetics,* Vol. 20, No. 8, (December 1999), pp. 497–511, ISSN 0197-8462

Lovisolo, G. A.; Apollonio, F., Ardoino, L., Liberti, M., Lopresto, V.; Marino, C.; Paffi, A. & Pinto, R. (2009). Specifications of in vitro exposure setups in the radiofrequency range. *Radio Science Bulletin*, No. 331, (December 2009), pp. 21–30, ISSN 1024-4530

Marchionni, I.; Paffi, A.; Pellegrino; M., Liberti; M., Apollonio, F.; Abeti, R.; Fontana, F.; d'Inzeo, G.; Mazzanti, M. (2006). Comparison between low-level 50 Hz and 900 MHz electromagnetic stimulation on single channel ionic currents and on firing frequency in dorsal root ganglion isolated neurons. *Biochimica et Biophysica Acta Biomembranes*, Vol. 1758, pp. 597-605, ISSN 0005-2736

Merla, C.; Ticaud, N.; Arnaud-Cormos, D.; Veyret, B.; Leveque, P. (2011). Real-Time RF Exposure Setup Based on a Multiple Electrode Array (MEA) for Electrophysiological Recording of Neuronal Networks. *IEEE Transactions on Microwave Theory And Techniques*, Vol. 59, No. 3, (March 2011), pp. 755-762, ISSN 0018–9480

Misfud, N.C.D.; Scott, I.R.; Green, A.C & Tattersall, J.E.H. (2007). Temperature effects in brain slices exposed to radiofrequency fields. in *Book of Abstract of 8th Int. Congress European BioElectromagnetics Association*, Bordeaux, France, Apr. 11–13, 2007

Neher, E.; Sakmann, B., (1998). *Single channel recording*, 2nd ed., Plenum Press, ISBN 0-306-41419-8, New York and London

Ohtani, N.; Yamakoshi, K.; Takahashi, A.; Hara, E. (2010). Real-time in vivo imaging of p16Ink4a gene expression: a new approach to study senescence stress signaling in living animals. *Cell Division*, Vol. 5, No. 1, ISSN 17471028

Paffi, A.; Pellegrino, M., Beccherelli, R.; Apollonio, F.; Liberti, M.; Platano, D.; Aicardi, G. & d'Inzeo, G. (2007). A real-time exposure system for electrophysiological recording in brain slices. *IEEE Transactions Microwave Theory Techique*, Vol. 55, No. 11, (November 2007), pp. 2463–2471, ISSN 0018–9480

Paffi, A.; Apollonio, F.; Lovisolo, G.; Marino, C.; Pinto, R.; Repacholi, M. & Liberti, M. (2010). Considerations for Developing an RF Exposure System: A Review for in vitro Biological Experiments. *IEEE Transactions Microwave Theory Techique*. Vol. 58, No. 10, (December 2010), pp. 2702–2714, ISSN 0018–9480

Paffi, A.; Apollonio, F.; Lovisolo, G.A.; Marino, C.; Liberti, M. (2011). Exposure Systems for Bioelectromagnetic Investigations in the Radiofrequency Range: Classification and Emerging Trends. in *Proceedings of the 5th European Conference on Antennas and Propagation*, pp. 3159-3163, ISBN 978-1-4577-0250-1, Rome, 11-15 April 2011

Pakhomov, A. G.; Mathur, S. P.; Doyle, J.; Stuck, B.E.; Kiel, J. L. & Murphy, M. R. (2000). Comparative effects of extremely high power microwave pulses and a brief CW irradiation on pacemaker function in isolated frog heart slices. *Bioelectromagnetics*, Vol. 21, No. 4, (May 2000), pp. 245–254, ISSN 0197-8462

Pakhomov, A. G.; Doyle, J.; Stuck, B. E. & Murphy, M. R. (2003). Effects of high power microwave pulses on synaptic transmission and long term potentiation in hippocampus. *Bioelectromagnetics*, Vol. 24, (April 2003), pp. 174–181, ISSN 0197-8462

Platano, D.; Mesirca, P.; Paffi, A.; Pellegrino, M.; Liberti, M.; Apollonio, F.; Bersani, F.; Aicardi, G. (2007). Acute exposure to 900 MHz CW and GSM-modulated radiofrequencies does not affect Ba^{2+} currents through voltage-gated calcium channels in rat cortical neurons. *Bioelectromagnetics*, Vol. 28, No. 8, (Dec. 2007), pp. 598-606, ISSN 0197-8462

Preece, A.W.; Goodfellow, S.; Wright, M.G.; Butler, S.R.; Dunn, E.J.; Johnson, Y.; Manktelow, T.C.; Wesnes, K. (2005). Effect of 902 MHz mobile phone transmission on cognitive function in children. *Bioelectromagnetics*, Suppl 7, pp. S138 - S143, ISSN 0197-8462

Ramundo-Orlando, A.; Liberti, M.; Mossa, G. & d'Inzeo, G. (2004). Effects of 2.45 GHz microwave fields on liposomes entrapping glycoenzyme ascorbate oxidase: Evidence for oligosaccaride side chain involvement. *Bioelectromagnetics*, Vol. 25, No. 5, (July 2004) pp. 338–345, ISSN 0197-8462

Samaras, T.; Kuster, N. & Nebovetic, S. (2005). Scientific report: Workshop on EMF health risk research lessons learned and recommendations for the future, presented at the Centro Stefano Franscini, Monte Verita, Switzerland, Nov. 20–24, 2005

Schönborn, F.; Pokovic, K. & Burkhardt, M. (1999). In vitro setups for HF exposure. in *Proc. 6th COST 244bis Exposure Syst. and Their Dosimetry Workshop*, pp. 12–23, Zurich, Switzerland, Feb. 1999

Schönborn, F.; Pokovic, K.; Kuster, N. (2004). Dosimetric Analysis of the Carousel Setup for the Exposure of Rats at 1.62 GHz. *Bioelectromagnetics*, Vol. 25, pp. 16-26, ISSN 0197-8462

Schuderer, J.; Samaras, T.; Oesch, W.; Spät, D.; Kuster, N. (2004). High peak SAR exposure unit with tight exposure and environmental control for *in vitro* experiments at 1800 MHz. *IEEE Trans. Microw. Theory Tech.*, Vol. 52, No. 8, (Aug. 2004), pp. 2057–2066, ISSN 0018–9480

Shutes, A.; Der, C.J. (2005). Real-time in vitro measurement of GTP hydrolysis. *Methods*, Vol. 37, pp. 183–189, ISSN 1046-2023

Seong, J.K.; Baek, N.; Kim, K.J. (2011). Real-time approximation of molecular interaction interfaces based on hierarchical space decomposition. *Computer-Aided Design*, Vol. 43, pp. 1598–1605, ISSN 0010-4485

Sienkiewicz, Z.J.; Blackwell, R.P.; Haylock, R.G.; Saunders, R.D.; Cobb, B.L. (2000). Low-level exposure to pulsed 900 MHz microwave radiation does not cause deficits in the performance of a spatial learning task in mice. *Bioelectromagnetics*, Vol. 21, No. 3, pp. 151 - 158, ISSN 0197-8462

Tattersall, J. E. H.; Scott, I. R.; Wood, S. J.; Nettel, J. J.; Bevir, M. K.; Wang, Z.; Somasiri, N. P. & Chen, X. (2001). Effects of low intensity radiofrequency electromagnetic fields on electrical activity in rat hippocampal slices. *Brain Research*, Vol. 904, No. 1, (June 2001), pp. 43–53, ISSN 0006-8993

Testylier, G.; Tonduli, L.; Malabiau, R.; Debouzy, J. C. (2002). Effects of Exposure to Low Level Radiofrequency Fields on Acetylcholine Release in Hippocampus of Freely Moving Rats. *Bioelectromagnetics*, Vol. 23, pp. 249-255, ISSN 0197-8462

Valberg, P.A.; van Deventer, T.E.; Repacholi, M.H. (2007). Workgroup report: base stations and wireless networks radiofrequency (RF) exposures and health consequences. *Environ Health Perspect.*, Vol. 115, pp. 416-424, ISSN 0091-6765

Voyvodic, J. T.; Glover, G.H.; Greve, D.; Gadde, S.; FBIRN (2011). Automated real-time behavioral and physiological data acquisition and display integrated with stimulus presentation for fMRI. *Frontiers in Neuroinformatics*, Vol. 5, pp. 1-9, ISSN 1662-5196

Wang, B.; Lai, H. (2000). Acute exposure to pulsed 2450 MHz microwaves affects water-maze performance of rats. *Bioelectromagnetics*, Vol. 21, No. 1, pp. 52 - 56, ISSN 0197-8462

Wang, H.; Ma, Y.; Pratx, G.; Xing, L. (2011). Toward real-time Monte Carlo simulation using a commercial cloud computing infrastructure. *Phys. Med. Biol.*, Vol. 56, pp. N175–N181, ISSN 0031-9155

WHO Int. EMF Project (1996). Health and environmental effects of exposure to static and time varying electric and magnetic fields: Guidelines for quality research, WHO, Geneva, Switzerland, Available from
www.who.int/peh-emf/research database/en/index.html

Wu, T.; Hadjem, A.; Wong, M.; Gati, A.; Picon, O.; Wiart J. (2010). Whole-body new-born and young rats' exposure assessment in a reverberating chamber operating at 2.4 GHz. *Phys. Med. Biol.*, Vol. 55, pp. 1619–1630, ISSN 0031-9155

Yoon, J.; Chatterjee, I.; McPherson, D. & Craviso, G. L. (2006). Design, characterization, and optimization of a broadband mini exposure chamber for studying catecholamine release from Chromaffin cells exposed to microwave radiation: Finite-difference time-domain technique. *IEEE Transactions Plasma Science*, Vol. 34, No. 4, (August 2006), pp. 1455–1469, ISSN 0093-3813

15

Real–Time Low–Latency Estimation of the Blinking and EOG Signals

Robert Krupiński and Przemysław Mazurek
Department of Signal Processing and Multimedia Engineering
West Pomeranian University of Technology, Szczecin
Poland

1. Introduction

Electrooculography biosignals (EOG) are very important for the eye orientation and eyelid movements (blinking) estimation. There are many applications of the EOG signals. Most important applications are related to the medical applications [Duchowski (2007)]. The EOG signal is used for the analysis of eye movement in the selected medical test of the eye related health problems. It is also important for the sleep analysis. The EOG signal has much higher level than the important EEG (electroencephalography) signals and should be removed from the EEG measurements [Duchowski (2007); Shayegh & Erfanian (2006)]. The reduction of the EOG artifacts from EEG is considered by many researchers and it is also important for the practical applications of the EEG–based Human–Computer Interfaces.

The EOG and blinking signals are used in Human–Computer Interfaces in: the ergonomics, the advertisement analysis [Poole & Ball (2005)], the human–computer interaction (HCI) systems (e.g. a virtual keyboard [Usakli at al. (2010)], the vehicle control [Barea et al. (2002); Firoozabadi (2008)], the wearable computers [Bulling et al. (2009)]), and the video compression driven by eye–interest [Khan & Komogortsev (2004)].

Many alternative oculography techniques are available. The applications of the EOG signals for the HCI applications should be considered as one of the available techniques. The most important disadvantage is the long–time stability of the measurements and the influences of the other factors like light sources. The video–oculography (VOG) is interesting alternative, but the long–time influence of the infrared illuminators usually used on the eye has not been well tested. The infrared oculography (IROG) applies a small set of the illuminators (IR LEDs) and IR sensors for the estimation of eye movements.

The recent application of the EOG signal is the computer animation. The estimated orientation and blinking signals are used for the control of eye and eyelid of the human–generated avatar [Deng et al. (2008)]. This is specific for the motion capture technique [Duchowski (2007); Krupiński & Mazurek (2009)] that, for instance, was used successfully in Beowulf movie [Sony et al. (2006); Warner Brothers (2008)]. Such a motion capture technique is alternative to the video–based motion capture systems fixed to the human head.

A measured biosignal has two important subsignals: electrooculography and blinking. Both of them should be separated and the interesting parameters should be estimated. The possibilities of application of the HCI system based on EOG depend on the biosignal measurement system and digital signal processing techniques applied to the obtained signals.

2. Electrooculography signal

2.1 Retina–cornea voltage source

The EOG measurement is based on the voltage measurement that depends on the eye orientation (Fig. 1). The voltage between retina–cornea is about ± 1 mV [Northrop (2002); Schlgöl et al. (2007)], which is a very high value in comparison to other biosignals, but it also depends on numerous factors, for instance, the light conditions [Denney & Denney (1984)], the contact between electrodes and skin, which is the source of amplitude instability [Augustyniak (2001); Krogh (1975)].

One of the advantages of the EOG measurements over other techniques is that the field–of–view is not reduced by the glasses that are used as mounting platform for video or other sensors and illuminators. The electrodes are placed around eyes and are distant for the eye safety reasons.

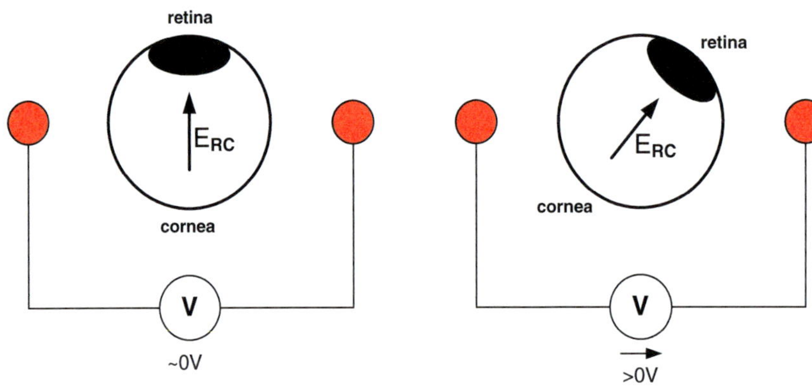

Fig. 1. Model of retina–cornea measurements for two different orientations

2.2 Measurement system configurations

There is no single unique electrodes placement, so many configurations are possible and used in practice [Brown et al. (2006)]. Such situation complicates the comparison of different algorithms used by researchers. The properties of the EOG signal change depending on the placement of electrodes, so the estimation technique should be robust. Additional calibration is necessary if the precise estimation is expected.

There are a few electrode configurations (Fig. 2) and in this chapter the 3/4 configuration is assumed: three main electrodes, for two differential measurements: LEFT–UP and RIGHT–UP, and an additional fourth reference electrode (REF).

The 3/4 configuration is minimal one for the full estimation of eye orientation in both directions and blinking too. Further reduction is possible if the single orientation is sufficient for a specific application. Another configuration 7/8 is the maximal variant [Thakor (1999)] that allows the measurement of very precise movement including every eye separately. It

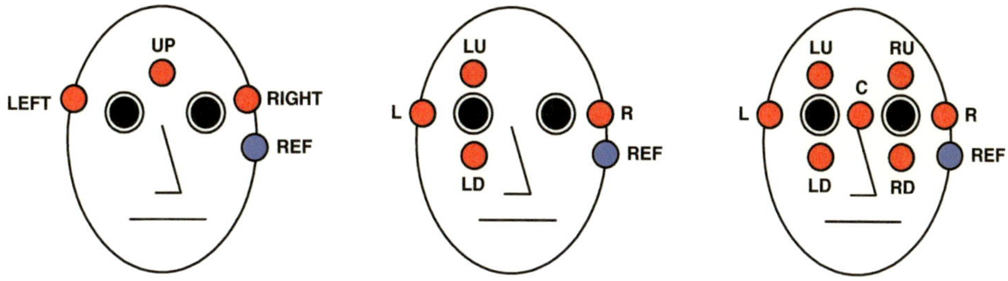

Fig. 2. Different measurement systems: 3/4, 4/5, and 7/8

is important especially for the medical purposes. The configuration 4/5 is the compromise between both mentioned configurations. The large number of electrodes reduces the long time reliability due to the degradation of skin contact. The reduced number of electrodes is preferred for the applications where the touching of the human face is possible. The wires located especially below eyes in the 4/5 and 7/8 configuration is one of disadvantage. The 3/4 configuration allows the placement of electrodes in less visible parts of a face.

The number of electrodes depends on the acquisition systems. The first number represents the number of active electrodes used for measurements and the second number is the total number of electrodes. The additional electrode (the number 4 in the 3/4 configuration) is the reference electrode (REF). The acquisition systems typically use differential inputs. Such input type is preferred due to better SNR. Two channels are used and the first one is the LEFT–UP and the second one is the RIGHT–UP. The example signals are shown in Fig. 3. High impedance inputs are necessary due to the high resistance of the voltage source. The additional suppression of the 50/60 Hz interference is necessary [Prutchi & Norris (2005)], because the power lines are the source of the biosignal disturbances for the EOG signal, which has bandwidth about 200 Hz. Filtering techniques and appropriate wiring are used for the reduction of power lines interference. High frequency power line interference is omitted if a measurement system has the low–pass properties. The main source of high frequency interference is an incandescent light source. The power line interference is additive to a biosignal, especially, if the measurement systems wires are not shielded. Some portion of the power line interference occurs between electrodes on the human body.

The long time stability of the skin contact is obtained using the adhesive electrodes or an electrogel. The Ag/Ag–Cl electrodes are used typically. Such electrode types are conductive, but the other types (e.g. capacitance–based) are also used. The conductive electrodes support a DC signal.

2.3 Measurements settings and signal processing

The EOG biosignal needs a much higher sampling rate in comparison to other biosignal measurement systems. The sampling rate should be about a few hundreds samples per second. The low–pass filtering property of the measurement system is necessary. The AC coupling application used for the suppression of the DC signal is not correct. The DC level and low–frequency components corresponds to the eye orientation. The band–pass filtering in some measurement systems makes the differentiation of signals and the correction of measurements very hard or not possible.

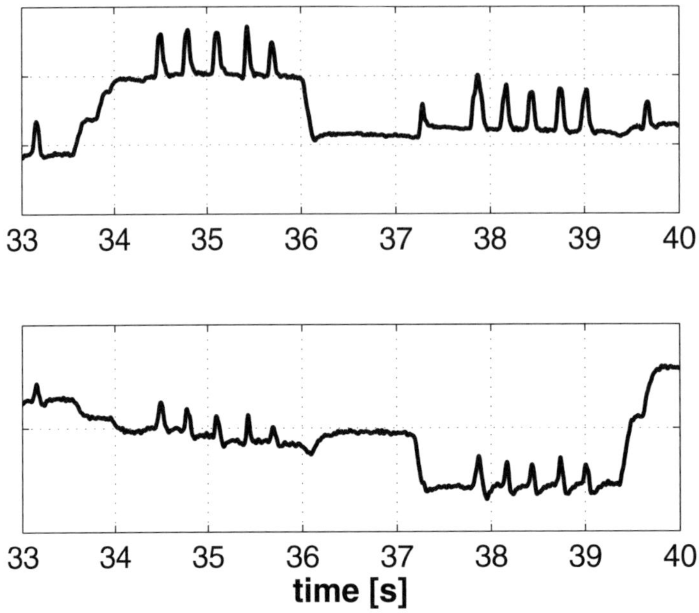

Fig. 3. Example of the EOG signal – two channels for the 3/4 configuration

The reliable measurements should be obtained using the flat band–pass filters (e.g. the Buttherworth filter), but the phase distortions are introduced by the analog filters. The combined filtering of a signal using the analog and digital filters and higher sampling rates is necessary.

The number of quantization levels (the number of bits per sample) for EOG should be carefully set depending on the DC level processing. Even a 8–bit per sample is enough for not demanding applications with correct DC level maintenance and 50/60 Hz interference suppression before sampling. The higher resolution of quantization is used (e.g. 12–16 bits per sample) if both mentioned components are hard to control by electronics. The higher resolution of quantization allows the signal processing using the digital signal processing algorithms.

The higher sampling rate and better quantization create the possibilities of precise observation of the EOG signal, which is important especially for the medical purposes.

The calibration of the system is necessary. A few extreme orientations of eyes are used and the intermediate orientations are interpolated. The HCI system requires the calibration before the beginning of measurements. The non real–time applications support the additional calibration at the end and intermediate calibration if they are necessary. More than single calibration allow the correction of the measurements and improve the acquisition results.

High quality measurements are recommended, but the signal processing of the obtained biosignal is necessary for the separation of the EOG and blinking signals. The estimation of parameters for both signals is necessary.

3. Signal properties

3.1 Blinking

The EOG signal has one important artifact and it is the blinking signal. The blinking occurs if the eyelid makes movements (vertical one). The disturbance depends on the electrode configuration and it is additive for the 3/4 configuration.

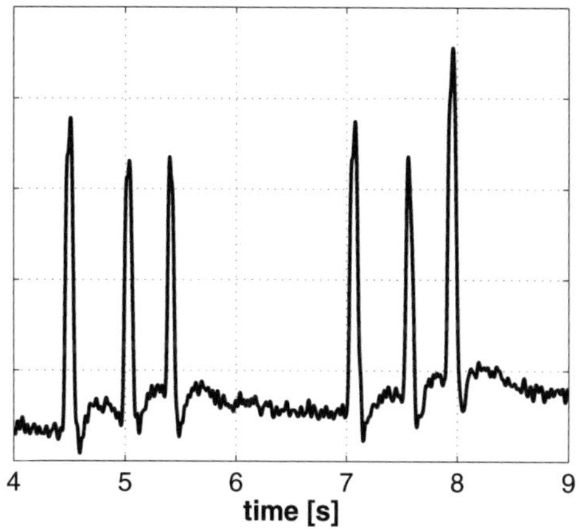

Fig. 4. Example of blinking pulses

The blinking pulse is similar to the Gaussian pulse for typical blinking (Fig. 4).

There are also atypical blinking cases when the eyelid moves very slowly or if the eyelid closing time is different than the eyelid opening time. There are much more cases when blinking is non–Gaussian, but they are not considered in typical systems. In this chapter typical blinking is assumed.

3.2 Saccades

The saccade is the rapid change (Fig. 5) of eye orientation [Becker (1989); Gu et al. (2008); Mosimann et al. (2005)]. The rapid changes require the acquisition of high frequency components of a signal. This is one of the reasons why the necessary sampling rate is higher in comparison to the other systems. The low–pass filtering for the removal of the 50/60 Hz component using the cut of frequency about 30–40 Hz disturbs a saccade signal.

There are also interesting cases, for instance, when the blinking is near to the saccades. This situation is not rare in real measurements, but it is very often not considered by researchers.

3.3 Smooth pursuits

During the tracking of a slowly moving object, the eyes move smoothly (Fig. 6). Such movements are named as smooth pursuits.

There are also other features of the EOG measurements, like the microsaccades that are rapid movements of eyes but in the smaller scale.

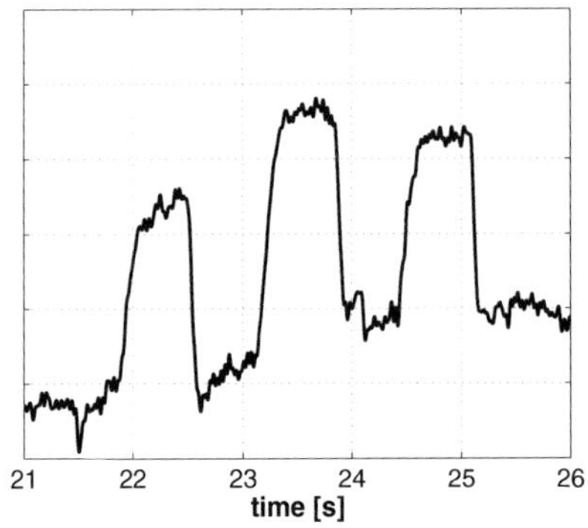

Fig. 5. Example of saccades

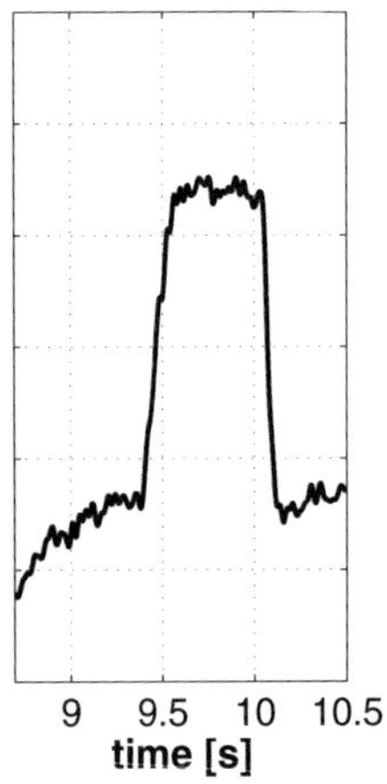

Fig. 6. Example of smooth pursuit with a two saccades

4. Signal separation techniques

4.1 Filtering techniques

There are many techniques for the separation of the EOG and blinking signals. The main techniques are based on the filtering (linear or non–linear) of blinking pulses. The signal with removed blinking pulses is the EOG one. The subtraction of EOG from the original signal gives a blinking signal. Such operation is applied independently to both channels in the 3/4 system. The pattern recognition techniques are used for the estimation of the position of the saccades (e.g. using differentiation and thresholding). The blinking pulses are detected using thresholding. The independent processing of both channels for blinking signal is necessary if the asymmetric blinking is possible. The typical blinking is related to both eyelids together, but the single eyelid blinking is possible too.

The typical filter used for the separation (Fig. 7) is a median filter and derivative filters that are used for the removal of the pulses [Bankman & Thakor (1990); Juhola (1991); Krupiński (2010); Krupiński & Mazurek (2010a); Martinez et al. (2008); Niemenlehto (2009)]. The filtering based on a median filter is the simplest technique but not reliable. There are many cases when the blink removal is not possible: a typical case if a blink is after a falling saccade step or before a saccade step.

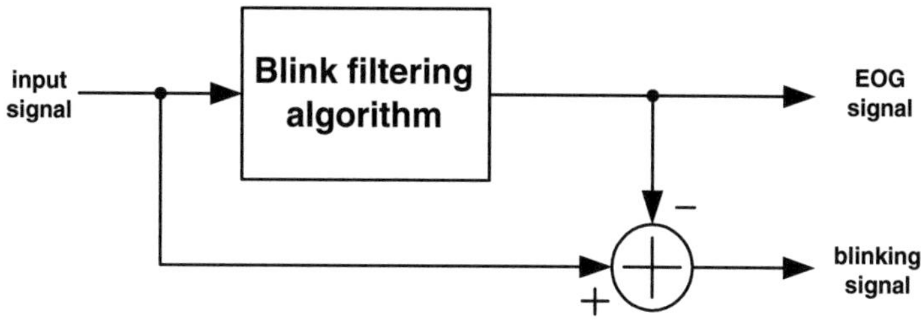

Fig. 7. Typical separation technique

Such techniques are useful for real–time systems. The latency is higher than the maximal blinking pulse width. The rising edge of blinking pulse is simple to detect, but without the falling edge of blinking it is not possible to recognize it correctly. The rising edge for saccadic movement is similar. The availability of both edges of blinking is necessary for correct detection. The median filter calculates a median value from available values and is used for the estimation of the EOG signal level. The expected value is obtained if more than 50% values are assigned to the signal part without blinking. The median filter size (a median moving window) determines the latency.

The implementation of the median filter is possible using more efficient way due to the moving window requirements and full sorting is not necessary [Arce (2005)].

4.2 Analysis by synthesis technique

The estimation of signal parameters using the synthesis technique is possible (Fig. 8). Such a technique is based on fitting a signal generator model to a signal using the optimization techniques [Krupiński & Mazurek (2010b;d;e; 2011)]. The additional constraints are added for improving results and for the reduction of computation time. A correct model related to the specific domain of synthesis is necessary.

The EOG signal and blinking one are well defined in time domain, so synthesis is performed by the comparison of the part (S) of selected signal (s) and synthesized one (m). The aim of optimization process is to reduce an error value using, for example, the following fitting criteria:

$$E\left(signalparameters\right) = \sum_{i \in S} \left(s_i - m_i\left(signalparameters\right)\right)^2. \tag{1}$$

The estimated parameters are related to the selected part of a signal and the number of them depend on the number of detected features.

The advantage of this technique is the parallel signal separation, estimation, filtering and detection. The signals are separated using the model of one of them or both of them. The estimated signals are properly obtained if the model of both signals (EOG and blinking) is applied. The artifacts that are not assigned to EOG or blinking are considered as noise, but depend on the model quality and may be still interesting, e.g. for further microsaccadic movement analysis. The models are based on discreet events (blinking pulses, saccades) and additional pattern recognition techniques are not necessary. The obtained results are based on

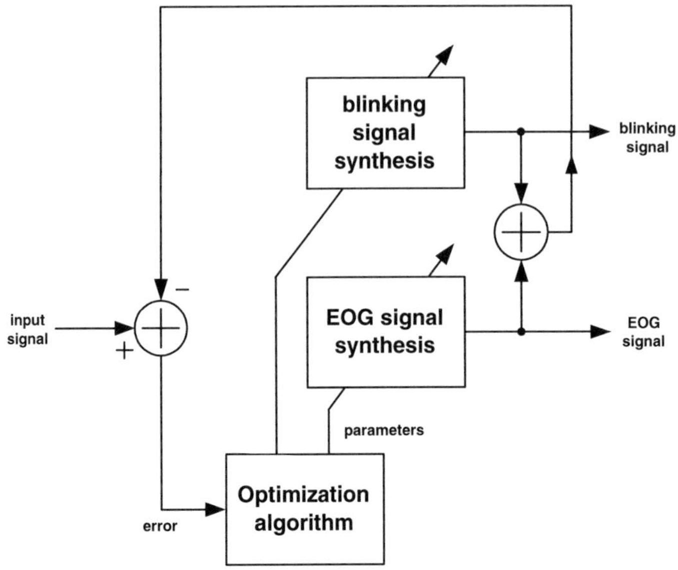

Fig. 8. Analysis by synthesis technique

the set of discreet events and the corresponding values like the height of a blink and an EOG level value.

The disadvantage of this technique is computation power requirements [Krupiński & Mazurek (2010c)]. Real–time processing is very difficult and additional latency occurs. Some applications does not need the detection of saccades and the EOG signal is a signal that is used directly (e.g. in the motion capture applications or the analysis of point–of–interest).

In [Krupiński & Mazurek (2011)] such a technique for the EOG and blinking signals is introduced. This algorithm uses evolutionary search with the mutation of a single child [Michalewicz (1996)]. The additional gradient optimization is used for the computation time reduction by the local improving of convergence for a blink position and height, a saccade position and the value of the EOG signal level between two saccades.

5. Waveletes separation technique

5.1 Singularity processing

Another method of the event detection (a saccade, a blink) is the wavelets transform [Ghandeharion & Ahmadi–Noubari (2009); Reddy et al. (2010)]. The saccade and blink are well defined in time domain and they have a limited length in time.

In [Bukhari et al. (2010a;b; 2011)] the signal analysis and filtering of eye movements using scalogram and 'db4' wavelets up to details level 10 are considered. In [Reddy et al. (2010)] a few wavelets are compared ('sym8','haar','db4','db10','coif3') for the blink detection, and the best is 'sym8'. The threshold based technique is applied for the blink detection. In [Bhandari et al. (2006)] the signal enhancement techniques using wavelets are proposed. The 'coiflet3' wavelet for denoising is applied. Blinks and saccades are enhanced using the 'haar' wavelet. Discussed wavelets techniques by the authors are not sufficient for HCI systems. Moreover, there is a lack of the analysis of the more complex scenarios, like a saccade near to a blink, what appears in real measurements.

The wavelets are useful for the processing of signals and depend on the applied wavelet so the selected properties of a signal are emphasized [Augustyniak (2003); Mallat (1999); Mallat & Zhang (1993)]. The selection of a particular wavelet defines the specific response for singularities too.

The non–isolated singularities need the multifractal analysis. The signals with singularities are analyzed using the singularity spectrum. The EOG signal with blinking is such a kind of signal that has the isolated singularities for most cases. The distance between events of any type is quite large, but both kinds of events may appear in short time and in such a case the limited multifractal properties exist. The analysis of the singularities is the basis of the detection and gives the possibility for real–time processing without median filtering (Fig. 9).

The singularities create the large amplitude values in their cone of influence what is observed in a singularity spectrum. The analysis of singularity spectrum is possible using the detection of local maximum for every scale. The maximal values of the wavelet transform coefficients $|Wf(u,s)|$ are obtained by differentiation and testing the values. The zero value is obtained if a maximum point is found.

$$\frac{\partial |Wf(u_0,s_0)|}{\partial u} = 0 \tag{2}$$

The additional conditions are necessary for the removal of non–strict maximum points that appear for the constant value of $|Wf(u,s)|$ for some cases.

The detected maximum points are connected on the every scale. The parameters of a line: a length, an accumulated value over a line, and a slope are used for the detection of the even type and the estimation of parameters.

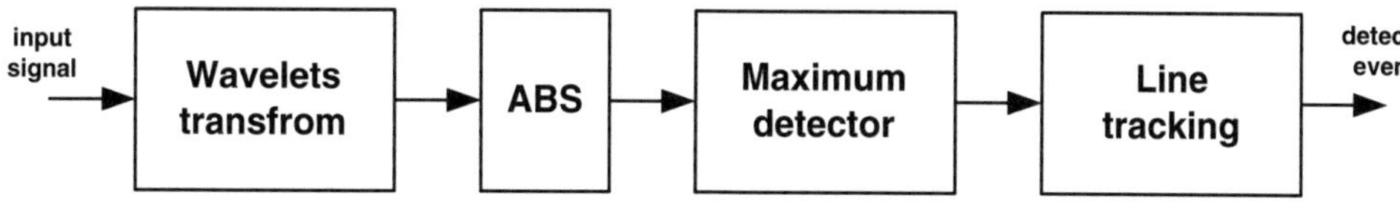

Fig. 9. Singularity analysis scheme

The singularity analysis needs the tracking of the lines starting from the small scale to the largest one. The line length depends on the fitting of the wavelets to the singularity (event). A small length corresponds to the less important feature. The longest lines are taken into account. The length of a line is not only one method for the detection of features. The accumulation of the values along trajectories of accumulated singularity spectra is a technique used in this work. The accumulated value should be higher than a predefined threshold and this value is set by the previous observation of signal behavior. The wavelet shape 'gaus2' (Fig. 10) is applied for the signal processing by the continuous wavelet transform (CWT).

The following CWT formula is used for the computations:

$$C(a,b;f(t),\psi(t)) = \int_{-\infty}^{\infty} f(t)\frac{1}{\sqrt{a}}\psi^*\left(\frac{t-b}{a}\right)dt \tag{3}$$

where $*$ denotes the complex conjugate, a is a scale parameter, b is a position, and ψ is the selected wavelet.

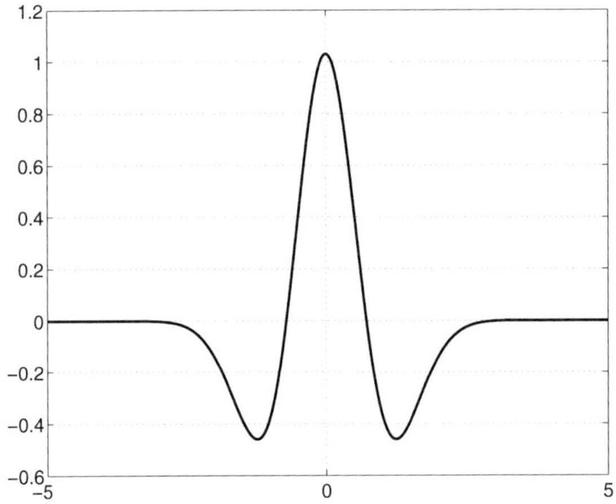

(a)

Fig. 10. Wavelets shape – 'gaus2'

5.2 Example 1 – two blinks and a single saccade

In this example the results of CWT for two blinks and a single saccade are shown.

First blink is slow and second one is fast (Fig. 11a). For the blinks and saccade positions the cones are visible and start from the smallest scale and they extend towards the larger scale (Fig. 11b). The local peaks are detected and multiplied by the wavelets coefficients and the results are shown in Fig. 11c. The accumulated values from the previous step are depicted in (Fig. 11d). The obtained positions are used as the starting positions for the tracking algorithm. The track–before–detect approach (TBD) is used and the simplified spatio–temporal track–before–detect algorithms are used with recurrent processing [Mazurek (2009; 2010a;b;c; 2011a;b)]. There are three motion vectors used due to the high resolution of the scale. There is not need for searching more motion vectors. The result of tracking is shown in Fig. 11e. The tracking of values along lines is important and the accumulated value corresponds to the strength of the event (a blinking height and saccade differential height). The motion trajectory vectors are accumulated too (Fig. 11f). The motion vector near zero corresponds to the blink signal, because a wavelet function is similar. The slope is oriented to the left or right direction depending on the saccade falling or rising edge. The slope counter measures the motion vector (Fig. 11h) and is used together with accumulated values (Fig. 11g) for the threshold–based detection of the event. The detection of the event is shown in (Fig. 11i) where a peak and the peak marks correspond to the event type.

5.3 Example 2 – two blinks and two saccades and smooth pursuit

The next example shows the influence of the smooth pursuit on the processing of a signal. The smooth pursuit is very low frequency component of a signal and a very large scale should be considered by the CWT algorithm. The limited scale range allows reducing the influence of the trend from smooth pursuit. The filtering behavior (Fig. 12) is similar to Example 1.

The verification of the algorithm needs the computation of many examples using the Monte Carlo approach.

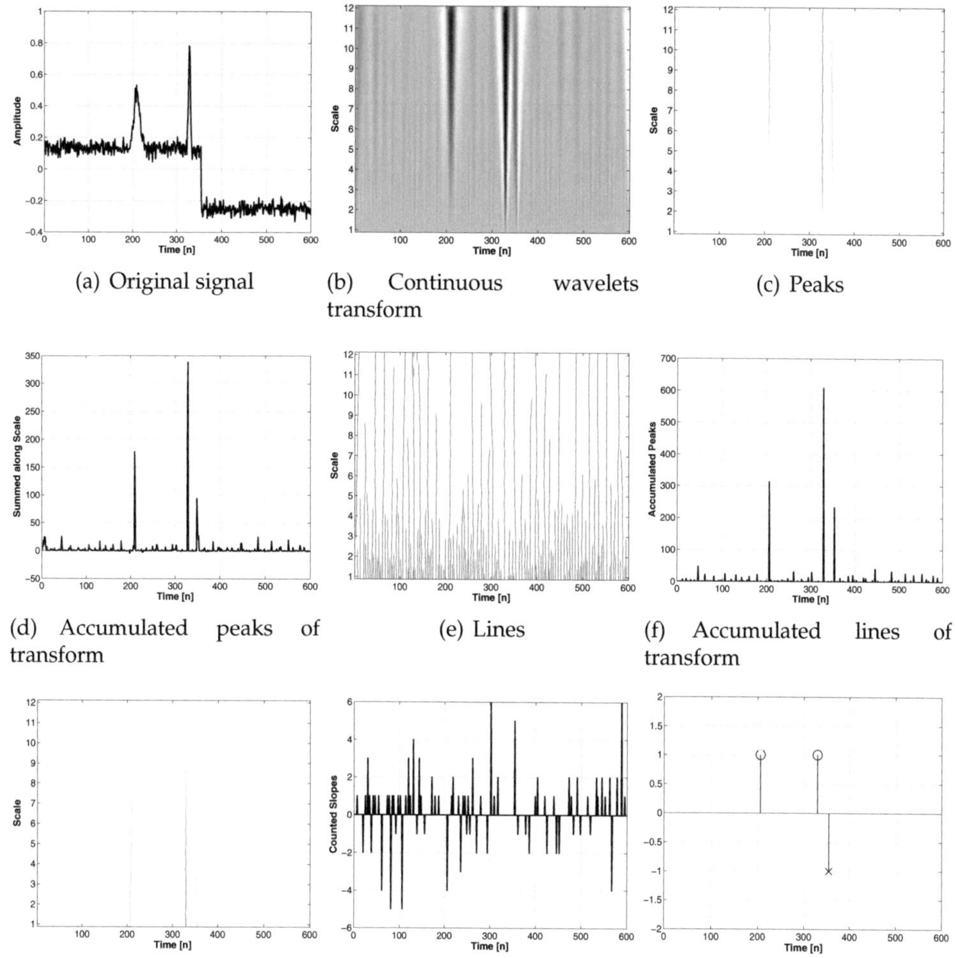

(a) Original signal (b) Continuous wavelets transform (c) Peaks

(d) Accumulated peaks of transform (e) Lines (f) Accumulated lines of transform

(g) Accumulated (h) Slope Counter (i) Detected signals

Fig. 11. Example 1 – two blinks and a single saccade

6. Performance analysis of wavelets separation technique

6.1 Monte Carlo approach and a signal generator

The Monte Carlo approach [Metropolis & Ulam (1949)] is applied for the tests of wavelets performance depending on a few conditions. The testing of the algorithms using synthetic EOG and blinking signals generator is necessary. Such approach is very good for the testing of algorithm. The tests based on the analysis of the recorded signal are limited by the number of available samples. The representative set of the real samples is necessary with the man–made description of every example. The synthetic technique needs a good generator, but the tests are much more reliable. The samples obtained by the real measurement process are related to the small set of humans. The EOG and blinking signals generator is described in [Krupiński & Mazurek (2010a)] and used in the papers [Krupiński & Mazurek (2010b;d;e; 2011)] with some additional extensions (the smooth pursuit support). There are two possible techniques

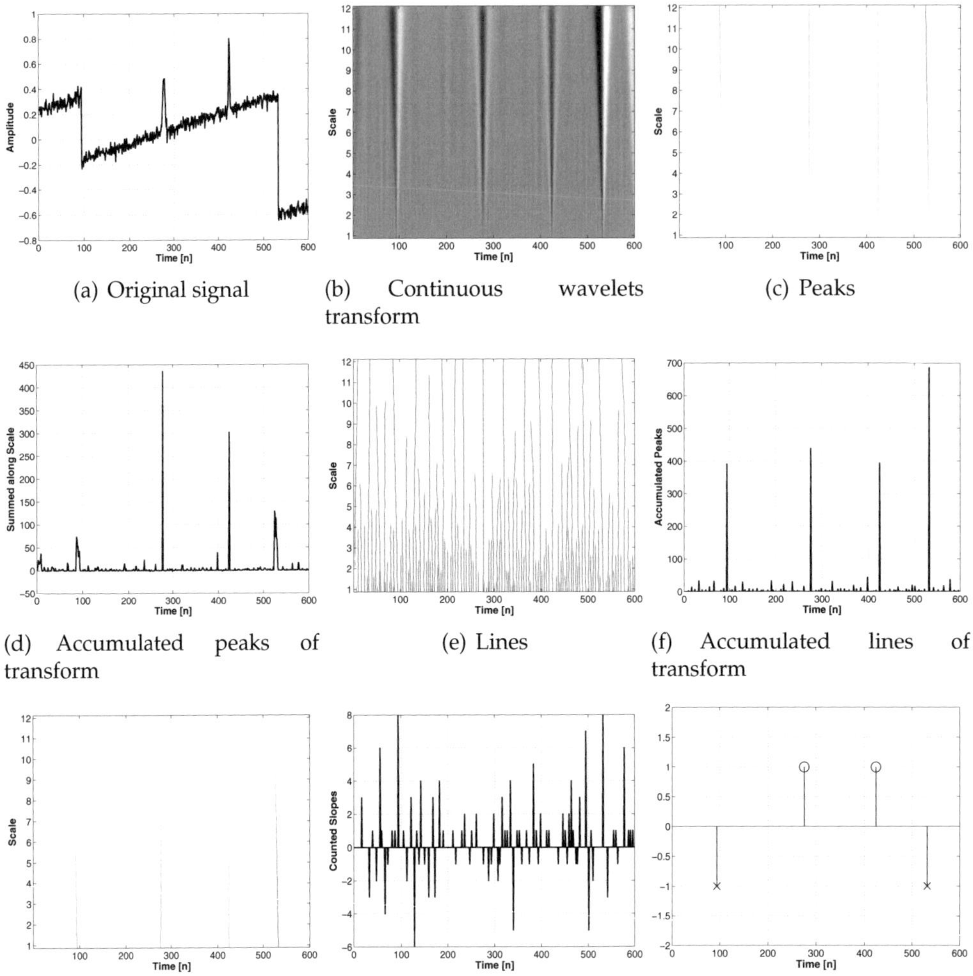

(a) Original signal (b) Continuous wavelets transform (c) Peaks

(d) Accumulated peaks of transform (e) Lines (f) Accumulated lines of transform

(g) Accumulated transform (h) Slope Counter (i) Detected signals

Fig. 12. Example 2 – two blinks, two saccades, smooth pursuit

for the application of the generator. The generator could be used for any possible values of parameters and also for the limited values of parameters. Additionally, it allows testing the specific cases more deeply.

6.2 Test 1 – three saccades and three blinks

This test shows the performance of the algorithm depending on the noise (Fig. 13).

The signal consists of three blinks, three saccades, and the smooth pursuit is not applied. The Gaussian additive noise disturbs the signal. There are many sources of the noises in biosignal measurement systems related to the electrical properties of human body, a contact type and the measurement system. The external radio frequency interference is also the important factor of noise.

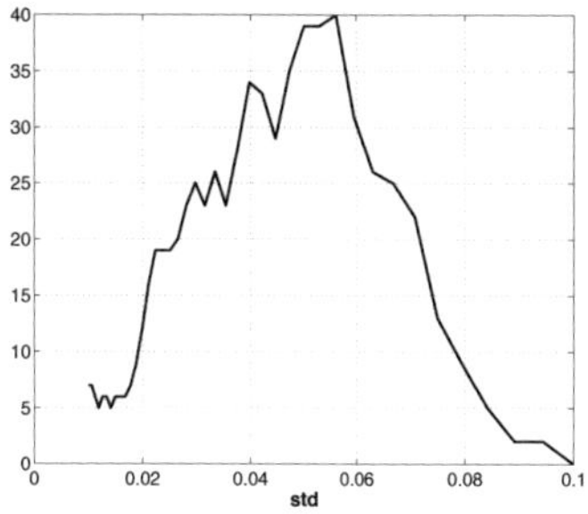

(a) Blinks missed

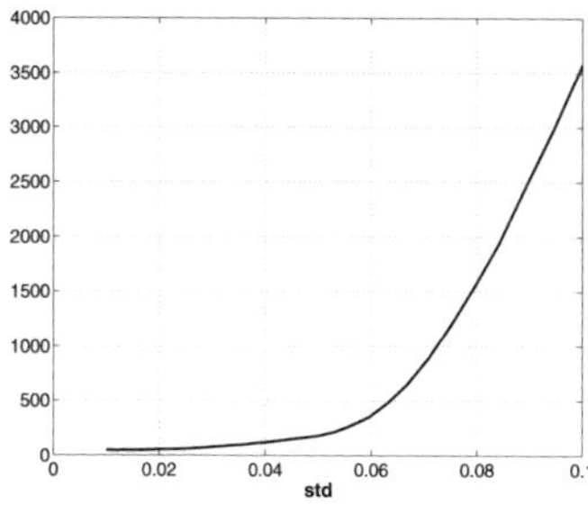

(b) Blinks overdetected

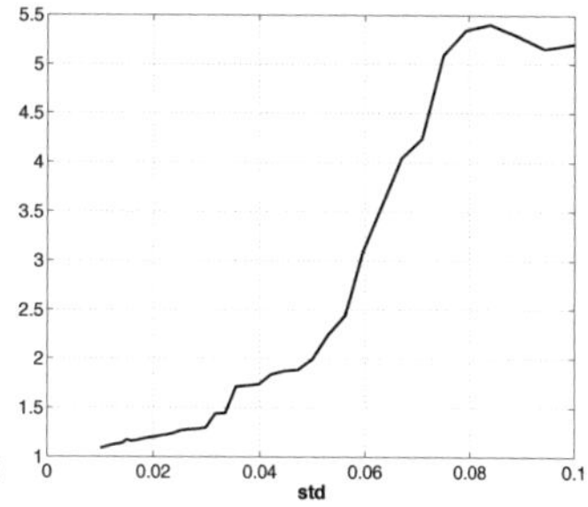

(c) Mean position error (in the number of samples) of detected blinks

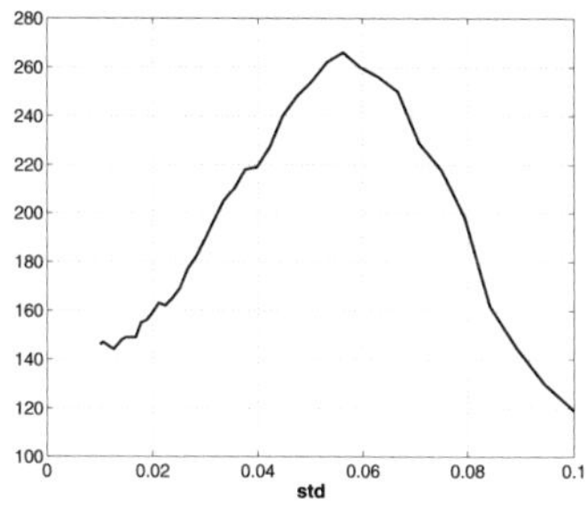

(d) Saccades (in the number of samples) missed

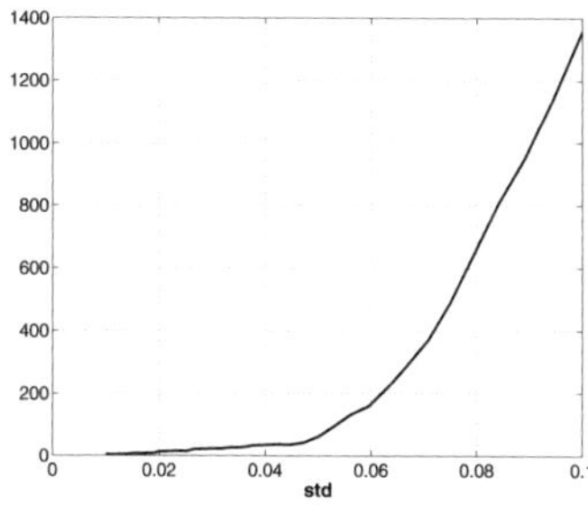

(e) Saccades overdetected

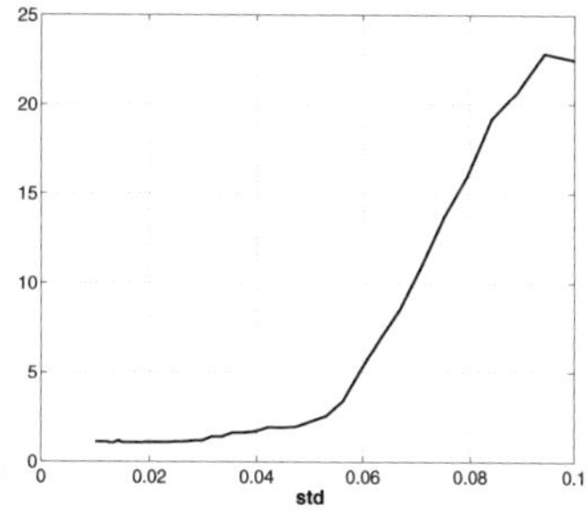

(f) Mean position error (in the number of samples) of detected saccades

Fig. 13. Monte Carlo performance Test 1

The 1000 tests were processed. The maximal number of missing blinks is less than 4% for the higher noised samples (Fig. 13a). This figure depicts the reduction of the missed blinks due to the higher probability of assignment the noise peaks to a blink. The amount of overdetected blinks is depicted in Fig. 13b. The estimated position of the blink is disturbed too (Fig. 13c). The noise level does not influence significantly the position error for the standard deviation for about 0.08. The saccade position detector is more sensitive (Fig. 13d). This is expected behavior, because a single noise value may disturb the position of a saccade. The large values of overdetected saccades due to higher standard deviation noise values, creates false saccades (Fig. 13e) or shifts existing ones (Fig. 13f). The curves for the corresponding quality plots are similar for the blinks and saccades.

6.3 Test 2 – three saccades, three blinks and smooth pursuit

This is similar test to Test 1. The smooth pursuit signal is added so a trend occurred (Fig. 14).

It is expected that the results are similar to the case without smooth pursuit. The wavelets transform does not support very long time scales so the influence of wavelets processing should not be observed. The smooth pursuit is very low frequency signal and should be processed in similar manner like the constant levels of the EOG signals between neighborhood saccades.

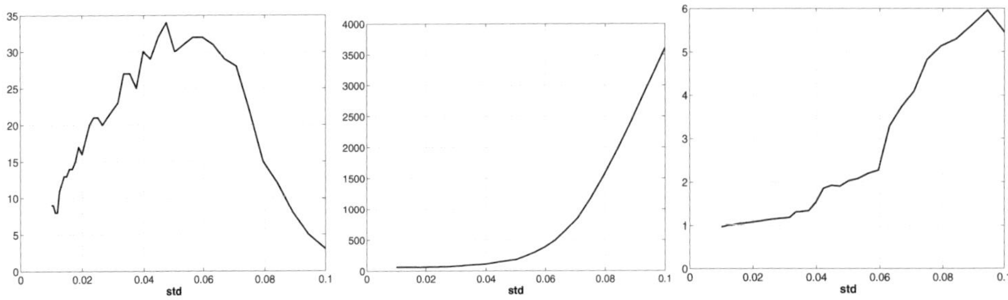

(a) Blinks missed (b) Blinks overdetected (c) Mean position error (in the number of samples) of detected blinks

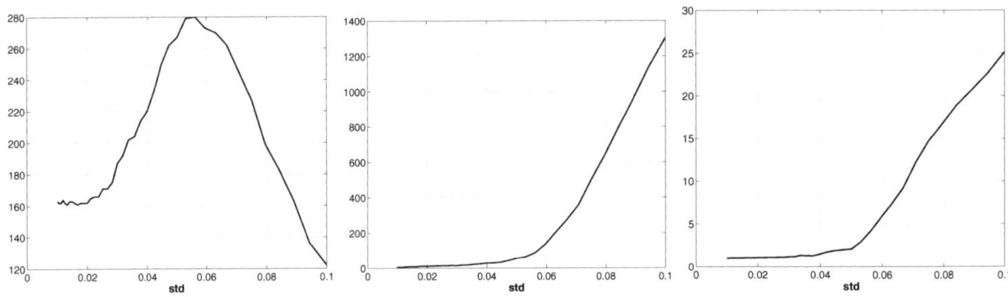

(d) Saccades missed (e) Saccades overdetected (f) Mean position error (in the number of samples) of detected saccades

Fig. 14. Monte Carlo performance Test 2

This test confirms that the trend does not affect significantly the results. This is very important for the applications, because no additional processing is necessary related to the smooth pursuit removal during estimation.

6.4 Test 3 – two blinks only

This test shows the influence of blinks (that are available) and saccades (that are absent) (Fig. 15).

The number of blinks missed is reduced proportionally in comparison to the previous Test 1. There is no influence due to false detected saccades.

6.5 Test 4 – two blinks, smooth pursuit

This similar test to Test 3 related to the influence of smooth pursuit (Fig. 16).

The results are similar to the previous test. The smooth pursuit does not influence significantly the algorithm.

6.6 Test 5 – two saccades

This is similar test to Test 3, but here exist only saccades without blinks (Fig. 17).

As expected there is no significant influence of blink detection on saccades.

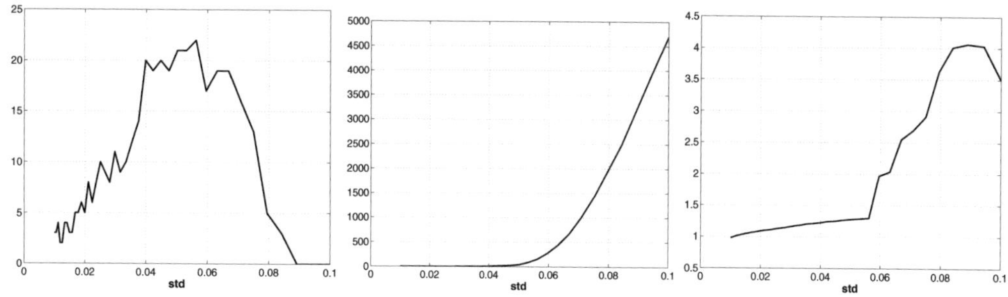

(a) Blinks missed

(b) Blinks overdetected

(c) Mean position error (in the number of samples) of detected blinks

Fig. 15. Monte Carlo performance Test 3

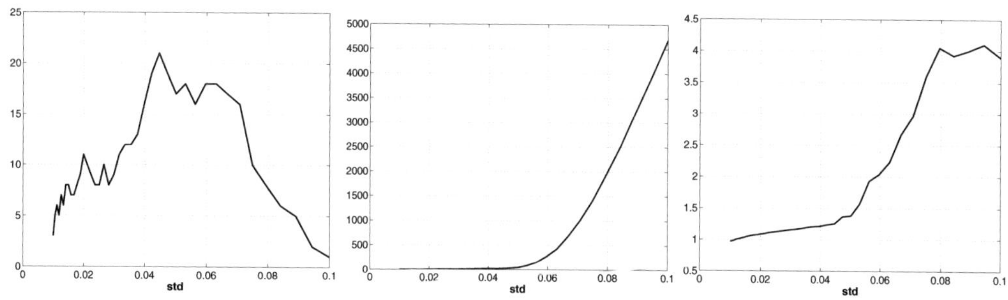

(a) Blink missed

(b) Blinks overdetected

(c) Mean position error (in the number of samples) of detected blinks

Fig. 16. Monte Carlo performance Test 4

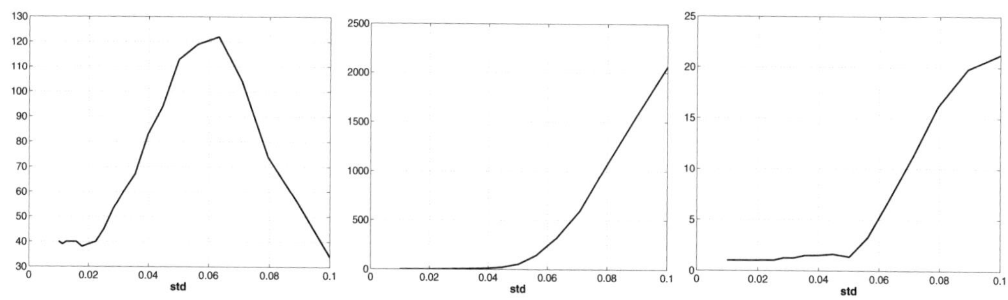

(a) Saccades missed

(b) Saccades overdetected

(c) Mean position error (in the number of samples) of detected saccades

Fig. 17. Monte Carlo performance Test 5

6.7 Test 6 – two saccades, smooth pursuit

In this test the influence of smooth pursuit on the detection of saccades is tested (Fig. 18).

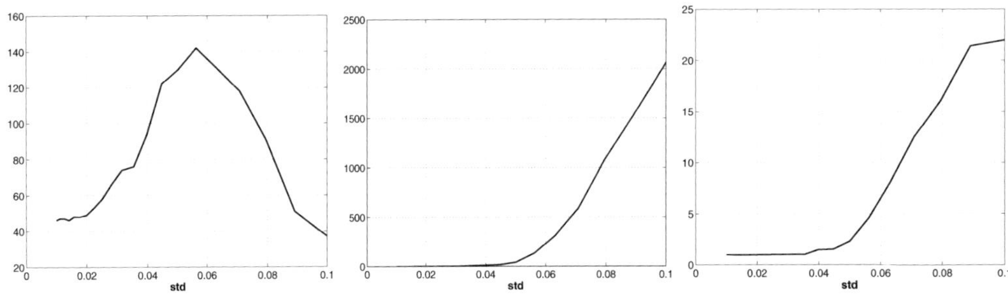

(a) Saccades missed (b) Saccades overdetected (c) Mean position error (in the number of samples) of detected saccades

Fig. 18. Monte Carlo performance Test 6

The plots are similar to the previous Test 5. It means that there is no significant influence of smooth pursuit.

Additionally, in all tests there is no one wrong detection of the saccade slope direction (falling or rising).

7. Latency of wavelets transform technique

The real–time processing is possible using CWT and signal events estimator algorithm. The most important is the latency of the algorithm for the real–time applications like HCI. It is possible to use the alone EOG signal directly to control a computer. The blinking pulses are used as the additional control signals. The applications of the 3/4 electrode system need the low–latency processing, but the median filters are not suitable. The wavelets transform–based approach discussed previously has important advantage over other discussed techniques.

The latency of the system is limited by two factors. The first factor is the blinking pulses width. The saccades are immediate signals that are detected using tens of samples, depending on the sampling rate. They are well defined in time domain and occupies a very short time periods.

The long width of blink means that a system is limited only to the typical blinking. The typical blinking takes about 300–400 ms. It means that the length of the wavelet for the largest scale of CWT should be similar in a value or larger. CWT may process data in real–time and update results for every new samples. The forbidden region of detection occurs for the latest samples and is well shown in the right part of the CWT result e.g. (Fig. 11b). The calculation of the correct values in the cone that starts in the boundary samples is not possible. The calculation results (false) are available due to zero padding. The width of half–cone (Fig. 19) is the half of the wavelets width at the largest scale. It means that for typical blinking the latency is about 150–200 ms appropriately.

The tracking algorithm used for the selection of the peak lines is very fast due to the limited number of motion vectors and the high resolution of CWT.

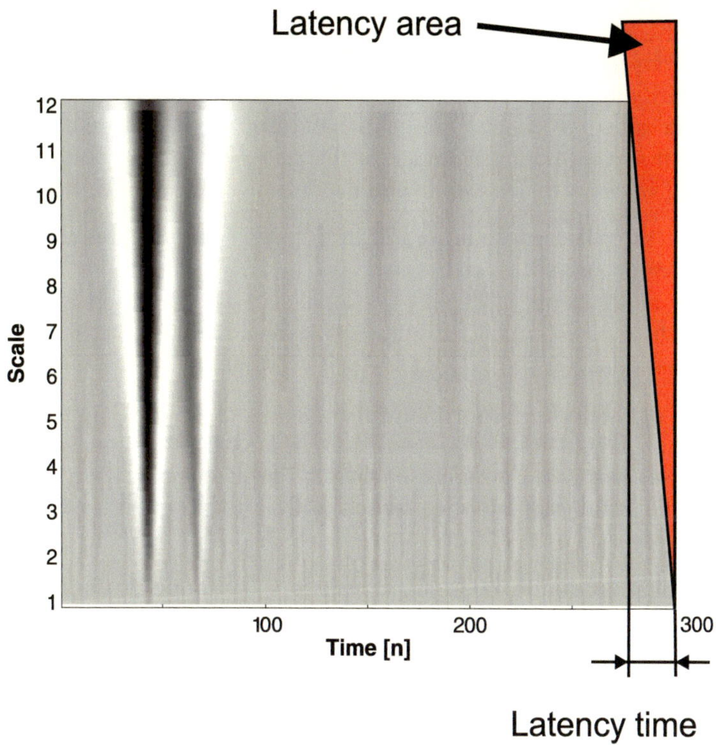

Fig. 19. Latency area and latency time

8. Conclusions and further work

The application of the EOG measurements system has been rising. The EOG systems are used in different and new application areas. The signal processing techniques for real–time processing with high accuracy and low–latency are necessary. There are many processing techniques for the detection and separation of blinking and EOG signals. Most of them are not suitable for more specific cases and new ones are necessary. The recent research shows the importance of the wavelets transform with carefully selected wavelets function.

In this chapter the new wavelets–based technique for the estimation of blinking and saccade time moments using CWT was proposed. The estimation of the blink and EOG signals is important for the real–time HCI systems. Previous work related to the optimization approach [Krupiński & Mazurek (2010b;d;e; 2011)], using the blinking and eye movement model, was not well fitted for the real–time processing. The computation requirements were high and not defined by the number of processing steps due to the applications of the random number generator in the optimization algorithm. The proposed techniques in those papers were based on the evolutionary approach. The reduction of computation time was obtained by the selection of more efficient evolutionary operators. The computation time was also reduced by the reduction of the number of processed samples. The blink and saccade positions were also considered as a starting point for the optimization process near the global minima [Krupiński & Mazurek (2010b)] and the sensitivity of this approach was considered in [Krupiński & Mazurek (2010e)]. Additionally, the estimation of the smooth pursuit movements was observed to improve the results [Krupiński & Mazurek (2010d)].

The proposed in this chapter technique for the EOG measurements was based on the basic idea of CWT analysis introduced in [Mallat (1999)]. The application of the spatio–temporal tracking of singularity improved the detection of the time moments and types of singularities like blinks and saccades. Wavelet techniques have well defined computation cost that is also constant, what is important advantage of this technique. The analysis of the slope of singularity in CWT image at all levels allowed the detection of a specific feature.

The application of the peak tracking algorithm allowed the detection of such event. The computation cost was quite low and nowadays available processing devices allow the processing signal at low cost. The EOG signal sampling frequency is usually small (100–400 Hz typically) so modern microcontrollers have enough computation power for signal processing, recommended are DSPs (Digital Signal Processors).

In the chapter the signal performance analysis of the algorithm and latency behavior due to wavelets and tracking algorithm were considered. The latency was obtained from the analysis of the blinking pulses and it was possible to reach 200 ms latency for a signal processing part, and if there were no additional latencies related to the measurement system it was also the overall system latency.

Future research will be related to the implementation of the proposed approach using DSP.

The reduction of latency using the pattern recognition techniques is possible and will be considered in further research.

The synthetic, generated signals may fill the extended range of possible cases, which is important for the estimation of algorithm performance and finding the incorrectly estimated cases. The knowledge about incorrect cases is the source of important information for researches and developers about the estimation algorithm and further improvements are possible by the analysis of such cases.

9. Acknowledgments

This work is supported by the UE EFRR ZPORR project Z/2.32/I/1.3.1/267/05 "Szczecin University of Technology – Research and Education Center of Modern Multimedia Technologies" (Poland).

10. References

Arce, G.R. (2005). Nonlinear Signal Processing: A Statistical Approach, Wiley, ISBN 0471676241.

Augustyniak, P. (2001). Przetwarzanie sygnałów elektrodiagnostycznych (textbook in Polish), Uczelniane Wydawnictwa Naukowo–Dydaktyczne AGH, Kraków, ISBN 8388408372.

Augustyniak, P. (2003). Transformacje falkowe w zastosowanich elektrodiagnostycznych (textbook in Polish), Uczelniane Wydawnictwa Naukowo–Dydaktyczne AGH, Kraków, ISBN 8389388103.

Bankman, I.N. & Thakor, N.V. (1990). Noise reduction in biological step signals: application to saccadic EOG, Med Biol Eng Comput, Vol.28, No.6, pp.544–549, ISSN 0140–0118.

Barea, R., Boquete, L., Mazo, M. & López, E. (2002). Wheelchair Guidance Strategies Using EOG. Journal of Intelligent and Robotic Systems, Vol.34, pp.279–299, ISSN 1573–0409.

Becker, W. (1989). The Neurobiology of Saccadic Eye Movements. Metric. Rev Oculomot Res., pp.13–67, Elsevier Science Publishers BV (Biomedical Division), ISSN 0168–8375.

Bhandari, A., Khare, V., Trikha, M.& Anand, S. (2006). Wavelet based Novel Technique for Signal Conditioning of Electro–Oculogram Signals, 2006 Annual IEEE India Conference, ISBN 1424403693.

Bukhari, W.M., Daud, W. & Sudirman, R. (2010a). A Wavelet Approach on Energy Distribution of Eye Movement Potential towards Direction, 2010 IEEE Symposium on Industrial Electronics and Applications (ISIEA 2010), October 3–5, 2010, Penang, Malaysia, ISBN 9781424476459.

Bukhari, W.M., Daud, W., Sudirman, R. & Al Haddad, A. (2010b). Wavelet Frequency Energy Distribution of Electrooculogram Potential Towards Vertical and Horizontal Movement, 2010 Second International Conference on Computational Intelligence, Modelling and Simulation (CiMSiM), pp.326–329, ISBN 9781424486526.

Bukhari, W.M., Daud, W., Sudirman, R. (2011). Time Frequency Analysis of Electrooculograph (EOG) Signal of Eye Movement Potentials Based on Wavelet Energy Distribution, 2011 Fifth Asia Modelling Symposium (AMS), pp.81–86, ISBN 9781457701931.

Brown, M., Marmor, M., Vaegan, Zrenner, E., Brigell, M. & Bach, M. (2006). ISCEV Standard for Clinical Electro–oculography (EOG), Doc Ophthalmol, Vol.113, pp.205–212, ISSN 1573–2622.

Bulling, A., Roggen, D. & Tröster, G. (2009). Wearable EOG goggles: Seamless sensing and context–awareness in everyday environments, Journal of Ambient Intelligence and Smart Environments (JAISE), Vol.1, No.2, pp.157–171, IOS Press, DOI: 10.3929/ethz-a-005783740, ISSN 1876–1364.

Deng, Z., Lewis, J.P. & Neumann, U. (2008). Realistic Eye Motion Synthesis by Texture Synthesis, in: Deng, Z. & Neumann, U. (Eds.), Data–Driven 3D Facial Animation, pp.98–112, Springer–Verlag, ISBN 1846289064.

Denney, D. & Denney, C. (1984). The eye blink electro–oculogram, British Journal of Ophthalmology, Vol.68, pp.225–228, ISSN 1468–2079.

Duchowski, A. (2007). Eye Tracking Methodology: Theory and Practice, Springer, ISBN 1846286085.

Firoozabadi, S.M.P., Oskoei, M.A. & Hu, H. (2008). A Human–Computer Interface based on Forehead Multi–channel Bio–signals to control a virtual wheelchair, Proceedings of the 14th Iranian Conference on Biomedical Engineering (ICBME), Shahed University, Iran, pp.272–277.

Ghandeharion, H. & Ahmadi–Noubari, H. (2009). Detection and removal of ocular artifacts using Independent Component Analysis and wavelets, 4th International IEEE/EMBS Conference on Neural Engineering, 2009. NER09, pp.653–656, DOI: 10.1109/NER.2009.5109381, ISBN: 1424420728.

Gu, E., Lee, S.P., Badler, J.B. & Badler, N.I. (2008). Eye Movements, Saccades, and Multiparty Conversations, in: Deng, Z. & Neumann, U. (Eds.), Data–Driven 3D Facial Animation, pp.79–97, Springer–Verlag, ISBN 1846289068.

Juhola, M. (1991). Median filtering is appropriate to signals of saccadic eye movements, Computers in Biology and Medicine, Vol.21, pp.43–49, DOI: 10.1016/0010–4825(91)90034–7, ISSN 0010–4825.

Khan, J.I. & Komogortsev, O. (2004). Perceptual video compression with combined scene analysis and eye–gaze tracking, in: Duchowski, A.T. & Vertegaal, R. (Eds.), ETRA

2004 – Proceedings of the Eye Tracking Research and Application Symposium, ACM Press, p.57, ISBN 1581138253.

Krogh, E. (1975). Normal values in clinical electrooculography, Acta Ophthalmol (Copenh), Vol.53, No.4, pp.563–575, ISSN 0001–639X.

Krupiński, R. (2010). Recursive polynomial weighted median filtering, Signal Processing, Vol.90, No.11, pp.3004–3013, Elsevier, ISSN 0165–1684.

Krupiński, R. & Mazurek, P. (2009). Estimation of Eye Blinking using Biopotentials Measurements for Computer Animation Applications, in: Bolc, L., Kulikowski, J.L. & Wociechowski, K. (Eds.), Lecture Notes in Computer Science, ICCVG 2008, Vol.5337, pp.302–310, Springer–Verlag, DOI: 10.1007/978–3–642–02345–3_30, ISBN 3642023446.

Krupiński, R. & Mazurek, P. (2010a). Median Filters Optimization for Electrooculography and Blinking Signal Separation using Synthetic Model, 14–th IEEE/IFAC International Conference on Methods and Models in Automation and Robotics MMARŚ2009, Miedzyzdroje, Poland, DOI: 10.3182/20090819–3–PL–3002.00057.

Krupiński, R. & Mazurek, P. (2010b). Convergence Improving in Evolution–Based Technique for Estimation and Separation of Electrooculography and Blinking Signals, Information Technologies in Biomedicine, Advances in Soft Computing, Vol.69, Springer, pp.293–302, DOI: 10.1007/978–3–642–13105–9_30, ISSN 1867–5662.

Krupiński, R. & Mazurek, P. (2010c). Towards to Real–time System with Optimization Based Approach for EOG and Blinking Signals Separation for Human Computer Interaction, Proceeding ICCHP'10 Proceedings of the 12th international conference on Computers helping people with special needs: Part I, Lecture Notes in Computer Science, Vol.6179, Springer, pp.154–161, DOI: 10.1007/978–3–642–14097–6_26, ISBN 3642140963.

Krupiński, R. & Mazurek, P. (2010d). Electrooculography signal estimation by using evolution–based technique for computer animation applications, Lecture Notes in Computer Science, ICCVG 2010 Part I, Vol.6374, Springer, pp.139–146, DOI: 10.1007/978–3–642–15910–7_16, ISBN 3642159091.

Krupiński, R. & Mazurek, P. (2010e). Sensitivity analysis of eye blinking detection using evolutionary approach, Procedings – International Conference on Signals and Electronic Systems ICSES'10, Gliwice, Poland, pp.81–84, ISBN 1424453078.

Krupiński, R. & Mazurek, P. (2011). Optimization–based Technique for Separation and Detection of Saccadic Movements and Eye–blinking in Electrooculography Biosignals, in: Arabnia, H.R. & Tran, Q.-N. (Eds.), Software Tools and Algorithms for Biological Systems, Advances in Experimental Medicine and Biology, Vol.696, Springer–Verlag pp.537–545, DOI: 10.1007/978–1–4419–7046–6_54, ISBN 9781441970459.

Mallat, S. (1999). A wavelet tour of signal processing, Academic Press, ISBN 012466606x.

Mallat, S.G. & Zhang, Z. (1993). Matching Pursuits with Time–Frequency Dictionaries, IEEE Transactions on Signal Processing, December (1993), pp.3397–3415, ISSN 1053–587X.

Martinez, M., Soria, E., Magdalena, R., Serrano, A.J., Martin, J.D. & Vila, J. (2008). Comparative study of several Fir Median Hybrid Filters for blink noise removal in Electrooculograms, WSEAS Transactions on Signal Processing, March 2008, Vol.4, pp.53–59, ISSN 2224–3488.

Mazurek, P. (2009). Implementation of spatio–temporal Track–Before–Detect algorithm using GPU, Measurement Automation and Monitoring, Vol 55, No.8, pp.657–659, ISSN 0032–4110.

Mazurek, P. (2010a). Optimization of bayesian Track–Before–Detect algorithms for GPGPUs implementations, Electrical Review, Vol.86, No.7, pp.187–189, ISSN 0033–2097.

Mazurek, P. (2010b). Optimization of Track–Before–Detect systems for GPGPU, Measurement Automation and Monitoring, Vol.56, No.7, pp.665–667, ISSN 0032–4110.

Mazurek, P. (2010c). Optimization of Track–Before–Detect Systems with Decimation for GPGPU, Measurement Automation and Monitoring, Vol.56, No.12, pp.1523–1525, ISSN 0032–4110.

Mazurek, P. (2011a). Comparison of Different Measurement Spaces for Spatio–Temporal Recurrent Track–Before–Detect Algorithm, Advances in Intelligent and Soft Computing – Image Processing and Communications Challenges 3, Vol.102, Springer Verlag, pp.157–164, DOI: 10.1007/978–3–642–23154–4_18, ISBN 3642231537.

Mazurek, P. (2011b). Hierarchical Track–Before–Detect Algorithm for Tracking of Amplitude Modulated Signals, Advances in Intelligent and Soft Computing – Image Processing and Communications Challenges 3, Vol.102, Springer Verlag, pp.511–518, DOI: 10.1007/978–3–642–23154–4_56, ISBN 3642231537.

Metropolis, N. & Ulam, S. (1949). The Monte Carlo Method, Journal of the American Statistical Association (American Statistical Association), Vol.247, No.44, pp.335–341. DOI: 10.2307/2280232, ISSN 0162–1459.

Michalewicz, Z. (1996). Genetic Algorithms + Data Structures = Evolution Programs, Springer–Verlag, ISBN 3540606769.

Mosimann, U.P., Mri, R.M., Burn, D.J., Felblinger, J., O'Brien, J.T., McKeith & I.G. (2005). Saccadic eye movement changes in Parkinson's disease dementia and dementia with Lewy bodies, Brain, Vol.128, No.6, pp.1267–1276, DOI: 10.1093/brain/awh484, ISSN 1460–2156.

Niemenlehto, P.H. (2009). Constant false alarm rate detection of saccadic eye movements in electro–oculography, Computer Methods and Programs in Biomedicine, Vol.96, No.2, pp.158–171, DOI: 10.1016/j.cmpb.2009.04.011, ISSN 0169–2607.

Northrop, R.B. (2002). Noninvasive Instrumentation and Measurement in Medical Diagnosis, CRC Press, ISBN 0849309611.

Poole, A. & Ball, L.J. (2005). Eye Tracking in Human–Computer Interaction and Usability Research: Current Status and Future Prospects, in: Ghaoui C. (Ed.), Encyclopedia of Human Computer Interaction, pp.211–219, Idea Group, ISBN 1591405629.

Prutchi, D. & Norris, M. (2005). Design and Development of Medical Electronic Instrumentation, Wiley, ISBN 0471676233.

Reddy, M.S., Narasimha, B., Suresh, E., Rao, K.S. (2010). Analysis of EOG signals using wavelet transform for detecting eye blinks, 2010 International Conference on Wireless Communications and Signal Processing (WCSP), pp.1–4, DOI: 10.1109/WCSP.2010.5633797, ISBN 1424475568.

Schlgöl, A., Keinrath, C., Zimmermann, D., Scherer, R., Leeb, R. & Pfurtscheller, G. (2007). A fully automated correction method of EOG artifacts in EEG recordings, Clinical Neurophysiology, Vol.118, pp.98–104, DOI: 10.1016/j.clinph.2006.09.003, ISSN 1744–4144.

Shayegh, F. & Erfanian, A. (2006). Real–time ocular artifacts suppression from EEG signals using an unsupervised adaptive blind source separation, Conf Proc IEEE Eng Med Biol Soc., DOI: 2006;1:5269–72. PMID: 17946689.

Sony Pictures Entertainment, Sony Corporation, Sagar, M., Remington, S. (2006). System and method for tracking facial muscle and eye motion for computer graphics animation, Patent US., International Publication Number WO/2006/039497 A2 (13.04.2006).

Thakor, N.V. (1999). Biopotentials and Electrophysiology Measurement, in: Webster J.G. (Ed.), The Measurement, Instrumentation, and Sensors Handbook, Vol.74, CRC Press, ISBN 0849383471.

Usakli, A.B., Gurkan, S., Aloise ,F., Vecchiato, G. & Babiloni, F. (2010). On the Use of Electrooculogram for Efficient Human Computer Interfaces, Computational Intelligence and Neuroscience, Vol.2010, 5 pages, DOI: 10.1155/2010/135629, ISSN 1687–5273.

Warner Brothers (2008). E.O.G Beowulf DVD 2'nd disc, Warner Brothers.